D1556468

Administrative
Subdivisions
of Countries

Administrative
Sudivisions
of Countries

A Comprehensive World Reference,
1900 through 1998

by
GWILLIM LAW

McFarland & Company, Inc., Publishers
Jefferson, North Carolina, and London

A.M.D.G.,
and for Janice

Library of Congress Cataloguing-in-Publication Data

Law, Gwillim, 1945–
Administrative subdivisions of countries : a comprehensive world
reference, 1900 through 1998 / by Gwillim Law.
p.   cm.
Includes bibliographical references and index.
ISBN 0-7864-0729-8 (library binding : 50# alkaline paper)
1. Administrative and political divisions — Handbooks, manuals, etc.
I. Title.
JS48.L39   1999   351— dc21
99-34429 CIP

British Library Cataloguing-in-Publication data are available

Manufactured in the United States of America

McFarland & Company, Inc., Publishers
Box 611, Jefferson, North Carolina 28640
www.mcfarlandpub.com

Contents

Introduction

The land area of the earth is entirely divided into countries, without overlap. Likewise, each country is entirely divided into units variously designated as states, provinces, governorates, regions, and so on. A comprehensive phrase for them all is "major administrative divisions." A synonymous phrase is "primary civil divisions."

The concept of a country is a powerful organizer in human geography. A grade-school child can understand that people who live in France speak French and spend francs. The reality is more complex; there are also many native speakers of Provençal, Breton, and Basque, and in a few years they will probably be spending euros. The fact remains that one of the first things one would want to know about a person or place is what country it is in.

Administrative divisions are useful for some of the same reasons as countries, though to a lesser degree. Knowing what country a city is in is the first step toward determining its precise location. Knowing the division helps still further. The subdivision may also imply something about the time zone, postal code, or telephone number of a location, and sometimes the laws that are in force there. Often, knowing the region a place is in permits a greater understanding of its terrain, climate, mores, ethnicity, and economy than would be so just knowing its country.

The goal of this book is to help determine the administrative division a place is in, using whatever clues are available. If a division name is encountered written in nonstandard form, or in another language, the standard English name can be found here. The division a place was in formerly can be traced up to the present, despite subsequent placename and boundary changes.

Some limits to the scope of this book have been set, of necessity. The period covered is from 1900 to the end of 1998. Translations of division names into most Western European languages are given. The only alphabet used is the Roman, although many non–Western placenames are transliterated from other alphabets. The divisions given are those generally recognized by the international community. In Africa in 1900, there may very well have been indigenous forms of territorial division that do not appear on maps drawn by Europeans; these have necessarily been left out.

Each country entry can be read independently. Use of the book will be enhanced, however, by an awareness of the information in the section titled "The Elements of the Entries," which follows.

The Elements of the Entries

This book is organized by countries. The list of countries used is adapted from an international standard called ISO 3166-1 (formerly simply ISO 3166). For more details about the selection of countries, or about ISO 3166-1, see section **A** of this key.

The country listings follow a single format, but most countries are missing one or more elements of the format which are not applicable or not available. Data pertaining to the country as a whole come first, followed by data on the country's administrative subdivisions.

Each entry begins with a header, containing the country's common name in English; ISO code (see section **A**); FIPS code (see section **B**); official language(s); time zone (see section **C**); capital; summary history; other names of the country (see section **D**); and origin or meaning of the country name. The summary history briefly explains the status of the country throughout the 20th century, if there have been any major changes.

The subdivisions-related data always begin with a table of the country's present-day divisions. This main table will contain different columns, based on the availability and relevance of data. If the divisions are of mixed status (e.g., several states and several territories), there will be a column for status. (The "status" is just a classification: state, province, territory, department, district, or some other type of administrative entity.) Next, there will be a column for every different set of standardized abbreviations available. Usually this includes ISO and FIPS codes. Sometimes I've found it necessary to define my own set of two-letter codes (see section **E**). If the whole country is not in the same time zone, there will be a column showing the main time zone for each subdivision. Next come population, area, and capital for each subdivision, followed by any additional information that might be useful for that country. A few countries are so small they have been treated as having only one division, consisting of the entire country.

At the end of this table there is a key to the column headings, with a summary description of the status of subdivisions, and the date of the census for population figures (see section **F**).

If available and suitable, the tables that follow this one will be "Further subdivisions," a discussion of smaller subdivisions of the country; "Territorial extent," notes about helpful or unusual features of the geographical configuration of the divisions (see section **G**); "Origins of names"; "Change history," explaining changes to the list of statoids that have occurred throughout the 20th century, with their dates (see section **F**); "Variant names of subdivisions" (see section **D**); and "Population history," showing the population of each division at intervals, usually since about 1900.

Many countries have multiple levels of administrative subdivision. The United States is divided into states, which are further divided into counties (or county equivalents, such as parishes in Louisiana). In many states, the counties are further divided into townships or the equivalent. For a book of international scope, it was not possible to give details at the county level or lower. However, there are a few countries where more than one level of subdivision seemed worthy of inclusion. For example, in France, the department has been the primary administrative subdivision ever since the Revolutionary period. In the 1970s, it was observed that several government ministries had adopted regional groupings of departments to organize their services; but the regions were slightly different in each case. France then adopted a uniform set of regions, and required every ministry to conform. The regions have also been given certain administrative functions of their own, along with budgets. The number of regions (22) is more manageable than the number of departments (95). Therefore, I felt it was necessary to give extensive information about both levels of subdivision in France.

A ISO is the symbol of the International Organization for Standardization. (It was not chosen as an acronym; rather, *iso-* is the Greek prefix for "equal.") ISO 3166-1 is entitled, "Code for the representation of names of countries." It provides a list of countries, and a two-letter code for each country (and other things of lesser significance). It was first issued in 1974. I have found this to be a widely accepted standard.

It is not, however, perfect for the present purpose. It

states clearly, "The list contains overlaps in those cases where entities are geographically separated from their main entity ... the entities are not mutually exclusive." (Entities simply means items on the list.) For example, Martinique is formally an integral part of the French Republic, but Martinique is in the Caribbean while the main part of France is in Europe. Therefore, ISO 3166-1 lists France (FR), Metropolitan France (FX), and Martinique (MQ) for three separate entries.

In some cases, the document explains the geographical scope of entries, especially in mentioning isolated islands included in the entry. In general it is, however, left up to the users of the standard to agree on what they mean by each entry. Therefore, I have usually had to make my own determination on the scope of each country. The only way in which my list differs from the complete list from ISO 3166-1 is that I've omitted Metropolitan France. I use France to mean all of European France, including Corsica, and not including overseas departments such as Martinique. (I have been privately informed that Metropolitan France will be dropped from a future version of ISO 3166-1, but I have yet to confirm this.)

The ISO recognized the need for a related list of administrative subdivision codes. In 1996 it issued ISO/DIS 3166-2, a draft international standard entitled "Codes for the representation of names of countries and their subdivisions." It contains exactly the same list of countries as does ISO 3166-1. For most of them, it then gives a list of subdivisions and codes. The codes all begin with the two-letter country code, followed by a hyphen and a specific code for the division. For example, the province of Balkh in Afghanistan is coded AF-BAL, where AF is the country code for Afghanistan. To save space in the tables, I have omitted the country code and the hyphen.

A representative of the working group that prepared ISO/DIS 3166-2 told me that the finished product, ISO 3166-2, was to have been published at the end of 1998 (unfortunately too late for this book) if all goes well. It "will be very different in content (many updates) and coverage (more countries with lists of subdivisions) from the Draft International Standard.... It is likely that yearly updates will be issued which will contain all the changes that have run up over that period."

B FIPS stands for Federal Information Processing Standards, promulgated by the United States Government. There are many such standards, but only two appear in this book: numbers 5-2 and 10-4. The FIPS PUB 5-2 is entitled, "Codes for the identification of the states, the District of Columbia and the outlying areas of the United States, and associated areas." It contains a two-letter code and a two-digit code for every major administrative division under U.S. sovereignty (states, territories, etc.). The two-letter codes are the familiar postal abbreviations for the states. The two-digit codes can be extended to make five-digit county codes (as listed in FIPS PUB 6-4); or they can be extended to make seven-digit codes for "populated places, primary county divisions, and other locational entities" (as listed in FIPS PUB 55-3). The FIPS PUB 10-4 is entitled, "Countries, dependencies, areas of special sovereignty, and their principal administrative divisions." It assigns a two-letter code to each country, and a two-character extension which can be used to form a four-character code for each subdivision. The extension is almost always two digits, but a few divisions have a letter and a digit. Thus, a typical FIPS code is aann, where the a's are letters and the n's are digits. (The numbers after the hyphens are version numbers; for example, FIPS PUB 5-2 is the second major version of the standard.)

The National Bureau of Standards recommends using FIPS country codes for State and Defense Department purposes, and ISO country codes for international commerce and for communicating with international organizations. It adds, "the existence of two sets of codes for the same purpose has been confusing to users, but neither set can be generally adopted throughout the Federal Government to the exclusion of the other."

The set of countries listed in FIPS 10-4 is very similar to that in ISO 3166-1. The main difference is that FIPS 10-4 lists some small island groups as separate countries, where ISO 3166-1 treats them as parts of another country.

There is another standard defined locally. This one applies to Europe. Eurostat has defined a hierarchical subdivision of the countries of the European Union (EU). The code is called NUTS, for Nomenclature des Unités Territoriales Statistiques (Nomenclature of Territorial Units for Statistics). The purpose is to divide the EU into entities which are statistically comparable to one another, despite the widely different sizes and structures of the individual countries. The highest-level subdivision is the country. Each country is identified by a two-letter code. The country codes match ISO 3166, except for Finland (NUTS = FL; ISO = FI) and the United Kingdom (NUTS = UK; ISO = GB). In most countries, an alphanumeric third character creates a NUTS 1 code, usually an unofficial grouping of subdivisions. Appending a fourth character makes a NUTS 2 code, which often represents an actual administrative division of a country, such as a region or state. The standard appends more characters, one at a time, to generate NUTS 3, NUTS 4, and NUTS 5 codes. These codes represent successively smaller geographical units, always based on the actual administrative divisions of the country.

C The time zone is identified by its standard time offset, which is the number of hours(:minutes) to be added to (+) or subtracted from (-) Greenwich Mean Time to obtain standard local time. This number is followed by a superscript [d] if daylight saving time is observed in the zone. Daylight saving time is called "summer time" in many areas. It is observed by setting the clocks forward during local summer, roughly April–October in the northern hemisphere or September–March in the southern hemisphere. The advance is one hour almost everywhere.

English	North	East	South	West	Center	Upper	Lower
Arabic	Ash Shamāl	Ash Sharq	Al Janūb	Al Gharb	Al Wusta		
French	du Nord	de l'Est	du Sud	de l'Ouest	Centre	Haut	Bas
French	Septentrional	Oriental	Méridional	Occidental	Central	Supérieur	Inférieur
German	Nord-	Ost-	Süd-	West-	Mittel-	Ober-	Nieder-
Indonesian	Utara	Timur	Selatan	Barat	Tengah		
Italian	Settentrionale	Orientale	Meridionale	Occidentale	Centrale	Superiore	Inferiore
Italian	Nord	Est	Sud	Ovest	Centro	Alto	Basso
Portuguese	Setentrional	Oriental	Meridional	Ocidental	Central	Superior	Inferior
Portuguese	Norte	Leste	Sul	Oeste	Médio	Alto	Baixo
Romance	Boreal	Levant	Austral	Ponent			
Russian	Sever	Vostok	Yug	Zapad	Tsentr		
Spanish	del Norte	del Este	del Sur	del Oeste	Centro-	Alta	Baja

D In the lists of "other names," foreign, obsolete, formal, informal, and variant names are labeled. Foreign names are provided for Danish, Dutch, Finnish, French, German, Icelandic, Italian, Norwegian, Portuguese, Spanish, Swedish, and the vernacular of the country itself, when they differ from the English name. (The vernacular name may have been transliterated from a non–Roman script.) Obsolete names are generally those that have been formally replaced by a new name. Formal names may be defined in a constitution. Informal names are usually shorter forms used conversationally. Variant names are interchangeable with the common name in most contexts, like Slovak Republic and Slovakia. A vernacular that must be transliterated, and for which there is more than one standard method, is another source of variants.

When a place name in one country has a translation into the language of another, the translated name is called an exonym. For example, the vernacular (Italian) name of Venice is Venezia. Its exonyms include Venice (English), Venise (French), Venedig (German), Veneza (Portuguese), and Venecia (Spanish). Many exonyms can be translated using the table of points of the compass at the top of this page. Most of the words will be inflected. The "Romance" row has fancy names occasionally used in French, Italian, Spanish, and Portuguese.

Most people through the ages have not used more than a few hundred placenames outside of their own country. As a result, most languages have fewer than a thousand true exonyms. That is why only the best-known administrative subdivisions have exonyms. The exonyms in this book are for purposes of identification. Translators should use them only with due caution. The United Nations Conference on the Standardization of Geographical Names, the chief international authority on geographical names, urges a minimal use of exonyms.

E Four-letter subdivision codes (4LSC) for international compatibility: Various groups have already created subdivision codes for many purposes. They can be used for filling out forms, in postal addresses, in electronic commerce, and so on. I believe these purposes would be better served by an international set of codes, based on common assumptions, and absolutely uniform in format. Accordingly, I have created a set of codes that are each four letters, where the first two letters are the ISO 3166-1 country code. In any country where the

ISO 3166-2 codes are each two letters, I used them. Elsewhere, I defined a new set of two-letter codes.

The point is that, thanks to this book, there is now a unique four-letter code for every subdivision in the world. They are related to existing standard codes wherever possible. Once the system is understood, they are fairly mnemonic. I intend to maintain these codes, posting changes on the "Statoids Web Page" at the URL <www.mindspring.com/~gwil/statoids.html>. When world changes occur, I will create a new code for every subdivision (or "statoid") that has a different territorial extent than before, except for minor boundary adjustments. I will avoid reusing codes for as long as possible.

For data interchange, by electronic means or printed forms, subdivisions can be represented using just the four letters. For ease of readability, I suggest separating the first two letters from the last two with a period. Thus, the abbreviation for New York State could be written "US.NY".

One advantage to this system is that it can be further extended. I hope in the future to create a worldwide system of city codes, formed by suffixing a three-letter code to the four-letter subdivision code. For example, Abergavenny, Wales, might be abbreviated "GB.GW.AGV", which breaks down as GB for United Kingdom (ISO code), GW for Gwent (from my 4LSC), and AGV for Abergavenny.

F All dates are written in the form yyyy-mm-dd (if available; alternatively, yyyy-mm or yyyy). There are several advantages to using this format. It is logical: like ordinary decimal notation, it puts the most significant digits first. A column of dates in this format can easily be checked for chronological order. Also, this format conforms to the international standard for representation of dates, ISO 8601, and is widely used throughout the world. A year preceded by a tilde (~yyyy) means an approximate date.

G An enclave is a small patch of some other country's territory that is completely surrounded by your country. An exclave is a patch of your country that is surrounded by another. In the country entries, I avoid the word exclave, which is rare in nontechnical usage. In the "territorial extent" sections, however, I have mentioned only exclaves. For example, to find Baarle-Hertog, a small part of Belgium surrounded by the Netherlands, look under Belgium, not Netherlands.

A Note to the Reader

The numerical data provided herein should be considered approximate. Different countries will, in general, use different methods for taking censuses or surveying areas. They may have different rules for the treatment of nomads, foreign nationals residing in the country, or students and military personnel who live in one administrative subdivision but vote in another. Some countries may use statistical methods to adjust for an undercount in the census. The areas reported may or may not include inland or coastal waters. Less developed countries may not have accurate data available. The reason for including these figures is primarily to help the reader resolve any doubt as to which subdivision, at which point in history, is being referred to by some other document.

For these reasons, and because of rounding, columns of figures may not add up to the total given. In those cases, the printed total is probably more accurate than the numerical sum would be.

Placename etymologies are often controversial. I have consulted reliable reference works for the etymologies provided, but many details and alternate hypotheses have been omitted. The value of the name origins is that they provide mental hooks to help in the retention of information; also, in some cases, they hint at geographical relationships. However, if completeness and accuracy are essential, one should use specialized reference books on the subject.

It is impossible for anyone writing a book such as this to rely entirely on direct observation. I had to depend largely on reference books. Most of the references I used were highly reliable, but probably none of them was 100 percent accurate. I was able to eliminate some of the errors by consulting multiple sources; by making informed judgments of their relative reliability; and even by comparing them to direct observation, in some cases. On the other hand, I may have introduced errors by miscopying or misinterpreting my sources. I would welcome corrections. For them to be useful, they must, however, be documented. Documentation could be a photocopy of a page from an official government publication, with bibliographic information; it could also be a current URL for a government-maintained Web page. You can communicate with me at the e-mail address gwil@mindspring.com, or by writing to me in care of McFarland. There will be a link to my e-mail address on my "Statoids Web Page."

Registry of Countries

This list contains current, obsolete, and foreign names of countries (exonyms). As far as possible, forms of names incorporating generics such as Republic or Islands have been omitted or inverted. When several names for the same country are adjacent in the list and are recognizably similar, I have chosen only the most common form.

Abyssinia	120	Amerikanische Jungferninseln	410
Aden	413	Amerikanische kleinere abgelegene	
Ækvatorialguinea	117	Inseln im Pazifik	399
Afars and Issas	107	Amerikanisch-Ozeanien	399
Afghanistan	19	Amerikanisch-Samoa	26
Africa del Sud	334	Andorra	27
Africa Occidental Española	412	Anglo-Egyptian Sudan	344
Africa Orientale Italiana	118, 120, 332	Angola	27
Africa Oriental, Estado de	251	Anguilla	29
Afrique du Sud	334	Antarctica	29
Afrique Équatoriale Française	138	Antigua and Barbuda	31
Afrique Occidentale Française	160, 233, 236, 324	Antilhas Holandesas	260
Ägypten	113	Antillas Neerlandesas	260
Alankomaat	257	A.O.F.	233, 324
Alaouites	354	Aotearoa	261
al-'Arabiya as-Sa'udiya	323	Äquatorialguinea	117
al-Bahrayn	43	Arab Federation	202
Albania	21	Arabia Saudita	323
Alemania	141	Arabiemiirikunnat	381
Algeria	23	Arabie Saoudite	323
al 'Iraqia	184	Argelia	23
al-Jazairiya	23	Argentina	31
al-Kuwait	210	Armenia	34
Allemagne	141	Aruba	35
al-Libiya	219	Ashanti	147
al-Lubnaniya	215	Ashmore and Cartier Islands	35
al-Maghrebia	247	Asir	323
al-Qumur	91	as-Suriya	354
Alsír	23	Ástralía	35
Alto Volta	65	Äthiopien	120
al Urduniya	202	at-Tunisiya	367
al-Yamaniya	413	Äussere Mongolei	245
American Samoa	26	Austerrike	38
Amerikaanse Maagdeneilanden	410	Australia	35
Amerikaans Samoa	26	Austria	38

Nýja-Sjáland	261	Reino Unido	382
Oekraine	378	Reunião	303
Oezbekistan	401	Réunion	303
Olanda	257	Rhodesia	417
Oman	274	Rhodesia and Nyasaland	416, 417
Omán de la Tregua	381	Rhodesia protectorate	416
Oostenrijk	38	Rijeka	190
Oost Timor	111	Río de Oro	412
Orange Free State	334	Río Muni	117
Orange River Colony	334	Romania	304
Österreich	38	Rossiiskaya Federatsiya	307
Østrig	38	Roumanie	304
Ottoman Empire	369	Royaume-Uni	382
Oubangui-Chari	76	Ruanda	317
Ouganda	376	Ruanda-Urundi	67, 317
Outer Mongolia	245	Rumänien	304
Ozbekiston Respublikasy	401	Ruotsi	349
Países Bajos	257	Russia	307
Päiväntasaajan Guinea	117	Russia Bianca	46
Pakistan	44, 174, 275	Russland	307
Palau	277	Rwanda	317
Palestine	188	Ryssland	307
Panama	278	Saara Ocidental	412
Papua New Guinea	279	Saarland	141
Paquistão	275	Sádi-Arabía	323
Paracel Islands	81	Saguia el Hamra	412
Paraguay	281	Sahara Español	412
Pays-Bas	257	Sahara Occidental	412
Pérou	283	Saint Christopher and Nevis	318
Persia	182	Sainte-Hélène	318
Peru	283	Sainte-Lucie	319
Philippines	285	Saint Helena	318
Pitcairn	292	Saint Kitts–Nevis	318
Pohjois-Korea	207	Saint Kitts–Nevis–Anguilla	29, 318
Poland	292	Saint Lucia	319
Polen	292	Saint-Marin	322
Polinesia Francesa	136	Saint Pierre and Miquelon	320
Pologne	292	Saint-Siège	404
Polska	292	Saint Vincent	320
Polynésie française	136	Sakartvelos Respublika	140
Pondicherry	174	Saksa	141
Portogallo	296	Salomón, Islas	331
Porto Rico	299	Salvador	116
Portugal	296	Sambia	416
Portuguese East Africa	251	Sameinuðu arabísku furstadæmin	381
Portuguese Guinea	161	Samoa	321
Portuguese India	174	Samoa Americana	26
Portuguese Timor	111	Samoa Estadounidense	26
Portuguese West Africa	27	Samoa i Sisifo	321
Puerto Rico	299	Samoa Occidentali	321
Puola	292	San Cristóbal y Nieves	318
Qatar	302	Sankt Helena	318
Quênia	205	Sankti Kristófer og Nevis	318
Quirguízia	211	Sankti Lúsía	319
Ranska	128	Sankt Kitts und Nevis	318

AFGHANISTAN

ISO = AF/FIPS = AF   Languages = Pashtu, Dari   Time zone = +4:30   Capital = Kabul

The external borders of Afghanistan have remained almost unchanged through the twentieth century. Its division into provinces, on the other hand, has changed frequently. The tendency has been to create more provinces over the years. Part of the border with Pakistan is in dispute.

Other names of country: Afeganistão (Portuguese); Afganistan (Dutch, Finnish, Icelandic); Afganistán (Spanish); Dowlat-e Eslami-ye Afghanestan (formal-Pashtu); Islamic State of Afghanistan (formal).

Meaning of name: Land of the Afghani (ethnic name).

division	abv	FIPS	ISO	population	area-km	area-mi	capital
Badakhshan	BD	AF01	BDS	520,620	46,710	18,035	Feyzabad
Badghis	BG	AF02	BDG	244,346	21,854	8,438	Qal'eh-ye Now
Baghlan	BL	AF03	BGL	516,921	17,106	6,605	Baghlan
Balkh	BK	AF30	BAL	609,590	11,833	4,569	Mazar-e Sharif
Bamian	BM	AF05	BAM	280,859	17,411	6,722	Bamian
Farah	FH	AF06	FRA	245,474	58,834	22,716	Farah
Faryab	FB	AF07	FYB	609,703	22,274	8,600	Meymaneh
Ghazni	GZ	AF08	GHA	676,416	32,902	12,704	Ghazni
Ghowr	GR	AF09	GHO	353,494	38,658	14,926	Chaghcharan
Helmand	HM	AF10	HEL	541,508	61,816	23,867	Lashgar Gah
Herat	HR	AF11	HER	808,224	51,711	19,966	Herat
Jowzjan	JW	AF31	JOW	615,877	25,548	9,864	Sheberghan
Kabul	KB	AF13	KAB	1,517,909	4,583	1,770	Kabul
Kandahar	KD	AF23	KAN	597,954	49,430	19,085	Kandahar
Kapisa	KP	AF14	KAP	262,039	1,871	722	Mahmud-e Eraqi
Konar	KO	AF15	KNR	261,604	10,477	4,045	Asadabad
Konduz	KZ	AF24	KDZ	582,600	7,825	3,021	Konduz
Laghman	LM	AF16	LAG	325,010	7,209	2,783	Mehtar Lam
Lowgar	LW	AF17	LOW	226,234	4,411	1,703	Baraki Barak
Nangarhar	NG	AF18	NAN	781,619	7,614	2,940	Jalalabad
Nimruz	NM	AF19	NIM	108,418	41,347	15,964	Zaranj
Oruzgan	OR	AF20	ORU	464,556	28,756	11,103	Tarin Kowt
Paktia	PA	AF21	PIA	506,264	17,528	6,768	Gardez
Paktika	PK	AF29	PKA	256,470	19,336	7,466	Orgun
Parvan	PR	AF22	PAR	527,987	9,399	3,629	Charikar
Samangan	SM	AF32	SAM	273,864	16,220	6,263	Aybak
Sar-e Pol	SP	AF33	SAR	— —	— —	— —	Sar-e Pol
Takhar	TK	AF26	TAK	543,818	12,373	4,777	Taloqan
Vardak	VR	AF27	WAR	300,796	9,638	3,721	Kowt-e-Ashrow
Zabol	ZB	AF28	ZAB	187,612	17,289	6,675	Qalat
				13,747,786	671,963	259,447	

Status: These divisions are all velayat (provinces).

Abv: Two-letter code for international compatibility (created by the author).

FIPS: Codes from FIPS PUB 10-4.

ISO: Codes from ISO 3166-2.

Population: 1982 estimates. More recent figures are unavailable or unreliable because of unsettled political conditions in Afghanistan. Thus, there are no solid data for the province of Sar-e Pol, which was created in about 1990.

Area-km: Square kilometers.

Area-mi: Square miles.

Territorial extent: Badakhshan province contains the Wakhan Corridor (Vakhan), a narrow strip of land extending eastward.

Change history:

~1970   Re-organization split 14 provinces into 29.

~1975   Name of Chakhansur province changed to Nimruz.

~1975   Katawaz-Urgun province merged with Paktia, forming a larger Paktia province.

~1978   Capital of Kapisa moved from Tagab to Mahmud-e-Eraqi.

~1982   Paktika formed from parts of Ghazni and Paktia.

~1990   Sar-e Pol formed from parts of Balkh, Jowzjan, and Samangan.

~1990   Many provincial boundaries adjusted. For example, northern Samangan, including the city of
         Kholm, transferred to Balkh.

~1991   The CIA World Factbook says there "may" be a new province named Nurestan.

~1995   The CIA World Factbook says there "may" be a new province named Khowst.

Other names of subdivisions: Place names in the vernacular are written in Arabic characters. There are various methods for transliteration from Arabic to Latin alphabets, producing fairly predictable variant names.

Badghis: Badghes, Badghisat (variant)

Baghlan: Kataghan (obsolete ↑)

Balkh: Mazar-i-Sharif, Mazar (obsolete ↑)

Bamian: Bamiyan, Bamyan (variant)

Faryab: Fariab (variant); Maimana (obsolete ↑)

Ghowr: Ghor, Ghur, Ghore (variant)

Helmand: Girishk (obsolete)

Jowzjan: Jawzjan, Jouzjan, Jozjan (variant); Shibarghan (obsolete ↑)

Kabul: Kabol (variant)

Kandahar: Qandahar (variant)

Konar: Konarha, Kunarha (variant)

Konduz: Kondoz, Qonduz, Kunduz (variant)

Lowgar: Logar (variant)

Nangarhar: Ningrahar (variant); Eastern Province (obsolete)

Nimruz: Nimrooz, Nimroze (variant); Chakhansur (obsolete)

Oruzgan: Uruzgan (variant)

Paktia: Paktiya, Paktya, Southern Province (obsolete)

Parvan: Parwan (variant); Charikar (obsolete ↑)

Sar-e Pol: Saripol (variant)

Vardak: Wardak (variant)

Zabol: Zabul (variant)

↑ = *name applied to a larger area containing the province*

ALBANIA

ISO = AL/FIPS = AL   Language = Albanian   Time zone = +1 [d]   Capital = Tirana

Albania was still part of Turkey at the beginning of the 20th century. It declared its independence in 1912. The country went through several forms of government, including occupation during the World Wars, until it became a republic on 1946-01-11.

Other names of country: Albanía (Icelandic); Albânia (Portuguese); Albanie (French); Albanië (Dutch); Albanien (Danish, German, Swedish); Republic of Albania (formal–English); Republika e Shqipërisë (formal); Shqipëria (Albanian = land of the men of the eagle).

Origin of name: Ancient inhabitants were called Albanoi by Ptolemy.

name	ISO	FIPS	population	area-km	area-mi	capital
Berat	BR	AL01	173,700	1,027	397	Berat
Bulqizë	BU	——	——	——	——	
Delvinë	DL	——	——	——	——	Delvinë
Devoll	DV	——	——	——	——	
Dibër	DI	AL02	148,200	1,568	605	Peshkopi
Durrës	DR	AL03	242,500	848	327	Durrës
Elbasan	EL	AL04	238,600	1,481	572	Elbasan
Fier	FR	AL05	239,700	1,175	454	Fier
Gjirokastër	GJ	AL06	65,500	1,137	439	Gjirokastër
Gramsh	GR	AL07	43,800	695	268	Gramsh
Has	HA	——	——	——	——	
Kavajë	KA	——	——	——	——	Kavajë
Kolonjë	ER	AL08	24,600	805	311	Ersekë
Korçë	KO	AL09	213,200	2,181	842	Korçë
Krujë	KR	AL10	105,300	607	234	Krujë
Kuçovë	KC	——	——	——	——	
Kukës	KU	AL11	99,400	1,330	514	Kukës
Laç	LA	——	——	——	——	Laç
Lezhë	LE	AL12	61,100	479	185	Lezhë
Librazhd	LB	AL13	70,800	1,013	391	Librazhd
Lushnjë	LU	AL14	132,200	712	275	Lushnjë
Malesia e Madhe	MM	——	——	——	——	
Mallakastër	MK	——	——	——	——	
Mat	MT	AL15	75,900	1,028	397	Burrel
Mirditë	MR	AL16	49,700	867	335	Rrëshen
Peqin	PQ*	——	——	——	——	Peqin
Përmet	PR	AL17	39,400	929	359	Përmet
Pogradec	PG	AL18	70,500	725	280	Pogradec
Pukë	PU	AL19	48,200	1,034	399	Pukë
Sarandë	SR	AL20	86,600	1,097	424	Sarandë
Shkodër	SH	AL21	233,000	2,528	976	Shkodër
Skrapar	SK	AL22	45,800	775	299	Çorovodë
Tepelenë	SP	AL23	49,100	817	315	Tepelenë
Tiranë	TR	AL28	363,100	1,238	478	Tiranë
Tropojë	BC	AL26	44,200	1,043	403	Bajram Curri
Vlorë	VL	AL27	174,000	1,609	621	Vlorë
			3,138,100	28,748	11,100	

* = *the draft standard lists PG for both Peqin and Pogradec; I changed the code for Peqin to make them distinct*

Status: All subdivisions are rrethet (districts; sing. rreth).

ISO: Codes from ISO 3166-2.

FIPS: Codes from FIPS PUB 10-4. (Data from the newest ten districts not yet available.)

Population: Average population of district in 1988.

Area-km: Square kilometers.

Area-mi: Square miles.

Note: Some sources mention two subdivisions named Tiranë: a district and a municipality (qytet). The FIPS standard merged them into a single district in 1991. There are no separate statistics available for the two entities.

Further subdivisions: There are about 3000 smaller divisions called lokalitet (pl. lokaliteteve).

Territorial extent: Vlorë includes Saseno (Sazan) Island.

Change history:

1912-11-28	Albania, consisting of the vilayet of Scutari and parts of Monastir and Yanina, declared independence from Turkey.
1923	Albania acquired a strip of territory in the south from Greece.
~1925	Albania had the following prefectures, further subdivided into 57 districts. Kukës was later renamed Kosovo. Populations are shown for the 1930 census and 1941 estimates.

name	capital	1930c	1941	area-km	later became these districts
Berat	Berat	142,616	169,431	3,666	Berat, Fier, Lushnjë, Skrapar
Dibër	Peshkopijë	86,992	83,491	2,151	Dibër, Mat
Durrës	Durrës	77,890	90,243	1,550	Durrës, Krujë
Elbasan	Elbasan	111,422	110,447	3,539	Elbasan, Gramsh, Librazhd
Gjinokastër	Gjinokastër	143,926	159,695	4,125	Gjirokastër, Përmet, Sarandë, Tepelenë
Korçë	Korçë	147,536	169,234	3,750	Kolonjë, Korçë, Pogradec
Kukës	Kukës	49,081	46,666	2,038	Kukës, Tropojë
Shkodër	Scutari	132,336	160,929	5,560	Lezhë, Mirditë, Pukë, Shkodër
Tirana	Tirana	57,808	59,160	911	Tiranë
Vlonë	Vlonë	53,461	56,607	1,448	Vlorë
		1,003,068	1,105,903	28,738	

1949   A new set of subdivisions was implemented. No details available.
1953   The ten prefectures were restored.
1958–1959   The ten prefectures were re-organized into 26 districts.
~1980   Ersekë renamed Kolonjë.
~1991–06   Bulqizë district split from Dibër; Delvinë district split from Sarandë; Devoll district split from Korçë; Has district split from Kukës; Kavajë district split from Durrës; Kuçovë district split from Berat; Laç district split from Krujë; Malesia e Madhe district split from Shkodër; Mallakastër district split from Fier; Peqin district split from Elbasan.

Origins of names:

Durrës: from Ancient Greek *dyrrachion*, possibly meaning dangerous cliffs
Elbasan: Turkish *el*: the people, *basan*: dominating (originally a fortress)
Korçë: South Slavic *gorica*: small mountain
Tiranë: from Ancient Greek *Tyrrenos*: Etruscans; or, named after Tehran, Iran, to commemorate a victory
Vlorë: from Ancient Greek *aulon*: narrow passage, strait

Other names of subdivisions: The Italian names are often used by Western Europeans in general.

Dibër: Dibra, Dibrë (variant)
Durrës: Durresi, Durrsi (variant); Durazzo (Italian)
Gjirokastër: Gjinokastër (variant); Argirocastro (Italian); Argyrocastro, Argyrokastron (Greek)
Kolonjë: Ersekë (obsolete); Kolonja (variant)
Korçë: Coriza, Corizza, Koritsa, Koritza (Italian); Korça (variant); Kortscha (German)
Kukës: Kosova, Kossovo (obsolete)
Lezhë: Alessio (Italian); Lezha (variant)
Lushnjë: Lushenjë, Lushnja (variant)
Shkodër: Shkodra, Skodër (variant); Scutari (Italian)
Tiranë: Tirana (Italian)
Vlorë: Vlona, Vlora, Vlonë (variant); Valona (Italian)

Population history:

name	1960c	1970c	1973	1978	1982	1988a
Berat	85,000	115,000	124,300	140,600	154,000	173,700
Dibrë	78,000	99,000	106,800	122,000	134,800	148,200
Durrës	127,000	169,000	182,400	202,000	217,000	242,500
Elbasan	105,000	142,000	154,700	187,700	208,000	238,600
Fier	112,000	158,000	171,500	195,000	212,000	239,700
Gjirokastër	44,000	51,000	53,500	57,100	60,300	65,500
Gramsh	20,000	27,000	29,400	34,500	38,000	43,800
Kolonjë	17,000	19,000	19,200	21,000	22,300	24,600
Korçë	139,000	168,000	175,400	187,500	199,000	213,200
Krujë	43,000	69,000	75,600	84,600	93,000	105,300
Kukës	48,000	65,000	71,400	75,400	86,000	99,400
Lezhë	27,000	37,000	40,500	48,200	53,000	61,100
Librazhd	36,000	44,000	48,500	56,300	63,000	70,800
Lushnjë	66,000	91,000	94,100	106,400	115,400	132,200
Mat	39,000	50,000	53,500	60,600	67,000	75,900
Mirditë	17,000	27,000	29,400	40,500	45,000	49,700
Përmet	27,000	30,000	31,700	34,100	36,400	39,400 ➤

name	1960c	1970c	1973	1978	1982	1988a
Pogradec	36,000	46,000	49,300	56,500	62,000	70,500
Pukë	23,000	29,000	32,800	40,100	45,000	48,200
Sarandë	48,000	62,000	66,500	72,000	76,700	86,600
Shkodër	128,000	167,000	178,500	191,400	206,200	233,000
Skrapar	20,000	28,000	30,800	37,800	42,000	45,800
Tepelenë	26,000	35,000	37,800	41,600	45,200	49,100
Tiranë	194,000	254,000	272,000	286,200	310,000	363,100
Tropojë	21,000	28,000	30,500	36,400	39,800	44,200
Vlorë	101,000	126,000	133,500	144,900	155,000	174,000
	1,627,000	2,136,000	2,293,600	2,560,400	2,786,100	3,138,100

a = *average population for the year;* c = *census*

ALGERIA

ISO = DZ/FIPS = AG   Language = Arabic   Time zone = +1   Capital = Algiers

At the beginning of the 20th century, Algeria was a French colony. The borders, except near the Mediterranean coast, were ill-defined. The administrative division into departments and territories was based on French practice. During much of the colonial period, Algerian departments had a legal status which was supposedly equal to that of the European departments of France. Algeria became independent in 1962. Since then, it has re-organized twice. After the most recent change, in 1984, the new subdivisions were called wilayas. The southern border has been clearly defined, but the southern parts of the Tunisian and Moroccan borders are still in dispute.

Under French administration, the official division names were in French. More recently, the official names have been in Arabic, and many different rules have been used to transliterate them into the Roman alphabet. The most common variants are shown in the table of variants. Names of capitals are always the same as the name of the subdivision, except as noted.

Other names of country: Algerie (Norwegian); Algérie (French); Algerien (German); Algeriet (Danish, Swedish); Algerije (Dutch); al-Jumhuriya al-Jazairiya ad-Dimuqratiya ash-Shabiya (formal); Alsír (Icelandic); Argelia (Spanish); Argélia (Portuguese); Democratic and Popular Republic of Algeria (formal–English); República Argelina Democrática y Popular (formal–Spanish).

Origin of name: Arabic *al-Jazairiya* from capital city Algiers, which comes from Arabic *al-jaza'ir:* the islands, for four islands in the harbor (now connected to the mainland by jetties).

division	ab	ISO	FIPS	population	division	ab	ISO	FIPS	population
Adrar	AR	01	AG34	216,931	Ghardaïa	GR	47	AG45	215,955
Aïn Defla	AD	44	AG35	536,205	Guelma	GL	24	AG23	353,329
Aïn Témouchent	AT	46	AG36	271,454	Illizi	IL	33	AG46	19,698
Alger	AL	16	AG01	1,687,579	Jijel	JJ	18	AG24	471,319
Annaba	AN	23	AG37	453,951	Khenchela	KH	40	AG47	243,733
Batna	BT	05	AG03	757,059	Laghouat	LG	03	AG25	215,183
Béchar	BC	08	AG38	183,896	Mascara	MC	29	AG26	562,806
Béjaïa	BJ	06	AG18	697,669	Médéa	MD	26	AG06	650,623
Biskra	BS	07	AG19	429,217	Mila	ML	43	AG48	511,047
Blida	BL	09	AG20	704,462	Mostaganem	MG	27	AG07	504,124
Bordj Bou Arréridj	BB	34	AG39	429,009	Msila	MS	28	AG27	605,578
Bouira	BU	10	AG21	525,460	Naama	NA	45	AG49	112,858
Boumerdès	BM	35	AG40	646,870	Oran	OR	31	AG09	916,578
Chlef	CH	02	AG41	679,717	Ouargla	OG	30	AG50	286,696
Constantine	CO	25	AG04	662,330	Oum el Bouaghi	OB	04	AG29	402,683
Djelfa	DJ	17	AG22	490,240	Relizane	RE	48	AG51	545,061
El Bayadh	EB	32	AG42	155,494	Saïda	SD	20	AG10	235,240
El Oued	EO	39	AG43	379,512	Sétif	SF	19	AG12	997,482
El Tarf	ET	36	AG44	276,836	Sidi Bel Abbès	SB	22	AG30	444,047 ➤

division	ab	ISO	FIPS	population	division	ab	ISO	FIPS	population
Skikda	SK	21	AG31	619,094	Tipaza	TP	42	AG55	615,140
Souk Ahras	SA	41	AG52	298,236	Tissemsilt	TS	38	AG56	227,542
Tamanghasset	TM	11	AG53	94,219	Tizi Ouzou	TO	15	AG14	931,501
Tébessa	TB	12	AG33	409,317	Tlemcen	TL	13	AG15	707,453
Tiaret	TR	14	AG13	574,786					22,971,558
Tindouf	TN	37	AG54	16,339					

Status: These divisions are wilayat (provinces). Capitals all have the same name as their province.

Ab: Two-letter code for international compatibility (created by the author).

ISO: Codes from ISO DIS 3166-2.

FIPS: Codes from FIPS PUB 10-4.

Population: 1987 census.

Further subdivisions: The provinces are subdivided into dayrat (municipalities). Under French administration, the country was divided into départements (departments), which were subdivided into arrondissements, which in turn were subdivided into communes.

Origins of names:

Adrar: Tamashek *adrar*: mountain

Alger: Arabic *al-jaza'ir*: the islands, for four islands in the harbor

Annaba: corruption of Arabic *madinat al-'unnab*: city of the jujube tree

Béchar: after Wadi Bashshar, possibly from Arabic *bashar*: to bring good news (i.e., finding water)

Béjaïa: ethnic name, possibly from Arabic *baqaya*: survivors

Constantine: rebuilt in 311 by Roman emperor Constantine the Great

El Oued: = the Wadi (intermittent stream)

Oran: Arabic *Wahran* (name of a Berber chief)

Sétif: ancient Sitifi, possibly from Berber *sedif*: black

Sidi Bel Abbès: Arabic *Saydi Bal-'A bbas* (a person's honorific and name)

Skikda: Arabic corruption of Latin Rusicade, from Punic *ruš*: cape

Tizi-Ouzou: Berber *tizi*: mountain pass, *uzzu*: prickly furze

Tlemcen: Arabic *tilimsan*: place of the rushes

Change history: At the beginning of the 20th century, the area roughly north of the Atlas Mountains was divided into three departments, whose status was nominally on a par with the departments of European France. Their names were Alger (English: Algiers), Constantine, and Oran. Each department also administered two territoires (territories) in the south.

1902-12-24 The six territories were consolidated into a unit called Territoires du Sud (no capital). The result was three departments and one territory. The departments were divided into arrondissements, as shown below.

name	area-km	arrondissements
Alger	54,861	Alger, Aumale, Blida, Médéa, Miliana, Orléansville, Tizi-Ouzou
Constantine	87,578	Batna, Bône, Bougie, Constantine, Guelma, Philippeville, Sétif
Oran	67,262	Mascara, Mostaganem, Oran, Sidi Bel Abbès, Tiaret, Tlemcen
Territoires du Sud	1,981,750	
	2,191,451	

1905-08-14 Territoires du Sud organized into four territories: Aïn Sefra, Ghardaia, Oasis (no capital), and Touggourt.

1955-08-07 Bône department formed by taking the eastern arrondissements of Constantine department: Bône and Guelma.

1956-06-28 The three northern departments of 1955 were restored and given the status of igamies. (An igamie is the jurisdiction of an igame, which is an acronym for *inspecteur général de l'administration en mission extraordinaire* = administrative inspector general on special mission.) Each igamie was subdivided into four new departments. The departments were further subdivided into arrondissements.

1957-05-20 More arrondissements were created.

1957-08-07 Territoires du Sud divided into two departments: Saoura and Oasis.

1959-11-07 Saïda split from Tiaret to form a new department. This table shows the resulting subdivision of Algeria. Note: total area has changed from 1902 because of border adjustments in desert areas. Arr56 = number of arrondissements after 1956-06-28; arr57 = number of arrondissements after 1957-05-20. FIPS = code from FIPS PUB 10-3.

department	igamie	area-km	arr56	arr57	FIPS
Alger	Alger	3,398	2	3	AG01
Batna	Constantine	37,179	3	6	AG03
Bône	Constantine	24,760	4	6	AG02
Constantine	Constantine	19,580	4	8	AG04
Médéa	Alger	61,264	3	6	AG06
Mostaganem	Oran	11,111	3	6	AG07
Oasis		1,301,561			AG08
Oran	Oran	16,799	3	5	AG09
Orléansville	Alger	12,261	4	6	AG05
Saïda	Oran	56,420			AG10
Saoura		779,797			AG11
Sétif	Constantine	18,117	3	9	AG12
Tiaret	Oran	25,659	2	5	AG13
Tizi-Ouzou	Alger	5,719	4	6	AG14
Tlemcen	Oran	8,120	2	5	AG15
		2,381,745	37	71	

1962-07-01	Algeria became independent from France.
~1962	Name of Bône department changed to Annaba.
1964	Name of Orléansville department changed to El Asnam.
~1978	Fifteen departments re-organized to form thirty-one. The resulting division was as shown. New FIPS codes were assigned to the departments with new names.

department	area-km	FIPS	formed from	department	area-km	FIPS	formed from
Adrar	422,498	AG16	Oasis, Saoura	Médéa	8,704	AG06	Médéa
Alger	786	AG01	Alger	Mostaganem	7,024	AG07	Mostaganem
Annaba	3,489	AG02	Annaba	M'Sila	19,825	AG27	Batna, Médéa, Sétif
Batna	14,882	AG03	Batna	Oran	1,820	AG09	Oran
Béchar	306,000	AG17	Saoura	Ouargla	559,234	AG28	Oasis
Béjaïa	3,444	AG18	Sétif	Oum el Bouaghi	8,123	AG29	Constantine
Biskra	109,728	AG19	Oasis, Batna	Saïda	106,777	AG10	Oran, Saïda, Saoura
Blida	3,704	AG20	Alger, El Asnam	Sétif	10,350	AG12	Sétif
Bouira	4,517	AG21	Médéa, Tizi-Ouzou	Sidi Bel Abbès	11,648	AG30	Oran
El Asnam	8,677	AG05	El Asnam	Skikda	4,748	AG31	Constantine
Constantine	3,562	AG04	Constantine	Tamanrasset	556,000	AG32	Oasis
Djelfa	22,905	AG22	Batna, Médéa, Oasis, Tiaret	Tébessa	16,575	AG33	Annaba, Batna
Guelma	8,624	AG23	Annaba	Tiaret	23,456	AG13	El Asnam, Tiaret
Jijel	3,704	AG24	Constantine, Sétif	Tizi-Ouzou	3,756	AG14	Tizi-Ouzou
Laghouat	112,052	AG25	Oasis, Tiaret	Tlemcen	9,284	AG15	Oran, Tlemcen
Mascara	5,846	AG26	Mostaganem, Oran		2,381,742		

~1980	Name of El Asnam department changed to Chlef.
1984-02-04	Thirty-one departments re-organized to form 48 provinces (as shown in the first table). The new provinces were predominantly formed by taking the old departments as they were, or by splitting them into two provinces. Aïn Defla split from Chlef; Aïn Témouchent split from Sidi Bel Abbès; Bordj Bou Arréridj split from Sétif; Boumerdès formed from parts of Alger and Tizi Ouzou; El Bayadh split from Saïda; El Oued split from Biskra; El Tarf formed from parts of Annaba and Guelma; Ghardaïa split from Laghouat; Illizi split from Ouargla; Khenchela formed from parts of Oum el Bouaghi and Tébessa; Mila formed from parts of Constantine, Jijel, Oum el Bouaghi, and Sétif; Naama split from Saïda; Relizane split from Mostaganem; Souk Ahras split from Guelma; Tindouf split from Béchar; Tipaza split from Blida; Tissemsilt formed from parts of Alger and Tiaret.

Other names of subdivisions: The boundaries of subdivisions have changed, although the names may have stayed the same. Since the subdivision name is usually the same as the name of its capital, the easiest way to track the changes is to consider them as city names. Also note that diacritical marks may be different, depending on the method of transliteration used.

Adrar: Duperré (obsolete)

Alger: Dzayer, Djezaïr (variant); Algeri (Italian); Algiers (English); Algier (Danish, German); Argel (Portuguese, Spanish); al-Jazair, al-Djazair (Arabic)

Annaba: Bône (obsolete)

Béchar: Colomb-Béchar (obsolete)

Béjaïa: Bougie, Bedjaya (French); Bidjaia (variant); Bugia (Italian)

Biskra: Beskra (variant)

Blida: El Boulaïda, al-Boulaida (variant)

Bordj Bou Arréridj: Bordj Bou Ariridj (variant)

Boumerdès: Boumerdas (variant)

Chlef: El Asnam, Orléansville (obsolete); Chelif, Ech Cheliff (variant)

Constantine: Costatina (Italian); Qoussantina, Qacentina (variant)

Djelfa: El Djelfa (variant)

El Bayadh: El Bayad, El Beyyadh (variant); Géryville (obsolete)

El Oued: El Ouadi, El Wad (variant)

El Tarf: Et Tarf (variant)

Ghardaïa: Ghardaya (variant)

Illizi: Polignac, Fort Polignac (obsolete); Ilizi (variant)

Jijel: Djidjel (variant); Djidjelli (obsolete)

Khenchela: Khenchla (variant)

Mascara: Mouaskar (variant)

Médéa: El Mediyya, Lemdiyya (variant)

Mostaganem: Mestghanem (variant)

Oasis: Oasis Sahariennes (variant); Saharan Oases (English)

Oran: Ouahran, Ouahrane, Wahran (variant); Orano (Italian)

Ouargla: Wargla (variant)

Oum el Bouaghi: Oum el Bouagui (variant); Canrobert (obsolete)

Relizane: Ghelizane, Ghilizane (variant)

Sétif: Stif (variant)

Skikda: Philippeville (obsolete); Skidda (variant)

Souk Ahras: Souq Ahras (variant)

Tamanghasset: Tamanrasset, Tamenghest (variant); Fort Laperrine (obsolete)

Tébessa: Tbessa (variant)

Tiaret: Tihert (variant)

Tissemsilt: Vialar (obsolete)

Tlemcen: Tilimsene, Tlemsane, Tilimsen (variant)

AMERICAN SAMOA

ISO = AS/FIPS = AQ   Languages = English, Samoan   Time zone = -11   Capital = Pago Pago

On 1900-02-19, the interested European powers recognized American Samoa as a territory of the United States. Swain's Island was added in 1925.

Other names of country: Amerikaans Samoa (Dutch); Amerikanisch-Samoa (German); Amerikansk Samoa (Norwegian); Amerika Samoa (Samoan); Samoa américaines (French); Samoa Americana (Portuguese, Spanish); Samoa americane (Italian); Samoa Estadounidense (Spanish); Territory of American Samoa (formal).

Meaning of name: American possessions in Samoan Islands.

division	ab	FIPS	population	km	mi	islands included
Eastern Tutuila	ET	010	17,311	65	25	Aunuu, Tutuila (part)
Manu'a	MA	020	1,732	57	22	Ofu, Olosega, Tau
Western Tutuila	WT	050	13,227	73	28	Tutuila (part)
Unorganized	UU	*	29	4	2	Swain's Island, Rose Island
			32,399	197	76	

* = in addition to the codes listed, 030 is used for Rose Island and 040 for Swain's Island

Status: The first three divisions are districts. The fourth division has no status.

Ab: Two-letter code for international compatibility (created by the author).

FIPS: Codes from FIPS PUB 6-4, representing second-level administrative divisions of the United States. The codes for American Samoa in FIPS PUB 5-2 are AS (alpha) and 60 (numeric). When the FIPS 5-2 and 6-4 codes are concatenated, as in 60020 for Manu'a, the result is a code that uniquely identifies a county-equivalent unit in the United States.

Population: 1980 census.
Km: Square kilometers.
Mi: Square miles.
Further subdivisions: The territory is further subdivided into 15 counties.

ANDORRA

ISO = AD/FIPS=AN   Language = Catalan   Time zone = +1 [d]   Capital = Andorra la Vella

Andorra has been a joint fief of France and Spain throughout the 20th century.

Other names of country: Andorre (French); Principado de Andorra (formal–Spanish); Principat d'Andorra (formal); Principality of Andorra (formal–English).

Origin of name: possibly Navarrian *andurrial*: land covered with bushes, or Basque *ama*: ten, *iturri*: springs.

division	ISO	FIPS	km	mi	capital
Andorra la Vella	AN	AN01	59	23	Andorra
Canillo	CA	AN02	121	47	Canillo
Encamp	EN	AN03	74	29	Encamp
Escaldes-Engordany	EE	—	—	—	Les Escaldes-Engordany
La Massana	MA	AN04	61	24	La Massana
Ordino	OR	AN05	89	34	Ordino
Sant Julià de Lòria	JL	AN06	60	23	Sant Julià de Lòria
			464	179	

Status: All divisions are parròquies (parishes).
ISO: Codes from ISO 3166-2.
FIPS: Codes from FIPS PUB 10-4.
Km: Area in square kilometers.
Mi: Area in square miles.
Change history:

    1978   Escaldes-Engordany split from Andorra.

Variant names:

Andorra la Vella: Andorra (informal); Andorre-la-Vieille (French); Andorra la Vieja (Spanish) [Note: Vella is Catalan for "city," but the French and Spanish names treat it as if it meant "old."]

Escaldes-Engordany: Les Escaldes (variant)

ANGOLA

ISO = AO/FIPS = AO   Language = Portuguese   Time zone = +1   Capital = Luanda

In 1900, the area now known as Angola was Portuguese West Africa. By 1906, its boundaries were almost exactly the same as Angola's are today. Angola was an overseas province of Portugal until its independence on 1975-11-11.

Other names of country: Angóla (Icelandic); People's Republic of Angola (formal–English); República Popular de Angola (formal).

Origin of name: From N'gola, 16th century king.

division	abv	ISO	FIPS	population	area-km	area-mi	capital	colonial name of capital
Bengo	BO	BGO	AO19	196,100	31,371	12,112	Caxito	
Benguela	BG	BGU	AO01	656,600	31,788	12,273	Benguela	
Bié	BI	BIE	AO02	1,119,800	70,314	27,148	Kuito	Silva Pôrto
Cabinda	CB	CAB	AO03	152,100	7,270	2,807	Cabinda	
Cuando Cubango	CC	CCU	AO04	139,600	199,049	76,853	Menongue	Serpa Pinto
Cuanza Norte	CN	CNO	AO05	385,200	24,190	9,340	N'dalatando	Salazar
Cuanza Sul	CS	CUS	AO06	694,500	55,660	21,490	Sumbe	Novo Redondo
Cunene	CU	CNN	AO07	241,200	89,342	34,495	Ondjiva	
Huambo	HM	HUA	AO08	1,521,000	34,274	13,233	Huambo	Nova Lisboa
Huíla	HL	HUI	AO09	885,100	75,002	28,958	Lubango	Sá da Bandeira
Luanda	LU	LUA	AO20	1,588,600	2,418	934	Luanda	São Paulo de Loanda
Lunda Norte	LN	LNO	AO17	305,900	102,783	39,685	Lucapa	
Lunda Sul	LS	LSU	AO18	169,100	45,649	17,625	Saurimo	Henrique de Carvalho
Malanje	ML	MAL	AO12	906,000	97,602	37,684	Malanje	
Moxico	MX	MOX	AO14	319,300	223,023	86,110	Luena	Luso
Namibe	NA	NAM	AO13	107,300	58,137	22,447	Namibe	Moçâmedes
Uíge	UI	UIG	AO15	802,700	58,698	22,663	Uíge	Carmona
Zaire	ZA	ZAI	AO16	237,500	40,130	15,494	M'banza Congo	São Salvador do Congo
				10,427,600	1,246,700	481,354		

Status: These divisions are all províncias (provinces).
Abv: Two-letter code for international compatibility (created by the author).
ISO: Codes from ISO 3166-2.
FIPS: Codes from FIPS PUB 10-4.
Population: 1992 estimates.
Area-km: Square kilometers.
Area-mi: Square miles.
Smaller subdivisions: The provinces are divided into 139 districts.
Territorial extent: Cabinda is an enclave, separated from the rest of Angola by part of Zaire.
Origins of names:

Cabinda: from an ethnic group of the same name.
Luanda: from a native word *luanda* = tax. Shellfish caught there were sent as tribute to the king of Congo.

Namibe: from the Namib Desert (see also Namibia).
Zaire: from the Zaïre River, from Kikongo *nzadi* = river (see also Zaire).

Change history:

1900	The provinces were Benguella, Kongo, Loanda, Lunda, and Mossamedes.
1950	The provinces were Benguela, Bié, Huíla, Luanda (or Congo), and Malange. The provincial capitals were, respectively, Benguela, Silva Pôrto, Mossâmedes, Uíge, and Malange.
1951	Name of country changed from Portuguese West Africa to Angola.
Between 1950 and 1967,	Benguela was split into Benguela, Cuanza Sul, and Huambo; Bié was split into Bié-Cuando Cubango and Moxico; Huíla was split into Moçâmedes and Huíla; Luanda was split into Cabinda, Cuanza Norte, Luanda, Uíge and Zaire; and Malange was split into Lunda and Malange.
~1971	Bié-Cuando Cubango province (capital Silva Pôrto) split into Bié and Cuando Cubango.
1975-11-11	Angola changed from overseas province of Portugal to independent country.
~1975	Huíla province (capital Sá da Bandeira) split into Cunene and Huíla.
~1976	Name of capital of Zaïre province changed from São Salvador do Congo to M'banza Congo; name of capital of Cuanza Norte province changed from Vila Salazar to N'dalatando; name of capital of Bié province changed from Silva Pôrto to Bié.
~1980	Lunda province (capital Saurimo) split into Lunda Norte and Lunda Sul; name of capital of Bié province changed from Bié to Kuito.
1985	Name of Moçâmedes (province and capital) changed to Namibe; name of Malange province and city changed to Malanje; Luanda province (capital Luanda) split into Bengo and Luanda.

There have also been minor boundary changes.

Other names of subdivisions:

Luanda: Loanda (obsolete)
Malanje: Malange (variant)

Namibe: Moçâmedes, Mossamedes (obsolete)

ANGUILLA

ISO = AI/FIPS = AV   Language = English   Time zone = -4   Capital = The Valley

At the beginning of the 20th century, Anguilla was part of the Leeward Islands, a British colony which consisted of five presidencies. On 1956-06-30, each presidency became a separate colony. Anguilla belonged to the colony of St. Kitts-Nevis-Anguilla. Anguilla seceded unilaterally on 1967-06-16 from this colony. It was fully recognized as a separate dependency by the mother country on 1980-12-19.

Other names of country: Anguila (Dutch, Spanish).
Origin of name: Named by Columbus < Spanish *anguila* = eel, from the shape of the island.

division	abv	population	area-km	area-mi	capital
Anguilla	AI	6,897	155	60	The Valley

Status: This division is the whole of the country, treated as a division for compatibility.
Abv: Two-letter code for international compatibility (defined by the author).
Population: 1984 census.
Area-km: Square kilometers.
Area-mi: Square miles.
Territorial extent: Includes a few small islands and cays, among the larger: Dog Island, Prickly Pear Cays, Scrub Island, Seal Islands, Sombrero Island.

ANTARCTICA

ISO = AQ/FIPS = AY   Languages = several   Time zones = see text below   Capital = none

Several countries have laid claim to territory in Antarctica. The Antarctic Treaty took effect on 1961-06-23, having been ratified by all the claimant nations and a number of others. By its terms, all territorial disputes in Antarctica were suspended. The claimants were not required to relax their claims. No new claims would be allowed. The treaty would be renewed periodically. Until further disposal of the claims, the continent was open to all legitimate uses. The area covered by the treaty is everything south of latitude 60 degrees South. This encompasses all of the Antarctic continent and adjacent islands.

Time zone note: Antarctic research stations generally observe the same time standard as their supply bases. Palmer Station follows mainland Chile time (-4 [d]). Amundsen-Scott Station (at the South Pole), McMurdo Station, and Scott Station on Ross Island all follow New Zealand time (+12 [d]). This leads to the paradox that at the South Pole, where there is no daylight in the winter and nothing but daylight in the summer, clocks are set forward each spring and backward each fall to "save daylight."

Other names of country: Antarctique (French); Antarktis (Danish, German, Norwegian); Antártida (Portuguese, Spanish); Antartide (Italian).
Origin of name: Antipode of the Arctic. Arctic < Greek *arktos*: bear (for the constellations of the Great and Little Bear).

claim	abv	West end	East end	claim	abv	West end	East end
Unclaimed	NT	150° W.	90° W.	Norway Claim	NO	20° W.	45° E.
Chile Claim	CL	90° W.	80° W.	Australia Claim	AU	45° E.	136° E.
Chile/UK Claim	CU	80° W.	74° W.	"		142° E.	160° E.
Chile/UK/Argentina Claim	CA	74° W.	53° W.	France Claim	FR	136° E.	142° E.
Argentina/UK Claim	AK	53° W.	25° W.	New Zealand Claim	NZ	160° E.	150° W.
United Kingdom Claim	UK	25° W.	20° W.				

Status: These divisions are obviously not the administrative divisions of a political whole. However, they appear to be the most useful way of subdividing Antarctica.

Abv: Two-letter code for international compatibility (defined by the author).

West end and East end are the lines of longitude which bound each claim.

Territorial extent: Unclaimed includes Marie Byrd Land, part of Ellsworth Land, and Peter I Island. Peter I Island is an exception to the unclaimed status. It is claimed by Norway as a dependency.

Chile Claim includes part of Ellsworth Land.

Chile/UK Claim includes part of Ellsworth Land.

Chile/UK/Argentina Claim includes part of Ellsworth Land and the Antarctic Peninsula (Graham Land, Palmer Land). There are also numerous islands, including the South Shetland Islands, of which King George Island is the largest. Prior to the Antarctic Treaty, the South Shetlands and South Orkneys were part of the Falkland Islands Dependencies.

Argentina/UK Claim includes part of Coats Land, part of Berkner Island, and the South Orkney Islands, of which the largest is Coronation Island.

United Kingdom Claim is part of Coats Land.

Norway Claim is Queen Maud Land.

Australia Claim includes Enderby Land, Wilkes Land, and part of Victoria Land.

France Claim is Adélie Land.

New Zealand Claim includes part of Victoria Land, most of the Ross Ice Shelf, the Balleny Islands, and Sturge Island.

The Argentine claim has an area of about 1,230,000 sq. km. If Argentina's claim were recognized, it would be part of the territory of Tierra del Fuego, Antártida e Islas del Atlántico Sur.

The Australian claim has an area of about 6,115,000 sq. km. If Australia's claim were recognized, this area would be an external territory of Australia, named Australian Antarctic Territory.

The Chilean claim has an area of 1,270,000 sq. km. If Chile's claim were recognized, this area would be part of the Chilean region of Magallanes.

The French claim has an area of about 430,000 sq. km. If France's claim were recognized, this area would be part of French Southern and Antarctic Territories (treated as a country in this book).

The New Zealander claim has an area of about 420,000 sq. km. If New Zealand's claim were recognized, it would be an overseas territory of New Zealand, named Ross Dependency.

If Norway's claim were recognized, it would be a dependency of Norway, named Queen Maud Land.

The British claim has an area of about 1,710,000 sq. km. If the United Kingdom's claim were recognized, it would be a territory named British Antarctic Territory.

The total area of Antarctica is about 14,000,000 sq. km.

Origins of names:

Adélie Land: named by the French explorer Jules Dumont d'Urville for his wife Adèle.

Ellsworth Land: named for American explorer Lincoln Ellsworth.

Enderby Land: named for the whaling company, Samuel Enderby & Sons, that financed the expedition which discovered it.

Queen Maud Land: named for Queen Maud, consort of Haakon VII of Norway, daughter of Edward VII of England.

Ross Dependency (New Zealand Claim): named for Sir James Clark Ross, a British Antarctic explorer.

Other names of subdivisions:

Adélie Land: Terra Adelia (Italian); Terre Adélie (French)

British Antarctic Territory: Falkland Islands Dependency (obsolete); Territorio Antartico Britannico (Italian)

Peter I Island: Peter I Øy (Norwegian)

Queen Maud Land: Dronning Maud Land (Norwegian); Königin-Maud-Land (German); Terra Regina Maud (Italian); Terre de la Reine-Maud (French)

ANTIGUA AND BARBUDA

ISO = AG/FIPS = AC   Language = English   Time zone = -4   Capital = Saint John's

At the beginning of the 20th century, Antigua was one of five presidencies of the Leeward Islands, a British colony. On 1956-06-30, each presidency became a separate colony. On 1981-11-01, Antigua was granted full independence, and renamed Antigua and Barbuda.

Other names of country: Antigua e Barbuda (Italian); Antígua e Barbuda (Portuguese); Antigua et Barbuda (French); Antigua ja Barbuda (Finnish); Antigua och Barbuda (Swedish); Antigua og Barbuda (Danish, Norwegian); Antigúa og Barbúda (Icelandic); Antigua und Barbuda (German); Antigua y Barbuda (Spanish).

Origin of name: Antigua was named by Columbus after Santa Maria la Antigua, a chapel in Seville (Spanish *antigua*: ancient).

division	abv	ISO	FIPS	division	abv	ISO	FIPS
Barbuda	BB	BAR	AC01	Saint Paul	PA	SPA	AC06
Saint George	GE	SGE	AC03	Saint Peter	PE	SPE	AC07
Saint John	JO	SJO	AC04	Saint Philip	PH	SPH	AC08
Saint Mary	MA	SMA	AC05				

Status: These divisions are parishes, except for Barbuda, which is sometimes said to be a dependency.
Abv: Two-letter code for international compatibility (defined by the author).
ISO: Codes from ISO 3166-2.
FIPS: Codes from FIPS PUB 10-4.
Territorial extent: Antigua Island, and several closely adjacent islands such as Guana Island and Long Island, are partitioned by the six parishes. Barbuda Island, with its adjacent islets, forms the dependency of Barbuda. Redonda Island is remote from both Antigua and Barbuda, uninhabited, and tiny. There is some disagreement about which parish or dependency it belongs to, but it is most often considered part of Barbuda.

ARGENTINA

ISO = AR/FIPS = AR   Language = Spanish   Time zone = -3 (see note)   Capital = Buenos Aires

Argentina has been an independent country throughout the 20th century. It has maintained its boundaries relatively unchanged during that period. It has had border disputes and adjustments with Chile. Argentina has also claimed the Islas Malvinas, or Falkland Islands, but was unable to enforce its claim in the 1982 war with Great Britain. It has claims in Antarctica which have been held in abeyance by the Antarctic Treaty. Areas and populations are given here without the claims.

Time zone note: As recently as 1994, Argentina has had several time zones. Mendoza and Jujuy provinces have experimented with using an offset of -4 for their standard time. There have always been some provinces that used standard time year-round, but until 1994 some of the provinces did observe daylight saving time from October to March.

Other names of country: Argentiina (Finnish); Argentína (Icelandic); Argentine (French); Argentine Republic (formal-English); Argentinië (Dutch); Argentinien (German); República Argentina (formal).

Origin of name: Explorers saw that natives had silver objects (Latin *argentum*: silver).

division	ab	ISO	FIPS	IATA	population	area-km	area-mi	capital
Buenos Aires	BA	B	AR01	BA	12,594,974	307,571	118,754	La Plata
Catamarca	CT	K	AR02	CA	264,234	102,602	39,615	(San Fernando del Valle de) Catamarca
Chaco	CC	H	AR03	CH	839,677	99,633	38,469	Resistencia
Chubut	CH	U	AR04	CB	357,189	224,686	86,752	Rawson
Córdoba	CB	X	AR05	CD	2,766,683	165,321	63,831	Córdoba
Corrientes	CN	W	AR06	CR	795,594	88,199	34,054	Corrientes ➤

division	ab	ISO	FIPS	IATA	population	area-km	area-mi	capital
Distrito Federal	DF	C	AR07		2,965,403	200	77	Buenos Aires
Entre Ríos	ER	E	AR08	ER	1,020,257	78,781	30,418	Paraná
Formosa	FM	P	AR09	FO	398,413	72,066	27,825	Formosa
Jujuy	JY	Y	AR10	PJ	512,329	53,219	20,548	(San Salvador de) Jujuy
La Pampa	LP	L	AR11	LP	259,996	143,440	55,382	Santa Rosa
La Rioja	LR	F	AR12	LR	220,729	89,680	34,626	La Rioja
Mendoza	MZ	M	AR13	MD	1,412,481	148,827	57,462	Mendoza
Misiones	MN	N	AR14	MI	788,915	29,801	11,506	Posadas
Neuquén	NQ	Q	AR15	NE	388,833	94,078	36,324	Neuquén
Río Negro	RN	R	AR16	RN	506,772	203,013	78,384	Viedma
Salta	SA	A	AR17	SA	866,153	155,488	60,034	Salta
San Juan	SJ	J	AR18	SJ	528,715	89,651	34,614	San Juan
San Luis	SL	D	AR19	SL	286,458	76,748	29,633	San Luis
Santa Cruz	SE	Z	AR20	SC	159,839	243,943	94,187	Río Gallegos
Santa Fe	SC	S	AR21	SF	2,798,422	133,007	51,354	Santa Fe
Santiago del Estero	SF	G	AR22	SE	671,988	136,351	52,645	Santiago del Estero
Tierra del Fuego	TF	V	AR23	TF	69,369	21,571	8,329	Ushuaia
Tucumán	TM	T	AR24	TU	1,142,105	22,524	8,697	(San Miguel de) Tucumán
					32,615,528	2,780,400	1,073,520	

Status: These divisions are provincias (provinces), except for Distrito Federal (a federal district) and Tierra del Fuego, a território nacional (national territory).

Ab: Subdomain codes, assigned by Argentina to identify Internet URLs by province. (I added the code for Distrito Federal, which is not covered by this standard.)

ISO: Codes from ISO 3166-2.

FIPS: Codes from FIPS PUB 10-4.

IATA: Codes from the IATA Airline Coding Directory, used to locate airports by province.

Population: 1991 census.

Area-km: Square kilometers.

Area-mi: Square miles.

Capital: Common name is not in parentheses; adding parenthetical parts gives formal name.

Postal codes: Argentina has four-digit postal codes (commonly called Código Postal, officially número postal), but they don't correlate to provinces well enough to list here.

Further subdivisions: The provinces are further subdivided into departamentos (departments), except for Distrito Federal, which has no internal divisions on this level, and Buenos Aires, which is divided into partidos (parts).

Territorial extent: Buenos Aires includes the Argentine claim to Isla Martín García. This island, situated in the Río de la Plata, is also claimed by Uruguay.

Tierra del Fuego includes the Argentine section of the island of Tierra del Fuego, as well as several unrecognized claims of Argentina. These claims are to the Islas Malvinas (Falkland Islands), its associated islands (South Georgia and South Sandwich Islands), and a sector of Antarctica. This book lists the Antarctic claim under Antarctica.

Argentina and Chile have had numerous boundary disputes and border adjustments over the years. They exercise shared sovereignty over a few small islands at the eastern end of the Beagle Channel, including Islas Lennox, Nueva, and Picton.

There is a four-corners boundary where the provinces of Mendoza, La Pampa, Neuquén, and Río Negro come together. The borders are defined by the Río Colorado and the meridian of 68° 15' W.

Origins of names:

Buenos Aires: = Good Winds. Former name Nuestra Señora Santa Maria de los Buenos Aires, after the Virgin Mary, revered in Seville as protectress of sailors.

Catamarca: from Quechua *qata*: slope and *marka*: region.

Chaco: from Guaraní *chako*: hunting ground.

Córdoba: named by Jerónimo Luis de Cabrera for his wife's home, the city of Córdoba, Spain.

Corrientes: = Currents. Originally the city was named Ciudad de San Juan de las Siete Corrientes (= City of Saint John of the Seven Currents), for seven branches of the Paraná River.

Distrito Federal: = Federal District.

Entre Ríos: = Between Rivers. The province lies between the Paraná and Uruguay Rivers where they meet to form the estuary of Río de la Plata.

Formosa: Portuguese = Beautiful.

Jujuy: named for Xuxuyoc, the last Inca governor of the area.

La Pampa: = The Prairie.

La Rioja: from the region of that name in Spain.

Los Andes: from the mountain range, which was probably named for an ethnic group called Anti.

Mendoza: after Pedro de Mendoza, early explorer, or Don Garcia Hurtado de Mendoza, Chilean governor.

Misiones: = Missions, for Jesuit missions to the natives.
Río Negro: from the river of that name (= Black River).
Santa Cruz: = Holy Cross; Magellan reached the site of the
  port on 1520-09-14, the feast day of the Exaltation of the
  Holy Cross.

Santa Fe: = Holy Faith.
Santiago del Estero: = Saint James of the Estuary.
Tierra del Fuego: = Land of Fire. Magellan saw fires burning
  on the island.
Tucumán: possibly Aymara *tucu man*: the place where it ends.

Change history:

~1920	Capital of Neuquén moved from Chos Malal to Neuquén.	
~1935	Capital of La Pampa moved from General Acha to Santa Rosa.	
1943-09-23	Los Andes territory (capital: San Antonio de los Cobres) divided among Catamarca, Jujuy, and Salta provinces. In the division, Catamarca received the departamento of Antofagasta de la Sierra, about 27,886 sq. km.; Jujuy got Susques departamento, 9,554 sq. km.; and Salta got Pastos Grandes and San Antonio de los Cobres departamentos, 25,200 sq. km.	
1946	Comodoro Rivadavia territory split from Chubut, taking approximately the southern half of the territory. They were reunited in ~1955.	
1950	Chaco territory renamed Presidente Juan Perón.	
1951	Presidente Juan Perón changed from territory to province.	
1952	La Pampa territory renamed Eva Perón and changed to province (unromantically, these provinces are about 750 km. apart at their closest).	
1953	Misiones changed from territory to province.	
1955	Presidente Juan Perón and Eva Perón provinces renamed Chaco and La Pampa, respectively.	
1955-07-27	Chubut, Formosa, Neuquén, Río Negro, and Santa Cruz changed from territories to provinces; name of Santa Cruz changed to Patagonia (but soon changed back to Santa Cruz).	

There have also been minor boundary adjustments over the years, both external (with Chile) and internal (between adjacent provinces, especially in the north and west).

Other names of subdivisions:

Buenos Aires: Baires (informal); Buenos Ayres (obsolete)
Chaco: El Chaco (obsolete); Presidente Juan Perón (obsolete)
Córdoba: Cordova (obsolete–English)
Distrito Federal: Capital Federal (variant); Distretto Federale (Italian)
La Pampa: El Pampa (obsolete); Eva Perón (obsolete)

Santa Fe: Santa Fé (variant)
Tierra del Fuego: Feuerland (German); Terra del Fuoco (Italian); Terre de Feu (French); Terra do Fogo (Portuguese); Tierra del Fuego, Antártida e Islas del Atlántico Sur (formal); Tierra del Fuego, Antarctica and South Atlantic Islands (formal-English)

Population history:

	1895	1914	1940	1947	1960	1970	1980	1991
Buenos Aires	921,168	2,066,165	3,486,430	4,408,373	7,139,000	8,775,000	10,796,036	12,594,974
Catamarca	90,161	100,391	149,766	145,216	179,000	172,000	206,204	264,234
Chaco	10,422	46,274	329,400	443,922	559,000	567,000	692,410	839,677
Chubut	3,748	23,065	86,100	105,500	151,000	190,000	262,196	357,189
Córdoba	351,223	735,472	1,271,494	1,455,222	1,829,000	2,060,000	2,407,135	2,766,683
Corrientes	239,618	347,055	516,671	570,967	559,000	564,000	657,716	795,594
Federal District	663,854	1,576,597	2,364,263	3,000,371	3,040,000	2,972,000	2,908,001	2,965,403
Entre Ríos	292,019	425,373	737,300	776,280	825,000	812,000	902,241	1,020,257
Formosa	4,829	19,281	56,900	112,056	189,000	234,000	292,479	398,413
Jujuy	49,713	76,631	113,144	166,783	253,000	302,000	408,514	512,329
La Pampa	25,914	101,338	148,700	167,562	161,000	172,000	207,132	259,996
La Rioja	69,502	79,754	110,537	109,386	133,000	136,000	163,342	220,729
Mendoza	116,136	277,535	513,527	590,548	869,000	973,000	1,187,305	1,412,481
Misiones	33,163	53,563	186,200	244,123	415,000	443,000	579,579	788,915
Neuquén	14,517	28,866	75,200	85,601	116,000	155,000	241,904	388,833
Río Negro	9,241	42,242	135,200	132,419	203,000	263,000	383,896	506,772 ➤

	1895	1914	1940	1947	1960	1970	1980	1991
Salta	118,015	140,927	212,307	290,063	435,000	510,000	662,369	866,153
San Juan	84,251	119,252	216,844	260,714	370,000	384,000	469,973	528,715
San Luis	81,450	116,266	196,677	167,620	180,000	183,000	212,837	286,458
Santa Cruz	1,058	9,948	18,700	24,651	55,000	84,000	114,479	159,839
Santa Fe	379,188	899,640	1,546,880	1,700,026	1,928,000	2,136,000	2,457,188	2,798,422
Santiago del Estero	161,502	261,678	484,649	538,383	489,000	495,000	652,318	671,988
Tierra del Fuego	— —	2,504	2,300	4,902	7,000	16,000	29,451	69,369
Tucumán	215,742	332,933	530,664	604,526	818,000	766,000	968,066	1,142,105
Los Andes	477	2,487	7,100	— —	— —	— —	— —	— —
	3,954,911	7,885,237	13,496,953	16,105,214	20,902,000	23,364,000	27,862,771	32,615,528

(1940 figures are estimated.)

ARMENIA

ISO = AM/FIPS = AM   Language = Armenian   Time zone = +3 [d]   Capital = Yerevan

Armenia has been under Russian domination for most of the 20th century. As part of Czarist Russia, it was the district of Erivan. It included some territory south of the Aras (Araks) River which was lost to Turkey in World War I. Armenia was independent from 1917 to 1920. For part of that time, it belonged to the Transcaucasian Federation, with Azerbaijan and Georgia. Armenia became part of the Transcaucasian Soviet Socialist Republic, on 1922-03-12. This became one of the constituent republics of the U.S.S.R. later that year. In 1936 the Transcaucasian S.S.R. was split into the three republics again. The Commonwealth of Independent States supplanted the U.S.S.R. on 1991-12-08. Armenia became a member of the C.I.S. that same month.

Other names of country: Armenía (Icelandic); Arménia (Portuguese); Armenian Soviet Socialist Republic (obsolete); Arménie (French); Armenië (Dutch); Armenien (Danish, German, Swedish); Armeniya (Russian); Armyanskaya Sovyetskaya Sotsialisticheskaya Respublika (obsolete–Russian); Haikakan Hanrapetoutioun, Hayastani Hanrapetut'yun (formal); Hayastan (Armenian); Republic of Armenia (formal–English).

Origin of name: From the legendary patriarch Armenak.

division	abv	ISO	FIPS	division	abv	ISO	FIPS
Aragacot'n	AG	01	AM01	Loři	LO	07	AM06
Ararat	AT	02	AM02	Širak	SR	08	AM07
Armavir	AM	03	AM03	Syunik'	SN	09	AM08
Erevan	ER	04	AM11	Tavuš	TA	10	AM09
Gelark'unik'	GE	05	AM04	Vayoc'Jor	VA	11	AM10
Kotayk'	KO	06	AM05				

Status: Each division is a gavař (province), except Erevan, which is a kaghak (city).

Abv: Two-letter code for international compatibility (defined by the author).

ISO: Codes from ISO 3166-2.

FIPS: Codes from FIPS PUB 10-4.

Territorial extent: The territory of Nagorno-Karabakh is currently part of Azerbaijan. For a long time it was an autonomous oblast, but Azerbaijan has now integrated it into the country. It has a large Armenian population which would like to unite with Armenia. Armenia and Nagorno-Karabakh have no common border, but are only a few kilometers apart. Armenia includes the small Artsvashen enclave, containing the town of Bashkend, enclosed within Azerbaijan.

Origins of names: Erevan: possibly from Armenian *erevan*: to appear or show, implying that it was the first place to appear after the Biblical flood.

Change history:

Under the Soviet Union, Armenia was the Armenian Soviet Socialist Republic (Armyanskaya Sovyetskaya Sotsialisticheskaya Respublika).

After independence, Armenia consisted of 37 shrjanner (regions): Akhuryan, Amasiya, Ani, Aparan, Aragats, Ararat, Armavir, Artashat, Art'ik, Ashots'k', Ashtarak, Baghramyan, Ejmiatsin, Goris, Gugark', Hrazdan, Ijevan, Kamo, Kapan, Kotayk', Krasnoselsk, Martuni, Masis, Meghri, Nairi, Noyemberyai, Sevan, Sisian, Spitak, Step'anavan, T'alin, Tashir, Taush, T'umanyan, Vardenik, Vayk', Yeghegnadzor; and 23 kaghakner (cities): Abovyan, Alaverdi, Ararat, Artashat, Art'ik, Ashtarak, Ch'arents'avan, Dilijan, Ejmiatsin, Goris, Gyumri, Hoktemberyan, Hrazdan, Ijevan, Jermuk, Kamo, Kapan, Metsamor, Sevan, Spitak, Step'anavan, Vanadzor, and Yerevan.

1995-07-05   Armenia re-organized into the current ten provinces and one city.

Other names of subdivisions:

Aragacot'n: Aragatsotn (variant)
Erevan: Erivan, Ierevan, Yerevan (variant); Eriwan (German)
Gelark'unik': Gegharkunik (variant)

Šırak: Shırak (variant)
Syunik': Syunk (variant)
Vayoc'Jor: Vayots Dzor (variant)

ARUBA

ISO = AW/FIPS = AA   Language = Dutch   Time zone = -4   Capital = Oranjestad

Aruba was part of the Netherlands Antilles, a colony of the Netherlands, until 1986-01-01. On that date it became a separate autonomous colony. It will eventually attain independence as a separate country.

division	abv	population	area-km	area-mi	capital
Aruba	AA	68,900	193	75	Oranjestad

Status: This division is the whole of the country, treated as a division for compatibility.
Abv: Two-letter code for international compatibility (defined by the author).
Population: 1991 estimate.
Area-km: Square kilometers.
Area-mi: Square miles.
Territorial extent: The country consists only of Aruba Island and islets immediately off its shore.

AUSTRALIA

ISO = AU/FIPS = AS   Language = English   Time zones = see **zone** text below   Capital = Canberra

In 1900, there were six British colonies on the Australian continent. On January 1, 1901, they united to form a single independent country, professing allegiance to the crown of England.
Other names of country: Ástalía (Icelandic); Austrália (Portuguese); Australie (French); Australië (Dutch); Australien (Danish, German, Swedish); Commonwealth of Australia (formal); Oz (informal).
Origin of name: Early cartographers used Latin *Terra Australis*: Southern Land.

division	typ	abv	ISO	IATA	FIPS	conv	zone	population	area-km	area-mi	capital
Australian Capital Territory	ty	CT	CT	AC	AS01	ACT	+10 [d]	280,085	2,432	939	Canberra
New South Wales	st	NS	NS	NS	AS02	NSW	+10 [d]	5,731,926	801,425	309,432	Sydney
Northern Territory	ty	NT	NT	NT	AS03	NT	+9:30	175,253	1,356,170	523,620	Darwin ➤

division	typ	abv	ISO	IATA	FIPS	conv	zone	population	area-km	area-mi	capital
Queensland	st	QL	QL	QL	AS04	Qld.	+10	2,976,617	1,736,587	670,500	Brisbane
South Australia	st	SA	SA	SA	AS05	SA	+9:30 d	1,400,656	984,377	380,070	Adelaide
Tasmania	st	TS	TS	TS	AS06	Tas.	+10 d	452,847	68,127	26,304	Hobart
Victoria	st	VI	VI	VI	AS07	Vic.	+10 d	4,243,719	227,619	87,884	Melbourne
Western Australia	st	WA	WA	WA	AS08	WA	+8	1,586,393	2,527,621	975,920	Perth
Ashmore and Cartier Islands	ty	AS			AT			0	5	2	Darwin
Coral Sea Islands Territory	ty	CR			CR			0	3	1	Kingston
								16,847,496	7,704,366	2,974,672	

Typ: These divisions are states (st) and territories (ty), as shown.

Abv: Two-letter code for international compatibility (defined by the author).

ISO: Codes from ISO 3166-2.

IATA: Codes used in the IATA Airline Coding Directory.

FIPS: Codes from FIPS PUB 10-4. The island territories are treated as countries by FIPS PUB 10-4.

Conv: Conventional abbreviations. In postal addresses, use all capitals and no period.

Zone: Time zone indication. Lord Howe Island is offset +10:30 from UTC, and advances only 30 minutes in the summer, the only place in the world that does so. A few resort islands in Queensland, and all of Western Australia, have observed daylight saving time in some recent summers. Broken Hill, New South Wales has sometimes followed South Australian time.

Population: 1991 census.

Area-km: Square kilometers.

Area-mi: Square miles.

Further subdivisions: There are about 900 units of local government. In different parts of the country, they are called boroughs, cities, district councils, municipalities, shires, or towns. There are also some unincorporated areas.

Territorial extent: Australian Capital Territory has two sections. The larger, that of Canberra, is completely surrounded by New South Wales. The smaller, that of Jervis Bay, is on the west coast of New South Wales.

New South Wales includes Lord Howe Island and nearby Ball's Pyramid.

Northern Territory includes Ashmore and Cartier Islands. These islands are referred to as a territory, but they are uninhabited and are administered as part of Northern Territory. I have given them a separate line in the table to be able to show their FIPS code.

Queensland includes islands in the Torres Strait as far north as the south coast of New Guinea, including Saibai Island, Boigu Island, Talbot Islands, and Bramble Cay, but excluding Bristow Island and Parama Island. Queensland's eastern border includes the Great Barrier Reef.

Tasmania includes Macquarie Island. The dividing line between the islands in the Bass Strait that belong to Victoria and those that belong to Tasmania is the parallel of 39° 15' South. Almost all of the islands, as far north as the Hogan Group, thus belong to Tasmania.

Western Australia includes reefs within about 400 km. of the Australian mainland, but not Ashmore and Cartier Islands.

Coral Sea Islands Territory includes the islands east of the Great Barrier Reef, west of the meridian of 157° East, and between the parallels of 12° and 24° South. The only settlement in this territory is a weather station on Willis Island. It is administered from Kingston, Norfolk Island. There is no indication in ISO 3166-2 of where this territory is assigned.

The following remote territories of Australia are treated as separate countries by ISO 3166-1, so they are not included here: Cocos (Keeling) Islands; Christmas Island [in the Indian Ocean]; Norfolk Island; and Heard and McDonald Islands. In addition, Australian Antarctic Territory is claimed by Australia but is listed under Antarctica in this book.

Postal and telephone area codes: The Australian telephone numbering system has recently been reformed. Effective in 1997, there are four area codes, each serving a whole state or states. All local telephone numbers are eight digits. This replaces the old system, in which both the city access codes and the local numbers were variable in length.

Australian postal codes are four digits. With a few exceptions, the state can be deduced from the first one or two digits. The exceptions are cases where a city is served from a distribution center in a neighboring state.

This table shows the codes for each of the major states and territories:

state	area code	regular postal codes	high-volume mailers
Australian Capital Territory	02	26xx, 29xx	02xx
New South Wales	02	20xx-25xx, 27xx-28xx	1xxx
Northern Territory	08	08xx	09xx
Queensland	07	4xxx	9xxx
South Australia	08	50xx-57xx	58xx-59xx ➤

state	area code	regular postal codes	high-volume mailers
Tasmania	03	70xx–77xx	78xx–79xx
Victoria	03	3xxx	8xxx
Western Australia	08	60xx–67xx	68xx–69xx

Origins of names:

New South Wales: named by Captain James Cook for its resemblance to the south coast of Wales.

Queensland: named in honor of Queen Victoria of England.

Tasmania: named for its discoverer, Abel Janszoon Tasman.

Victoria: also named for Queen Victoria of England.

Change history:

1901-01-01	Commonwealth of Australia formed by the union of six British colonies: New South Wales, Queensland, South Australia, Tasmania, Victoria, and Western Australia.
1905-11	British New Guinea became an external territory of Australia.
1906-09-01	Name of British New Guinea changed to Papua.
1911-01-01	Northern Territory split from South Australia as a territory. Name of capital of Northern Territory changed from Palmerston to Darwin.
1911-01-01	Australian Capital Territory (Canberra section) split from New South Wales as a territory.
1914-07-01	Norfolk Island (q.v.) became a federal territory.
1915	Jervis Bay section (73 sq. km.) transferred from New South Wales to Australian Capital Territory.
1921-05-09	New Guinea Territory, consisting of the part of New Guinea Island north of Papua and east of Indonesia (Irian Jaya) and nearby islands, mandated to Australia by the League of Nations.
1927-02-01	Northern Territory split into two territories, North Australia and Central Australia, along the parallel of 20° South.
1927	National capital moved from Melbourne to Canberra. Some sources say that Bombala, south of Canberra in New South Wales, was capital for part of the period 1901–1927.
1931-06-12	North Australia and Central Australia reunited into the territory of Northern Territory.
1931-07-23	Ashmore and Cartier Islands became part of Australia as external territory.
1938	Ashmore and Cartier Islands placed under Northern Territory administration.
1946-12-13	Australian mandate for New Guinea Territory renewed by the United Nations as a trusteeship.
1969-09-30	Coral Sea Islands Territory became an external territory of Australia.
1975-09-16	Papua and New Guinea Territories became independent.

Other names of subdivisions:

Australian Capital Territory: Territoire de la Capitale Australienne (French); Território da Capital (Portuguese); Territorio della Capitale Federale (Italian)

Canton and Enderbury Islands: Canton und Enderbury Inseln (German); Îles Canton et Enderbury (French); Ilhas Cantão e Enderbury (Portuguese); Islas Canton y Enderbury (Spanish)

Coral Sea Islands Territory: Territoire des Îles de la Mer de Corail (French)

New South Wales: Neusüdwales (German); Nieuw Zuid-Wales (Dutch); Nouvelle-Galles du Sud (French); Nova Gales do Sul (Portuguese); Nueva Gales del Sur (Spanish); Nuovo Galles del Sud (Italian)

Northern Territory: Noordelijk Territorium (Dutch); Nordterritorium, Nord-Australien (German); Territoire du Nord (French); Territorio del Nord (Italian); Territorio del Norte (Spanish); Território do Norte (Portuguese)

South Australia: Australia del Sur (Spanish); Austrália do Sul (Portuguese); Australia Meridionale (Italian); Australie méridionale (French); Südaustralien (German); Zuid-Australië (Dutch)

Tasmania: Tasmânia (Portuguese); Tasmanie (French); Tasmanië (Dutch); Tasmanien (German)

Victoria: Vitória (Portuguese)

Western Australia: Australia Occidental (Spanish); Austrália Ocidental (Portuguese); Australia Occidentale (Italian); Australie occidentale (French); West-Australië (Dutch); Westaustralien (German)

Population history:

	Australian Capital Territory	New South Wales	Northern Territory	Queensland	South Australia	Tasmania	Victoria	Western Australia	Totals
1901	— —	1,355,355	4,811	498,129	358,346	172,475	1,201,070	184,124	3,774,310
1911	1,714	1,646,734	3,310	605,813	408,558	191,211	1,315,551	282,114	4,455,005
1921	2,572	2,100,371	3,867	755,972	495,160	213,780	1,531,280	332,732	5,435,734
1933	8,947	2,600,847	4,850	947,534	580,949	227,599	1,820,261	438,852	6,629,839
1947	16,905	2,984,838	10,868	1,106,415	646,073	257,078	2,054,701	502,480	7,579,358
1954	30,315	3,423,529	16,469	1,318,259	797,094	308,752	2,452,341	639,771	8,986,530
1961	58,828	3,917,013	27,095	1,518,828	969,340	350,340	2,930,113	736,629	10,508,186
1966	96,032	4,237,901	37,433	1,674,324	1,094,984	371,436	3,220,217	848,100	11,580,427
1971	144,063	4,601,180	86,390	1,827,065	1,173,707	398,100	3,520,351	1,053,834	12,804,690
1976	197,622	4,914,300	97,090	2,037,197	1,244,756	412,300	3,646,975	1,178,342	13,728,582
1981	221,609	5,126,217	115,900	2,295,123	1,285,033	427,200	3,832,443	1,300,056	14,603,581
1986	264,400	5,401,881	154,000	2,587,315	1,345,945	436,353	4,019,478	1,459,019	15,668,391
1991	280,085	5,731,926	175,253	2,976,617	1,400,656	452,847	4,243,719	1,586,393	16,847,496

Censuses up to and including 1961 did not count the aboriginal population. The 1901 census was taken as of March 31, the 1911 census as of April 2, the 1921 census as of April 4, and all subsequent censuses as of June 30.

AUSTRIA

ISO = AT/FIPS = AU   Language = German   Time zone = +1 [d]   Capital = Vienna

At the beginning of the 20th century, Austria was part of the Austro-Hungarian Empire, or Austria-Hungary. This country included most or all of present-day Austria, Hungary, Czech Republic, Slovakia, Slovenia, and Croatia, about half of Romania, and parts of Southern Poland, Western Ukraine, Northern Yugoslavia, and Northern Italy. It also had administrative control of Bosnia-Herzegovina. At the end of World War I, the treaties of Saint-Germain and Trianon redrew the map of Europe, and Austria emerged looking almost exactly as it does today. During World War II, Austria was annexed by Germany, but the Allies never recognized the annexation, and at the end of the war, the status quo ante was restored.

Other names of country: Austerrike (Norwegian nynorsk); Áustria (Portuguese); Austurríki (Icelandic); Autriche (French); Itävalta (Finnish); Oostenrijk (Dutch); Österreich (German); Østerrike (Norwegian bokmål); Österrike (Swedish); Østrig (Danish); Republic of Austria (formal–English); Republik Österreich (formal).

Origin of name: German *Österreich*: Eastern empire. Created by Charlemagne as a buffer state.

division	abv	ISO	FIPS	NUTS	conv	population	area-km	area-mi	capital	postal codes
Burgenland	BU	1	AU01	AT11	Bgl.	273,541	3,965	1,531	Eisenstadt	7xxx
Carinthia	KA	2	AU02	AT21	Ktn.	552,421	9,533	3,681	Klagenfurt	90xx to 98xx
Lower Austria	NO	3	AU03	AT12	NÖ.	1,480,927	19,170	7,402	Vienna	2xxx, 3xxx
Salzburg	SZ	5	AU05	AT32	Sbg.	483,880	7,154	2,762	Salzburg	5xxx
Styria	ST	6	AU06	AT22	Stm.	1,184,593	16,386	6,327	Graz	8xxx
Tyrol	TR	7	AU07	AT33	Tirol	630,358	12,648	4,883	Innsbruck	60xx to 66xx (a)
Upper Austria	OO	4	AU04	AT31	OÖ.	1,340,076	11,978	4,625	Linz	4xxx
Vienna	WI	9	AU09	AT13	Wien	1,533,176	415	160	Vienna	1xxx
Vorarlberg	VO	8	AU08	AT34	Vbg.	333,128	2,601	1,004	Bregenz	67xx to 69xx
						7,812,100	83,850	32,375		

Status: These divisions are Bundesländer, or simply Länder (singular Land: state).
Abv: Two-letter code for international compatibility (defined by the author).
ISO: Codes from ISO 3166-2.
FIPS: Codes from FIPS PUB 10-4.
NUTS: Nomenclature of Territorial Units for Statistics. Note: by taking the first three characters of the NUTS codes, the states can be grouped into three regions: AT1 Ostösterreich, AT2 Südösterreich, and AT3 Westösterreich.

Conv: Conventional abbreviations used in Austria.

Population: 1991 census.

Area-km: Square kilometers.

Area-mi: Square miles.

Postal codes: Austrian *Postleitzahlen* (postal codes, abbreviated PLZ) are four digits. With a few exceptions, the state can be deduced from the first one or two digits. The exceptions are cases where a city is served from a distribution center in a neighboring state. (a) Also 99xx for East Tyrol. Note: postal codes for Austrian addresses can be identified by prefixing them with "A-".

Further subdivisions: Each state is further subdivided into entities of two types: Politischer Bezirk (district) and Statutarstadt (statutory city, or urban district). (Vienna has only one such subdivision.) The number of districts in Austria was 98 in 1987, and had grown to 102 in 1993. These districts are further subdivided into Gemeinden (communes).

Territorial extent: Tyrol consists of two sections, separated by a strip of land belonging to Salzburg. The smaller part, commonly called Osttirol (East Tyrol), is equivalent to the Politischer Bezirk of Lienz. Vienna is completely surrounded by Lower Austria.

Origins of names:

Burgenland: Named for the three Hungarian counties, known in German as Eisenburg, Ödenburg, and Wieselburg, which were cut up to make this state: the *Land* of the "-burgs."

Carinthia: The inhabitants of this region were known as Carantani to the ancient Romans.

Lower Austria: Area of Austria which lies downstream along the Danube.

Salzburg: German *Salz*: salt, *Burg*: castle. Salt was mined and stored here.

Styria: German Steiermark from Steyr, a city name, and Old High German *marcha*: boundary land.

Tyrol: Named for Tyrol Castle near Merano.

Upper Austria: Area of Austria which lies upstream along the Danube.

Vienna: Latin Vindobona from Indo-European *vindo*: whiteness and Celtic *bona*: citadel.

Vorarlberg: = Before the Arlberg, a mountain (pass) which divides this state from the rest of Austria.

Change history:

1918	The official names of the provinces of Österreich ober der Enns and Österreich unter der Enns were changed to Oberösterreich and Unterösterreich, respectively, to conform to popular usage.
1920-07-16	By the Treaty of Saint-Germain, Austria was created as a fragment of Austria-Hungary. In principle, Austria was to include the ethnic German areas of Austria-Hungary, but some of these areas were given to other countries for political reasons. The southern part of Tyrol was given to Italy, and is now the region of Trentino-Alto Adige. (The loss of this area left Tyrol in two fragments.) The provinces of Coastland, Carniola, Dalmatia, and the southern part of Styria (6,032 sq. km.) were incorporated in the new Kingdom of Serbs, Croats, and Slovenes, which later became Yugoslavia. Carinthia lost 777 sq. km., part to Italy and part to Yugoslavia. The provinces of Bohemia, Moravia, and most of Silesia became part of Czechoslovakia. Galicia and the rest of Silesia were given to Poland. Bukowina was given to Romania. By the Treaty of Trianon, the western parts of three Hungarian counties were transferred from Hungary to Austria, forming the state of Burgenland. For other transfers of territory, see Hungary.
1921-12-14	Part of Burgenland restored to Hungary, including the city of Ödenburg, now known as Sopron.
1938-03-13	Austria was annexed by Germany in the Anschluss. The Allies never recognized the legality of this act. The German government called the Austrian territory Ostmark. Tirol and Vorarlberg were unified into a single entity called Tirol-Vorarlberg. Burgenland was entirely divided between Lower Austria and Styria. The names of Lower and Upper Austria were changed to Niederdonau and Oberdonau (Lower and Upper Danube), respectively. The divisions of Ostmark were classified as Reichsgaue (provinces or districts of the empire). An area of 800 sq. km. around Vienna was transferred from Lower Austria to Vienna.
1945-04-29	A provisional government was set up for a liberated Austria, restored to its pre-war borders

(both external and internal, except for Vienna). The Allied Council recognized this government on 1945-10-20.

1954   Vienna was restored to its pre-war borders.

Other names of subdivisions:

Carinthia: Carinthie (French); Caríntia (Portuguese); Carintia (Spanish); Carinzia (Italian); Karintië (Dutch); Kärnten (German); Koroško (Slovenian)

Lower Austria: Austria Inferiore (Italian); Baixa-Áustria (Portuguese); Baja Austria (Spanish); Basse-Autriche (French); Niederdonau, Österreich unter der Enns (obsolete–German); Niederösterreich (German)

Salzburg: Salisburgo (Italian); Salzbourg (French); Salzburgo (Portuguese, Spanish)

Styria: Estíria (Portuguese); Estiria (Spanish); Steiermark (German); Stiermarken (Dutch); Stiria (Italian); Styrie (French)

Tyrol: Tirol (Dutch, German, Portuguese, Spanish); Tiròlo (Italian)

Upper Austria: Alta-Áustria (Portuguese); Alta Austria (Spanish); Austria Superiore (Italian); Haute-Autriche (French); Oberdonau, Österreich ober der Enns (obsolete–German); Oberösterreich (German)

Vienna: Viena (Portuguese, Spanish); Vienne (French); Wien (Danish, German)

Population history:

	1900	1923	1939	1951	1961	1971	1981	1991
Burgenland	— —	286,299	— —	276,136	271,001	272,119	269,771	273,541
Carinthia	367,324	370,432	460,946	474,764	495,226	525,728	536,179	552,421
Lower Austria	3,100,493	1,478,697	1,708,237	1,400,471	1,374,012	1,414,161	1,427,849	1,480,927
Salzburg	192,763	222,731	267,169	327,232	347,292	401,766	442,301	483,880
Styria	1,356,494	977,350	1,119,374	1,109,335	1,137,865	1,192,100	1,186,525	1,184,593
Tyrol	981,949	313,699	484,165	427,465	462,899	540,771	586,663	630,358
Upper Austria	810,246	873,702	1,040,931	1,108,720	1,131,623	1,223,444	1,269,540	1,340,076
Vienna	— —	1,863,783	1,918,462	1,616,125	1,627,566	1,614,841	1,531,346	1,533,176
Vorarlberg	— —	139,968	— —	193,657	226,323	271,473	305,164	333,128
	6,809,269	6,526,661	6,999,284	6,933,905	7,073,807	7,456,403	7,555,338	7,812,100

Dates of censuses, where known: 1900-12-31, 1923-03-07, 1951-06-01, 1971-05-12, 1981-05-12.

In 1900, Burgenland was not part of Austria. In 1939, Burgenland was included in Lower Austria and Styria. In 1900 and 1939, Vorarlberg was included in Tyrol. Austria had additional provinces in 1900.

AZERBAIJAN

ISO = AZ/FIPS = AJ   Language = Azeri   Time zone = +4   Capital = Baku

Modern Azerbaijan corresponds quite closely to the Russian districts of Baku, Elizabethpol, and Zakataly at the beginning of the 20th century. The Democratic Republic of Azerbaijan declared its independence on 1918-05-28. It was reconquered and incorporated into the Soviet Union on 1922-12-30, becoming part of the Transcaucasian Soviet Socialist Republic. Under the Soviets, the territory of Zangezur (27,400 sq. km.) was transferred from Azerbaijan to Armenia, separating Nakhichevan from the rest of Azerbaijan. In 1936, Azerbaijan became a separate republic within the U.S.S.R. Azerbaijan declared its independence from the U.S.S.R. on 1991-08-30. Later that year, it abolished the Nagorno-Karabakh Autonomous Region as a separate entity.

Other names of country: Aserbaidschan (German); Aserbaídsjan (Icelandic); Aserbajdsjan (Danish, Norwegian); Azerbaiyán (Spanish); Azerbaïdjan (French); Azerbaidjão (Portuguese); Azerbaidžan (Finnish); Azerbaidzjan (Dutch); Azerbaigian (Italian); Azerbaijani Republic (formal–English); Azerbajdzjan (Swedish); Azarbaycan Respublikasi, Azarbaijchan Respublikasy (formal); Azerbaydzhan (Russian); República Azerbaiyana (formal–Spanish).

Origin of name: Named for Atropates, one of Alexander the Great's generals.

division	abv	population	area-km	area-mi	capital
Azerbaijan (Baku)	AZ	6,800,000	81,100	31,300	Baku
Naxçıvan	NX	300,000	5,500	2,100	Naxçıvan
		7,100,000	86,600	33,400	

Status: Azerbaijan is a country. Naxçıvan is an autonomous republic. I chose this method of subdividing Azerbaijan because it can be seen on any map, and it reflects the situation that prevailed for most of the past eighty years. (See note below.)

Abv: Two-letter code for international compatibility (defined by the author).

Population: 1990 estimated.

Area-km: Square kilometers.

Area-mi: Square miles.

Note: The CIA World Factbook (1996), and recent editions of FIPS 10-4, list a division of Azerbaijan into 59 rayons, 11 cities, and one autonomous republic. ISO 3166-2 lists the same 71 divisions, plus six more rayons.

Territorial extent: Nakhichevan is separated from the rest of Azerbaijan by a strip of Armenian territory. It includes a tiny enclave inside Armenia, near Ararat. Azerbaijan (Baku) is the main section of the country. It includes the former autonomous region of Nagorno-Karabakh, claimed by Armenia. It also includes two small enclaves inside Armenia, north of Idzhevan.

Change history:

Under the Soviet Union, Azerbaijan was the Azerbaijan Soviet Socialist Republic (Azerbaydzhanskaya Sovyetskaya Sotsialisticheskaya Respublika). Nakhichevan was an Autonomous Soviet Socialist Republic (Nakhichevanskaya Avtonomnaya Sovyetskaya Sotsialisticheskaya Respublika). Nagorno-Karabakh was an autonomous oblast (Nagorno-Karabakhskaya Avtonomnaya Oblast') with Stepanakert as its capital.

Origins of names:

Nakhichevan: = City of Nakhich (man's name)

BAHAMAS

ISO = BS/FIPS = BF   Language = English   Time zone = -5 [d]   Capital = Nassau

The Bahama Islands were a British possession until 1973-07-10, when they gained independence.

Other names of country: Bahama (Finnish, Italian); Bahama eilanden (Dutch); Bahamaeyjar (Icelandic); Bahama-Inseln (German); Bahamaøyene (Norwegian); Commonwealth of the Bahamas (formal); Lucayas (obsolete).

Origin of name: Spanish *baja mar*: low sea.

division	abv	FIPS	population	area-km	area-mi	chief town
Abaco	AB	BF01	10,061	1,681	649	Marsh Harbour
Acklins Island	AK	BF02	428	389	150	Masons Bay
Andros	AN	BF03	8,155	5,957	2,300	Nicholls' Town
Berry Islands	BR	BF04	634	31	12	Bullocks Harbor
Biminis	BI	BF05	1,638	23	9	Alice Town
Cat Island	CI	BF06	1,678	388	150	Arthur's Town
Cay Lobos	CL	BF07	25	18	7	Cay Lobos
Crooked Island	CK	BF08	423	238	92	Colonel Hill
Eleuthera	EL	BF09	9,300	518	200	Governor's Harbour
Exuma	EX	BF10	3,539	290	112	Georgetown
Grand Bahama	GB	BF11	41,035	1,373	530	Freeport
Harbour Island	HB	BF12	(a)	4	2	Dunmore Town
Inagua	IN	BF13	985	1,671	645	Matthew Town
Long Cay	LC	BF14	(b)	23	9	Albert Town
Long Island	LI	BF15	3,107	448	173	Clarence Town
Mayaguana	MG	BF16	308	110	42	Abraham's Bay ▶

division	abv	FIPS	population	area-km	area-mi	chief town
New Providence	NW	BF17	171,542	207	80	Nassau
Ragged Island	RI	BF18	89	23	9	Duncan Town
Rum Cay	RC	BF19	(c)	78	30	Port Nelson
San Salvador	SS	BF20	539	163	63	Cockburn Town
Spanish Wells	SW	BF21	(a)	1	0	Spanish Wells
			253,486	13,634	5,264	

Status: These divisions are districts.

Abv: Two-letter code for international compatibility (defined by the author).

FIPS: Codes from FIPS PUB 10-4.

Population: 1990 census. Population included in: (a) Eleuthera. (b) Crooked Island. (c) San Salvador.

Area-km: Square kilometers.

Area-mi: Square miles.

Territorial extent: The Bahamas are separated from Cuba by the Nicholas Channel and Old Bahama Channel. Cay Sal Bank, Guinchos Cay, Cay Lobos, Cay Santo Domingo, and Great Inagua Island are among the closest points to Cuba in the Bahamas. They are separated from the United States by the Straits of Florida. Cay Sal Bank, Ocean Cay, Bimini Islands, and Grand Bahama Island are among the closest to the United States. The Caicos Passage separates the Bahamas from the Turks and Caicos Islands on the east. Mayaguana and Little Inagua Islands are among the easternmost of the Bahamas.

Abaco includes Moore's Island (Mores Island).

Biminis includes Cay Sal Bank.

Origins of name: Eleuthera: Greek for place of freedom; named by Puritans from Bermuda

Change history:

In February, 1993, a new release of FIPS PUB 10-3 showed changes to many of the districts of the Bahamas. When ISO DIS 3166-2 was released in 1996, it used the same districts. Areas and populations are not available for the new districts. This table shows how they probably relate to the old ones.

division	ISO	FIPS	before change, was:
Acklins and Crooked Islands	AC	BF24	BF02, BF08, and BF14
Bimini	BI	BF05	BF05
Cat Island	CI	BF06	BF06
Exuma	EX	BF10	BF10
Freeport	FP	BF25	Part of BF11
Fresh Creek	FC	BF26	Part of BF03
Governor's Harbour	GH	BF27	Part of BF09
Green Turtle Cay	GT	BF28	Part of BF01
Harbour Island	HI	BF22	BF12, BF21, and possibly part of BF09
High Rock	HR	BF29	Part of BF11
Inagua	IN	BF13	BF13
Kemps Bay	KB	BF30	BF07 and part of BF03
Long Island	LI	BF15	BF15
Marsh Harbour	MH	BF31	Part of BF01
Mayaguana	MG	BF16	BF16
New Providence	NP	BF23	Part of BF17
Nichollstown and Berry Islands	NB	BF32	BF04 and part of BF03
Ragged Island	RI	BF18	BF18
Rock Sound	RS	BF33	Part of BF09
Sandy Point	SP	BF34	Part of BF01
San Salvador and Rum Cay	SR	BF35	BF19 and BF20

Other names of subdivisions:

Biminis: Bimini (new)

Eleuthera: Eleutéria (Portuguese); Eleutère (French)

Inagua: Inague (French)

Long Cay: Fortune Island (variant)

New Providence: Nova Providência (Portuguese); Nueva Providencia (Spanish)

San Salvador: Watling Island (variant)

BAHRAIN

ISO = BH/FIPS = BA   Language = Arabic   Time zone = +3   Capital = Manama

Bahrain was a British protectorate until 1971-08-15, when it became independent.

Other names of country: Bahrein (Italian, Portuguese, Spanish); Bahreïn (French); Barein (Icelandic, Portuguese); Dawlat al-Bahrayn (formal); State of Bahrain (formal–English).

Origin of name: Arabic *al-bahrayn*: the two seas.

division	abv	ISO	FIPS	population	capital
Al Hadd	HD	01	BA01	5,300	Al Hadd
Al Manamah	MN	03	BA02	89,400	Manama
Al Mintaqah al Gharbiyah	MG	10	BA08	8,700	
Al Mintaqah al Wusta	MW	07	BA11	6,700	
Al Mintaqah ash Shamaliyah	MS	05	BA10	10,600	
Al Muharraq	MQ	02	BA03	44,200	Al Muharraq
Ar Rifa' wa al Mintaqah al Janubiyah	RF	09	BA13	12,600	Ar Rifa al Gharbi
Jidd Hafs	JH	04	BA05	19,500	Jidd Hafs
Madinat Hamad	MH	12	BA14		
Madinat 'Isa	MI	08	BA12	7,500	
Mintaqat Juzur Hawar	MJ	11	BA09		
Sitrah	ST	06	BA06	11,300	Sitrah
				215,800	

Status: These divisions are manatiq (sing. mintaqah: regions).

Abv: Two-letter code for international compatibility (defined by the author).

ISO: Codes from ISO 3166-2.

FIPS: Codes from FIPS PUB 10-4.

Population: 1971 census.

Territorial extent: Bahrain consists entirely of islands in the Gulf of Bahrain, an arm of the Persian Gulf. The largest is Bahrain itself. Near it are Al Muharraq, Sitrah, and Umm Nasan, all connected to it by causeways. Just off the coast of Qatar is Hawar Island and some neighboring islets. Qatar also claims this group.

Meanings of names:

Al Manamah: Arabic *al-manama*: the place of dreams
Al Mintaqah al Gharbiyah: = Western Region
Al Mintaqah al Wusta: = Central Region
Al Mintaqah ash Shamaliyah: = Northern Region

Madinat Hamad: = Hamad Town
Madinat 'Isa: = Isa Town
Mintaqat Juzur Hawar: = Hawar Islands Region

Change history:

In 1960, Bahrain was divided into four municipalities: Al Hadd, Al Manamah, Al Muharraq, and Ar Rifa'. They had divided into nine regions by about 1984.

~1985   Al Hadd split from Al Muharraq.

~1988   Madinat 'Isa split from Al Mintaqah al Wusta.

~1991   Madinat Hamad split from Ar Rifa' wa al Mintaqah al Janubiyah.

Other names of subdivisions:

Al Hadd: Hedd, Hidd (variant)
Al Manamah: Manama (variant)
Ar Rifa' wa al Mintaqah al Janubiyah: Rifaa, Rufaa, Rifa'a (variant)

Jidd Hafs: Judd Hafs (variant)
Mintaqat Juzur Hawar: Huwar Islands, Howar Islands (English)
Sitrah: Sitra (variant)

BANGLADESH

ISO = BD/FIPS = BG   Language = Bengali   Time zone = +6   Capital = Dhaka

At the beginning of the 20th century, India was the jewel in the crown of the British Empire. It consisted of provinces directly under British control and Native States with feudal allegiance to the British crown. After World War II, Mahatma Gandhi's campaign of passive resistance induced Britain to grant India its independence. In an attempt to avoid ethnic conflict, the country was partitioned into a Hindu section (India) and a Muslim section (Pakistan). Pakistan became a Dominion of the British Commonwealth on 1947-08-14. It consisted of two separate areas of Muslim concentration. The eastern section corresponded to the prewar district of East Bengal, plus a small part of Assam. On 1955-08-14, the two sections became the provinces of West Pakistan and East Pakistan. The two sections suffered from mutual distrust. On 1971-03-26, East Pakistan declared its independence from Pakistan. A war ensued between India and Pakistan. On 1971-12-15, Pakistan accepted defeat, and East Pakistan became a separate country, aligned with India. The new nation was initially known as Bangla Desh.

Other names of country: Bangladesch (German); Bangladess (Icelandic); East Pakistan (obsolete); Gama Prajatantri Bangladesh (formal); Pakistán oriental (Spanish-obsolete); People's Republic of Bangladesh (formal–English).

Origin of name: Bengali *bongo*: Bengali, *desh*: land.

division	abv	ISO	FIPS	population	area-km	area-mi	no. regions
Barisal	BA	1	— —	— —	11,394	4,399	2
Chittagong	CH	2	BG80	22,565,556	45,414	17,534	6
Dhaka	DA	3	BG81	26,248,864	30,772	11,881	5
Khulna	KH	4	BG82	17,149,792	22,181	8,564	3
Rajshahi	RJ	5	BG83	21,087,812	34,238	13,219	5
				87,052,024	143,999	55,598	21

Status: These divisions are bibhag (divisions).
Abv: Two-letter code for international compatibility (defined by the author).
ISO: Codes from ISO 3166-2.
FIPS: Codes from FIPS PUB 10-4.
Population: 1981 census. (Barisal was part of Khulna division at that time.)
Area-km: Square kilometers.
Area-mi: Square miles.
Capitals: All capitals have the same name as their division.
Further subdivisions: The five divisons are subdivided into 21 entities which are now called anchal (regions). Before about 1985, they were called zila (districts). The 21 regions are divided into 64 entities called districts; earlier, they were divided into nearly 500 entitites called upazila (subdistricts) or thana. In 1996, there were the following regions:

region	division	abv	ISO	FIPS	population	area-km	area-mi	u/t	districts
Bandarban	Chittagong	CB	2A	BG04	171,000	4,501	1,738	7	1
Barisal	Barisal	BB	1B	BG01	4,667,000	7,299	2,818	27	4
Bogra	Rajshahi	RB	5C	BG02	2,728,000	3,888	1,501	16	2
Chittagong	Chittagong	CC	2D	BG03	5,491,000	7,457	2,879	27	2
Chittagong Hill Tracts	Chittagong	CT	2E	BG21	580,000	8,679	3,351	17	2
Comilla	Chittagong	CO	2F	BG05	6,881,000	6,599	2,548	25	3
Dhaka	Dhaka	DD	3G	BG06	10,014,000	7,470	2,884	48	6
Dinajpur	Rajshahi	RD	5H	BG07	3,198,000	6,566	2,535	23	3
Faridpur	Dhaka	DF	3I	BG08	4,764,000	6,882	2,657	26	5
Jamalpur	Dhaka	DJ	3J	(a)	2,452,000	3,349	1,293	11	2
Jessore	Khulna	KJ	4K	BG09	4,020,000	6,573	2,538	21	4
Khulna	Khulna	KK	4L	BG10	4,329,000	12,168	4,698	25	3
Kushtia	Khulna	KU	4M	BG11	2,292,000	3,440	1,328	12	3
Mymensingh	Dhaka	DM	3N	BG12	6,568,000	9,668	3,733	34	3
Noakhali	Chittagong	CN	2O	BG13	3,816,000	5,460	2,108	16	3
Pabna	Rajshahi	RP	5P	BG14	3,424,000	4,732	1,827	17	2
Patuakhali	Barisal	BP	1Q	BG15	1,843,000	4,095	1,581	11	2
Rajshahi	Rajshahi	RR	5R	BG16	5,270,000	9,456	3,651	32	4
Rangpur	Rajshahi	RN	5S	BG17	6,510,000	9,593	3,704	35	5
Sylhet	Chittagong	CS	2T	BG18	5,656,000	12,718	4,910	36	4 ➤

region	division	abv	ISO	FIPS	population	area-km	area-mi	u/t	districts
Tangail	Dhaka	DT	3U	BG19	2,444,000	3,403	1,314	11	1
					87,118,000	143,996	55,596	477	64

Abv: Two-letter code for international compatibility (defined by the author).

FIPS: When FIPS PUB 10-3 came out, Mymensingh and Jamalpur (note a) were joined as a single region.

U/t: number of upazilas or thanas in each region as of 1981.

Districts: number of districts in each region as of 1996.

Capitals: All capitals have the same name as their region, except that Rangamati is the capital of Chittagong Hill Tracts. These are the districts listed in ISO 3166-2. They are the same as the ones listed in FIPS PUB 10-3 after 1991.

district	ISO	FIPS	region	district	ISO	FIPS	region
Bagerhat	05	BG22	Khulna	Magura	37	BG53	Jessore
Bandarban	01	BG04	Bandarban	Manikganj	33	BG54	Dhaka
Barguna	02	BG25	Patuakhali	Meherpur	39	BG55	Kushtia
Barisal	06	BG01	Barisal	Moulvibazar	38	BG56	Sylhet
Bhola	07	BG23	Barisal	Munshiganj	35	BG57	Dhaka
Bogra	03	BG24	Bogra	Mymensingh	34	BG12	Mymensingh
Brahmanbaria	04	BG26	Comilla	Naogaon	48	BG58	Rajshahi
Chandpur	09	BG27	Comilla	Narail	43	BG59	Jessore
Chittagong	10	BG29	Chittagong	Narayanganj	40	BG60	Dhaka
Chuadanga	12	BG30	Kushtia	Narsingdi	42	BG61	Dhaka
Comilla	08	BG05	Comilla	Natore	44	BG62	Rajshahi
Cox's Bazar	11	BG31	Chittagong	Nawabganj	45	BG28	Rajshahi
Dhaka	13	BG32	Dhaka	Netrakona	41	BG63	Mymensingh
Dinajpur	14	BG33	Dinajpur	Nilphamari	46	BG64	Rangpur
Faridpur	15	BG34	Faridpur	Noakhali	47	BG13	Noakhali
Feni	16	BG35	Noakhali	Pabna	49	BG65	Pabna
Gaibandha	19	BG36	Rangpur	Panchagarh	52	BG66	Dinajpur
Gazipur	18	BG37	Dhaka	Parbattya			
Gopalganj	17	BG38	Faridpur	Chattagram	56	BG67	Chittagong Hill Tracts
Habiganj	20	BG39	Sylhet	Patuakhali	51	BG15	Patuakhali
Jaipurhat	24	BG40	Bogra	Pirojpur	50	BG68	Barisal
Jamalpur	21	BG41	Jamalpur	Rajbari	53	BG69	Faridpur
Jessore	22	BG42	Jessore	Rajshahi	54	BG70	Rajshahi
Jhalakati	25	BG43	Barisal	Rangpur	55	BG71	Rangpur
Jhenaidah	23	BG44	Jessore	Satkhira	58	BG72	Khulna
Khagrachari	29	BG45	Chittagong Hill Tracts	Shariatpur	62	BG73	Faridpur
Khulna	27	BG46	Khulna	Sherpur	57	BG74	Jamalpur
Kishorganj	26	BG47	Mymensingh	Sirajganj	59	BG75	Pabna
Kurigram	28	BG48	Rangpur	Sunamganj	61	BG76	Sylhet
Kushtia	30	BG49	Kushtia	Sylhet	60	BG77	Sylhet
Lakshmipur	31	BG50	Noakhali	Tangail	63	BG78	Tangail
Lalmonirhat	32	BG51	Rangpur	Thakurgaon	64	BG79	Dinajpur
Madaripur	36	BG52	Faridpur				

Territorial extent: Sandwip Island, and other coastal islands to the south and east, down to Saint Martin's Island, are in Chittagong region.

Hatia Island and South Hatia Island are in Noakhali region.

Origins of names:

Chittagong: Hindi *chitta*: white, *ganv*: village   Dhaka: Bengali *dhak*: name of a papilionaceous tree

Change history:

   Divisions:

   ~1993   Barisal split from Khulna, consisting of Barisal and Patuakhali regions.

   Regions:

   ~1972   Nasirabad and Quaidabad districts merged to form Mymensingh.

   ~1974   Jamalpur district split from Mymensingh. Jamalpur consisted of the western part of the former district of Nasirabad, not including the city of Mymensingh itself.

   ~1980   Bandarban split from Chittagong Hill Tracts.

1981   Khagrachhari split from Chittagong Hill Tracts, but was reintegrated again.
1983   Name of capital of country, and the divisions containing it, changed from Dacca to Dhaka.

Other names of subdivisions:

Barisal: Bakerganj (obsolete)
Chittagong: Chattagram (Bengali)
Chittagong Hill Tracts: Parbattya Chattagram (Bengali); Rangamati (variant)
Dhaka: Daca (Portuguese); Dacca (obsolete)
Khagrachhari: Ramgarh (variant)
Lakshmipur: Laksmipur (variant)

Moulvibazar: Moulavibazar (variant)
Mymensingh: Nasirabad (obsolete)
Natore: Nator (variant)
Nawabganj: Chapai Nawabganj (variant)
Panchagarh: Panchagar (variant)
Shariatpur: Shariyatpur (variant)

BARBADOS

ISO = BB/FIPS = BB   Language = English   Time zone = -4   Capital = Bridgetown

Barbados was a British possession, until it achieved independence on 1966-11-30.
Other names of country: Barbade (French); Barbadoes (obsolete); Barbadoseyjar (Icelandic).
Origin of name: Portuguese: the bearded ones, from beard-shaped fig tree leaves.

division	abv	ISO	FIPS	population	area-km	area-mi
Christ Church	CC	C	BB01	40,790	57	22
Saint Andrew	AN	A	BB02	6,731	36	14
Saint George	GE	G	BB03	17,361	44	17
Saint James	JM	S	BB04	17,255	31	12
Saint John	JN	J	BB05	10,330	34	13
Saint Joseph	JS	O	BB06	7,211	26	10
Saint Lucy	LU	L	BB07	9,264	36	14
Saint Michael	MI	M	BB08	99,953	39	15
Saint Peter	PE	E	BB09	10,717	34	13
Saint Philip	PH	P	BB10	18,662	60	23
Saint Thomas	TH	T	BB11	11,000	34	13
				249,274	431	166

Status: These divisions are parishes. Some sources show Bridgetown as an independent city, but the most authoritative indicate that it's just part of Saint Michael parish.
Abv: Two-letter code for international compatibility (defined by the author).
ISO: Codes from ISO 3166-2.
FIPS: Codes from FIPS PUB 10-4.
Population: 1980 census.
Area-km: Square kilometers.
Area-mi: Square miles.

BELARUS

ISO = BY/FIPS = BO   Language = Byelorussian   Time zone = +2 [d]   Capital = Minsk

At the beginning of the 20th century, Belarus was part of the Russian Empire, in the area named West Russia. In the course of two World Wars and the Russian Revolution, its map was repeatedly redrawn. When the Soviet Union disintegrated, Belarus declared independence on 1991-08-25. Soon afterward, it adopted a new system of Romanization, changing the preferred transliteration of many place names.

Other names of country: Bélarus (French); Bielo-Rússia (Portuguese); Belarús, Bielorrusia, Rusia Blanca (Spanish); Biélorussie (French); Byelarus (obsolete); Hviderusland (Danish); Hvíta-Rússland (Icelandic); Hviterussland (Norwegian bokmål); Kviterussland (Norwegian nynorsk); Republic of Belarus (formal–English); Respublika Belarus (formal); Russia Bianca (Italian); Valko-Venäjä (Finnish); Vitryssland (Swedish); Weißrußland (German); White Russia (obsolete); Wit-Rusland (Dutch)

Meaning of name: Byelorussian for White Russia.

division	abv	ISO	FIPS	population	area-km	area-mi
Brest	BR	BR	BO01	1,386,000	32,000	12,000
Homyel'	HO	HO	BO02	1,636,000	40,000	15,000
Horad Minsk	HM	MSQ	BO04	1,385,000		
Hrodna	HR	HR	BO03	1,140,000	25,000	10,000
Mahilyow	MA	MA	BO06	1,261,000	29,000	11,000
Minsk	MI	MI	BO05	1,545,000	41,000	16,000
Vitsyebsk	VI	VI	BO07	1,391,000	40,000	15,000
				9,744,000	207,600	80,150

Status: Each division is a voblasts' (region), except Horad Minsk, which is a horad (municipality). Under the Soviet Union, the divisions were called oblasts.

Capitals: Capitals have the same name as their regions. (Minsk is the capital of Horad Minsk.)

Abv: two-letter abbreviations for international compatibility (defined by the author).

ISO: Codes from ISO 3166-2.

FIPS: Codes from FIPS PUB 10-4.

Population: 1982-01-01 census.

Area-km: Square kilometers.

Area-mi: Square miles.

Further subdivisions: The regions are subdivided into rayoni (districts). There were 172 districts in 1958.

Origins of names:

Brest (also Brest-Litovsk, i.e., Lithuanian Brest): from Old Russian *bieriest*: elm

Hrodno: from Slavonic *grad*: city

Mahilyow: from Russian *mogila*: tomb

Minsk: Men for Menka River + -sk: city suffix

Change history:

At the beginning of the century, the present-day area of Belarus corresponded roughly to the guberniy (governments) of Minsk, Mogilev, most of Grodno, part of Vitebsk, and part of Vilna.

1918-03-03 Russia and Germany signed the Treaty of Brest-Litovsk, allowing Germany to occupy Byelorussia. Both Germany and Russia later renounced this treaty. Since the Allies were slow to recognize the Soviet regime in Russia, they neglected to set the border between Poland and Russia in their division of European territory after World War I. Lord Curzon proposed a boundary, the Curzon Line, which nearly matched the pre-war border, but the Russo-Polish War (1919–20) left it a dead letter.

1919-01-01 The Byelorussian Soviet Socialist Republic (Byelorusskaya Sovyetskaya Sotsialisticheskaya Respublika) was declared. Its territory remained in dispute for two years.

1921-03-18 Peace treaty between Poland and Russia divided Byelorussia into a western section, annexed to Poland, and an eastern section, the Byelorussian S.S.R. The latter contained what is now all of Minsk except a western fringe, plus the western part of Homyel', a western slice of Mahilyow, and a small part of Vitsyebsk. Brest-Litovsk was renamed to Brześč nad Bugiem.

1924-03-03 By decree of the All-Russian Central Executive Committee, the Byelorussian S.S.R. was augmented by the rest of Mogilev and Vitebsk, and a central strip of Gomel'.

1926-12-06 Another decree annexed the rest of Gomel' to Byelorussia.

1939 Brześč nad Bugiem renamed to Brest.

1939-09-17 The Soviet Union invaded Poland. By November, Poland had been divided between Germany and the Soviet Union. West Byelorussia and East Byelorussia were reunited to form Byelorussia. The territory changed hands back and forth during the war. By 1946, Byelorussia had essentially the same territory that it does now. Its oblasts were:

oblast	capital	later became part of
Baranovichi	Baranovichi	Brest, Grodno, Minsk
Bobruysk	Bobruysk	Minsk, Mogilev
Brest	Brest	Brest
Gomel	Gomel	Gomel'
Grodno	Grodno	Grodno
Minsk	Minsk	Minsk
Mogilev	Mogilev	Mogilev
Molodechno	Molodechno	Molodechno
Pinsk	Pinsk	Brest
Polesye	Mozyr'	Gomel'
Polotsk	Polotsk	Molodechno, Vitebsk
Vitebsk	Vitebsk	Vitebsk

~1955 Byelorussia reorganized into the oblasts of Brest, Gomel', Grodno, Minsk, Mogilev, Molodechno, and Vitebsk.

~1960 Byelorussia reorganized. Molodechno split up among Grodno, Minsk, and Vitebsk. Begoml' rayon transferred from Minsk to Vitebsk. Glusk rayon transferred from Minsk to Mogilev.

~1993 Horad Minsk split from Minsk. Names changed to modern transliteration.

Other names of subdivisions:

Brest: Brestskaya Voblasts' (formal)
Homyel': Gomel' (obsolete); Homyel'skaya Voblasts' (formal)
Hrodna: Grodno (obsolete); Hrodzenskaya Voblasts' (formal)
Mahilyow: Mahilyowskaya Voblasts' (formal); Mogilev (obsolete)

Minsk: Minskaya Voblasts' (formal)
Vitsyebsk: Vitebsk (obsolete); Vitsyebskaya Voblasts' (formal); Witebsk (German)

BELGIUM

ISO = BE/FIPS = BE   Languages = Flemish, French   Time zone = +1 [d]   Capital = Brussels

Belgium has been independent throughout the 20th century, except during the German invasions of the two World Wars. It has undergone relatively minor transfers of territory in the aftermath of those wars. The provinces trace their origins to nine departments imposed by France in 1795. The regions originated with a constitutional reform in 1967–1971.

Other names of country: Belgia (Finnish, Norwegian); Belgía (Icelandic); Bélgica (Portuguese, Spanish); België (Dutch, Flemish); Belgien (Danish, German, Swedish); Belgio (Italian); Belgique (French); Kingdom of Belgium (formal–English); Koninkrijk België (formal–Flemish); Reino de Bélgica (formal–Spanish); Royaume de Belgique (formal–French).

Origin of name: Called Gallia Belgica by Romans, after an ethnic name.

division	abv	ISO	FIPS	NUTS	INS	population	area-km	area-mi	capital	region	postal codes
Antwerp	AN	VAN	BE01	BE21	10	1,637,857	2,867	1,107	Antwerp	VLG	2xxx
Brussels	BU	BXL	BE02	BE1	21	953,175	161	62	Brussels	BXL	10xx–12xx
East Flanders	OV	VOV	BE08	BE23	40	1,357,576	2,982	1,151	Ghent	VLG	9xxx
Flemish Brabant	VB	VBR	BE02	BE24	20	1,007,882	2,106	814	Leuven	VLG	9xxx
Hainaut	HT	WHT	BE03	BE32	50	1,282,783	3,787	1,462	Mons	WAL	60xx–62xx and 7xxx
Liege	LG	WLG	BE04	BE33	60	1,016,762	3,862	1,491	Liege	WAL	4xxx ➤

division	abv	ISO	FIPS	NUTS	INS	population	area-km	area-mi	capital	region	postal codes
Limburg	LI	VLI	BE05	BE22	70	783,927	2,422	935	Hasselt	VLG	35xx–39xx
Luxembourg	LX	WLX	BE06	BE34	80	243,790	4,441	1,715	Arlon	WAL	66xx–67xx
Namur	NA	WNA	BE07	BE35	90	438,864	3,665	1,415	Namur	WAL	5xxx
Walloon Brabant	BW	WBR	BE02	BE31	20	344,508	1,091	421	Wavre	WAL	1xxx and 30xx-33xx
West Flanders	WV	VWV	BE09	BE25	30	1,125,140	3,134	1,210	Brugge	VLG	8xxx
						10,192,264	30,518	11,783			

Status: These divisions are provinces (Flemish: provincies), except for Brussels, which is a capital region.

Abv: Two-letter code for international compatibility (defined by the author).

ISO: Codes from ISO 3166-2.

FIPS: Codes from FIPS PUB 10-4.

NUTS: Nomenclature of Territorial Units for Statistics.

INS: Codes assigned by the National Statistics Institute for the 1991 census.(Brabant was a single province then, coded 20.)

Population: 1998-01-01 estimate.

Area-km: Square kilometers.

Area-mi: Square miles.

Postal codes: Belgian postal codes are four digits. Postal codes in the provinces recently formed from Brabant don't correspond neatly to the new province boundaries. Note: postal codes for Belgian addresses can be identified by prefixing them with "B-".

Further subdivisions: Belgium is also divided into three régions (gewesten, régions). When they were created in 1970, Brabant was divided among all three regions; in 1995, it was split, and now each region contains provincial-level units as shown in the region colum in the table above. Here is a list of the regions.

ISO	region	NUTS	predominant language
BXL	Brussels Capital Region	BE1	Bilingual
VLG	Flemish Region	BE2	Flemish
WAL	Wallonia	BE3	French

Below the provinces, there are 43 arrondissements. In this list, each province name is followed by its level-2 NUTS code; after the colon, the arrondissements in the province are listed. The level-3 NUTS code for each arrondissement is formed by appending the given digit to the level-2 NUTS code. There are also two-digit INS codes for each arrondissement. If they are not listed in brackets, they may be formed by adding the given digit to the provincial INS code shown above.

Antwerp BE21: Antwerp 1, Mechelen 2, Turnhout 3

Brussels BE1: Brussels [no level-3 NUTS code; INS 21]

East Flanders BE23: Aalst 1, Dendermonde 2, Eeklo 3, Gent 4, Oudenaarde 5, Sint Niklaas 6

Flemish Brabant BE24: Halle-Vilvoorde 1 [INS 23], Leuven 2 [INS 24]

Hainaut BE32: Ath 1, Charleroi 2, Mons 3, Mouscron 4, Soignies 5, Thuin 6, Tournai 7

Liege BE33: Huy 1, Liège 2, Verviers 3, Waremme 4

Limburg BE22: Hasselt 1, Maaseik 2, Tongeren 3

Luxembourg BE34: Arlon 1, Bastogne 2, Marche-en-Famenne 3, Neufchâteau 4, Virton 5

Namur BE35: Dinant 1, Namur 2, Philippeville 3

Walloon Brabant BE31: Nivelles [INS 25]

West Flanders BE25: Brugge 1, Diksmuide 2, Ieper 3, Kortrijk 4, Oostende 5, Roeselare 6, Tielt 7, Veurne 8

On a deeper level, there are communes. Before 1977, they were changed often, but the number of communes remained close to 2500. On 1977-01-01, an act for the amalgamation of communes took effect. The old communes were merged in various ways, creating 589 new and larger communes.

Territorial extent: There is an enclave belonging to Antwerp inside the Netherlands, about 2 km. from the Belgian border. Its main town is Baarle-Hertog.

Hainaut is split into two parts by a strip of French territory. The western part is much smaller. Comines is its largest city.

Limburg is split into two parts by a strip of Dutch territory. The eastern part is much smaller. It is the commune of Fourons.

Origins of names:

Antwerp: from Germanic *anda werpum*: at the jetty
Brabant: Old High German *bracha*: new country, *bant*: region
Brussels: Middle Dutch *broec*: swamp, *sele*: castle
Flanders: possibly from Flemish *vlakte*: plain, *wanderen*: wander.
Hainaut: Haine River, with German suffix *-gau*: district

Liege: from Latin *lætica*: plantations owned by *læti* (immigrants)
Limburg: Germanic *lindo*: linden, *burg*: fort.
Luxembourg: Germanic *luttila*: little, *burg*: fort.
Wallonia: land of Walloons, from Germanic *walhon*: foreigner.

Change history:

1920-01-20	The Treaty of Versailles granted three German cantons (Eupen, Malmédy, and Saint Vith) to Belgium. Although geographically separated from it, they were annexed to Limburg. Also annexed was a sliver of land which had been neutral territory since the Napoleonic Wars. This was Moresnet, adjacent to Eupen.
1923	Two communes were transferred from East Flanders to Antwerp, constituting all of the present territory of Antwerp west of the Scheldt River.
~1932	Eupen, Malmédy, and Saint Vith transferred from Limburg to Liege.
1962-11-08	Administrative reform law changed numerous boundaries. The arrondissement of Mouscron was created and transferred from West Flanders to Hainaut. The town of Landen was transferred from Liege to Brabant. Fourons was transferred from Liege to Limburg. The arrondissement of Brussels was split into Brussels-Capital, Brussels-Suburbs, and Halle-Vilvoorde. The provinces of East Flanders and Limburg were also affected.
1970	Brussels-Suburbs arrondissement annexed to Halle-Vilvoorde arrondissement. The three modern regions were defined geographically, but not given administrative functions.
1980	Regional governments formed for the Flemish Region and Wallonia.
1989	Regional government formed for Brussels capital region.
1995-01-01	Brabant province divided into Brussels capital region, Flemish Brabant province, and Walloon Brabant province.

Other names of subdivisions:

Note: the Flemish language is basically the same as Dutch.
Antwerp: Amberes (Spanish); Antuérpia (Portuguese); Antwerpen (Dutch, German); Anvers (French); Anversa (Italian)
Brabant: Brabante (Italian, Portuguese, Spanish)
Brussels: Bruselas (Spanish); Brussel Hoofstadt, Brusselse Hoofdstedelijke Gewest (Dutch); Brüssel (German); Bruxelas (Portuguese); Région de Bruxelles-Capital (French)
East Flanders: Fiandra Orientale (Italian); Flandes Oriental (Spanish); Flandre orientale (French); Flandres Oriental (Portuguese); Oost-Vlaanderen (Dutch); Ost Flandern (German)
Flemish Brabant: Brabant Flamand (French); Vlaams Brabant (Dutch)
Flemish Region: Flandre, Région Flamande (French); Vlaanderen, Vlaams Gewest (Dutch)
Hainaut: Henegouwen (Dutch); Hennegau (German)

Liege: Liège (French, Portuguese); Liegi (Italian); Lieja (Spanish); Luik (Dutch); Lüttich (German)
Limburg: Limbourg (French); Limburgo (Italian, Portuguese, Spanish)
Luxembourg: Lussemburgo (Italian); Luxemburg (Dutch, German); Luxemburgo (Portuguese, Spanish)
Namur: Namen (Dutch)
Wallonia: Walenland (obsolete–Dutch); Wallonië (Dutch); Wallonie, Région Wallonne (French)
Walloon Brabant: Brabant Wallon (French); Waals Brabant (Dutch)
West Flanders: Fiandra Occidentale (Italian); Flandes Occidental (Spanish); Flandre occidentale (French); Flandres Ocidental (Portuguese); West Flandern (German); West-Vlaanderen (Dutch)

Population history:

division	1910c	1930c	1938e	1947c	1955e	1961c	1970c	1982e	1992e
Antwerp	968,677	1,173,363	1,254,242	1,281,333	1,362,908	1,443,000	1,533,249	1,577,246	1,610,695
Brabant	1,469,677	1,680,065	1,771,038	1,798,468	1,887,782	2,009,000	2,176,373	2,221,383	2,253,794
East Flanders	1,120,335	1,149,199	1,192,034	1,217,280	1,249,435	1,272,000	1,310,117	1,332,265	1,340,056
Hainaut	1,232,867	1,270,231	1,238,537	1,224,800	1,261,125	1,317,000	1,317,453	1,291,610	1,283,252
Liege	888,341	973,031	972,481	963,851	994,185	992,000	1,008,905	995,576	1,006,081
Limburg	275,691	367,642	416,547	460,446	528,123	572,000	652,547	724,032	755,593 ➤

division	1910c	1930c	1938e	1947c	1955e	1961c	1970c	1982e	1992e
Luxembourg	231,215	220,920	219,566	213,478	216,394	217,000	217,310	222,784	234,664
Namur	362,846	355,965	356,198	356,090	394,125	369,000	380,561	408,741	426,305
West Flanders	874,135	901,588	965,910	996,449	1,032,169	998,000	1,054,429	1,084,380	1,111,557
	7,423,784	8,092,004	8,386,553	8,512,195	8,926,246	9,189,000	9,650,944	9,858,017	10,021,997

c = census; e = estimate

Dates (where known): 1910-12-31, 1955-12-31, 1970-01-01, 1992-01-01.

BELIZE

ISO = BZ/FIPS = BH   Language = English   Time zone = -6   Capital = Belmopan

Belize started the 20th century as a British colony, under the name of British Honduras (although the region had long been known as Belize). It achieved full independence on 1981-09-21. Guatemala has asserted a claim to its territory through most of the century.

Other names of country: Belice (Spanish); Belís (Icelandic); Britisch-Honduras (obsolete–German); British Honduras (obsolete–English); Honduras Británica (obsolete–Spanish); Honduras britannico (obsolete–Italian); Honduras britannique (obsolete–French).

Origin of name: Named for Peter Wallace, Scottish buccaneer, Hispanicized as Belice.

division	abv	ISO	FIPS	population	area-km	area-mi	capital
Belize	BZ	BZ	BH01	50,801	4,204	1,623	Belize City
Cayo	CY	CY	BH02	22,337	5,338	2,061	Belmopan
Corozal	CZ	CZL	BH03	22,902	1,860	718	Corozal
Orange Walk	OW	OW	BH04	22,870	4,737	1,829	Orange Walk
Stann Creek	SC	SC	BH05	14,181	2,176	840	Dangriga
Toledo	TO	TOL	BH06	11,762	4,649	1,795	Punta Gorda
				144,853	22,964	8,866	

Status: These divisions are all districts.
Abv: Two-letter code for international compatibility (defined by the author).
ISO: Codes from ISO 3166-2.
FIPS: Codes from FIPS PUB 10-4.
Population: 1980 census.
Area-km: Square kilometers.
Area-mi: Square miles.
Territorial extent: Includes barrier islands and reefs from Ambergris Cay at the north to Sapodilla Cays at the south, and as far east as Lighthouse Reef (Half Moon Cay).
Change history:

~1955	Northern district split into Corozal and Orange Walk districts.
~1960	An area of 854 sq. km. was transferred from Toledo to Cayo.
1970-08-03	National capital moved to Belmopan from Belize City.
1974	Country name changed from British Honduras to Belize.
~1990	Capital of Cayo district moved from San Ignacio to Belmopan.

BENIN

ISO = BJ/FIPS = BN   Language = French   Time zone = +1   Capital = Porto-Novo

Benin began the 20th century under the name of Dahomey, as a French colony. On 1960-08-01, it became an independent member of the French Community. It has retained its borders virtually unchanged throughout the 20th century, bearing in mind that its northern (inland) borders were ill-defined in the early years.

Other names of country: Benín (Icelandic); Bénin (French); Dahomey (obsolete); Republic of Benin (formal–English); République du Bénin (formal).

Origin of name: Named for Bini, an ancient kingdom on the Gulf of Guinea.

division	ISO	FIPS	population	area-km	area-mi	capital
Atacora	AK	BN01	479,604	31,200	12,046	Natitingou
Atlantique	AQ	BN02	686,258	3,220	1,236	Cotonou
Borgou	BO	BN03	490,669	51,000	19,691	Parakou
Mono	MO	BN04	477,378	3,800	1,467	Lokossa
Ouémé	OU	BN05	626,868	4,700	1,815	Porto-Novo
Zou	ZO	BN06	570,433	18,700	7,220	Abomey
			3,338,240	112,622	43,484	

Status: These divisions are provinces (sometimes referred to as départements).
ISO: Codes from ISO 3166-2.
FIPS: Codes from FIPS PUB 10-4.
Population: 1979 census.
Area-km: Square kilometers.
Area-mi: Square miles.
Further subdivisions: The six provinces are further divided into 84 districts, which are categorized as urban or rural. Before independence, the provinces were subdivided into 29 préfectures.
Origins of names:

Atacora: From Atacora mountain range

Atlantique: From Atlantic Ocean

Change history:

1904	French colony of Dahomey incorporated into French West Africa as a territory.
1920	In the aftermath of World War I, the former German colony of Togo was split from north to south. The western third was mandated to Great Britain, and the eastern two-thirds to France. For part of the period between the wars, Dahomey and the French mandate of Togo were combined under the name Dahomey for administrative purposes.
~1923	Capital moved from Abomey to Porto-Novo.
1975-11-30	Country name changed from Dahomey to People's Republic of Benin.

Other names of subdivisions:

Atacora: Atakora, Nord-Ouest (obsolete)
Atlantique: Sud (obsolete)
Borgou: Nord-Est (obsolete)

Mono: Sud-Ouest (obsolete)
Ouémé: Sud-Est (obsolete)
Zou: Centre (obsolete)

BERMUDA

ISO = BM/FIPS = BD Language = English Time zone = -4 [d] Capital = Hamilton

Bermuda is a British dependency. It is an isolated island group in the Atlantic Ocean. For convenience, although not actually in the West Indies, it is sometimes included with them.

Other names of country: Bermuda-Inseln (German); Bermudas (Portuguese, Spanish); Bermude (Italian); Bermudes (French).

Origin of name: For discoverer Juan de Bermúdez (1515).

division	abv	ISO	FIPS	population	area-km	area-mi
Devonshire	DE	DEV	BD01	6,800	4.90	1.89
Hamilton	HA	HAM	BD02	3,800	5.10	1.97
Hamilton municipality	HC	HA	BD03	1,600	0.70	0.27
Paget	PA	PAG	BD04	4,500	5.28	2.04
Pembroke	PE	PEM	BD05	10,400	5.44	2.10
Saint George municipality	SG	SG	BD06	1,600	1.37	0.53
Saint George's	SC	SGE	BD07	2,900	9.30	3.59
Sandys	SA	SAN	BD08	6,300	6.75	2.61
Smiths	SM	SMI	BD09	4,500	4.90	1.89
Southampton	SO	SOU	BD10	4,600	5.75	2.22
Warwick	WA	WAR	BD11	7,000	5.72	2.21
				54,000	55.21	21.32

Status: These divisions are parishes, except for Hamilton municipality and Saint George municipality.
Abv: Two-letter code for international compatibility (defined by the author).
ISO: Codes from ISO 3166-2.
FIPS: Codes from FIPS PUB 10-4.
Population: 1980 census.
Area-km: Square kilometers.
Area-mi: Square miles.
Territorial extent:

Hamilton: Eastern end of Bermuda Island, separated from Hamilton city

Saint George's: Coney Island, Saint David's Island (including the U.S. Naval Air Station), Saint George's Island (except for Saint George city)

Sandys: Boaz Island, Ireland Island, Somerset Island, Watford Island, and the western tip of Bermuda Island (including the U.S. Naval Air Station Annex)

The sequence of parishes along the south shore of Bermuda Island from west to east is: Sandys, Warwick, Paget, Devonshire, Smith's, Hamilton, and Saint George's. Along the north shore, also from west to east: Pembroke, Devonshire, Smith's, and Hamilton. Hamilton Harbour separates Pembroke from Paget. Hamilton city lies on the north shore of Hamilton Harbour, surrounded on its other three sides by Pembroke.

Other names of subdivisions:

Saint George municipality: Saint Georges, Saint George's (variant)
Saint George's: Saint Georges (variant)

Sandys: Sandy's (variant)
Smiths: Smith's (variant)

BHUTAN

ISO = BT/FIPS = BT Language = Tibetan (Dzongkha) Time zone = +6 Capital = Thimphu

Bhutan has been an independent kingdom throughout the 20th century.

Other names of country: Bhoutan (French); Bhután (Spanish); Butão (Portuguese); Bútan (Icelandic); Druk-yul (formal); Kingdom of Bhutan (formal–English).

Origin of name: from Sanskrit *bhotas*: Tibet, *antas*: edge (i.e. land on the edge of Tibet). Druk-yul is Tibetan for Land of the Dragon.

division	abv	ISO	FIPS	rgn	population	capitals
Bumthang	BU	33	BT05	1	— —	Jakar
Chhukha	CK	12	BT06	1	97,200	Chhukha
Chirang	CR	21	BT07	2	104,500	Damphu
Daga	DA	22	BT08	2	27,700	Daga
Geylegphug	GE	31	BT09	3	112,800	Geylegphug
Ha	HA	13	BT10	1	17,100	Ha
Lhuntshi	LH	44	BT11	4	36,900	Lhuntshi
Mongar	MO	42	BT12	4	71,300	Mongar
Paro	PR	11	BT13	1	39,800	Paro
Pemagatsel	PM	43	BT14	4	35,100	Pemagatsel
Punakha	PN	23	BT15	2	34,500	Punakha
Samchi	SM	14	BT16	1	138,900	Samchi
Samdrup Jongkhar	SJ	45	BT17	4	72,200	Samdrup Jongkhar
Shemgang	SG	34	BT18	3	43,300	Shemgang
Tashigang	TA	41	BT19	4	170,000	Tashigang
Thimphu	TM	15	BT20	1	64,600	Thimphu
Tongsa	TO	32	BT21	3	28,600	Tongsa
Wangdi Phodrang	WP	24	BT22	2	47,700	Wangdi Phodrang
					1,142,200	

Status: These divisions are dzongkhag (districts).
Abv: Two-letter code for international compatibility (defined by the author).
ISO: Codes from ISO 3166-2.
FIPS: Codes from FIPS PUB 10-4.
Rgn: Region to which this district belongs, according to the ISO code below.
Population: 1980 census.

region	ISO	region	ISO
Central	1	Southern	3
Eastern	2	Western	4

Change history:

1949-08-08	India restored an area of 83 sq. km. around Dewangiri, which it had annexed in 1865, to Bhutan. It is now part of Samdrup Jongkhar.
~1964	National capital moved from Punakha to Thimphu, through a transition period when Punakha was the winter capital and Thimphu the summer capital.
1965	Bhutan had nine penlop (provinces): Byakar, Dukye, Ha, Paro, Punakha, Tagana, Thimbu, Tongsa, and Wangü-Phodrang.
~1979	Gasa district split up among Punakha and Thimphu; Chhukha district formed from parts of Samchi, Paro, and Thimphu.

Other names of subdivisions:

Chirang: Tsirang (variant)
Daga: Dagana, Tagana (variant)
Geylegphug: Gaylegphug (variant)
Lhuntshi: Lhuentse, Lhuntsi (variant)
Paro: Rinpung (variant)
Pemagatsel: Pemagatshel (variant)
Punakha: Punaka (variant)
Samchi: Samtse (variant)

Samdrup Jongkhar: Samdrup, Samdrup Jongkha (variant)
Shemgang: Zhemgang (variant)
Tashigang: Trashigang (variant)
Thimphu: Tashi Chho Dzong, Thimbu (variant)
Tongsa: Trongsa (variant)
Wangdi Phodrang: Andguphodang, Wangdue Phodrang, Wangdupotrang, Wangü-Phodrang (variant)

BOLIVIA

ISO = BO/FIPS = BL   Language = Spanish   Time zone = -4   Capitals = La Paz, Sucre

Bolivia has been independent for the whole 20th century. It has had numerous boundary disputes with its neighbors, usually losing. Its boundaries have remained quite stable since 1950.

Other names of country: Bolívia (Portuguese); Bólivía (Icelandic); Bolivie (French); Bolivien (German); Republic of Bolivia (formal–English); República de Bolivia (formal).

Origin of name: Named in honor of Simón Bolívar (1783–1830), independence fighter.

division	abv	ISO	FIPS	population	area-km	area-mi	capital
Chuquisaca	CQ	H	BL01	451,722	51,524	19,894	Sucre
Cochabamba	CB	C	BL02	1,093,625	55,631	21,479	Cochabamba
El Beni	EB	B	BL03	251,390	213,564	82,458	Trinidad
La Paz	LP	L	BL04	1,883,122	133,985	51,732	La Paz
Oruro	OR	O	BL05	338,893	53,588	20,690	Oruro
Pando	PA	N	BL06	37,785	63,827	24,644	Cobija
Potosí	PO	P	BL07	645,817	118,218	45,644	Potosí
Santa Cruz	SC	S	BL08	1,351,191	370,621	143,098	Santa Cruz (de la Sierra)
Tarija	TR	T	BL09	290,851	37,623	14,526	Tarija
				6,344,396	1,098,581	424,164	

Status: These divisions are departamentos (departments).

Abv: Two-letter code for international compatibility (defined by the author).

ISO: Codes from ISO 3166-2.

FIPS: Codes from FIPS PUB 10-4.

Population: 1992 census (preliminary).

Area-km: Square kilometers.

Area-mi: Square miles.

Further subdivisions: The departments are divided into about 100 provincias (provinces). The provinces, in turn, are subdivided into over 1,000 cantones (cantons). New provinces and cantons are often created.

Territorial extent: The border between Cochabamba and El Beni is still not defined.

Origins of names:

El Beni: from the River Beni. Beni is Pano (native dialect) for river.

La Paz: earlier name Pueblo Novo de Nuestra Señora de la Paz, Spanish for "New City of Our Lady of Peace." So named to encourage an end to internecine strife among the conquistadores.

Oruro: native word for "black and white," referring to petroglyphs.

Potosí: probably from Quechua *potojchi*: rumbling noise

Santa Cruz: city founded by missionaries on 1560-09-14, festival of the Exaltation of the Holy Cross.

Change history:

1900-03-23	Acre reconquered by Bolivia after proclaiming its independence on 1899-07-14.
1903-11-17	Brazil purchased the Acre territory from Bolivia for two million pounds in the Treaty of Petrópolis; border demarcated 1909-09-08.
~1924	Madre de Dios territory split from La Paz department.
1925	Bolivia (Potosí department) acquired land from Argentina (Jujuy province).
~1938	Madre de Dios renamed Colonial Territories.
1938	Bolivia and Paraguay had a long-standing dispute over the Gran Chaco, which lay between the Paraguay and Pilcomayo Rivers north into Santa Cruz. Until 1932, it was divided along a line roughly from the split of the Pilcomayo River to Fuerte Olimpo. Oil was discovered. Both countries tried to assert their rights. They fought the Chaco War from 1932 to 1935. In the eventual peace settlement, Bolivia lost most of the disputed territory — parts of Chuquisaca, Santa Cruz, and Tarija departments — to Paraguay.

~1943   Colonial Territories became Pando department.

~1943   There was a short-lived Chaco department, capital Villa Montes, later annexed to Tarija.

There have been minor adjustments to the department boundaries.

Other names of subdivisions:

El Beni: Beni (variant)

Pando: Colonial Territories, Madre de Dios (obsolete); Ter-

ritorio Nacional de Colonias (obsolete–Spanish)

Population history:

	1900	1940	1950	1971	1976	1982	1990
Chuquisaca	196,434	400,000	282,980	474,000	358,516	435,406	498,000
Cochabamba	326,163	642,000	490,475	822,000	720,952	908,674	1,098,000
El Beni	25,680	63,000	119,770	200,900	168,367	217,700	278,000
La Paz	426,930	872,000	948,446	1,590,000	1,456,078	1,913,184	2,409,000
Oruro	86,081	169,000	210,260	352,600	310,409	385,121	461,000
Pando	7,228	62,000	19,804	33,200	34,493	42,594	59,000
Potosí	325,615	638,000	534,399	896,000	657,743	823,485	967,000
Santa Cruz	171,592	410,000	286,145	479,800	710,724	942,986	1,237,000
Tarija	67,887	201,000	126,752	212,600	186,704	246,691	315,000
	1,633,610	3,457,000	3,019,031	5,061,100	4,603,986	5,915,841	7,322,000

Census details:

1940 — estimate

1950 — August–September

1971 — estimate

1990 — estimate

BOSNIA AND HERZEGOVINA

ISO = BA/FIPS = BK   Language = Serbo-Croatian   Time zone = +1 [d]   Capital = Sarajevo

At the beginning of the 20th century, Bosnia and Herzegovina had been occupied by the Austro-Hungarian Empire, but was still de jure part of the Ottoman Empire. It was formally annexed by Austria-Hungary in 1908. In the aftermath of World War I, it was allocated to the Kingdom of Serbs, Croats, and Slovenes, which soon became Yugoslavia. It remained one of the six constituent republics of Yugoslavia until the federation broke up in 1992. The situation in Bosnia has been unstable since then. This listing assumes that the subdivisions that existed in Bosnia as a part of Yugoslavia have remained in effect.

Other names of country: Bosnia (informal); Bosnia ed Erzegovina (Italian); Bosnia-Hercegovina (Norwegian); Bósnia-Herzegóvina (Portuguese); Bosnia ja Hertsegovina (Finnish); Bosnía og Hersegóvína (Icelandic); Bosnia y Herzegovina (Spanish); Bosnie-Herzégovine (French); Bosnien-Hercegovina (Danish, Swedish); Bosnien und Herzegowina (German); Republika Bosna i Hercegovina (formal).

Origin of name: Bosnia from the Bosna River; Old Serbian *Herzegovina*: duchy, named by governor Stepan Vukčić on taking the title herzeg.

division	abv	population	area-km	area-mi	division	abv	population	area-km	area-mi
Banja Luka	BL	338,196	4,720	1,822	Mostar	MO	347,516	9,425	3,639
Bihać	BH	195,573	3,868	1,493	Prijedor	PR	250,078	3,660	1,413
Brčko	BR	256,467	2,375	917	Sarajevo	SA	424,472	5,212	2,012
Doboj	DO	319,125	3,356	1,296	Tuzla	TU	452,107	5,067	1,956
Goražde	GO	155,890	3,384	1,307	Zenica	ZE	267,662	2,800	1,081
Jajce	JJ	137,702	2,650	1,023			3,277,935	51,129	19,741
Livno	LI	133,147	4,500	1,737					

Status: These divisions are kotari (counties).
Abv: Two-letter code for international compatibility (defined by the author).
Population: 1961 estimate.
Area-km: Square kilometers.
Area-mi: Square miles.
Capitals: All capitals have the same name as their kotar.
Further subdivisions: The kotari are subdivided into 105 opčine (communes).
Origins of names:

Banja Luka: probably Serbo-Croat *banja*: governor's, *luka*: prairie
Mostar: Serbo-Croat *most*: bridge, *star*: old. Unfortunately,

the old bridge was destroyed by civil war.
Sarajevo: From Turkish *saray*: palace

BOTSWANA

ISO = BW/FIPS = BC   Languages = English, Setswana   Time zone = +2   Capital = Gaborone

Bechuanaland was a British protectorate at the beginning of the 20th century. It became independent, and took the name Botswana, on 1966-09-30. Its borders have remained almost the same.

Other names of country: Bechuanaland (obsolete); Bechuania (obsolete–Spanish); Botsuana (German, Portuguese); Botsvana (Icelandic); Republic of Botswana (formal–English).

Meaning of name: Land of the Bechuana, or Tswana (ethnic name).

division	ISO	FIPS	population	area-km	area-mi	capital
Central	CE	BC01	373,497	147,730	57,039	Serowe
Chobe	CH	BC02	7,934	20,800	8,031	Kasane
Ghanzi	GH	BC03	19,096	117,910	45,525	Ghanzi
Kgalagadi	KG	BC04	24,059	106,940	41,290	Tshabong
Kgatleng	KL	BC05	44,461	7,960	3,073	Mochudi
Kweneng	KW	BC06	117,127	35,890	13,857	Molepolole
Ngamiland	NG	BC07	68,063	109,130	42,135	Maun
North-East	NE	BC08	67,701	5,120	1,977	Francistown
South-East	SE	BC09	109,340	1,780	687	Gaborone
Southern	SO	BC10	109,749	28,470	10,992	Kanye
			941,027	581,730	224,606	

Status: These divisions are districts.
ISO: Codes from ISO 3166-2.
FIPS: Codes from FIPS PUB 10-4.
Population: 1981 census.
Area-km: Square kilometers.
Area-mi: Square miles.
Further subdivisions: There are town councils and townships which are reported in various ways. Some sources place them on the same level with the districts. To conform to the standards, I have made them subordinate to the districts.
Territorial extent: Central includes the town councils or townships of Malalapye, Orapa, Selebi-Pikwe, and Serowe.
North-East includes the town council of Francistown.
South-East includes the town councils of Gaborone and Lobatse.
Change history:

1969   Name of national capital changed from Gaberones to Gaborone.

Other names of subdivisions:

Central: Ngwato (Setswana)

Southern: Ngwakets, Ngwaketse (Setswana)

BOUVET ISLAND

ISO = BV/FIPS = BV   Language = Norwegian   Time zone =   Capital = none

British possession until 1930-02-27, when it was amicably transferred to Norway as a dependency. Included here only to conform to the standards.

Other names of country: Bouvetinsel (German); Bouvetøya (formal); Île Bouvet (French).

Origin of name: Discovered by French navigator Jean-Baptiste Bouvet de Lozier.

division	abv	population	area-km	area-mi
Bouvet Island	BV	0	58	22

Status: This division is the whole of the country, treated as a division for compatibility.

Abv: Two-letter code for international compatibility (defined by the author).

Area-km: Square kilometers.

Area-mi: Square miles.

BRAZIL

ISO = BR/FIPS = BR   Language = Portuguese   Time zones (see table)   Capital = Brasília, DF

Brazil has been an independent country for the whole 20th century.

Other names of country: Brasil (Norwegian, Portuguese, Spanish); Brasile (Italian); Brasilia (Finnish); Brasilía (Icelandic); Brasilien (Danish, German, Swedish); Brazilië (Dutch); Brésil (French); Estados Unidos do Brasil (obsolete; formal until 1969); Federative Republic of Brazil (formal–English); República Federativa do Brasil (formal).

Origin of name: Brazil wood was a major export in early colonial times.

division	abv	FIPS	zone	population	area-km	area-mi	capital	region	adjective	CEP range
Acre	AC	BR01	-5	417,100	152,589	58,915	Rio Branco	N	acreano	69900–69999
Alagoas	AL	BR02	-3	2,512,661	27,731	10,707	Maceió	NE	alagoano	57000–57999
Amapá	AP	BR03	-3	289,041	140,276	54,161	Macapá	N	amapaense	68500–68999
Amazonas	AM	BR04	-4a[d]	2,102,771	1,564,445	604,037	Manaus	N	amazonense	69000–69899
Bahia	BA	BR05	-3 [d]	11,867,328	561,026	216,614	Salvador	NE	baiano	40000–48999
Ceará	CE	BR06	-3	6,366,117	148,016	57,149	Fortaleza	NE	cearense	60000–63999
Distrito Federal	DF	BR07	-3 [d]	1,601,095	5,814	2,245	Brasília	CO	brasiliense	70000–70999
Espírito Santo	ES	BR08	-3 [d]	2,600,624	45,296	17,489	Vitória	NE	capixaba	29000–29999
Goiás	GO	BR29	-3 [d]	4,017,510	340,166	131,339	Goiânia	CO	goiano	74000–77499
Maranhão	MA	BR13	-3	4,929,687	328,663	126,898	São Luís	NE	maranhense	65000–65999
Mato Grosso	MT	BR14	-4 [d]	2,026,078	881,001	340,157	Cuiabá	CO	matogrossense	78000–78899
Mato Grosso do Sul	MS	BR11	-4 [d]	1,780,370	350,548	135,348	Campo Grande	CO	sul-mato-grossense	79000–79999
Minas Gerais	MG	BR15	-3 [d]	15,743,561	587,172	226,709	Belo Horizonte	SD	mineiro	30000–39999
Pará	PA	BR16	-3b	4,949,217	1,248,042	481,873	Belém	N	paraense	66000–68499
Paraíba	PB	BR17	-3	3,201,319	56,372	21,765	João Pessoa	NE	paraibano	58000–58999
Paraná	PR	BR18	-3 [d]	8,448,600	199,554	77,048	Curitiba	S	paranaense	80000–86999
Pernambuco	PE	BR30	-3c	7,127,942	98,307	37,957	Recife	NE	pernambucano	50000–56999
Piauí	PI	BR20	-3	2,582,077	250,934	96,886	Teresina	NE	piauiense	64000–64999
Rio de Janeiro	RJ	BR21	-3 [d]	12,807,220	44,258	17,088	Rio de Janeiro	SD	fluminense	20000–28999
Rio Grande do Norte	RN	BR22	-3	2,415,092	53,015	20,469	Natal	NE	potiguar	59000–59999
Rio Grande do Sul	RS	BR23	-3 [d]	9,138,453	287,189	110,885	Porto Alegre	S	gaúcho	90000–99999
Rondônia	RO	BR24	-4	1,133,268	243,044	93,840	Porto Velho	N	rondoniano	78900–78999
Roraima	RR	BR25	-4	217,584	230,104	88,844	Boa Vista	N	roraimense	69000–69899
Santa Catarina	SC	BR26	-3 [d]	4,542,044	95,985	37,060	Florianópolis	S	catarinense	87000–89999

➤

division	abv	FIPS	zone	population	area-km	area-mi	capital	region	adjective	CEP range
São Paulo	SP	BR27	-3 [d]	31,588,801	247,898	95,714	São Paulo	SD	paulista	00000–19999
Sergipe	SE	BR28	-3	1,491,871	21,994	8,492	Aracaju	NE	sergipano	49000–49999
Tocantins	TO	BR31	-3	918,387	277,322	107,075	Palmas	N	tocantinense	77500–77999
				146,815,818	8,486,761	3,276,757				

a = *Amazonas is divided between zones -4 and -5. Zone -5 comprises only the part west of a geodesic connecting Tabatinga to Porto Acre, excluding those two towns.* b = *Pará is divided between zones -3 and -4. Zone -3 lies east of the line formed by Rio Jari and Rio Xingu, and a short segment of the Amazon River connecting them.* c = *Fernando de Noronha, although part of Pernambuco, is in zone -2.*

Status: Each of these divisions is an estado (state), except for one. Distrito Federal, as its name indicates, is a federal district. Formerly, some divisions were territórios (territories).

Abv: These codes, defined by the Brazilian government, are widely used and recognized in Brazil. They are called siglas. ISO 3166-2 uses these same codes as the second element (after BR-) of the subdivision codes. These are the same as the codes used by IATA in the Airline Coding Directory to locate airports by state.

FIPS: Codes from FIPS PUB 10-4.

Zone: Time zones. Convert from UTC to local time by adding this number of hours. Superscript ([d]) indicates areas where daylight saving time is in effect during summer.

Population: 1991 census.

Area-km: Square kilometers.

Area-mi: Square miles.

CEP range: Brazilian códigos de endereçamento postal (postal codes) are five digits, with an optional three-digit extension. With a few exceptions, postal codes for each state fall into a defined range. The exceptions are cases where a city is served from a distribution center in a neighboring state. Also, Amazonas and Roraima share a block of codes.

Region:

CO = Centro-Oeste (Center-West)
N = Norte (North)
NE = Nordeste (North-East)
S = Sul (South)
SD = Sudeste (South-East)

Regions (região, pl. regiões, sometimes grande região) seem to have no administrative purpose but are often used for statistical analysis. Abbreviations used here are unofficial. This regional division dates from 1971; a different division was in effect from 1941 to 1970.

Further subdivisions: The states are subdivided into municípios (municipalities). There were 4,493 municípios in 1992; 3,950 in 1976. The municípios are subdivided into distritos (districts). The federal district is subdivided into 13 administrative regions.

Territorial extent: Several areas are or were in dispute between neighboring states:

Amazonas/Pará: some islands in the Amazon, including the town of Nhamunda, totaling 2,680 sq.km. Now part of Amazonas.

Ceará/Piauí: three sections, including the town of Macambira (or Mocambira), totaling 3,382 sq.km.

Espírito Santo/Minas Gerais: Serra dos Aimorés, briefly treated as a separate region in the 1950s. Largest towns: Mantena and Barra de São Francisco. Area 10,137 sq. km. Later divided, with about 5,719 sq. km. going to Espírito Santo.

Pernambuco includes the former territory of Fernando de Noronha, consisting of the Atlantic islands of Fernando de Noronha, Penedos de São Pedro e São Paulo, and Atol das Rocas.

Espírito Santo includes the Atlantic islands of Martin Vaz and Trindade.

Distrito Federal and Minas Gerais have a short border along the Rio Preto, which is hard to see on a small-scale map.

Tocantins contains Ilha do Bananal, a lozenge of land lying between two arms of the Araguaia River. It is said to be the largest river island in the world.

Pará contains Ilha de Marajó in the Amazon delta. It is said to be the largest island in the world partly surrounded by fresh water.

Origins of names:

Acre: from Acre River (formerly Aquiri River)
Alagoas: from large number of lakes (Portuguese *as lagoas*: the lakes)

Amazonas: from Amazon River. Amazon comes from the Greek for "without breast." Greek legend said that the Amazons were a race of female warriors in Scythia who cut off their right breasts to be able to draw their bows unencumbered. When early explorer Francisco de Orellana encountered beardless warriors, he named the river after the legendary women.

Bahia: formed around All Saints' Bay (Portugese Baía de Todos os Santos; Bahia is another spelling of Baía). The bay was discovered by Amerigo Vespucci on All Saints' Day, 1501-11-01.

Ceará: Guaraní *ceara*: shouts

Distrito Federal: = Federal District

Espírito Santo: = Holy Spirit

Fernando de Noronha: named for Portuguese navigator Fernando de Noronha, who discovered the island on 1502-08-29, Saint John's Day, and named it Ilha de São Johão

Goiás: from an ethnic name

Maranhão: Guaraní *para*: river, *na*: parent, *jho*: come out

Mato Grosso: = Large Brushland

Mato Grosso do Sul: = Southern Mato Grosso

Minas Gerais: from government-owned gold mines in the area (Portuguese *Minas Gerais*: General Mines)

Pará: Guaraní *para*: variegated

Paraíba: from Paraíba River (Tupí *para hiba*: arm of the river, or Guaraní *para ai*: bad river)

Paraná: from Paraná River (Guaraní *parana*: father of waters)

Pernambuco: Guaraní *parana*: great river, *mbuku*: arm

Rio de Janeiro: = River of January. When Gaspar de Lemos and Amerigo Vespucci discovered the mouth of Guanabara Bay on 1502-01-01, they named it Rio de Janeiro in the mistaken belief that it was a large river.

Rio Grande do Norte: = Big River of the North

Rio Grande do Sul: = Big River of the South

Rondônia: named for Marshal Cândido Mariano da Silva Rondon, soldier and explorer

Roraima: from Mount Roraima

Santa Catarina: reportedly named by Sebastian Cabot after Saint Catherine of Alexandria

São Paulo: = Saint Paul. Founded by Jesuits on 1554-01-25, festival day of Saint Paul's conversion.

Sergipe: from Serigy, a native chief

Tocantins: from Tocantins River, which came from an ethnic name

Change history:

1867-03-27	Acre granted to Bolivia in the Treaty of Ayacucho.
1895	Name of capital of Santa Catarina changed from (Nossa Senhora do) Desterro to Florianópolis in memory of Marshal Floriano Peixoto.
1897-10-12	Capital of Minas Gerais moved from Ouro Preto to Belo Horizonte.
1900-01-01	Geneva Commission awarded present-day Amapá to Brazil in a boundary dispute with France.
1900-03-23	Acre reconquered by Bolivia after proclaiming its independence on 1899-07-14.
1901	Name of capital of Minas Gerais changed from Cidade de Minas to Belo Horizonte.
1903-11-17	Acre purchased from Bolivia for two million pounds in the Treaty of Petrópolis, organized as a territory; border demarcated 1909-09-08.
1904	A district named Pirara was taken from Amazonas (in the area that is now Roraima) and annexed to British Guiana through arbitration.
1904	Ecuador ceded land between the Japurá and Amazon Rivers, as far west as the modern border between Brazil and Colombia, to Brazil.
1907	Colombia ceded a large, remote area around the Uaupés River to Brazil, where it became part of Amazonas.
1930-09-04	Name of capital of Paraíba changed from Paraíba to João Pessoa in memory of an assassinated president-elect.
1937	Capital of Goiás moved from Goiás to the newly built city of Goiânia.
1942-09-02	Fernando de Noronha and several smaller Atlantic islands split from Pernambuco to become Fernando de Noronha territory. Officially, the capital was the whole island of Fernando de Noronha. There is only one city on the island: Vila dos Remedios.
1943-09-13	Ponta Porã split from Mato Grosso as territory.
1943-09-13	Iguaçu formed from parts of Paraná and Santa Catarina as territory.
1943-09-13	Rondônia formed from parts of Amazonas and Minas Gerais as Guaporé territory.
1943-09-13	Roraima split from Amazonas as Rio Branco territory.
1943-09-13	Amapá split from Pará as territory.
1943-09-13?	Name changed from Goiáz to Goiás.
1943-09-13?	Name changed from Baía to Bahia.
1944-05-31	Macapá becomes capital of Amapá.
1946-09-18	Ponta Porã restored to Mato Grosso.

1946-09-18   Iguaçu restored to Paraná and Santa Catarina.
1956-02-17   Name of Rondônia changed from Guaporé to Rondônia.
1960-04-21   Capital of Brazil changed from Rio de Janeiro to Brasília.
1960-04-21   (New) Distrito Federal split from Goiás as federal district.
1960-04-21   Name and status of (old) Distrito Federal changed to Guanabara state.
1962-06-15   Acre changed from territory to state.
1962-12-13   Name changed from Rio Branco to Roraima.
1975-03-15   Guanabara merged with Rio de Janeiro; capital of Rio de Janeiro changed from Niterói
             to Rio de Janeiro.
1979-01-01   Mato Grosso do Sul split from Mato Grosso as state (FIPS: BR12 -> BR11 + BR14 [con-
             jectural]).
1981-12-22   Rondônia changed from territory to state.
1989-01-01   Fernando de Noronha merged with Pernambuco (FIPS: BR09 + BR19 -> BR30).
1989-01-01   Amapá changed from territory to state.
1989-01-01   Roraima changed from territory to state.
1989-01-01   Tocantins state split from Goiás, with Miracema do Tocantins as its capital. At the same
             time, it was transferred from Centro-Oeste region to Norte. (FIPS: BR10 -> BR29
             + BR31).
1990-01   Capital of Tocantins moved from Miracema do Tocantins to Palmas.

Other names of subdivisions:

Amazonas: Amazone (French)
Bahia: Baía (obsolete)
Goiás: Goiáz, Goyáz (obsolete)
Maranhão: São Luíz de Maranhão (obsolete)
Mato Grosso: Matto Grosso (variant)
Minas Gerais: Minas (informal); Minas Geraes (variant)

Paraíba: Parahyba (obsolete)
Pernambuco: Pernambouc (French)
Piauí: Piauhy (obsolete)
Rondônia: Guaporé (obsolete)
Roraima: Rio Branco (obsolete)
Santa Catarina: Santa Catharina (variant)

Population history:

abv	1900-12-31	1920-01-01	1940-01-01	1950-07-01	1960-09-01	1970-09-01	1980-09-01	1991-09-01
AC	——	92,379	79,768	114,755	160,208	215,299	301,303	417,100
AL	649,273	978,748	951,300	1,093,137	1,271,062	1,588,109	1,982,591	2,512,661
AP	——	——	——	37,477	68,889	114,359	175,257	289,041
AM	249,756	363,166	438,008	514,099	721,215	955,235	1,430,089	2,102,771
BA	2,117,956	3,334,465	3,918,112	4,834,575	5,990,605	7,493,470	9,454,346	11,867,328
CE	849,172	1,319,228	2,091,032	2,695,450	3,337,856	4,361,603	5,288,253	6,366,117
DF	——	——	——	——	141,742	537,492	1,176,935	1,601,095
ES	209,783	457,328	790,149	957,238	1,418,348	1,599,333	2,023,340	2,600,624
FN	——	——	——	581	1,389	1,241	1,279	——
GB	811,443	1,157,873	1,764,141	2,377,451	3,307,163	4,251,918	——	——
GO	255,284	511,919	826,414	1,214,921	1,954,862	2,938,677	3,859,602	4,017,510
MA	499,308	874,337	1,235,169	1,583,248	2,492,139	2,992,686	3,996,404	4,929,687
MT	118,025	246,612	432,265	522,044	910,262	1,597,090	1,138,691	2,026,078
MS	——	——	——	——	——	——	1,369,567	1,780,370
MG	3,594,471	5,888,174	6,763,368	7,782,188	9,960,040	11,487,415	13,378,553	15,743,561
PA	445,356	983,507	944,644	1,123,273	1,550,935	2,167,018	3,403,391	4,949,217
PB	490,784	961,106	1,422,282	1,713,259	2,018,023	2,382,617	2,770,176	3,201,319
PR	327,136	685,711	1,236,276	2,115,547	4,296,375	6,929,868	7,629,392	8,448,600
PE	1,178,150	2,154,835	2,688,240	3,395,185	4,136,900	5,160,640	6,143,272	7,127,942
PI	334,328	609,003	817,601	1,045,696	1,263,368	1,680,573	2,139,021	2,582,077
RJ	926,035	1,559,371	1,847,857	2,297,194	3,402,728	4,742,884	11,291,520	12,807,220
RN	274,317	537,135	768,018	967,921	1,157,258	1,550,244	1,898,172	2,415,092
RS	1,149,070	2,182,713	3,320,689	4,164,821	5,448,823	6,664,891	7,773,837	9,138,453
RO	——	——	——	36,935	70,783	111,064	491,069	1,133,268
RR	——	——	——	18,116	29,489	40,885	79,159	217,584
SC	320,289	668,743	1,178,340	1,560,502	2,146,909	2,901,734	3,627,933	4,542,044
SP	2,282,279	4,592,188	7,180,316	9,134,423	12,974,699	17,771,948	25,040,712	31,588,801 ▶

abv	1900-12-31	1920-01-01	1940-01-01	1950-07-01	1960-09-01	1970-09-01	1980-09-01	1991-09-01
SE	356,264	477,064	542,326	644,361	760,273	900,744	1,140,121	1,491,871
TO	——	——	——	——	——	——	——	918,387

Note: GB = Guanabara = (old) Distrito Federal (unofficial abbreviation).

BRITISH INDIAN OCEAN TERRITORY

ISO = IO/FIPS = IO   Language = English   Time zone = +5   Capital = none

A British possession, created in 1965 for mutual military use by the United Kingdom and the United States.

Other names of country: Britisches Territorium im Indischen Ozean (German); Territoire britannique de l'Océan Indien (French); Territorio Británico del Océano Índico (Spanish); Território Britânico do Oceano Indico (Portuguese); Territorio Britannico dell'oceano Indiano (Italian).

Origin of name: Descriptive: British possession in Indian Ocean.

division	abv	population	area-km	area-mi
British Indian Ocean Territory	IO	0	60	23

Status: This division is the whole of the country, treated as a division for compatibility.

Abv: Two-letter code for international compatibility (defined by the author).

Area-km: Square kilometers.

Area-mi: Square miles.

Territorial extent: Territory includes the atolls of Diego Garcia, Eagle, Egmont, Peros Banhos, and Salomon. These are collectively known as the Chagos Archipelago (formerly, the Oil Islands). Although there is no permanent population, there is a U.S. naval facility on Diego Garcia.

Change history:

1965-11-08	Territory was created from parts of Mauritius and Seychelles.
1976-06-29	Aldabra Island, Desroches Island, and Farquhar Island restored to Seychelles.

BRUNEI DARUSSALAM

ISO = BN/FIPS = BX   Language = Malay   Time zone = +8   Capital = Bandar Seri Begawan

The Sultanate of Brunei was a British protectorate at the beginning of the 20th century. It became independent on 1983-12-31.

Other names of country: Brúnei (Icelandic); Brunei (informal); Brunéi Darussalam (French); Negara Brunei Darussalam (formal); State of Brunei Darussalam (formal–English).

Origin of name: Possibly from Sanskrit *bhumi:* land.

division	ISO	FIPS	population	area-km	area-mi	capital
Belait	BE	BX01	56,000	2,725	1,052	Kuala Belait
Brunei and Muara	BM	BX02	147,300	570	220	Bandar Seri Begawan
Temburong	TE	BX03	9,000	1,166	450	Bangar
Tutong	TU	BX04	28,500	1,303	503	Tutong
			240,800	5,765	2,226	

Status: These divisions are districts.
ISO: Codes from ISO 3166-2.
FIPS: Codes from FIPS PUB 10-4.
Population: 1988 estimate.
Area-km: Square kilometers.
Area-mi: Square miles.
Territorial extent: Temburong is separated from the rest of Brunei by part of Sarawak (Malaysia) and Brunei Bay. However, the bay is only about 10 km. wide, and Brunei claims a 12-mile limit. Therefore, it's possible to go from Temburong to the rest of Brunei without leaving the country's territorial waters.

Brunei and Muara contains the island of Pulau Muara Besar.

Change history:

1970   Name of national capital changed from Brunei to Bandar Seri Begawan.

Other names of subdivisions:

Brunei and Muara: Brunei-Muara (variant)

BULGARIA

ISO = BG/FIPS = BU   Language = Bulgarian   Time zone = +2 ^{d} Capital = Sofiya

Bulgaria began the 20th century as a tributary principality of the Ottoman Empire. It consisted of Bulgaria proper and Eastern Rumelia. On 1908-10-05 it became an independent kingdom. In 1913, as a result of the First Balkan War, Bulgaria acquired territory from the Ottoman Empire in what is now southern Bulgaria, Greek Thrace, and a small part of the Former Yugoslav Republic of Macedonia. In the northeast, however, it ceded territory around Bazargic (Dobitsch) to Romania. In 1915, it acquired another small slice of the Ottoman Empire around Orestias and Dimotika, now in Greece. In the Peace of Sèvres (1920), Bulgaria lost part of Thrace to Greece. The Peace of Lausanne (1923) gave more of Thrace to Greece, resulting in the present-day border between Bulgaria and Greece. The Treaty of Craiova (1940-09-08) transferred Durostor (Silistra) and Caliacra (Tolbukhin) provinces (together known as Southern Dobruja) from Romania to Bulgaria. After World War II, the peace treaty restored Bulgaria to its borders of 1941-01-01, canceling out its conquests in Thrace and southern Yugoslavia. In a referendum, voters chose to end the monarchy and form a republic. The first general election went to the Communists. Bulgaria remained in the Communist bloc until the Iron Curtain fell in 1991.

Other names of country: Bulgária (Portuguese); Búlgaría (Icelandic); Bulgarie (French); Bulgarien (Danish, German, Swedish); Bulgarije (Dutch); Republic of Bulgaria (formal–English); Republika Bulgaria (formal).

Meaning of name: Land of the Bulgars. Bulgar comes from the Turkish word for mixed, since the Bulgars had mixed origins.

division	abv	ISO	FIPS	population	area-km	area-mi	communes
Burgas	BU	2	BU29	875,319	14,657	5,659	21
Grad Sofiya	GS	1	BU30	1,221,436	1,311	506	25
Khaskovo	HA	9	BU31	1,054,442	13,892	5,364	27
Lovech	LO	4	BU32	1,053,895	15,150	5,849	32
Montana	MO	5	BU33	658,284	10,607	4,095	33
Plovdiv	PL	6	BU34	1,279,381	13,628	5,262	34
Razgrad	RA	7	BU35	848,742	10,842	4,186	27
Sofiya	SO	8	BU36	1,013,875	18,979	7,328	51
Varna	VA	3	BU37	986,942	11,929	4,606	29
				8,992,316	110,994	42,855	279

Status: These divisions are oblasti (regions).
Abv: Two-letter code for international compatibility (defined by the author).
ISO: Codes from ISO 3166-2.
FIPS: Codes from FIPS PUB 10-4.

Population: 1998 estimate.
Area-km: Square kilometers.
Area-mi: Square miles.
Communes: Number of communes in each region.
Capitals always have the same name as their divisions, except that the capital of Grad Sofiya is Sofiya.
Further subdivisions: In 1959, there were 13 okruzhi (provinces; sing. okrug), divided into 105 okolii (counties; sing. okolia), which were further divided into 2,142 obshchini (communes; sing. obshchina). A reform that year eliminated the counties, cut the provinces into 28 smaller provinces, and cut the number of communes roughly in half. A reform of 1979 cut the number of communes from 1,374 to 291. There were 300 communes by 1986. In 1987, the provinces were merged to form nine oblasti (regions; sing. oblast). In 1992, these were subdivided into a total of 279 communes.
Origins of names:

Blagoevgrad: Bulgarian: city of Blagoev, for Dimitar Blagoev, Bulgarian politician and writer
Burgas: possibly from Ancient Greek *pyrgos*: walled city
Dimitrovgrad: Bulgarian: city of Dimitrov, for Gyorgy Mikhailovich Dimitrov, Bulgarian politician
Khaskovo: possibly from Turkish *has*: dwelling place

Plovdiv: the city was named Philippopolis by Philip II of Macedonia. The inhabitants corrupted Philip into Pulpu, and replaced -opolis (city) with their own name for city, *diva*.
Sofiya: Named by Turks for the church of Saint Sophia, which they changed to a mosque

Change history:

1909	Before the first Balkan war, the districts of Bulgaria were Bourgas, Choumen, Kustendil, Pléven, Plovdiv, Ruse, Sophia, Stara Zagora, Turnovo, Varna, Vidin, and Vratsa.
1945	Bulgaria had nine regions at the end of World War II: Burgas, Gorna Dzhumaya, Plovdiv, Pleven, Ruse, Sofiya, Stara Zagora, Varna, and Vratsa.
1949-09-22	Nine regions replaced by 15 provinces: Blagoevgrad, Burgas, Gorna Oryahovitsa, Haskovo, Pleven, Plovdiv, Ruse, Shumen, Sofiya, Sofiya City, Stalin, Stara Zagora, Vidin, Vratsa, and Yambol.
1950	Shumen province and its capital renamed to Kolarovgrad.
1950	Capital of Blagoevgrad province renamed from Gorna Djumaya to Blagoevgrad.
1951-01-02	Vidin province merged into Vratsa, and Yambol merged into Burgas.
~1953	Capital of Gorna Oryahovitsa moved to Veliko Turnovo, and province renamed accordingly.
1956	Stalin province and its capital renamed to Varna.
1959	The thirteen provinces were regrouped into 28 provinces.
1965	Kolarovgrad province and its capital renamed back to Shumen.
1987-08	Nine regions formed by consolidating the 28 provinces. Topolovgrad commune was moved from Yambol province to Khaskovo region.
~1991	Name of Mikhaylovgrad region changed to Montana.

Other names of subdivisions: The Bulgarian language uses a Cyrillic alphabet, so all names are transliterated into the Roman alphabet. Some of the variant names are due to different transliteration schemes. Also note that oblasti and okruzhi come and go, but cities stay. Variant names are shown for capitals, which have the same name as their division whenever the division exists.

Blagoevgrad: Gorna Dzhumaya (obsolete)
Burgas: Bourgas (variant)
Grad Sofiya: Sofia City (English)
Khaskovo: Haskovo (variant)
Kurdzhali: Kurdjali, Kârdžali, Kirjali (variant)
Kyustendil: Keustendil, Kjustendil (variant)
Lovech: Loveč (variant)
Montana: Mikhaylovgrad, Mihailovgrad (obsolete)
Pazardzhik: Pazardjik (variant); Tatar Pazardžik (obsolete)
Pleven: Plevila, Plevna (obsolete); Plyeven (variant)

Plovdiv: Philippopolis (obsolete)
Shumen: Kolarovgrad, Šumla (obsolete); Šumen (variant)
Sliven: Slivno (obsolete)
Smolyan: Smoljan (variant)
Sofiya: Sofia, Sofija (variant)
Ruse: Russe, Ruščuk, Rustchuk (obsolete)
Tolbukhin: Bazargic, Bazardzhik, Dobritch, Dobrici, Hagi Oglu (obsolete); Tolbuhin (variant)
Turgovishte: Torgovishte, Tâgovište (variant)
Veliko Turnovo: Gorna Oryahovitsa, Gorna Orjahovica

(obsolete); Turnovo, Tirnovo, Trnova, Veliko Tarnovo (variant)

Vratsa: Vraca (variant)

Yambol: Jambol (variant); Jamboli (obsolete)

Population history:

province	FIPS	area-km	1965	1975	1985	region (after 1987)
Blagoevgrad	BU01	6,478	303,000	324,000	346,000	Sofiya
Burgas	BU02	7,618	381,000	421,000	446,000	Burgas
Gabrovo	BU03	2,053	169,000	176,000	178,000	Lovech
Grad Sofiya	BU20	1,119	895,000	1,066,000	1,193,000	Grad Sofiya
Khaskovo	BU04	4,033	290,000	293,000	300,000	Khaskovo
Kurdzhali	BU05	4,032	284,000	288,000	298,000	Khaskovo
Kyustendil	BU06	3,027	197,000	199,000	193,000	Sofiya
Lovech	BU07	4,134	217,000	217,000	204,000	Lovech
Mikhaylovgrad	BU08	3,595	241,000	236,000	226,000	Mikhaylovgrad
Pazardzhik	BU09	4,393	297,000	314,000	326,000	Plovdiv
Pernik	BU10	2,377	181,000	175,000	176,000	Sofiya
Pleven	BU11	4,216	352,000	359,000	367,000	Lovech
Plovdiv	BU12	5,588	645,000	721,000	758,000	Plovdiv
Razgrad	BU13	2,648	198,000	204,000	197,000	Razgrad
Ruse	BU14	2,616	273,000	294,000	303,000	Razgrad
Shumen	BU15	3,365	243,000	254,000	256,000	Varna
Silistra	BU16	2,862	171,000	177,000	174,000	Razgrad
Sliven	BU17	3,646	227,000	238,000	239,000	Burgas
Smolyan	BU18	3,532	160,000	163,000	171,000	Plovdiv
Sofiya	BU19	7,277	318,000	322,000	304,000	Sofiya
Stara Zagora	BU21	4,959	352,000	390,000	415,000	Khaskovo
Tolbukhin	BU22	4,700	236,000	250,000	256,000	Varna
Turgovishte	BU23	2,735	178,000	179,000	172,000	Razgrad
Varna	BU24	3,847	367,000	430,000	466,000	Varna
Veliko Turnovo	BU25	4,684	339,000	350,000	338,000	Lovech
Vidin	BU26	3,071	181,000	179,000	165,000	Mikhaylovgrad
Vratsa	BU27	4,098	309,000	312,000	288,000	Mikhaylovgrad
Yambol	BU28	4,209	223,000	207,000	204,000	Burgas
		110,912	8,227,000	8,738,000	8,959,000	

Census dates: 1975-12-02, 1985-12-04.

BURKINA FASO

ISO = BF/FIPS = UV   Language = French   Time zone = 0   Capital = Ouagadougou

The area now known as Burkina Faso was part of French Sudan at the beginning of the 20th century. French colonial control was not yet firmly established, and borders were indefinite. In 1904, the colony of Upper Senegal and Niger was created. In 1919, it was broken up, and Upper Volta was one of the parts thus formed. On 1932-09-06, it was partitioned among Ivory Coast, French Sudan, and Niger, but this change was nullified on 1947-09-04. The country gained its independence on 1960-08-05.

Other names of country: Alto Volta (obsolete–Italian, obsolete–Spanish); Burkina (informal); Búrkína Fasó (Icelandic); Haute Volta (obsolete–French); People's Democratic Republic of Burkina Faso (formal–English); République Démocratique Populaire de Burkina Faso (formal); Upper Volta (obsolete); Voltaic Republic (obsolete).

Meaning of name: fatherland of honest men (Moré *burkina*: worthy, Dioula *faso*: fatherland).

division	abv	ISO	FIPS	population	area-km	area-mi	capital
Bam	BM	BAM	UV15	164,263	4,017	1,551	Kongoussi
Bazèga	BZ	BAZ	UV16	306,976	5,313	2,051	Kombissiri
Bougouriba	BB	BGR	UV17	221,522	7,087	2,736	Diébougou ➤

division	abv	ISO	FIPS	population	area-km	area-mi	capital
Boulgou	BL	BLG	UV18	403,358	9,033	3,488	Tenkodogo
Boulkiemdé	BK	BLK	UV19	363,594	4,138	1,598	Koudougou
Ganzourgou	GZ	GAN	UV20	196,006	4,087	1,578	Zorgo
Gnagna	GG	GNA	UV21	229,249	8,600	3,320	Bogandé
Gourma	GM	GOU	UV22	294,123	26,613	10,275	Fada-N'Gourma
Houet	HO	HOU	UV23	585,031	16,472	6,360	Bobo-Dioulasso
Kadiogo	KA	KAD	UV24	459,138	1,169	451	Ouagadougou
Kénédougou	KN	KEN	UV25	139,722	8,307	3,207	Orodara
Komoé	KM	KOM	UV26	250,510	18,393	7,102	Banfora
Kossi	KS	KOS	UV27	330,413	13,177	5,088	Nouna
Kouritenga	KR	KOT	UV28	197,027	1,627	628	Koupéla
Mouhoun	MO	MOU	UV29	289,213	10,442	4,032	Dédougou
Namentenga	NM	NAM	UV30	198,798	7,755	2,994	Boulsa
Naouri	NR	NAO	UV31	105,273	3,843	1,484	Pô
Oubritenga	OB	OUB	UV32	303,229	4,693	1,812	Ziniaré
Oudalan	OD	OUD	UV33	105,715	10,046	3,879	Gorom-Gorom
Passoré	PA	PAS	UV34	225,115	4,078	1,575	Yako
Poni	PO	PON	UV35	234,501	10,361	4,000	Gaoua
Sanguié	SG	SNG	UV36	218,289	5,165	1,994	Réo
Sanmatenga	ST	SMT	UV37	368,365	9,213	3,557	Kaya
Séno	SE	SEN	UV38	230,043	13,473	5,202	Dori
Sissili	SS	SIS	UV39	246,844	13,736	5,303	Léo
Soum	SM	SOM	UV40	190,464	13,350	5,154	Djibo
Sourou	SR	SOR	UV41	267,770	9,487	3,663	Tougan
Tapoa	TA	TAP	UV42	159,121	14,780	5,707	Diapaga
Yatenga	YT	YAT	UV43	537,205	12,292	4,746	Ouahigouya
Zoundwéogo	ZW	ZOU	UV44	155,142	3,453	1,333	Manga
				7,976,019	274,200	105,868	

Status: These divisions are provinces.
Abv: Two-letter code for international compatibility (defined by the author).
ISO: Codes from ISO 3166-2.
FIPS: Codes from FIPS PUB 10-4.
Population: 1985 census.
Area-km: Square kilometers.
Area-mi: Square miles.

The ISO 3166-2 documents shows 15 additional provinces for which no other data are available. They are listed below, along with the codes to be used if their existence is confirmed.

province	abv	ISO		province	abv	ISO
Balé	BA	BAL		Loroum	LO	LOR
Banwa	BW	BAN		Nayala	NY	NAY
Ioba	IO	IOB		Noumbiel	NB	NOU
Komondjari	KJ	KMD		Tui	TU	TUI
Kompienga	KP	KMP		Yagha	YG	YAG
Koulpélogo	KL	KOP		Ziro	ZR	ZIR
Kourwéogo	KW	KOW		Zondoma	ZM	ZON
Léraba	LE	LER				

Further subdivisions: The provinces are subdivided into 250 districts.
Origins of names of the old departments:

Centre, Centre-Est, Centre-Nord, Centre-Ouest, Est, Nord, Sud-Ouest: Describe their position within the country (central, east of central, ..., southwest)

Hauts-Bassins: High [River] Basins

Ouagadougou: Possibly from Moré *ouaga*: come here, Dioula *dougou*: village

Sahel: originally Arabic *sahil*: seacoast, applied by mistake to the region north of Timbuktu, and later to any semi-arid land near the Sahara. The French botanist Auguste Chevalier asked natives what lay to the north; they thought he meant at the end of the caravan trails to the Mediterranean.

Volta-Noire: Black Volta, from the name of a branch of   turn
the Volta River, whose name comes from Portuguese *volta*:

Change history:

~1970	Five départements (departments): Est, Centre, Sahel, Hauts-Bassins, and Volta-Noire, reorganized into ten.
1984-08-03	Name of country changed to Burkina Faso. Note: ISO code was HV before name change.
1984-08-15	Ten departments reorganized into thirty provinces. The following list shows the departments before the change, and how they were split up.

département	capital	FIPS	population	area-km	divided into these provinces in 1984
Centre	Ouagadougou	UV05	944,706	21,952	Bazèga, part of Boulkiemdé, Ganzourgou, Kadiogo, Naouri, Oubritenga, Zoundwéogo
Centre-Est	Tenkodogo	UV06	404,602	11,266	Boulgou, Kouritenga
Centre-Nord	Kaya	UV07	632,285	21,578	Bam, Namentenga, part of Passoré, Sanmatenga
Centre-Ouest	Koudougou	UV08	788,962	26,324	most of Boulkiemdé, most of Passoré, Sanguié, Sissili
Est	Fada-N'Gourma	UV09	407,215	49,992	Gnagna, Gourma, Tapoa
Hauts-Bassins	Bobo-Dioulasso	UV10	582,810	43,172	Houet, Kénédougou, Komoé
Nord	Ouahigouya	UV11	530,192	12,293	Yatenga
Sahel	Dori	UV12	354,079	36,869	Oudalan, Séno, Soum
Sud-Ouest	Gaoua	UV13	357,592	17,448	Bougouriba, Poni
Volta-Noire	Dédougou	UV14	635,760	33,106	Kossi, Mouhoun, Sourou
			5,638,203	274,000	

Population: 1975 census.
Other names of subdivisions:

Bazèga: Bazéga (variant)
Houet: Houé (variant)
Komoé: Comoé (variant)

Kouritenga: Kourittenga (variant)
Naouri: Nahouri (variant)

BURUNDI

ISO = BI/FIPS = BY   Languages = Kirundi, French   Time zone = +2   Capital = Bujumbura

The territory which is now Burundi was part of German East Africa at the beginning of the century. In 1919, Ruanda-Urundi was mandated to Belgium. It consisted of two counties or residencies, Ruanda in the north and Urundi in the south. It became administratively part of the Belgian Congo on 1925-08-21, and remained so until the Congo's independence in 1960. On 1962-07-01, when Ruanda-Urundi attained independence, the two counties became the countries of Rwanda and Burundi. The capital of Ruanda-Urundi, which had been known as Usumbura, became the capital of Burundi under its new name, Bujumbura.

Other names of country: Búrúndí (Icelandic); Republic of Burundi (formal–English); Republika y'Uburundi (formal); Urundi (obsolete).

Origin of name: ethnic name Barundi, applied to a country.

division	ISO	FIPS	population	area-km	area-mi	comm	formerly
Bubanza	BB	BY09	222,953	1,093	422	5	Bubanza
Bujumbura	BJ	BY02	608,931	1,334	515	10	Bujumbura
Bururi	BR	BY10	385,490	2,515	971	9	Bururi
Cankuzo	CA	BY11	142,797	1,940	749	5	Ruyigi
Cibitoke	CI	BY12	279,843	1,639	633	6	Bubanza ➤

division	ISO	FIPS	population	area-km	area-mi	comm	formerly
Gitega	GI	BY13	565,174	1,989	768	10	Gitega
Karuzi	KR	BY14	287,905	1,459	563	7	Gitega
Kayanza	KY	BY15	443,116	1,229	475	9	Ngozi
Kirundo	KI	BY16	401,103	1,711	661	7	Muyinga
Makamba	MA	BY17	223,799	1,972	761	6	Bururi*
Muramvya	MU	BY05	441,653	1,530	591	11	Muramvya
Muyinga	MY	BY18	373,382	1,825	705	7	Muyinga
Ngozi	NG	BY19	482,246	1,468	567	9	Ngozi
Rutana	RT	BY20	195,834	1,898	733	6	Ruyigi*
Ruyigi	RY	BY21	238,567	2,365	913	8	Ruyigi
			5,292,793	25,967	10,026	115	

* = except for Gitanga and Bukemba communes (see below under change history)

Status: These divisions are provinces.
ISO: Codes from ISO 3166-2.
FIPS: Codes from FIPS PUB 10-4.
Population: 1990–08 census.
Area-km: Square kilometers.
Area-mi: Square miles.
Comm: Number of communes.
Formerly: Province containing this area before 1979.
Capitals have the same names as their provinces.
Further subdivisions: The regions are subdivided into 114 districts, and the districts are subdivided into communes. Before 1979, there were eight provinces, subdivided into 18 arrondissements, which were further divided into 78 communes.
Change history:

1962   Name of Usumbura changed to Bujumbura.
~1979   Eight provinces were regrouped to form 15. The provinces before the change were as follows. All capitals have the same name as their provinces. Populations are from the 1978 census.

province	FIPS	population	area-km	arrondissements
Bubanza	BY01	293,221	2,670	Bubanza, Cibitoke
Bujumbura	BY02	386,041	1,255	Bujumbura, Mwisare
Bururi	BY03	398,614	4,680	Bururi, Makamba
Gitega	BY04	612,118	3,320	Bukirasazi, Gitega, Karuzi
Muramvya	BY05	342,722	1,510	Muramvya, Mwaro
Muyinga	BY06	494,140	3,535	Kirundo, Muyinga
Ngozi	BY07	714,476	2,595	Kayanza, Ngozi
Ruyigi	BY08	348,102	5,445	Cankuzo, Rutana, Ruyigi
		3,589,434	25,010	

At first glance, it may appear that the new provinces are the same as the old arrondissements. This is not quite accurate. Bukirasazi has disappeared, almost all of it absorbed into Gitega. Mwaro has merged into Muramvya, and Mwisare has merged into Bujumbura. There were also a number of minor adjustments. The commune of Gihogaze was transferred from Gitega to Karuzi. Almost all of Giteranyi commune was transferred from Kirundo to Muyinga. Gitanga and Bukemba communes were transferred from Makamba to Rutana. Busiga commune was transferred from Kayanza to Ngozi. About half of Bukinanyana commune was transferred from Bubanza to Cibitoke.
Other names of subdivisions:

Bujumbura: Usumbura (obsolete)
Gitega: Kitega (obsolete)

Muyinga: Muhinga (obsolete)

CAMBODIA

ISO = KH/FIPS = CB   Language = Khmer   Time zone = +7   Capital = Phnom Penh

At the beginning of the 20th century, most of Cambodia was part of French Indo-China, a French protectorate; the rest of it was in Siam. In 1907, the British and French delimited their respective "spheres of influence" in Siam. The French part, consisting of most of what are now the provinces of Bântéay Méanchey, Bătdâmbâng, and Siĕmréab-Ŏtdâr Méanchey, was quickly annexed to French Indo-China. French Indo-China at that time comprised the territories of Annam, Cambodge (Cambodia), Cochinchine (Cochin-China), Kouang-Tchéou-Wan (Kwangchowan), Laos, and Tongking. Kwangchowan was leased from China. In 1946, France surrendered its lease. On 1949-07-19, French Indo-China was granted independence as three Associate States of the French Union: Cambodia, Laos, and Vietnam. On 1970-10-09, Cambodia changed its name to the Khmer Republic. On 1979-01-08, it changed once again, to Kampuchea. In the 1980s, each political faction wanted to impose its preferred name, and the rest of the world has quietly gone back to using Cambodia.

Other names of country: Cambodge (French); Cambogia (Italian); Cambodja (Danish); Camboja (Portuguese); Camboya (Spanish); Kambódía (Icelandic); Kambodja (Swedish); Kambodscha (German); Kambodsja (Norwegian); Kambodža (Finnish); Kampuchea (obsolete); Roat Kampuchea (formal); Khmer Republic (obsolete); State of Cambodia (formal–English)

Origin of name: Named for Kambu, legendary patriarch.

division	ISO	FIPS	population	area-km	area-mi	capital
Bântéay Méanchey	OM	——	——	——	——	Sisŏphŏn
Bătdâmbâng	BA	CB01	671,000	19,184	7,407	Bătdâmbâng
Kâmpóng Cham	KM	CB02	999,000	9,799	3,783	Kâmpóng Cham
Kâmpóng Chhnăng	KG	CB03	333,000	5,521	2,132	Kâmpóng Chhnăng
Kâmpóng Saôm	KA*	——	8,000	68	26	Kâmpóng Saôm
Kâmpóng Spœ	KS	CB04	374,000	7,017	2,709	Kâmpóng Spœ
Kâmpóng Thum	KT	CB05	390,000	27,602	10,657	Kâmpóng Thum
Kâmpôt	KP	CB06	414,000	5,962	2,302	Kâmpôt
Kândal	KN	CB07	859,000	3,812	1,472	Ta Khmau
Kaôh Kŏng	KK	CB08	48,000	11,161	4,309	Krŏng Kaôh Kŏng
Krâchéh	KH*	CB09	154,000	11,094	4,283	Krâchéh
Môndól Kiri	MK	CB10	18,000	14,288	5,516	Senmonorom
Phnom Penh	PP	CB11	479,000	46	18	Phnom Penh
Poŭthĭsăt	PO	CB12	219,000	12,692	4,900	Poŭthĭsăt
Preăh Vihéar	PH	CB13	——	——	——	Phnum Tbêng Méanchey
Prey Vêng	PY	CB14	592,000	4,883	1,885	Prey Vêng
Rôtânôkiri	RO	CB15	60,000	10,782	4,163	Lumphăt
Siĕmréab-Ŏtdâr Méanchey	SI	CB16	380,000	16,457	6,354	Siĕmréab
Stœng Trêng	ST	CB17	42,000	11,092	4,283	Stœng Trêng
Svay Riĕng	SR	CB18	352,000	2,966	1,145	Svay Riĕng
Takêv	TA	CB19	566,000	3,563	1,376	Takêv
			6,968,000	181,035	69,898	

* = *In the draft standard, the codes KK and KS were used twice. To provide uniqueness, I changed Kâmpóng Saôm from KS to KA and Krâchéh from KK to KH.*

Status: These divisions are khêt (provinces), except for Kâmpóng Saôm and Phnom Penh, which are autonomous municipalities.

ISO: Codes from ISO 3166-2.

FIPS: Codes from FIPS PUB 10-4.

Population: 1971 estimate.

Area-km: Square kilometers.

Area-mi: Square miles.

Territorial extent: Thmei Island, Tônsay Island, and Set Island (Sês) are in Kâmpôt province, Cambodia. Facing them across the border from the Vietnamese side are Phu Quoc Island and the Hai Tac Islands. Farther out in the Gulf of Thailand, the islands of Poulo Wai (Ko Way), Kaoh Prins (Prins Island), and Kaoh Tang (Tang Island) belong to Cambodia.

Bokor (Bok Koŭ) and Krŏng Kêb (Kep), two cities in Kâmpôt province according to this list, were said by some sources from the early 1980s to be autonomous municipalities.

Origins of names:

Bătdâmbâng: Khmer *tampan*: stick (houses in the city were made of bamboo sticks)

Kâmpóng Chhnăng: Malay *kamban*: port, Khmer *chhnang*: pots

Kâmpóng Saôm: Malay *kamban*: port, Sanskrit *saumya*: pleasant

Phnom Penh: Khmer *phnom*: mountain, *penh*: full (i.e. mountain of abundance)

Change history:

1904   Stœ̆ng Trêng province transferred from Laos to Cambodge.

1949   At independence, Cambodia had fourteen provinces: Battambang, Kompong Cham, Kompong Chhnang, Kompong Speu, Kompong Thom, Kampot, Kandal, Kratie, Pursat, Prey Veng, Siem Reap, Stung Treng, Svay Rieng, and Takeo.

~1962   Môndól Kiri, Rôtânôkiri, and Kaôh Kŏng provinces, and Phnom Penh autonomous municipality, split from neighboring provinces. At about that time, the capital of Kândal moved from Phnom Penh to Ta Khmau.

~1980   Preăh Vihéar province split from Stœ̆ng Trêng.

~1983   Kâmpóng Saôm autonomous municipality (formerly Sihanoukville) split from Kâmpôt province.

~1989   Bântéay Méanchey formed from part of Bătdâmbâng and a small part of Siĕmréab-Ŏtdâr Méanchey province.

~1995   If recent changes to the FIPS PUB 10-4 list are accurate, the following changes, not shown in the table above, can be inferred. Status of autonomous municipalities changed to krong (municipalities). Siĕmréab-Ŏtdâr Méanchey split into Siĕmréab and Ŏtdâr Méanchey; Krŏng Kêb (Kâmpôt province) became a municipality. Name of Kâmpóng Saôm changed to Krŏng Preăh Seihanu.

Other names of subdivisions:

Bătdâmbâng: Battambang, Băt Dâm Bâng (variant)

Bântéay Méanchey: Banteay Mean Cheay (variant)

Kâmpóng Cham: Kompong Cham (variant)

Kâmpóng Chhnăng: Kompong Chhnang (variant)

Kâmpóng Saôm: Kompong Som (variant)

Kâmpóng Spœ: Kompong Speu (variant)

Kâmpóng Thum: Kompong Thom (variant)

Kaôh Kŏng: Koh Kong (variant)

Krâchéh: Kratié, Kratiĕ, Krâ Chéh, Krachen (variant)

Môndól Kiri: Mondolkiri, Môndŭl Kiri (variant)

Ŏtdâr Méanchey: Oddâr Méanchey (variant)

Phnom Penh: Phnum Pénh (variant)

Poŭthĭsăt: Pursat (variant)

Rôtânôkiri: Râtanăkiri, Rotanah Kiri (variant)

Siĕmréab: Siem Reap, Siĕm Réab, Siemreap (variant)

Stœ̆ng Trêng: Stung Treng (variant)

Takêv: Takeo (variant)

Some sources show the name of the capital of Kaôh Kŏng as Krong Khemarak Phoumin, or Khemarak Phouminville.

Andaung Pich, also known as Ândong Péch or Ba Kev, may have been the capital of Rôtânôkiri at some time.

CAMEROON

ISO = CM/FIPS = CM   Languages = French, English   Time zone = +1   Capital = Yaoundé

In 1900, the German protectorate of Kamerun covered a little more territory than Cameroon does now. On 1911-11-04, it was augmented by a cession of 270,000 sq. km. taken from French Equatorial Africa. In 1916-01, during World War I, France and England seized Kamerun from Germany. France immediately re-integrated its 1911 cession into French Equatorial Africa. On 1922-07-20, former Kamerun was mandated partly to England (90,000 sq. km.) and partly to France (700,000 sq. km.). The British mandate (British Cameroons) was treated as two parts: Northern and Southern Cameroons. After World War II, the mandate was converted to a trust territory under the aegis of the United Nations. The French mandate became the territory of Cameroun. Cameroun gained its independence from France on 1960-01-01. Southern Cameroons united with it on 1961-10-01.

Other names of country: Camarão (Portuguese); Cameroons (obsolete); Cameroun (Danish, French, obsolete); Camerun (Italian); Camerún (Spanish); Kameroen (Dutch); Kamerun (Finnish, German, Norwegian, Swedish, obsolete); Kamerún (Icelandic); Republic of Cameroon (formal–English); République du Cameroun (formal).

Origin of name: from the Cameroon River, Portuguese *Rio dos Camarões*: Crayfish River.

division	ISO	FIPS	population	area-km	area-mi	depts	capital	former
Adamaoua	AD	CM10	359,227	63,691	24,591	5	Ngaoundéré	Nord
Centre	CE	CM11	1,176,206	68,926	26,612	8	Yaoundé	Centre-Sud
Est	ES	CM04	366,235	109,011	42,089	4	Bertoua	Est
Extrême-Nord	EN	CM12	1,394,958	34,246	13,222	6	Maroua	Nord
Littoral	LT	CM05	935,166	20,239	7,814	4	Douala	Littoral
Nord	NO	CM13	479,072	65,576	25,319	4	Garoua	Nord
Nord-Ouest	NW	CM07	980,531	17,812	6,877	5	Bamenda	Nord-Ouest
Ouest	OU	CM08	1,035,597	13,872	5,356	6	Bafoussam	Ouest
Sud	SU	CM14	315,739	47,110	18,189	3	Ebolowa	Centre-Sud
Sud-Ouest	SW	CM09	620,515	24,571	9,487	4	Buéa	Sud-Ouest
			7,663,246	465,054	179,556	49		

Status: These divisions are provinces.
ISO: Codes from ISO 3166-2.
FIPS: Codes from FIPS PUB 10-4.
Population: 1976 census.
Area-km: Square kilometers.
Area-mi: Square miles.
Depts: Number of départements in each province (1987).
Former: Pre–1982 province containing this area.
Further subdivisions: The provinces are subdivided into départements, which are in turn subdivided into arrondissements. The number of départements has changed from time to time. There were 33 in ~1965, 39 in ~1982, and 49 in ~1987.
Origins of names:

Adamaoua: conquered by Moddibo (King) Adama in the early 19th century

Extrême-Nord: French for Far North

Littoral: French for Coastal

Change history:

1908	Germany ceded a duck-bill-shaped region east of the Logone River to French Kongo (Chad).
~1950	The French territory of Cameroun consisted of the following regions: Adamaoua, Bamiléké, Bamoun, Benoué, Haut-Nyong, Kribi, Lom et Kadei, M'Bam, Mungo, Nord-Cameroun, N'Tem, Nyong et Sanaga, Sanaga-Maritime, and Wouri.
1961-10-01	Southern Cameroons united with Cameroon. It became Nord-Ouest and Sud-Ouest provinces.
1982	Centre-Sud province split into two provinces: Centre and Sud. Nord province split into three provinces: Adamaoua, Nord, and Extrême-Nord. This list shows the provinces, their FIPS codes, and compatibility codes from before the change. Their areas and populations can be computed by totaling the figures for the modern-day provinces.

province	capital	abv	FIPS	province	capital	abv	FIPS
Centre-Sud	Yaoundé	CS	CM03	Nord-Ouest	Bamenda	NW	CM07
Est	Bertoua	ES	CM04	Ouest	Bafoussam	OU	CM08
Littoral	Douala	LT	CM05	Sud-Ouest	Buéa	SW	CM09
Nord	Garoua	ND	CM06				

Other names of subdivisions: All the directional names (Centre, Est, etc.) can be translated.

Adamaoua: Adamawa (English)

Littoral: Litoral (Portuguese, Spanish)

CANADA

ISO = CA/FIPS = CA   Languages = English, French   Time zones = see table   Capital = Ottawa, Ontario

Canada became an independent nation and member of the British Commonwealth in 1867, and has remained so ever since. It began with four provinces. There have been territorial acquisitions since then, but only one during the 20th century: Newfoundland, in 1949.

Other names of country: Canadá (Portuguese, Spanish); Kanada (Finnish, German, Icelandic).

Origin of name: native word *kanata*: settlements; named by Jacques Cartier in 1536.

division	ISO	FIPS	IATA	conv-E	conv-F	post	zone	population	area-km	area-mi	capital
Alberta	AB	CA01	AL	Alta.	Alb.	T	-7:00 [d]	2,545,553	655,029	252,908	Edmonton
British Columbia	BC	CA02	BC	B.C.	C.-B.	V	-8:00f[d]	3,282,061	910,745	351,641	Victoria
Manitoba	MB	CA03	MN	Man.	Man.	R	-6:00 [d]	1,091,942	649,296	250,695	Winnipeg
New Brunswick	NB	CA04	NB	N.B.	N.-B.	E	-4:00 [d]	723,900	72,913	28,152	Fredericton
Newfoundland	NF	CA05	NF	Nfld.	T.-N.	A	-3:30a[d]	568,474	405,667	156,629	Saint John's
Northwest Territories	NT	CA06	NT	N.W.T.	T.N.-O.	X	-7:00e[d]	57,649	3,379,683	1,304,903	Yellowknife
Nova Scotia	NS	CA07	NS	N.S.	N.-É.	B	-4:00 [d]	899,942	55,491	21,425	Halifax
Ontario	ON	CA08	OT	Ont.	Ont.	KLMNP	-5:00c[d]	10,084,885	1,095,123	422,829	Toronto
Prince Edward Island	PE	CA09	PE	P.E.I.	Î-P.-É.	C	-4:00 [d]	129,765	5,660	2,185	Charlottetown
Quebec	QC	CA10	QU	Que.	Qué.	GHJ	-5:00b[d]	6,895,963	1,541,544	595,193	Quebec
Saskatchewan	SK	CA11	SA	Sask.	Sask.	S	-6:00d	988,928	651,744	251,640	Regina
Yukon Territory	YT	CA12	YT	Y.T.	Yn.	Y	-8:00 [d]	27,797	536,324	207,076	Whitehorse
								27,296,859	9,959,219	3,845,276	

[d] = indicates areas where daylight saving time is in effect during summer. a = Except Labrador, which is on -4:00 [d]. b = A small part of Quebec, including part of Anticosti Island and the north bank of the Gulf of Saint Lawrence (east of about longitude 64° W.), observes -4:00 [d]. c = Western Ontario (west of longitude 90° W.) observes -6:00 [d]. d = Small areas in western and northern Saskatchewan observe -7:00 [d]. e = Eastern Northwest Territories (east of the Manitoba-Saskatchewan border) observe -4:00 [d], -5:00 [d], and -6:00 [d]. f = Small areas in eastern British Columbia observe -7:00 [d].

Status: These divisions are provinces, except for Northwest Territories and Yukon Territory, which are territories.

ISO: Codes from ISO 3166-2. These are also the abbreviations used by the Canadian post office and other government agencies. Unofficially, PQ is often used for Quebec, and LB for Labrador (part of Newfoundland).

FIPS: Codes from FIPS PUB 10-4.

IATA: Codes from the IATA Airline Coding Directory, used to locate airports by province.

Conv-E: Conventional abbreviations used by Anglophone Canadians before standardization. Sometimes Newf. for Newfoundland, P.Q. for Quebec (Province of Quebec).

Conv-F: Conventional abbreviations used by Francophone Canadians before standardization.

Postal code: Canadian postal codes have the format "ana nan," where each a is a letter and each n is a digit. The first letter in a postal code can be used to identify the province. Some provinces have more than one letter. This column shows the letters for each province.

Zone: Time zones. Convert from UTC to local time by adding this number of hours. Canada has a national standard (CAN/CSA-Z234.4-89) for time zone abbreviations in English and French. Reading from east to west, the standard time offset from UTC, English abbreviation, French abbreviation, and short English name for standard time in each of the time zones are: -3:30/NST/HNT/Newfoundland, -4:00/AST/HNA/Atlantic, -5:00/EST/HNE/Eastern, -6:00/CST/HNC/Central, -7:00/MST/HNR/Mountain, -8:00/PST/HNP/Pacific, -9:00/YST/HNY/Yukon. (Yukon time is no longer observed in Canada.)

Population: 1991 census.

Area-km: Square kilometers

Area-mi: Square miles.

Further subdivisions: The subdivisions of the Canadian provinces and territories are varied in size, status, and stability. The eastern provinces tend to be divided into counties; the western provinces, sections, divisions, or districts; and Yukon Territory is only subdivided for electoral or census purposes. Prince Edward Island appears to have been subdivided into Prince, Queens, and Kings Counties for as long as it has been a province. Northwest Territory had been subdivided into the districts of Franklin, Keewatin, and Mackenzie since 1912, although their borders had been somewhat modified; then, about 1980, it was changed to five districts (Baffin, Fort Smith, Inuvik, Keewatin, and Kitikmeot).

Other provinces are more complex. The units of local government include cantons, cities, community councils, counties, districts, divisions, muncipalities, parishes, sections, towns, and villages. There are sub-varieties, including county regional municipalities, district municipalities, metropolitan municipalities, and municipal townships. Many provinces have more than one level of subdivision. Most of them have changed their subdivisions several times.

Territorial extent: British Columbia is separated from Alaska by an indefinite boundary in coastal waters. It contains the Queen Charlotte Islands and Dundas Island, but not Dall Island, Prince of Wales Island, or Sitklan Island. The boundary with Washington follows the Strait of Juan de Fuca between Vancouver Island and the Olympic Peninsula, then turns north between Canada's Sidney Island, South Pender Island, and Saturna Island, and the United States's San Juan Island, Stuart Island, and Waldron Island, until it meets the longitude of 49° N.

New Brunswick is divided from Maine by a line that runs down the Saint Croix River and passes between Deer Island, Campobello Island, Grand Manan Island, and adjacent islets on the Canadian side, across from West Quoddy Head, the easternmost point in the United States.

Newfoundland consists of the large island of Newfoundland, a large mainland area on the northeast coast (Labrador), and adjacent islands. Labrador is always considered part of Newfoundland province, but it is sometimes abbreviated LB as if it were a province name.

Northwest Territories includes all Canadian islands in Hudson Bay, James Bay, the Hudson Strait, Ungava Bay, and the Arctic Ocean between the eastern border of Yukon Territory and the northern tip of Labrador. The border between Labrador and Northwest Territories runs along Killiniq Island. The division between Northwest Territories and Greenland follows the Robeson Channel, Kennedy Channel, Kane Basin, Baffin Bay, Davis Strait, and Labrador Bay.

Nova Scotia includes Sable Island in the Atlantic Ocean.

Ontario includes Main Duck Island in Lake Ontario, and Pelee Island in Lake Erie. One of the islets lying off Pelee Island is the southernmost point of land in Canada. Ontario also includes Manitoulin Island, between Lake Huron and Georgian Bay, the largest lake island in the world. In Lake Superior, Caribou Island belongs to Ontario.

Quebec includes Anticosti Island and the Îles de la Madeleine (Magdalen Islands) in the Gulf of Saint Lawrence.

Yukon Territory includes Herschel Island in the Arctic Ocean.

Origins of names:

Alberta: Named for Princess Louise Caroline Alberta, wife of the then-Governor General of Canada and daughter of Queen Victoria of England.

British Columbia: British possession, on the Columbia River, named by Capt. Robert Gray for his vessel Columbia, in turn named for Cristopher Columbus.

Labrador: Portuguese *lavrador*: laborer, farmer. Probably for João Fernandes, an explorer and farmer.

Manitoba: Probably from Cree *maniotwapow*: the strait of the spirit, from a belief that a natural noise caused by pebbles on Manitoba Island was caused by a spirit beating a drum.

New Brunswick: Named in honor of King George III of England, a descendant of the House of Brunswick (Germany).

Newfoundland: Called a "new found isle" by discoverer, John Cabot.

Northwest Territories: Descriptive.

Nova Scotia: Latin for New Scotland.

Ontario: Named for Lake Ontario. From native word, possibly *onittariio*: beautiful lake.

Prince Edward Island: Named for Prince Edward, Duke of Kent, father of Queen Victoria of England.

Quebec: From the Algonquian word for narrow passage, referring to the Saint Lawrence River at Cape Diamond.

Saskatchewan: Named for the Saskatchewan River. From Cree *Kisiskatchewani Sipi*: swift-flowing river.

Yukon Territory: Named for the Yukon River. From native name *Yu-kun-ah*: great river.

Change history:

1905-09-01   Alberta province formed from Alberta district and part of Athabaska district; Saskatchewan province formed from Assiniboia district and parts of Athabaska and Saskatchewan districts; remainder of Saskatchewan district annexed by Manitoba province; Keewatin district merged with Northwest Territories. (All districts mentioned here had been part of Northwest Territories.)

1912   The section of Keewatin district south of latitude 60° N. (also known as New South Wales) removed from Northwest Territories and divided between Manitoba and Ontario provinces. Ungava district transferred in entirety from Northwest Territories to Quebec province.

1927   Border delineated between Labrador and Quebec. (Quebec disputes the division.)

1949-03-31   Newfoundland merged with Canada, becoming a province. Labrador, formerly its dependency, became part of the new province.

1967-01-18   Yellowknife became capital of Northwest Territories. Formerly, the region had been administered from Ottawa.

1999-04-01   Northwest Territories is due to be split into two territories. The western section will still be called Northwest Territories, and its capital will still be Yellowknife. The eastern section will be called Nunavut. Its capital will be Iqaluit on Baffin Island. Its present population is about 22,000. It includes Arctic islands east of longitude 110° W., plus the part of Victoria Island south of latitude 70° N.; on the mainland, it includes all of Northwest Territories east of longitude 102° W., plus an irregularly shaped area in the far north.

Other names of subdivisions:

British Columbia: Britisch Kolumbien (German); Colombie britannique (French); Columbia Británica (Spanish); Colúmbia Britânica (Portuguese); Columbia Britannica (Italian); New Caledonia (obsolete)

New Brunswick: Neubraunschweig (German); Nueva Brunswick (Spanish); Nouveau-Brunswick (French); Nova Brunswick (Portuguese)

Newfoundland: Neufundland (German); Terra Nova (Portuguese); Terranova (Italian, Spanish); Terre-Neuve (French)

Northwest Territories: Nordwestgebiete, Nordwest-Territorien (German); Territoires du Nord-Ouest (French); Territori di Nordovest (Italian); Territorios del Noroeste (Spanish); Territórios do Noroeste (Portuguese)

Nova Scotia: Acadia (obsolete, also refers to New Brunswick); Neuschottland (German); Nouvelle-Écosse (French); Nova Escócia (Portuguese); Nueva Escocia (Spanish)

Ontario: Ontário (Portuguese); Upper Canada (obsolete)

Prince Edward Island: Île de Saint-Jean (obsolete); Île du Prince-Édouard (French); Ilha do Príncipe Eduardo (Portuguese); Isla Príncipe Eduardo (Spanish); Isola Principe Edoardo (Italian); Prinz Edward-Insel (German)

Quebec: Québec (French, Italian, Portuguese); Lower Canada (obsolete)

Yukon Territory: Territoire du Yukon (French); Yukon (informal); Yukón (Spanish)

Population history:

	1901	1911	1921	1931	1941	1951	1961	1971	1981	1991
Alberta	73,022	374,295	588,454	731,605	796,169	939,501	1,331,944	1,627,874	2,237,724	2,545,553
British Columbia	178,657	392,480	524,582	694,263	817,861	1,165,210	1,629,082	2,184,621	2,744,467	3,282,061
Manitoba	255,211	461,394	610,118	700,139	729,744	776,541	921,686	988,247	1,026,241	1,091,942
New Brunswick	331,120	351,889	387,876	408,219	457,401	515,697	597,936	634,557	696,403	723,900
Newfoundland	——	——	——	——	——	361,416	457,853	522,104	567,681	568,474
Northwest Territories	20,129	6,507	8,143	9,316	12,028	16,004	22,998	34,807	45,471	57,649
Nova Scotia	459,574	492,338	523,837	512,846	577,962	642,584	737,007	788,960	847,442	899,942
Ontario	2,182,947	2,527,292	2,933,662	3,431,683	3,787,655	4,597,542	6,236,092	7,703,106	8,625,107	10,084,885
Prince Edward Island	103,259	93,728	88,615	88,038	95,047	98,429	104,629	111,641	122,506	129,765
Quebec	1,648,898	2,005,776	2,360,510	2,874,662	3,331,882	4,055,681	5,259,211	6,027,764	6,438,403	6,895,963
Saskatchewan	91,279	492,432	757,510	921,785	895,992	831,728	925,181	926,242	968,313	988,928
Yukon Territory	27,219	8,512	4,157	4,230	4,914	9,096	14,628	18,388	23,153	27,797
	5,371,315	7,206,643	8,787,949	10,376,786	11,506,655	14,009,429	18,238,247	21,568,311	24,342,911	27,296,859

Census dates: 1901-04-01, 1911-06-01, 1921-06-01, 1931-06-01, 1941-06-02; the census has been quinquennial since 1951. Prior to 1949, Newfoundland had a separate census. Its population was 289,588 in 1935, and 321,819 in 1945.

CAPE VERDE

ISO = CV/FIPS = CV   Language = Portuguese   Time zone = -1   Capital = Praia

Cape Verde had been a Portuguese colony for more than five centuries when it was granted its independence on 1975-07-05.

Other names of country: Cabo Verde (Portuguese, Spanish); Capo Verde (Italian); Cap-Vert (French); Grænhöfðaeyjar (Icelandic); Kaapverdië (Dutch); Kapp Verde (Norwegian); Kap Verde (Danish, Finnish, German, Swedish); Kapverden (Swiss German); Republic of Cape Verde (formal–English); República de Cabo Verde (formal).

Origin of name: After Cap Vert, Senegal (Portuguese *Cabo Verde:* green cape).

division	ISO	FIPS	population	area-km	area-mi	capital	district
Boa Vista	BV	CV01	3,110	620	239	Sal Rei	B
Brava	BR	CV02	6,610	67	26	Nova Sintra	S
Fogo	FO	CV03	34,580	476	184	São Felipe	S
Maio	MA	CV04	4,560	269	104	Porto Inglês	S
Paúl	PA	CV05	9,080	54	21	Pombas	B
Porto Novo	PN		13,650	558	215	Porto Novo	B
Praia	PR	CV06	94,250	396	153	Praia	S
Ribeira Grande	RG	CV07	22,300	167	64	Ponta Sol	B
Sal	SL	CV08	8,150	216	83	Santa Maria	B
Santa Catarina	CA	CV09	48,000	243	94	Assomada	S
Santa Cruz	CR		27,730	149	58	Pedra Badejo	S
São Nicolau	SN	CV10	12,630	388	150	Ribeira Brava	B
São Vicente	SV	CV11	62,710	227	88	Mindelo	B
Tarrafal	TA	CV12	29,330	203	78	Tarrafal	S
			376,690	4,033	1,557		

Status: These divisions are concelhos (counties).

ISO: Codes from ISO 3166-2.

FIPS: Codes from FIPS PUB 10-4.

Population: 1990 estimate.

Area-km: Square kilometers.

Area-mi: Square miles.

District: Cape Verde is also divided into two distritos (districts): Barlavento (B) and Sotavento (S). This column indicates which district each county belongs to.

Territorial extent:

Boa Vista contains Boa Vista Island.

Brava contains Brava Island, Rei Island, and Rombo Island.

Fogo contains Fogo Island.

Maio contains Maio Island.

Paúl is part of Santo Antão Island.

Porto Novo is part of Santo Antão Island

Praia is part of São Tiago Island.

Ribeira Grande is part of Santo Antão Island.

Sal contains Sal Island.

Santa Catarina is part of São Tiago Island.

Santa Cruz is part of São Tiago Island.

São Nicolau contains São Nicolau Island.

São Vicente contains São Vicente and Santa Luzia Islands.

Tarrafal is part of São Tiago Island.

Meanings of names:

Barlavento: Portuguese for windward. Prevailing winds are from the northeast, and these islands are to the north.

Boa Vista: Portuguese for good view.

Fogo: Portuguese for fire. Island has an active volcano.

Maio: Portuguese for May (the month).

Praia: Portuguese for beach.

Sal: Portuguese for salt.

Sotavento: Portuguese for leeward.

Change history:

~1968   Porto Novo county split from Paúl.

~1975   Santa Cruz county formed from parts of Praia and Santa Catarina.

CAYMAN ISLANDS

ISO = KY/FIPS = CJ   Language = English   Time zone = -5   Capital = George Town

The Cayman Islands were a dependency of Jamaica until 1959-07-04, when they became a separate British colony.

Other names of country: Caymaneilanden (Dutch); Îles Caïmanes (French); Ilhas Cayman (Portuguese); Islas Caimán (Spanish); Isole Cayman (Italian); Kaimaninseln (German).

Origin of name: Caimans (crocodilian reptiles) lived there.

division	ISO	FIPS		division	ISO	FIPS
Creek	CR	CJ01		Spot Bay	SP	CJ05
Eastern	EA	CJ02		Stake Bay	ST	CJ06
Midland	MI	CJ03		West End	WD	CJ07
South Town	SO	CJ04		Western	WN	CJ08

Status: These divisions are districts.

ISO: Codes from ISO 3166-2.

FIPS: Codes from FIPS PUB 10-4.

Population: 25,355 (1989 census).

Area: 259 square kilometers, or 100 square miles.

Territorial extent: It appears that Stake Bay district corresponds to Cayman Brac Island, and Spot Bay to Little Cayman Island. The other districts are all on Grand Cayman Island.

Change history:

> In the censuses of 1921 and 1934, the districts were Bodden Town, East End, George Town, North Side, Prospect, West Bay, Cayman Brac, and Little Cayman. The first six constituted Grand Cayman Island; the other two were separate islands.
>
> In 1957, Grand Cayman was divided into three districts and seven sub-districts. The sub-districts were the six districts from before, plus Savannah. The districts were Eastern, Midland, and Western. Eastern district contained East End sub-district and parts of Bodden Town and Northside. Midland contained the rest of Bodden Town and Northside, plus part of Savannah, and Western contained all the rest.

CENTRAL AFRICAN REPUBLIC

ISO = CF/FIPS = CT   Languages = French, Sango   Time zone = +1   Capital = Bangui

In 1900, the territory of Ubangi-Shari, part of French Kongo, corresponded most closely to the present-day Central African Republic. On 1910-01-15, the Kongo became French Equatorial Africa. In 1911, France ceded part of this area to German-owned Kamerun, but during World War I (1916), the land was restored to its previous status. For part of the colonial period, Chad was administered jointly with Ubangi-Shari. In one week in August, 1960, all of the territories of French Equatorial Africa gained complete independence. The Central African Republic's turn came on 1960-08-13, and it took its name then. During the reign of Jean-Bedel Bokassa (1976-12-04 to 1979-09-21), the country was called the Central African Empire.

Other names of country: Centrafrikaanse Republiek (Dutch); Centrafrikanske Republik (Danish); Central African Empire (obsolete); Centralafrikanska republiken (Swedish); Den sentralafrikanske republikken (Norwegian); Imperio Centroafricano, Ubangui-Chari (obsolete–Spanish); Keski-Afrikan tasavalta (Finnish); Mið-Afríkulýðveldið (Icelandic); Oubangui-Chari (obsolete–French); Repubblica Centrafricana (Italian); República Centro-Africana (Portuguese); República Centroafricana (Spanish); République Centrafricaine (French); Ubangi-Shari (obsolete); Zentralafrikanische Republik (German).

Origin of name: Descriptive.

division	abv	ISO	FIPS	population	area-km	area-mi	capital
Bamingui-Bangoran	BB	BB	CT01	28,643	58,200	22,471	Ndélé
Bangui	BG	BGF	CT18	451,690	67	26	Bangui
Basse-Kotto	BK	BK	CT02	194,750	17,604	6,797	Mobaye
Haute-Kotto	HK	HK	CT03	58,838	86,650	33,456	Bria
Haut-Mbomou	HM	HM	CT05	27,113	55,530	21,440	Obo
Kémo	KG	KG	CT06	82,884	17,204	6,643	Sibut
Lobaye	LB	LB	CT07	30,179	19,235	7,427	Mbaïki ➤

division	abv	ISO	FIPS	population	area-km	area-mi	capital
Mambéré-Kadéï	HS	HS	CT04	230,364	30,203	11,661	Berbérati
Mbomou	MB	MB	CT08	119,252	61,150	23,610	Bangassou
Nana-Grébizi	KB	KB	CT15	95,497	19,996	7,720	Kaga Bandoro
Nana-Mambéré	NM	NM	CT09	191,970	26,600	10,270	Bouar
Ombella-Mpoko	MP	MP	CT17	180,857	31,835	12,292	Boali
Ouaka	UK	UK	CT11	208,332	49,900	19,266	Bambari
Ouham	AC	AC	CT12	262,950	50,250	19,402	Bossangoa
Ouham-Pendé	OP	OP	CT13	287,653	32,100	12,394	Bozoum
Sangha-Mbaéré	SE	SE	CT16	65,961	19,412	7,495	Nola
Vakaga	VK	VK	CT14	32,118	46,500	17,954	Birao
				2,549,051	622,436	240,324	

Status: These divisions are préfectures, except for Bangui, which is a commune autonome (autonomous commune), and Nana-Grébizi and Sangha-Mbaéré, which are préfectures économiques (economic prefectures).

Abv: Two-letter code for international compatibility (defined by the author).

ISO: Codes from ISO 3166-2. The code for Bangui is the same as the IATA airport code.

FIPS: Codes from FIPS PUB 10-4.

Population: 1989 census.

Area-km: Square kilometers.

Area-mi: Square miles.

Further subdivisions: The prefectures are subdivided into sous-préfectures (sub-prefectures). There were 36 sub-prefectures in 1965, and 51 of them in 1984.

Origins of names:

The prefectures are named for the major rivers of the area: Ubangui, Nana, Mambéré, Kadéï, Lobaye, Mpoko, Ombella, Sangha, Kémo, Ouaka, Kotto, and M'Bomou all flow into the Congo; Pendé, Ouham, Gribingui, Bamingui, Bangoran, and Vakaga all flow into the Chari, and thus to Lake Chad. Basse (Lower) means downstream, and Haut or Haute (Upper) means upstream.

Bangui: in the Bobangui language, it means "the rapids." Bangui is located at the first great rapid of the Ubangi River.

Change history:

~1975   Name of Ndélé changed to Bamingui-Bangoran. Name of Obo-Zemio changed to Haut-Mbomou. Name of Bouar-Baboua changed to Nana Mambéré. Name of Birao changed to Vakaga. Along with the name changes, the status of Birao and Ndélé changed from sous-préfectures autonomes (autonomous sub-prefectures) to prefectures. Capital of Ombella-Mpoko moved from Bangui to Boali.

~1982   Bangui split from Ombella-Mpoko; Gribingui-Économique (the economic prefecture of Gribingui) split from Kémo-Gribingui; Sangha-Économique (the economic prefecture of Sangha) formed by taking about 14,150 sq. km. of Haute-Sangha, plus 5,250 sq. km. of Lobaye. Name of the capital of Gribingui-Économique changed from Fort-Crampel to Kaga Bandoro. Name of the capital of Kémo-Gribingui changed from Fort-Sibut to Sibut. Capital of Ombella-Mpoko moved from Boali to Bimbo.

~1992   Name of Sangha changed to Sangha-Mbaéré. Name of Gribingui changed to Nana-Grébizi. Name of Haute-Sangha changed to Mambéré-Kadéï. Name of Kémo-Gribingui changed to Kémo.

Other names of subdivisions:

Bamingui-Bangoran: N'Délé, Ndélé (obsolete)

Haut-Mbomou: Haut-M'bomou (variant); Obo-Zemio (obsolete)

Kémo: Kémo-Gribingui, Kémo-Ibingui (obsolete)

Mambéré-Kadéï: Haute-Sangha (obsolete); Mambéré Kadéi (variant)

Mbomou: M'Bomou (variant)

Nana-Grébizi: Gribingui, Gribingui-Économique, Ibingui (obsolete); Nana Gribizi (variant)

Nana-Mambéré: Bouar-Baboua, Buar-Baboua (obsolete); Nana Nambéré (variant)

Ombella-Mpoko: Ombella-M'Poko (variant)

Sangha-Mbaéré: Sangha, Sangha-Économique (obsolete); Sangha M'baéré (variant)

Vakaga: Birao (obsolete)

CHAD

ISO = TD/FIPS = CD   Languages = French, Arabic   Time zone = +1   Capital = N'Djamena

In 1900, Chad was a territory, administered as part of French Kongo. On 1910-01-15, French Kongo's name was changed to French Equatorial Africa. During the period around World War II, Chad was called a military territory, and was subordinate to Ubangi-Shari-Chad. In one week in August, 1960, the four territories of French Equatorial Africa became independent, one by one. Chad was first, on 1960-08-11.

Other names of country: Ciad (Italian); Republic of Chad (formal–English); République du Tchad (formal); Tchad (Danish, French, Norwegian, Portuguese, Swedish); Tschad (German); Tsjaad (Dutch); Tsjad (Icelandic); Tšad (Finnish).

Origin of name: after Lake Chad, which came from Bornu *tsade*: lake.

division	abv	ISO	FIPS	population	area-km	area-mi	capital
Batha	BA	BA	CD01	470,900	88,800	34,286	Ati
Biltine	BI	BI	CD02	238,400	46,850	18,089	Biltine
Borkou-Ennedi-Tibesti	BT	BET	CD03	119,200	600,350	231,796	Faya-Largeau
Chari-Baguirmi	CB	CB	CD04	924,000	82,910	32,012	N'Djamena
Guéra	GR	GR	CD05	280,200	58,950	22,761	Mongo
Kanem	KA	KA	CD06	268,200	114,520	44,216	Mao
Lac	LC	LC	CD07	178,800	22,320	8,618	Bol
Logone Occidental	LO	LO	CD08	399,400	8,695	3,357	Moundou
Logone Oriental	LR	LR	CD09	417,300	28,035	10,824	Doba
Mayo-Kébbi	MK	MK	CD10	941,900	30,105	11,624	Bongor
Moyen-Chari	MC	MC	CD11	709,400	45,180	17,444	Sarh
Ouaddaï	OD	OD	CD12	465,000	76,240	29,436	Abéché
Salamat	SA	SA	CD13	143,000	63,000	24,324	Am Timan
Tandjilé	TA	TA	CD14	405,300	18,045	6,967	Laï
				5,961,000	1,284,000	495,755	

Status: These divisions are préfectures.

Abv: Two-letter code for international compatibility (defined by the author).

ISO: Codes from ISO 3166-2.

FIPS: Codes from FIPS PUB 10-4.

Population: 1992 estimates.

Area-km: Square kilometers.

Area-mi: Square miles.

Further subdivisions: The prefectures are subdivided into sous-préfectures (sub-prefectures). There were 47 in 1982, 53 in 1990.

Territorial extent: The Aozou strip, an area of some 100,000 sq. km. along the Libyan border, is claimed and occupied by Libya. It lies within Borkou-Ennedi-Tibesti.

Origins of names: Some of the prefectures are named for the major rivers of the area. The Mayo Kébi River drains into the Bénoué, and thus finally to the Gulf of Guinea. The Chari, and its tributaries, including the Logone (with two branches, Logone Occidental and Logone Oriental) and Bahr Salamat, flows into Lake Chad. The Batha is an intermittent river, ending at Lake Fitri. Lakes Chad and Fitri grow and shrink according to the amount of rainfall. Bas (Lower) means downstream. Moyen means middle. Chari is a local word meaning river.

Change history:

~1968   Logone prefecture split into Logone Occidental and Logone Oriental. Lac and Tandjilé prefectures created.

1973   Name of national capital changed from Fort Lamy to N'Djamena (sometimes spelled Ndjamena or N'djamena). Name of capital of Moyen-Chari changed from Fort Archambault to Sahr.

Other names of subdivisions:

Chari-Baguirmi: Bas-Chari (obsolete)

Guéra: Baguirmi (obsolete)

Mayo-Kébbi: Maio-Kebbi, Mayo-Kabbi, Mayo Kébi, Mayokerbi (variant)

CHILE

ISO = CL/FIPS = CI   Language = Spanish   Time zone = -4 (see note)   Capital = Santiago

Chile has been an independent nation throughout the 20th century. It has revamped its administrative division several times. Chile makes a distinction between administrative and political subdivisions, but the geographic areas are the same for both types.

Time zone note: Easter Island and Sala y Gómez are in the -6 time zone.

Other names of country: Chili (Dutch, French); Cile (Italian); Republic of Chile (formal–English); República de Chile (formal); Síle (Icelandic).

Origin of name: named Chile mapu by the Incas (Quechua *chile*: cold, *mapu*: land).

division	ISO	FIPS	Rom	population	area-km	area-mi	capital
Aisén del General Carlos Ibáñez del Campo	AI	CI02	XI	82,071	107,153	41,372	Coihaique
Antofagasta	AN	CI03	II	407,409	125,306	48,381	Antofagasta
Araucanía	AR	CI04	IX	774,959	32,472	12,538	Temuco
Atacama	AT	CI05	III	230,786	78,268	30,219	Copiapó
Bío-Bío	BI	CI06	VIII	1,729,920	36,007	13,902	Concepción
Coquimbo	CO	CI07	IV	502,460	39,647	15,308	La Serena
Libertador General Bernardo O'Higgins	LI	CI08	VI	688,385	15,950	6,158	Rancagua
Los Lagos	LL	CI09	X	953,330	69,039	26,656	Puerto Montt
Magallanes y Antártica Chilena	MA	CI10	XII	143,058	112,310	43,363	Punta Arenas
Maule	ML	CI11	VII	834,053	30,518	11,783	Talca
Región Metropolitana de Santiago	RM	CI12		5,170,293	15,782	6,093	Santiago
Tarapacá	TA	CI13	I	341,112	58,073	22,422	Iquique
Valparaíso	VS	CI01	V	1,373,967	16,378	6,324	Valparaíso
				13,231,803	736,903	284,519	

Status: These divisions are regiones (regions). For convenience, I will use shortened forms of the four longest region names in the tables that follow.

ISO: Codes from ISO 3166-2.

FIPS: Codes from FIPS PUB 10-4.

Rom: Roman numerals used by Chile to designate the regions other than Santiago.

Population: 1992 census.

Area-km: Square kilometers.

Area-mi: Square miles.

According to the Encyclopedia Britannica, Chile is conventionally divided into seven "regions" with no administrative status. From north to south, they are:

Norte Grande (Big North): Antofagasta, Tarapacá

Norte Chico (Little North): Atacama, Coquimbo

Núcleo Central (Central Nucleus): Libertador, Maule, Santiago, Valparaíso

Bío-Bío: Bío-Bío, Malleco province of Araucanía region

La Frontera (the Border): Cautín province of Araucanía region

Los Lagos (the Lakes): Los Lagos region, except for Chiloé province

Las Canales (the Canals): Aisén, Magallanes, Chiloé province of Los Lagos region

Further subdivisions: The 13 regions are subdivided into 40 provincias (provinces), which are further subdivided into 334 comunas (municipalities). This table shows the modern provinces contained in each of the regions.

Antofagasta: Antofagasta, El Loa, Tocopilla

Araucanía: Cautín, Malleco

Atacama: Chañaral, Copiapó, Huasco

Aisén: Aisén, Capitán Prat, General Carrera

Bío-Bío: Arauco, Bío-Bío, Concepción, Ñuble

Coquimbo: Choapa, Elqui, Limarí

Libertador: Cachapoal, Colchagua

Los Lagos: Chiloé, Llanquihue, Osorno, Valdivia

Magallanes: Magallanes, Tierra del Fuego, Ultima Esperanza

Maule: Curicó, Linares, Talca

Santiago: Santiago

Tarapacá: Arica, Iquique

Valparaíso: Ísla de Pascua, Los Andes, Petorca, Quillota, San Antonio, San Felipe, Valparaíso

Territorial extent: Valparaíso includes Chile's remote Pacific islands: Ísla de Pascua (Easter Island, or Rapa Nui), the Íslas Juan Fernández (Más a Tierra, Más Afuera, and some smaller islands), Ísla Sala y Gómez, and Íslas de los Desventurados (San Félix, San Ambrosio, and some smaller islands). Más a Tierra (Spanish for "closer to land") is sometimes called Ísla Róbinson Crusoe, and Más Afuera (Spanish for "farther out"), Ísla Alejandro Selkirk. Alexander Selkirk, the real-life prototype for Robinson Crusoe, was marooned on Más a Tierra from 1704 to 1709.

Magallanes y Antártica Chilena includes the Chilean section of the island of Tierra del Fuego, the Íslas Diego Ramírez, and Chile's claim in Antarctica. This book lists the Antarctic claim under Antarctica.

Chile and Argentina have had numerous boundary disputes and border adjustments over the years. They exercise shared sovereignty over a few small islands at the eastern end of the Beagle Channel, including Islas Lennox, Nueva, and Picton.

Origins of names:

Aisén del General Carlos Ibáñez del Campo: Named for President Carlos Ibáñez del Campo (1877–1960).

Araucanía: For the native Araucanian or Mapuche Indians.

Atacama: For the Atacama Desert, from an ethnic name, possibly from Quechua *tacama*: black duck

Bío-Bío: For the Bío-Bío River (Río Bío-Bío).

Coquimbo: Quechua *cullqui*: silver, *tampu*: inn

Libertador General Bernardo O'Higgins: Named for Bernardo O'Higgins (1776–1842), the liberator of Chile. His birth surname, Chillán, is the name of a former department of Chile in Ñuble province.

Los Lagos: Spanish for "the lakes."

Magallanes y Antártica Chilena: Spanish for "Magellan and the Chilean Antarctic." Named for the Strait of Magellan, which was named for Ferdinand Magellan (Portuguese: Fernão de Magalhães, ~1480–1521), the navigator who discovered the Strait of Magellan, which passes through this region.

Región Metropolitana de Santiago: Spanish for "Metropolitan Region of Santiago." The city was founded in 1541 by Pedro de Valdivia, who named it Santiago del Nuevo Extremo: Santiago in honor of Saint James, patron saint of Castile; Nuevo Extremo as the farthest point of the conquest at that time.

Valparaíso: After the city, which was named in 1536 by its founder, Juan de Saavedra, for his birthplace in Spain.

Change history:

1902   Border between Chile and Argentina in Patagonia and Tierra del Fuego settled through British arbitration.

1927   At the beginning of the century, Chile was divided into 23 provinces. By 1927, one additional territory had been created. There were 82 departamentos (departments) at that time. In 1927, President Carlos Ibáñez del Campo carried out a reform which left sixteen provinces and two territories on the highest administrative level, and 75 departments at the next level. However, the bureaucracy opposed the changes, and gradually reversed them until in 1940 there were 25 provinces (the earlier 23, plus Aysén and Osorno), subdivided into 85 departments, which were further subdivided into 278 municipalities. The 25 provinces remained quite steady, although the departments rose to 89.

1929   Dispute between Chile and Peru over the area around Arica and Tacna resolved: Tacna province transferred from Chile to Peru; Arica remained part of Tarapacá province.

~1979 In another reform, the provinces were re-organized into the 13 regions described above.

1985   Name of Aconcagua region changed to Valparaíso.

Other names of subdivisions:

Aisén del General Carlos Ibáñez del Campo: Aisén, Aysén (informal); Aysén del General Carlos Ibáñez del Campo (variant)

Bío-Bío: Bíobío (obsolete)

Libertador General Bernardo O'Higgins: Libertador (informal)

Magallanes y Antártica Chilena: Región de Magallanes y de la Antártica Chilena (formal)

Región Metropolitana de Santiago: Región Metropolitana

Valparaíso: Aconcagua (obsolete)

Population history:

	1982	1992	former provinces
Aisén	65,478	82,071	Aysén, small part of Chiloé
Antofagasta	341,203	407,409	most of Antofagasta ▶

	1982	1992	former provinces
Araucanía	692,924	774,959	Cautín, Malleco
Atacama	183,071	230,786	most of Atacama
Bío-Bío	1,516,552	1,729,920	Arauco, Bío-Bío, Concepción, Ñuble
Coquimbo	419,178	502,460	Coquimbo, small part of Atacama
Libertador	584,989	688,385	Colchagua, O'Higgins, small part of Santiago
Los Lagos	843,430	953,330	Llanquihue, Osorno, Valdivia, most of Chiloé
Magallanes	132,333	143,058	Magallanes
Maule	723,224	834,053	Curicó, Linares, Maule, Talca
Santiago	4,294,938	5,170,293	most of Santiago
Tarapacá	273,427	341,112	Tarapacá, small part of Antofagasta
Valparaíso	1,204,693	1,373,967	Aconcagua, Valparaíso, part of Santiago
	11,275,440	13,231,803	

	area-km	1910	1940	1957	1972	capital
Aconcagua	10,204	132,730	118,049	154,075	181,660	San Felipe
Antofagasta	123,063	118,718	145,147	221,820	283,029	Antofagasta
Arauco	5,756	62,259	66,107	86,758	110,401	Lebu
Atacama	79,883	65,118	84,312	96,152	174,634	Copiapó
Aysén	88,984	42,925	17,014	31,518	55,201	Puerto Aysén
Bío-Bío	11,248	100,495	127,312	165,975	216,789	Los Ángeles
Cautín	17,370	161,935	374,659	438,149	465,695	Temuco
Chiloé	23,446	91,657	101,706	120,844	124,442	Ancud
Colchagua	8,431	159,421	131,248	167,459	184,837	San Fernando
Concepción	5,701	225,054	308,241	493,950	723,630	Concepción
Coquimbo	39,889	178,731	245,609	314,647	377,372	La Serena
Curicó	5,737	108,120	81,185	107,333	126,565	Curicó
Linares	9,820	111,773	134,968	175,534	210,766	Linares
Llanquihue	18,407	113,285	117,225	168,005	225,821	Puerto Montt
Magallanes	135,418	23,650	48,813	66,258	101,368	Punta Arenas
Malleco	14,277	113,020	154,174	191,330	200,894	Angol
Maule	5,626	115,568	70,497	86,629	92,336	Cauquenes
Ñuble	14,211	169,858	243,185	301,654	351,277	Chillán
O'Higgins	7,112	94,257	200,297	269,549	346,258	Rancagua
Osorno	9,083	— —	107,341	147,693	179,652	Osorno
Santiago	17,422	546,599	1,268,505	2,106,249	3,724,540	Santiago
Talca	9,640	132,730	157,141	208,463	257,937	Talca
Tarapacá	55,287	115,940	104,097	123,365	204,745	Iquique
Valdivia	20,934	131,751	191,642	279,215	304,106	Valdivia
Valparaíso	4,818	299,466	425,065	597,990	820,985	Valparaíso
	741,767	3,415,060	5,023,539	7,120,614	10,044,940	

Census details:

1957: estimate of 1957-06
1972: census of 1972-06-30

Population of Tacna province for 1910 is listed under Aysén.

CHINA

ISO = CN/FIPS = CH   Language = Chinese   Time zone = +8   Capital = Beijing

At the beginning of the 20th century, an emperor ruled China. It was riddled with European spheres of influence and leased territories. On 1912-01-01, the emperor was overthrown and a republic was proclaimed. In 1931, Japan occupied Manchuria. During World War II, Japan overran a substantial part of China. All of its conquests were nullified by the Allied victory in 1945. Meanwhile, Mao Zedong was leading a Communist revolution which, by 1950, had conquered all of China except Taiwan. In recent years, all concerned parties have agreed that there is only one China, without resolving which is the legitimate government thereof: the People's Republic of China which exercises power on the mainland, or the Republic of China which rules Taiwan. Taiwan is just one province of this theoretically unified country. This book follows ISO standard 3166 in offering two listings, under the names China and Taiwan.

Spelling note: Because of the many systems used to transliterate Chinese characters into the Roman alphabet, there are an inordinate number of variant spellings for place names within China. The Pinyin system, devised by Chinese scholars in the 1950s and used as the standard Romanization of the People's Republic of China since 1979, is now widely accepted. The Wade-Giles system was commonly used in English texts before then. Western conventional spelling is not a system, but refers to naive transcriptions that have been in common use. In the main table of divisions, the Pinyin and conventional transcriptions of province names are listed, with the Pinyin form of capitals. In the change history, the transcriptions shown are those most likely to be found in historical sources in English. Pinyin equivalents are given with "p:". The list of other names of subdivisions attempts to communicate a feel for the kind of variations that occur. In that table, some variants are translations rather than transliterations. Note how each language uses its own phonetic conventions to render similar sounds.

Other names of country: Chine (French); Cina (Italian); Kiina (Finnish); Kina (Danish, Norwegian, Swedish); Kína (Icelandic); People's Republic of China (formal–English); Zhonghua Renmin Gonghe Guo (formal).

Origin of name: Latin *Sina*, ancient form of the province name Shaanxi (controversial).

division	abv	ISO	FIPS	type	population	area-km	area-mi	conventional	capital
Anhui	AH	34	CH01	p*	52,290,000	139,900	54,016	Anhwei	Hefei
Beijing	BJ	11	CH22	m	10,870,000	17,800	6,873	Peking	Beijing
Fujian	FJ	35	CH07	p*	30,610,000	123,100	47,529	Fukien	Fuzhou
Gansu	GS	62	CH15	p*	22,930,000	530,000	204,634	Kansu	Lanzhou
Guangdong	GD	44	CH30	p*	63,210,000	197,400	76,217	Kwangtung	Guangzhou
Guangxi Zhuang	GX	45	CH16	a*	42,530,000	220,400	85,097	Kwangsi Chuang	Nanning
Guizhou	GZ	52	CH18	p*	32,730,000	174,000	67,182	Kweichow	Guiyang
Hainan	HA	00	CH31	p	6,420,000	34,000	13,127	Hainan	Haikou
Hebei	HB	13	CH10	p*	60,280,000	202,700	78,263	Hopeh	Shijiazhuang
Heilongjiang	HL	23	CH08	p	34,770,000	463,600	178,997	Heilungkiang	Harbin
Henan	HE	41	CH09	p*	86,140,000	167,000	64,479	Honan	Zhengzhou
Hubei	HU	42	CH12	p*	54,760,000	187,500	72,394	Hupeh	Wuhan
Hunan	HN	43	CH11	p*	60,600,000	210,500	81,275	Hunan	Changsha
Jiangsu	JS	32	CH04	p*	68,170,000	102,200	39,460	Kiangsu	Nanjing
Jiangxi	JX	36	CH03	p*	38,280,000	164,800	63,630	Kiangsi	Nanchang
Jilin	JL	22	CH05	p	25,150,000	187,000	72,201	Kirin	Changchun
Liaoning	LN	21	CH19	p	39,980,000	151,000	58,301	Liaoning	Shenyang
Nei Mongol	NM	15	CH20	a	21,110,000	450,000	173,746	Inner Mongolia	Hohhot
Ningxia Hui	NX	64	CH21	a	4,660,000	170,000	65,637	Ningsia Hui	Yinchuan
Qinghai	QH	63	CH06	p	4,430,000	721,000	278,380	Tsinghai	Xining
Shaanxi	SA	61	CH26	p*	32,470,000	195,800	75,599	Shensi	Xian
Shandong	SD	37	CH25	p*	83,430,000	153,300	59,189	Shantung	Jinan
Shanghai	SH	31	CH23	m	13,510,000	5,800	2,239	Shanghai	Shanghai
Shanxi	SX	14	CH24	p*	28,180,000	157,100	60,657	Shansi	Taiyuan
Sichuan	SC	51	CH27	p*	106,370,000	569,000	219,692	Szechwan	Chengdu
Tianjin	TJ	12	CH28	m	8,830,000	4,000	1,544	Tientsin	Tianjin
Xinjiang Uygur	XJ	65	CH13	a	15,370,000	1,646,800	635,833	Sinkiang Uighur	Urumqi
Xizang	XZ	54	CH14	a	2,220,000	1,221,600	471,662	Tibet	Lhasa
Yunnan	YN	53	CH29	p*	36,750,000	436,200	168,418	Yunnan	Kunming
Zhejiang	ZJ	33	CH02	p*	40,840,000	101,800	39,305	Chekiang	Hangzhou
					1,127,890,000	9,105,300	3,515,576		

* = the traditional "eighteen provinces"

Abv: Two-letter code for international compatibility (defined by the author).
ISO: Codes from ISO 3166-2. These are based on Chinese National Standard GB2260-86, except for Hainan (see below).
FIPS: Codes from FIPS PUB 10-4.
Type: China currently has 22 sheng (p = provinces), 5 zizhiqu (a = autonomous regions), and 3 shih (m = municipalities) under direct control of the central government).
Population: 1990 census.
Area-km: Square kilometers.
Area-mi: Square miles.
Note: The Chinese National Bureau of Standards has created a hierarchical set of codes for the first-, second-, and third-

level administrative subdivisions. In a six-digit code, the first two digits indicate a province, the next two a prefecture or munic-ipality on the prefecture level, and the last two a county or municipality on the county level. The standard is designated GB2260, where GB stands for Guobiao, and the codes are called Guobiao codes. (They should not be confused with the Guo-biao codes for Chinese characters, which are defined by standard GB12345.) Exceptions and additions: the Guobiao code for Hainan is 46; for Xianggang (Hong Kong), 81; Macau will be coded 82 when it reverts to Chinese control; and Taiwan is 71 according to Beijing's reckoning.

Further subdivisions: First-level subdivisions of China are provinces, autonomous regions, and municipalities, as shown. There are about 350 second-level divisions, including municipalities under direct provincial control, t'i-ch'ü (prefectures, or areas), chuan-ch'ü (special districts), tzu-chih-chou (autonomous districts), hsing-cheng-ch'ü (administrative districts), and (in Nei Mongol only) meng (leagues). There are about 2,800 third-level divisions: hsien (counties), municipalities, tzu-chih-hsien (autonomous counties), etc. The fourth-level divisions were formerly hsiang (villages) and chen (towns). In 1958, they were all replaced by communes.

China's government uses adjustments to administrative divisions as a policy tool, and approximately 1% of the county-level units are changed each year.

Territorial extent: Although Hong Kong and Taiwan are part of China, this book, following ISO 3166, treats them as separate entities.

China claims the Paracel Islands and Spratly Islands in the South China Sea. These groups have been given FIPS 10-4 country codes of PF and PG, respectively.

China has long-standing border disputes with most of its Asian neighbors. In the Karakoram Range of the Himalayas, there is an area, mostly in Xinjiang Uygur but partly in Xizang, possessed by China but claimed by India. In Eastern India, most of Arunachal Pradesh state is claimed by China.

Jilin is blocked from access to the Sea of Japan by North Korea and Russia.

Fujian province includes islands to the middle of the Taiwan Strait, with some exceptions. Taiwan claims, and occupies, two island groups in what would otherwise be the territorial waters of the People's Republic. The main islands are Quemoy, near Xiamen, and Matsu, near Fuzhou.

Hebei province has an unusual sort of enclave. As the municipalities of Beijing and Tianjin grew, their borders met on the east and the west, leaving an undigested area in the middle. Sanhe and Zizhixian are towns in this enclave.

Shanghai municipality includes the island of Chongming Dao, north of the main channel of the Yangtze River.

Origins of names:

Anhui: Chinese *an*: tranquil, *hui*: excellent; name derived from the first syllables of An-Ch'ing and Hweichow cities.

Beijing: Chinese *bei*: north, *jing*: capital (i.e. northern capital).

Fujian: Chinese *fu*: happiness, *jian*: establish (i.e. happy establishment).

Gansu: Chinese *gan*: benevolent, *su*: respectful; name derived from the first syllables of Kan-chou and Su-chou districts.

Guangdong: Chinese *guang*: wide, *dong*: east; province was formed long ago as the eastern part of an area known as Kwang-nan Hsi-lu ("Wide south, western route").

Guangxi: Chinese *guang*: immense, *xi*: west (western part of Kwang-nan Hsi-lu).

Guizhou: Chinese *gui*: precious, *zhou*: region.

Hainan: Chinese *hai*: sea, *nan*: south (island in the South China Sea).

Hebei: Chinese *he*: river, *bei*: north (i.e. north of the Hwang Ho).

Heilongjiang: Chinese *hei*: black, *long*: dragon, *jiang*: river; named for the river which forms its northern border.

Henan: Chinese *he*: river, *nan*: south (south of the Hwang Ho).

Hubei: Chinese *hu*: lake, *bei*: north (north of a chain of lakes along the Yangtze River).

Hunan: Chinese *hu*: lake, *nan*: south (south of the same lakes).

Jiangsu: Chinese *jiang*: river, *su*: bounty, or thyme, or relive; name derived from the first syllables of Chiang-ning and Su-chou prefectures.

Jiangxi: Chinese *jiang*: river, *xi*: west (originally west of the Yangtze River).

Jilin: Chinese *ji*: good luck, *lin*: forest; but the name derives from Manchu kirin ula: riverbank

Liaoning: Chinese *liao*: distant, *ning*: peace; named for the Liao River.

Nei Mongol: Inner Mongolia

Ningxia: Chinese *ning*: peace; named for the Hsi Hsia, or Tangut, tribe, then at peace.

Qinghai: Chinese *qing*: blue, *hai*: sea; named for a lake in its northeast. Both the lake and the province were formerly called Koko Nor.

Shaanxi: west of the pass.

Shandong: Chinese *shan*: mountains, *dong*: east (i.e. eastern mountains).

Shanghai: on the sea.

Shanxi: Chinese *shan*: mountains, *xi*: west (i.e. west of the mountains).

Sichuan: four rivers (referring to four tributaries of the Yangtze River).

Tianjin: Chinese *tian*: celestial, *jin*: ford; originially Tien-chin-wei: defense of the heavenly ford.

Xinjiang: new frontier, new dominion.

Xizang: Chinese *xi*: west, *zang*: storehouse.

Yunnan: Chinese *yun*: clouds, *nan*: south; region is south of the Yun-ling Shan, or cloudy mountains.

Zhejiang: From the province's main river, formerly named Che Chiang (crooked river).

Change history: The change history of Chinese subdivisions is somewhat confusing. It is best understood by separately examining each of the components of the Chinese empire, as of 1900: China, Manchuria, Mongolia, Sinkiang, and Tibet. The external borders of this region were roughly the same as present-day China and Mongolia combined.

China in 1900 consisted of eighteen provinces, the traditional heartland of the empire. There were several independent states in the southern mountains, completely surrounded by China: Lolos, Seng-Miaotse (two enclaves), and Choang Kolao (also two enclaves). Territories leased to other nations included Kwangchowan (French: Kouang-Tchéou-Wan, on modern Donghai Island and adjacent land on the Leizhou Peninsula), Macao (Portuguese: Macau), Hong Kong (British), Kiao-Chow (p:Jiaozhou) Bay (German: Tsing-tao [p:Qingdao]), Weihai (British: Wei-hai-wei, on the Shandong Peninsula), and Kwantung (p:Guandong, not to be confused with Kwangtung (p:Guangdong) province in South China) in Manchuria (Russian: Port Arthur). Japan had acquired Taiwan and the adjacent Penghu Islands in the Sino-Japanese War of 1895.

1914	Japan acquired the lease to Kiao-Chow Bay from Germany.
1922	Kiao-Chow Bay reverted to China.
1928	Nanking replaced Peking as capital of China. (Note: Nanking is from *nan*: south, *jing*: capital; Peking is from *bei*: north, *jing*: capital.) Peking renamed Pei-p'ing (peace in the north). Its province renamed from Chihli to Hopeh.
1930-10-01	Wei-hai-wei restored to China by Great Britain.
~1938	Capital of Kiangsu moved from Nanking to Chinkiang (p:Zhenjiang).
~1939	Capital of Kwangsi moved from Kweilin (p:Guilin) to Nanning.
1945-08-18	Kwangchowan restored to China by France.
1949-04-23	As the Communists advanced, the Nationalist government retreated to a temporary capital at Chungking (p:Chongqing) in Szechuan.
1949	A set of regional administrative areas (see table below) temporarily replaced provincial government under the Communist regime.
1949-10-01	Peking replaced Nanking as capital of China, re-assuming its former name.
1952	Capital of Kiangsu moved from Chinkiang back to Nanking.
~1952	Peking municipality split from Hopeh province; Shanghai municipality split from Kiangsu province.
1954	The administrative areas were abolished and provincial government resumed.
~1955	Capital of Honan renamed from K'ai-feng to Cheng-chou (p:Zhengzhou).
1957-06	Guangxi province became Guangxi Zhuang autonomous region.
~1958	Capital of Anhwei moved from Anking (p:Anqing) to Hefei.
1958	Capital of Hopeh moved from Paoting (p:Baoding) to Tientsin.
1958	Kwangsi changed from province to autonomous region.
1967	Capital of Hopeh moved from Tientsin to Shih-chia-chuang (p:Shijiazhuang). Tientsin became a provincial-level municipality.
~1970	Triangle of land around Beihai transferred from Guangdong province to Guangxi Zhuang autonomous region, giving the latter a seacoast.
1988-04	Hainan province split from Guangdong province.
1997-07-01	Hong Kong (not listed here) reverted to China, on the expiration of Great Britain's lease.
~1997	A recent FIPS PUB 10-4 list implies that Chongqing (not shown on the list above) has been split from Sichuan province. Logically, it should be a municipality.

Manchuria in 1900 had three provinces: Heilungkiang, Kilin, and Shengching. Their respective capitals were Tsitsihar (p:Qiqihar), Kirin (p:Jilin), and Mukden (now named p:Shenyang). Russian armed forces occupied Manchuria during the course of 1900. After Japan won the Russo-Japanese war in 1905, the Russian forces withdrew and were supplanted by Japanese. Japan also acquired the lease to Kwantung. By 1925, Japan's military occupation was confined to Kwantung. On 1931-09-18, two bombings in Mukden gave the Japanese a pretext to invade Manchuria. On 1932-03-09, the nominally independent country of Manchukuo was declared. In actuality, it was a Japanese puppet state. Its capital was Hsinking (p:Changchun). Japan extended its control, enlarging Manchukuo with territory seized from Inner Mongolia (the Chearim area) and China (the northern part of Chihli province, which became Jehol province of Manchuria). At the end of World War II, Manchuria reverted de facto to Chinese sovereignty. The de jure restoration was completed about 1951. Since then, the Chinese have called the region the Northeast, rather than Manchuria. It now consists of three provinces which roughly match the ones in 1900, with Liaoning corresponding to Shengching.

1903	Name of Shengching province changed to Feng-t'ien.
1905	Japan won the Kwantung lease from Russia in the Russo-Japanese War.
1928	Name of Feng-t'ien province changed to Liao-ning, with altered boundaries.
1931-09-18	Japan occupied Manchuria.
1932-03-09	Creation of Manchukuo announced.
1933	Jehol province created as a buffer state between Manchukuo and China. Its capital was Jehol (p:Chengde).
1945-09-02	Japan surrendered, ending World War II. Manchuria, Taiwan, and the Penghu Islands were restored de facto to China. The Soviet Union took possession of Kwantung.
1947	During the period between 1947 and 1955-08, Manchuria split into as many as eleven provinces. Jehol and Cherim provinces, in the west, were historically part of Inner Mongolia, but had been annexed to Manchukuo during the war. In place of the prewar Heilungkiang, there were now the provinces of Heilungkiang, Hsingan, and northern parts of Nunkiang, Sungkiang, and Hokiang. Prewar Kirin corresponded to the southern parts of those three provinces, plus Kirin. Prewar Liaoning was divided into Liaohsi (west), Liaoning, and Liaotung (east). Then it was resectioned into Liaoning, Antung (east), and Liaopeh (north), with much of Cherim province attached to Liaopeh. Finally, Hsingan and much of Jehol and Liaopeh became part of Inner Mongolia; Heilungkiang, Hokiang, Nunkiang, and Sungkiang became modern Heilungkiang; Kirin acquired parts of Antung and Liaopeh; another part of Jehol was annexed to Hopeh; and what was left became Liaoning.
1954	Capital of Kirin province moved from Kirin to Changchun.
1955	Kwantung territory returned to China by the Soviet Union.

Mongolia in 1900 included what is now Mongolia, most of Nei Mongol, and parts of Heilongjiang, Jirin, and Liaoning. It acquired independence from China by stages, losing Inner Mongolia and Tannu Tuva in the process. During this period, it was sometimes called Outer Mongolia, to help distinguish it from Inner Mongolia. For internal divisions, see the listing for Mongolia.

1912	Mongolia became autonomous.
1919	Mongolia reintegrated with China.
1921-03-13	Outer Mongolia declared independence from China. The Mongolian provinces of Ala-Shan (roughly equivalent to Ningsia), Ordos, Silin Gol, and Chearim remained part of China.
~1930	Ordos (south of the Hwang Ho) and Silin Gol merged to form Suiyuan province, with capital Kweisui (now named p:Hohhot).
1946-01-05	China recognized Mongolia's independence.
1947-05	Inner Mongolia autonomous region formed by the Communist regime from parts of Chahar and Heilungkiang provinces.
1954-02	A long strip of southern Mongolia was annexed by Inner Mongolia.
1954	Ningsia province merged with Kansu.
1954-06	Suiyuan province merged with Inner Mongolia autonomous region. Hohhot (also known as Hu-ho-hao-t'e, Huhehot, etc.) became capital of Inner Mongolia.
1956	Part of Kansu transferred to Inner Mongolia (northern part of former Ningsia province).
1958	Ningsia Hui autonomous region (southern part of former Ningsia province) split from Kansu province.
1969	Hu-lun-pei-erh-meng transferred from Nei Mongol to Heilongjiang.

| 1969 | Ala-Shan East transferred from Nei Mongol to Ningsia Hui. |
| ~1970 | Part of Pa-yen-nao-erh-meng transferred from Nei Mongol to Kansu. |

In 1900, Sinkiang had almost the same extent that it does now. Its northern part was called Sungaria or Jungaria. Its western part was called East Turkestan, or Chinese Turkestan.

| 1956 | Sinkiang province became Sinkiang Uighur autonomous region. |

In 1900, Tibet occupied approximately the territory of modern Xizang and Qinghai. Its relationship to China has fluctuated between subjugation and independence. Between 1912 and 1950, the scale tilted toward independence. In 1950-10, China invaded Tibet, and has remained sovereign there ever since. The status of Tibet's subdivisions has also been variable over the years. As a rule, the Tibetan region has comprised Tibet proper, in the west; Koko Nor, later called Tsinghai, in the northeast; and Kham, later called Sikang, in the southwest.

1914	"Inner Tibet" created as a buffer zone between Tibet itself ("Outer Tibet") and China, but its boundaries were never agreed on.
1928	Tsinghai became a province of China.
1950-10	Chinese troops occupied Tibet.
1951-05-23	Tibet and China signed an agreement formalizing the occupation.
1955-08	Sikang province (capital Yaan) merged into Sichuan province.
1965-09-09	Xizang became autonomous region.

Administrative areas 1949–1954:

Central South: Honan, Hunan, Hupeh, Kiangsi, Kwangsi, Kwangtung

East China: Anhwei, Chekiang, Fukien, Kiangsu, Shantung

Inner Mongolia: Northern Chahar, Suiyuan

North China: Southern Chahar, Hopei, Shansi

Northeast China: Antung, Heilungkiang, Jehol, Kirin, Liaohsi

Northwest China: Kansu, Ningsia, Shensi, Sinkiang, Tsinghai

Southwest China: Kweichow, Sikang, Szechuan, Yunnan

Other names of subdivisions:

Anhui: An-hui (Wade-Giles); Ngan-houei (French); Ngan-hui (obsolete)

Beijing: Pechino (Italian); Pei-ching (Wade-Giles); Pei-p'ing (obsolete); Pékin (French); Pekín (Spanish); Pequim (Portuguese)

Fujian: Foekien (Dutch); Fokien (German); Fou-kien (French); Fu-chien (Wade-Giles); Min Sheng (informal)

Gansu: Kansoe (Dutch); Kan-sou (French); Kan-su (Wade-Giles)

Guangdong: Kouang-tong, Kuan-tung (French); Kuangtung (Portuguese); Kuang-tung (Wade-Giles); Kwangtoeng (Dutch)

Guangxi Zhuang: Guangxi (informal); Kouang-si (French); Kuang-hsi (Wade-Giles); Kuangsi (Portuguese); Kwangsi (Dutch, German); Kwangsi-Chuang (conventional)

Guizhou: Kouei-tcheou (French); Kueichau (Portuguese); Kuei-chou (Wade-Giles); Kweitschou (German); Kweitsjou (Dutch)

Hainan: Hai-nan (French, Wade-Giles)

Hebei: Ho-pei (French, Wade-Giles); Hopei (Dutch, German, Portuguese)

Heilongjiang: Heiloengkiang (Dutch); Hei-long-kiang (French); Hei-lung-chiang (Wade-Giles)

Henan: Ho-nan (French, Wade-Giles)

Hubei: Hoepeh (Dutch); Hou-pei (French); Hu-pei (Wade-Giles); Hupei (German, Portuguese)

Hunan: Hoenan (Dutch); Hou-nan (French); Hu-nan (Wade-Giles)

Jiangsu: Chiang-su (Wade-Giles); Kiangsoe (Dutch); Kiang-sou (French)

Jiangxi: Chiang-hsi (Wade-Giles); Kiang-si (French)

Jilin: Chi-lin (Wade-Giles); Ki-lin (French)

Liaoning: Fengtien (obsolete); Leao-ning (French); Liao-ning (Wade-Giles)

Nei Mongol: Binnen-Mongolië (Dutch); Indre Mongolia (Norwegian); Innere Mongolei (German); Mongolia Interior (Spanish); Mongólia Interior (Portuguese); Mongolia Interna (Italian); Mongolie-Intérieure (French); Neimeng (variant); Nei-meng-ku (Wade-Giles); Nei Monggol (variant)

Ningxia Hui: Ninchsia (German); Ning-hia (French); Ning-hsia (Wade-Giles); Ninghsia (German, Portuguese); Ningsia (informal-conventional)

Qinghai: Ch'ing-hai (Wade-Giles); Chinghai (Portuguese); Tschinghai (German); Ts'ing-hai (French)

Shaanxi: Chen-si (French); Schensi (German); Shen-hsi (Wade-Giles); Sjensi (Dutch)

Shandong: Chan-tong (French); Schantung (German); Shan-tung (Wade-Giles); Sjantoeng (Dutch)

Shanghai: Chang-haï (French); Schanghai (German); Sjanghai (Dutch); Xangai (Portuguese)

Shanxi: Chan-si (French); Schansi, Shansi (German); Shan-hsi (Wade-Giles); Shansi (Portuguese); Sjensi (Dutch)

Sichuan: Setchouan, Seu-tch'ouan, Sseu-tch'ouan (French); Setsuan (Portuguese); Sezuan, Szechuan, Szetschuan (German); Ssu-ch'uan (Wade-Giles); Szetsjwan (Dutch)

Tianjin: T'ien-tsin (French)

Xinjiang Uygur: Hsin-chiang (Wade-Giles); Sin-kiang (French); Sinkiang (informal-conventional); Sinkiang-Oeigoer (Dutch); Uigurische Autonome Region Xinjiang (German); Xinjiang (informal)

Xizang: Hsi-tsang (Wade-Giles); Sitsang (German); Thibet (French-obsolete); Tibete (Portuguese)

Yunnan: Junnan (Dutch); Jünnan, Yünnan (German); Yunnan (French, Wade-Giles)

Zhejiang: Che-chiang (Wade-Giles); Chekiang (German, Portuguese); Tchö-kiang (French); Tschekiang (German); Tsjekiang (Dutch)

Population history:

	1898	1936	1953	1982	1990
Anhui	20,596,288	23,265,368	30,343,637	49,665,000	52,290,000
Beijing	——	——	2,768,149	9,230,000	10,870,000
Chahar	——	2,035,957	——	——	——
Chinghai	——	1,196,054	11,676,534	——	——
Fujian	22,790,556	11,755,625	13,142,721	25,873,000	30,610,000
Gansu	9,285,377	6,705,446	12,928,102	19,569,000	22,930,000
Guangdong	29,706,249	32,385,215	34,770,059	59,299,000	63,210,000
Guangxi Zhuang	5,151,327	13,385,215	19,560,822	36,420,000	42,530,000
Guizhou	7,669,181	9,043,207	15,037,310	28,553,000	32,730,000
Hainan	——	——	——	——	6,420,000
Hebei	17,937,000	28,644,737	35,984,644	53,006,000	60,280,000
Heilongjiang	——	——	11,897,309	32,665,000	34,770,000
Henan	22,115,827	34,289,848	44,214,594	74,422,000	86,140,000
Hubei	33,365,005	25,541,636	27,789,693	47,804,000	54,760,000
Hunan	21,002,604	28,293,735	33,226,954	54,008,000	60,600,000
Jiangsu	20,905,171	36,469,321	41,252,192	60,521,000	68,170,000
Jiangxi	24,534,118	15,820,403	16,772,865	33,184,000	38,280,000
Jilin	——	——	11,290,073	22,560,000	25,150,000
Liaoning	——	——	18,545,147	35,721,000	39,980,000
Manchuria	——	43,233,954	——	——	——
Nei Mongol	——	——	——	19,274,000	21,110,000
Ningxia Hui	——	1,023,143	——	3,895,000	4,660,000
Qinghai	——	——	11,676,534	3,895,000	4,430,000
Shaanxi	8,432,193	7,717,881	15,881,281	28,904,000	32,470,000
Shandong	36,247,835	38,029,294	48,876,548	74,419,000	83,430,000
Shanghai	——	——	6,204,417	11,859,000	13,510,000
Shanxi	12,211,453	11,601,026	14,314,485	25,291,000	28,180,000
Sichuan	67,712,897	52,963,269	62,303,999	99,713,000	106,370,000
Sikang	——	968,187	3,381,064	——	——
Suiyuan	——	2,083,693	——	——	——
Tianjin	——	——	2,693,831	7,764,000	8,830,000
Xinjiang Uygur	——	4,360,020	4,873,608	13,081,000	15,370,000
Xizang	——	——	1,273,969	1,892,000	2,220,000
Yunnan	11,721,576	11,994,549	17,472,737	32,553,000	36,750,000
Zhejiang	11,588,692	21,230,749	22,865,747	38,884,000	40,840,000
	382,973,349	464,037,532	593,019,025	1,003,924,000	1,127,890,000

Census details: 1898, 1936 estimates.

1953: census of 1953-06-30.

CHRISTMAS ISLAND

ISO = CX/FIPS = KT   Language = English   Time zone = +7   Capital = Flying Fish Cove

Christmas Island was part of the Straits Settlements (the precursor of Malaysia). In 1900, the settlement of Singapore brought it into the colony of Singapore. On 1958-10-01, it was transferred to Australia as an external territory.

Other names of country: Christmaseilanden (Dutch); Île Christmas (French); Ilha Christmas (Portuguese); Isla Christmas (Spanish); Isola Christmas (Italian); Territory of Christmas Island (formal–English); Weihnachtsinsel (German).

Origin of name: Discovered on Christmas Day.

division	abv	population	area-km	area-mi	capital
Christmas Island	CX	1,275	135	52	Flying Fish Cove

Status: This division is the whole of the country, treated as a division for compatibility.
Abv: Two-letter code for international compatibility (defined by the author).
Population: 1991 census.
Area-km: Square kilometers.
Area-mi: Square miles.
Territorial extent: Christmas Island is an isolated island in the Indian Ocean. It should not be confused with Christmas Island in the Pacific Ocean, which is part of Kiribati, and is now more properly called Kiritimati (the Micronesian rendering of "Christmas"). Flying Fish Cove is not officially a capital, but is the only settlement shown on most maps of Christmas Island.

COCOS (KEELING) ISLANDS

ISO = CC/FIPS = CK   Language = English   Time zone = +6:30   Capital = Bantam Village

Cocos (Keeling) Islands was part of the Straits Settlements (the precursor of Malaysia). In 1903, it became part of the colony of Singapore. On 1955-11-23, it was transferred to Australia as an external territory. The parenthetical expression in its name expresses the fact that either name, Cocos Islands or Keeling Islands, is equally acceptable.

Other names of country: Îles des Cocos (Keeling) (French); Ilhas Cocos (Keeling) (Portuguese); Islas Cocos (Keeling) (Spanish); Isole Cocos (Keeling) (Italian); Kokosinseln (Keeling-Inseln) (German); Territory of Cocos (Keeling) Islands (formal–English)

Origin of name: Discovered 1609 by Capt. William Keeling; coconut palms found there.

division	abv	population	area-km	area-mi	capital
Cocos (Keeling) Islands	CC	647	14	5	Bantam Village

Status: This division is the whole of the country, treated as a division for compatibility.
Abv: Two-letter code for international compatibility (defined by the author).
Population: 1991 census.
Area-km: Square kilometers.
Area-mi: Square miles.
Territorial extent: Cocos (Keeling) Islands consists of two atolls in the Indian Ocean. North Keeling Island is the only significant island in one of the atolls; the other one comprises Home Island and West Island, which are inhabited, and several others. Bantam Village, on Home Island, is not officially a capital, but it appears to be the main settlement.

COLOMBIA

ISO = CO/FIPS = CO   Language = Spanish   Time zone = -5   Capital = Bogotá

Colombia has been an independent country during the entire 20th century, but its territory has undergone some adjustments. The first and most notorious was the loss of its department of Panama, in a revolution encouraged by the United States to ease the way for the leasing of the Panama Canal Zone.

Other names of country: Colômbia (Portuguese); Colombie (French); Kolumbia (Finnish); Kólumbía (Icelandic); Kolumbien (German); Republic of Colombia (formal–English); República de Colombia (formal).

Origin of name: Named in honor of Christopher Columbus (1451?–1506).

division	abv	ISO	FIPS	typ	population	area-km	area-mi	capital
Amazonas	AM	AMA	CO01	c	39,937	109,665	42,342	Leticia
Antioquia	AN	ANT	CO02	d	4,067,664	63,612	24,561	Medellín
Arauca	AR	ARA	CO03	i	89,972	23,818	9,196	Arauca
Atlántico	AT	ATL	CO04	d	1,478,213	3,388	1,308	Barranquilla
Bolívar	BL	BOL	CO35	d	1,288,985	25,978	10,030	Cartagena
Boyacá	BY	BOY	CO36	d	1,209,739	23,189	8,953	Tunja
Caldas	CL	CAL	CO37	d	883,024	7,888	3,046	Manizales
Caquetá	CQ	CAQ	CO08	i	264,507	88,965	34,350	Florencia
Casanare	CS	CAS	CO32	i	147,472	44,640	17,236	Yopal
Cauca	CA	CAU	CO09	d	857,731	29,308	11,316	Popayán
Cesar	CE	CES	CO10	d	699,428	22,905	8,844	Valledupar
Chocó	CH	CHO	CO11	d	313,567	46,530	17,965	Quibdó
Córdoba	CO	COR	CO12	d	1,013,427	25,020	9,660	Montería
Cundinamarca	CU	CUN	CO33	d	1,512,928	22,478	8,679	Bogotá
Distrito Especial	DC	DC	CO34	e	4,227,706	1,732	669	Bogotá
Guainía	GN	GUA	CO15	c	12,345	72,238	27,891	Puerto Inírida
Guaviare	GV	GUV	CO14	c	47,073	42,327	16,343	San José del Guaviare
Huila	HU	HUI	CO16	d	693,713	19,890	7,680	Neiva
La Guajira	LG	LAG	CO17	d	299,995	20,848	8,049	Riohacha
Magdalena	MA	MAG	CO38	d	890,934	23,188	8,953	Santa Marta
Meta	ME	MET	CO19	d	474,046	85,635	33,064	Villavicencio
Nariño	NA	NAR	CO20	d	1,085,173	33,268	12,845	Pasto
Norte de Santander	NS	NSA	CO21	d	913,491	21,658	8,362	Cúcuta
Putumayo	PU	PUT	CO22	i	174,219	24,885	9,608	Mocoa
Quindío	QD	QUI	CO23	d	392,208	1,845	712	Armenia
Risaralda	RI	RIS	CO24	d	652,872	4,140	1,598	Pereira
San Andrés y Providencia	SA	SAP	CO25	i	35,818	44	17	San Andrés
Santander	ST	SAN	CO26	d	1,511,392	30,537	11,790	Bucaramanga
Sucre	SU	SUC	CO27	d	561,649	10,917	4,215	Sincelejo
Tolima	TO	TOL	CO28	d	1,142,220	23,562	9,097	Ibagué
Valle del Cauca	VC	VAC	CO29	d	3,027,247	22,140	8,548	Cali
Vaupés	VP	VAU	CO30	c	26,178	65,268	25,200	Mitú
Vichada	VD	CID	CO31	c	18,702	100,242	38,704	Puerto Carreño
					30,053,575	1,141,748	440,831	

Status: These divisions are departamentos, except for Distrito Especial (see also the typ column).

Abv: Two-letter code for international compatibility (defined by the author).

ISO: Codes from ISO 3166-2.

FIPS: Codes from FIPS PUB 10-4.

Typ: Until 1991, the divisions of Colombia were of four types. They were departamentos (d: departments), comisarías (c: commissaries), intendencias (i: intendancies), and a distrito especial (e: special district).

Population: 1985 census (officially adjusted).

Area-km: Square kilometers.

Area-mi: Square miles.

Further subdivisions: Subdivisions of the departments are called municipalities.

Territorial extent: San Andrés y Providencia consists of a few small islands in the Caribbean Sea: Isla de San Andrés and its neighbors, Cayos del E.S.E. and Cayos de Albuquerque; Isla de Providencia; and some islets used jointly by the United

States and Colombia, such as Roncador Cay, Quita Sueño Bank, and Serrana Bank. Colombia also owns Malpelo Island, in the Pacific Ocean west of Valle del Cauca.

Origins of names:

Amazonas: From the Amazon River

Arauca: From the Arauca River

Atlántico: On the Caribbean Sea, considered part of the Atlantic Ocean

Bolívar: For Simón Bolívar (1783–1830), Colombia's liberator from Spain

Caquetá: From the Caquetá River

Casanare: From the Casanare River

Cauca: From the Cauca River

Distrito Especial: = Special District

Guainía: From the Guainía River

Guaviare: From the Guaviare River

Huila: From Nevado de Huila, a mountain

Magdalena: From the Magdalena River

Meta: From the Meta River

Nariño: For Antonio Nariño (1765–1823), revolutionary leader

Norte de Santander: Formed from the north part of Santander

Putumayo: From the Putumayo River

Santander: For Francisco de Paula Santander (1792–1840), Simón Bolívar's co-revolutionist and vice-president.

Sucre: For Antonio José de Sucre (1795–1830), Simón Bolívar's co-revolutionist.

Tolima: From Nevado de Tolima, a mountain

Valle del Cauca: Spanish for "Cauca Valley," which runs through the department.

Vaupés: From the Vaupés River (called Uaupés in Brazil)

Vichada: From the Vichada River

Change history: In 1900, Colombia had nine departments. Their approximate relation to the present divisions is shown here.

Antioquia: Antioquia, Caldas

Bolívar: Atlántico, Bolívar, Córdoba, Sucre

Boyacá: Arauca, Boyacá, Casanare

Cauca: Cauca, Chocó, Nariño, Putumayo, Quindío, Risaralda, Valle del Cauca, and Territorio de Caquetá (Amazonas, Caquetá, Guainía, Guaviare, Vaupés, and some territory ceded to Brazil in 1907)

Cundinamarca: Cundinamarca, Distrito Especial, and Territorio de San Martin (Meta, Vichada)

Magdalena: Cesar, La Guajira, Magdalena

Panamá: Panamá, now a different country

Santander: Santander, Norte de Santander

Tolima: Huila, Tolima

These are the approximate dates of the changes.

1903-11-03	Panama declared its independence from Colombia.
1907	Colombia ceded a large area in southeastern Cauca department to Brazil.
~1935	Territory transferred from Cauca to Antioquia, giving it a corridor of access to the Caribbean Sea. Atlántico department split from Bolívar; Arauca commissary split from Boyacá; Caldas formed from parts of Antioquia and Cauca; Cauca split into the departments of Cauca, Chocó, Nariño, Valle del Cauca; the commissaries of Caquetá, Putumayo, and Vaupés; and part of Caldas; Huila split from Tolima; La Guajira commissary split from Magdalena; Meta intendancy split from Cundinamarca (approximately the area of San Martin territory); Norte de Santander split from Santander.
~1942	Vichada split from Meta; Amazonas commissary split from Caquetá; also, territory transferred from Caquetá to Putumayo.
~1950	Córdoba split from Bolívar.
~1955	Arauca, Caquetá, and La Guajira changed from commissaries to intendancies.
~1964	Guainía split from Vaupés.
~1966	La Guajira changed from intendancy to department.
~1971	Cesar split from Magdalena; Quindío and Risaralda split from Caldas; Sucre split from Bolívar.
~1974?	Distrito Especial split from Cundinamarca. (Distrito Especial is a separate division for some purposes, and an integral part of Cundinamarca for others. Sources started listing it as a separate entity around 1970.)
~1974	Putumayo changed from commissary to intendancy.
~1978	Casanare split from Boyacá.

1982   Guaviare split from Vaupés.
1991-07-05   All commissaries and intendancies changed to departments.

Other names of subdivisions:

Cesar: El Cesar (variant)
Distrito Especial: Distrito Capital de Santa Fe de Bogotá (variant)
La Guajira: Goagira, Guajira, La Goajira (variant)
Magdalena: La Magdalena (variant)

Norte de Santander: Santander del Norte (variant)
San Andrés y Providencia: San Andres; San Andres, Providencia y Santa Catalina (variant)
Valle del Cauca: Valle (variant)

Population history:

division	1912	1938	1951	1964	1973	1985
Amazonas	——	6,414	7,619	12,962	16,500	39,937
Antioquia	740,937	1,188,587	1,570,197	2,477,299	2,826,900	4,067,664
Arauca	——	11,156	13,221	24,148	32,000	89,972
Atlántico	114,887	268,409	428,429	717,406	949,850	1,478,213
Bolívar	425,975	765,194	665,195	1,006,347	758,400	1,288,985
Boyacá	586,499	737,368	801,436	1,058,152	1,054,475	1,209,739
Caldas	341,498	769,968	1,068,180	1,455,872	650,325	883,024
Caquetá	99,576	20,914	46,588	103,718	158,000	264,507
Casanare	——	——	——	——	——	147,472
Cauca	211,756	356,040	443,439	607,197	527,675	857,731
Cesar	——	——	——	——	321,850	699,428
Chocó	60,653	111,216	131,101	181,863	169,125	313,567
Córdoba	——	——	326,263	585,714	633,675	1,013,427
Cundinamarca	715,610	1,174,607	1,624,044	2,817,436	3,888,236	1,512,928
Distrito Especial	——	——	——	——	——	4,227,706
Guainía	——	——	——	3,602	48,000	12,345
Guaviare	——	——	——	——	——	47,073
Huila	158,191	216,676	293,692	416,289	465,800	693,713
La Guajira	53,018	53,409	52,346	147,140	127,775	299,995
Magdalena	140,106	342,322	457,393	789,410	510,475	890,934
Meta	29,299	51,674	67,492	165,530	238,100	474,046
Nariño	293,918	465,868	569,790	705,611	747,125	1,085,173
Norte de Santander	204,381	346,181	387,450	534,486	675,850	913,491
Putumayo	——	15,688	——	56,284	76,000	174,219
Quindío	——	——	——	——	300,075	392,208
Risaralda	——	——	——	——	431,925	652,872
San Andrés y Providencia	——	6,528	5,675	16,731	22,719	35,818
Santander	400,084	615,710	747,706	1,001,213	1,114,425	1,511,392
Sucre	——	——	——	——	355,925	561,649
Tolima	282,426	547,796	712,490	841,424	866,950	1,142,220
Valle del Cauca	217,147	613,230	1,106,927	1,733,053	2,129,350	3,027,247
Vaupés	——	7,767	9,169	13,403	17,700	26,178
Vichada	——	9,094	12,330	10,130	9,200	18,702
	5,075,961	8,701,816	11,548,172	17,482,420	20,124,405	30,053,575

COMOROS

ISO = KM/FIPS = CN   Language = Comoran   Time zone = +3   Capital = Moroni

These islands, along with Mayotte, were a French protectorate at the start of the 20th century. On 1912-07-25, they became French colonies. They gained full independence on 1975-07-06, leaving Mayotte behind as a French possession (by a local vote).

Other names of country: Comorerna (Swedish); Comorerne (Danish); Comoras (Spanish); Comore (Italian); Comores (French, Portuguese); Federal Islamic Republic of the Comoros (formal–English); Jumhuriyat al-Qumur al-Itthadiyah al-Islamiyah (formal); Kamaran (Dutch); Komorane (Norwegian nynorsk); Komoren (German); Komorene (Norwegian bokmål); Kómoreyjar (Icelandic); Komorit (Finnish); República Federal Islámica de las Comoras (formal–Spanish); République Fédérale Islamique des Comores (formal–French).

Origin of name: Arabic *qamar*: moon.

division	abv	ISO	FIPS	population	area-km	area-mi	capital
Anjouan	AN	A	CN01	137,621	424	164	Mutsamudu
Grande Comore	GC	G	CN02	192,177	1,148	443	Moroni
Mohéli	MO	M	CN03	17,194	290	112	Fomboni
				346,992	1,862	719	

Status: These divisions are governorates.

Abv: Two-letter code for international compatibility (defined by the author).

ISO: Codes from ISO 3166-2.

FIPS: Codes from FIPS PUB 10-4.

Population: 1980 census.

Area-km: Square kilometers.

Area-mi: Square miles.

Territorial extent: Each governorate includes one major island of the Comoro Archipelago and the islets in its immediate vicinity.

Other names of subdivisions:

Anjouan: Johanna (obsolete); Ndzouani (Arabic); Nzwani (Comoran)

Grande Comore: Ngazidja (Arabic); Njazídja (Comoran)

Mohéli: Moili (Arabic); Mwali (Comoran)

CONGO, DEMOCRATIC REPUBLIC OF THE

ISO = CD/FIPS = CG   Languages = French, Lingala, Kiswahili, Tshiluba, Kikongo   Time zones (see table)   Capital = Kinshasa

At the start of the 20th century, the État Indépendant du Congo (Congo Free State) was the personal domain of King Léopold II of Belgium. In 1908, Leopold ceded it to Belgium. As a Belgian colony, it was called Belgian Congo. It became independent on 1960-06-30 and took the name République du Congo. A month and a half later, the French colony on the other side of the Congo River, Moyen Congo, gained its independence and likewise took the name République du Congo. Most people distinguished the two countries by calling them Congo-Léopoldville and Congo-Brazzaville, according to their capitals. In 1964, the former Belgian colony changed its official name to République democratique du Congo. On 1971-10-27 it was renamed to Zaire (or Zaïre). On 1997-05-19, it changed back to République democratique du Congo.

Other names of country: Belgian Congo (obsolete); Belgisch Congo (obsolete–Dutch); Congo Belga (obsolete–Spanish); Congo Belge, Zaïre (obsolete–French); Congo Free State (obsolete); Congo-Kinshasa (obsolete-informal); Congo-Léopoldville (obsolete-informal); Democratic Republic of the Congo (English); Kongo Free State (obsolete); Demokratische Republik Kongo (German); Repubblica Democratica del Congo (Italian); República Democrática del Congo (Spanish); République démocratique du Congo (French); Zaire (obsolete).

Origin of name: from the Congo river, which came from the ethnic name Kikongo.

district	abv	ISO	FIPS	tz	population	area-km	area-mi	zones	capital	former name
Bandundu	BN	BN	CG01	+1	5,201,000	295,658	114,154	23	Bandundu	Banningville
Bas-Congo	BC	BZ	CG08	+1	2,835,000	53,920	20,819	16	Matadi	
Équateur	EQ	EQ	CG02	+1	4,820,000	403,292	155,712	28	Mbandaka	Coquilhatville
Haut-Congo	HC	HZ	CG09	+2	5,566,000	503,239	194,302	30	Kisangani	Stanleyville
Kasai-Occidental	KC	KW	CG03	+2	3,337,000	154,742	59,746	15	Kananga	Luluabourg
Kasai-Oriental	KR	KE	CG04	+2	3,830,000	170,302	65,754	21	Mbuji-Mayi	Bakwanga ▶

district	abv	ISO	FIPS	tz	population	area-km	area-mi	zones	capital	former name
Katanga	KT	SH	CG05	+2	4,125,000	496,877	191,845	35	Lubumbashi	Élisabethville
Kinshasa	KN	KN	CG06	+1	4,787,000	9,965	3,848	24	Kinshasa	Léopoldville
Maniema	MN	—	——	+2	1,246,787	132,250	51,062	7	Kindu	
Nord-Kivu	NK	—	——	+2	3,564,434	59,483	22,967	6	Goma	
Sud-Kivu	SK	—	——	+2	2,837,779	65,070	25,124	11	Bukavu	Costermansville
					42,150,000	2,344,798	905,333	216		

Status: These divisions are régions, except for Kinshasa, which is a ville neutre (neutral city).

Abv: Two-letter code for international compatibility (defined by the author).

ISO: Codes from ISO 3166-2. Two codes added for completeness.

FIPS: Codes from FIPS PUB 10-4.

Tz: Time zone (offset from GMT).

Population: 1998 estimate.

Area-km: Square kilometers.

Area-mi: Square miles.

Zones: Number of administrative zones in each region.

Further subdivisions: The regions are divided into 41 sous-régions (sub-regions), which are further divided into 216 zones administratives (administrative zones), which are in turn subdivided into collectivités.

Territorial extent: Sud-Kivu includes Île Idjwi, an island in Lake Kivu.

Origins of names:

Bas-Congo: French for lower Congo. Region lies along the lower reaches of the Congo River.

Haut-Congo: French for upper Congo

Kinshasa: named after a nearby pre-colonial village, Kikongo for salt market

Kivu: for Lake Kivu, whose name is Rwandese for large body of water

Shaba: Swahili for copper, which is mined there

Zaïre: From a native word *n'zai*: river, a traditional name for the Congo River. It was the river's official name, and the country's, from 1971 to 1997.

Change history:

1929   National capital moved from Boma to Léopoldville.

1935   Belgian Congo reorganized from four provinces (Congo Kasai, Équateur, Katanga, and Orientale) into six provinces as shown in the following table:

province	population	area-km	post–1947	post–1997
Coquilhatville	1,557,972	403,290	Équateur	Équateur
Costermansville	1,302,432	230,209	Kivu	Maniema, Nord-Kivu, Sud-Kivu
Élisabethville	1,023,060	496,962	Katanga	Katanga
Léopoldville	1,997,796	362,953	Léopoldville	Bas-Zaïre, Bandundu, Kinshasa
Lusambo	1,953,931	321,534	Kasai	Kasai-Occidental, Kasai-Oriental
Stanleyville	2,382,217	528,925	Orientale	Haut-Zaïre
	10,217,408	2,343,873		

Names of capitals are the same as the names of provinces shown in the first column. Populations are from the 1938 census. In 1947, the province names were changed to the ones shown in the fourth column. They correspond closely in extent to the modern regions shown in the fifth column.

~1957   Capital of Kasai province moved from Lusambo to Luluabourg.

1960   After independence there were changes of all sorts. New provinces were created repeatedly. By 1963-06-25, when Katanga-Oriental was formed, the list was as shown here.

province	capital	modern equivalent
Congo-Central	Matadi	Bas-Congo
Cuvette-Centrale	Coquilhatville	Équateur
Haut-Congo	Stanleyville	Haut-Congo
Katanga-Oriental	Élisabethville	Katanga ▶

province	capital	modern equivalent
Kibali-Ituri	Bunia	Haut-Congo
Kivu-Central	Bukavu	Sud-Kivu
Kwango	Kenge	Bandundu
Kwilu	Kikwit	Bandundu
Léopoldville	Léopoldville	Kinshasa
Lomami	Kabinda	Kasai-Oriental
Lualaba	Kolwezi	Katanga
Luluabourg	Luluabourg	Kasai-Occidental
Mai-Ndombe	Inongo	Bandundu
Maniema	Kindu-Port Empain	Maniema
Moyen-Congo	Lisala	Équateur
Nord-Katanga	Albertville	Katanga
Nord-Kivu	Luofu	Nord-Kivu
Sankuru	Lodja	Kasai-Occidental, Kasai-Oriental
Sud-Kasai	Bakwanga	Kasai-Oriental
Ubangi	Gemena	Équateur
Uele	Paulis	Haut-Congo
Unité-Kasaïenne	Tshikapa	Kasai-Occidental

1966-07-01	Country reorganized into Bandundu, Bas-Zaïre, Équateur, Haut-Zaïre, Kasai-Occidental, Kasai-Oriental, Kinshasa, Kivu, and Shaba regions. National capital renamed from Léopoldville to Kinshasa; Stanleyville renamed to Kisangani; Élisabethville renamed to Lubumbashi; Coquilhatville renamed to Mbandaka; Banningville renamed to Bandundu; Bakwanga renamed to Mbuji-Mayi; Luluabourg renamed to Kananga; Costermansville renamed to Bukavu.
1972	Katanga region renamed to Shaba.
-1975	Kongo-Central region renamed to Bas-Zaïre.
~1980	An area of 7,949 sq. km. transferred from Bas-Zaïre region to Kinshasa.
~1996	Kivu region (ISO code KV, FIPS code CG07, capital Bukavu) split into Maniema, Nord-Kivu, and Sud-Kivu.
1997-05-19	Name of Bas-Zaïre changed to Bas-Congo, Haut-Zaïre to Haut-Congo, and Shaba to Katanga.

Other names of subdivisions:

Bas-Congo: Bas-Zaïre, Kongo-Central (obsolete); Lower Zaire (English)
Équateur: Equator, Equatorial (English)
Haut-Congo: Haut-Zaïre, Orientale (obsolete); Upper Zaire (English)
Kasai: Kassai (variant)

Kasai-Occidental: Kasai West, West Kasai (English)
Kasai-Oriental: East Kasai, Kasai East (English)
Kinshasa: Léopoldville (obsolete)
Kivu: Kivou (variant)
Katanga: Shaba (obsolete)

CONGO, REPUBLIC OF

ISO = CG/FIPS = CF   Languages = French, Lingala, Monokutuba   Time zone = +1   Capital = Brazzaville

Congo was one of the territories of French Equatorial Africa until 1960, under the name Moyen Congo. (For further details, see Central African Republic.) It gained independence on 1960-08-15. In 1970-01, the name was changed to People's Republic of Congo, but this change was later reversed. For further information on name changes, see Congo, Democratic Republic of the.

Other names of country: Congo-Brazzaville (obsolete); Kongo (Dutch, Finnish, German, Norwegian, Swedish); Kongó (Icelandic); Middle Congo (obsolete); Moyen Congo (obsolete–French); Republic of Congo (formal–English); République du Congo (formal).

Origin of name: from the Congo river, which came from the ethnic name Kikongo

division	abv	ISO	FIPS	population	area-km	area-mi	capital
Bouenza	BO	11	CF01	205,986	12,266	4,736	Madingou
Brazzaville	BR	BZV	CF12	760,300	100	39	Brazzaville
Cuvette	CU	8	CF03	144,427	74,850	28,900	Owando
Kouilou	KO	5	CF04	470,930	13,694	5,287	Pointe-Noire
Lékoumou	LE	2	CF05	71,248	20,950	8,089	Sibiti
Likouala	LI	7	CF06	61,358	66,044	25,500	Impfondo
Niari	NI	9	CF07	197,700	25,940	10,015	Loubomo
Plateaux	PL	14	CF08	114,629	38,400	14,826	Djambala
Pool	PO	12	CF11	188,285	33,955	13,110	Kinkala
Sangha	SA	13	CF10	49,438	55,800	21,545	Ouesso
				2,264,301	341,999	132,047	

Status: These divisions are régions, except for Brazzaville. Brazzaville is described variously as a commune, capital district, or federal district.

Abv: Two-letter code for international compatibility (defined by the author).

ISO: Codes from ISO 3166-2. (BZV is the IATA airport code for Brazzaville.)

FIPS: Codes from FIPS PUB 10-4.

Population: 1991 census.

Area-km: Square kilometers.

Area-mi: Square miles.

Further subdivisions: The regions are subdivided into sub-prefectures, administrative control posts, and communes. The sub-prefectures are further subdivided into cantons and communes.

Origins of names:

Brazzaville: Named for Count Pietro Paolo Savorgnan di Brazza (1852–1905), the city's founder

Cuvette: French *cuvette*: basin (in either the hydrological or utensil sense)

Plateaux: French for plateaus

Pool: For Stanley Pool, an enlargement in the Congo River

Change history:

1977	Capital of Cuvette renamed from Fort-Rousset to Owando.
~1980	Capital of Niari renamed from Dolisie to Loubomo.
~1980	Brazzaville commune split from Pool (former FIPS code: CF09).
1996	ISO 3166-2 implies that a new region, Cuvette-Ouest, has been split from Cuvette. The ISO code for this region is "15." No further information on this region is yet available.

COOK ISLANDS

ISO = CK/FIPS = CW   Language = English   Time zone = -10   Capital = Avarua

On 1901-06-11, the Cook Islands changed from a British protectorate to an integral part of New Zealand. On 1965-08-04, they became autonomous, but New Zealand retains some responsibility for their governance.

Other names of country: Cookeilanden (Dutch); Cookinseln (German); Cooks øyer (Norwegian); Îles Cook (French); Ilhas Cook (Portuguese); Islas Cook (Spanish); Isole Cook (Italian).

Origin of name: Discovered by Capt. James Cook (1728–1779) in 1773.

division	abv	population	area-km	area-mi	capital
Cook Islands	CK	17,463	293	113	Avarua

Status: This division is the whole of the country, treated as a division for compatibility.
Abv: Two-letter code for international compatibility (defined by the author).
Population: 1986 census.
Area-km: Square kilometers.
Area-mi: Square miles.
   Territorial extent: Cook Islands includes the Pacific islands in the rectangle defined by roughly 7° to 23° latitude south, and 156° to 167° longitude west. These islands can be divided into a northern group and a southern group. The northern group includes Manihiki, Nassau, Penrhyn, Pukapuka, Rakahanga, and Suwarrow Islands. The southern group includes a number of islands in a triangle with Aitutaki, Mauke, and Rarotonga Islands at the vertices, and some isolated islands like Mangaia Island and Palmerston Atoll. Avarua, the capital, is located on Rarotonga Island.

COSTA RICA

ISO = CR/FIPS = CS   Language = Spanish   Time zone = -6   Capital = San José

Costa Rica has been an independent country for the whole period of this study. There have been minor territorial transfers, but the names and capitals of its provinces have lasted the whole century.
   Other names of country: Costa-Rica (Italian); Kostaríka (Icelandic); Republic of Costa Rica (formal–English); República de Costa Rica (formal).
   Origin of name: Spanish for rich coast. Columbus thought there was gold to be found there.

division	abv	ISO	FIPS	population	area-km	area-mi	capital
Alajuela	AL	A	CS01	539,375	9,754	3,766	Alajuela
Cartago	CA	C	CS02	340,298	3,125	1,206	Cartago
Guanacaste	GU	G	CS03	242,681	10,141	3,915	Liberia
Heredia	HE	H	CS04	243,679	2,657	1,026	Heredia
Limón	LI	L	CS06	219,485	9,189	3,548	Puerto Limón
Puntarenas	PU	P	CS07	338,384	11,266	4,350	Puntarenas
San José	SJ	SJ	CS08	1,105,844	4,960	1,915	San José
				3,029,746	51,090	19,726	

Status: These divisions are provincias (provinces).
Abv: Two-letter code for international compatibility (defined by the author).
ISO: Codes from ISO 3166-2.
FIPS: Codes from FIPS PUB 10-4.
Population: 1991 estimate.
Area-km: Square kilometers.
Area-mi: Square miles.
Further subdivisions: The provinces are subdivided into cantons, which in turn are subdivided into districts.
Territorial extent: Costa Rica owns Isla del Coco in the Pacific Ocean.
   Puntarenas includes the southeastern part of Península de Nicoya; Isla Chira and other islands in the Gulf of Nicoya; and Isla del Caño.
Change history:

   ~1990   Name of the capital of Limón changed from Limón to Puerto Limón.

CÔTE D'IVOIRE

ISO = CI/FIPS = IV   Language = French   Time zone = +0   Capital = Abidjan

Ivory Coast, as it was called by English speakers until recently, was a French colony in 1900. In 1904, it became a territory, as part of French West Africa. On 1932-09-06, Upper Volta (Haute Volta) was partitioned among Ivory Coast, French Sudan, and Niger, but this change was nullified on 1947-09-04. Ivory Coast became independent on 1960-08-07.

Other names of country: Costa d'Avorio (Italian); Costa de Marfil (Spanish); Costa do Marfim (Portuguese); Elfenbeinküste (German); Elfenbeinskysten (Norwegian nynorsk); Elfenbenskusten (Swedish); Elfenbenskysten (Danish, Norwegian bokmål); Fílabeinsströndin (Icelandic); Ivoorkust (Dutch); Ivory Coast (obsolete), Norsunluurannikko (Finnish); Republic of the Ivory Coast (formal–English); République de la Côte d'Ivoire (formal).

Origin of name: French for Ivory Coast. Trade in ivory was conducted there.

division	abv	ISO	FIPS	region	division	abv	ISO	FIPS	region
Abengourou	AG	ABE	IV59	2	Guiglo	GU	GUI	IV46	8
Abidjan	AJ	ABI	IV35	9	Issia	IS	ISS	IV28	4
Aboisso	AS	ABO	IV04	9	Katiola	KA	KAT	IV20	3
Adzopé	AZ	ADZ	IV05	9	Korhogo	KO	KOR	IV21	5
Agboville	AV	AGB	IV06	9	Lakota	LA	LAK	IV29	9
Agnibilékrou	AK	AGN	IV60	2	Man	MA	MAN	IV47	8
Bangolo	BA	BAN	IV36	8	Mankono	MK	MNK	IV30	7
Béoumi	BE	BEO	IV37	3	Mbahiakro	MB	MBA	IV48	3
Biankouma	BI	BIA	IV07	8	Odienné	OD	ODI	IV23	7
Bondoukou	BD	BON	IV38	6	Oumé	OU	OUM	IV31	4
Bongouanou	BG	BAN	IV27	1	Sakassou	SK	SAK	IV49	3
Bouaflé	BF	BOF	IV39	2	San-Pédro	SP	SAP	IV50	10
Bouaké	BK	BOK	IV40	3	Sassandra	SS	SAS	IV51	10
Bouna	BO	BON	IV11	6	Séguéla	SG	SEG	IV25	7
Boundiali	BL	BOD	IV12	5	Sinfra	SN	SIN	IV52	4
Dabakala	DB	DAB	IV03	3	Soubré	SO	SOU	IV32	10
Daloa	DL	DAL	iV41	4	Tabou	TA	TAB	IV53	10
Danané	DN	DAN	IV14	8	Tanda	TD	TAN	IV54	6
Daoukro	DA	DAO	IV42	1	Tiassalé	TI	TIA	IV55	9
Dimbokro	DM	DIM	IV43	1	Tingréla	TG	TEN	IV33	5
Divo	DV	DIV	IV16	9	Touba	TO	TOB	IV26	7
Duékoué	DK	DUE	IV44	8	Toumodi	TM	TOM	IV56	1
Ferkessédougou	FE	FER	IV17	5	Vavoua	VA	VAV	IV57	4
Gagnoa	GA	GAG	IV18	4	Yamoussoukro	YA	YAM	IV58	1
Grand-Lahou	GL	GRL	IV45	9	Zuénoula	ZU	ZUE	IV34	4

Status: These divisions are départements (departments).

Capitals: The capitals have the same name as their departments.

Abv: Two-letter code for international compatibility (defined by the author).

ISO: Codes from ISO 3166-2.

FIPS: Codes from FIPS PUB 10-4.

Population: Apparently only one census has been taken since independence. It was taken in 1975, when the division into departments was different from the present.

Region: Keyed to the following list of regions, also from ISO 3166-2. There is probably a mistake in ISO 3166-2, because Bouaflé is geographically remote from Centre-Est.

1	Centre		6	Nord-Est
2	Centre-Est		7	Nord-Ouest
3	Centre-Nord		8	Ouest
4	Centre-Ouest		9	Sud
5	Nord		10	Sud-Ouest

Further subdivisions: The departments are subdivided into sous-préfectures (sub-prefectures). The number of sub-prefectures was 108 in 1967, 127 in 1972, 162 in 1977, and 183 in 1993. When departments are split, the division almost always preserves sub-prefectures intact.

Origins of names:

Abidjan: Supposedly, when the first colonists asked native women the name of the place, the women misunderstood and replied "T'chan m'bi djan": "I've just been cutting leaves."

Bouaké: Named for Gbouéké, native king, founder of the city. The name elements Centre, Est, Nord, Ouest, and Sud can be translated with Center, East, North, West, and South respectively.

Change history: At independence, Côte d'Ivoire was subdivided into six régions. In ~1970, a new subdivision into 24 departments was adopted. This list shows the regions with their capitals, and the departments that were formed from each region.

region	capital	departments
Centre	Bouaké	Bouaflé, Bouaké, Dimbokro, Katiola
Centre Ouest	Daloa	Daloa, Gagnoa, part of Sassandra
Est	Abengourou	Abengourou, Bondoukou
Nord	Korhogo	Boundiali, Ferkessédougou, Korhogo, Odienné, Séguéla, Touba
Ouest	Man	Biankouma, Danané, Guiglo, Man
Sud	Abidjan	Abidjan, Aboisso, Adzopé, Agboville, Divo, part of Sassandra

In ~1974, Bouna department was split from Bondoukou, and Dabakala department was split from Katiola.

In ~1980, the number of departments was increased to 34. Bongouanou was split from Dimbokro; Issia was split from Daloa; Lakota was split from Divo; Mankono was split from Séguéla; Oumé was split from Gagnoa; Soubré was split from Sassandra; Tingréla was split from Boundiali; and Zuénoula was split from Bouaflé.

1986-01-01: Côte d'Ivoire declared that the only correct form of its name in any language was the French one. This wish has been honored, for the most part, by those who are aware of it.

In ~1988, 15 more departments were created by fission. The FIPS codes of departments that lost part of their territory were changed to reflect that fact. (The former FIPS codes of those departments are shown in parentheses.) Grand-Lahou and Tiassalé were split from Abidjan (IV02); Tanda was split from Bondoukou (IV08); Sinfra was split from Bouaflé (IV09); Béoumi, Mbahiakro, Sakassou, Toumodi, and Yamoussoukro were split from Bouaké (IV10); Vavoua was split from Daloa (IV13); Daoukro was split from Dimbokro (IV15); Duékoué was split from Guiglo (IV19); Bangolo was split from Man (IV22); and San-Pédro and Tabou were split from Sassandra (IV24).

According to ISO 3166-2, in ~1995, Agnibilékrou was split from Abengourou. There are plans to move the national capital to Yamoussoukro.

Other names of subdivisions:

Sakassou: Sakasso (variant)

Tingréla: Tengréla (variant)

CROATIA

ISO = HR/FIPS = HR   Language = Serbo-Croatian   Time zone = +1 [d]   Capital = Zagreb

The area constituting modern Croatia was part of the Austro-Hungarian Empire in 1900. It was distributed among the Austrian provinces of Coastland and Dalmatia, and the Hungarian province of Croatia and Slavonia. In the aftermath of World War I, it was allocated to the Kingdom of Serbs, Croats, and Slovenes, which soon became Yugoslavia. The peace treaties didn't settle the border between Italy and Yugoslavia, which was eventually negotiated in 1924. Italy received all of the Istrian peninsula (including Rijeka, which had been an independent city from 1918 to 1924), an enclave around Zadar (Zara), and two groups of Adriatic islands: in the north, Cres (Cherso), Lošinj (Lussin), and some smaller islands; in the south, Lastovo (Lagosta), Palagruža (Pelagosa), and others. Yugoslavia was occupied by the axis powers in World War II. When the war ended, Istria, Zadar, and Lastovo were restored to Yugoslavia. Trieste became an independent city in 1947. Its territory was divided into a northern A Zone, under British-American military administration, and a B Zone run by Yugoslavia. In 1954, the A Zone was annexed to Italy, and the B Zone to Yugoslavia; most of it went to Croatia. Croatia was one of the six constituent republics of Yugoslavia from 1946 until the federation broke up. Its claim to independence was recognized by the European Union on 1992-01-15.

Other names of country: Croacia (Spanish); Croácia (Portuguese); Croatie (French); Croazia (Italian); Hrvatska (Serbo-Croatian); Kroatia (Finnish, Norwegian); Króatía (Icelandic); Kroatië (Dutch); Kroatien (Danish, German, Swedish); Republic of Croatia (formal–English); Republika Hrvatska (formal).

Origin of name: perhaps from Slavonic *khrebet*: mountain range.

division	abv	ISO	division	abv	ISO
Bjelovar–Bilagora	BB	07	Primorje–Gorski Kotar	PG	08
Dubrovnik–Neretva	DN	19	Sisak–Moslavina	SM	03
Grad Zagreb	GZ	21	Slavonski Brod–Posavina	SP	12
Istra	IS	18	Split–Dalmacia	SD	17
Karlovac	KA	04	Šibenik	SK	15
Koprivnica–Križevci	KK	06	Varaždin	VA	05
Krapina–Zagorje	KZ	02	Virovitica–Podravina	VP	10
Lika–Senj	LS	09	Vukovar–Srijem	VS	16
Medimurje	ME	20	Zadar–Knin	ZK	13
Osijek–Baranja	OB	14	Zagreb	ZG	01
Požega–Slavonija	PS	11			

Status: These divisions are kotari (counties).

Abv: Two-letter code for international compatibility (defined by the author).

ISO: Codes from ISO 3166-2.

Further subdivisions: The counties are further subdivided into 116 opčine (communes).

Territorial extent: Croatia owns almost all of the islands along the Adriatic coast of the Balkan Peninsula. Near the center of the gulf, the Palagruža group belongs to Croatia, while Pianosa belongs to Italy. Bosnia has one outlet to the sea, along a 10-km. stretch of coast near Neum, between Dubrovnik and Split. This divides the Croatian coastline into two separate sections, but when Croatian islands and territorial waters are taken into account, the two sections are connected.

Meanings of names:

Dalmacia: originally a Roman province, from ethnic name Dalmatae

Dubrovnik: from Serbo-Croat *dubrova*: oak grove

Grad Zagreb: = City of Zagreb

Istra: apparently named in the mistaken belief that a branch of the Danube (Ister in Latin) lay nearby

Rijeka: Serbo-Croat for river (likewise, fiume is Italian for river)

Split: from Ancient Greek *aspalathos*: a thorny bush

Change history: In the 1950s, Croatia consisted of 27 counties: Bjelovar, Čakovec, Daruvar, Dubrovnik, Gospić, Karlovac, Koprivnica, Krapina, Križevci, Kutina, Makarska, Našice, Nova Gradiška, Ogulin, Osijek, Pula, Rijeka, Sisak, Slavonski Brod, Slavonska Požega, Split, Šibenik, Varaždin, Vinkovci, Virovitica, Zadar, and Zagreb.

Other names of subdivisions:

Dalmacia: Dalmatia (variant); Dalmatie (French); Dalmazia (Italian)

Dubrovnik: Ragusa (Italian)

Istra: Istria (Italian); Istrie (French)

Osijek: Esseg, Eszek (Hungarian)

Pula: Pola (Italian)

Rijeka: Fiume (Italian)

Šibenik: Sebenico (Italian)

Sisak: Saiszek (Hungarian)

Split: Spalato (Italian)

Varaždin: Varasd (Hungarian)

Virovitica: Veröcze (Hungarian)

Zadar: Zara (Italian)

Zagreb: Agram (German); Zagabria (Italian)

CUBA

ISO = CU/FIPS = CU   Language = Spanish   Time zone = -5 [d]   Capital = Havana

Cuba was liberated from Spanish rule in the Spanish-American War, just before the beginning of the 20th century. The United States dominated the Cuban administration for about a decade, but Cuba has been considered an independent country throughout the century.

Other names of country: Kuba (German); Kúba (Icelandic); Kuuba (Finnish); Republic of Cuba (formal–English); República de Cuba (formal).

Origin of name: A native called the island Colba when questioned by Columbus, possibly misunderstanding him.

division	abv	ISO	FIPS	population	area-km	area-mi	mun	capital
Camagüey	CM	09	CU05	732,056	14,134	5,457	13	Camagüey
Ciego de Ávila	CA	08	CU07	358,059	5,962	2,302	10	Ciego de Ávila
Cienfuegos	CF	06	CU08	358,589	4,149	1,602	9	Cienfuegos
Ciudad de la Habana	CH	03	CU02	2,077,938	740	286	15	Havana
Granma	GR	12	CU09	781,331	8,452	3,263	13	Manzanillo
Guantánamo	GU	14	CU10	491,422	6,366	2,458	10	Guantánamo
Holguín	HO	11	CU12	982,722	9,105	3,516	14	Holguín
Isla de la Juventud	IJ	99	CU04	71,097	2,199	849	1	Nueva Gerona
La Habana	LH	02	CU11	636,889	5,669	2,189	19	Havana
Las Tunas	LT	10	CU13	485,136	6,373	2,461	8	Victoria de Las Tunas
Matanzas	MA	04	CU03	602,996	11,669	4,505	14	Matanzas
Pinar del Río	PR	01	CU01	684,725	10,860	4,193	13	Pinar del Río
Sancti Spíritus	SS	07	CU14	424,243	6,737	2,601	8	Sancti Spíritus
Santiago de Cuba	SC	13	CU15	980,002	6,343	2,449	9	Santiago de Cuba
Villa Clara	VC	05	CU16	801,456	8,069	3,115	13	Santa Clara
				10,468,661	106,827	41,246	169	

Status: These divisions are provincias (provinces), except for Isla de la Juventud, which is a municipio especial (special municipality).

Abv: Two-letter code for international compatibility (defined by the author).

ISO: Codes from ISO 3166-2.

FIPS: Codes from FIPS PUB 10-4.

Population: 1989 estimate.

Area-km: Square kilometers.

Area-mi: Square miles.

Mun: Number of municipios in each province.

Further subdivisions: The provinces are subdivided into municipios (municipalities). Their number has stayed quite constant since 1976. Just before 1976, there were six provinces, divided into 51 regiones (regions), which in turn were divided into 326 municipalities. The provinces had been quite stable, but the lower-level subdivisions had undergone extensive changes over the years. In 1906, the six provinces had been subdivided into 83 términos municipales (municipal boundaries).

Territorial extent: Cuba is separated from the Bahamas by the Nicholas Channel and Old Bahama Channel; from Haiti by the Windward Channel; from Jamaica by the Cayman Trench; from the Cayman Islands and Mexico by the Yucatan Channel and Yucatan Basin. Some of the smaller, uninhabited islands and cays belonging to Cuba are not part of any province.

Ciego de Ávila includes, along its south shore, islands in the Archipiélago de los Jardines de la Reina from its western end to Cayo Caballones, and the Cayos de Ana María. Along its north shore, it contains Cayo Coco and a number of small islands, mostly west of Cayo Coco and east of Cayo Santa María.

Camagüey includes, along its south shore, islands in the Archipiélago de los Jardines de la Reina from Cayo Anclitos to its eastern end, and Cayo Media Luna. Along its north shore, it includes islands in the Archipiélago de Camagüey as far west as Cayo Romano.

Guantánamo surrounds an enclave leased to the United States, containing the Guantánamo Bay Naval Station.

Isla de la Juventud includes the adjacent small islands in the Archipiélago de los Canarreos as far east as Cayo Largo, and as far north as Islas de Mangles.

La Habana includes most islands in the Ensenada de la Broa and the Golfo de Batabanó as far south as Cayos del Hambre.

Matanzas includes about the western third of the Archipiélago de Sabana.

Pinar del Río includes the Cayos de San Felipe.

Villa Clara includes islands in the Archipiélago de Sabana and the Archipiélago de Sabana Camagüey as far east as Cayo Santa María.

Meanings of names:

Cienfuegos: Spanish *cien fuegos*: a hundred fires, but named after an inhabitant.

Ciudad de La Habana: City of Havana (considered a province, despite its name). In common usage, La Habana is translated when it refers to the city (Havana in Dutch, English, and Portuguese; La Havane in French; L'Avana in Italian; Habana in German), but not when it refers to either of the provinces.

Granma: Named for the yacht which brought Fidel Castro back to Cuba on 1956-12-02.

Isla de la Juventud: Island of youth, because of a cohort of young settlers.

La Habana: named San Cristóbal de la Habana by Diego Velásquez. Habana may be an ethnic name, or related to Middle Dutch *havene*: port.

Matanzas: Killings

Oriente: East

Sancti Spíritus: Latin for Holy Spirit.

Change history:

~1930	Name of Puerto Príncipe province changed to Camagüey.
1940	Name of Santa Clara province changed to Las Villas.
1976-06-05	Cuba reorganized from six provinces to fifteen. The following table shows data for the six provinces of Cuba from 1900 to 1976, along with the new provinces formed from each of them.

province	capital	area-km	divided into
Camagüey	Camagüey	20,623	Camagüey, Ciego de Ávila, parts of Las Tunas and Sancti Spíritus
La Habana	Havana	8,252	Ciudad de La Habana, Isla de Pinos, most of La Habana
Las Villas	Santa Clara	18,837	Cienfuegos, Villa Clara, most of Sancti Spíritus, part of Matanzas
Matanzas	Matanzas	12,033	most of Matanzas
Oriente	Santiago de Cuba	36,601	Granma, Guantánamo, Holguín, Santiago de Cuba, most of Las Tunas
Pinar del Río	Pinar del Río	10,859	Pinar del Rio, part of La Habana
		107,205	

1978-06-28	Name of Isla de Pinos changed to Isla de la Juventud.

Population history:

	1899	1914	1943	1953	1970
Camagüey	88,243	154,567	487,701	618,256	813,204
La Habana	427,614	651,266	1,235,939	1,538,803	2,335,344
Las Villas	356,536	567,277	938,581	1,030,162	1,362,179
Matanzas	202,214	270,483	361,079	395,780	501,273
Oriente	327,715	567,639	1,356,489	1,797,606	2,998,972
Pinar del Río	170,254	257,893	398,794	448,422	542,423
	1,572,576	2,469,125	4,778,583	5,829,029	8,553,395

CYPRUS

ISO = CY/FIPS = CY   Languages = Greek, Turkish, English   Time zone = +2 [d]   Capital = Nicosia

Cyprus, a bone of contention between Greece and Turkey for centuries, was under British administration in 1900. On 1925-05-01 it became a crown colony; on 1960-08-16 it became an independent republic. Turkish forces invaded in 1974, and between 1974-07-20 and 1974-08-16 occupied the northern, Turkish-majority half of the island. Since that time, Cyprus has dwelt in uneasy equilibrium as a divided country. The Turkish Republic of Northern Cyprus is a de facto government which neither seeks nor has received international recognition, except from Turkey.

Other names of country: Chipre (Portuguese, Spanish); Chypre (French); Cipro (Italian); Cypern (Danish, Swedish); Kibris Çumhuriyeti (formal–Turkish); Kípur (Icelandic); Kypriaki Dimokratia (formal–Greek); Kypros (Finnish, Norwegian); Republic of Cyprus (formal–English); Zypern (German).

Origin of name: probably from Sumerian *kabar*: bronze

division	abv	ISO	FIPS	population	area-km	area-mi	postal codes
Famagusta	FA	04	CY01	123,856	1,979	764	5000–5999
Kyrenia	KY	06	CY02	32,586	640	247	9000–9999
Larnaca	LA	03	CY03	60,714	1,129	436	6000–7999
Limassol	LI	02	CY05	124,855	1,396	539	3000–4999
Nicosia	NI	01	CY04	232,702	2,714	1,048	1000–2999
Paphos	PA	05	CY06	57,065	1,393	538	8000–8999
				631,778	9,251	3,572	

Status: These divisions are districts.
Abv: Two-letter code for international compatibility (defined by the author).
ISO: Codes from ISO 3166-2.
FIPS: Codes from FIPS PUB 10-4.
Population: 1973 census.
Area-km: Square kilometers.
Area-mi: Square miles.
Postal codes: Cyprus uses four-digit postal codes. The range of codes assigned to each district is shown. The system is fully implemented in the Greek-controlled area, but only partly in the Turkish-controlled north. Note: postal codes for Cypriot addresses can be identified by prefixing them with "CY-".
Capitals: The capitals have the same name as their districts.
Territorial extent: Two small coastal enclaves of Cyprus are British military bases, sovereign soil of the United Kingdom. One of them is surrounded by Limassol. The other borders on Famagusta and Larnaca. This book treats them as part of the neighboring districts of Cyprus.

The border between the Greek and Turkish sectors of Cyprus is a buffer strip, administered by the United Nations. The Turkish sector contains all of Kyrenia district, most of Famagusta, part of Nicosia, and a tiny bit of Larnaca. The British sovereign areas lie entirely within the Greek sector.

Origins of names:

Famagusta: Latin *Fama Augusta*.

Other names of subdivisions:

Famagusta: Ammochostos (Greek); Famagosta (Italian); Famagouste (French); Gazimagosa, Gazimağusa, Mağusa (Turkish)
Kyrenia: Kerineia, Kirínia (Greek); Girne (Turkish)
Larnaca: Larnaka (Greek); Lárnax (variant)
Limassol: Lemesós (Greek); Limasol (variant)
Nicosia: Levkosía (Greek); Lefkoşa (Turkish); Nicosie (French); Nikosia (German)
Paphos: Baf (Turkish); Pafos (variant)

Population history:

division	1901	1921	1931	1946	1960	1973
Famagusta	48,508	63,755	71,472	94,474	114,309	123,856
Kyrenia	16,808	21,615	22,659	28,174	30,946	32,586
Larnaca	26,073	34,918	42,208	52,189	58,619	60,714
Limassol	39,139	54,332	57,841	75,421	107,262	124,855
Nicosia	71,289	93,765	110,010	145,965	204,283	232,702
Paphos	35,205	42,330	43,769	53,891	58,147	57,065
	237,022	310,715	347,959	450,114	573,566	631,778

CZECH REPUBLIC

ISO = CZ/FIPS = EZ   Language = Czech   Time zone = +1   Capital = Prague

The Czech Republic is the latest manifestation of Bohemia and Moravia. Those two ethnic and political groupings, along with Slovakia and Ruthenia, have been combined in various ways in the past. Under the Austro-Hungarian Empire, Bohemia, Moravia, and Silesia were provinces of Austria, and covered almost exactly the same territory as the modern Czech Republic. (Bohemia is most closely identified with the Czech people. Austrian Silesia is only a fraction of the area known as Silesia, the bulk of which is now in Poland.) At the end of World War I, shortly before the Armistice, the Czechs organized a new government for the three Austrian provinces. The Slovaks, meanwhile, were doing the same thing in northern Hungary. At the initiative of the Slovaks, the two infant states merged to form Czechoslovakia on 1918-11-14. The Treaty of Saint-Germain (1919-09-10) ratified this fait accompli. The western fringe of Bohemia, known as the Sudetenland, still contained a German-speaking majority. Hitler seized on that pretext to annex the Sudetenland by the Munich Pact of 1938-09-30. Germany, Hungary, and Poland nibbled away at the rest of the country in a series of moves not recognized by the Allies. At the end of World War II, Czechoslovakia was reconstituted almost as it had been before 1938. The Soviet Union annexed Transcarpathian Ukraine, also known as Ruthenia, at the eastern end. A small area east of Ostrava was transferred from Poland to Moravia, splitting in two the city known as Cieszyn in Polish, Těšín in Czech, and Teschen in German. Czechoslovakia's constitution of 1948-06-09 made it a "people's democratic republic," whose primary divisions were two socialist republics: the Czech and the Slovak Socialist Republic. This status prevailed until after the fall of communism. Then, on 1993-01-01, the two republics became separate countries. What had been the second-level subdivisions of Czechoslovakia were now first-level subdivisions of the Czech Republic and of Slovakia.

Other names of country: Česká Republika (formal); Česko, Czechia (informal); Repubblica Ceca (Italian); República Checa (Spanish); República Tcheca (Portuguese); République tchèque (French); Tékkland (Icelandic); Tjeckien (Swedish); Tjekkiet (Danish); Tschechische Republik (German); Tsjekkia (Norwegian); Tšekki (Finnish).

Origin of name: unknown.

division	abv	ISO	population	area-km	area-mi	capital	Czech name	PSC
Prague	PR	PRG	1,214,772	496	192	Prague	Praha	10xxx-24xxx
Central Bohemia	ST	CST	1,118,232	10,994	4,245	Prague	Středočeský	25xxx-29xxx
South Bohemia	JC	CJC	699,564	11,345	4,380	České Budějovice	Jihočeský	37xxx-39xxx
West Bohemia	ZC	CZC	869,461	10,875	4,199	Pilsen	Západočeský	33xxx-36xxx
North Bohemia	SC	CSC	1,190,442	7,819	3,019	Ústí nad Labem	Severočeský	40xxx-47xxx
East Bohemia	VC	CVC	1,239,726	11,240	4,340	Hradec Králové	Východočeský	50xxx-57xxx
South Moravia	JM	CJM	2,058,156	15,028	5,802	Brno	Jihomoravský	58xxx-69xxx
North Moravia	SM	CSM	1,972,200	11,067	4,273	Ostrava	Severomoravský	70xxx-79xxx
			10,362,553	78,864	30,450			

Status: These divisions are kraj (regions), except for Prague, which is a hlavni město (city).

Abv: Two-letter code for international compatibility (defined by the author).

ISO: Codes from ISO 3166-2.

Population: 1990 estimate.

Area-km: Square kilometers.

Area-mi: Square miles.

PSC: Approximate ranges of Postovní Smerovací Čísla (postal codes). Note: postal codes for Czech addresses can be identified by prefixing them with "CZ-". They are written with a space after the third digit.

Further subdivisions: Prague is subdivided into obvodi (10 in 1978). The regions are subdivided into 75 okresi (districts). FIPS PUB 10-4 lists the okresi and Prague as divisions. The regions have fallen into disuse since 1993.

Origins of names:

Bohemia: Germanic *Baihaimoz*: Land of the Boii (ethnic name)

Prague: Old Czech *Praga*: doorsill

Change history:

1949-01-01   The země (provinces) of Bohemia and Moravia-Silesia were replaced by thirteen regions. This table shows populations as of 1957-01-01. The capitals have the same names as their regions. The German names of the capitals are also shown. The subsequent reorganization in 1960 did not follow the same boundaries as this division; to give a rough idea of the correspondence between the two sets of regions, the last column lists the modern region for the capital cities.

region	population	area-km	German name	modern region
Brno	1,001,091	7,449	Brünn	South Moravia
České Budějovice	521,894	8,968	Budweis	South Bohemia
Gottwaldov	655,207	5,107	Gottwaldov	South Moravia
Hradec Králové	583,868	5,145	Königgrätz	East Bohemia
Jihlava	436,982	6,651	Iglau	South Moravia
Karlovy Vary	337,890	4,579	Karlsbad	West Bohemia
Liberec	505,371	4,237	Reichenberg	North Bohemia
Olomouc	650,646	6,214	Olmütz	North Moravia
Ostrava	948,225	4,526	Ostrau	North Moravia
Pardubice	456,819	4,232	Pardubitz	East Bohemia
Plzeň	578,085	7,887	Pilsen	West Bohemia
Prague	2,188,221	9,730	Prag	Prague
Ústí nad Labem	675,907	4,145	Aussig	North Bohemia
	9,540,206	78,870		

1960   The thirteen regions were replaced by the present eight regions. The Austrian province of Silesia is now entirely within North Moravia.

1993-01-01   Czechoslovakia split into two countries, the Czech Republic and Slovakia. The Czech Republic consisted of the eight divisions listed above, all of which had been divisions of Czechoslovakia with the same boundaries.

Other names of subdivisions:

Bohemia: Boemia (Italian); Boêmia (Portuguese); Bohême (French); Böhmen (German); Čechy (Czech)

Moravia: Mähren (German); Morava (Czech); Moravie (French); Morávia (Portuguese)

Prague: Prag (German, Swedish); Praga (Italian, Portuguese, Spanish); Praha (Czech, Norwegian)

Silesia: Schlesien (German); Silésia (Portuguese); Silésie (French); Sleszko (Czech)

Population history:

	1900	1921	1930	1950	1961	1970	1982	1990
Prague	516,000	678,000	853,000	940,000	1,003,000	1,078,000	1,185,693	1,214,772
Central Bohemia	1,186,000	1,228,000	1,320,000	1,202,000	1,270,000	1,192,000	1,147,104	1,118,232
South Bohemia	835,000	836,000	810,000	626,000	650,000	653,000	693,165	699,564
West Bohemia	1,082,000	1,156,000	1,212,000	772,000	829,000	849,000	878,044	869,461
North Bohemia	1,387,000	1,455,000	1,570,000	1,027,000	1,085,000	1,103,000	1,173,782	1,190,442
East Bohemia	1,396,000	1,383,000	1,411,000	1,155,000	1,199,000	1,202,000	1,247,994	1,239,726
South Moravia	1,569,000	1,730,000	1,835,000	1,751,000	1,900,000	1,938,000	2,051,662	2,058,156
North Moravia	1,401,000	1,543,000	1,663,000	1,423,000	1,631,000	1,800,000	1,944,661	1,972,200
	9,372,000	10,009,000	10,674,000	8,896,000	9,567,000	9,815,000	10,322,105	10,362,553

(Populations for 1900–1950 are supposed to correspond to regional boundaries as of 1961.)

DENMARK

ISO = DK/FIPS = DA   Language = Danish   Time zone = +1 [d]   Capital = Copenhagen

Denmark remained neutral in World War I. At the end of the war, a plebiscite was held in Schleswig. As a result, the northern part of Schleswig (Danish: Slesveg) was transferred from Germany to Denmark on 1920-02-10. It corresponds fairly well with the modern county of South Jutland. In World War II, Denmark was occupied by Germany, but its pre-war borders were restored in the peace.

Spelling note: The Danes carried out a spelling reform in 1948. Before that time, "aa" was often used instead of "å."

Other names of country: Danemark (French); Dänemark (German); Danimarca (Italian); Danmark (Danish, Norwegian, Swedish); Danmörk (Icelandic); Denemarken (Dutch); Dinamarca (Portuguese, Spanish); Kingdom of Denmark (formal–English); Kongeriget Danmark (formal); Reino de Dinamarca (formal–Spanish); Tanska (Finnish).

Origin of name: Dansk (ethnic name) + *mark*: field.

division	abv	ISO	FIPS	NUTS	population	area-km	area-mi	capital	postal codes
Århus	AR	070	DA01	DK00D	605,447	4,561	1,761	Århus	8000–8699
Bornholm	BO	040	DA02	DK007	45,541	588	227	Rønne	3700–3799
Copenhagen	KH	101	DA05	DK002	603,179	526	203	Copenhagen	2600–2699
Copenhagen City	SK	015	DA06	DK001	464,566	88	34	Copenhagen	1000–2599
Frederiksberg	SF	147	DA16	DK001	86,372	9	3	Frederiksberg	
Frederiksborg	FR	020	DA03	DK003	344,559	1,347	520	Hillerød	3000–3599
Fyn	FY	042	DA04	DK008	463,241	3,486	1,346	Odense	5300–5999
North Jutland	NJ	080	DA07	DK00F	485,787	6,173	2,383	Ålborg	9300–9999
Ribe	RB	055	DA08	DK00A	219,800	3,131	1,209	Ribe	6700–6899
Ringkøbing	RK	065	DA09	DK00C	268,398	4,853	1,874	Ringkøbing	7400–7899
Roskilde	RS	025	DA10	DK004	220,129	891	344	Roskilde	4000–4099
South Jutland	SJ	050	DA11	DK009	250,756	3,938	1,521	Åbenrå	6200–6599
Storstrøm	ST	035	DA12	DK006	256,987	3,398	1,312	Nykøbing (Falster)	4700–4999
Vejle	VJ	060	DA13	DK00B	332,707	2,997	1,157	Vejle	6000–6099, 7000–7399
Vestsjælland	VS	030	DA14	DK005	285,098	2,984	1,152	Sorø	4100–4699
Viborg	VB	076	DA15	DK00E	229,559	4,122	1,592	Viborg	8800–8899
					5,162,126	43,092	16,638		

Status: These divisions are amter (counties; singular: amt), except for Copenhagen City and Frederiksberg. Those two are kommuner (municipalities). Some sources call Frederiksberg a borough, or omit it completely.

Abv: Two-letter code for international compatibility (defined by the author).

ISO: Codes from ISO 3166-2.

FIPS: Codes from FIPS PUB 10-4.

NUTS: Nomenclature of Territorial Units for Statistics.

Population: 1992 estimate.

Area-km: Square kilometers.

Area-mi: Square miles.

Postal codes: Danish postal codes are four digits. In most cases, the county can be deduced from the first two digits. Note: postal codes for Danish addresses can be identified by prefixing them with "DK-".

Further subdivisions: The counties are further subdivided into 275 municipalities.

Territorial extent: Århus lies mostly on Jutland, but also includes some islands, such as Anholt and Samsø.

Bornholm includes the island of Bornholm and the smaller Ertholmene Islands.

Copenhagen occupies part of the island of Sjælland (Zealand), most of Amager, and all of Saltholm.

Copenhagen City lies mainly on the islands of Sjælland and Amager. It surrounds Frederiksberg, and in return it is surrounded by Copenhagen (the county), if water territory is taken into account.

Frederiksberg is entirely surrounded by Copenhagen City. It has no direct relationship to Frederiksborg.

Frederiksborg is almost entirely on the island of Sjælland.

Fyn contains the islands of Fyn, Æbelø, Ærø (on the Bay of Kiel), Bågø, Brandsø, Langeland, Romsø, Tåsinge, and other smaller ones.

North Jutland includes only a few islands. The largest is Læsø in the Kattegat. It also includes an area known as Vendsyssel. Vendsyssel and Thy (see Viborg) are connected to one another, but separated from the rest of Jutland by a variable strip of water called Limfjorden. Nonetheless, they are considered part of Jutland.

Ribe contains the North Sea islands of Fanø and Mandø; the rest of it is part of Jutland.

Ringkøbing is part of Jutland, containing only a few islands in fjords.

Roskilde is almost entirely on Sjælland.

South Jutland is mostly on Jutland, but includes some islands, such as Als, Årø, and Barsø in the Little Belt, and Rømø in the North Sea.

Storstrøm occupies part of Sjælland, and the entirety of a number of islands, such as Bogø, Falster, Fejø, Femø, Lolland, Møn, and Vejrø.

Vejle is mostly on Jutland, but includes a few islands, such as Endelave and Hjarnø.

Vestsjælland lies almost entirely on Sjælland, but also contains some small islands, such as Hesselø in the Kattegat, Orø in Isefjord, Agersø, Omø, Scjerø, Sprogø, etc.

Viborg contains part of Jutland, including Thy (see North Jutland) and some islands in Limfjorden, notably Mors.

The Faroe Islands and Greenland, remote territories of Denmark with limited home rule, are treated as separate countries by ISO 3166-1, so they are not included here. Iceland had a similar status at the beginning of the 20th century. In 1918 it nominally became a sovereign state, but it remained subordinate to Denmark in international affairs. On 1944-06-17, it officially became an independent republic.

Origins of names:

Ålborg: probably from Old Norse *áll*: channel, *borg*: fort

Århus: from Old Danish *å*: river and *os*: mouth

Bornholm: Old Danish for Islet of the Burgundar (ethnic name, also found in the old province of Burgundy in France)

Copenhagen: Danish *København*: merchants' port

Fyn: from Old Norwegian *fjón*: pasturage

Jutland: land of the Jutes, an ethnic name

Roskild: Old Danish *Hroarskilde*: origin of Hroar (a king)

Vestsjælland = West Zealand, from Old Danish *sjæ*: sea, *land*: land (Zealand is the island on which most of Copenhagen sits)

Change history: In 1900, Denmark (excluding the Faroes, Greenland, and Iceland) contained 19 counties: Aalborg, Aarhus, Bornholm, Frederiksborg, Hjörring, Holbæk, Kjöbenhaven, Maribo, Odense, Præstö, Randers, Ribe, Ringkjöbing, Skanderborg, Sorö, Svendborg, Thisted, Vejle, and Viborg. All of these counties except Bornholm (Rönne) had capitals with the same names.

It appears that Aarhus, Kjöbenhaven, Odense, and (after 1920) Aabenraa counties were each subdivided into two districts. Some sources show the counties whole; others show the districts rather than the counties. The districts are listed below, with their counties.

1920-02-10	Northern Schleswig, consisting of the counties of Aabenraa, Haderslev, and Tönder, transferred from Germany to Denmark.
~1923	Frederiksborg province and its capital renamed to Hilleröd.
1948	Spelling reform changed Aa to Å, ö to ø, Kjöbenhaven to København, and Ringkjöbing to Ringkøbing.
1970-04-01	The 21 counties were reorganized into the present 14 counties and two municipalities. The following table lists the old counties, broken up into districts where applicable, with population according to the 1955 census, area in sq. km., and their disposition in the creation of the new counties. Capitals have the same name as their counties or districts, except for Bornholm (Rönne).

county	district	population	area-km	disposition
Åbenrå	Åbenrå	48,676	790	South Jutland
"	Sønderborg	49,604	441	South Jutland
Ålborg		232,885	2,914	North Jutland
Århus	Århus	210,409	804	Århus, *Vejle
"	Skanderborg	136,495	1,719	Århus, Vejle
Bornholm		48,632	588	Bornholm
Frederiksborg		162,889	1,344	Frederiksborg, *Vestsjælland
Haderslev		71,715	1,342	South Jutland
Hjørring		173,233	2,865	North Jutland
Holbæk		127,127	1,752	Vestsjælland, Århus
København	København	1,269,366	584	Copenhagen, Copenhagen City, Frederiksberg
"	Roskilde	82,223	690	Roskilde
Maribo		133,870	1,798	Storstrøm
Odense	Odense	196,213	1,149	Fyn
"	Assens	58,005	667	Fyn
Præstø		122,919	1,693	Storstrøm, Roskilde
Randers		170,802	2,466	Århus, *North Jutland
Ribe		178,501	3,069	Ribe, *South Jutland
Ringkøbing		198,389	4,660	Ringkøbing
Sorø		128,639	1,478	Vestsjælland
Svendborg		150,365	1,667	Fyn
Thisted		86,703	1,774	Vejle, *North Jutland ➤

county	district	population	area-km	disposition
Tønder		42,842	1,390	South Jutland
Vejle		207,881	2,348	Vejle, *Ribe, *Ringkøbing, *South Jutland
Viborg		160,018	3,050	Viborg, *Århus, *Ringkøbing
		4,448,401	43,042	

* = only a very small part (usually a single municipality or less) of the old county went into the new county under this name

Other names of subdivisions:

Århus: Arósar (Icelandic); Aarhus (Danish-obsolete)

Bornholm: Borgundarhólmur (Icelandic); Bornholms (variant)

Copenhagen: Copenaghen (Italian); Copenhague (French, Portuguese, Spanish); Kaupmannahöfn (Icelandic); Kjöbenhavn (Danish-obsolete); København, Københavns (Danish); Kopenhagen (German)

Copenhagen City: Staden København (Danish)

Fyn: Fionia (Spanish); Fionie (French); Fjón (Icelandic); Fünen (German); Fyen (Danish-obsolete); Fyns (variant)

North Jutland: Nord-Jütland (German); Nordjylland, Nordjyllands (Danish); Norður-Jótland (Icelandic)

Ringkøbing: Ringkjöbing (Danish-obsolete)

Roskilde: Roschild (German); Roskild (French)

South Jutland: Sønderjylland, Sønderjyllands (Danish); Süd-Jütland (German); Suður-Jótland (Icelandic)

Storstrøm: Storstrøms (variant)

Vestsjælland: Vestsjaland (Icelandic); Vestsjællands (variant); West-Seeland (German)

DJIBOUTI

ISO = DJ/FIPS = DJ   Language = French   Time zone = +3   Capital = Djibouti

In 1900, French Somaliland was a freshly-minted French colony. It became an overseas territory in 1947. The name was changed to Afars and Issas, after the two major ethnic groups, in 1967. On 1977-06-27, the country became independent, changing its name to the Republic of Djibouti at the same time. There have been moderate border changes during the century.

Other names of country: Afars and Issas, French Somaliland (obsolete–English); Côte Française des Somalis (obsolete); Djiboutí (Spanish); Djíbútí (Icelandic); Djibuti (Portuguese); Dschibuti (German); Französisch Somali-Küste (obsolete–German); Gibuti (Italian); Jibuti (obsolete); Jumhouriyya Djibouti (formal); Republic of Djibouti (formal–English); Somalia Francesa, Territorio de los Afares y los Issas (obsolete–Spanish); Territoire Français des Afars et des Issas (obsolete–formal).

Origin of name: Afar *gabod*: basketwork tray, which Arabic traders adapted to Gabuti to refer to a cape with a similar shape.

division	ISO	FIPS	population	area-km	area-mi
'Ali Sabieh	AS	DJ01	13,000	2,600	1,000
Dikhil	DI	DJ02	32,000	7,800	3,000
Djibouti	DJ	DJ03	127,000	600	250
Obock	OB	DJ04	14,000	5,700	2,200
Tadjoura	TA	DJ05	30,000	7,300	2,800
			216,000	24,000	9,250

Status: These divisions are cercles (districts).

ISO: Codes from ISO 3166-2.

FIPS: Codes from FIPS PUB 10-4.

Population: 1976 estimate.

Area-km: Square kilometers.

Area-mi: Square miles.

Capitals have the same names as their districts.

Origin of names:

Djibouti: after the city, which was named for the cape (Ras   Tadjoura: from Arabic *tidjare*: marketplace
Gabuti in Arabic)

Change history:

~1981   Obock, formerly a subdistrict of Tadjoura, became a separate district.

Other names of subdivisions:

'Ali Sabieh: 'Ali Sabîh (variant)

DOMINICA

ISO = DM/FIPS = DO   Language = English   Time zone = -4   Capital = Roseau

At the beginning of the 20th century, Dominica was one of five presidencies of the Leeward Islands, a British colony. On 1940-01-01, it became a separate British colony. On 1958-04-22, it joined the West Indies Federation. The Federation was dissolved on 1962-05-31. Dominica became independent on 1978-11-03.
   Other names of country: Commonwealth of Dominica (formal–English); Dóminíka (Icelandic); Dominique (French).
   Origin of name: discovered by Christopher Columbus on Sunday 1493-11-03 (Spanish *domingo*: Sunday).

division	ISO	FIPS	population	area-km	area-mi	division	ISO	FIPS	population	area-km	area-mi
Saint Andrew	AN	DO02	12,748	165	64	Saint Mark	MA	DO08	1,921	15	6
Saint David	DA	DO03	7,337	120	46	Saint Patrick	PK	DO09	9,780	100	39
Saint George	GO	DO04	20,501	55	21	Saint Paul	PL	DO10	6,386	65	25
Saint John	JN	DO05	5,412	65	25	Saint Peter	PR	DO11	1,601	40	15
Saint Joseph	JH	DO06	6,606	110	42				73,795	750	289
Saint Luke	LU	DO07	1,503	15	6						

Status: These divisions are parishes.
ISO: Codes from ISO 3166-2.
FIPS: Codes from FIPS PUB 10-4.
Population: 1981 census.
Area-km: Square kilometers.
Area-mi: Square miles.
The parishes do not have capitals.
Territorial extent: The country consists of the island of Dominica.

DOMINICAN REPUBLIC

ISO = DO/FIPS = DR   Language = Spanish   Time zone = -4   Capital = Santo Domingo

The Dominican Republic shares the island of Hispaniola with Haiti. The boundary between these two countries has remained fairly stable throughout the 20th century. Unfortunately, the same can't be said about their system of government. The Dominican Republic was dominated by Rafael Trujillo from 1930 to 1961. He and his family attempted to impose their names on several geographical features.

Other names of country: Den dominikanske republikken (Norwegian); Dominicaanse Republiek (Dutch); Dominikaaninen tasavalta (Finnish); Dominikanische Republik (German); Dominikanska republiken (Swedish); Dominikanske Republik (Danish); Dóminíska lýðveldið (Icelandic); Repubblica Dominicana (Italian); República Dominicana (Portuguese, Spanish); République dominicaine (French).

Origin of name: from Santo Domingo, the capital, which was named by Columbus in 1496 in honor of his father's patron saint.

division	ISO	FIPS	population	area-km	area-mi	capital
Azua	AZ	DR01	195,420	2,430	938	Azua (de Compostela)
Bahoruco	BR	DR02	87,376	1,376	531	Neiba
Barahona	BH	DR03	152,405	2,528	976	(Santa Cruz de) Barahona
Dajabón	DA	DR04	64,123	890	344	Dajabón
Distrito Nacional	DN	DR05	2,411,895	1,477	570	Santo Domingo
Duarte	DU	DR06	261,725	1,292	499	San Francisco de Macorís
Elías Piña	EP	DR11	72,651	1,788	690	Comendador
El Seibo	SE	DR28	97,590	1,714	662	(Santa Cruz de) El Seibo
Espaillat	ES*	DR08	182,248	1,000	386	Moca
Hato Mayor	HM	DR29	77,823	1,276	493	Hato Mayor (del Rey)
Independencia	IN	DR09	43,077	1,861	719	Jimaní
La Altagracia	AL	DR10	111,241	3,084	1,191	(Salvaleón de) Higüey
La Romana	RO	DR12	169,223	541	209	La Romana
La Vega	VE	DR30	303,047	2,287	883	(Concepción de) la Vega
María Trinidad Sánchez	MT	DR14	125,148	1,310	506	(Trinidad Sánchez) Nogua
Monseñor Nouel	MN	DR31	124,794	1,004	388	Bonao
Monte Cristi	MC	DR15	92,678	1,989	768	(San Fernando de) Monte Cristi
Monte Plata	MP	DR32	174,799	2,613	1,009	Monte Plata
Pedernales	PN	DR16	18,896	967	373	Pedernales
Peravia	PR	DR17	186,810	1,622	626	Baní
Puerto Plata	PP	DR18	229,738	1,881	726	(San Felipe de) Puerto Plata
Salcedo	SC	DR19	110,216	533	206	Salcedo
Samaná	SM	DR20	73,000	989	382	(Santa Bárbara de) Samaná
Sánchez Ramírez	SZ	DR21	140,635	1,174	453	Cotuí
San Cristóbal	CR	DR33	320,921	1,244	480	San Cristóbal
San Juan	JU	DR23	266,628	3,561	1,375	San Juan (de la Maguana)
San Pedro de Macorís	PM	DR24	197,862	1,666	643	San Pedro de Macorís
Santiago	ST	DR25	704,835	3,122	1,205	Santiago (de los Caballeros)
Santiago Rodríguez	SR	DR26	61,570	1,020	394	(San Ignacio de) Sabaneta
Valverde	VA	DR27	111,470	569	220	Mao
			7,169,844	48,808	18,845	

* = The draft standard lists EP for both Elías Piña and Espaillat; I changed the code for Espaillat to make them distinct.

Status: These divisions are provincias (provinces), except for Distrito Nacional, which is a national district, as its name implies.

ISO: Codes from ISO 3166-2.

FIPS: Codes from FIPS PUB 10-4.

Population: 1990 estimate.

Area-km: Square kilometers.

Area-mi: Square miles.

Capitals: When part of the name of a capital is in parentheses, that means that the capital has a short, informal name, and a formal name including the parenthetical part. The shorter form is commonly used.

Further subdivisions: The provinces are subdivided into comunes (municipalities). There were 61 of them in 1935, rising to 97 in 1993. Municipalities are further subdivided into secciones (sections).

Territorial extent: Independencia contains most of Lago Enriquilla, including all of Isla Cabritos.

La Altagracia includes Isla Saona.

Pedernales includes Isla Beata and Cayo los Frailes.

Origins of names:

Distrito Nacional = national district

Duarte: named for Juan Pablo Duarte, 19th-century revolutionary.

Espaillat: named for Ulises F. Espaillat (1823–1878), 19th-century author and governor.

Pedernales = flints

Puerto Plata = silver port

Sánchez Ramírez: named for General Juan Sánchez Ramírez, who led the fight to expel the French and restore the country to Spanish rule in 1809.

Valverde: named for José D. Valverde, 19th-century governor.

Change history:

The provinces in 1935 were Azua, Barahona, Duarte, Espaillat, La Vega, Montecristi, Puerto Plata, Samaná, San Pedro de Macorís, Santiago, Santo Domingo (modern Distrito Nacional), Seibo (modern El Seibo), and Trujillo (modern San Cristóbal). Note that the correspondence with modern provinces is not exact, because of later splitting. As a rule, the capital of the old province will be the same as the capital of the corresponding modern province.

1936 Name of national capital changed from Santo Domingo to Ciudad Trujillo. The name of the district of Santo Domingo remained unchanged.

1938 Benefactor province (modern San Juan) split from Azua; Libertador province (modern Dajabón) split from Montecristi; Monseñor de Meriño province (modern Monte Plata) split from Trujillo.

1942 San Rafael province (modern Elías Piña) split from Benefactor.

1943 Bahoruco province split from Barahona.

1944 José Trujillo Valdez province split from Azua.

~1950 La Altagracia province (capital La Romana) split from Seibo.

~1950 Monseñor de Meriño province merged back into Trujillo.

~1955 Independencia province split from Bahoruco; Salcedo province split from Espaillat; Sánchez Ramírez province split from Duarte; Santiago Rodríguez province split from Montecristi, now spelled Monte Cristi.

~1955 Name of Distrito de Santo Domingo changed to Distrito Nacional.

1961 Name of national capital restored to Santo Domingo; name of Trujillo province changed to San Cristóbal; name of José Trujillo Valdez province changed to Peravia; name of Benefactor province changed to San Juan; name of Libertador province changed to Dajabón.

~1963 María Trinidad Sánchez province (at first also known as Trinidad Sánchez Nagua province) split from Samaná; Pedernales province split from Barahona; Valverde province split from Santiago.

1965 Name of San Rafael province changed to Elías Piña. (It was temporarily called La Estrelleta in later years.)

~1968 La Romana province split from La Altagracia.

~1979 Name of capital of Santiago Rodríguez province changed from Santiago Rodríguez to Sabaneta (restoring the name previously changed in 1936).

~1992 Hato Mayor province split from El Seibo; Monseñor Nouel province split from La Vega; Monte Plata province split from San Cristóbal. The FIPS codes of these three provinces prior to the change were DR07, DR13, and DR22, respectively.

Other names of subdivisions:

Bahoruco: Baoruco (variant)

Dajabón: Libertador (obsolete)

Distrito Nacional: Santo Domingo (obsolete)

Elías Piña: La Estrelleta, San Rafael (obsolete)

El Seibo: Seibo (obsolete)

María Trinidad Sánchez: Trinidad Sánchez Nagua (obsolete)

Peravia: José Trujillo Valdez (obsolete)

San Cristóbal: Trujillo (obsolete)

San Juan: Benefactor (obsolete)

EAST TIMOR

ISO = TP/FIPS = ID27   Languages = Portuguese, Indonesian   Time zone = +8   Capital = Dili

At the beginning of the 20th century, part of the East Indian island of Timor was a Portuguese territory. The Portuguese inhabitants called it simply Timor. In English, it was more often referred to as Portuguese Timor. In 1951, East Timor became an overseas province of Portugal. In 1976, Indonesia unilaterally annexed the area. Portugal still refuses to recognize Indonesia's sovereignty. In an attempt to accommodate both sides, ISO 3166-1 includes a code for the entity, TP, presumably derived from "Timor Portugues." Indonesia still preserves the boundaries of the former country as those of its province Timor Timur. In conformance with ISO 3166, this book lists East Timor as a separate country. See Indonesia for additional information.

Other names of country: Loro Sae (Indonesian-obsolete); Oost Timor (Dutch); Timor oriental (French); Timor Oriental (Spanish); Timor Portugues (Portuguese-obsolete); Timor Timur (Indonesian).

Origin of name: Eastern part of the island of Timor.

division	FIPS	population	area-km	area-mi	capital
Timor Timur	ID27	747,750	14,874	5,743	Dili

Status: This division is the whole of the country, treated as a division for compatibility.
Abv: Use ID.TT for international compatibility (see Indonesia entry).
FIPS: Codes from FIPS PUB 10-4.
Population: 1990 census.
Area-km: Square kilometers.
Area-mi: Square miles.
Territorial extent: East Timor includes a small enclave near the western end of the island of Timor, known as Oé-Cussi, and formerly called Okusi Ambeno or other similar names. Atauro (or Kambing) Island is also included. The division of Timor between Portugal and the Netherlands was settled by treaty on 1904-10-01.
Origin of names:

Timor: Malay for east. Thus, the name of the country or
   province is literally "East East."

Change history:
Under Portuguese administration, East Timor was divided into eight circunscrições.

ECUADOR

ISO = EC/FIPS = EC   Language = Spanish   Time zone = -5 (see note)   Capital = Quito

Ecuador has been an independent country throughout the whole 20th century. It has also been involved in territorial disputes throughout the century. Provincial borders have undergone extensive changes. Ecuador and Peru have fought repeatedly over disputed territories in the Región Oriental.

Time zone note: The Galapagos Islands are in time zone -6.
Other names of country: Ekvador (Icelandic); Equador (Portuguese); Équateur (French); Equatore (Italian); Republic of Ecuador (formal–English); República del Ecuador (formal).
Origin of name: Spanish *ecuador*: equator, from location on equator.

division	abv	ISO	FIPS	population	area-km	area-mi	capital
Azuay	AZ	A	EC02	506,090	8,125	3,137	Cuenca
Bolívar	BO	B	EC03	155,088	3,940	1,521	Guaranda ➤

division	abv	ISO	FIPS	population	area-km	area-mi	capital
Cañar	CN	F	EC04	189,347	3,122	1,205	Azogues
Carchi	CR	C	EC05	141,482	3,605	1,392	Tulcán
Chimborazo	CB	H	EC06	364,682	6,569	2,536	Riobamba
Cotopaxi	CT	X	EC07	276,324	6,072	2,344	Latacunga
El Oro	EO	O	EC08	412,572	5,850	2,259	Machala
Esmeraldas	ES	E	EC09	306,628	15,239	5,884	Esmeraldas
Galápagos	GA	W	EC01	9,785	8,010	3,093	Puerto Baquerizo Moreno
Guayas	GU	G	EC10	2,515,146	20,503	7,916	Guayaquil
Imbabura	IM	I	EC11	265,499	4,559	1,760	Ibarra
Loja	LJ	L	EC12	384,698	11,027	4,258	Loja
Los Ríos	LR	R	EC13	527,559	7,175	2,770	Babahoyo
Manabí	MN	M	EC14	1,031,927	18,879	7,289	Portoviejo
Morona-Santiago	MS	S	EC15	84,216	25,690	9,919	Macas
Napo	NA	N	EC21	103,387	33,931	13,101	Tena
Pastaza	PA	Y	EC17	41,811	29,774	11,496	Puyo
Pichincha	PI	P	EC18	1,756,228	12,915	4,987	Quito
Sucumbíos	SU	U	EC22	76,952	18,328	7,076	Nueva Loja
Tungurahua	TU	T	EC19	361,980	3,335	1,288	Ambato
Zamora-Chinchipe	ZC	Z	EC20	66,167	23,111	8,923	Zamora
				9,648,189	272,048	105,038	

Status: These divisions are provincias (provinces).

Abv: Two-letter code for international compatibility (defined by the author).

ISO: Codes from ISO 3166-2.

FIPS: Codes from FIPS PUB 10-4.

Population: 1990 census.

Area-km: Square kilometers.

Area-mi: Square miles.

Further subdivisions: The provinces are subdivided into cantones (cantons), which are further subdivided into parroquias (parishes). The parishes are classified as parroquias urbanas (urban) and parroquias rurales (rural). There are almost a thousand all told, and the number tends to rise.

Territorial extent: Ecuador's territorial claim extended as far as the Marañón River before 1942. In that year, the Protocol of Rio de Janeiro drew the border between Ecuador and Peru shown on most modern maps. However, Ecuador still claims some of the region adjudicated to Peru. This area was part of the Región Oriental, which in 1942 consisted of Napo Pastaza and Santiago Zamora provinces.

Galápagos consists of an isolated island group in the Pacific, including the islands of Fernandina, Isabela (the largest), San Cristóbal (site of the capital), San Salvador, and Santa Cruz.

Guayas contains Isla Puná and other smaller islands in the mouth of the Guayas River.

Origins of names:

Archipiélago de Colón: named for Christopher Columbus (Cristóbal Colón in Spanish)

Bolívar: named for Simón Bolívar (1783–1830), liberator of Ecuador from Spanish rule

Chimborazo: after Chimborazo, the highest mountain in the world (as measured by its summit's distance from the center of the earth)

Cotopaxi: after the volcano Cotopaxi, from Quechua *q'utu*: smokes, *p'asi*: mouth.

El Oro: Spanish for The Gold

Esmeraldas: Spanish for Emeralds

Galápagos: Spanish *galápago*: river tortoise

Guayas: ethnic name

Los Ríos: Spanish for The Rivers

Change history:

1904   Ecuador ceded land between the Japurá and Amazon Rivers, as far west as the modern border between Brazil and Colombia, to Brazil.

~1935   Oriente region (capital Archidona) split into the provinces of Napo Pastaza (capital Tena) and Santiago Zamora (capital Macas). The name Región Oriental is still applied to the group of provinces descended from these.

1939   Name of León province changed to Cotopaxi.

~1965   Santiago Zamora province split into Morona-Santiago and Zamora-Chinchipe; Napo Pastaza province split into Napo and Pastaza.

~1965   Capital of Archipiélago de Colón moved from San Cristóbal to nearby Puerto Baquerizo
         Moreno (sometimes shortened to either Puerto Baquerizo or Baquerizo Moreno).
~1987   Territorio Insular del Archipiélago de Colón territory became Galápagos province.
 1989   Sucumbíos province split from Napo (former FIPS code EC16).

Other names of subdivisions:

Cotopaxi: León (obsolete)   Galápagos: Archipiélago de Colón (variant)

EGYPT

ISO = EG/FIPS = EG   Language = Arabic   Time zone = +2 ᵈ   Capital = Cairo

Egypt had been part of the Ottoman Empire before 1879. The British military occupied it in 1882, setting up a government subservient to British interests, although it remained technically a tributary state of the Ottoman Empire. On 1914-11-18, Great Britain declared Egypt to be a protectorate. After World War I, with Turkey defeated, Egypt was granted a large measure of independence, effective as of 1922-02-28. A constitutional monarchy was established. In 1952, the monarchy fell to a coup led by Gamal Abdel Nasser. Nasser's government formed a union with Syria, the United Arab Republic (U.A.R.), on 1958-02-01. Egypt and Syria became regions of the U.A.R. Syria withdrew from the union on 1961-09-29. Egypt continued to call itself the U.A.R. until 1971-09-01. On that date, a loose federation was formed, the Federation of Arab Republics, comprising Egypt, Syria, and Libya. Egypt's official name became the Arab Republic of Egypt. In the Six-Day War of 1967, Israel occupied the Sinai Peninsula up to the banks of the Suez Canal, later withdrawing to a cease-fire line a few kilometers to the east. The canal remained closed from 1967 to 1975. The Sinai was restored to Egypt in stages by the terms of the peace treaty negotiated at Camp David and signed on 1979-03-26.

Spelling notes: Place names are officially written in Arabic script. City names, and governorate names derived from city names, may be translated, but in general, names must be transliterated or transcribed into the Roman alphabet. There are many possible methods of transliteration. Some of this variety is shown in the table of variant names. The initial elements Ad, Al, As, Ash, Aṭ, and Az are articles. Sometimes, especially in older sources, they are spelled Ed, El, Es, and so on. Sometimes they are connected to the following word with hyphens. A few sources omit them entirely.

Other names of country: Ägypten (German); Arab Republic of Egypt (formal–English); Egiptaland (Icelandic); Egipto (Spanish); Egito (Portuguese); Egitto (Italian); Egypte (Dutch); Égypte (French); Egypten (Danish, Swedish); Egypti (Finnish); Jumhuriyat Misr al-Arabiya (formal); Miṣr (Arabic); República Árabe de Egipto (formal–Spanish); United Arab Republic (obsolete).

Origin of name: Ancient Greek *Aigyptios*, from Egyptian *hut-ka-ptah*: castle of the soul of Ptah.

division	abv	ISO	FIPS	reg	population	area-km	area-mi	capital	Anglicized
Ad Daqahlīyah	DQ	DK	EG01	L	3,500,470	3,471	1,340	Al Manṣūrah	Dakahlia
Al Baḥr al Aḥmar	BA	BA	EG02	D	90,491	203,685	78,643	Al Ghurdaqah	Red Sea
Al Buḥayrah	BH	BH	EG03	L	3,257,168	10,129	3,911	Damanhūr	Beheira
Al Fayyūm	FY	FYM	EG04	U	1,544,047	1,827	705	Al Fayyūm	Fayyum
Al Gharbīyah	GH	GH	EG05	L	2,870,960	1,942	750	Ṭanṭā	Gharbia
Al Iskandarīyah	IK	ALX	EG06	C	2,917,327	2,679	1,035	Al Iskandarīyah	Alexandria
Al Ismāʿīlīyah	IS	IS	EG07	C	544,427	1,442	557	Al Ismāʿīlīyah	Ismailia
Al Jīzah	JZ	GZ	EG08	U	3,700,054	85,105	32,859	Al Jīzah	Giza
Al Minūfīyah	MF	MNF	EG09	L	2,227,087	1,532	592	Shibīn al Kawm	Minufia
Al Minyā	MN	MN	EG10	U	2,648,043	2,262	873	Al Minyā	Minya
Al Qāhirah	QH	C	EG11	C	6,052,836	214	83	Al Qāhirah	Cairo
Al Qalyūbīyah	QL	KB	EG12	L	2,514,244	1,001	387	Banhā	Kalyubia
Al Wādī al Jadīd	WJ	WAD	EG13	D	113,838	376,505	145,369	Al Khārijah	New Valley
Ash Sharqīyah	SQ	SHR	EG14	L	3,420,119	4,180	1,614	Az Zaqāzīq	Sharkia
As Suways	SW	SUZ	EG15	C	326,820	17,840	6,888	As Suways	Suez
Aswān	AN	ASN	EG16	U	801,408	679	262	Aswān	Aswan
Asyūṭ	AT	AST	EG17	U	2,223,034	1,553	600	Asyūṭ	Asyut
Banī Suwayf	BN	BNS	EG18	U	1,442,981	1,322	510	Banī Suwayf	Beni Suef ➤

division	abv	ISO	FIPS	reg	population	area-km	area-mi	capital	Anglicized
Būr Sa'īd	BS	PTS	EG19	C	399,793	72	28	Būr Sa'īd	Port Said
Dumyāṭ	DT	DT	EG20	L	741,264	589	227	Dumyāṭ	Damietta
Janūb Sīnā'	JS	JS	EG26	D	28,988	33,140	12,795	Aṭ Ṭur	South Sinai
Kafr ash Shaykh	KS	KFS	EG21	L	1,800,129	3,437	1,327	Kafr ash Shaykh	Kafr el Sheikh
Maṭrūḥ	MT	MT	EG22	D	160,567	212,112	81,897	Maṭrūḥ	Matruh
Qinā	QN	KN	EG23	U	2,252,315	1,851	715	Qinā	Kena
Shamal Sīnā'	SS	SIN	EG27	D	171,505	27,574	10,646	Al 'Arish	North Sinai
Sūhāj	SJ	SHG	EG24	U	2,455,134	1,547	597	Sūhāj	Suhag
					48,205,049	997,690	385,210		

Status: These divisions are muḥāfaẓāt (governorates).

Abv: Two-letter code for international compatibility (defined by the author).

ISO: Codes from ISO 3166-2.

FIPS: Codes from FIPS PUB 10-4.

Reg: These have been called regions, but they are actually classes of governorate.

    C: (City) urban governorates

    D: (Desert) frontier governorates

    L: Governorates of Lower (downstream) Egypt

    U: Governorates of Upper Egypt

Population: 1986 census.

Area-km: Square kilometers.

Area-mi: Square miles.

Anglicized: Versions of the governorate names that might be more comfortable for English speakers.

Territorial extent: Egypt ceded two sparsely inhabited areas to Libya in 1919 and 1926. These cessions left the border in its modern position, following the meridian of 25° East quite closely.

The legal boundary between Egypt and Sudan follows the parallel of 22° North, except for a small jog where the Nile crosses it. At the Nile, Sudan owns territory north of that parallel, mostly inundated by Lake Nasser. However, near the Red Sea, the administrative boundary deviates from the legal boundary. There is a small region in Sudan, south of 22°, administered by Egypt, and a larger area in Egypt, north of the parallel, administered by Sudan.

Egypt owns some islands in the Red Sea. They belong to Al Baḥr al Aḥmar governorate. The largest of them include Jazīrat Shākir and Jazīrat Zabarjad.

Origins of names:

Al Fayyūm: from Coptic *Fiom*: the lake

Al Gharbīyah: Arabic for Western

Al Iskandarīyah: founded by Alexander the Great in 332 B.C.

Al Ismā'īlīyah: named for Ismail Pasha (1830–1895), viceroy of Egypt during the building of the Suez Canal

Al Jīzah: Egyptian *er-ges-her*: beside the great pyramid

Al Qāhirah: Arabic for the victorious one, an epithet of the planet Mars, which was in the ascendant when construction began on 969-07-06

Ash Sharqīyah: Arabic for Eastern

As Suways: after a nearby spring, Bīr Suweis

Aswān: Ancient Egyptian *suanit*: market

Asyūṭ: Ancient Egyptian *syawt*: guardian

Būr Sa'īd: Arabic for Port Said, which was named for Mohammed Said Pasha, viceroy of Egypt when work began on the Suez Canal

Change history:

There have been numerous border adjustments. Typically, one of the smaller governorates annexes adjacent territory from a frontier governorate.

~1952   Kafr ash Shaykh governorate split from Al Gharbīyah.

~1960   Capital of Girga governorate moved from Girga to Sūhāj, and name changed to match.

~1963   Al Ismā'īlīyah governorate split from Būr Sa'īd.

1980s   Several sources show a governorate named Aṭ Taḥrīr (Liberation), capital Naṣr. This governorate was apparently swallowed up by the growth of the governorates of Al Iskandarīyah and Al Buḥayrah.

~1984   Sīnā' governorate split into Janūb Sīnā' (South) and Shamal Sīnā' (North).

~1987   Name of Marsā Maṭrūḥ governorate, and its capital, changed to Maṭrūḥ.

Other names of subdivisions:

Ad Daqahlīyah: Dacahlia, Dagahlia, Dakahlieh, Dakalieh, Daqahlīya (variant)

Al Baḥr al Aḥmar: Mar Rojo (Spanish); Mar Rosso (Italian); Mar Vermelho (Portuguese); Mer Rouge (French); Red Sea (variant); Röda havet (Swedish); Rødehavet (Norwegian); Rotes Meer (German)

Al Buḥayrah: Behera (variant)

Al Fayyūm: El Faiyum, el Fayoum, Faium, Faiyūm, Fayoum, Fayum (variant)

Al Gharbīyah: Garbia, Gharbieh, Gharbīya (variant)

Al Iskandarīyah· Alejandría (Spanish); Alessandria (Italian); Alexandrie (French)

Al Ismāʿīlīyah: Ismaïlia (French)

Al Jīzah: El Giza, El Gīzah, Gizeh (variant); Guizèh (French)

Al Minūfīyah: Menoufia, Menoufieh, Menufia, Menūfīya, Minūfīya, Munufia (variant)

Al Minyā: Menia, Minia, Minieh (variant)

Al Qāhirah: El Cairo (Spanish); Il Cairo (Italian); Kairo (Danish, German, Norwegian, Swedish); Le Caire (French)

Al Qalyūbīyah: Caliubia, Kalioubiya, Kalioubieh, Kalyoubia, Qaliyubia, Qalyubiya (variant)

Al Wādī al Jadīd: El-Wadi El-Gidid (variant); Southern Desert (obsolete); Novo Vale (Portuguese)

Ash Sharqīyah: Charkieh, Sharqia, Sharqīya, Sharquia (variant)

As Suways: Es Suweis (variant)

Aswān: Assouan (French); Assuã (Portuguese); Assuan (Italian, Norwegian); Assuán (Spanish); Syene (ancient)

Asyūṭ: Assiut, Assyut, Asyout (variant); Assiout (French)

Banī Suwayf: Beni Souef (variant)

Būr Saʿīd: Canal (obsolete); Port-Saïd (French)

Dumyāṭ: Dumiāt (variant); Damietta (Italian); Damiette (French)

Janūb Sīnā: Sinai al Janūbīa (variant)

Kafr ash Shaykh: Kafr ash Shaikh, Kafr el Sheik (variant)

Maṭrūḥ: Marsā Matrūḥ, Matrouh, Mersa Matruh, Western Desert (obsolete)

Qinā: Qena, Quena (variant)

Shamal Sīnāʾ: Sinai ash Shamālīya

Sūhāj: Girga, Girgeh (obsolete); Sawhāj, Sohag (variant)

Population history:

	1937	1947	1957	1966	1976	1986
Ad Daqahlīyah	1,218,502	1,413,905	1,849,000	2,285,000	2,732,756	3,500,470
Al Baḥr al Aḥmar	9,914	15,929	N/A	38,000	56,191	90,491
Al Buḥayrah	1,061,596	1,244,495	1,484,000	1,979,000	2,517,292	3,257,168
Al Fayyūm	602,122	669,696	765,000	935,000	1,140,245	1,544,047
Al Gharbīyah	1,967,894	2,327,031	1,567,000	1,901,000	2,294,303	2,870,960
Al Iskandarīyah	685,736	919,024	1,290,000	1,801,000	2,318,655	2,917,327
Al Ismāʿīlīyah	— —	— —	— —	345,000	351,889	544,427
Al Jīzah	685,331	818,168	1,117,000	1,650,000	2,419,247	3,700,054
Al Minūfīyah	1,159,701	1,165,015	1,260,000	1,458,000	1,710,982	2,227,087
Al Minyā	928,259	1,044,201	1,476,000	1,706,000	2,055,739	2,648,043
Al Qāhirah	1,312,096	2,090,654	1,726,000	4,220,000	5,084,463	6,052,836
Al Qalyūbīyah	610,157	693,908	758,000	1,212,000	1,674,006	2,514,244
Al Wādī al Jadīd	29,109	32,503	N/A	59,000	84,645	113,838
Ash Sharqīyah	1,120,826	1,345,829	1,635,000	2,108,000	2,621,208	3,420,119
As Suways	49,686	107,244	163,000	264,000	194,001	326,820
Aswān	305,096	290,842	340,000	521,000	619,932	801,408
Asyūṭ	1,205,321	1,374,454	1,203,000	1,418,000	1,695,378	2,223,034
Banī Suwayf	561,312	612,027	793,000	928,000	1,108,615	1,442,981
Būr Saʿīd	161,146	245,932	416,000	283,000	262,620	399,793
Dumyāṭ	40,332	53,631	333,000	432,000	557,115	741,264
Janūb Sīnāʾ	— —	— —	— —	— —	— —	28,988
Kafr ash Shaykh	— —	— —	832,000	1,118,000	1,403,468	1,800,129
Maṭrūḥ	52,576	74,839	N/A	124,000	112,772	160,567
Qinā	1,017,569	1,106,302	1,219,000	1,471,000	1,705,594	2,252,315
Shamal Sīnāʾ	18,011	37,670	N/A	131,000	10,104	171,505
Sūhāj	1,118,402	1,283,468	1,449,000	1,689,000	1,924,960	2,455,134
	15,920,694	18,966,767	21,675,000	30,076,000	36,656,180	48,205,049

EL SALVADOR

ISO = SV/FIPS = ES   Language = Spanish   Time zone = -6   Capital = San Salvador

El Salvador has been an independent country since 1841. There has been no change to the names, number, or capitals of its departments in the 20th century. The capital of La Libertad has had two names, but they have both been in use throughout the century.

Other names of country: República de El Salvador (formal); Republic of El Salvador (formal–English); Salvador (obsolete).

Origin of name: After the city of San Salvador, Spanish for Holy Savior, in honor of Christ.

division	ISO	FIPS	population	area-km	area-mi	capital
Ahuachapán	AH	ES01	260,563	1,240	479	Ahuachapán
Cabañas	CA	ES02	136,293	1,104	426	Sensuntepeque
Chalatenango	CH	ES03	180,627	2,017	779	Chalatenango
Cuscatlán	CU	ES04	167,290	756	292	Cojutepeque
La Libertad	LI	ES05	522,071	1,653	638	Nueva San Salvador (Santa Tecla)
La Paz	PA	ES06	246,147	1,224	472	Zacatecoluca
La Unión	UN	ES07	251,143	2,074	801	La Unión
Morazán	MO	ES08	166,772	1,447	559	San Francisco Gotera
San Miguel	SM	ES09	380,442	2,077	802	San Miguel
San Salvador	SS	ES10	1,477,766	886	342	San Salvador
Santa Ana	SA	ES11	451,620	2,023	781	Santa Ana
San Vicente	SV	ES12	135,471	1,184	457	San Vicente
Sonsonate	SO	ES13	354,641	1,226	473	Sonsonate
Usulután	US	ES14	317,079	2,130	823	Usulután
			5,047,925	21,041	8,124	

Status: These divisions are departamentos (departments).
ISO: Codes from ISO 3166-2.
FIPS: Codes from FIPS PUB 10-4.
Population: 1992 census.
Area-km: Square kilometers.
Area-mi: Square miles.
Territorial extent: There are long-standing boundary disputes between El Salvador and Honduras.

La Unión includes some islands in the Gulf of Fonseca, of which the largest are Isla Meanguera, Isla Conchagüita, and Isla Zacatillo.

Origins of names:

Cabañas: Spanish for huts, cabins.
La Libertad: Spanish for liberty.
La Paz: Spanish for peace.
La Unión: Spanish for union, unity.

Morazán: Named for Francisco Morazán (1799–1842), Central American revolutionary.
San Salvador: Spanish for Holy Savior.

Population history:

division	1930	1945	1961	1971	1981	1992
Ahuachapán	79,033	109,495	131,000	183,682	241,323	260,563
Cabañas	59,081	88,162	95,000	139,312	179,909	136,293
Chalatenango	83,216	120,568	130,000	186,003	235,757	180,627
Cuscatlán	83,363	112,186	113,000	158,458	203,978	167,290
La Libertad	118,360	154,620	203,000	293,076	388,538	522,071
La Paz	85,632	120,729	131,000	194,196	249,635	246,147
La Unión	74,568	113,645	148,000	230,103	309,879	251,143
Morazán	75,661	111,526	119,000	170,706	215,163	166,772
San Miguel	126,582	180,565	232,000	337,325	434,047	380,442
San Salvador	191,125	245,599	463,000	681,656	979,683	1,477,766 ➤

division	1930	1945	1961	1971	1981	1992
Santa Ana	154,493	207,237	259,000	375,186	445,462	451,620
San Vicente	77,724	107,400	113,000	160,534	206,959	135,471
Sonsonate	100,217	130,717	167,000	239,688	321,989	354,641
Usulután	125,306	175,400	207,000	304,369	399,912	317,079
	1,434,361	1,977,849	2,511,000	3,654,294	4,812,234	5,047,925

EQUATORIAL GUINEA

ISO = GQ/FIPS = EK   Language = Spanish   Time zone = +1   Capital = Malabo

At the start of the 20th century, there were three Spanish colonies called Elobey, Annobón y Corisco; Fernando Póo; and Guinea Continental Española. In 1909 they were united under one administration, forming Territorios Españoles del Golfo de Guinea. The more convenient name Guinea Española was used increasingly, and finally became official. On 1935-04-16, the colony was subdivided into two districts: Fernando Póo (capital Santa Isabel, included Annobón Island) and Guinea Continental (capital Bata, included Corisco and Elobey). On 1960-04-01, the two districts became Spanish overseas provinces under the names Fernando Póo and Río Muni. On 1963-12-20 the provinces were combined once more into Guinea Ecuatorial, an autonomous region. On 1968-10-12 it became an independent country.

Other names of country: Ækvatorialguinea (Danish); Äquatorialguinea (German); Ekvatorial-Guinea (Norwegian); Ekvatorialguinea (Swedish); Equatoriaal Guinee (Dutch); Guinea Ecuatorial (Spanish); Guinea Equatoriale (Italian); Guinée équatoriale (French); Guiné Equatorial (Portuguese); Miðbaugs-Gínea (Icelandic); Päiväntasaajan Guinea (Finnish); Republic of Equatorial Guinea (formal–English); República de Guinea Ecuatorial (formal).

Origin of name: Descriptive: lies near the equator and on the Gulf of Guinea (see Guinea).

division	ISO	FIPS	reg	population	area-km	area-mi	capital
Annobón	AN	EK03	I	2,006	17	7	San Antonio de Palea
Bioko Norte	BN	EK04	I	46,221	776	300	Malabo
Bioko Sur	BS	EK05	I	10,969	1,241	479	Luba
Centro Sur	CS	EK06	C	52,393	9,931	3,834	Evinayong
Kié-Ntem	KN	EK07	C	70,202	3,943	1,522	Ebebiyín
Litoral	LI	EK08	C	66,370	6,665	2,573	Bata
Wele-Nzás	WN	EK09	C	51,839	5,478	2,115	Mongomo
				300,000	28,051	10,830	

Status: These divisions are provinces.
ISO: Codes from ISO 3166-2.
FIPS: Codes from FIPS PUB 10-4.
Reg: Equatorial Guinea is also divided into two regions. ISO 3166-2 lists them, assigning them the one-letter codes shown in the reg column. These regions were the former provinces of the country. Their codes and names according to FIPS are shown.

reg	name	FIPS	FIPS name	reg	name	FIPS	FIPS name
C	Región Continental	EK02	Río Muni	I	Región Insular	EK01	Bioko

Population: 1983 census.
Area-km: Square kilometers.
Area-mi: Square miles.
Further subdivisions: Before 1963, Fernando Póo was subdivided into four regional districts, and Río Muni was subdivided into 11 municipios.
Territorial extent: Litoral province contains the islands of Corisco, Elobey Chico, and Elobey Grande in the Muni estuary.
Origins of names:

Annobón: From Portuguese *anno bom*: happy new year, discovered on 1471-01-01.

Bioko: After Adolfo Bioco, who in turn was born in a village named Bioko. Norte: North. Sur: South.

Centro Sur: Spanish for Center-South.

Fernando Póo: after the Portuguese navigator Fernando Póo, who discovered it and called it Ilha Formosa (beautiful island).

Litoral: Spanish for Coastal.

Macías Nguema Biyogo: After Francisco Macías (later Masie) Nguema Biyogo Ñegue Ndong, dictator from 1968 until his overthrow in 1979.

Río Muni: From the estuary at the southwestern corner of the territory, misnamed as a river by early explorers. Muni is a Pamue word for big.

Change history:

1973   Name of Fernando Póo island and province changed to Macías Nguema Biyogo (sometimes given as just Macías Nguema); name of Río Muni province changed to Mbini; name of national capital changed from Santa Isabel to Malabo; name of Annobón island changed to Pagalu.

1979   Name of Macías Nguema Biyogo changed to Bioko; name of Mbini restored to Río Muni; name of Pagalu restored to Annobón.

~1990   The provinces became regions, and were subdivided into the seven new provinces.

Other names of subdivisions:

Fernando Póo: Fernando Po (variant)

ERITREA

ISO = ER/FIPS = ER   Languages = Tigrinya, Arabic, and others   Time zone = +3   Capital = Asmara

In 1889, Italy consolidated its possessions on the Red Sea coast, and declared Eritrea to be a colony on 1890-01-01. In 1936 it became a province of Italian East Africa (Africa Orientale Italiana), along with Ethiopia and Italian Somaliland. The British expelled the Italians in 1941. Eritrea remained a British protectorate until 1952-09-15. The United Nations voted to create a federation of Eritrea and Ethiopia, which lasted uneasily until 1962-11-14, when Ethiopia took full control. Eritrea regained its independence by force of arms. The separation was ratified by a referendum, and independence became official on 1993-05-27. The boundaries of Eritrea have changed somewhat during the century.

Other names of country: Dewlet Eritrea (formal–Arabic); Erítrea (Icelandic); Eritréia (Portuguese); Érythrée (French); Hagare Eretra (formal–Tigrinya); State of Eritrea (formal–English).

Origin of name: From Italian *mare Eritreo*, a name for the Red Sea.

division	ISO	capital	division	ISO	capital
Akele Guzai	AG	Adi K'eyih (Adi Caieh, Adi Qayeh)	Hamasien	HA	Asmara (Asmera, Asmra)
Asmara	AS	Asmara (Asmera, Asmra)	Sahel	SA	Nakfa
Barka	BA	Ak'ordat (Agordat)	Semhar	SM	Massawa (Massaua, Mesewa, Mits'iwa)
Denkalia	DE	Assab (Aseb, Asseb)	Senhit	SN	Keren (Karen)
Gash-Setit	GS	Barentu	Seraye	SR	Mendefera (Mendeferas)

Status: Each division is an awraja (province).

ISO: Codes from ISO 3166-2.

FIPS: No FIPS codes have been assigned to Eritrean provinces yet. The code ER covers the country.

Capitals: Followed by variant spellings.

Territorial extent: Eritrea includes Red Sea islands near its coast. The main group is the Dahlak Archipelago, whose largest island is Dehalak Deset, offshore from Massawa. There are a number of smaller islands near Assab, the largest of which is Halba Deset. The Hanish Islands are disputed between Eritrea and Yemen; the International Court of Justice is arbitrating. These include Jazirat Jabal Zuqar (Mount Zuqar Island), also spelled Zugur or Zugura; Jazirat al Hanish al Kabir (Great Hanish Island); Jazirat al Hanish al Sqier, and a number of smaller islands.

Origins of names:

Asmara: Tigrinya for blooming woods; or, Amharic for good pasture

Change history:

1936   As part of Italian East Africa, Eritrea was subdivided into five commisariats (Bassopiano Occidentale, Bassopiano Orientale e Dancalia, Cheren, Confine Meridionale, Hamasien) and one autonomous residence (Dancalia Meridionale).

When the new constitution takes effect, Eritrea is supposed to be reorganized into six provinces. The following list shows their names with variants, capitals, and relation to the existing provinces.

name	capital	corresponds roughly to
Anseba (Ansaba)	Keren	Barka, Senhit
Debub (South)	Mendeferas	Akele Guzai, Seraye
Debubawi Keyh Bahri (Southern Red Sea)	Assab	Denkalia
Gash Barka	Barentu	Barka, Gash-Setit, Seraye
Maekel (Central)	Asmara	Asmara, Hamasien
Semenawi Keyh Bahri (Northern Red Sea)	Massawa	Akele Guzai, Denkalia, Sahel, Semhar

Other names of subdivisions:

Akele Guzai: Akale Guzay, Akole Guzay (variant)

Barka: Baraka (variant)

Denkalia: Aseb, Denakil (variant)

Gash-Setit: Gash and Setit (English); Gashe na Setit (variant)

Hamasien: Hamasen, Hamassien (variant)

Sahel: Sahil (variant)

Semhar: Mits'iwa, Samhar (variant)

ESTONIA

ISO = EE/FIPS = EN   Language = Estonian   Time zone = +2 [d]   Capital = Tallinn

Modern Estonia corresponds to the Russian government (guberniya) of Estonia, plus the northern part of the government of Livonia, as they stood in 1900. In 1918-02, it declared its independence, with essentially its present borders. Estonia was occupied by the army of the Soviet Union in 1940, and became a constituent republic of the U.S.S.R., the Estonian Soviet Socialist Republic, on 1940-08-06. The annexation was never recognized by the United States. Estonia once again proclaimed its independence, this time from a disintegrating Soviet Union, on 1991-08-20.

Other names of country: Eesti Vabariik (formal); Eistland (Icelandic); Esthonia (obsolete); Esthonie (obsolete–French); Estland (Danish, Dutch, German, Norwegian, Swedish); Estlandija (obsolete–Estonian); Estônia (Portuguese); Estonie (French); Republic of Estonia (formal–English); Viro (Finnish).

Origin of name: Possibly meaning shore dwellers, from Baltic *aueist*: water dweller.

division	abv	ISO	FIPS	capital	division	abv	ISO	FIPS	capital
Harju	HA	37	EN01	Tallinn	Põlva	PL	65	EN12	Põlva
Hiiu	HI	39	EN02	Kärdla	Rapla	RA	70	EN13	Rapla
Ida-Viru	IV	44	EN03	Jõhvi	Saare	SA	74	EN14	Kuressaare
Järva	JR	51	EN04	Paide	Tartu	TA	78	EN18	Tartu
Jõgeva	JN	49	EN05	Jõgeva	Valga	VG	82	EN19	Valga
Lääne	LN	57	EN07	Haapsalu	Viljandi	VD	84	EN20	Viljandi
Lääne-Viru	LV	59	EN08	Rakvere	Võru	VR	86	EN21	Võru
Pärnu	PR	67	EN11	Pärnu					

Status: These divisions are maakonnad (sing. maakond: counties).

Abv: Two-letter code for international compatibility (defined by the author).

ISO: Codes from ISO 3166-2.

FIPS: Codes from FIPS PUB 10-4.

Further subdivisions: The counties are divided into linnad (sing. linn: towns) and vallad (sing. vald: parishes). In 1997 there were 254 towns and parishes. The parishes are further subdivided into alevid (alev: borough), alevikud (alevik: small borough), and külad (küla: village). Some of the towns are subdivided into linnaosad (linnaosa: district).

Territorial extent: Estonia includes many islands. The largest ones are Saaremaa (Saare county), Hiiumaa (Hiiu county), Muhu, and Vormsi in the Baltic Sea, Ruhnu and Kihnu in the Gulf of Riga, Nais, Osmus, and Prangli in the Gulf of Finland, and Piiri in Lake Peipus.

Change history:

1917	Name of capital of Estonia changed from Revel to Tallinn.
1918–1940	During its period of independence, Estonia was divided into eleven provinces. This table shows them, with their populations according to the 1934 census, and the approximate correspondence between them and the present-day divisions. The Soviet Union apparently used these divisions, but modified them soon after the end of World War II.

province	population	area-km	capital	modern counties
Harju	243,122	5,682	Tallinn	Harju, Rapla
Järva	58,954	2,761	Paide	Järva
Lääne	75,039	4,779	Haapsalu	Lääne
Pärnu	94,653	5,457	Pärnu	Pärnu
Petseri	64,712	1,891	Petseri	— —
Ösel	55,851	2,963	Kuressaare	Hiiu, Saare
Tartu	181,296	7,016	Tartu	Jõngeva, Tartu
Valga	39,278	1,510	Valga	Valga
Viljandi	74,993	4,059	Viljandi	Viljandi
Viru	146,318	7,384	Rakvere	Ida-Viru, Lääne-Viru
Võru	83,145	4,043	Võru	Põlva, Võru
	1,117,361	47,545		

1944	Petseri province annexed to Pskov Oblast of the Russian Republic.
1990	The Soviet-era divisions, rajoonid (rayoni, or districts), became counties, and their Estonian names were restored.
1992	Under new constitution, six independent cities merged with the surrounding counties: Kohtla-Järve (FIPS code EN06), Narva (EN09), and Sillamäe (EN15) merged with Ida-Viru county; Pärnu (EN10) merged with Pärnu; Tallinn (EN16) merged with Harju; and Tartu (EN17) merged with Tartu.

Other names of subdivisions: All of the counties may be written with -maa suffixed to their names, especially Hiiumaa and Saaremaa, which are also island names. Officially preferred, but less common, are the forms "Harju maakond," "Hiiu maakond," etc.

Hiiu: Dagö (German)   Tartu: Dorpat (German)
Saare: Ösel (German)   Viljandi: Vilyandi (variant)

ETHIOPIA

ISO = ET/FIPS = ET   Language = Amharic   Time zone = +3   Capital = Addis Ababa

Europeans have used the names Ethiopia and Abyssinia interchangeably for the country in this location. Italy had territorial ambitions over the region in the 19th century. However, as of 1900, Italy in fact controlled only Eritrea. Ethiopia's independence was recognized by the European powers in 1906. In 1935, Italy invaded, and in 1936-06 Ethiopia was made part of Italian East Africa (Africa Orientale Italiana), along with Eritrea and Italian Somaliland. The British expelled the Italians in

1941 and liberated Ethiopia. The United Nations voted to create a federation of Eritrea and Ethiopia, which lasted from 1952 until 1962, when Ethiopia annexed Eritrea. Eritrea became an independent country again on 1993-05-27. The boundaries of Ethiopia have changed somewhat during the century, and the border with Somalia has never been finally established.

Other names of country: Äthiopien (German); Ethiopië (Dutch); Éthiopie (French); Etiopia (Finnish, Italian, Norwegian); Etiopía (Spanish); Etiópia (Portuguese); Etíópía (Icelandic); Etiopien (Danish, Swedish); Ityopia (formal); People's Democratic Republic of Ethiopia (formal–English).

Origin of name: Greek Aithiopis, from *aithe*: burn, *opsis*: appearance (i.e. dark-skinned natives appeared burnt).

division	ISO	division	ISO
Addis Ababa	AA	Harari People	HA
Afar	AF	Oromia	OR
Amhara	AM	Somali	SO
Benshangul-Gumaz	BE	Southern Nations, Nationalities and Peoples	SN
Gambela Peoples	GA	Tigray	TI

Status: These divisions are astedader akababiwach (administrative regions), except for Addis Ababa, which is a federal capital district.

ISO: Codes from ISO 3166-2.

Further subdivisions: As of 1953, there were twelve teklay ghizatoch (provinces), subdivided into 76 awraji ghizatoch (subprovinces), which were subdivided into wereda (districts), which were subdivided into mikitil wereda (subdistricts). By 1965, the number of provinces had increased to 14, and the number of subprovinces to 82. In 1974, the new military government changed the status of the fourteen provinces to kifle hager (regions), and reorganized their subdivisions. As a result, there were 102 awraja subdivided into 556 wereda. Another reorganization in 1991 left twelve rasgez akababiwach (autonomous regions) and two chartered cities, which were subdivided into about 600 wereda.

Territorial extent: In the territorial division which prevailed up until 1987, Gojam contained the island of Daga, or Dek, in Lake Tana. Eritrea contained many Red Sea islands, as described in the country listing for Eritrea.

Origins of names:

Addis Ababa: Amharic for the new flower

Harar: Amharic *harar*, corruption of a word meaning commercial station

Somali: see Somalia

Change history:

1936	As part of Italian East Africa, Ethiopia was subdivided into four governments: Amhara, Galla and Sidama, Harar, and Shoa.
1952-09-15	Eritrea joined Ethiopia in a federation.
1962	Eritrea became province.
~1963	Bale province split from Hararge.
~1965	Capital of Gamo Gofa province moved from Chencha to Arba Minch.
1974	Provinces changed to regions.
~1978	Capital of Ilubabor province moved from Gore to Metu; capital of Sidamo province moved from Yirgalem to Awasa.
1981	Addis Ababa region split from Shewa; Aseb region split from Eritrea.

This was the division of Ethiopia prevailing in 1987:

division	FIPS	population	area-km	area-mi	awr	capital
Addis Ababa		1,654,327	218	100		Addis Ababa
Arsi	ET01	1,860,606	23,500	9,100	3	Asela
Aseb		101,352				Aseb
Bale	ET03	1,126,697	124,600	48,100	5	Goba
Eritrea	ET04	2,938,113	117,600	45,400	9	Asmara
Gamo Gofa	ET05	1,395,331	39,500	15,300	4	Arba Minch
Gojam	ET06	3,632,276	61,600	23,800	7	Debre Markos
Gonder	ET02	3,270,440	74,200	28,600	7	Gonder
Harerge	ET07	4,657,859	259,700	100,300	13	Harer
Ilubabor	ET08	1,078,308	47,400	18,300	5	Metu
Kefa	ET09	2,740,773	54,600	21,100	6	Jima ➤

division	FIPS	population	area-km	area-mi	awr	capital
Shewa	ET10	9,059,917	85,200	32,900	11	Addis Ababa
Sidamo	ET11	4,241,827	117,300	45,300	6	Awasa
Tigray	ET12	2,700,921	65,900	25,400	8	Mekele
Welega	ET13	2,770,598	71,200	27,500	6	Nekemte
Welo	ET14	4,075,959	79,400	30,700	12	Dese
		47,305,304	1,221,918	471,900	102	

FIPS: Codes from FIPS PUB 10-4.
Population: 1988 estimate.
Awr: number of awraja by province.

1987-09   Ethiopia reorganized into 25 administrative regions and five autonomous regions; however, the new administrative structure may never have been fully implemented. Here is a table describing the new divisions.

division	FIPS	population	area-km	area-mi	alternate names
Addis Ababa	ET15	2,379,500	5,200	2,000	
Ārsī	ET01	1,984,000	23,700	9,200	Arusi
Āseb	ET16	451,900	69,800	26,900	Assab
Assosa	ET17	525,900	23,100	8,900	Āsosa
Balē	ET38	977,300	67,300	26,000	Mendebo
Borena	ET18	668,800	94,000	36,300	
Dirē Dawa	ET22	476,000	29,300	11,300	
East Gojam	ET28	1,563,200	13,900	5,400	Misrak Gojam
East Hārergē	ET29	2,552,300	90,600	35,000	Misrak Hārergē
East Shewa		934,500	12,800	4,900	Misrak Shewa
Eritrea	ET36	3,138,600	93,700	36,200	Ērtra
Gambēla	ET23	179,400	26,100	10,100	Gambella
Gamo Gofa	ET39				Gemu Gwefa
Īlubabor	ET40	2,867,900	35,100	13,600	Illubabor
Kefa	ET41	1,057,900	40,100	15,500	Keffa
Metekel	ET24	383,300	30,500	11,800	Metekel Nazaret
Nazrēt	ET30				
North Gonder	ET19	1,873,000	62,000	23,900	Debub Gonder
North Omo	ET32	2,806,000	29,900	11,500	Debub Omo
North Shewa	ET20	2,364,300	27,000	10,400	Debub Shewa
North Welo	ET21	1,491,700	30,800	11,900	Debub Welo
Ogadēn	ET31	833,200	179,300	69,200	
Sīdamo	ET42	2,741,700	20,700	8,000	
South Gonder	ET33	1,719,900	17,100	6,600	Semēn Gonder
South Omo		248,000	22,000	8,500	Semēn Omo
South Shewa	ET34	2,977,500	16,800	6,500	Semēn Shewa
South Welo	ET35	2,461,700	20,700	8,000	Semēn Welo
Tigray	ET37	2,757,100	53,400	20,600	Tigre
Welega	ET43	2,460,300	42,600	16,400	Walaga
West Gojam	ET25	2,032,800	17,300	6,700	Mirab Gojam
West Hārergē	ET26	1,364,200	33,200	12,800	Mirab Hārergē
West Shewa	ET27	2,702,000	23,200	9,000	Mirab Shewa
		50,973,900	1,251,200	483,100	

Status: Āseb, Dirē Dawa, Eritrea, Ogadēn, and Tigray are autonomous regions. The rest are all administrative regions. Note that this table shows 27 autonomous regions instead of the 25 expected. The Central Statistical Authority of Ethiopia doesn't mention Gamo Gofa or Nazrēt. The FIPS document doesn't mention East Shewa or South Omo, and uses the name Omo rather than North Omo.
FIPS: Codes from FIPS PUB 10-4.
Population: 1982 estimate.

1991   Ethiopia reorganized into twelve autonomous regions and two chartered cities. This division did not last long enough to be recognized by the FIPS standard. Sources differ about the names of these divisions. Apparently Addis Ababa and Harer were the chartered cities, and the autonomous regions were Afar, Agew, Amhara, Benishangul, Gambela, Gurage-Hadiya-Kambata, Kefa, Omo, Oromo, Sidamo, Somali, and Tigray.

1993-05-27   Eritrea became independent. Āseb and Eritrea ceased being regions of Ethiopia.
~1995   Ethiopia reorganized into nine administrative regions and one federal capital district.

Other names of subdivisions: Many of the variants shown here are just different transliterations from the Amharic alphabet.

Addis Ababa: Ādīs Ābaba, Addis Abeba, Adis-Abeba, Ādīs Ābeba (variant)

Amhara: Amara (variant)

Arsi: Arssi, Arusi, Arussi, Ārsı (variant)

Bale: Balē, Mendebo (variant)

Benishangul: Beni Shangul, Bénishangul, Benshangul-Gumaz (variant)

Eritrea: Ertra (variant; see also country listing for Eritrea)

Gamo Gofa: Gamu Gofa, Gemu Gefa, Gemu Gofa, Gemu Goffa, Gemu Gwefa (with or without hyphen) (variant)

Gojam: Gojjam, Gwejam (variant)

Gonder: Bagemder, Begemder, Begemdir, Begemdir and Simen, Gondar (variant)

Gurage-Hadiya-Kambata: Gurage-Hadiya-Wolayta, Gurage Kembatahadiya (variant)

Harerge: Harar, Hararge, Harer, Hārergē (variant)

Ilubabor: Illabobor, Illubabor, Ilubbabor, Īlubabor (variant)

Kefa: Kafa, Kaffa (variant)

Shewa: Shawa, Shoa (variant)

Sidamo: Sidama, Sīdamo, Sidamo-Boran, Sidamo-Borana (variant)

Tigray: Tegré, Tigrai, Tigre (variant)

Welega: Walaga, Wallaga, Wallega, Wellega, Wollega (variant)

Welo: Elo, Wallo, Wollo (variant)

FALKLAND ISLANDS

ISO = FK/FIPS = FK   Language = English   Time zone = -4 [d]   Capital = Stanley

The Falkland Islands have been a British colony throughout the 20th century. The relationship between the Falkland Islands and other British possessions in the area has varied. From 1908 to 1962, Falkland Islands Dependencies consisted of South Georgia, the South Orkney Islands, the South Shetland Islands, the Antarctic Peninsula, and the Palmer Archipelago. On 1962-03-03, the United Kingdom formed a new colony called British Antarctic Territory, incorporating that part of the territories south of the parallel of 60° South. Since the Antarctic Treaty had already been ratified, the British Antarctic Territory should be considered part of the Antarctica listing at that point. Under a new constitution which took effect on 1985-10-03, South Georgia and the South Sandwich Islands are no longer a dependency of the Falkland Islands. FIPS reflected this change by creating a new country entry and code for South Georgia and the South Sandwich Islands, and also by changing the code for Falkland Islands from FA to the present FK.

Argentina, which calls them the Islas Malvinas, has claimed them since the 19th century. It asserted its claim by invasion in 1982, but was defeated. If Argentina's claim were accepted, the islands would be part of the territory of Tierra del Fuego.

Other names of country: Falklandeilanden (Dutch); Falklandinseln, Malwinen (German); Falklandsöarna (Swedish); Falklandsøyene (Norwegian); Îles Falkland, Îles Malouines (French); Islas Malvinas (Spanish); Isole Falkland, Isole Malvine (Italian).

Origin of name: after Falkland Sound (between East and West Falkland), which was named in 1690 for Viscount Lucius Cary Falkland, treasurer of British Navy. 18th-century seal hunters called them "Îles Malouines" after their home port, Saint-Malo.

division	abv	population	area-km	area-mi
Falkland Islands	FK	2,121	12,200	4,700

Status: This division is the whole of the country, treated as a division for compatibility.

Abv: Two-letter code for international compatibility (defined by the author).

Population: 1991 census.

Area-km: Square kilometers.

Area-mi: Square miles.

Territorial extent: Falkland Islands includes the main islands of East Falkland and West Falkland, and a number of nearby smaller islands, of which the farthest out are Beauchêne Island and the Jason Islands.

FAROE ISLANDS

ISO = FO/FIPS = FO   Languages = Faroese, Danish   Time zone = +0 [d]   Capital = Thorshavn

The Faroes are a county of Denmark with limited autonomy.

Other names of country: Færeyjar (Icelandic); Faeroer (Dutch); Faeroes (obsolete); Færøerne (Danish); Færøyane (Norwegian nynorsk); Færøyene (Norwegian bokmål); Färöarna (Swedish); Färöer (German); Färsaaret (Finnish); Føroyar (Faroese); Föroyari, Isole Färöer (Italian); Ilhas Faroë (Portuguese); Îles Féroé (French); Islas Feroé (Spanish).

Origin of name: Faroese *Føroyar*: sheep islands.

division	abv	population	area-km	area-mi	division	abv	population	area-km	area-mi
Norderøerne	NO	5,931	241	93	Suderø Nordre	SN	3,102	97	37
Østerø	OS	10,093	286	111	Suderø Søndre	SS	2,778	70	27
Sandø	SA	1,757	125	48	Vågø	VG	2,966	188	73
Strømø	ST	32,698	456	176			59,325	1,462	565

Status: These divisions are syssel (regions).

Abv: Two-letter code for international compatibility (defined by the author).

Population: 1985 estimate.

Area-km: Square kilometers.

Area-mi: Square miles.

Further subdivisions: The counties are further subdivided into kommunur (communes).

Territorial extent: Norderøerne includes the islands of Bordø (Borðoy), Fuglø (Fugloy), Kalsø (Kalsoy), Kunø (Kunoy), Svinø (Svínoy), Viderø (Viðoy), and adjacent islets.

Østerø includes the island of Østerø and adjacent islets.

Sandø includes the islands of Sandø, Skuø (Skúvoy, Skuva), Store Dimon (Stóra Dímun, Great Dimon), and adjacent islets.

Strømø includes the islands of Strømø, Hestø (Hestur), Kolter (Koltur), Nolsø (Nólsoy), and adjacent islets.

Suderø Nordre includes the northern part of Suderø, Lille Dimon (Lítla Dímun, Little Dimon), and adjacent islets.

Suderø Søndre includes the southern part of Suderø and adjacent islets.

Vågø includes the islands of Vågø, Myggenæs (Mykines), and adjacent islets.

Other names of subdivisions:

Norderøerne: Norðoyar, Norderøer (variant)
Østerø: Eysturoy (variant)
Strømø: Stremoy, Streymoy (variant)

Vågø: Vágoy, Vágar, Vaagø (variant)
Sandø: Sandoy (variant)
Suderø: Suðuroy, Syderø (variant)

FIJI

ISO = FJ/FIPS = FJ   Languages = English, Fijian   Time zone = +12   Capital = Suva

Fiji was a British colony from 1874 until it was granted independence on 1970-10-10.

Other names of country: Fidji (French); Fídjieyjar (Icelandic); Fidschi (German); Fidži (Finnish); Figi (Italian); Fiyi, Viti (obsolete–Spanish); Republic of Fiji (formal–English).

Origin of name: from Viti (native name).

Spelling note: sometimes the letters -mb- are written as -b-, -nd- as -d-, and -ng- as -g-.

division	abv	ISO	FIPS	population	area-km	area-mi	capital
Central	CE	C	FJ01	154,000	4,293	1,658	Suva
Eastern	EA	E	FJ02	38,000	1,376	531	Levuka
Northern	NO	N	FJ03	84,000	6,199	2,393	Lambasa
Rotuma	RO	R	FJ04	3,000	46	18	Motusa
Western	WE	W	FJ05	195,000	6,360	2,456	Lautoka
				474,000	18,274	7,056	

Status: These divisions are actually called divisions, except for Rotuma, which is a dependency.

Abv: Two-letter code for international compatibility (defined by the author).

ISO: Codes from ISO 3166-2.

FIPS: Codes from FIPS PUB 10-4.

Population: 1966 census.

Area-km: Square kilometers.

Area-mi: Square miles.

Further subdivisions: Fiji is also subdivided into provinces. The following table shows the provinces, and their relationship to the divisions. The capitals of the provinces have the same names as the provinces themselves. (Rotuma is not a province, but is included for completeness.)

province	population	area-km	division code	province	population	area-km	division code
Kandavu	9,000	478	EA	Nandronga-Navosa	37,000	2,385	WE
Lau	16,000	487	EA	Ra	22,000	1,341	WE
Lomaiviti	13,000	411	EA	Rewa	70,000	272	CE
Mathuata	44,000	2,004	NO	Rotuma	3,000	46	RO
Mba	136,000	2,634	WE	Serua	8,000	830	CE
Mbua	10,000	1,379	NO	Tailevu	34,000	955	CE
Naitasiri	39,000	1,666	CE	Thakaundrove	30,000	2,816	NO
Namosi	3,000	570	CE				

Territorial extent: Central contains the southeastern part of the main island of Viti Levu and the small islands of Mbengga and Yanutha.

Eastern contains the Lau Group (Lakemba, Fulanga, Kambara, Ongea Levu, etc.), the Lomaiviti Group (Koro, Ngau, Ovolau, and the Exploring Islands [Vanua Mbalavu, Mango, etc.]), Kandavu, Matuku, Moala, Ono-i-lau, and Totoya.

Northern contains Vanua Levu (the second-largest in the group), Cikobia, Kioa, Nggamea, Rambi, Taveuni, Yandua, and Yathata.

Rotuma contains Rotuma and nearby islets, and is isolated from the rest of the group.

Western contains the northern and western parts of Viti Levu, the Yasawa Group (Nathula, Naviti, Waya, and Yasawa), Vatulele, and the isolated Ceva-i-Ra (Conway Reef).

FINLAND

ISO = FI/FIPS = FI   Languages = Finnish, Swedish   Time zone = +2 [d]   Capital = Helsinki

Finland was a grand duchy of the Russian Empire in 1900, enjoying a good measure of autonomy. It declared its independence on 1917-07-20. During World War II, Finland and the Soviet Union fought each other. Finland had to make several territorial concessions. Since 1947, Finland's borders have remained intact. Swedish is an official language, but is spoken by a small minority, so names given here are Finnish unless otherwise stated.

Other names of country: Finlande (French); Finlandia (Italian, Spanish); Finlândia (Portuguese); Finnland (German,

Icelandic); Republic of Finland (formal–English); Republiken Finland (Swedish); Suomen Tasavalta (formal); Suomi (Finnish).

Origin of name: Land of Finns, from Germanic *finna*: fish scale, since *suomu* is Finnish for fish scale.

division	abv	population	area-km	area-mi	capital
Åland	AV	25,392	1,552	599	Mariehamn
Eastern Finland	IS	603,724	60,720	23,444	Mikkeli
Lapland	LP	199,051	98,946	38,203	Rovaniemi
Oulu	OU	452,942	61,572	23,773	Oulu
Southern Finland	ES	2,037,147	34,378	13,273	Hämeenlinna
Western Finland	LS	1,829,093	80,975	31,265	Turku
		5,147,349	338,143	130,557	

Status: These divisions are läänit (sing. lääni, Swedish län: provinces), except for Åland, which is an itsehallinnollinen maakunta (autonomous province).

Abv: Two-letter code for international compatibility (defined by the author).

Population: 1997-12-31 estimate.

Area-km: Square kilometers.

Area-mi: Square miles.

Post codes: Finland has five-digit postal codes, but they do not correlate to provinces well enough to list here.

Further subdivisions: The provinces are divided into twenty regional councils, which are further subdivided into kaupunki (Swedish stad: urban communes) and kunta (rural communes). The total number of communes has been decreasing, from 475 in 1976 to 452 in 1998. The following list shows the regional councils for each province. In parentheses are the English name of the region if different, and its NUTS code.

Åland: Ahvenanmaa (FL2)
Eastern Finland: Etelä-Savo (South Savo, FL13), Pohjois-Karjala (North Karelia, FL13), Pohjois-Savo (Savo, FL13)
Lapland: Lappi (FL15)
Oulu: Kainuu (FL13), Pohjois-Pohjanmaa (North Ostrobothnia, FL15)
Southern Finland: Etelä-Karjala (South Karelia, FL12), Häme (FL12), Itä-Uusimaa (Eastern Uusimaa, FL11), Kymenlaakso (FL12), Päijät-Häme (FL12), Uusimaa (FL11)

Western Finland: Etelä-Pohjanmaa (South Ostrobothnia, FL14), Keski-Pohjanmaa (Central Ostrobothnia, FL14), Keski-Suomi (Central Finland, FL14), Pirkanmaa (Tampere Region, FL12), Satakunta (FL12), Vaasan Rannikkoseuta (Ostrobothnia, FL14), Varsinais-Suomi (Southwest Finland, FL12)

The overall descriptions of NUTS regions are FL11 = Uusimaa, FL12 = Etelä-Suomi, FL13 = Itä-Suomi, FL14 = Väli-Suomi, FL15 = Pohjois-Suomi, and FL1 (includes FL11–FL15) = Manner-Suomi (continental Finland).

Unfortunately, some of the administrative divisions have the same names but different areas.

Territorial extent: Åland includes islands west of the Skiftet, or Kihti (channel), and east of Ålands Hav. The largest is Åland island. Among the easternmost are Kökar and Brändö.

Oulu includes the island of Hailuoto.

Southern Finland includes the island of Haapasaari and other small islands in the Gulf of Finland north of Ostrov Gogland.

Western Finland includes islands east of the Skiftet and north of Åland up to the midline of the Gulf of Bothnia. Among them are Kimito, Nagu, Bergö, and Vallgrund.

Origins of names:

Ahvenanmaa: Finnish *ahven*: perch (the fish) + *maa*: land. Åland comes from Swedish *å*: river, *land*: land.
Lappi: from Norse *Lappland*: the land at the end.
Mikkeli: named for the city, which was named for Saint Michael.
Pohjois-Karjala: Karjala (Karelia) comes from Finnish *karja*: herd.

Turku ja Pori: named for its two main cities (Finnish *ja*: and). Turku is a word for marketplace in the regional lingua franca.
Uusimaa: Finnish for new land. Its Swedish name, Nyland, means the same.
Vaasa: probably from King Gustavus Vasa I of Sweden (1496–1560), who created the Grand Duchy of Finland.

Change history:

1918	Ahvenanmaa split from Turku ja Pori province.
1921-10	Ahvenanmaa granted autonomous status by a decision of the League of Nations.
1938	Lappi province split from Oulu province.
1940-03-12	In peace treaty ending Finnish-Russian War, Finland ceded several border territories to the Soviet Union, including about half of Kymen province (with the port of Viborg), and part of Kuopio.
1945	Name of Viipuri province (Viborg in Swedish) changed to Kymi.
1947	In Paris peace treaty, Finland reaffirmed the cessions of 1940 (some of which it had temporarily reconquered), and ceded more land to the Soviet Union, including the strip of Lappi that had connected Finland to the Arctic Ocean around Petsamo.
1960-03-01	Pohjois-Karjala province split from Kuopio; Keski-Suomi province formed from parts of Häme, Kuopio, Mikkeli, and Vaasa.
1997-09-01	Finland reorganized. Before the reorganization, the divisions were as follows. Division names are shown in Finnish. They were all provinces except for Ahvenanmaa, which was an autonomous province.

division	ISO	FIPS	population	area-km	area-mi	capital	now
Ahvenanmaa	AL	FI01	25,008	1,552	599	Maarianhamina/Mariehamn	Åland
Häme	H	FI02	688,355	19,104	7,376	Hämeenlinna	Southern, Western
Keski-Suomi	X	FI03	255,879	19,357	7,474	Jyväskylä	Western
Kuopio	K	FI04	258,712	19,953	7,704	Kuopio	Eastern
Kymi	R	FI05	335,093	12,828	4,953	Kouvola	Southern
Lappi	L	FI06	202,434	98,937	38,200	Rovaniemi	Lapland
Mikkeli	M	FI07	207,875	21,660	8,363	Mikkeli	Eastern, Southern
Oulu	O	FI08	445,632	61,582	23,777	Oulu/Uleåborg	Oulu
Pohjois-Karjala	S	FI09	177,803	21,585	8,334	Joensuu	Eastern
Turku ja Pori	T	FI10	731,792	23,863	9,214	Turku/Åbo	Western
Uusimaa	U	FI11	1,277,800	10,404	4,017	Helsinki/Helsingfors	Southern
Vaasa	V	FI12	448,363	27,319	10,548	Vaasa/Vasa	Western
			5,054,746	338,144	130,559		

ISO: Codes from ISO 3166-2.
FIPS: Codes from FIPS PUB 10-4.
Population: 1993 estimate.
Capital: Finnish/Swedish names, where different.
Now: Modern province(s) in the same area.
Other names of subdivisions:

Åland: Ahvenanmaa maakunta (Finnish); Åland-Inseln (German); Álandseyjar (Icelandic); Ålands län (Swedish)
Eastern Finland: Itä-Suomen lääni (Finnish); Östra Finlands län (Swedish)
Lapland: Lapin lääni, Lappi (Finnish); Laponia (Spanish); Lapônia (Portuguese); Laponie (French); Lappland (Icelandic); Lapplands län (Swedish)

Oulu: Oulun lääni (Finnish); Uleåborgs län (Swedish)
Southern Finland: Etelä-Suomen lääni (Finnish); Södra Finlands län (Swedish)
Western Finland: Länsi-Suomen lääni (Finnish); Västra Finlands län (Swedish)

Former provinces:

Häme: Hämeen lääni (Finnish); Tavastehus län (Swedish)
Keski-Suomi: Central Finland (English); Keski-Suomen lääni (Finnish); Mellersta Finlands län (Swedish)
Kuopio: Kuopio län (Swedish); Kuopion lääni (Finnish)
Kymi: Kymen lääni (Finnish); Kymmene län (Swedish); Viborg (Swedish-obsolete); Viipuri (obsolete)
Mikkeli: Mikkelin lääni (Finnish); Saint Michels län (Swedish)
Pohjois-Karjala: Carelia del Norte (Spanish); North Karelia

(English); Pohjois-Karjalan lääni (Finnish); Norra Karelens län (Swedish)
Turku ja Pori: Turku-Pori, Turun ja Porin lääni (Finnish); Åbo-Björneborg, Åbo och Björneborgs län (Swedish)
Uusimaa: Nyland (Icelandic); Nylands län (Swedish); Uudenmaan lääni (Finnish)
Vaasa: Vaasan lääni (Finnish); Vasa län (Swedish); Wasa (obsolete)

FRANCE

ISO = FR/FIPS = FR Language = French Time zone = +1 ^d Capital = Paris

Alsace-Lorraine has changed hands several times between France and Germany. In the Franco-Prussian War of 1870, Germany won the territory. France recovered it in the Treaty of Versailles after World War I, and it has remained part of France ever since.

Other names of country: Frakkland (Icelandic); França (Portuguese); Francia (Italian, Spanish); Frankreich (German); Frankrig (Danish); Frankrijk (Dutch); Frankrike (Norwegian, Swedish); French Republic (formal–English); Ranska (Finnish); República Francesa (formal–Spanish); République Française (formal).

Origin of name: Land of the Franks.

division	abv	ISO	FIPS	NUTS	reg	population	area-km	area-mi	arr	capital
Ain	AI	01	FR01	FR711	V	471,000	5,762	2,225	4	Bourg-en-Bresse
Aisne	AS	02	FR02	FR221	S	537,300	7,369	2,845	5	Laon
Allier	AL	03	FR03	FR721	C	357,700	7,340	2,834	3	Moulins
Alpes-de-Haute-Provence	AP	04	FR12	FR821	U	130,900	6,925	2,674	4	Digne
Alpes-Maritimes	AM	06	FR04	FR823	U	971,800	4,299	1,660	2	Nice
Ardèche	AH	07	FR05	FR712	V	277,600	5,529	2,135	3	Privas
Ardennes	AN	08	FR06	FR211	G	296,400	5,229	2,019	4	Charleville-Mézières
Ariège	AG	09	FR07	FR621	N	136,500	4,890	1,888	3	Foix
Aube	AB	10	FR08	FR212	G	289,200	6,004	2,318	3	Troyes
Aude	AD	11	FR09	FR811	K	298,700	6,139	2,370	3	Carcassonne
Aveyron	AV	12	FR10	FR622	N	270,100	8,735	3,373	3	Rodez
Bas-Rhin	BR	67	FR11	FR421	A	953,100	4,755	1,836	7	Strasbourg
Bouches-du-Rhône	BD	13	FR15	FR824	U	1,759,400	5,087	1,964	4	Marseille
Calvados	CV	14	FR16	FR251	P	618,500	5,548	2,142	4	Caen
Cantal	CL	15	FR17	FR722	C	158,700	5,726	2,211	3	Aurillac
Charente	CT	16	FR18	FR531	T	342,000	5,956	2,300	3	Angoulême
Charente-Maritime	CM	17	FR19	FR532	T	527,100	6,864	2,650	5	La Rochelle
Cher	CH	18	FR20	FR241	F	321,600	7,235	2,793	3	Bourges
Corrèze	CZ	19	FR21	FR631	L	237,900	5,857	2,261	3	Tulle
Corse-du-Sud	CS	2A	FR90	FR831	H	118,200	4,014	1,550	2	Ajaccio
Côte-d'Or	CO	21	FR22	FR261	D	493,900	8,763	3,383	3	Dijon
Côtes-d'Armor	CA	22	FR23	FR521	E	538,400	6,878	2,655	4	Saint-Brieuc
Creuse	CR	23	FR24	FR632	L	131,300	5,565	2,149	2	Guéret
Deux-Sèvres	DS	79	FR25	FR533	T	346,000	5,999	2,316	3	Niort
Dordogne	DD	24	FR26	FR611	B	386,400	9,060	3,498	4	Périgueux
Doubs	DB	25	FR27	FR431	I	484,800	5,234	2,021	3	Besançon
Drôme	DM	26	FR28	FR713	V	414,100	6,530	2,521	3	Valence
Essonne	ES	91	FR79	FR104	J	1,084,800	1,804	697	3	Évry
Eure	EU	27	FR29	FR231	Q	513,800	6,040	2,332	3	Évreux
Eure-et-Loir	EL	28	FR30	FR242	F	396,100	5,880	2,270	4	Chartres
Finistère	FI	29	FR31	FR522	E	838,700	6,733	2,600	4	Quimper
Gard	GA	30	FR32	FR812	K	585,000	5,853	2,260	3	Nîmes
Gers	GE	32	FR33	FR624	N	174,600	6,257	2,416	3	Auch
Gironde	GI	33	FR34	FR612	B	1,213,500	10,000	3,861	5	Bordeaux
Haute-Corse	HC	2B	FR96	FR832	H	131,600	4,666	1,801	3	Bastia
Haute-Garonne	HG	31	FR35	FR623	N	926,000	6,309	2,436	3	Toulouse
Haute-Loire	HL	43	FR36	FR723	C	206,600	4,977	1,922	3	Le Puy
Haute-Marne	HM	52	FR37	FR214	G	204,100	6,211	2,398	3	Chaumont
Hautes-Alpes	HA	05	FR38	FR822	U	113,300	5,549	2,142	2	Gap
Haute-Saône	HN	70	FR39	FR433	I	229,700	5,360	2,070	2	Vesoul
Haute-Savoie	HS	74	FR40	FR718	V	568,300	4,388	1,694	4	Annecy
Hautes-Pyrénées	HP	65	FR41	FR626	N	224,800	4,464	1,724	3	Tarbes
Haute-Vienne	HV	87	FR42	FR633	L	353,600	5,520	2,131	3	Limoges
Haut-Rhin	HR	68	FR43	FR422	A	671,300	3,525	1,361	6	Colmar
Hauts-de-Seine	HD	92	FR77	FR105	J	1,391,700	176	68	3	Nanterre
Hérault	HE	34	FR44	FR813	K	794,600	6,101	2,356	3	Montpellier
Ille-et-Vilaine	IV	35	FR45	FR523	E	798,700	6,775	2,616	4	Rennes
Indre	IN	36	FR46	FR243	F	237,500	6,791	2,622	4	Châteauroux ➤

division	abv	ISO	FIPS	NUTS	reg	population	area-km	area-mi	arr	capital
Indre-et-Loire	IL	37	FR47	FR244	F	529,300	6,127	2,366	3	Tours
Isère	IS	38	FR48	FR714	V	1,016,200	7,431	2,869	3	Grenoble
Jura	JU	39	FR49	FR432	I	248,800	4,999	1,930	3	Lons-le-Saunier
Landes	LD	40	FR50	FR613	B	311,500	9,243	3,569	2	Mont-de-Marsan
Loire	LR	42	FR51	FR715	V	746,300	4,781	1,846	3	Saint-Étienne
Loire-Atlantique	LA	44	FR52	FR511	R	1,052,200	6,815	2,631	4	Nantes
Loiret	LT	45	FR53	FR246	F	580,600	6,775	2,616	3	Orléans
Loir-et-Cher	LC	41	FR54	FR245	F	305,900	6,343	2,449	3	Blois
Lot	LO	46	FR55	FR625	N	155,800	5,217	2,014	3	Cahors
Lot-et-Garonne	LG	47	FR56	FR614	B	306,000	5,361	2,070	4	Agen
Lozère	LZ	48	FR57	FR814	K	72,800	5,167	1,995	2	Mende
Maine-et-Loire	ML	49	FR58	FR512	R	705,900	7,166	2,767	4	Angers
Manche	MH	50	FR59	FR252	P	479,600	5,938	2,293	4	Saint-Lô
Marne	MR	51	FR60	FR213	G	558,200	8,162	3,151	5	Châlons-Sur-Marne
Mayenne	MY	53	FR61	FR513	R	278,000	5,175	1,998	3	Laval
Meurthe-et-Moselle	MM	54	FR62	FR411	M	711,800	5,241	2,024	4	Nancy
Meuse	MS	55	FR63	FR412	M	196,300	6,216	2,400	3	Bar-Le-Duc
Morbihan	MB	56	FR64	FR524	E	619,800	6,823	2,634	3	Vannes
Moselle	MO	57	FR65	FR413	M	1,011,300	6,216	2,400	9	Metz
Nièvre	NI	58	FR66	FR262	D	233,300	6,817	2,632	4	Nevers
Nord	NO	59	FR67	FR301	O	2,531,900	5,743	2,217	6	Lille
Oise	OI	60	FR68	FR222	S	725,600	5,860	2,263	4	Beauvais
Orne	OR	61	FR69	FR253	P	293,200	6,103	2,357	3	Alençon
Pas-de-Calais	PC	62	FR70	FR302	O	1,433,200	6,671	2,576	7	Arras
Puy-de-Dôme	PD	63	FR71	FR724	C	598,200	7,970	3,077	5	Clermont-Ferrand
Pyrénées-Atlantiques	PA	64	FR13	FR615	B	578,500	7,645	2,952	3	Pau
Pyrénées-Orientales	PO	66	FR72	FR815	K	363,800	4,116	1,589	3	Perpignan
Rhône	RH	69	FR73	FR716	V	1,509,000	3,249	1,254	2	Lyon
Saône-et-Loire	SL	71	FR74	FR263	D	559,400	8,575	3,311	5	Mâcon
Sarthe	ST	72	FR75	FR514	R	513,700	6,206	2,396	3	Le Mans
Savoie	SV	73	FR76	FR717	V	348,300	6,028	2,328	3	Chambéry
Seine-et-Marne	SE	77	FR78	FR102	J	1,078,200	5,915	2,284	4	Melun
Seine-Maritime	SM	76	FR80	FR232	Q	1,223,400	6,278	2,424	3	Rouen
Seine-Saint-Denis	SS	93	FR91	FR106	J	1,381,200	236	91	2	Bobigny
Somme	SO	80	FR81	FR223	S	547,800	6,170	2,382	4	Amiens
Tarn	TA	81	FR82	FR627	N	342,700	5,758	2,223	2	Albi
Tarn-et-Garonne	TG	82	FR83	FR628	N	200,200	3,718	1,436	2	Montauban
Territoire de Belfort	TB	90	FR14	FR434	I	134,100	609	235	1	Belfort
Val-de-Marne	VM	94	FR92	FR107	J	1,215,500	245	95	3	Créteil
Val-d'Oise	VO	95	FR93	FR108	J	1,049,600	1,246	481	3	Pontoise
Var	VR	83	FR84	FR825	U	815,400	5,973	2,306	3	Toulon
Vaucluse	VC	84	FR85	FR826	U	467,100	3,567	1,377	3	Avignon
Vendée	VD	85	FR86	FR515	R	509,400	6,720	2,594	3	La Roche-sur-Yon
Vienne	VN	86	FR87	FR534	T	380,000	6,990	2,699	3	Poitiers
Ville de Paris	VP	75	FR94	FR101	J	2,152,400	105	41	1	Paris
Vosges	VG	88	FR88	FR414	M	386,300	5,874	2,268	3	Épinal
Yonne	YO	89	FR89	FR264	D	323,100	7,427	2,868	3	Auxerre
Yvelines	YV	78	FR95	FR103	J	1,307,200	2,284	882	4	Versailles
						56,614,900	543,965	210,028	327	

Status: These divisions are départements (departments).

Abv: Two-letter code for international compatibility (defined by the author).

ISO: Codes from ISO 3166-2. These are standard department codes for France, and are also the first two digits of the five-digit French postal codes, except for 2A (Corse-du-Sud, postal codes 200xx–201xx) and 2B (Haute-Corse, postal codes 202xx). Note: postal codes for French addresses can be identified by prefixing them with "F-".

FIPS: Codes from FIPS PUB 10-4.

NUTS: Nomenclature of Territorial Units for Statistics.

Reg: ISO code of the region the department belongs to (see below).

Population: 1990 census (provisional).

Area-km: Square kilometers.

Area-mi: Square miles.

Arr: Number of arrondissements in the department.

Note on collation sequence: In French usage, Bas, Haut, and their feminine and plural forms are not considered part of the collation object. For example, Haute-Marne is alphabetized as if it were "Marne, Haute," and comes between Marne and Mayenne.

ISO code note: ISO standard 3166 contains a specific disclaimer stating that the scope of different codes may overlap. It even gives France and Martinique as an example, explaining that although Martinique is part of France (and presumably covered by the code FR), it also has its own code MQ. However, the only cases of overlap seem to follow the same paradigm as Martinique. The remote territories of a colonial power have their own listings, but can also be considered as covered under the mother country. Until 1993, it was possible to use the standard as if its countries were disjoint, by ignoring the disclaimer and making the mental proviso that codes like FR applied to the mother country only. In 1993, the code FX was added to the standard. FX is described as referring to Metropolitan France, excluding territories such as Martinique. To adhere strictly to the standard, I should use FX for the France listings given here. In practice, though, people are still using FR and not FX. Even ISO 3166-2 quietly ignores FX. It appears that FX is going to be used primarily for technical purposes.

Regions: Various ministries of the French government found it convenient to group the departments into régions. Each one used a slightly different grouping. In 1960, the present set of regions was adopted as a standard. The regions have gradually taken on an administrative structure, including councils, elections, and budgets. For a country the size of France, 96 departments is an unwieldy number, and it's possible that the regions will eventually become the basic administrative divisions.

region	ISO	FIPS	NUTS	population	area-km	capital
Alsace	A	FRC1	FR42	1,624,400	8,280	Strasbourg
Aquitaine	B	FR97	FR61	2,795,800	41,308	Bordeaux
Auvergne	C	FR98	FR72	1,321,200	26,013	Clermont-Ferrand
Basse-Normandie	P	FR99	FR25	1,391,300	17,589	Caen
Bourgogne	D	FRA1	FR26	1,609,700	31,582	Dijon
Bretagne	E	FRA2	FR52	2,795,600	27,208	Rennes
Centre	F	FRA3	FR24	2,371,000	39,151	Orléans
Champagne-Ardenne	G	FRA4	FR21	1,347,800	25,606	Châlons-sur-Marne
Corse	H	FRA5	FR83	249,700	8,680	Ajaccio
Franche-Comté	I	FRA6	FR43	1,097,300	16,202	Besançon
Haute-Normandie	Q	FRA7	FR23	1,737,200	12,317	Rouen
Île-de-France	J	FRA8	FR1	10,660,600	12,012	Paris
Languedoc-Roussillon	K	FRA9	FR81	2,115,000	27,376	Montpellier
Limousin	L	FRB1	FR63	722,900	16,942	Limoges
Lorraine	M	FRB2	FR41	2,305,700	23,547	Metz
Midi-Pyrénées	N	FRB3	FR62	2,430,700	45,348	Toulouse
Nord-Pas-de-Calais	O	FRB4	FR3	3,965,100	12,414	Lille
Pays de la Loire	R	FRB5	FR51	3,059,100	32,082	Nantes
Picardie	S	FRB6	FR22	1,810,700	19,399	Amiens
Poitou-Charentes	T	FRB7	FR53	1,595,100	25,810	Poitiers
Provence-Alpes-Côte d'Azur	U	FRB8	FR82	4,257,900	31,400	Marseille
Rhône-Alpes	V	FRB9	FR71	5,350,700	43,698	Lyon
				56,614,500	543,964	

NUTS: Nomenclature of Territorial Units for Statistics. The six regions whose NUTS codes begin with FR2 form a group which the NUTS standard designates as Bassin Parisien. Similarly, FR4 is Est; FR5 is Ouest; FR6 is Sud-Ouest; FR7 is Centre-Est; and FR8 is Méditerranée. The NUTS codes beginning with FR9 are assigned to the départements d'outre-mer (overseas departments).

Further subdivisions: The departments of France are subdivided into arrondissements, which are subdivided into cantons, which are (in general) subdivided into communes. (The same words are generally used in English. The basic meaning of arrondissement is a rounding off, or rounding out.) In densely populated areas, there may be several cantons in a commune. Paris is divided into 20 arrondissements, but they are treated as if they were cantons. On 1988-01-01, there were 22 regions, 96 departments, 326 arrondissements, 3,827 cantons, and 36,538 communes in metropolitan France (France in Europe, including Corsica). The word circonscription (circumscription, constituency) is used in France and its former colonies to describe an administrative division at any level.

Territorial extent: Charente-Maritime includes the Île d'Oléron and Île de Ré.

Corse-du-Sud includes Île Cavallo in the Strait of Bonifacio.

Côte-d'Or includes an enclave that lies between Nièvre and Saône-et-Loire, consisting of the commune of Ménessaire.

Finistère includes the Île d'Ouessant and Île de Sein.

Hautes-Pyrénées includes two enclaves within Pyrénées-Atlantiques, containing five communes, including Luquet and Séron.

Manche includes the Îles Chausey in the Gulf of Saint-Malo.

Meurthe-et-Moselle includes an enclave within Meuse, consisting of the commune of Othe.

Morbihan includes the Île de Groix and Belle-Île.

Nord includes an enclave within Pas-de-Calais, containing three communes, including Boursies.

Île des Faisans, in the Bidassoa River, is a condominium of France and Spain. It lies in Pyrénées-Atlantiques.

Var includes the Îles d'Hyères.

Vaucluse includes an enclave within Drôme, containing the canton of Valréas.

Vendée includes the Île d'Yeu.

The following remote territories of France are treated as separate countries by ISO 3166-1, so they are not included here: French Guiana, French Polynesia, French Southern Territories, Guadeloupe, Martinique, Mayotte, New Caledonia, Reunion, Saint Pierre and Miquelon, and Wallis and Futuna. Each of the overseas departments (French Guiana, Guadeloupe, Martinique, and Reunion) has also been a region since 1974.

Origins of names: When the departments of France were created in 1790, they were named fairly systematically after the geographic features that marked them. The following 51 rivers have all contributed to department names: Ain, Aisne, Allier, Ardèche, Ariège, Aube, Aude, Aveyron, Charente, Cher, Corrèze, Creuse, Dordogne, Doubs, Drôme, Eure, Gard, Garonne, Gers, Gironde, Hérault, Ille, Indre, Isère, Loir, Loire, Loiret, Lot, Maine, Marne, Mayenne, Meurthe, Meuse, Moselle, Nièvre, Oise, Orne, Rhin (Rhine), Rhône, Saône, Sarthe, Seine, Sèvre Nantaise, Sèvre Niortaise, Somme, Tarn, Var, Vendée, Vienne, Vilaine, and Yonne. Topographic features used in department names include five mountain ranges (Alpes (Alps), Jura, Lozère, Pyrénées, and Vosges); two individual mountains (Cantal and Puy de Dôme); and a range of hills (the Côte d'Or). There are also departments named for forests (Ardennes and Yvelines), a gulf (Morbihan), two straits (Pas-de-Calais and Manche), rocky islets (Calvados), a spring (Vaucluse), and a sandy plain (Landes).

Since France so often re-uses name elements (there are six departments and one region containing Loire in their names), I have given the probable origins of name elements rather than the full names.

Alpes: probably from an Indo-European root meaning mountain, high place

Alsace: from ethnic name, probably Germanic for "those of foreign parts"; or, land of the Ill (River)

Aquitaine: from ethnic name Aquitani; or, Latin *Aquitania*: land of water

Ardennes: said to come from Celtic *ardu-*: high

Atlantique: for the Atlantic Ocean, which was probably named for Atlas, a Titan of Greek mythology

Aube: from Latin *alba*: white

Auvergne: from ethnic name Arverni, from Gallic *are verno*: at the alders

Bas, Basse: French for low (m., f.), usually applied to downstream regions

Belfort: Latin *Bellofortis*: beautiful and strong

Bouches-du-Rhône: French: Mouths of the Rhône River

Bourgogne: Germanic Burgundja, either from Indo-European *bhrghu*: tall, or from Gothic *baurgjans*: inhabitants of fortified places

Bretagne: Land of the Bretons

Calvados: from the rocks of Calvados. When the department was founded in 1790, Delaunay, a deputy from the area, stated that the rocks had been named for the galleon San Salvador (misspelled Çalvador) of the Spanish Armada, which foundered on them. This theory has not been confirmed.

Cantal: Mediterranean root *kanto*: stone, mountain

Centre: French for center

Champagne: Latin *campania*: countryside

Charente: from Gallic word for sandy

Corrèze: Latin Curretia, from pre–Latin *cur*: stream

Corse: from ethnic name Corsi, possibly from Phoenician *horsi*: wooded

Corse-du-Sud: French for Southern Corsica

Côte-d'Azur: French: blue coast (coined by Stephen Liégeard in his 1887 book, *La Côte d'Azur*)

Côte-d'Or: French: golden hillside (from color of grapevines, or their monetary value)

Côtes-d'Armor: coasts of Armorica (ancient name of Bretagne)

Côtes-du-Nord: French: northern coasts

Creuse: French: hollow (adj. f.), describing the river's course through gorges. (The adjective and the name of the river haven't always been the same, but have undergone parallel evolution.)

Deux-Sèvres: French: two Sèvres, referring to the rivers Sèvre Nantaise and Sèvre Niortaise

Doubs: from Celtic *dubis*: black

Finistère: Latin *finis terrae*: end of the earth

Franche-Comté: French for free county. From 1361 to 1678, Bourgogne was divided into a duchy, which belonged to France, and the free county, which was exempt from tribute to the king.

Gascogne: Latin *Vasconia*: land of the Basques

Gironde: the estuary of the Garonne River. In ancient times they had the same name.

Haut, Haute: French for high (m., f.; f. pl. Hautes), usually used for upstream regions

Île-de-France: French: Island of France (the area around Paris, once the only territory of the King of France)

Indre: Latin *Angerum*, from Frankish *anger*: prairie

Jura: from Celtic *juris*: wooded heights

Isère: from pre–Celtic Isara, in which ara means river

Landes: from Gallic *landa*: flatlands

Languedoc: French *Langue d'Oc*: language of "oc" (in the local dialect, "oc" was used for "yes")

Limousin: province of Limoges, from ethnic name Lemovices, from Gallic *lemo*: elm, *vices*: warrior

Lorraine: from Lotharingie, the domain given to Lothaire in the partition of Charlemagne's realm (843)

Lot: the river's Latin name was Ulta, which became Olt in the Middle Ages. The definite article in the expression "l'Olt" became absorbed into the name itself.

Maine: see Mayenne

Manche: = sleeve, from the French name for the English Channel, which resembles a sleeve; or from a Celtic word for channel

Maritime: French: seaside (adjective)

Marne: Gallic, apparently from Matrona, a goddess of motherhood

Mayenne: from Celtic Meduana, in which *medu-* means mead. The name formerly applied to both the Mayenne and the Maine, but underwent divergent evolution. (The Mayenne meets the Sarthe near Angers, forming the Maine, which flows into the Loire 10 km. further downstream.)

Midi: French for South (as a region rather than a compass point), from Latin *meridies*: midday (sun stands in the south at midday in those latitudes)

Morbihan: Breton *mor*: sea, *bihan*: little, by contrast with the Atlantic Ocean, a great sea

Moselle: from Latin Mosella, a diminutive form of Mosa, the Latin name for the Meuse. The Moselle was being likened to a smaller Meuse.

Nord: French for North

Normandie: from ethnic name Normand (people from the North)

Orientales: French for eastern (feminine plural), from Latin *oriens*: rising (direction of the rising sun)

Paris: from ethnic name Parisii; shortened from Latin name Lutetia Parisiorum

Pas-de-Calais: French: Strait of Calais. Calais comes from the ethnic name Caleti.

Pays de la Loire: French for land of the Loire River

Poitou: province of Poitier, from ethnic name Pictones

Provence: Latin *Provincia*: the province

Puy-de-Dôme: Puy comes from Latin *podium*: high place. The mountain had a temple dedicated to Mercury Dumias, whence Dôme

Pyrénées: Mountains named for a village named Pyrene.

Rhin: from the Celtic root *renos*: river

Rhône: came through Latin Rhodanus from an old root *Rhod-*: river

Roussillon: from Ruscino, name of a city in the province (modern Château-Roussillon)

Somme: from Celtic *samara*: tranquil

Val-de, Val-d': French for "valley of"

Var: from a Celtic root meaning river

Vaucluse: after the source of the Sorgue River at a place called, in Latin, *Vallis clusa*: enclosed valley

Vendée: from Gallic *vindo*: white, clear, describing the river

Vosges: named for the god Vosegus

Yonne: for a tutelary goddess named Icauna

Change history: There have been numerous minor boundary adjustments between departments.

The basic set of departments dates back to 1790, when the French National Assembly abolished the old provinces and established 83 departments to replace them. This may have been the first attempt to create a reasoned, methodical set of administrative divisions for any country. Each department was to be small enough that all its citizens could reach its capital in a day's journey.

The departments were defined as sets of communes. Since the drafters had inaccurate maps, it often happened that a commune was placed in a department with which it was not contiguous. The resulting enclaves were gradually eliminated in the early 19th century, although some still remain.

When France was defeated by Prussia in 1871, it ceded Bas-Rhin and parts of Haut-Rhin, Meurthe, Moselle, and Vosges, as those departments stood then. The retained parts of Meurthe and Moselle formed the department of Meurthe-et-Moselle, as it still stands now. The section of Haut-Rhin which remained in France eventually became known as the Territoire de Belfort.

1919-10-17	Alsace-Lorraine restored to France, as the departments of Bas-Rhin, Haut-Rhin, and Moselle. These were known as Unterelsaß, Oberelsaß, and Lothringen respectively under German administration.
1922	Territoire de Belfort given the status of department.
1941-09-04	Charente-Inférieure department renamed to Charente-Maritime, to avoid the negative connotations of "Inférieure" (lower, or inferior).
1947-02-10	A few villages formerly in Italy were annexed to Alpes-Maritimes by the peace treaty.
1955-01-18	Seine-Inférieure department renamed to Seine-Maritime.
1957-03-09	Loire-Inférieure department renamed to Loire-Atlantique.
1964-07-10	Seine (capital Paris) and Seine-et-Oise (capital Versailles) departments reorganized, forming the departments of Essonne, Hauts-de-Seine, Seine-Saint-Denis, Val-de-Marne,

Val-d'Oise, Ville de Paris, and Yvelines. Of these, Ville de Paris was formed entirely from Seine. Essonne, Val-d'Oise, and Yvelines were formed entirely from Seine-et-Oise. The other three contain parts of both former departments.

1965	Capital of Essonne renamed from Évry-Petit-Bourg to Évry.
1966	Capital of Ardennes renamed from Mézières to Charleville-Mézières because of the merging of the two cities.
1967-12-29	Territory transferred from Ain and Isère departments to Rhône, in order to unite the Lyon metropolitan area into one department.
1969-10-10	Basses-Pyrénées department renamed to Pyrénées-Atlantiques, to avoid the negative connotations of "Basses" (low).
1970-04-13	Basses-Alpes department renamed to Alpes-de-Haute-Provence.
1974	Capital of Var moved from Draguignan to Toulon.
1976-01-01	Corse department (capital Ajaccio) split into Corse-du-Sud and Haute-Corse.
1990-02-27	Côtes-du-Nord department renamed to Côtes-d'Armor, to avoid the supposedly negative connotations of "North" for tourism.
1991-05-13	Status of Corse region changed to collectivité territoriale (territorial collectivity).

Note: Vilaine is the feminine of the French adjective *vilain*, which means disreputable, vile, offensive. Can it be long before the name of Ille-et-Vilaine department is expurgated?

Other names of subdivisions:

Alpes-de-Haute-Provence: Alpes da Alta Provença (Portuguese); Basses-Alpes (obsolete)

Alsace: Alsacia (Spanish); Alsazia (Italian); Elsaß (German)

Aquitaine: Aquitania (Italian); Aquitanien (German)

Auvergne: Alvernia (Italian)

Bas-Rhin: Unterelsaß (German-obsolete)

Basse-Normandie: Baja Normandía (Spanish); Bassa Normandia (Italian); Lower Normandy (English)

Bourgogne: Borgogna (Italian); Borgoña (Spanish); Burgund (German); Burgundy (English)

Bretagne: Bretagna (Italian); Bretaña (Spanish); Brittany (English)

Centre: Centro (Italian)

Champagne-Ardenne: Champaña-Ardenne (Spanish)

Charente-Maritime: Charente-Inférieure (obsolete)

Corse: Córcega (Spanish); Córsega (Portuguese); Corsica (English, Italian, Swedish); Korsika (German, Norwegian)

Côtes-d'Armor: Côtes-du-Nord (obsolete)

Franche-Comté: Franca Contea (Italian); Franco-Condado (Spanish)

Haute-Garonne: Alto Garona (Spanish)

Haute-Normandie: Alta Normandia (Italian); Alta Normandía (Spanish); Upper Normandy (English)

Hautes-Pyrénées: Altos Pirineos (Spanish)

Haut-Rhin: Oberelsaß (German-obsolete)

Île-de-France: Regione Parigina (Italian)

Landes: Landas (Spanish)

Languedoc-Roussillon: Languedoc-Rosellon (Spanish); Linguadoca e Rossiglione (Italian)

Limousin: Lemosin (Spanish); Limosino (Italian)

Loire-Atlantique: Loire-Inférieure (obsolete)

Lorraine: Lorena (Italian, Spanish); Lothringen (German)

Midi-Pyrénées: Midi e Pirinei (Italian)

Moselle: Lothringen (German-obsolete)

Pays de la Loire: Regione della Loira (Italian)

Picardie: Picardía (Spanish); Piccardia (Italian)

Provence-Alpes-Côte d'Azur: Provenza-Alpes-Costa de Azul (Spanish); Provenza e Costa Azzurra (Italian)

Pyrénées-Atlantiques: Basses-Pyrénées (obsolete); Pirinio Atlantiarrak (Basque)

Pyrénées-Orientales: Pirineos Orientales (Spanish); Pirineus Orientais (Portuguese)

Rhône-Alpes: Rodano e Alpi (Italian)

Savoie: Sabóia (Portuguese), Savoia (Italian)

Seine-Maritime: Seine-Inférieure (obsolete); Sena Marítimo (Portuguese)

Vendée: Vendéia (Portuguese)

Population history:

department	1891	1913	1936-03	1946-03	1954-05	1962-03	1968-03	1975-04	1982	1990
Ain	356,907	350,420	316,710	306,778	311,941	327,146	339,262	376,477	418,000	471,000
Aisne	545,493	535,590	484,647	453,411	487,068	512,920	526,346	533,862	534,000	537,300
Allier	424,382	422,000	368,778	373,481	372,689	380,221	386,533	378,406	369,000	357,700
Alpes-de-Haute-Provence	124,285	115,000	85,090	83,354	84,335	91,843	104,813	112,178	119,000	130,900
Alpes-Maritimes	258,571	293,250	513,714	452,546	515,484	618,265	722,070	816,681	881,000	971,800
Ardèche	371,269	353,570	272,698	254,598	249,077	248,516	256,927	257,065	268,000	277,600 ▶

department	1891	1913	1936-03	1946-03	1954-05	1962-03	1968-03	1975-04	1982	1990
Ardennes	324,923	315,600	288,632	245,335	280,490	300,247	309,380	309,306	302,000	296,400
Ariège	227,491	210,550	155,134	145,956	140,010	137,192	138,478	137,857	136,000	136,500
Aube	255,548	246,200	239,563	235,237	240,797	255,099	270,325	284,823	289,000	289,200
Aude	317,372	310,520	285,115	268,889	268,254	269,782	278,323	272,366	281,000	298,700
Aveyron	400,467	382,100	314,682	307,717	292,727	290,442	281,568	278,306	279,000	270,100
Bas-Rhin	— —	— —	711,830	673,281	707,934	770,150	827,367	882,121	918,000	953,100
Bouches-du-Rhône	630,622	734,400	1,224,802	971,935	1,048,762	1,248,355	1,470,271	1,632,974	1,725,000	1,759,400
Calvados	428,945	410,200	404,901	400,026	442,991	480,686	519,695	560,967	590,000	618,500
Cantal	239,601	230,500	190,888	186,843	177,065	172,977	169,330	166,549	163,000	158,700
Charente	360,259	350,300	309,279	311,137	313,635	327,658	331,016	337,064	341,000	342,000
Charente-Maritime	456,202	452,200	419,021	416,187	447,973	470,897	483,622	497,859	513,000	527,100
Cher	359,276	346,000	288,695	286,070	284,376	293,514	304,601	316,350	320,000	321,600
Corrèze	328,119	318,500	262,770	254,574	242,798	237,926	237,858	240,363	241,000	237,900
Corse-du-Sud	288,596	295,600	322,854	267,873	246,995	275,465	269,831	289,842	109,000	118,200
Côte-d'Or	376,866	362,000	334,386	335,602	356,839	387,869	421,192	456,070	473,000	493,900
Côtes-d'Armor	618,652	610,000	531,840	526,955	503,178	501,923	506,102	525,556	539,000	538,400
Creuse	284,660	278,000	201,844	188,669	172,702	163,515	156,876	146,214	140,000	131,300
Deux-Sèvres	354,282	342,500	308,841	312,756	312,842	321,118	326,462	335,829	343,000	346,000
Dordogne	478,471	453,000	386,963	387,643	377,870	375,455	374,073	373,179	377,000	386,400
Doubs	303,081	299,000	304,812	298,255	327,187	384,881	426,363	471,082	477,000	484,800
Drôme	306,419	297,500	267,281	268,233	275,280	304,227	342,891	361,847	390,000	414,100
Essonne	— —	— —	— —	— —	— —	— —	807,463	923,061	998,000	1,084,800
Eure	349,471	335,000	303,829	315,902	332,514	361,904	383,375	422,952	462,000	513,800
Eure-et-Loir	284,683	276,000	252,690	258,110	261,035	277,546	302,207	335,151	363,000	396,100
Finistère	727,012	773,000	756,793	724,735	727,847	749,558	768,929	804,088	828,000	838,700
Gard	419,388	421,000	395,299	380,837	396,742	435,482	478,544	494,575	530,000	585,000
Gers	261,084	239,000	192,451	190,431	185,111	182,264	181,577	175,366	174,000	174,600
Gironde	793,528	822,000	850,567	858,381	896,517	935,448	1,009,390	1,061,474	1,128,000	1,213,500
Haute-Corse	— —	— —	— —	— —	— —	— —	— —	— —	131,000	131,600
Haute-Garonne	472,383	450,000	458,647	512,260	525,669	594,633	690,712	777,431	824,000	926,000
Haute-Loire	316,735	314,000	245,271	228,076	215,577	211,036	208,337	205,491	206,000	206,600
Haute-Marne	243,533	226,500	188,471	181,840	197,147	208,446	214,336	212,304	211,000	204,100
Hautes-Alpes	115,522	109,500	88,210	84,932	85,067	87,436	91,790	97,358	105,000	113,300
Haute-Saône	280,856	267,000	212,829	202,573	209,303	208,440	214,176	222,254	232,000	229,700
Haute-Savoie	268,267	264,000	259,961	270,565	293,852	329,230	378,550	447,795	494,000	568,300
Hautes-Pyrénées	225,861	216,000	188,604	201,954	203,544	211,433	225,730	227,222	278,000	224,800
Haute-Vienne	372,878	382,000	333,589	336,313	324,429	332,514	341,589	352,149	356,000	353,600
Haut-Rhin	— —	— —	507,551	471,705	509,647	547,920	585,018	635,209	650,000	671,300
Hauts-de-Seine	— —	— —	— —	— —	— —	— —	1,472,835	1,438,930	1,387,000	1,391,700
Hérault	461,651	490,000	502,043	461,100	471,429	516,658	591,397	648,202	706,000	794,600
Ille-et-Vilaine	626,875	614,000	565,766	578,246	586,812	614,268	652,722	702,199	750,000	798,700
Indre	292,868	335,500	245,622	252,075	247,436	251,432	247,178	248,523	243,000	237,500
Indre-et-Loire	337,298	335,000	343,276	349,685	364,706	395,210	437,870	478,601	506,000	529,300
Isère	572,145	569,000	572,742	574,019	626,116	729,789	768,451	860,378	937,000	1,016,200
Jura	273,028	261,000	220,797	216,386	220,202	225,682	233,547	238,856	243,000	248,800
Landes	297,842	291,600	251,436	248,395	248,943	260,495	277,381	288,323	297,000	311,500
Loire	616,227	648,000	650,226	631,591	654,482	696,348	722,383	742,396	740,000	746,300
Loire-Atlantique	645,263	665,000	659,428	665,064	733,575	803,372	861,462	934,499	995,000	1,052,200
Loiret	377,718	367,000	343,865	346,918	360,523	389,372	430,629	490,189	536,000	580,600
Loir-et-Cher	280,358	276,000	240,908	242,419	239,824	250,741	267,896	283,686	296,000	305,900
Lot	253,885	226,800	162,572	154,897	147,754	149,929	151,198	150,725	155,000	155,800
Lot-et-Garonne	295,360	279,000	252,761	265,449	265,549	275,028	290,592	292,616	298,000	306,000
Lozère	135,527	129,000	98,480	90,523	82,391	81,868	77,258	74,825	74,000	72,800
Maine-et-Loire	518,589	515,000	477,690	496,068	518,241	556,272	584,709	629,849	675,000	705,900
Manche	513,815	491,500	438,539	435,468	446,860	446,878	451,939	451,662	466,000	479,600
Marne	434,692	433,000	410,238	386,926	415,141	442,195	485,388	530,399	544,000	558,200
Mayenne	332,387	313,000	251,348	256,317	251,522	250,030	252,762	261,789	272,000	278,000
Meurthe-et-Moselle	444,150	485,000	576,041	528,805	607,002	678,078	705,413	722,587	717,000	711,800
Meuse	292,253	284,000	216,934	188,786	207,106	215,985	209,513	203,904	200,000	196,300
Morbihan	544,470	563,000	542,248	506,884	520,978	530,833	540,474	563,588	591,000	619,800
Moselle	— —	— —	696,246	622,145	769,388	919,412	971,314	1,006,373	1,007,000	1,011,300
Nièvre	343,581	324,000	249,673	248,559	240,078	245,921	247,702	245,212	240,000	233,300
Nord	1,736,341	1,867,000	2,022,167	1,917,452	2,098,545	2,293,112	2,417,899	2,510,738	2,521,000	2,531,900

➤

department	1891	1913	1936-03	1946-03	1954-05	1962-03	1968-03	1975-04	1982	1990
Oise	401,835	408,000	402,569	396,724	435,308	481,289	540,988	606,320	662,000	725,600
Orne	354,387	327,000	269,331	273,181	274,862	280,549	288,524	293,523	295,000	293,200
Pas-de-Calais	874,364	955,000	1,179,467	1,168,545	1,276,833	1,366,282	1,397,159	1,403,035	1,412,000	1,433,200
Puy-de-Dôme	564,266	544,000	486,103	478,876	481,380	508,928	547,743	580,033	594,000	598,200
Pyrénées-Atlantiques	425,027	426,000	413,411	415,797	420,019	466,038	508,734	534,748	556,000	578,500
Pyrénées-Orientales	210,125	212,000	233,347	228,776	230,285	251,231	281,976	299,506	335,000	363,800
Rhône	806,737	843,000	1,028,379	918,866	966,782	1,116,664	1,325,611	1,429,647	1,445,000	1,509,000
Saône-et-Loire	619,523	620,000	525,676	506,749	511,182	535,772	550,381	569,810	572,000	559,400
Sarthe	429,737	423,000	388,519	412,214	420,393	443,019	461,839	490,385	505,000	513,700
Savoie	263,297	255,000	239,010	235,939	252,192	266,678	288,921	305,118	324,000	348,300
Seine-et-Marne	356,709	358,300	409,311	407,137	453,438	524,486	604,340	755,762	887,000	1,078,200
Seine-Maritime	839,876	854,000	915,628	846,131	941,684	1,035,844	1,113,977	1,172,743	1,193,000	1,223,400
Seine-Saint-Denis	— —	— —	— —	— —	— —	— —	1256,884	1,322,127	1,324,000	1,381,200
Somme	546,495	538,000	467,479	441,368	464,153	488,225	512,113	538,462	544,000	547,800
Tarn	346,739	332,000	297,871	298,117	308,197	319,560	332,011	338,024	339,000	342,700
Tarn-et-Garonne	206,596	196,000	164,629	167,664	172,379	175,847	183,572	183,314	190,000	200,200
Territoire de Belfort	83,670	92,300	99,497	86,648	99,427	109,371	118,450	128,125	132,000	134,100
Val-de-Marne	— —	— —	— —	— —	— —	— —	1,121,340	1,215,674	1,194,000	1,215,500
Val-d'Oise	— —	— —	— —	— —	— —	— —	701,644	840,885	921,000	1,049,600
Var	288,336	326,000	398,662	370,688	413,012	469,557	555,926	626,093	708,000	815,400
Vaucluse	235,411	237,000	245,508	249,838	268,318	303,536	353,966	390,446	427,000	467,100
Vendée	442,355	441,000	389,211	393,787	395,641	408,928	421,250	450,641	483,000	509,400
Vienne	344,355	336,500	306,820	313,932	319,208	331,619	340,256	357,366	371,000	380,000
Ville de Paris	3,141,595	3,670,000	4,962,967	4,775,711	5,154,834	5,646,446	2,590,771	2,299,830	2,176,000	2,152,400
Vosges	410,196	421,000	376,926	342,315	372,523	380,676	388,201	397,957	396,000	386,300
Yonne	334,688	321,000	271,685	266,014	266,410	269,826	290,818	299,851	311,000	323,100
Yvelines	628,590	707,300	1,413,472	1,414,910	1,708,791	2,298,931	871,743	1,082,255	1,196,000	1,307,200
	38,333,192	39,015,300	41,907,056	40,506,059	42,777,154	46,519,789	49,845,344	52,655,802	54,393,000	56,614,900

Population of Corse listed under Corse-du-Sud before 1976.
Population of Seine listed under Ville de Paris before 1964.
Population of Seine-et-Oise listed under Yvelines before 1964.

FRENCH GUIANA

ISO = GF/FIPS = FG   Language = French   Time zone = -3   Capital = Cayenne

French Guiana has been linked to France throughout the 20th century, first as a colony, then as a remote but integral part of the country. French Guiana has a NUTS code of FR93, a department code of 973, and postal codes of the form 973xx, all of which are extensions of the French system.

Other names of country: Department of Guiana (formal–English); Frans Guyana (Dutch); Franska Guyana (Swedish); Französisch-Guayana (German); Guaiana Francese (Italian); Guayana Francesa (Spanish); Guiana (Norwegian); Guiana Francesa (Portuguese); Guyane française (French).

Origin of name: Descriptive: French colony in the Guyana area.

division	abv	population	area-km	area-mi	capital
Cayenne	CY	45,892	49,500	19,100	Cayenne
Saint-Laurent-du-Maroni	SL	9,233	40,500	15,600	Saint-Laurent-du-Maroni
		55,125	90,000	34,700	

Status: These divisions are arrondissements.
Abv: Two-letter code for international compatibility (defined by the author).
Population: 1974 census.
Area-km: Square kilometers.
Area-mi: Square miles.
Further subdivisions: The arrondissements are further subdivided into 22 communes and 19 cantons.
Territorial extent: Most of French Guiana's islands belong to Cayenne. They include the Îles Connétable, Îles Rémire, and Îles du Salut, one of which is Devil's Island (Île du Diable).
Origins of names:

Cayenne: Old French *cayenne*: seaport hostelry.

Change history:

1930-07-06   French Guiana divided into two territories, French Guiana (along the Atlantic coast; 20,000 sq. km.) and Inini (inland; 70,000 sq. km.).
1947-01-01   French Guiana and Inini reunited, changed from colony to département d'outre-mer (overseas department). Nominally, this status is on a par with the metropolitan French departments.
1951-09-14   French Guiana subdivided into two arrondissements, Cayenne and Inini.
1969-03-17   French Guiana reorganized into two arrondissements, Cayenne and Saint-Laurent-du-Maroni. Both began at the coast and extended inland to the southern end of the country; thus, new Cayenne was neither a subdivision nor an enlargement of old Cayenne.

FRENCH POLYNESIA

ISO = PF/FIPS = FP   Languages = French, Tahitian   Time zone = -10   Capital = Papeete

Formed in 1903 under the name French Establishments in Oceania (Établissements français de l'Océanie), by uniting several French colonies. In 1958-11, it changed its status to overseas territory and its name to French Polynesia.
Other names of country: Établissements français de l'Océanie (French-obsolete); Frans Polynesië (Dutch); Fransk Polynesia (Norwegian); Französisch-Polynesien (German); Polinesia Francesa (Spanish); Polinésia Francesa (Portuguese); Polinesia Francese (Italian); Polynésie française (French); Territory of French Polynesia (formal–English).
Origin of name: Descriptive: French possessions in Polynesia. Polynesia comes from the Greek words for "many islands."

division	abv	population	area-km	area-mi	capital	island
Clipperton Island	CI	0	5	2	none	
Leeward Islands	LI	22,232	430	166	Utorua	Raiatea
Marquesas Islands	MI	7,538	997	385	Taiohae	Nuku Hiva
Tuamotu and Gambier Islands	TG	12,374	877	339	Rangiroa	Rangiroa
Tubuai Islands	TI	6,509	142	55	Mataura	Tubuai
Windward Islands	WI	140,341	1,196	462	Papeete	Tahiti
		188,995	3,647	1,408		

Status: These divisions are circonscriptions (circumscriptions).
Abv: Two-letter code for international compatibility (defined by the author).

Population: 1988 estimates.
Area-km: Square kilometers.
Area-mi: Square miles.
Postal codes: Postal codes for French Polynesia have the form F-988xx, an extension of the French system.
Further subdivisions: French Polynesia is also divided into 48 communes.
Territorial extent: A note in ISO standard 3166 states that French Polynesia includes Clipperton Island. FIPS PUB 10-4, on the other hand, lists Clipperton Island as a separate country (code IP). Clipperton is over 3,000 km. from the nearest part of French Polynesia.

Leeward Islands extends from Bellinghausen Island and the Îles Scilly in the west to Raiatea and Huahine in the east. It also includes Bora Bora.

Marquesas Islands extends from Eiao and Hatutu in the northwest to Fatu Hiva in the southeast. It also includes Hiva Oa.

Tuamotu and Gambier Islands includes several smaller island groups: the Actaeon Islands, Disappointment Islands, Duke of Gloucester Islands, Gambier Islands, and King George Islands. Some of its outlying members are Hereheretue, Timoe (Temoe), Pukapuka, and Matahiva.

Tubuai Islands extends from Îles Maria in the west to Îles Marotiri (Îlots de Bass) in the east. It also includes Tubuai and Rurutu.

Windward Islands extends from Maiao (Tubuai Manu) in the west to Mehetia in the east. It also includes Tahiti and Moorea.

Origins of names:

Clipperton Island: named for discoverer
Leeward Islands, Windward Islands: named for their relative locations in the Society Islands with respect to the prevailing easterly winds. The Society Islands, in turn, were named by Captain James Cook in honor of the Royal Society of Sciences, which had subsidized his journey.

Marquesas Islands: named by Alvaro de Mendana de Neyra in honor of his uncle, Marquis Antonio de Mendoza, viceroy of Peru.
Tuamotu and Gambier Islands: Tahitian *tua*: high sea, *motu*: islands; Gambier Islands named for James Gambier of the British Admiralty by discoverer, Captain Wilson.

Change history:

1931	Clipperton Island, disputed between France and Mexico, awarded to France by arbitration.
1936-06-12	Clipperton Island attached to French Establishments in Oceania.

Other names of subdivisions:

Clipperton Island: Île Clipperton (French)
Leeward Islands: Îles sous le Vent (French)
Marquesas Islands: Îles Marquises (French); Isole Marchesi (Italian); Markesasinseln, Marquesasinseln (German); Marquezas Islands (obsolete)
Tuamotu and Gambier Islands: Îles Tuamotu et Gambier (French); Low Archipelago (obsolete); Paumotu Islands (obsolete)
Tubuai Islands: Austral Islands (variant); Îles Australes, Îles Tubuai (French)
Windward Islands: Îles du Vent (French)

FRENCH SOUTHERN TERRITORIES

ISO = TF/FIPS = FS   Language = French   Time zone = +5   Capital = none

On 1955-08-06, several island dependencies of Madagascar in the Indian Ocean, along with the French Antarctic claim of Adélie Land, were united to form an overseas territory of France, called French Southern and Antarctic Lands.

Other names of country: Französische Süd- und Antarktisgebiete (German); Sør- og antarktiske territorier (Norwegian); Terras Austrais e Antárticas Francesas (Portuguese); Terres australes et antartiques françaises (French); Territori Australi e Antartici (Italian); Territory of the French Southern and Antarctic Lands (formal–English); Tierras Australes y Antárticas Francesas (Spanish); Zuidelijke en Antarctische Franse Gebieden (Dutch).

Origin of name: Descriptive.

division	abv
French Southern Territories	TF

Status: This division is the whole of the country, treated as a division for compatibility.

Abv: Two-letter code for international compatibility (defined by the author).

Territorial extent: France claims Adélie Land in Antarctica as part of French Southern Lands. In this book, Adélie Land is listed under Antarctica.

French Southern Lands includes the islands of Kerguelen, Amsterdam, the Crozet Archipelago, and Saint-Paul.

GABON

ISO = GA/FIPS = GB   Language = French   Time zone = +1   Capital = Libreville

Gabon began the 20th century as part of French Kongo (Congo). On 1910-01-15, it became one of four colonies making up Afrique Équatoriale Française (French Equatorial Africa). When the four gained their independence in a single week, Gabon was the last one, on 1960-08-17.

Other names of country: Gabão (Portuguese); Gabón (Spanish); Gabonese Republic (formal–English); Gaboon (obsolete); Gabun (German); República Gabonesa (formal–Spanish); République Gabonaise (formal).

Origin of name: Portuguese *gabao*: hooded cloak, named for the shape of the Gabon estuary.

division	abv	ISO	FIPS	population	area-km	area-mi	dep	capital
Estuaire	ES	1	GB01	359,000	20,740	8,008	3	Libreville
Haut-Ogooué	HO	2	GB02	213,000	36,547	14,111	6	Masuku
Moyen-Ogooué	MO	3	GB03	49,000	18,535	7,156	2	Lambaréné
Ngounié	NG	4	GB04	118,000	37,750	14,575	7	Mouila
Nyanga	NY	5	GB05	98,000	21,285	8,218	4	Tchibanga
Ogooué-Ivindo	OI	6	GB06	53,000	46,075	17,790	4	Makokou
Ogooué-Lolo	OL	7	GB07	49,000	25,380	9,799	3	Koulamoutou
Ogooué-Maritime	OM	8	GB08	194,000	22,890	8,838	3	Port-Gentil
Woleu-Ntem	WN	9	GB09	166,000	38,465	14,851	5	Oyem
				1,299,000	267,667	103,346	37	

Status: These divisions are provinces.

Abv: Two-letter code for international compatibility (defined by the author).

ISO: Codes from ISO 3166-2.

FIPS: Codes from FIPS PUB 10-4.

Population: 1978 estimates.

Area-km: Square kilometers.

Area-mi: Square miles.

Dep: Number of départements in each province.

Further subdivisions: The provinces are further subdivided into 37 départements.

Origins of names:

The provinces are predominantly named for rivers which flow through them: the Ivindo, Lolo, N'Gounié, Ntem, Nyanga, Ogooué, and Woleu.

Estuaire: Named for the Gabon Estuary.

Change history:

  1915   Capital of Ogooué-Maritime renamed from Mandji to Port-Gentil.

  ~1975   Gabon had previously been divided into nine prefectures and subdivided into 28 sub-prefectures.

The status of the prefectures was now changed to that of provinces, and the sub-prefectures were reorganized into 37 departments.

~1985   Capital of Haut-Ogooué renamed from Franceville to Masuku.

Other names of subdivisions:

Ngounié: N'Gounié (variant)   Ogooué-Maritime: Ogooué Marittimo (Italian)

GAMBIA

ISO = GM/FIPS = GA   Language = English   Time zone = +0   Capital = Banjul

The Gambia was a British colony until its independence on 1965-02-18. With Senegal, it formed a federation called Senegambia from 1982-02-01 to 1989-09-21. In text, the country name is often given as The Gambia; on maps, it usually appears as just Gambia. The country's stamps were inscribed Gambia until 1966, when The Gambia came into use. In alphabetized lists, it invariably appears under G.

Other names of country: Gambía (Icelandic); Gambie (French); Republic of The Gambia (formal–English); The Gambia (variant).

Origin of name: from Gambia River, corruption of native name *Ba-Dimma*: river.

division	abv	ISO	FIPS	population	area-km	area-mi	capital
Banjul	BJ	B	GA01	39,473	88	34	Banjul
Lower River	LR	L	GA02	42,652	1,618	625	Mansa Konko
MacCarthy Island	MC	M	GA03	100,818	2,895	1,118	Georgetown
North Bank	NB	N	GA07	93,536	2,256	871	Kerewan
Upper River	UR	U	GA04	87,074	2,070	799	Basse Santa Su
Western	WE	W	GA05	129,641	1,764	681	Brikama
				493,194	10,691	4,128	

Status: These divisions are actually called divisions, except for Banjul, which is a city.
Abv: Two-letter code for international compatibility (defined by the author).
ISO: Codes from ISO 3166-2.
FIPS: Codes from FIPS PUB 10-4.
Population: 1973 census.
Area-km: Square kilometers.
Area-mi: Square miles.
Further subdivisions: The country is subdivided into 35 districts.
Origins of names:

Banjul: native *bangjulo*: rope mats (informants thought
    they were being asked, what are you making?)

Change history: Before independence, the country was divided into the Colony (a small area containing present-day Banjul) and the Protectorate. The Protectorate had five divisions: Kombo Saint Mary, MacCarthy Island, North Bank, South Bank, and Upper River.

1973   Name of national capital and its division changed from Bathurst to Banjul.

Other names of subdivisions:

Lower River: Central (obsolete)
Kombo Saint Mary: Kombo, Kombo North and Saint Mary
    (variant)

GEORGIA

ISO = GE/FIPS = GG   Language = Georgian   Time zone = +3 [d]   Capital = Tbilisi

Modern Georgia corresponds to the Russian districts of Kars, Kutais, and Tiflis at the start of the 20th century. A substantial part of Kars was lost to Turkey in World War I. Georgia declared independence on 1918-05-26. Russia invaded and annexed it on 1921-02-25. It became part of the Transcaucasian Soviet Federal Socialist Republic on 1922-12-15, and remained so until the dissolution of that republic in 1936. Georgia declared its independence once again on 1991-04-09, in the collapse of the Soviet Union.

Other names of country: Georgía (Icelandic); Geórgia (Portuguese); Géorgie (French); Georgien (Danish, German, Swedish); Grusinien (German); Gruziya (Russian); Republic of Georgia (formal–English); Sakartvelos Respublika (formal).

Origin of name: Persians called the inhabitants "Gorj."

division	abv	ISO	population	area-km	area-mi	capital
Abkhazia	AB	AB	538,000	8,600	3,300	Sukhumi
Adjaria	AJ	AJ	382,000	3,000	1,200	Batumi
Georgia (Tbilisi)	GE		4,437,000	54,200	20,900	Tbilisi
South Ossetia	SO		99,000	3,900	1,500	Tskhinvali
			5,456,000	69,700	26,900	

Status: Abkhazia and Adjaria are autonomous republics. South Ossetia is an autonomous region. Georgia (Tbilisi) is not an actual division, but is included simply to represent the rest of the area.

Abv: Two-letter code for international compatibility (defined by the author).

ISO: Codes from ISO 3166-2.

Population: 1990-01-01.

Area-km: Square kilometers.

Area-mi: Square miles.

Further subdivisions: Georgia (Tbilisi) is further subdivided into prefectures. FIPS shows a division into 53 raioni (regions), 9 cities, and the two autonomous republics.

Origins of names:

Abkhazia: Georgian *abkhazi*: good men, or from Ancient Greek *Abaskos*: ethnic name

South Ossetia: Southern part of Ossetia, from Georgian *osi*: ethnic name

Tbilisi: Georgian *tbili*: hot, for hot springs

Change history: During the Stalin regime, the name of the capital of South Ossetia was temporarily changed to Stalinir. In the past, Tbilisi was often rendered into European languages as Tiflis.

Other names of subdivisions:

Abkhazia: Abkhásia (Portuguese); Abkhazie (French); Sukhum, Sukhumskiy Okrug (obsolete)

Adjaria: Adjarie (French); Batum, Batumskaya Oblast' (obsolete)

South Ossetia: Ossétia Meridional (Portuguese); Süd-Ossetien (German); Yugo-Ossetiya (Russian)

GERMANY

ISO = DE/FIPS = GM   Language = German   Time zone = +1 ^{d} Capital = Berlin

In the last part of the 19th century, hundreds of small Germanic kingdoms, princedoms, duchies, margravates, etc., were finally united into the German Empire (Deutsches Reich). The more important units became Länder (states); others became Provinzen (provinces) within the states. In 1900, the Empire comprised all of modern Germany, Alsace-Lorraine, some communes now in Belgium, some counties now in Denmark, about half of modern Poland, the Kaliningrad oblast of Russia, and a strip of Lithuania, plus overseas colonies in Africa and the South Pacific. As a result of World War I (1914–1918), Germany became a republic in 1919, somewhat diminished in extent. The Allies stripped it of its overseas possessions and made a number of territorial alterations (see change history). In 1933, Hitler and his supporters proclaimed the Third Reich (so called in reference to the earlier Holy Roman Empire and the Deutsches Reich of 1871–1918). Germany made a number of territorial gains at the expense of its neighbors before and during World War II. These gains were all annulled in its defeat. After the war, an even smaller Germany was partitioned among the Big Four Allies. This was intended to be a temporary arrangement, in order to handle the transition to a reconstructed postwar Germany. However, mistrust and tension between the Western Allies and the Soviet Union delayed the fulfillment of the plan for over 40 years. The Russian (Soviet) zone became East Germany (officially Deutsche Demokratische Republik, German Democratic Republic, or DDR; capital East Berlin), in effect a separate country, while the other three zones became West Germany (officially Bundesrepublik Deutschland, Federal Republic of Germany, or BRD; capital Bonn). Berlin was sometimes treated as a separate sovereignty, because there had been no peace treaty to formalize its status. The two Germanies (and Berlin) were finally united, under the name and administration of the BRD, as the Cold War ended.

Note on spelling: the German-speaking lands have agreed on a spelling reform to be complete early in the 21st century. Among other things, the character 'ß', called "scharfes s" or "eszet," will in many cases be replaced by 'ss'. The state names containing eszet are obsolete.

Other names of country: Alemanha (Portuguese); Alemania (Spanish); Allemagne (French); Bundesrepublik Deutschland (formal); Deutsche Demokratische Republik (German-obsolete–part); Deutsches Reich (German-obsolete); Deutschland (German); Duitsland (Dutch); East Germany (obsolete–part); Federal Republic of Germany (formal–English); Germania (Italian); Repubblica Federale Tedesca (Italian-formal); Saksa (Finnish); Tyskland (Danish, Norwegian, Swedish); Þýskaland (Icelandic); West Germany (obsolete–part).

Origin of name: Latin *germanus*: original, native. Alemania, etc.: ancient tribe of Alamans, from Germanic: all men. Deutschland, etc.: ancient tribe of Teutons, from Germanic *theud*: people.

division	ISO	FIPS	NUTS	population	area-km	area-mi	capital	German name
Baden-Wurttemberg	BW	GM01	DE1	10,001,840	35,751	13,804	Stuttgart	Baden-Württemberg
Bavaria	BY	GM02	DE2	11,595,970	70,554	27,241	Munich	Bayern
Berlin	BE	GM16	DE3	3,434,000	889	343	Berlin	Berlin
Brandenburg	BR	GM11	DE4	2,542,723	29,056	11,219	Potsdam	Brandenburg
Bremen	HB	GM03	DE5	683,684	404	156	Bremen	Bremen
Hamburg	HH	GM04	DE6	1,668,700	755	292	Hamburg	Hamburg
Hesse	HE	GM05	DE7	5,837,330	21,114	8,152	Wiesbaden	Hessen
Lower Saxony	NI	GM06	DE9	7,475,790	47,351	18,282	Hanover	Niedersachsen
Mecklenburg-West Pomerania	MV	GM12	DE8	1,923,959	23,559	9,096	Schwerin	Mecklenburg-Vorpommern
North Rhine-Westphalia	NW	GM07	DEA	17,509,866	34,070	13,155	Dusseldorf	Nordrhein-Westfalen
Rhineland-Palatinate	RP	GM08	DEB	3,821,235	19,849	7,664	Mainz	Rheinland-Pfalz
Saarland	SL	GM09	DEC	1,072,963	2,570	992	Saarbrucken	Saarland
Saxony	SN	GM13	DED	4,678,877	18,341	7,081	Dresden	Sachsen
Saxony-Anhalt	ST	GM14	DEE	2,823,324	20,607	7,956	Magdeburg	Sachsen-Anhalt
Schleswig-Holstein	SH	GM10	DEF	2,648,532	15,731	6,074	Kiel	Schleswig-Holstein
Thuringia	TH	GM15	DEG	2,637,261	16,251	6,275	Erfurt	Thüringen
				80,356,054	356,852	137,782		

Status: These divisions are Länder (sing. Land: state).
ISO: Codes from ISO 3166-2.
FIPS: Codes from FIPS PUB 10-4.
NUTS: Codes from Nomenclature for Statistical Territorial Units (European standard).

Population: 1991-12-31 estimate.

Area-km: Square kilometers.

Area-mi: Square miles.

Capitals: listed in English, but the only name difference in German is München = Munich.

Further subdivisions: Seven of the 16 states—generally, the larger ones—are subdivided into Regierungsbezirke (sing. Regierungsbezirk: administrative district). All of the states and districts are subdivided into Kreise (sing. Kreis: county), which are further subdivided into Gemeinden (sing. Gemeinde: commune). The Kreise are of two kinds: Landkreise (rural counties) and kreisfreie Städte (urban counties). On 1992-01-01, there were 29 administrative districts, 543 counties, and 16,095 communes.

Here is a list of administrative districts for those states that have them. For each district, the name is given in English, followed by the NUTS code, the name in German (if different), and the ☆capital name in German.

Baden-Württemberg: Freiburg, DE13, ☆Freiburg im Breisgau; Karlsruhe, DE12, ☆Karlsruhe; Stuttgart, DE11, ☆Stuttgart; Tübingen, DE14, ☆Tübingen

Bavaria: Lower Bavaria, DE22, Niederbayern, ☆Landshut; Lower Franconia, DE26, Unterfranken, ☆Würzburg; Middle Franconia, DE25, Mittelfranken, ☆Ansbach; Swabia, DE27, Schwaben, ☆Augsburg; Upper Bavaria, DE21, Oberbayern, ☆München; Upper Franconia, DE24, Oberfranken, ☆Bayreuth; Upper Palatinate, DE23, Oberpfalz, ☆Regensburg

Hesse: Darmstadt, DE71, ☆Darmstadt; Giessen, DE72, Gießen, ☆Gießen; Kassel, DE73, ☆Kassel

Lower Saxony: Brunswick, DE91, Braunschweig, ☆Braunschweig; Hanover, DE92, Hannover, ☆Hannover; Lüneburg, DE93, ☆Lüneburg; Weser-Ems, DE94, ☆Oldenburg

North Rhine-Westphalia: Arnsberg, DEA5, ☆Arnsberg; Cologne, DEA2, Köln, ☆Köln; Detmold, DEA4, ☆Detmold; Düsseldorf, DEA1, ☆Düsseldorf; Münster, DEA3, ☆Münster

Rhineland-Palatinate: Koblenz, DEB1, ☆Koblenz; Rhenish Hesse-Palatinate, DEB3, Rheinhessen-Pfalz, ☆Neustadt an der Weinstrasse; Trier, DEB2, ☆Trier

Saxony-Anhalt: Dessau, DEE1, ☆Dessau; Halle, DEE2, ☆Halle; Magdeburg, DEE3, ☆Magdeburg

Territorial extent: In the 19th century, Germany was a crazy quilt of tiny fiefs, with enclaves everywhere. Each successive change of administrative divisions has tended to reduce the number of enclaves, until now there are hardly any left.

Baden-Württemberg state (Freiburg district) includes the small enclave of Büsingen, surrounded by Schaffhausen canton in Switzerland.

Bremen state has two separate parts, containing the cities of Bremen and Bremerhaven. Both parts are completely surrounded by Lower Saxony, if territorial waters are taken into account.

Hamburg includes the North Sea islands of Neuwerk and Scharhörn. The part of Hamburg containing the city itself lies on the border between Lower Saxony and Schleswig-Holstein.

Lower Saxony includes the East Frisian Islands, from Borkum in the west to Hoher Knechtsand in the east.

Mecklenburg-Vorpommern includes the Baltic island of Rügen, and Usedom except for a small area around Swinoujscie, Poland.

Schleswig-Holstein includes the North Sea island of Helgoland and the North Frisian Islands, from Trischen in the south to Sylt in the north. On the Baltic coast, it contains the island of Fehmarn.

Origins of names:

Baden-Württemberg: Germanic *badun*: at the baths; possibly *wirten*: innkeepers, *berg*: mountain

Bavaria (Bayern): Germanic *Bai*: Boii (ethnic name), *warioz*: defender

Berlin: origin unknown, but the coat of arms displays a bear because of a folk etymology from *Bärlein*: bear cub

Brandenburg: Slavic *brenna*: swamp, influenced by Germanic *brand*: heath; *burg*: fort

Bremen: Old High German *brem*: swampy coast

Hamburg: possibly Germanic *hamma*: spit of land (between the Alster and Elbe Rivers), *burg*: fort

Hesse: Latin *Hassi*: ethnic name

Mecklenburg-West Pomerania: Old German *mikilal*: big, *burg*: city; Slavic *po more*: [dwellers] by the sea

North Rhine-Westphalia: Rhine is from Celtic *renos*: river; Westphalia is a plain west of the Weser River, from Old German *falen*: plain.

Rhineland-Palatinate: Land by the Rhine, and German *Pfalz*: royal palace, from Latin *palatium*: palace.

Saarland: Land by the Saar River

Saxony: Germanic *sahsa*: short sword

Saxony-Anhalt: Saxony + fief of Counts von Anhalt; German *anhalten*: hold on to

Schleswig-Holstein: Old Norse *slie*: rushes, reeds, *vik*: bay; Germanic *holt*: woods, *sittan*: to be situated (i.e. dwellers in the woods)

Change history: From 1871 to 1918, the German Empire was divided into 26 units. They were heterogeneous in population, size, and status (duchies, principalities, kingdoms, etc.). The word Land, however, could be applied to any of them. The list is shown under Population history.

1919-06-28	Treaty of Versailles signed. Poland's independence, which it had proclaimed on 1918-11-09, was recognized. Germany lost most of Posen and West Prussia provinces of Prussia to Poland, leaving East Prussia and a small section of West Prussia isolated from the rest of Germany by the "Polish Corridor." The Reichsland Elsaß-Lothringen (imperial state of Alsace-Lorraine) was restored to France. Memelgebiet (or Memelland, a section of East Prussia province of Prussia, north of the Memel River, containing the port of Memel (modern Klaipeda)) detached from Germany and placed under French administration. Saar Territory (Saarland) split from the southern part of Rhine province of Prussia as a French protectorate. The entities remaining to Germany changed their status to that of states.
1920-01-20	Following a plebiscite ordained by the Versailles Treaty, the cantons of Eupen, Malmédy, and Saint Vith transferred from Rhine province of Prussia to Belgium.
1920-02-10	Another Versailles plebiscite transferred the northern part of Schleswig province of Prussia from Germany to Denmark.
1920	The states of Reuss (elder and junior branches), Saxe-Altenburg, Saxe-Coburg-Gotha, Saxe-Meiningen, Saxe-Weimar-Eisenach, Schwarzburg-Rudolstadt, and Schwarzburg-Sondershausen merged to form the state of Thuringia. However, part of Saxe-Coburg-Gotha (containing the city of Coburg) was transferred to Bavaria.
1920	Silesia province of Prussia divided into the provinces of Lower Silesia (Niederschlesien, capital Breslau) and Upper Silesia (Oberschlesien/Oppeln, capital Oppeln).
1921-05-21	Plebiscite held in most of Upper Silesia province of Prussia. A few eastern cantons voted for union with Poland, which took place in 1922.
1923-02-16	Memelgebiet placed under Lithuanian administration.
1929-04-01	Waldeck state merged into Hessen-Nassau province of Prussia.
1932	Bautzen and Dresden districts merged to form the district of Dresden-Bautzen, capital Dresden.
~1932	Niederbayern and Oberpfalz districts merged to form the district of Niederbayern und Oberpfalz, capital Regensburg.
1934	Mecklenburg-Schwerin and Mecklenburg-Strelitz states merged to form Mecklenburg state.
1935-03-01	Saarland annexed to Germany after a plebiscite. It became part of Rhine province again.
1937	Birkenfeld (near Trier) and Eutin (near Lübeck), remote enclaves of Oldenburg state, merged with Prussia. Lübeck free city merged into Schleswig-Holstein province of Prussia.
1938	Hamburg annexed a number of districts from adjacent provinces of Prussia.
1938-03-13	Austria annexed by Germany in the Anschluss. The German government called the Austrian territory Ostmark.
1938-09-30	The Sudetenland, a fringe of Czechoslovakia, transferred to Germany by the Munich Pact.
1939	Bremerhaven transferred from Bremen to Hannover province of Prussia.
1939-03-23	Memelgebiet transferred from Lithuania to Germany in response to a German ultimatum.
1945-05-09	Germany's unconditional surrender to the Allies took effect. The German Empire ceased to exist. The Allies, following preconceived plans, restored Germany to its borders of 1937-12-31, and divided it into four administrative zones: American, British, French, and Russian. Berlin, completely surrounded by the Russian zone, was partitioned in the same way. During the next few years, the administrative division of Germany was gradually redefined by the occupying forces.
1945-07-16	Potsdam Conference began. It transferred large parts of Pomerania, Brandenburg, Silesia, East and West Prussia provinces to Poland, except that the northern part of East

Prussia became Kaliningrad Oblast of Russia. The new eastern border of Germany was called the Oder-Neisse Line, as it generally followed the course of the Oder and Neisse Rivers.

1945–1946   Germany (excluding Berlin) divided into 17 states. The delineation of these states, and the establishment of their governmental institutions, was a gradual process. The following table shows the states and Berlin circa 1950. In the last column, in order to show sufficient detail, I list provinces of Prussia (indicated by PR:) and Bavaria (BA:).

division	capital	zone	from earlier division
Bavaria	Munich	Amer	Bavaria (except BA:Palatinate)
Berlin	Berlin	joint	PR:Brandenburg (part)
Brandenburg	Potsdam	Russ	PR:Brandenburg (part)
Bremen	Bremen	Amer	Bremen
Hamburg	Hamburg	Brit	Hamburg
Hesse	Wiesbaden	Amer	Hesse (part), PR:Hesse-Nassau
Lower Saxony	Hannover	Brit	Brunswick, Oldenburg, Lippe, Schaumburg-Lippe, PR:Hanover
Mecklenburg-Vorpommern	Schwerin	Russ	Mecklenburg, PR:Pomerania (part)
North Rhine-Westphalia	Düsseldorf	Brit	PR:Rhine (part), PR:Westphalia
Rhineland-Palatinate	Mainz	Frch	PR:Rhine (part), BA:Palat, Hesse (part), PR:Hess-Nass (part)
Saarland	Saarbrücken	Frch	PR:Rhine (part)
Saxony	Dresden	Russ	Saxony, PR:Silesia (part)
Saxony-Anhalt	Halle	Russ	Anhalt, PR:Saxony, PR:Bdbg (part), Brswk (part), Thrg (part)
Schleswig-Holstein	Kiel	Brit	Schleswig-Holstein
Südbaden	Freiburg	Frch	Baden (part)
Thuringia	Weimar	Russ	Thuringia, PR:Saxony (part), PR:Hesse-Nassau (part)
Württemberg-Baden	Stuttgart	Amer	Baden (part), Württemberg (part)
Württemberg-Hohenzollern	Tübingen	Frch	Württemberg (part), PR:Hohenzollern

1946-11-01   Lower Saxony state established by British military government by merging Hanover province of Prussia, and the states of Braunschweig, Oldenburg, and Schaumburg-Lippe.

1946-12-02   British and American zones merged, forming the Bizone (also called Bizonia).

1947   Schleswig-Holstein state organized.

1947   Bremerhaven transferred from Lower Saxony to Bremen state.

1947-12-15   Saarland (slightly enlarged on the north side) became a protectorate of France, after a plebiscite favored economic union with France.

1948-07-01   Separate municipal government formed for East Berlin under aegis of the Soviet Union.

1952   Baden-Württemberg state formed by merging Württemberg-Baden, Südwürttemberg-Hohenzollern, and Südbaden, following a plebiscite held 1951-12-09.

1952-07-23   East Germany reorganized from five states into 14 Bezirke (sing. Bezirk: district), plus East Berlin. This table shows the districts at that time, and how they were formed.

district	formed from state(s)	district	formed from state(s)
Chemnitz	Saxony	Leipzig	Saxony, Saxony-Anhalt, Thuringia
Cottbus	Brandenburg, Saxony-Anhalt, Saxony	Magdeburg	Saxony-Anhalt, Brandenburg
Dresden	Saxony	Neubrandenburg	Mecklenburg, Brandenburg
East Berlin	Berlin	Potsdam	Brandenburg, Saxony-Anhalt
Erfurt	Thuringia, Saxony-Anhalt	Rostock	Mecklenburg
Frankfurt an der Oder	Brandenburg	Schwerin	Mecklenburg, Brandenburg
Gera	Thuringia, Saxony-Anhalt, Saxony	Suhl	Thuringia
Halle	Saxony-Anhalt, Thuringia		

1953   Chemnitz district of East Germany, and its capital, renamed to Karl-Marx-Stadt.

1957-01-01   Saar transferred to West Germany as the result of a new plebiscite.

1959-06-07   Saar became a state of West Germany.

1990-07-01   Name of Karl-Marx-Stadt restored to Chemnitz.

1990-10-03   East Germany (ISO = DD/FIPS = GC) and West Germany (ISO = DE/FIPS = GE) merged to form Germany. Also on this date, the 14 districts of East Germany reverted to the five postwar states. The capital of the unified country is to be Berlin, but Bonn remains the seat of government until the governing institutions can be moved.

Other names of subdivisions:

Baden-Württemberg: Bade-Wurtemberg (French)

Bavaria: Baviera (Italian, Portuguese, Spanish); Bavière (French); Bayern (German, Danish); Beieren (Dutch)

Berlin: Berlim (Portuguese); Berlín (Spanish); Berlino (Italian)

Brandenburg: Brandebourg (French); Brandeburgo (Italian)

Bremen: Brema (Italian); Brême (French); Freie Hansestadt Bremen (formal)

Hamburg: Amburgo (Italian); Freie und Hansestadt Hamburg (formal); Hamborg (Danish); Hambourg (French); Hamburgo (Portuguese, Spanish)

Hesse: Assia (Italian); Hessen (German, Spanish)

Lower Saxony: Baixa Saxônia (Portuguese); Bassa Sassonia (Italian); Basse-Saxe (French); Niedersachsen (German)

Mecklenburg-Vorpommern: Mecklembourg-Poméranie (French); Mecklenburg (variant); Meclemburgo (Italian)

North Rhine-Westphalia: Noordrijn-Westfalen (Dutch); Nordrhein-Westfalen (German); Renania del Norte-West-falia (Spanish); Renânia do Norte-Vestfália (Portuguese); Renania Settentrionale-Vestfalia (Italian); Rhénanie du Nord-Westphalie (French)

Rhineland-Palatinate: Renania-Palatinado (Spanish); Renânia-Palatinado (Portuguese); Renania-Palatinato (Italian); Rheinland-Pfalz (German); Rhénanie-Palatinat (French); Rijnland-Palts (Dutch)

Saarland: Saar (Italian); Saargebiet (German-obsolete); Saarland (German); Sarre (French, Portuguese, Spanish)

Saxony: Freistaat Sachsen (formal); Sachsen (Danish, German); Saksen (Dutch); Sajonia (Spanish); Sassonia (Italian); Saxe (French)

Saxony-Anhalt: Sachsen-Anhalt (German); Sassonia e Anhalt (Italian); Saxe-Anhalt (French)

Schleswig-Holstein: Sleeswijk-Holstein (Dutch); Slesvig-Holsten (Danish); Sleswig-Holstein (obsolete)

Thuringia: Thuringe (French); Thüringen (German); Turingia (Italian, Spanish)

Population history (pre–World War I):

division	population	area-km	capital	full German name
Alsace-Lorraine	1,874,014	14,504	Straßburg	Reichsland Elsaß-Lothringen
Anhalt	331,128	2,347	Dessau	Herzogtum Anhalt
Baden	2,142,833	15,076	Karlsruhe	Großherzogtum Baden
Bavaria	6,887,291	75,840	München	Königreich Bayern
Bremen	295,715	256	Bremen	Freie Stadt Bremen
Brunswick	494,339	3,688	Brunswick	Herzogtum Braunschweig
Hamburg	1,014,664	409	Hamburg	Freie Stadt Hamburg
Hesse	1,282,219	7,679	Darmstadt	Großherzogtum Hessen
Lippe	150,937	1,215	Detmold	Fürstentum Lippe-Detmold
Lubeck	116,599	298	Lübeck	Freie Stadt Lübeck
Mecklenburg-Schwerin	639,958	13,300	Schwerin	Großherzogtum Mecklenburg-Schwerin
Mecklenburg-Strelitz	106,442	2,929	Neu-Strelitz	Großherzogtum Mecklenburg-Strelitz
Oldenburg	483,042	6,421	Oldenburg	Großherzogtum Oldenburg
Prussia	40,165,219	348,258	Berlin	Königreich Preußen
Reuss, elder branch	72,769	316	Greiz	Fürstentum Reuß-Greiz (ältere Linie)
Reuss, junior branch	152,752	826	Gera	Fürstentum Reuß-Gera (jüngere Linie)
Saxe-Altenburg	216,128	1,323	Altenburg	Herzogtum Sachsen-Altenburg
Saxe-Coburg-Gotha	257,177	1,955	Coburg, Gotha	Herzogtum Sachsen-Coburg-Gotha
Saxe-Meiningen	278,762	2,468	Meiningen	Herzogtum Sachsen-Meiningen
Saxony, Kingdom of	4,806,661	14,988	Dresden	Königreich Sachsen
Saxony, Grand Duchy of	417,149	3,595	Weimar	Großherzogtum Sachsen-Weimar-Eisenach
Schaumburg-Lippe	46,652	339	Buckeburg	Fürstentum Schaumburg-Lippe
Schwarzburg-Rudolstadt	100,702	940	Rudolstadt	Fürstentum Schwarzburg-Rudolstadt
Schwarzburg-Sondershausen	89,917	862	Sondershausen	Fürstentum Schwarzburg-Sondershausen
Waldeck	61,707	1,121	Arolsen	Fürstentum Waldeck
Württemberg	2,437,574	19,497	Stuttgart	Königreich Württemberg
	64,922,350	540,450		

Population: 1910-12-01 census.

Capitals: listed in German (Straßburg = Strasbourg, München = Munich).

Full German names: the status is part of the name. Freie Stadt = free city, Fürstentum = principality, Großherzogtum = grand duchy, Herzogtum = duchy, Königreich = kingdom, Reichsland = imperial state. The generic term for all these divisions was Länder.

Some of the Länder were further subdivided into Provinzen (provinces). The German names of the provinces are given, followed by (the English names if different) and the ☆capitals. The slash (/) indicates an alternate form of the name. The Saxony which was a province of Prussia is not the same as any of the Saxonies listed above.

Alsace-Lorraine: Lothringen (Lorraine) ☆Metz; Oberelsaß (Upper Alsace) ☆Colmar; Unterelsaß (Lower Alsace) ☆Straßburg. These provinces are now French departments.

Bavaria: Mittelfranken (Middle Franconia) ☆Ansbach; Niederbayern (Lower Bavaria) ☆Landshut; Oberbayern (Upper Bavaria) ☆München; Oberfranken (Upper Franconia) ☆Bayreuth; Oberpfalz und Regensburg (Upper Palatinate and Ratisbon) ☆Regensburg; Pfalz/Rheinbayern (Palatinate/Rhenish Bavaria) ☆Speyer; Schwaben und Neuburg (Swabia and Neuburg) ☆Augsburg; Unterfranken und Aschaffenburg (Lower Franconia and Aschaffenburg) ☆Würzburg

Kingdom of Saxony: Bauzen; Chemnitz; Dresden; Leipzig; Zwickau. Capitals have same names.

Prussia: Brandenburg ☆Potsdam; Hannover (Hanover) ☆Hannover; Hessen-Nassau (Hesse-Nassau) ☆Kassel; Hohenzollern ☆Sigmaringen; Ostpreußen (East Prussia) ☆Königsberg; Pommern (Pomerania) ☆Stettin; Posen ☆Posen; Rheinprovinz/Rheinpreußen (Rhine Province/Rhenish Prussia) ☆Koblenz; Sachsen (Saxony) ☆Magdeburg; Schleswig-Holstein ☆Kiel; Schlesien (Silesia) ☆Breslau; Westfalen (Westphalia) ☆Münster; Westpreußen (West Prussia) ☆Danzig

Württemberg: Donau (Danube) ☆Ulm; Jagst ☆Ellwangen; Neckar ☆Stuttgart; Schwarzwald (Black Forest) ☆Reutlingen. These divisions were counties.

(as of late 1935)

division	population	area-km	capital	from earlier division
Anhalt	364,415	2,314	Dessau	Anhalt
Baden	2,412,951	15,070	Karlsruhe	Baden
Bavaria	7,681,584	75,996	Munich	Bavaria, SCG (part)
Bremen	371,558	258	Bremen	Bremen
Brunswick	512,989	3,672	Brunswick	Brunswick
Hamburg	1,218,447	415	Hamburg	Hamburg
Hesse	1,429,048	7,692	Darmstadt	Hesse
Lippe	175,538	1,215	Detmold	Lippe
Lubeck	136,413	298	Lubeck	Lubeck
Mecklenburg	805,213	16,056	Schwerin	M-Sch, M-Str
Oldenburg	573,853	6,427	Oldenburg	Oldenburg
Prussia	40,760,011	294,688	Berlin	Prussia (part), Waldeck
Saxony	5,196,652	14,986	Dresden	Kingdom of Saxony
Schaumburg-Lippe	49,955	340	Bückeburg	Schaumburg-Lippe
Thuringia	1,659,510	11,763	Weimar	Reuss (e/j), SA, SCG (part), SM, SWE, SL, SR, SS
Württemberg	2,696,324	19,508	Stuttgart	Württemberg
	66,044,461	470,698		

Population: 1933-06-16.

From earlier division: shows which pre-war states were included in each of the 1935 states (using abbreviations which should be self-explanatory).

(Cold War period)

division	FIPS	area-km	1957	1971	1986
East Berlin	BZ	403	1,110,016	1,094,000	1,223,300
Cottbus	GC01	8,262	799,160	872,000	883,300
Dresden	GC02	6,738	1,902,702	1,845,000	1,771,600
Erfurt	GC03	7,349	1,264,400	1,247,000	1,235,000
Frankfurt	GC04	7,186	661,106	689,000	707,600
Gera	GC05	4,004	727,576	739,000	740,500
Halle	GC06	8,771	1,995,879	1,890,000	1,785,800
Karl-Marx-Stadt	GC07	6,009	2,144,191	1,994,000	1,870,000
Leipzig	GC08	4,966	1,544,316	1,458,000	1,373,800
Magdeburg	GC09	11,526	1,400,616	1,298,000	1,250,000
Neubrandenburg	GC10	10,894	667,521	629,000	619,200
Potsdam	GC12	12,568	1,187,637	1,125,000	1,120,300 ▶

division	FIPS	area-km	1957	1971	1986
Rostock	GC13	7,074	828,440	868,000	903,000
Schwerin	GC14	8,672	634,057	592,000	592,100
Suhl	GC15	3,856	543,053	550,000	549,200
total East		108,278	17,410,670	16,890,000	16,624,700
West Berlin	BZ	480	2,228,500	2,197,000	1,867,700
Baden-Württemberg	GE01	35,751	7,301,900	7,759,000	9,295,100
Bavaria	GE02	70,547	9,192,800	9,515,000	10,993,400
Bremen	GE03	404	664,100	706,000	675,500
Hamburg	GE04	748	1,786,800	1,832,000	1,575,700
Hesse	GE05	21,113	4,599,700	4,814,000	5,531,300
Lower Saxony	GE06	47,415	6,496,100	6,641,000	7,149,300
North Rhine-Westphalia	GE07	34,069	15,193,300	15,912,000	16,665,300
Rhineland-Palatinate	GE08	19,839	3,313,800	3,417,000	3,610,400
Saarland	GE09	2,568	1,019,100	1,073,000	1,043,400
Schleswig-Holstein	GE10	15,696	2,264,300	2,317,000	2,612,700
total West		248,630	54,060,400	56,183,000	61,019,800
total Germany		356,908	71,471,070	78,471,766	77,644,500

FIPS: Codes from FIPS PUB 10-4 (1984 edition).
Area-km: Square kilometers.

1957: Population estimate 1957-12-31.
1971: East—1970 census; West—1971 census

1986: Population estimate 1986-06-30

GHANA

ISO = GH/FIPS = GH   Language = English   Time zone = 0   Capital = Accra

In 1900, the coastal region of Ghana had been colonized by the United Kingdom as the Gold Coast. In 1901, Ashanti, already a British protectorate, was annexed. The Northern Territories Protectorate followed in 1902. After World War I, the Allies divided Germany's African possessions among them. The League of Nations mandated Togoland to Great Britain and France. They split it longitudinally. Britain received the smaller western strip, which became Transvolta-Togoland territory. This territory was administered from the Gold Coast until 1956-12-13, when it formally merged with the Gold Coast. The country was granted independence on 1957-03-06, and took the name Ghana.

    Other names of country: Côte de l'Or (French-obsolete); Gana (Icelandic, Portuguese); Gold Coast (obsolete); Gold Küste (German-obsolete); Republic of Ghana (formal–English).

    Origin of name: after an ancient West African kingdom, from Sarakolé *ghana*: king.

division	ISO	FIPS	population	area-km	area-mi	capital
Ashanti	AH	GH02	2,090,100	24,390	9,417	Kumasi
Brong-Ahafo	BA	GH03	1,206,608	39,557	15,273	Sunyani
Central	CP	GH04	1,142,335	9,826	3,794	Cape Coast
Eastern	EP	GH05	1,680,890	19,977	7,713	Koforidua
Greater Accra	AA	GH01	1,431,099	2,593	1,001	Accra
Northern	NP	GH06	1,164,583	70,383	27,175	Tamale
Upper East	UE	GH10	772,744	8,842	3,414	Bolgatanga
Upper West	UW	GH11	438,008	18,477	7,134	Wa
Volta	TV	GH08	1,211,907	20,572	7,943	Ho
Western	WP	GH09	1,157,807	23,921	9,236	Sekondi-Takoradi
			12,296,081	238,538	92,100	

Status: These divisions are regions.
ISO: Codes from ISO 3166-2.
FIPS: Codes from FIPS PUB 10-4.

Population: 1984 census.
Area-km: Square kilometers.
Area-mi: Square miles.
Further subdivisions: The regions are subdivided into 110 districts.
Origins of names:

Accra: corruption of Bantu *nkran*: ants (forest dwellers likened city to an anthill)

Volta: from the Volta River, from Portuguese *volta*: turn

Change history:

1902	Gold Coast consisted of three regions: Ashanti, Gold Coast, and Northern Territories Protectorate.
1922	Transvolta Togoland became affiliated with Gold Coast.
1956-12-13	Transvolta Togoland became part of Gold Coast.
1957-03-06	Gold Coast renamed Ghana.
~1958	Gold Coast region (capital Accra) split into Eastern (capital Koforidua) and Western (capital Cape Coast).
~1961	Ashanti region (capital Kumasi) split into Ashanti and Brong-Ahafo regions. Northern Territories (capital Tamale) split into Northern and Upper regions. Western region split into Western (capital Sekondi) and Central. Transvolta Togoland (capital Ho) split in two; the southern part became Volta region, and the northern part was annexed to Northern and Upper regions.
~1971	Sekondi and Takoradi merge to form the city of Sekondi-Takoradi, the new capital of Western.
~1975	Eastern region split into Eastern and Greater Accra regions.
~1988	Upper region (FIPS code GH07) split into Upper East and Upper West regions.

GIBRALTAR

ISO = GI/FIPS = GI   Language = English   Time zone = +1 ^d   Capital = Gibraltar

Gibraltar has been a British colony since 1713.
Other names of country: Gibilterra (Italian).
Origin of name: Arabic *jabal Tariq*: mountain of Tariq, for Tariq ibn Ziyad, Berber chieftain who conquered the peninsula in 711.

division	abv	population	area-km	area-mi	capital
Gibraltar	GI	31,265	6	2	Gibraltar

Status: This division is the whole of the country, treated as a division for compatibility.
Abv: Two-letter code for international compatibility (defined by the author).
Population: 1991 census.
Area-km: Square kilometers.
Area-mi: Square miles.
Territorial extent: Gibraltar occupies a small peninsula with a very short border with Spain. There is a narrow neutral zone along the border.

GREECE

ISO = GR/FIPS = GR   Language = Greek   Time zone = +2 [d]   Capital = Athens

Greece in 1900 occupied only a fraction of its present extent. Crete was independent until 1913, when it was annexed to Greece. The Dodecanese Islands, after a number of changes, became part of Greece in 1947. The Northern Aegean Islands and most of Epirus and Macedonia were transferred from the waning Ottoman Empire to Greece in 1913 at the conclusion of the Balkan Wars. At the same time, most of Thrace was annexed by Bulgaria. The parts of Thrace which now belong to Greece were acquired from Bulgaria in the Treaties of Sèvres and Lausanne. Greece was occupied by the Axis during World War II.

Other names of country: Elliniki Dimokratia (formal); Grækenland (Danish); Grèce (French); Grecia (Italian, Spanish); Grécia (Portuguese); Grekland (Swedish); Griechenland (German); Griekenland (Dutch); Grikkland (Icelandic); Hellas (Norwegian); Hellenic Republic (formal–English); Kreikka (Finnish); República Helénica (formal–Spanish).

Origin of name: through Latin, originally from Greek *Graikos*: inhabitant in a section of Epirus.

district	abv	ISO	FIPS	population	area-km	area-mi	reg	capital
Achaea	AK	13	GR38	297,318	3,209	1,239	GW	Patras (Patrai)
Aitolia and Akarnania	AA	01	GR31	230,688	5,447	2,103	GW	Missolongi (Mesolongion)
Arcadia	AD	12	GR41	103,840	4,419	1,706	PP	Tripolis (Tripolitza)
Argolis	AG	11	GR36	97,250	2,214	855	PP	Nauplion
Arta	AR	31	GR20	78,884	1,612	622	EP	Arta
Attica	AT	02*	GR35	3,522,769	3,808	1,470	AT	Athens (Athenai)
Boeotia	BT	03	GR33	134,034	3,211	1,240	GC	Levadeia
Corfu	CF	22	GR25	105,043	641	247	II	Corfu (Kerkyra)
Corinth	CN	15	GR37	142,365	2,290	884	PP	Corinth (Korinthos)
Cyclades	CY	82	GR49	95,083	2,572	993	AS	Hermoupolis (Ermoupole)
Dodecanese	DO	81	GR47	162,439	2,705	1,044	AS	Rhodes (Rodos)
Drama	DR	52	GR04	96,978	3,468	1,339	MT	Drama
Euboea	EU	04	GR34	209,132	3,908	1,509	GC	Khalkis (Chalkida)
Evritania	ET	05	GR30	23,535	2,045	790	GC	Karpenissi (Karpenesion)
Evros	ES	71	GR01	143,791	4,242	1,638	MT	Alexandroupolis
Florina	FL	63	GR08	52,854	1,863	719	MW	Florina
Fokis	FK	07	GR32	43,889	2,121	819	GC	Amfissa
Fthiotis	FT	06	GR29	168,291	4,368	1,686	GC	Lamia
Grevena	GR	51	GR10	37,017	2,338	903	MW	Grevena
Heraklion	IR	91	GR45	263,868	2,641	1,020	CR	Heraklion (Candia, Megalokastron)
Ilia	IL	14	GR39	174,021	2,681	1,035	GW	Pyrgos
Imathia	IM	53	GR12	138,068	1,712	661	MC	Veroia
Ioannina	IO	33	GR17	157,214	4,990	1,927	EP	Ioannina (Yannina)
Karditsa	KT	41	GR23	126,498	2,576	995	TS	Karditsa
Kastoria	KS	56	GR09	52,721	1,685	651	MW	Kastoria
Kavala	KV	55	GR14	135,747	2,109	814	MT	Kavala (Cavalla)
Kefallinia	KF	23	GR27	32,314	935	361	II	Argostoli (Argostolion)
Khalkidiki	KD	64	GR15	91,654	2,945	1,137	MC	Polygyros
Khania	KN	94	GR43	133,060	2,376	917	CR	Khania (Canea)
Khios	KH	85	GR50	52,691	904	349	AN	Khios
Kilkis	KK	57	GR06	81,845	2,614	1,009	MC	Kilkis
Kozani	KZ	58	GR11	150,159	3,562	1,375	MW	Kozani
Laconia	LC	16	GR42	94,916	3,636	1,404	PP	Sparta (Sparte)
Larisa	LR	42	GR21	269,300	5,351	2,066	TS	Larisa (Larissa)
Lasithi	LT	92	GR46	70,762	1,823	704	CR	Agios Nikolaos
Lesvos	LS	83	GR51	103,700	2,154	832	AN	Mytilene
Levkas	LV	24	GR26	20,900	325	125	II	Levkas (Leucadia)
Magnesia	MG	43	GR24	197,613	2,636	1,018	TS	Volos (Nea Ionia)
Messinia	MS	17	GR40	167,292	2,991	1,155	PP	Kalamata (Kalamai)
Mount Athos	MA	69	GR15	1,472	336	130	MC	Karyai (Karyes)
Pella	PL	59	GR07	138,261	2,506	968	MC	Edessa
Pieria	PI	61	GR16	116,820	1,506	581	MC	Katerini
Preveza	PV	34	GR19	58,910	1,086	419	EP	Preveza
Rethymnon	RT	93	GR44	69,290	1,496	578	CR	Rethymnon (Rethymni)
Rodopi	RD	73	GR02	103,295	2,543	982	MT	Komotini ▶

district	abv	ISO	FIPS	population	area-km	area-mi	reg	capital
Samos	SM	84	GR48	41,850	778	300	AN	Samos (Limin Vatheos, Vathy)
Serrai	SR	62	GR05	191,890	3,970	1,533	MC	Serrai (Serres)
Thesprotia	TP	32	GR18	44,202	1,515	585	EP	Hegoumenitsa
Thessaloniki	TN	54	GR13	977,528	3,560	1,375	MC	Thessaloniki (Salonica)
Trikala	TR	44	GR22	137,819	3,367	1,300	TS	Trikala (Trikkala)
Xanthi	XN	72	GR03	90,450	1,793	692	MT	Xanthi
Zakynthos	ZK	21	GR28	32,746	406	157	II	Zakynthos (Zante)
				10,264,076	131,989	50,961		

* = *There are actually two codes for Attica: A1 = Attiki, and 02 = Attiki (ypoloipo — rest of). Probably A1 is meant to represent Greater Athens, and 02 is Attica except for Greater Athens.*

Status: These divisions are nomoi (sing. nomos; usually translated prefectures, but also departments), except for Mount Athos, which is an autonomous monastic community.

Abv: Two-letter code for international compatibility (defined by the author).

ISO: Codes from ISO 3166-2.

FIPS: Codes from FIPS PUB 10-4. Note: Mount Athos is not specifically mentioned in the standard, so I assume it's included in GR15 Khalkidiki.

Population: 1991-03-17 census.

Area-km: Square kilometers.

Area-mi: Square miles.

Reg: Region, as coded below.

Capital: Where two names are given, the first is the name most commonly found in English text. The second is a variant transliteration, a more Greek-like version, or an older name for the same city.

Greece has been divided up into larger units called diamerismata (regions). The regions have few or no administrative functions. Their purposes include education, tourism, and historic pride. The current division into regions is shown in the following table.

reg	region name	ISO	NUTS	population	area-km	capital	Greek name
AN	Aegean North	IV	GR41	198,241	3,836	Mytilene	Voreio Aigaio
AS	Aegean South	III	GR42	257,522	5,286	Hermoupolis	Notio Aigaio
AT	Attica	I	GR3	3,522,769	3,808	Athens	Attiki
CR	Crete	II	GR43	536,980	8,336	Heraklion	Kriti
EP	Epirus	V	GR21	339,210	9,203	Ioannina	Ipeiros
GC	Greece Central	VI	GR24	578,881	15,549	Lamia	Sterea Ellada
GW	Greece West	VII	GR23	702,027	11,350	Patras	Dytiki Ellada
II	Ionian Islands	VIII	GR22	191,003	2,307	Corfu	Ionioi Nisoi
MC	Macedonia Central	IX	GR12	1,736,066	19,147	Thessaloniki	Kentriki Makedonia
MT	Macedonia East and Thrace	XI	GR11	570,261	14,157	Comotini	Anatoliki Makedonia kai Thraki
MW	Macedonia West	X	GR13	292,751	9,451	Kozani	Dytiki Makedonia
PP	Peloponnese	XII	GR25	605,663	15,490	Tripolis	Peloponnisos
TS	Thessaly	XIII	GR14	731,230	14,037	Larissa	Thessalia

Reg: Arbitrary codes defined by the author.

ISO: ISO 3166-2 attributes these codes to an official map of Greece.

NUTS: Nomenclature of Territorial Units for Statistics. Truncating these codes to the first three characters defines a still higher-level subdivision: GR1 = Voreia Ellada (North Greece), GR2 = Kentriki Ellada (Central Greece), GR3 = Attiki, GR4 = Nisia Aigaiou, Kriti (Aegean Islands and Crete).

Capital: Not an administrative center for the region, but the chief town.

Further subdivisions: Greece is divided into 13 regions, which are subdivided into 51 prefectures and one autonomous community, which are further subdivided into 147 eparchia (provinces), which are further subdivided into 272 demoi (municipalities), which are further subdivided into localities.

Territorial extent: The prefectures all include tiny islets adjacent to their shores, too numerous to mention.

Attica includes a string of islands down the Peloponnese coast, as well as a fragment of the coast itself around the Methana Peninsula, along the coast of Argolis. The islands are Salamis, Aegina, Idra (Hydra), Spetses, Kythera (Cythera, Cerigo), Antikythera, Dokos, Poros, and Angistri.

Corfu consists of the islands of Corfu (Kerkyra), Paxi, Othoni, Erikoussa, Antipaxi, and Mathraki.

Cyclades consists of the islands of Naxos, Andros, Amorgos, Tinos, Paros, Mykonos, Siros, Kea, Thira (Santorini), Kithnos, Ios, Serifos, Sifnos, Folegandros, Anafi, Makronissi, Reneia, Kimolos, Polyaigos, Antiparos, Donousa, Herakleia, Thirasia, and Skhinousa.

Dodecanese consists of the islands of Rhodes, Karpathos, Kos, Kalymnos, Leros, Patmos, Nisyros, Telos, Symi, Kassos, Khalke, and Saria (the "twelve islands"), as well as small islands as far west as Kinaros and Ofidoussa, as far east as Megiste, and as far north as Agathonesi and Farmakonesi.

Euboea consists of the islands of Euboea, Skyros, Megalonisos Petalion, and Stira.

Evros includes the island of Samothraki (Samothrace)

Heraklion occupies an east-of-center part of the island of Crete, and includes the island of Dia.

Imathia includes an enclave surrounded by Pieria, containing the village of Elafos.

Kavala includes the island of Thasos.

Kefallinia consists of the islands of Kefallinia, Ithaki (Ithaca), Kalamos, Kastos, Atokos, Petalas, and Oxia.

Khalkidiki includes the island of Amoliani.

Khania is at the west end of Crete.

Khios consists of the islands of Khios, Psara, Oinousses, and Antipsara.

Laconia includes the island of Elafonesi.

Lasithi is at the east end of Crete, and includes the islands of Koufonesi, Elasa, and Dragonada.

Lesvos consists of the islands of Lesvos (Lesbos), Limnos, and Agios Eustratios.

Levkas consists of the islands of Levkas, Meganissi, and Arkoudi.

Magnesia includes most of the islands of the Northern Sporades: Skopelos, Alonnisos, Skiathos, Pelagos, Gioura, Skantzoura, and Piperi.

Messinia includes the islands of Sapientza, Shiza, Prote, and Venetiko.

Mount Athos occupies the easternmost of three rocky peninsulas off Khalkidiki.

Rethymnon occupies a west-of-center part of the island of Crete, and includes the island of Gaudos.

Samos consists of the islands of Samos, Ikaria, Fourni, and Thimena.

Zakynthos consists of the island of Zakynthos and the Strofades islands.

Origins of names:

Achaea: new application of the name of Agamemnon's kingdom in Homeric epics

Agion Oros (Mount Athos): Greek: Holy Mountain

Aitolia and Akarnania: from legendary patriarch Aitolos; pre-Indo-European *akarna*: rocky, *-anes*: dwellers

Arcadia: from Arkas, legendary king, changed into a bear (*arktos*)

Argolis: probably from Ancient Greek *argos*: white, brilliant, or Pelagic for high fortress

Attica: ancient Greek *Attike*: Athenian (region)

Boeotia: from ethnic name *Boiwtoi*: battler

Corfu: Greek *stous Koruphous*: with peaks, for two peaks on the island. Kerkyra: European root *kerk*: bend

Corinth: Greek Korinthos, from Pelagic *kar*: peak, or Ancient Greek *koruthos*: of the helmet

Cyclades: Ancient Greek *kyklos*: circle (islands supposedly arranged in a circle around Delos)

Dodecanese: Greek *dodeka*: twelve, *nesos*: island (twelve main islands in nomos)

Euboea: Greek *eu*: good, *bous*: bull (i.e. rich in cattle)

Heraklion: Modern Greek for sanctuary of Hercules

Ilia: possibly from Greek *elos*: swamp

Kefallinia: Ancient Greek *kefale*: head (i.e. mountain)

Khalkidike: Colonized from Khalkis, in Euboea. Ancient Greek *khalkos*: bronze, for local industry

Khania: Arabic *khniyah*: wine-seller's cabaret

Laconia: from ethnic name Lakones, from a word for lowlands or basin

Levkas: Ancient Greek *leukos*: white, for a white cliff near the city

Messenia: related to Greek *mesos*: middle (between Pylos and Sparta)

Samos: pre-Hellenic for upland

Thessalonika: after Thessalonike, wife of Kassandros, a general under Alexander the Great. The name means victorious over Thessaly, and commemorates a conquest by her father, Philip II

Regions:

Aegean: after Aegeus, legendary king of Athens, father of Theseus. In the legend, Aegeus drowned himself in this sea.

Epirus: new application of Ancient Doric *Apeiros*: shore, originally meaning all of continental Greece

Macedonia: probably from ethnic name

Peloponnese: Greek *nesos*: island: island of Pelops, a mythical king, son of Tantalus

Thessaly: from ethnic name Thessalos

Thrace: from ethnic name Thrax

Change history: At the turn of the century, there were several prefectures with compound names: Achaea and Ilia, Aitolia and Acarnania, Argolis and Corinth, Attica and Boeotia, Fthiotis and Fokis. They appear to have been composed of two divisions each, on a lower level than the prefecture. When they were split into two prefectures, in effect the lower-level divisions were simply promoted to prefecture status. In the same way, Messinia seems to have been composed of two lower-level divisions named Messinia and Triphylia, and Laconia composed of Laconia and Lacedæmonia, but these lower-level divisions never became prefectures.

1913	Crete, the Northern Aegean Islands, and most of Epirus and Macedonia annexed to Greece. This added the prefectures of Heraklion, Rethymnon, Khania, Lasithi, Lesbos, Khios, Samos, Yannina, Florina, Kozani, Salonica, Serres, and Drama, and the autonomous community of Mount Athos. Under the Ottoman Empire, Epirus had been the vilayet of Yannina (Ioannina); Macedonia, the vilayet of Salonica and part of Monastir; and the Northern Aegean Islands, part of the vilayet of Archipelago.
1920	Bulgarian territory annexed to Greece, becoming the prefecture of Thrace (about equivalent to the modern prefectures of Xanthi and Rodopi).
1923	More Bulgarian territory annexed to Thrace prefecture (modern Evros). Greece lost a section of Epirus to Albania.
1926-09-10	Greece officially recognized the status of Mount Athos as an autonomous community.
~1930	Pella prefecture split from Thessaloniki. Thrace prefecture divided into Evros and Rodopi.
~1937	Thesprotia prefecture formed from parts of Ioannina and Preveza (?).
~1939	Kilkis prefecture split from Thessaloniki. Achaea and Ilia prefecture split into Achaea prefecture and Ilia prefecture.
~1947	Attica and Boeotia prefecture split into Attica prefecture and Boeotia prefecture. Fthiotis and Fokis prefecture split into Fthiotis prefecture and Fokis prefecture. Imathia and Pieria prefectures split from Thessaloniki. Kastoria prefecture split from Florina (?). Argolis and Corinth prefecture split into Argolis prefecture and Corinth prefecture. Xanthi prefecture split from Rodopi. Magnesia prefecture split from Larissa. Karditsa prefecture split from Trikala. Evritania prefecture split from Aitolia and Acarnania.
1947	Dodecanese prefecture annexed to Greece. This area was the southern part of Archipelago vilayet under the Ottoman Empire. It was occupied by Italy in 1912, and granted to Italy by the Treaty of Sèvres in 1922. It became the colony of Isole Italiane dell'Egeo in 1930.
~1955	Levkas prefecture split from Preveza, and transferred from Epirus region to Ionian Islands.
~1968	Attica prefecture divided into Attica and Piraeus. At the same time, Greater Athens region split from Central Greece and Euboea. Greater Athens consisted of the urban parts of Attica and Piraeus prefectures.
~1969	Grevena prefecture split from Kozani.
~1987	Ten regions reorganized to make 13 regions. At the same time, Attica and Piraeus prefectures merged once again to form Attica. Regions before the reorganization were:

region	ISO	corresponds to modern regions
Aegean Islands	80	Aegean North, Aegean South
Crete	90	Crete
Epirus	30	Epirus
Greater Athens	A	Attica (Athens and Piraeus only)
Central Greece and Euboea	0	Attica (remainder), Greece Central, Greece West (Aitolia and Akarnania)
Ionian Islands	20	Ionian Islands
Macedonia	50, 60	Macedonia Central, Mac. East and Thrace (Drama, Kavala), Mac. West
Peloponnese	10	Greece West (Achaea, Ilia), Peloponnese
Thrace	70	Macedonia East and Thrace (remainder)
Thessaly	40	Thessaly

ISO: Codes from ISO 3166-2, attributed to a source in the Hellenic Organization for Standardization (ELOT). Many references give the same list of regions. Only ISO 3166-2 divides Macedonia into two regions: Macedonia I (code 50) and Macedonia II (code 60). It gives no indication of which prefectures belong to each of the Macedonian regions.

Other names of subdivisions: These names are officially spelled with the Greek alphabet. There are many transliteration schemes, giving rise to many variant names. For English names, the spellings that are most often met in literature or news reports are used here. A knowledge of the variations in transliteration schemes makes it easier to recognize variant names. The pronunciation of the letter Beta in Ancient Greek was like our B, but in Modern Greek more like V, so it may be transliterated either way. Likewise, Eta is usually E for Ancient Greek words, I for Modern. Gamma-Gamma is a diphthong, pronounced (and usually transliterated) "NG." Delta may be represented as D or DH; Gamma as G or Y; Phi as F or PH; Rho as R or RH; Kappa as K or C; Chi as KH or CH; and Upsilon as Y or I, or occasionally V or F. There is a diacritical mark similar to a reversed apostrophe called "rough breathing." In transliteration, it may be ignored, or may be shown as H. For example, it comes at the start of Ellas/Hellas, meaning Greece.

Prefectures:

Achaea: Acaia (Portuguese); Achaïa, Ahaïa, Akhaïa (variants); Achaïe (French)

Aitolia and Akarnania: Acarnania and Ætolia, Aetolia and Acarnania, Aitolia kai Akarnania, Aitolia-Akarnania, Etolía Akarnanía (variants); Atolien und Akarnien (German); Etólia e Acarnania (Portuguese); Étolie-Acarnanie (French)

Arcadia: Arcadie (French); Arkadhía, Arkadía (variants); Arkadien (German)

Argolis: Argolída (variant); Argolide (French); Argolide (Portuguese)

Attica: Atica (Portuguese); Atikí, Attikí (variants); Attika (German); Attique (French)

Boeotia: Beócia (Portuguese); Béotie (French); Böotien (German); Viotía, Voiotía (variants)

Corfu: Corcyra (obsolete); Corcyre (French-obsolete); Corfou (French); Kérkira, Kérkira, Kérkyra (variants); Korfu (German)

Corinth: Corinthia, Korinthía (variants); Corinthie (French); Corínzia (Portuguese); Korinth (German)

Cyclades: Cicladas (Portuguese); Cicladi (Italian); Cyclades (French); Kikládes, Kikladhes, Kykládes (variants); Kykladen (German)

Dodecanese: Dhodhekanisos, Dodekánis, Dodekánisos, Dodekánissa, Dodekánissos, Dodekánnisos (variants); Dodécanèse (French); Dodecanésia (Portuguese); Dodecaneso (Italian); Dodekanes (German); Sporades du Sud (French-variant)

Drama: Dhráma (German)

Euboea: Eubea (Italian); Eubée (French); Eubéia (Portuguese); Euböa, Ewwia (German); Euripos, Negropont (obsolete); Évia, Évvoia (variants); Nègrepont (French-obsolete)

Evritania: Euritanía (Portuguese); Eurytanie (French); Evrytanía (variant)

Evros: Euros (Portuguese); Hevros (variant); Héwros (German)

Fokis: Fócida (Portuguese); Fokída, Phocis, Phokis (variants); Phocide (French)

Fthiotis: Fthiótida, Phthiotis (variants); Ftiótida (Portuguese); Phthiotide, Phtiotide (French)

Grevena: Grewena (German)

Heraklion: Candia (obsolete); Candie (French-obsolete); Héracleion, Héraclion (French); Herákleion, Irákleion, Iráklio, Iráklion (variants)

Ilia: Elia, Elis, Ileía, Ilís (variants); Élida (Portuguese); Élide (French)

Imathia: Eimathía (variant); Emathia (Portuguese); Émathie (French)

Ioannina: Ianina (French-variant); Janina (Serbian); Jannina, Yanina, Yannina (variants)

Karditsa: Carditsa (French-variant); Kardhítsa (variant)

Kavala: Cavalla (French); Cavalla, Kavalla (variants); Kawála (German)

Kefallinia: Cefalonia (Italian); Cefalônia (Portuguese); Cephalonia, Kefallenia, Kefalloniá, Kefaloniá, Kephalonia (variants); Céphalonie (French)

Khalkidiki: Chalcidice, Chalcidice, Chalkidikí, Halkidikí, Khalkidhikí (variants); Chalcidique (French); Chalkidhikí (German); Kalkídica (Portuguese)

Khania: Canea, Chaniá, Haniá (variants); Canée (French); Canéia (Portuguese)

Khios: Chio (French-variant); Chios, Híos (variants); Sakis Adası (Turkish); Scio (Italian)

Kozani: Kosáni (German); Kozáne (variant)

Laconia: Lacônia (Portuguese); Laconie (French); Lakonía (variant); Lakonien (German)

Larisa: Lárissa (variant)

Lasithi: Lasithion, Lassíthi, Lassithion (variants)

Lesvos: Lesbos, Mytilène (variants)

Levkas: Lefkáda, Lefkás, Leucas (variants); Leucade (French, Italian); Leucádia (Portuguese); Sainte-Maure (French-obsolete); Santa Maura (obsolete)

Magnesia: Magnésia (Portuguese); Magnésie (French); Magnessia, Magnisía, Magnissía (variants)

Messinia: Messênia (Portuguese); Messenia (variant); Messénie (French); Messenien (German)

Mount Athos: Ághion Óros, Ágio Óros, Ágion Óros, Ágios Óros, Áyion Óros, Hágion Óros, Hágion Óros (variants); Mont Athos (French)

Pella: Péla, Pelli (variants)

Pieria: Piérie (French)

Preveza: Prévesa (Portuguese); Préwesa (German)

Rethymnon: Rethímni, Réthimno, Réthymno, Rethýmne (variants); Rethýmni (German)

Rodopi: Rhodope, Rodhópi (variants); Rhodopen (German); Rodope (French)

Samos: Susam Adası (Turkish)

Serrai: Séres, Sérres (variants)

Thessaloniki: Salônica (Portuguese); Salonica, Salonika, Thes- salonike (variants); Salonicco, Tessalonica (Italian); Saloniki (German); Salonique, Thessalonique (French)

Trikala: Tríkkala (variant)

Xanthi: Xante (French-variant)

Zakynthos: Jacinto (Portuguese); Sákynthos (German); Zacinthe (French-obsolete); Zákinthos, Zákintos, Zante (variants)

Regions:

Aegean Islands: Ägäische Inseln (German); Îles de la Mer Égée (French); Nísoi Aigaíou, Nísoi Aiyaíou, Nissiá Egeou, Níssoi Aigaíou (variants)

Aegean North: Nordägäis (German)

Aegean South: Südägäis (German)

Central Greece and Euboea: Attica and the Islands, Central Greece and Évvoia, Kentrikí Ellás kaí Évvoia, Kentrikí Hellás kaí Évia, Loipi Sterea Ellas kai Evvoia, Stereá Eláda (variants); Grèce centrale et Eubée (French); Grecia Central y Eubea (Spanish); Mittelgriechenland, Zentral- griechenland (German)

Crete: Candia (obsolete); Candie (French-obsolete); Creta (Italian, Spanish); Crète (French); Kreta (German); Kríti (variant)

Epirus: Épire (French); Epiro (Spanish); Ípeiros, Ípiros (vari- ants)

Greater Athens: Perifereia Proteuosis (variant)

Greece Central: Mittel-Hellas (German)

Greece West: West-Hellas (German)

Ionian Islands: Îles Ioniennes (French); Iónia Nissiá, Iónioi Nísoi, Iónioi Níssoi (variants); Ionische Inseln (German); Islas Jónicas (Spanish); Isole Ionie (Italian)

Macedonia: Macédoine (French); Makedhonía, Makedonía (variant); Makedonien, Mazedonien (German)

Macedonia Central: Zentralmakedonien (German)

Macedonia East and Thrace: Ostmakedonien und Thrakien (German)

Macedonia West: Westmakedonien (German)

Peloponnese: Morea (obsolete); Morée (French-obsolete); Peloponeso (Spanish); Pelopónissos, Peloponnesus, Pelopónnisos, Pelopónnissos (variants); Peloponnes (Ger- man); Péloponnèse (French); Peloponeso (Italian)

Thessaly: Tesalia (Spanish); Tessaglia (Italian); Thessalía (vari- ant); Thessalie (French); Thessalien (German)

Thrace: Thráki (variant); Thrakien, Thrazien (German); Tra- cia (Italian, Spanish)

Population history:

	1896	1940	1951	1971	1981	1991
Achaea	210,713	222,060	228,871	239,859	275,193	297,318
Aitolia/Akarnania	162,020	251,442	220,138	228,989	219,764	230,688
Arcadia	148,285	170,306	154,361	111,263	107,932	103,840
Argolis	144,836	199,148	85,389	88,698	93,020	97,250
Arta	32,890	65,175	72,717	78,376	80,044	78,884
Attica	257,764	1,394,021	1,556,029	2,797,849	3,369,424	3,522,769
Boeotia	——	——	106,838	114,675	117,175	134,034
Corfu	114,535	111,548	105,414	92,933	99,477	105,043
Corinth	——	——	113,358	113,115	123,042	142,365
Cyclades	131,508	129,015	125,959	86,337	88,458	95,083
Dodecanese	——	——	121,480	121,017	145,071	162,439
Drama	——	145,089	120,492	91,009	94,772	96,978
Euboea	103,442	177,076	164,542	165,369	188,410	209,132
Evritania	——	——	39,678	29,533	26,182	23,535
Evros	——	154,773	141,340	138,988	148,486	143,791
Florina	——	156,168	69,391	52,264	52,430	52,854
Fokis	——	——	51,472	41,361	44,222	43,889
Fthiotis	136,470	213,079	148,322	154,542	161,995	168,291
Grevena	——	——	——	35,275	36,421	37,017
Heraklion	——	167,918	189,637	209,670	243,622	263,868
Ilia	——	186,945	188,274	165,056	160,305	174,021
Imathia	——	——	96,439	118,103	133,750	138,068
Ioannina	——	162,150	153,748	134,688	147,304	157,214
Karditsa	——	——	138,786	133,776	124,930	126,498
Kastoria	——	——	46,407	45,711	53,169	52,721
Kavala	——	138,133	136,337	121,593	135,218	135,747
Kefallinia	80,178	66,849	47,369	36,742	31,297	32,314
Khalkidiki	——	81,180	75,735	73,850	79,036	91,654 ➤

	1896	1940	1951	1971	1981	1991
Khania	––	126,093	126,524	119,797	125,856	133,060
Khios	––	75,853	66,823	53,948	49,865	52,691
Kilkis	––	99,389	89,475	84,375	81,562	81,845
Kozani	––	197,476	177,838	135,709	147,051	150,159
Laconia	126,088	144,156	130,898	95,844	93,218	94,916
Larisa	168,034	322,273	208,120	232,226	254,295	269,300
Lasithi	––	71,172	73,784	66,226	70,053	70,762
Lesvos	––	159,031	154,795	114,802	104,620	103,700
Levkas	––	––	37,752	24,581	21,863	20,900
Magnesia	––	––	153,808	161,392	182,222	197,613
Messinia	183,232	240,987	227,871	173,077	159,818	167,292
Mount Athos	––	4,746	3,086	1,732	1,472	1,552
Pella	––	127,597	116,969	126,085	132,386	138,261
Pieria	––	––	86,161	91,728	106,859	116,820
Preveza	––	72,550	56,779	56,586	55,915	58,910
Rethymnon	––	73,056	72,179	60,949	62,634	69,290
Rodopi	––	205,150	105,723	107,677	107,957	103,295
Samos	––	69,138	59,709	41,709	40,519	41,850
Serrai	––	232,224	222,549	202,898	196,247	191,890
Thesprotia	––	62,457	47,299	40,684	41,278	44,202
Thessaloniki	––	577,128	459,956	710,352	871,580	977,528
Trikala	143,143	251,144	128,227	132,519	134,207	137,819
Xanthi	––	––	89,891	82,917	88,777	90,450
Zakynthos	44,070	41,165	38,062	30,187	30,014	32,746
	2,187,208	7,344,860	7,632,801	8,768,641	9,740,417	10,264,156

Census dates: 1928-05-16 (N/A), 1951-04-07, 1961-03-19 (N/A), 1971-03-14, 1981-04-05.

GREENLAND

ISO = GL/FIPS = GL   Languages = Inuit, Danish   Time zone = (see note)   Capital = Nuuk

Greenland began the 20th century as a Danish colony. On 1953-06-05 it became constitutionally part of Denmark as an overseas county. It still retains that status, although it has a great measure of autonomy. Places in Greenland usually have both Danish and Inuit names, which are not in the least similar, and can cause confusion.

Time zone note: Most of Greenland is currently on -3 ^{d} (three hours earlier than GMT, with daylight saving time in the summer). The far northwest, around Thule, is on -4 ^{d}; a small part of the east coast, around Scoresbysund and Constable Pynt, is on -1 ^{d}.

Other names of country: Grænland (Icelandic); Groenland (Dutch, French); Groenlandia (Italian, Spanish); Groenlân-dia (Portuguese); Grönland (German, Swedish); Grønland (Danish, Norwegian); Grönlanti (Finnish); Kalaallit Nunaat (Inuit)

Origin of name: Icelandic *grænland*: green land, named by Erik the Red to attract settlers.

division	abv	FIPS	population	area-km	area-mi	capital (Inuit/Danish)
East Greenland	EG	GL02	3,443	115,900	44,700	Ammassalik
North Greenland	NG	GL01	843	106,700	41,200	Qaanaaq/Thule
West Greenland	VG	GL03	50,217	119,100	46,000	Nuuk/Godthåb
			55,558	2,175,600	840,000	

Status: These divisions are called lansdele (parts, or provinces).
Abv: Two-letter code for international compatibility (defined by the author).
FIPS: Codes from FIPS PUB 10-4.
Population: 1991-01-01 estimate.
Area-km: Square kilometers.
Area-mi: Square miles.

Further subdivisions: The three parts are further subdivided into 18 municipalities or townships.

Territorial extent: The parts are only defined along the coast. The ice-covered interior is not organized territorially. Going clockwise, West Greenland extends about from Kap Farvel to the middle of Melville Bay; North Greenland, from there to Nordostrundingen; and East Greenland goes on around to Kap Farvel again. North Greenland includes Kaffeklubben Island, said to be the northernmost point of land in the world. West Greenland includes the island of Disko.

Other names of subdivisions:

East Greenland: Østgrønland (Danish); Tunu (Inuit)

North Greenland: Avannaa (Inuit); Nordgrønland (Danish)

West Greenland: Kitaa (Inuit); Vestgrønland (Danish)

GRENADA

ISO = GD/FIPS = GJ   Language = English   Time zone = -4   Capital = Saint George's

Grenada was a British colony at the beginning of the 20th century. It became a territory of the West Indies Federation on 1958-01-03. The Federation was dissolved on 1962-05-31. Some plans were proposed for a federation of the Windward Islands, but they came to nothing. Grenada became an independent country on 1974-02-07.

Other names of country: Granada (Spanish); Grenade (French).

Origin of name: Named by Columbus after the city in Spain, to commemorate its recapture from the Moors.

division	abv	ISO	FIPS	population	area-km	area-mi
Carriacou	CA			4,671	34	13
Saint Andrew	AN	A	GJ01	22,425	91	35
Saint David	DA	D	GJ02	10,195	47	18
Saint George	GE	G	GJ03	29,369	67	26
Saint John	JO	J	GJ04	8,328	39	15
Saint Mark	MA	M	GJ05	3,968	23	9
Saint Patrick	PA	P	GJ06	10,132	44	17
				89,088	345	133

Status: These divisions are parishes, except for Carriacou, which is a dependency.

Abv: Two-letter code for international compatibility (defined by the author).

ISO: Codes from ISO 3166-2. (The standards have omitted Carriacou. If you must give it an ISO or FIPS code, use the code for Saint Patrick, which is closest.)

FIPS: Codes from FIPS PUB 10-4.

Population: 1981 estimate.

Area-km: Square kilometers.

Area-mi: Square miles.

Territorial extent: Carriacou consists of several islands, of which the largest are Carriacou itself and Petit Martinique (sometimes called Petite Martinique or Little Martinique). It extends from Petit Martinique to Large Island.

Saint George includes Glover Island.

Saint Patrick includes some small islands in the Southern Grenadines. The largest of them is Ronde Island; the farthest north are Diamond Island and Les Tantes.

Other names of subdivisions:

Saint George: Saint George's (variant)

GUADELOUPE

ISO = GP/FIPS = GP   Language = French   Time zone = -4   Capital = Basse-Terre

Guadeloupe, formerly a French colony, became an overseas department of France on 1946-03-19. Its status is theoretically on a par with the European French departments. Guadeloupe has a NUTS code of FR91, a department code of 971, and postal codes of the form 971xx, all of which are extensions of the French system.

Other names of country: Department of Guadeloupe (formal–English); Guadalupa (Italian); Guadalupe (Portuguese, Spanish).

Origin of name: Named by Christopher Columbus for the monastery Santa Maria de Guadalupe in Estremadura.

division	abv	population	area-km	area-mi
Basse-Terre	BT	153,589	881	369
Pointe-à-Pitre	PP	191,033	748	289
Saint-Martin et Saint-Barthélémy	SS	33,556	75	28
		378,178	1,704	686

Status: These divisions are arrondissements.

Abv: Two-letter code for international compatibility (defined by the author).

Population: 1990 preliminary census figures.

Area-km: Square kilometers.

Area-mi: Square miles.

Further subdivisions: The three arrondissements are further subdivided into 34 communes and 42 cantons.

Territorial extent: The main island of Guadeloupe is split into two parts by a channel called Rivière Salée (Salty River). These parts are called Grande-Terre and Basse-Terre (French for Big-Land and Low-Land). Ironically, Basse-Terre is bigger than Grande-Terre, and Grande-Terre is lower than Basse-Terre.

Pointe-à-Pitre arrondissement consists of Grande-Terre in Guadeloupe, La Désirade, and Îles de la Petite Terre.

Basse-Terre arrondissement consists of Basse-Terre in Guadeloupe, Marie-Galante Island, and the Îles des Saintes.

Saint-Martin et Saint-Barthélémy arrondissement consists of Saint-Barthélémy Island and the northern part of Saint-Martin Island, which is partitioned between Guadeloupe and the Netherlands Antilles. (Dutch-speaking inhabitants call it Sint Maarten.)

Change history:

1946-03-19   Guadeloupe became a département d'outre-mer (overseas department) of France.
1963-02-01   Saint-Martin et Saint-Barthélémy annexed to Guadeloupe as a third arrondissement.

GUAM

ISO = GU/FIPS = GQ   Languages = English, Chamorro   Time zone = +10   Capital = Agana

Guam became an unincorporated territory of the United States as a result of the Spanish-American War in 1898. It still retains that status. It was occupied by Japan during World War II.

Other names of country: Territory of Guam (formal–English).

Origin of name: Possibly a corruption of Chamorro, ethnic name.

division	abv	population	area-km	area-mi
Agana	AN	1,139	3	1
Agana Heights	AH	3,646	3	1
Agat	AT	4,960	26	10
Asan	AS	2,070	16	6 ▶

division	abv	population	area-km	area-mi
Barrigada	BA	8,846	23	9
Chalan-Pago-Ordot	CP	4,451	16	6
Dededo	DD	31,728	78	30
Inarajan	IN	2,469	49	19
Mangilao	MA	10,483	26	10
Merizo	ME	1,742	16	6
Mongmong-Toto-Maite	MT	5,845	5	2
Piti	PI	1,827	18	7
Santa Rita	SR	11,857	44	17
Sinajana	SJ	2,658	3	1
Talofofo	TF	2,310	44	17
Tamuning	TM	16,673	16	6
Umatac	UM	897	16	6
Yigo	YG	14,213	91	35
Yona	YN	5,338	52	20
		133,152	545	209

Status: These divisions are municipalities.

Abv: Two-letter code for international compatibility (defined by the author).

FIPS: FIPS PUB 5-2 assigns Guam an alphabetic code of GU and a numeric code of 66. FIPS PUB 6-4, which ordinarily has three-digit codes for each of the second-level subdivisions of the United States, only lists one code in Guam: 010. When the FIPS 5-2 and 6-4 codes are concatenated, the result (66010) is a code that represents Guam as a county-equivalent unit.

Population: 1990-04-01 census.

Area-km: Square kilometers.

Area-mi: Square miles.

Territorial extent: Guam occupies a moderately large island, the southernmost in the Marianas group; and some adjacent islets. All of the municipalities lie mainly on Guam Island. In addition, Agat municipality includes Alutom, Anae, Bangi, and Facpi Islands; Merizo includes Agrigan and Cocos Islands; Piti includes Cabras Island; Santa Rita includes Neye and Udall Islands; and Tamuning includes Alupat Island.

Change history: The municipalities were first established in the 1920's. The original set consisted of Agana, Agat, Asan, Inarajan, Merizo, Piti, Sumay, and Yona.

In 1950, the list of municipalities was Agana, Agat, Asan, Barrigada, Dededo, Inarajan, Machanao, Merizo, Piti, Sinajana, Sumay, Talofofo, Umatac, Yigo, and Yona.

GUATEMALA

ISO = GT/FIPS = GT   Language = Spanish   Time zone = -6   Capital = Guatemala City

Guatemala has been an independent country for the whole of the 20th century to date. It has also asserted a claim to possession of Belize (formerly called British Honduras) during the entire period.

Other names of country: Gvatemala (Icelandic); Republic of Guatemala (formal–English); República de Guatemala (formal).

Origin of name: Theory 1: Aztec *quauhtemallan*: rotten tree; theory 2: Mayan *guhatezmalha*: mountain of vomiting water.

division	ISO	FIPS	population	area-km	area-mi	capital
Alta Verapaz	AV	GT01	591,911	8,686	3,354	Cobán
Baja Verapaz	BV	GT02	184,462	3,124	1,206	Salamá
Chimaltenango	CM	GT03	343,818	1,979	764	Chimaltenango
Chiquimula	CQ	GT04	252,052	2,376	917	Chiquimula
El Progreso	PR	GT05	108,399	1,922	742	Guastatoya
Escuintla	ES	GT06	542,091	4,384	1,693	Escuintla
Guatemala	GU	GT07	2,018,179	2,126	821	Guatemala City
Huehuetenango	HU	GT08	716,666	7,400	2,857	Huehuetenango
Izabal	IZ	GT09	326,402	9,038	3,490	Puerto Barrios ➤

division	ISO	FIPS	population	area-km	area-mi	capital
Jalapa	JA	GT10	190,847	2,063	797	Jalapa
Jutiapa	JU	GT11	354,337	3,219	1,243	Jutiapa
Petén	PE	GT12	253,326	35,854	13,843	Flores
Quetzaltenango	QZ	GT13	557,831	1,951	753	Quetzaltenango
Quiché	QC	GT14	574,746	8,378	3,235	Santa Cruz del Quiché
Retalhuleu	RE	GT15	238,857	1,856	717	Retalhuleu
Sacatepéquez	SA	GT16	180,155	465	180	Antigua Guatemala
San Marcos	SM	GT17	702,288	3,791	1,464	San Marcos
Santa Rosa	SR	GT18	267,790	2,955	1,141	Cuilapa
Sololá	SO	GT19	242,067	1,061	410	Sololá
Suchitepéquez	SU	GT20	361,678	2,510	969	Mazatenango
Totonicapán	TO	GT21	297,483	1,061	410	Totonicapán
Zacapa	ZA	GT22	161,644	2,690	1,039	Zacapa
			9,467,029	108,889	42,045	

Status: These divisions are departamentos (departments).
ISO: Codes from ISO 3166-2.
FIPS: Codes from FIPS PUB 10-4.
Population: 1991 estimate.
Area-km: Square kilometers.
Area-mi: Square miles.
Further subdivisions: The departments are further subdivided into municipios (municipalities).
Origins of names:

El Progreso: Spanish for progress.
Guatemala: same as the country name.

Huehuetenango: Nahuatl for city of the ancients.

Change history:

~1920 El Progreso formed from parts of Baja Verapaz, Jalapa, Zacapa, and Guatemala.
~1962 Amatitlán merged with Guatemala.
~1988 Name of Quezaltenango department changed to Quetzaltenango (perhaps to make the spelling more phonetic).
~1991 Name of capital of El Progreso department changed from El Progreso to Guastatoya, restoring it to its name from before 1920.

Other names of subdivisions:

Petén: El Petén (variant)
Quetzaltenango: Quezaltenango (obsolete)

Quiché: El Quiché (variant)

Population history:

	1898	1940	1964	1973	1983	1991
Alta Verapaz	110,936	282,562	259,873	279,880	386,636	591,911
Amatitlán	35,954	——	——	——	——	——
Baja Verapaz	50,874	96,182	95,663	106,440	155,083	184,462
Chimaltenango	61,013	177,123	163,753	197,780	272,685	343,818
Chiquimula	66,823	144,011	151,214	161,980	272,685	252,052
El Progreso	——	65,302	66,734	72,840	102,832	108,399
Escuintla	31,302	176,280	269,813	275,600	518,525	542,091
Guatemala	143,581	319,197	813,696	1,114,120	1,870,277	2,018,179
Huehuetenango	136,114	176,480	286,965	384,400	539,971	716,666
Izabal	5,067	83,153	114,404	169,960	303,123	326,402
Jalapa	35,954	124,855	97,996	119,960	165,763	190,847
Jutiapa	50,058	200,416	199,053	234,580	335,408	354,337
Petén	8,604	11,475	26,720	67,020	107,691	253,326
Quetzaltenango	107,324	233,655	268,962	308,880	457,498	557,831
Quiché	90,300	158,662	247,775	303,880	440,157	574,746 ➤

	1898	1940	1964	1973	1983	1991
Retalhuleu	25,009	69,974	122,829	124,580	213,673	238,857
Sacatepéquez	41,375	83,024	80,479	99,160	141,336	180,155
San Marcos	93,181	204,208	332,303	391,360	564,595	702,288
Santa Rosa	38,950	169,774	155,488	179,540	254,275	267,790
Sololá	85,591	86,625	108,815	128,120	176,192	242,067
Suchitepéquez	36,849	182,162	186,299	238,000	312,340	361,678
Totonicapán	160,942	92,292	139,636	168,700	240,340	297,483
Zacapa	44,216	145,797	97,976	105,100	151,341	161,644
	1,460,017	3,283,209	4,286,446	5,231,880	7,982,426	9,467,029

GUINEA

ISO = GN/FIPS = GV   Language = French   Time zone = +0   Capital = Conakry

Guinea was known as French Guinea in 1900. In 1943, it and seven other French colonies were combined to form French West Africa (Afrique Occidentale Française, capital Dakar). Guinea became independent on 1958-10-02.

Other names of country: French Guinea (obsolete–English); Gínea (Icelandic); Guiné (Portuguese); Guinea Francesa (obsolete–Spanish); Guinee (Dutch); Guinée (French); Guinée Française (obsolete–French); Republic of Guinea (formal–English); République de Guinée (formal).

Origin of name: Tuareg *aginaw*: speechless people, applied by Berbers to blacks speaking unknown tongues.

division	ISO	FIPS	population	area-km	area-mi	gov
Beyla	BE	GV01	170,000	17,452	6,738	N
Boffa	BF	GV02	90,000	6,003	2,318	B
Boké	BK	GV03	105,000	11,053	4,268	B
Conakry	CK*	GV04	172,000	308	119	C
Coyah	CO	— —	— —	— —	— —	D
Dabola	DB	GV05	54,000	6,000	2,317	F
Dalaba	DL	GV06	105,000	5,750	2,220	M
Dinguiraye	DI	GV07	67,000	11,000	4,247	F
Dubréka	DU	GV08	86,000	5,676	2,192	D
Faranah	FA	GV09	94,000	12,397	4,787	F
Forécariah	FO	GV10	98,000	4,265	1,647	D
Fria	FR	GV11	27,000	— —	— —	B
Gaoual	GA	GV12	81,000	11,503	4,441	B
Guéckédou	GU	GV13	130,000	4,157	1,605	N
Kankan	KA	GV14	176,000	27,488	10,613	K
Kérouané	KE	GV15	— —	— —	— —	K
Kindia	KI*	GV16	152,000	8,828	3,409	D
Kissidougou	KS	GV17	133,000	8,872	3,425	F
Koubia	KB	— —	— —	— —	— —	L
Koundara	KD	GV18	55,000	5,500	2,124	B
Kouroussa	KO	GV19	93,000	16,405	6,334	K
Labé	LA	GV20	283,000	7,616	2,941	L
Lélouma	LE	— —	— —	— —	— —	L
Lola	LO	— —	— —	— —	— —	N
Macenta	MC	GV21	123,000	8,710	3,363	N
Mali	ML	GV22	152,000	8,800	3,398	L
Mamou	MM	GV23	162,000	6,159	2,378	M
Mandiana	MD	— —	— —	— —	— —	K
Nzérékoré	NZ	GV24	195,000	10,183	3,932	N
Pita	PI	GV25	154,000	4,000	1,544	M
Siguiri	SI	GV26	179,000	23,377	9,026	K
Télimélé	TE	GV27	147,000	8,055	3,110	D ➤

division	ISO	FIPS	population	area-km	area-mi	gov
Tougué	TO	GV28	75,000	6,200	2,394	L
Yomou	YO	GV29	––	––	––	N
			3,358,000	245,757	94,890	

* = *The draft standard omits Conakry, and lists KD for both Kindia and Koundara. I made these changes for completeness and uniqueness.*

Status: These divisions are régions administratives (administrative regions). ISO calls them préfectures, except Conakry, which it calls a gouvernorat (governorate).

ISO: Codes from ISO 3166-2.

FIPS: Codes from FIPS PUB 10-4.

Population: 1963 estimate.

Area-km: Square kilometers.

Area-mi: Square miles.

Capitals: Names are the same as the administrative region names.

Gov: Code for the governorate to which the administrative region belongs, as defined by ISO: B = Boké; C = Conakry; F = Faranah; K = Kankan; D = Kindia; L = Labé; M = Mamou; N = Nzérékoré.

Further subdivisions: The administrative regions are further subdivided into 175 districts. The regions are now grouped into eight governorates. Before ~1988, the administrative regions were grouped into these "supra-regions":

name (English)	name (French)	population	area-km	capital
Conakry	Conakry	705,280	308	Conakry
Lower Guinea	Guinée-Maritime	1,147,301	43,980	Kindia
Fouta Djallon	Moyenne-Guinée	1,595,007	51,710	Labé
Upper Guinea	Haute-Guinée	1,086,679	92,535	Kankan
Forest-Guinea	Guinée-Forestière	1,246,747	57,324	Nzérékoré
		5,781,014	245,857	

Population: 1983 census.

Origins of names:

Conakry: local word *konakri*: across the water

Change history:

1904	Îles de Los transferred from Sierra Leone to French Guinea by cession.
~1980	Name of Youkoukoun region changed to Koundara.
~1985	Coyah region split from Dubréka; Koubia and Lélouma regions split from Labé; Lola region split from Nzérékoré; Mandiana region formed from parts of Kankan and Siguiri.

Other names of subdivisions:

Conakry: Conacri (Portuguese); Konakry (obsolete)   Koundara: Youkoukoun, Youkounkoun (obsolete)
Guéckédou: Guékédou (variant)

GUINEA-BISSAU

ISO = GW/FIPS = PU   Language = Portuguese   Time zone = +0   Capital = Bissau

The area now known as Guinea-Bissau was a Portuguese colony, Portuguese Guinea, in 1900. It gained its independence on 1973-09-24 and was recognized by Portugal on 1974-09-10.

Other names of country: Gínea-Bissá (Icelandic); Guinea Portuguesa (obsolete–Spanish); Guiné-Bissau (Portuguese); Guiné Portuguesa (obsolete–Portuguese); Guinee Bissau (Dutch); Guinée-Bissau (French); Portuguese Guinea (obsolete); Republic of Guinea-Bissau (formal–English); Republica da Guiné-Bissau (formal).

Origin of name: distinguished from Guinea by specifying the capital.

division	ISO	FIPS	population	area-km	area-mi	capital
Bafatá	BA	PU01	116,032	5,981	2,309	Bafatá
Biombo	BM	PU12	56,463	838	324	Quinhámel
Bissau	BS	PU11	109,214	729	281	Bissau
Bolama	BL	PU05	25,473	2,624	1,013	Bolama
Cacheu	CA	PU06	130,227	5,175	1,998	Cacheu
Gabú	GA	PU10	104,315	9,150	3,533	Gabú
Oio	OI	PU04	135,114	5,403	2,086	Farim
Quinara	QU	PU02	35,532	3,138	1,212	Buba
Tombali	TO	PU07	55,099	3,736	1,442	Catió
			767,469	36,774	14,198	

Status: These divisions are regiões (sing. região: regions), except for Bissau, which is a sector autonomo (autonomous sector).
ISO: Codes from ISO 3166-2.
FIPS: Codes from FIPS PUB 10-4.
Population: 1979 census.
Area-km: Square kilometers.
Area-mi: Square miles.
Further subdivisions: The regions are further subdivided into 37 sectors.
Territorial extent: Bolama includes the Bissagos (Bijagos) Archipelago. Some of the larger islands are Orango, Formosa, Roxa, and Caravela.
Origins of names:

Bissau: from ethnic name Bijagós or Bissagos

Change history:

1942   Capital of country moved from Bolama to Bissau.
~1976   Regions reorganized. Before the change, Guinea-Bissau was divided into concelhos (councils) and circunscrições (circumscriptions). Their names were Bafatá, Bijagós, Bissau, Bissorá, Bolama, Cacheu, Catió, Farim, Fulacunda, Gabú, Mansoa, and São Domingos.
~1990   Bissau region (PU03) split into Bissau and Biombo; name of Buba region changed to Quinara.

Other names of subdivisions:

Bolama: Bolama-Bijagós (variant)   Quinara: Buba (obsolete)

GUYANA

ISO = GY/FIPS = GY   Language = English   Time zone = -4   Capital = Georgetown

At the beginning of the 20th century, this territory was the British colony of British Guiana. It was locked in a dispute with Venezuela over possession of more than half of its area, the part to the west of the Essequibo River. The boundary was settled in 1904 at approximately its current position, although both Venezuela and Surinam still have claims. The country became independent on 1966-05-26, changing its name to Guyana at the same time.

Other names of country: British Guiana (obsolete); Co-operative Republic of Guyana (formal); Guayana Inglesa (obsolete–Spanish); Guiana (Portuguese); Gvæjana (Icelandic).

Origin of name: from native word *guiana:* land of waters, or possibly from native word for respectable.

division	ISO	FIPS	population	capital	formerly
Barima-Waini	BA	GY10	18,516	Mabaruma	North West
Cuyuni-Mazaruni	CU	GY11	17,941	Bartica	Mazaruni-Potaro (most) ▶

division	ISO	FIPS	population	capital	formerly
Demerara-Mahaica	DE	GY12	310,758	Paradise	EDem (part), WDem (part)
East Berbice-Corentyne	EB	GY13	148,967	New Amsterdam	EBer (most), Rupununi (part)
Essequibo Islands-West Demerara	ES	GY14	102,760	Vreed en Hoop	EssIs (most), WDem (part)
Mahaica-Berbice	MA	GY15	55,556	Fort Wellington	WBer, EBer (part), WBer (part)
Pomeroon-Supenaam	PM	GY16	41,966	Anna Regina	Ess (most), EssIs (part), NW (part)
Potaro-Siparuni	PT	GY17	5,672	Mahdia	MazP (part), Rupununi (part)
Upper Demerara-Berbice	UD	GY18	38,598	Linden	WDem (most); EBer, MazP, Rup (parts)
Upper Takutu-Upper Essequibo	UT	GY19	15,338	Lethem	Rupununi (part)
			756,072		

Status: These divisions are administrative regions.

ISO: Codes from ISO 3166-2.

FIPS: Codes from FIPS PUB 10-4.

Population: 1991 census.

Area: Areas of individual districts have not been published. The entire country is 214,969 sq. km. or about 83,000 sq. mi.

Formerly: shows the relationship between these regions and the administrative districts of 1970-80. I hope the abbreviations will be self-explanatory.

Territorial extent: Essequibo Islands-West Demerara includes islands in the mouth of the Essequibo River, such as Leguan and Wakenaam Islands.

Origins of names: The following are rivers of Guyana: Barima, Berbice, Courantyne, Cuyuni, Demerara, Essequibo, Mahaica, Mazaruni, Pomeroon, Potaro, Rupununi, Siparuni, Takutu, and Waini.

Change history: In the colonial period, Guyana was divided into the three counties of Berbice (40,077 sq. km.), Demerara (12,432 sq. km.), and Essequibo (156,749 sq. km.). (Essequibo corresponds approximately to the area in dispute with Venezuela.)

~1970   Guyana reorganized into nine administrative districts:

district	FIPS	population	capital	formerly
East Berbice	GY01	115,511	New Amsterdam	Berbice
East Demerara	GY02	256,908	Enmore	Demerara
Essequibo	GY03	29,729	Suddie	Essequibo
Essequibo Islands	GY04	15,728	Enterprise	Essequibo
Mazaruni-Potaro	GY05	12,029	Bartica	Essequibo
North West	GY06	12,809	Mabaruma	Essequibo
Rupununi	GY07	10,031	Lethem	Essequibo, Berbice, tiny part of Demerara
West Berbice	GY08	26,524	Fort Wellington	Berbice
West Demerara	GY09	81,061	Vreed en Hoop	Demerara
		560,330		

Population: 1960 census.

Formerly: county or counties from which this district was formed.

~1980   Guyana reorganized into six districts:

district	FIPS	capital	formerly
East Berbice-Corentyne	GY01	New Amsterdam	EBer (most), Rup (part)
East Demerara-West Coast Berbice	GY02	Mahaicony Village	EDem, WBer, EBer (part), MazP (part), WDem (most)
Mazaruni-Potaro	GY05	Matthews Ridge	MazP (most)
North West	GY06	Mabaruma	North West
Rupununi	GY07	Lethem	Rup (most)
West Demerara-Essequibo Coast	GY09	Anna Regina	Ess, EssIs, WDem (part)

~1986   Guyana reorganized into 10 administrative regions, as listed above.

HAITI

ISO = HT/FIPS = HA   Language = French   Time zone = -5 [d]   Capital = Port-au-Prince

Haiti has been an independent country for the whole of the 20th century, in theory. In actuality, it was under the control of U.S. marines from 1915 to 1934.

Other names of country: Haití (Spanish); Haítí (Icelandic); Haïti (French, German); Hayti (obsolete); Republic of Haiti (formal–English); République d'Haïti (formal).

Origin of name: Carib, either *haiti*: mountainous land, or *jhaiti*: nest.

division	ISO	FIPS	population	area-km	area-mi	capital	formerly
L'Artibonite	AR	HA06	732,932	4,895	1,890	Gonaïves	L'Artibonite
Centre	CE	HA07	361,470	3,597	1,389	Hinche	L'Artibonite, Ouest, Nord
Grand' Anse	GA	HA08	489,957	3,100	1,197	Jérémie	Sud
Nord	ND	HA09	564,002	2,175	840	Cap Haïtien	Nord
Nord-Est	NE	HA10	189,573	1,698	656	Fort-Liberté	Nord
Nord-Ouest	NO	HA03	293,531	2,094	808	Port-de-Paix	Nord-Ouest
Ouest	OU	HA11	1,551,792	4,595	1,774	Port-au-Prince	Ouest
Sud	SD	HA12	502,624	2,602	1,005	Les Cayes	Sud
Sud-Est	SE	HA13	367,911	2,077	802	Jacmel	Ouest
			5,053,792	26,833	10,361		

Status: These divisions are départements (departments).
ISO: Codes from ISO 3166-2.
FIPS: Codes from FIPS PUB 10-4.
Population: 1982 census.
Area-km: Square kilometers.
Area-mi: Square miles.
Formerly: Lists pre–1962 department(s) corresponding to each present-day department.
Further subdivisions: The departments are subdivided into arrondissements, which are further subdivided into communes.
Territorial extent: Grand' Anse includes Île Grande Cayemite.
Nord-Ouest includes Île de la Tortue (Tortuga Island).
Ouest includes Île de la Gonâve.
Sud includes Île à Vache.
Origins of names:

L'Artibonite: for the Artibonite River   Grand' Anse: = big cove

Change history:

1962   Haiti reorganized from five departments to nine. Apparently this reorganization was passed into law in 1962, but not implemented until around 1980. Here are data for the old departments:

department	FIPS	population	area-km	capital	department	FIPS	population	area-km	capital
L'Artibonite	HA01	756,000	6,800	Gonaïves	Ouest	HA04	1,611,000	7,900	Port-au-Prince
Nord	HA02	698,000	4,100	Cap-Haïtien	Sud	HA05	967,000	6,200	Les Cayes
Nord-Ouest	HA03	212,000	2,750	Port-de-Paix			4,244,000	27,750	

Population: 1971 census (rounded).
Other names of subdivisions:

Grand' Anse: Grande Anse (variant)   L'Artibonite: Artibonite (variant)

HEARD AND MCDONALD ISLANDS

ISO = HM/FIPS = HM   Language = English   Time zone = 0   Capital = none

These isolated islands were British possessions until 1947-12-26, when they were transferred to Australian control. They are now an Australian external territory. They are only visited by research expeditions.

Other names of country: Heard Island and McDonald Islands (variant); Heard- und McDonaldinseln (German); Îles Heard et MacDonald (French); Isole Heard e Macdonald (Italian); Territory of Heard Island and McDonald Islands (formal–English).

Origin of name: Heard Island was named in 1853 for an American, Captain John J. Heard.

division	abv	area km	area-mi
Heard and McDonald Islands	HM	412	159

Status: This division is the whole of the country, treated as a division for compatibility.

Abv: Two-letter code for international compatibility (defined by the author).

Population: No permanent residents.

Area-km: Square kilometers.

Area-mi: Square miles.

Territorial extent: The territory includes Heard Island, Shag Island, and the McDonald Islands (Flat Island and McDonald Island).

HONDURAS

ISO = HN/FIPS = HO   Language = Spanish   Time zone = -5   Capital = Tegucigalpa

Honduras has been an independent country during the entire 20th century.

Other names of country: Hondúras (Icelandic); Republic of Honduras (formal–English); República de Honduras (formal).

Origin of name: Spanish *honduras*: depths, after Cape Honduras.

division	ISO	FIPS	population	area-km	area-mi	capital
Atlántida	AT	HO01	238,742	4,251	1,641	La Ceiba
Choluteca	CH	HO02	295,484	4,211	1,626	Choluteca
Colón	CL	HO03	149,677	8,875	3,427	Trujillo
Comayagua	CM	HO04	239,859	5,196	2,006	Comayagua
Copán	CP	HO05	219,455	3,203	1,237	Santa Rosa de Copán
Cortés	CR	HO06	662,772	3,954	1,527	San Pedro Sula
El Paraíso	EP	HO07	254,295	7,218	2,787	Yuscarán
Francisco Morazán	FM	HO08	828,274	7,946	3,068	Tegucigalpa
Gracias a Dios	GD	HO09	34,970	16,630	6,421	Puerto Lempira
Intibucá	IN	HO10	124,681	3,072	1,186	La Esperanza
Islas de la Bahía	IB	HO11	22,062	261	101	Roatán
La Paz	LP	HO12	105,927	2,331	900	La Paz
Lempira	LE	HO13	177,055	4,290	1,656	Gracias
Ocotepeque	OC	HO14	74,276	1,680	649	Nueva Ocotepeque
Olancho	OL	HO15	283,852	24,351	9,402	Juticalpa
Santa Bárbara	DB	HO16	278,868	5,115	1,975	Santa Bárbara
Valle	VA	HO17	119,645	1,565	604	Nacaome
Yoro	YO	HO18	333,508	7,939	3,065	Yoro
			4,443,402	112,088	43,278	

Status: These divisions are departamentos (departments).
ISO: Codes from ISO 3166-2.
FIPS: Codes from FIPS PUB 10-4.
Population: 1988 census.
Area-km: Square kilometers.
Area-mi: Square miles.
Further subdivisions: There is a special district called Distrito Central, which is included in Francisco Morazán in the table above. It has an area of 1,648 sq. km., and contains the cities of Tegucigalpa and Comayaguela. Distrito Central ranks as a department in some ways, but in others it is subordinate to Francisco Morazán. The standards don't list it as a separate department. Aside from that, the departments are further subdivided into 282 municipalities.
Territorial extent: Islas de la Bahía consists of islands in the Gulf of Honduras, of which the largest are Roatán, Guanaja, Utila, Barbareta; and, farther offshore, the Islas Santanilla.

Valle includes Isla el Tigre in the Gulf of Fonseca.

Origins of names:

El Paraíso: Spanish for paradise
Francisco Morazán: named for Francisco Morazán (1799–1842), Central American revolutionary
Gracias a Dios: for Cape Gracias a Dios, Spanish for "Thanks to God"

Islas de la Bahía: Spanish for islands of the bay
Valle: Spanish for valley

Change history:

~1901	Cortés department formed from parts of Santa Bárbara and Yoro; El Paraíso department split from Tegucigalpa; Valle department split from Choluteca.
~1907	Ocotepeque department split from Gracias.
1943	Name of Gracias department changed to Lempira; name of Tegucigalpa department changed to Francisco Morazán.
1957-02	Gracias a Dios department formed from all of Mosquitia territory and parts of Colón and Olancho departments.
~1975	Name of capital of Ocotepeque department changed from Ocotepeque to Nueva Ocotepeque; capital of Gracias a Dios department moved from Brus Laguna to Puerto Lempira.

Other names of subdivisions:

Cortés: Cortez (obsolete)
Lempira: Gracias (obsolete)

Francisco Morazán: Tegucigalpa (obsolete)

Population history:

	1910	1916	1930	1940	1950	1961	1974	1988
Atlántida	11,372	20,905	32,506	43,862	63,582	92,914	148,440	238,742
Choluteca	45,817	47,771	69,096	88,245	107,271	149,175	192,145	295,484
Colón	11,191	12,918	31,787	30,644	35,465	41,904	77,239	149,677
Comayagua	26,339	31,199	42,987	54,046	68,171	96,442	135,455	239,859
Copán	40,282	47,827	66,208	82,053	95,880	126,183	151,331	219,455
Cortés	23,559	30,314	58,273	87,269	125,728	200,099	373,629	662,772
El Paraíso	42,118	40,857	56,300	67,742	82,572	106,823	140,840	254,295
Francisco Morazán	81,844	86,119	113,483	158,918	190,359	284,428	451,778	828,274
Gracias a Dios	— —	— —	— —	— —	— —	10,905	21,079	34,970
Intibucá	27,285	31,173	39,002	52,650	59,362	73,138	81,685	124,681
Islas de la Bahía	4,893	5,599	5,480	7,025	8,058	8,961	13,227	22,062
La Paz	28,764	30,601	39,140	48,516	51,220	60,600	65,390	105,927
Lempira	49,955	51,740	64,947	78,977	90,908	111,546	127,465	177,055
Ocotepeque	28,190	29,787	37,494	46,020	45,673	52,540	51,161	74,276
Olancho	43,368	45,904	53,412	64,521	83,910	110,744	151,923	283,852
Santa Bárbara	39,064	43,020	61,260	80,366	96,397	146,909	185,163	278,868 ➤

	1910	1916	1930	1940	1950	1961	1974	1988
Valle	30,479	28,723	40,254	53,666	65,349	80,907	90,954	119,645
Yoro	18,926	21,540	42,555	63,339	98,700	130,547	194,953	333,508
	553,446	605,997	854,184	1,107,859	1,368,605	1,884,765	2,653,857	4,443,402

Population of Mosquitia territory included in Colón until 1950.

HONG KONG

ISO = HK/FIPS = HK   Language = Chinese, English   Time zone = +8   Capital = Victoria

In 1900, Hong Kong proper (the island and Kowloon) was a British crown colony, and the British also had a 99-year lease on the New Territories. The Japanese occupied the territory during World War II. On 1984-12-19, the British and Chinese governments agreed that Hong Kong would become a Special Administrative Region of China on 1997-07-01, and so it did.

Other names of country: Xianggang (Chinese-Pinyin).

Origin of name: Chinese *xiang*: perfume, *gang*: port (i.e. the port of perfumes).

division	abv	population	area-km	area-mi	sec	capital
Central and Western	CW	260,000	12	5	H	Central (Victoria)
Eastern	EA	599,000	19	7	H	Sai Wan Ho
Islands	IS	63,100	174	67	I	Mui Wo, Cheung Chau
Kowloon City	KC	378,000	10	4	K	Hung Hom
Kwai Tsing	KI	470,700	23	9	N	Kwai Chung
Kwun Tong	KU	587,000	11	4	K	Kwun Tong
North	NO	232,000	134	52	N	Fanling
Sai Kung	SK	208,000	135	52	N	Tseung Kwan O
Sham Shui Po	SS	366,000	9	3	K	Sham Shui Po
Sha Tin	ST	583,000	69	26	N	Shatin Station
Southern	SO	288,000	40	15	H	Aberdeen
Tai Po	TP	284,600	148	57	N	Tai Po
Tsuen Wan	TW	271,000	62	24	N	Tsuen Wan
Tuen Mun	TM	466,700	85	33	N	Tuen Mun
Wan Chai	WC	172,000	10	4	H	Wan Chai
Wong Tai Sin	WT	396,000	9	4	K	San Po Kong
Yau Tsim Mong	YT	260,600	7	3	K	Mongkok
Yuen Long	YL	341,000	138	53	N	Yuen Long
		6,226,700	1,095	422		

Status: These divisions are districts.

Abv: Two-letter code for international compatibility (defined by the author).

Population: 1997 estimate.

Area-km: Square kilometers.

Area-mi: Square miles.

Sec: The sections of Hong Kong are Hong Kong Island (H), Kowloon Area (K), New Territories (N), and Islands (I). The districts in H and K are urban districts; the others are rural.

Capital: Location of the district board office.

Further subdivisions: In Hong Kong's local government structure, municipal councils are under the district boards.

Territorial extent: The sections of Kowloon Area and New Territories are attached to the Chinese mainland.

Islands includes Lantau, Lamma, Tsing Yi, Kau Sai Chau, Tung Lung, Po Toi, and other islands.

Origins of names:

Kowloon: Chinese for nine dragons.

Change history: The district boards were established in 1982.

~1983　Kwai Chung/Tsing Yi district (later called Kwai Tsing) split from Tsuen Wan.
~1991　Mong Kok and Yau Ma Tei districts merged to form Yau Tsim Mong.

HUNGARY

ISO = HU/FIPS = HU　Language = Hungarian　Time zone = 1 ^{d}　Capital = Budapest

In 1900, Hungary was part of the Austro-Hungarian Empire. A much smaller, independent Hungary, almost equivalent to the present-day country, emerged from the peace negotiations at the end of World War I. Hungary reconquered some of its old ground as World War II began, but its defeat cancelled all its gains.

At different times, Hungary has had varying numbers of urban counties. These are administrative divisions that appear geographically to be cities, but that are treated administratively as counties. Budapest has been of this type for the whole of the twentieth century. Others have come and gone. In 1921, there were thirty-five ordinary counties and twelve urban counties. In 1950, a territorial reform eliminated all of the urban counties. In 1954, four of them were created; in 1971, they were all abolished again. There were five of them in 1991. An additional 15 were created by 1993, and two more (making 22 in all) by 1996. In reference works, the urban counties are sometimes ignored, or treated as if they were part of the surrounding ordinary county.

Other names of country: Hongarije (Dutch); Hongrie (French); Hungarian Republic (formal–English); Hungria (Portuguese); Hungría (Spanish); Magyar Köztársaság (formal); Magyarország (Hungarian); Ungarn (Danish, German, Norwegian); Ungern (Swedish); Ungheria (Italian); Ungverjaland (Icelandic); Unkari (Finnish).

Origin of name: from Turkish *Onogur*: ten tribes, referring to tribes which later settled in Hungary.

division	ISO	FIPS	typ	population	area-km	area-mi	capital (county)
Bács-Kiskun	BK	HU01	m	574,009	8,362	3,229	Kecskemét
Baranya	BA	HU02	m	424,857	4,487	1,732	Pécs
Békés	BE	HU03	m	446,405	5,632	2,175	Békéscsaba
Borsod-Abaúj-Zemplén	BZ	HU04	m	779,424	7,247	2,798	Miskolc
Budapest	BU	HU05	f	2,016,132	525	203	Budapest
Csongrád	CS	HU06	m	441,399	4,263	1,646	Szeged
Fejér	FE	HU08	m	390,655	4,373	1,688	Székesfehérvár
Győr-Moson-Sopron	GS	HU09	m	403,860	4,012	1,549	Győr
Hajdú-Bihar	HB	HU10	m	531,508	6,211	2,398	Debrecen
Heves	HE	HU11	m	347,270	3,637	1,404	Eger
Jász-Nagykun-Szolnok	JN	HU20	m	449,001	5,607	2,165	Szolnok
Komárom-Esztergom	KE	HU12	m	301,760	2,251	869	Tatabánya
Nógrád	NO	HU14	m	240,129	2,544	982	Salgótarján
Pest	PE	HU16	m	875,462	6,394	2,469	Budapest
Somogy	SO	HU17	m	363,075	6,036	2,331	Kaposvár
Szabolcs-Szatmár-Bereg	SZ	HU18	m	590,211	5,938	2,293	Nyíregyháza
Tolna	TO	HU21	m	258,789	3,704	1,430	Szekszárd
Vas	VA	HU22	m	280,125	3,337	1,288	Szombathely
Veszprém	VE	HU23	m	412,298	4,689	1,810	Veszprém
Zala	ZA	HU24	m	266,779	3,784	1,461	Zalaegerszeg
Békéscsaba	BC	HU26	v				(Békés)
Debrecen	DE	HU07	v				(Hajdú-Bihar)
Dunaújváros	DU	HU27	v				(Fejér)
Eger	EG	HU28	v				(Heves)
Győr	GY	HU25	v				(Győr-Moson-Sopron)
Hódmezővásárhely	HV	HU29	v				(Csongrád)
Kaposvár	KV	HU30	v				(Somogy)
Kecskemét	KM	HU31	v				(Bács-Kiskun)
Miskolc	MI	HU13	v				(Borsod-Abaúj-Zemplén)
Nagykanizsa	NK	HU32	v				(Zala)
Nyíregyháza	NY	HU33	v				(Szabolcs-Szatmár-Bereg) ➤

division	ISO	FIPS	typ	population	area-km	area-mi	capital (county)
Pécs	PS	HU15	v				(Baranya)
Salgótarjan	ST		v				(Nógrád)
Sopron	SN	HU34	v				(Győr-Moson-Sopron)
Szeged	SD	HU19	v				(Csongrád)
Székesfehérvár	SF	HU35	v				(Fejér)
Szekszárd	SS		v				(Tolna)
Szolnok	SK	HU36	v				(Jász-Nagykun-Szolnok)
Szombathely	SH	HU37	v				(Vas)
Tatabánya	TB	HU38	v				(Komárom-Esztergom)
Veszprém	VM	HU39	v				(Veszprém)
Zalaegerszeg	ZE	HU40	v	10,393,148	93,033	35,920	(Zala)

ISO: Codes from ISO 3166-2.

FIPS: Codes from FIPS PUB 10-4.

Typ: These divisions are m: megyék (sing. megye; counties), f: föváros (capital city), and v: megyei jogu város (urban counties, county boroughs, cities of county right).

Population: 1990-01-01 estimate.

Area-km: Square kilometers.

Area-mi: Square miles.

Capital: Names in parentheses are the counties in which these cities were located before being made into county boroughs

Postal codes: Hungarian postal codes are four digits. Postal codes for Hungarian addresses can be identified by prefixing them with "H-".

Further subdivisions: Until 1984, the top-level divisions of Hungary were counties and urban counties; the second-level divisions were jaras (districts); below these were közseg (councils, villages). The number of each type of division varied with successive reforms. On 1984-01-01, the districts were done away with, replaced by 105 town-regions and 34 large villages with town rank.

Territorial extent: In 1990, Budapest capital city was an enclave entirely surrounded by Pest county. Likewise, the urban counties of Debrecen, Pécs, and Szeged were enclaves within their respective counties. The creation of new urban counties since then may have changed this state of affairs.

Origins of names:

Budapest: the cities Buda and Pest were united in 1872.

Győr: after Jewr, a man's name

Hódmezővásárhely: Hungarian *hód*: beaver, *mező*: field, *vásár*: fair, *hely*: place

Transylvania: Latin *trans*: beyond, *silva*: forest (i.e. the land beyond the forest, although earlier called simply Erdély, Hungarian for forested land)

Change history: Before World War I, the Kingdom of Hungary was one of the major divisions of the Austro-Hungarian Empire. The Kingdom of Hungary consisted of Hungary proper, the province of Croatia and Slavonia, and the tiny province of Fiume (Rijeka). The eastern part of Hungary, now in Romania, was called Transylvania. Hungary was subdivided into 64 comitate (counties):

county	capital	modern
Abauj-Torna	Kassa (Kaschau, Košice SK)	SK,HU
Also-Feher (Unter-Weissenburg)	Nagy-Enyed (Strassburg, Aiud RO)	RO*
Árad	Árad RO	RO
Árva	Kubin (Dolný Kubín SK)	SK
Bács-Bodrog	Zombor (Sombor YU)	YU,HU
Baranya	Pécs HU (Fünfkirchen)	HU,HR
Bars	Aranyos-Marot (Zlaté Marovce SK)	SK
Bekes	Gyula HU	HU
Bereg	Beregszász (Beregove UA)	UA,HU
Besztercze Naszod (Bistritz)	Besztercze (Bistritz, Bistriţa RO)	RO*
Bihar	Nagy-Várad (Großwardein, Oradea RO)	RO,HU
Borsod	Miskolc HU	HU
Brasso (Kronstadt)	Brasso (Kronstadt, Braşov RO)	RO*
Budapest	Budapest HU	HU
Csanád	Makó HU	HU ➤

county	capital	modern
Csik	Csik Szereda (Miercurea-Ciuc RO)	RO*
Csongrád	Szegedin (Szeged HU)	HU,YU
Esztergom (Gran)	Esztergom HU (Gran)	HU
Fogaras	Fogaras (Făgăras RO)	RO*
Gömör	Rima Szombath (Rimavská Sobota SK)	SK,HU
Györ (Raab)	Györ HU (Raab)	HU,SK
Hajdu (Hajduken)	Debrecen HU	HU
Háromszék	Sepsi-Szent-György (Sfîntu Gheorghe RO)	RO*
Heves	Eger HU (Erlau)	HU
Hont	Ipolyság (Šahy SK)	SK,HU
Hunyad	Deva RO	RO*
Jász-Nagykun-Szolnok	Szolnok HU	HU
Kis-Küküllö	Elisabethstadt (Dumbrăveni RO)	RO*
Kolozsvár (Klausenburg)	Kolozsvár (Klausenburg, Cluj-Napoca RO)	RO*
Komárom (Komorn)	Komárom (Komorn, Komarno SK)	HU,SK
Krasso-Szörény	Lugos (Lugoj RO)	RO
Lipto (Liptau)	Lipto-Szent-Miklos (Liptau, Liptov Mikuláš SK)	SK
Máramaros (Mármaros)	Máramaros-Sziget (Sighetu Marmaţiei RO)	UA,RO
Maros-Torda	Maros-Vásárhely (Neumarkt am Maros, Tîrgu Mures RO)	RO*
Mozsony (Wieselburg)	Ungarisch-Altenburg (Mosonmagyaróvar HU)	HU,AT,SK
Nagy-Küküllö	Segesvár (Schäßburg, Sighisoara RO)	RO*
Nógrád (Neograd)	Balassagyarmat HU	SK,HU
Nyitra (Neutra)	Nyitra (Neutra, Nitra SK)	SK
Pest-Pilis-Solt-Kiskun	Budapest HU	HU
Pozsony (Preßburg)	Pozsony (Preßburg, Bratislava SI)	SK
Saros	Eperies (Preschau, Prešov SK)	SK
Somogy	Kaposvar HU	HU
Sopron (Ödenburg)	Sopron HU (Ödenburg)	HU,AT
Szabolcs	Nyíregyháza HU	HU
Szatmar	Nagy-Károly (Carei RO)	RO,HU
Szeben (Hermannstadt)	Nagy-Szeben (Hermannstadt, Sibiu RO)	RO*
Székes-Fejervár (Stuhlweißenburg)	Székes-Fejervár (Stuhlweißenburg, Székesfehérvar HU)	HU
Szepes (Zips)	Leutschau (Locse, Levoča SK)	SK
Szilágy	Zilah (Zalău RO)	RO
Szolnok-Doboka	Des (Dej RO)	RO*
Temes	Temesvar (Timişoara RO)	RO,YU
Tolna (Tolnau)	Szegszárd (Szekszard HU)	HU
Torda-Aranyos	Torda (Thörenburg, Turda RO)	RO*
Torontál	Nagy-Becskerek (Zrenjanin YU)	YU,RO,HU
Trencsen	Trencsen (Trenschin, Trenčin SK)	SK
Turocz (Turoz)	Turócz-Szent-Marton (Turoz-Sankt-Martin, Martin SK)	SK
Udvarhely	Szent Egyhazas-Olahfalu (Odorheiu Secuiesc RO)	RO*
Ugocsa	Nagy-Szöllös (Vynogradiv UA)	UA,RO
Ung	Ungvár (Uzhgorod UA)	UA,SK
Vasvár (Eisenburg)	Szombathely HU (Steinamanger)	HU,AT,SI
Veszprém	Veszprém HU	HU
Zala	Zala-Egerszeg HU	HU,HR
Zemplen	Sátoraljaúhely HU	SK,HU
Zólyom (Sohl)	Besztercze-Banya (Neusohl, Banská Bystrica SK)	SK

* = counties in Transylvania.

County: county name in Hungarian, followed by German equivalent in parentheses, if any.

Capital: county town in Hungarian, followed by German equivalent and modern vernacular name, if different. The modern name is always immediately followed by the ISO code for the country in which the county town now lies.

Modern: ISO codes for the countries which now occupy part or all of the county territory, listed in descending order of share. AT = Austria, HR = Croatia, HU = Hungary, RO = Romania, SI = Slovenia, SK = Slovakia, UA = Ukraine, YU = Yugoslavia.

1920-06-04   The Treaty of Trianon reduced Hungary to approximately its present area. No change was made to the counties. Many of them were now divided between two or more countries by the newly drawn borders.

1923	Hungary reorganized into 25 counties. Their relationship to the pre-war counties listed above is as follows. Cities shown in parentheses are capitals of the new counties, where they differ from the pre-war capitals. Bekes, Budapest, Hajdu, Heves, Jász-Nagykun-Szolnok, Pest-Pilis-Solt-Kiskun, Somogy, Szabolcs, Tolna, and Veszprém were essentially unchanged. Székes-Fejervár was renamed Fejér, but otherwise unchanged. Bács-Bodrog (Baja), Baranya, Bihar (Berettyóújfalu), Csongrád, Sopron, Zala, and Zemplen lost fragments of their territory, but were otherwise unchanged. Two counties lost part of their territory and part of their names: Abauj-Torna was renamed Abaúj (Szikszó), and Vasvár was renamed Vas. Finally, a number of county fragments merged with their neighbors. Borsod merged with the part of Gömör that remained in Hungary to form Borsod-Gömör (Miskolc); Csanád merged with part of Torontál to form Csanád (Makó); parts of Györ and Mozsony merged to form Györ Moson (Győr); parts of Komárom and Esztergom merged to form Komárom-Esztergom (Esztergom); parts of Nógrád and Hont merged to form Nógrád-Hont (Balassagyarmat); and parts of Szatmar and Bereg merged to form Szatmár-Bereg (Mátészalka).
1938-11-02	Strip of territory in southern Slovakia transferred to Hungary.
1939-03-23	Carpatho-Ukraine (also known as Ruthenia) annexed by Hungary.
~1940	Hungary annexed about 20% of Rumania.
1945-01-20	Borders of Hungary as of 1938-01-01 restored by armistice agreement.
1947-02-10	Small (61 sq. km.) area west of the Danube near Bratislava transferred to Czechoslovakia.
1950	Under the new Constitution of 1949 and the Council Act of 1950, Hungary reorganized from 25 counties and one capital city to 19 counties and one capital city, thus: Budapest enlarged by annexation of surrounding suburbs in Pest-Pilis-Solt-Kiskun county; Bács-Kiskun county formed from southern half of Pest-Pilis-Solt-Kiskun and all of Bács-Bodrog; Békés county formed from almost all of old Békés county plus fragments of Bihar, Csongrád, Jász-Nagykun-Szolnok, and eastern half of Csanád; Borsod-Abaúj-Zemplén county formed from Borsod-Gömör, Abaúj, and Zemplén; western half of Csanád county annexed to Csongrád; Győr-Sopron county formed by merging Győr-Moson with Sopron; Hajdú-Bihar county formed by merging Bihar and Hajdú; Komárom-Esztergom county renamed to Komárom; Nógrád county formed from Nógrád-Hont by removing a strip of land on the west and annexing a strip from Heves on the east; Pest county formed from northern half of Pest-Pilis-Solt-Kiskun plus a fragment of Nógrád-Hont; name of Jász-Nagykun-Szolnok county changed to Szolnok; Szabolcs-Szatmár county formed by merging Szabolcs and Szatmár-Bereg, minus a fragment which was annexed by Hajdú-Bihar; a sizable chunk of Zala county transferred to Vesprém; along with many minor border adjustments.
1954	The urban counties of Debrecen, Miskolc, Pécs, and Szeged created (by splitting them from their former counties, resp. Hajdú-Bihar, Borsod-Abaúj-Zemplén, Baranya, and Csongrád).
1971	The four urban counties merged with the ordinary counties surrounding them.
~1975	Five urban counties created: the same four as in 1954, plus Győr.
1990	Győr-Sopron county renamed to Győr-Moson-Sopron; Komárom county renamed to Komárom-Esztergom; Szabolcs-Szatmár county renamed to Szabolcs-Szatmár-Bereg; Szolnok county renamed to Jász-Nagykún-Szolnok.
~1992	Fifteen more urban counties created.
~1995	Two more urban counties, Salgótarjan and Szekszárd, created.

Other names of subdivisions:

Budapest: Budapeste (Portuguese)
Bács-Kiskun: Bács-Bodrog-Kiskun (variant)
Győr-Moson-Sopron: Győr-Sopron (obsolete)
Jász-Nagykún-Szolnok: Szolnok (obsolete)

Komárom-Esztergom: Komárom (obsolete)
Szabolcs-Szatmár-Bereg: Szabolcs-Szatmár (obsolete)
Transylvania: Siebenbürgen (German); Transilvania (Italian); Transylvanie (French)

ICELAND

ISO = IS/FIPS = IC   Language = Icelandic   Time zone = 0   Capital = Reykjavik

Iceland was part of Denmark until 1918-12-01. After its independence, it retained its allegiance to the Danish crown until 1944-06-17, when it became a republic.

Other names of country: IJsland (Dutch); Island (Danish, German, Norwegian, Swedish); Ísland (Icelandic); Islanda (Italian); Islande (French); Islandia (Spanish); Islândia (Portuguese); Islanti (Finnish); Lyðveldið Ísland (formal); Republic of Iceland (formal–English).

Origin of name: Icelandic *is*: ice, *land*: country.

Spelling note: The Icelandic language uses the letters edh and thorn. The capital and small edh are printed Ð and ð; thorn is Þ and þ. Edh is used to represent the voiced 'th' sound (as in 'this'), and thorn the unvoiced (as in 'thing'). When place names are transcribed into a typeface that lacks these letters, edh is normally transcribed 'dh', and thorn 'th'. However, because of their superficial resemblance, thorn is sometimes erroneously transcribed 'p'.

division	abv	ISO	FIPS	population	area-km	area-mi	capital	reg
Árnessýsla	AR	87	IC03	10,073	8,810	3,402	Selfoss	SL
Austur-Barðastrandarsýsla	AB	45	IC04	416	1,150	444	Patreksfjörður (Vatneyri)	VF
Austur-Húnavatnssýsla	AH	56	IC05	2,571	4,920	1,900	Blönduós	NV
Austur-Skaftafellssýsla	AS	77	IC06	2,177	6,080	2,348	Vík i Mýrdal	AL
Borgarfjarðarsýsla	BF	35	IC07	6,648	1,950	753	Borgarnes	VL
Dalasýsla	DS	38	IC08	1,102	2,110	815	Búðardalur	VL
Eyjafjarðarsýsla	EY	65	IC09	18,545	4,150	1,602	Akureyri	NE
Gullbringusýsla	GU	25	IC10	30,416	1,050	405	Hafnarfjörður	RR
Kjósarsýsla	KJ	16	IC15	104,584	870	336	Kópavogur	RR
Mýrasýsla	MY	36	IC17	2,537	3,270	1,263	Borgarnes	VL
Norður-Ísafjarðarsýsla	NI	48	IC19	5,124	3,060	1,181	Ísafjörður	VF
Norður-Múlasýsla	NM	75	IC20	3,294	12,430	4,799	Seyðisfjörður	AL
Norður-Þingeyjarsýsla	NT	67	IC21	1,768	5,380	2,077	Húsavík	NE
Rangárvallasýsla	RA	86	IC23	8,220	8,280	3,197	Hvolsvöllur	SL
Skagafjarðarsýsla	SG	57	IC28	6,489	5,380	2,077	Sauðarkrókur	NV
Snæfellsnes- og Hnappadalssýsla	SH	37	IC29	4,597	2,190	846	Stykkishólmur (Helgafell)	VL
Strandasýsla	SD	49	IC30	1,184	2,630	1,015	Hólmavík	VF
Suður-Múlasýsla	SM	76	IC31	7,385	3,980	1,537	Eskifjörður	AL
Suður-Þingeyjarsýsla	ST	66	IC32	5,387	12,150	4,691	Húsavík	NE
Vestur-Barðastrandarsýsla	VB	46	IC34	2,045	1,550	598	Patreksfjörður (Vatneyri)	VF
Vestur-Húnavatnssýsla	VH	55	IC35	1,571	2,580	996	Blönduós	NV
Vestur-Ísafjarðarsýsla	VI	47	IC36	1,710	1,130	436	Ísafjörður	VF
Vestur-Skaftafellssýsla	VS	85	IC37	1,344	7,900	3,050	Vik i Mýrdal	SL
				229,187	103,000	39,768		

town	abv	ISO	FIPS	reg	county
Akranes	AK	30	IC01	VL	Borgarfjarðarsýsla
Akureyri	AY	60	IC02	NE	Eyjafjarðarsýsla
Bolungarvík	BL	41		VF	Norður-Ísafjarðarsýsla
Dalvík	DV	63		NE	Eyjafjarðarsýsla
Eskifjörður	ES	72		AL	Suður-Múlasýsla
Garðabær	GA	13		RR	Gullbringusýsla
Grindavík	GR	23		RR	Gullbringusýsla
Hafnarfjörður	HF	14	IC11	RR	Gullbringusýsla
Húsavík	HS	61	IC12	NE	Suður-Þingeyjarsýsla
Ísafjörður	IS	40	IC13	VF	Norður-Ísafjarðarsýsla
Keflavík	KF	22	IC14	RR	Gullbringusýsla
Kópavogur	KP	10	IC16	RR	Kjósarsýsla
Neskaupstaður	NK	71	IC18	AL	Suður-Múlasýsla
Njarðvík	NJ	24		RR	Gullbringusýsla
Ólafsfjörður	OF	62	IC22	NE	Eyjafjarðarsýsla
Olafsvík	OV	32		RR	Kjósarsýsla
Reykjavik	RK	00	IC24	RR	Kjósarsýsla ▶

town	abv	ISO	FIPS	reg	county
Sauðárkrókur	SK	51	IC25	NV	Skagafjarðarsýsla
Selfoss	SS	81		SL	Árnessýsla
Seltjarnarnes	SN	11		RR	Kjósarsýsla
Seyðisfjörður	SY	70	IC26	AL	Norður-Múlasýsla
Siglufjörður	SI	50	IC27	NV	Skagafjarðarsýsla
Vestmannaeyjar	VM	80	IC33	SL	Rangárvallasýsla

Status: These divisions are sýslur (sing. sýsla; counties, districts, or provinces —first list, above) and kaupstaðir (sing. kaupstaður; independent towns — second list).

Abv: Two-letter code for international compatibility (defined by the author).

ISO: Codes from ISO 3166-2.

FIPS: Codes from FIPS PUB 10-4.

Population: 1980 census (including independent towns within each county).

Area-km: Square kilometers (including towns).

Area-mi: Square miles (including towns).

County: Tells which county the independent town would presumably belong to if it weren't independent.

Reg: Code for the landsvædun (region) to which the town or county belongs (see below).

Roads: The first digit of a highway number determines the region in which the road is located. Highway number 1 is the ring road which encircles the whole island.

reg	name	roads	population	area-km	Icelandic name
AL	East	9	13,180	21,991	Austurland
NE	Northland East	8	26,382	22,368	Norðurland eystra
NV	Northland West	7	10,340	13,093	Norðurland vestra
RR	Reykjavík and Reykjanes Area	4	164,839	1,982	Reykjavíkursvaedi og Reykjanessvaedi
SL	South	2, 3	20,548	25,214	Suðurland
VF	Western Peninsula	6	9,756	9,470	Vestfirðir
VL	West	5	14,532	8,711	Vesturland
			259,577	102,829	

Further subdivisions: Iceland is divided into eight regions. Two of the regions are usually grouped together: Capital Area, also called Reykjavík, and Southwest Peninsula, also called Reykjanes. The regions are subdivided into 23 counties (1977, 1981-17; 1959-16) and 23 independent towns. These are further subdivided into 201 communes. Each of the independent towns coincides with a commune. The number of communes has been steadily decreasing, while the number of independent towns has generally been increasing.

Territorial extent: Rangárvallasýsla includes the Vestmannaeyjar, sometimes called the Westman Islands.

Origins of names:

Akureyri: Icelandic *akur*: field and *eyri*: alluvium

Reykjavik: Icelandic for smoky bay

Hafnarfjörður: Old Icelandic *hafnar*: port, *fjörður*: fjord

Change history: In 1900, Iceland consisted of three amter (counties) in the Danish administrative system: North, South, and West. North corresponded to the present-day regions of Northland East, Northland West, and most of East (all but part of Austur-Skaftafellssýsla); West corresponded to the present-day regions of West (excluding Borgarfjarðarsýsla) and Western Peninsula; and South comprised the rest of the country. These counties evolved into regions. The number of divisions was changed to five ~1937 and to eight ~1960.

There were 16 counties in 1958. Some of them have split since then. Specifically, Gullbringu- og Kjósarsýsla split into Gullbringusýsla and Kjósarsýsla, and Mýra- og Borgarfjarðarsýsla split into Mýrasýsla and Borgarfjarðarsýsla, both ~1964.

Other names of subdivisions:

Snæfellsnes- og Hnappadalssýsla: Snæfellsnessýsla (obsolete)

Population history:

region	1940	1950	1970	1980	1991
East	10,123	9,705	11,315	12,856	13,180 ➤

region	1940	1950	1970	1980	1991
Northland East	27,406	28,632	22,225	25,700	26,382
Northland West	——	——	9,909	10,631	10,340
Reykjavík and Reykjanes Area	——	——	119,822	135,000	164,839
South	13,596	13,847	18,052	19,637	20,548
Western Peninsula	57,396	80,623	10,050	10,479	9,756
West	12,953	11,166	13,205	14,884	14,532
	121,474	143,973	204,578	229,187	259,577

Census date is December 1. Before 1970, Northland is included in Northland East, and Reykjavík-Reykjanes is included in Western Peninsula.

INDIA

ISO = IN/FIPS = IN   Languages = Hindi, English, et al.   Time zone = +5:30   Capital = New Delhi

India in 1900 was a hodge-podge of British provinces under the direct sovereignty of the British crown, and small states ruled by Indian princes under British hegemony. The British position was called paramountcy, meaning simply that Britain had the power to overrule the native princes' actions. India at that time included present-day Pakistan, Bangladesh, Myanmar, and Aden (now part of Yemen). On the other hand, it excluded a few small enclaves in the possession of France and Portugal, and Sikkim, then a kingdom under British protection. When India obtained its independence on 1947-08-15, the area hitherto known as India was divided into two countries, India and Pakistan. The principle guiding the division was to allocate majority-Hindu areas to India and majority-Muslim areas to Pakistan. In the implementation, the large provinces of Bengal and Punjab were split between the two countries, and Pakistan was created as two pieces on opposite sides of the Indian subcontinent.

Other names of country: Bharat (formal); Hindustan, Hindoostan (obsolete); Inde (French); Indian Union, Republic of India (formal–English); Indien (German, Swedish); Indland (Icelandic); Intia (Finnish).

Origin of name: from Sanskrit *sindhu*: river, after the Indus River.

division	ISO	FIPS	typ	dist	population	area-km	area-mi	PIN	capital
Andaman and Nicobar Islands	AN	IN01	ut	2	280,661	8,249	3,185	744	Port Blair
Andhra Pradesh	AP	IN02	st	23	66,508,008	275,068	106,204	50-53	Hyderabad
Arunachal Pradesh	AR	IN30	ut	9	864,558	83,743	32,333	790-792	Itanagar
Assam	AS	IN03	st	10	22,414,322	78,438	30,285	78	Dispur
Bihar	BR	IN04	st	31	86,374,465	173,877	67,134	80-85	Patna/w, Ranchi/s
Chandigarh	CH	IN05	ut	1	642,015	114	44	16	Chandigarh
Dadra and Nagar Haveli	DN	IN06	ut	1	138,477	491	190	396	Silvassa
Daman and Diu	DD	IN32	ut	2	101,586	112	43	396	Daman, Diu
Delhi	DL	IN07	ut	1	9,420,644	1,483	573	11	Delhi
Goa	GA	IN33	st	1	1,169,793	3,702	1,429	403	Panaji
Gujarat	GJ	IN09	st	19	41,309,582	196,024	75,685	36-39	Gandhinagar
Haryana	HR	IN10	st	12	16,463,648	44,212	17,070	12-13	Chandigarh
Himachal Pradesh	HP	IN11	st	12	5,170,877	55,673	21,495	17	Simla
Jammu and Kashmir	JK	IN12	st	14	7,718,700	222,236	85,806	18-19	Srinagar/s, Jammu/w
Karnataka	KA	IN19	st	19	44,977,201	191,791	74,051	56-59	Bangalore
Kerala	KL	IN13	st	12	29,098,518	38,863	15,005	67-69	Trivandrum
Lakshadweep	LD	IN14	ut	1	51,707	32	12	673	Kavaratti
Madhya Pradesh	MP	IN15	st	45	66,181,170	443,446	171,215	45-49	Bhopal
Maharashtra	MH	IN16	st	26	78,937,187	307,690	118,800	40-44	Mumbai
Manipur	MN	IN17	st	6	1,837,149	22,327	8,621	795	Imphal
Meghalaya	ML	IN18	st	5	1,774,778	22,429	8,660	793-794	Shillong
Mizoram	MZ	IN31	ut	3	689,756	21,081	8,139	796	Aizawl
Nagaland	NL	IN20	st	7	1,209,546	16,579	6,401	797-798	Kohima
Orissa	OR	IN21	st	13	31,659,736	155,707	60,119	75-77	Bhubaneswar
Pondicherry	PY	IN22	ut	4	807,785	492	190	605	Pondicherry ▶

division	ISO	FIPS	typ	dist	population	area-km	area-mi	PIN	capital
Punjab	PB	IN23	st	12	20,281,969	50,362	19,445	14-15	Chandigarh
Rajasthan	RJ	IN24	st	26	44,005,990	342,239	132,139	30-34	Jaipur
Sikkim	SK	IN29	st	4	406,457	7,096	2,740	737	Gangtok
Tamil Nadu	TN	IN25	st	16	55,858,946	130,058	50,216	60-64	Chennai
Tripura	TR	IN26	st	3	2,757,205	10,486	4,049	799	Agartala
Uttar Pradesh	UP	IN27	st	56	139,112,287	294,411	113,673	20-28	Lucknow
West Bengal	WB	IN28	st	16	68,077,965	88,752	34,267	70-74	Calcutta
				412	846,302,688	3,287,263	1,269,218		

Typ: These divisions are states (st) and union territories (ut).

ISO: Codes from ISO 3166-2.

FIPS: Codes from FIPS PUB 10-4.

Dist: Number of districts in each division.

Population: 1991 census (Jammu and Kashmir includes only the part under Indian administration).

Area km: Square kilometers (Jammu and Kashmir includes areas claimed by Pakistan and China).

Area-mi: Square miles.

PIN: Indian postal codes (postal index numbers) are six digits. The first three digits generally determine a district. Ranges listed are the first two or three digits of the PIN.

Capital: Summer (s) and winter (w) capitals: primary capital named first.

Further subdivisions: The states and union territories are subdivided into districts.

Territorial extent: Andaman and Nicobar Islands is separated from islands belonging to Myanmar by the Coco Channel. Landfall Island is the northernmost of the Andamans. Narcondam Island is the easternmost. The Nicobar Islands lie to the south, Great Nicobar Island being southernmost. It is separated from Sumatra, Indonesia, by Great Channel.

Arunachal Pradesh is the object of a territorial claim by China.

Daman and Diu consists of two separate parts: the enclave of Daman, and the island of Diu with small adjacent coastal tracts. Both lie on the coast of Gujarat, but they are on opposite sides of the Gulf of Khambhat.

Goa consists of a coastal region and the islands of Angediva, Morcegos, and Saint George's.

Jammu and Kashmir is occupied partly by India and partly by Pakistan. Both countries have claims to more land. India also claims adjacent land occupied by China.

Lakshadweep consists of a number of islands and reefs in the Indian Ocean. Towards the Indian mainland, the easternmost are Androth, Cheriyam, and Kalpeni Islands. Towards the Maldive Islands, the southernmost is Minicoy Island. The Amindivi and Cannanore island groups make up most of the territory.

Pondicherry consists of four districts, each of which is a separate coastal enclave: Karaikal and Pondicherry, both surrounded by Tamil Nadu; Yanam, within Andhra Pradesh; and Mahé, within Kerala. The district of Pondicherry itself consists of several enclaves within Tamil Nadu.

Origins of names:

Ahmedabad: City of Shah Ahmad I, its founder

Andaman Islands: Sanskrit *Hanumant,* name of the king of the monkeys in the Ramayana

Andhra Pradesh: Hindi *andhra,* from Telugu *andhramu:* Telugu, and *pradesh:* state

Assam: probably from the Ahamiya clan (or Ahoms), who invaded in the 13th century

Bihar: Sanskrit *vihara:* monastery. Old capital had a major Buddhist monastery.

Chandigarh: Punjabi *Candi:* terrible goddess (the Hindu goddess Durga); *garh:* home

Delhi: named for the traditional founder, Raja Dhilu

Goa: from native words *goe mat:* fertile land

Gujarat: Sanskrit *Gurjara,* ethnic name

Haryana: Hari (a Hindu god) + Hindi *ayana:* home

Himachal Pradesh: Hindi *himachal:* Himalayas, *pradesh:* land

Kashmir: from Sanskrit *kasyapamara:* land of Kasyapa (Hindu god)

Lakshadweep: Sanskrit *laksha:* one hundred thousand, *dvipa:* islands

Madhya Pradesh: Hindi for central state

Maharashtra: Sanskrit for great kingdom (akin to maharaja)

Meghalaya: *megha:* cloud, *alaya:* home, i.e. home of the clouds

Orissa: Sanskrit *Odrah:* ethnic name, *deshah:* state

Pondicherry: Tamil *pudu:* new, *cheri:* town

Punjab: Persian *panj:* five, *ab:* river (the area is drained by five tributaries of the Indus)

Rajasthan: Hindi *raja:* king, *sthan:* land (formed by the union of 19 small kingdoms)

Uttar Pradesh: Sanskrit *uttarah:* upper or northern, *pradeshah:* state

West Bengal: Western part of Bengal, from Bengali *bangla:* ethnic name

Change history: In 1900, India included over 500 native states (also called princely states); the British provinces of Assam, Bengal, Berar, Bihar, Burma, Central Provinces, Orissa, Punjab, and North Western Provinces and Oudh; and the presidencies of Bombay and Madras. The presidency of Bombay contained the provinces of Bombay, Sind, and Aden. Burma was divided into Lower Burma and Upper Burma. The United Provinces of Agra and Oudh contained Oudh province and North Western Provinces.

1901	North-West Frontier Area (not to be confused with North Western Provinces) split from Punjab.
1902	Name of North Western Provinces and Oudh changed to United Provinces of Agra and Oudh.
1902-10-01	Berar merged with Central Provinces to form Central Provinces and Berar.
1905-10-16	Bengal and Assam provinces reorganized into Eastern Bengal and Assam province and West Bengal province.
1910	Native state of Benares formed by merging a number of smaller fiefs.
1911-12-12	1905 partition of Bengal was nullified.
1912-10-01	Delhi province split from Punjab; Indian capital moved from Calcutta to Delhi.
1912	Bihar and Orissa province split from Bengal.
1931-02-10	New Delhi officially replaced Delhi as capital.
1932	Aden province split from Bombay presidency.
1935	Name of United Provinces of Agra and Oudh changed to United Provinces.
1936-04-01	Orissa province formed from parts of Bihar and Orissa province, Central Provinces and Berar province, and Madras presidency; remaining part of Bihar and Orissa renamed Bihar; status of Sind division of Bombay presidency changed to province.
1937-04-01	Aden (now in Yemen) and Burma (now Myanmar) split from India as crown colonies.
1947-08-15	Indian independence. The British provinces became part of India immediately. The native states and agencies became effectively independent. Some of them were allowed to decide whether to accede to (merge with) India or Pakistan. Others combined to form new states in the Indian Union, or merged directly with existing provinces. The process was essentially complete when the new Constitution took effect, less than 2½ years later. On this date, Bengal split into West Bengal (India) and East Pakistan; Punjab split into East Punjab (India) and West Punjab (Pakistan); the presidency of Bombay, which had consisted of Bombay and Sind provinces, split, with Sind going to Pakistan; Banaras, Rampur, and Tehri-Garhwal states merged with United Provinces; Central Provinces and Berar became Madhya Pradesh.
1947-10	France ceded its loges, the sites of French-owned factories (trading posts) in Bombay, Madras, and Orissa provinces, totaling 526 sq. km., to India.
1947-10-26	Jammu and Kashmir state became part of India by the signing of the Instrument of Accession. However, Pakistani fighters invaded the area, bringing about a de facto partition which has been in dispute ever since.
1947-11-08	India annexed the native states of Junagadh and Manavadar to Rajputana, even though they had acceded to Pakistan.
1948	Native states merged to form seven unions: Greater Rajasthan (corresponding to an area called Rajputana before independence), Madhya Bharat (also called the Malwa Union), Patiala and East Punjab States Union (PEPSU for short), Saurashtra (also called the United State of Kathiawar), Travancore-Cochin, United Deccan State, and Vindhya Pradesh.
1948	15 native states merged with Madhya Pradesh.
1948	Native states of Banganapalle and Pudukottai merged with Madras state.
1948	174 native states merged with Bombay, including Baroda, Cambay, Idar, Janjira, Kolhapur, Palanpur, Radhanpur, Rajpipla, Sirohi, and the states of the United Deccan State.
1948	Native states of Dujana, Loharu, and Pataudi merged with East Punjab.
1948-04-15	Himachal Pradesh state formed from 30 former Hill States, including Chamba, Mandi, Nahan, Sirmur, and Suket.
1948-05	Native states of Saraikela and Kharsawan merged with Bihar.

1949-04-01   Native state of Sandar merged with Madras state.
1949-08-01   24 former native states merged with Orissa.
1949-10-15   Tripura merged with India as a centrally administered area.
1949-10-15   Manipur merged with India as a union territory.
1950-01-01   Cooch Behar state merged with West Bengal.
1950-01-24   Name of United Provinces changed to Uttar Pradesh.
1950-01-26   The Constitution took effect. The divisions of India were classified as follows: nine Part
              A states, formerly governors' provinces; eight Part B states, formerly native states or
              groups of states; ten Part C states, formerly chief commissioners' provinces; and two
              Part D territories. Name of East Punjab state changed to Punjab (India). Greater
              Rajasthan union became Rajasthan state.
1950-05-02   Chandernagore transferred from French possession to India.
1950-12-05   Sikkim became an Indian protectorate.
1951   Territory in Assam around Dewangiri ceded to Bhutan.
1953-10-07   Capital of Punjab moved to the new city of Chandigarh.
1953-10-01   Andhra Part A state split from Madras.
1954   Bilaspur state merged with Himachal Pradesh.
1954-10-02   Chandernagore merged with West Bengal.
1956   Capital of Hyderabad moved from Kurnool to Hyderabad.
1956-05-28   France ceded Pondicherry to India as a union territory.
1956-09-01   Status of Tripura changed from centrally administered area to union territory.
1956-11-01   States Reorganization Act took effect. The distinction among Part A, B, and C states
              was abolished. States were reorganized largely on linguistic lines. Andhra Pradesh
              state formed by merging Andhra with part of Hyderabad. Bombay state formed by
              merging Kutch, Saurashtra union, and part of former Bombay state. Status of Delhi
              and Himachal Pradesh changed from states to union territories. Kerala state formed
              by merging most of Travancore-Cochin union and part of Madras. Laccadive, Mini-
              coy, and Amindivi Islands union territory split from Madras. Madhya Pradesh state
              formed by merging Bhopal and Vindhya Pradesh union, all of Madhya Bharat union
              but one enclave, most of former Madhya Pradesh, and an enclave of Rajasthan. Madras
              state lost large areas to other states, but gained part of Travancore-Cochin union.
              Mysore state formed by merging Coorg and former Mysore states and parts of Bom-
              bay, Hyderabad, and Madras states. Punjab state formed by merging Patiala and East
              Punjab States Union and former Punjab. Rajasthan state gained Ajmer state and small
              parts of Bombay and Madhya Bharat union, and lost an enclave to Madhya Pradesh.
              8,177 sq. km. transferred from Bihar state to West Bengal.
1957-12-01   Naga Hills-Tuensang Area split from Assam as a centrally administered area.
1960-04-01   Madras state ceded 573 sq. km. of territory to Andhra Pradesh in exchange for another
              territory of 1,062 sq. km.
1960-05-01   Bombay state split into Gujarat and Maharashtra by the Bombay Reorganization
              Act.
1961-08-11   Dadra and Nagar Haveli, formerly a Portuguese colony and independent since 1954-07,
              merged with India as a union territory.
1961-12-19   Portuguese India (India Portuguesa, later called Estado da India) annexed by India and
              became the territory of Goa, Daman and Diu.
1962-09   Nagaland state split from Assam.
1966-11-01   By the Punjab Reorganization Act, Punjab state split into a smaller Punjab state, a new
              Haryana state and Chandigarh union territory, and a section which merged with
              Himachal Pradesh. Chandigarh, formerly capital of Punjab, became joint capital of
              Punjab and Haryana states and its own union territory.
1968-08   Name of Madras state changed to Tamil Nadu.
1970   Capital of Gujarat moved from Ahmedabad to Gandhinagar.
1971-01-25   Status of Himachal Pradesh changed from union territory to state.
1972-01-21   Arunachal Pradesh union territory, Meghalaya state, and Mizoram union territory split
              from Assam; capital of Assam moved from Shillong to Dispur; status of Manipur and

Tripura changed from union territories to states. Before the split, Arunachal Pradesh had been the North East Frontier Agency.

1972-12-17	A new line of control between India and Pakistan in the area of Jammu and Kashmir took effect.
1973	Name of Mysore state changed to Karnataka.
1973-11	Name of Laccadive, Minicoy, and Amindivi Islands union territory changed to Lakshadweep.
1975-04-26	Status of Sikkim changed from protectorate to state.
1986-07	Status of Mizoram changed from union territory to state.
1986-12	Status of Arunachal Pradesh changed from union territory to state.
1987-05-30	Goa, Daman, and Diu union territory split into Goa state and Daman and Diu union territory.
1996	Name of the capital of Tamil Nadu state changed from Madras to Chennai; name of the capital of Maharashtra state changed from Bombay to Mumbai.
1998	The governing coalition resolved to create three new states and change the status of Delhi, but no implementation date has been set. If and when the reform is passed, the status of Delhi will change from union territory to state; the city of New Delhi (about 43 sq. km.) will be split from Delhi and become National Capital Territory; about 146,361 sq. km. will be split from Madhya Pradesh and become the state of Chhattisgarh (capital: Raipur); about 51,125 sq. km. of Uttar Pradesh will be split off as the state of Uttaranchal (also called Uttarakhand; capital: Nainital); and about 74,677 sq. km. of Bihar will become Vananchal state (also called Jharkhand; capital: Ranchi).

Other names of subdivisions:

Andaman and Nicobar Islands: Îles Andaman et Nicobar (French); Ilhas de Andamã e Nicobar (Portuguese); Inseln Andamanen und Nikobaren (German); Isole Andamane e Nicobare (Italian)

Arunachal Pradesh: Agence de la Frontière du Nord-Est (French-obsolete); North East Frontier Agency (obsolete)

Daman and Diu: Daman e Diu (Italian); Damân et Diu (French); Damão e Diu (Portuguese)

Dadra and Nagar Haveli: Dâdra et Nagar Haveli (French); Dadra e Nagar Haveli (Italian)

Goa: Gôa (Portuguese)

Gujarat: Goudjerate, Gujerat (French), Gujerate (Portuguese)

Haryana: Hariana (French)

Jammu and Kashmir: Jammu e Cashemira (Portuguese); Jammu e Kashmir (Italian); Jammu et Cachemire (French); Jammu und Kaschmir (German); Kashmir, Kashmir and Jammu (variant)

Karnataka: Maisur (obsolete-variant); Mysore (obsolete)

Lakshadweep: Îles Laquedives (French); Laccadive, Minicoy, and Amindivi Islands, Laccadives (obsolete); Lackadiverna (Swedish); Lakkadiven (German); Lakkadivene (Norwegian); Lakshadivi (variant)

Punjab: Panjab (German, variant); Pendjab, Penjab (French); Pundjabe (Portuguese); East Punjab (obsolete)

Pondicherry: Pondichéry (French); Puduchcheri (variant)

Rajasthan: Greater Rajasthan, Rajputana (obsolete)

Tamil Nadu: Madras (obsolete); Tamilnad (variant)

Uttar Pradesh: United Provinces (obsolete)

West Bengal: Bengala Occidentale (Italian); Bengala Ocidental (Portuguese); Bengale occidental (French)

Population history: British Imperial period

province	area-km	1891	1901	1911	1921	1931	1941
Ajmer-Merwara	7,021	542,358	477,000	501,395	495,271	560,567	583,693
Andamans and Nicobars	8,140	16,000	25,000	26,459	27,086	29,463	33,768
Assam	126,920	5,476,833	5,842,000	6,714,000	7,606,230	8,784,943	10,204,733
Baluchistan	140,450	— —	382,000	414,412	420,648	463,492	501,631
Bengal	392,495	71,346,987	42,141,000	52,668,269	46,695,536	49,997,376	21,837,295
Bihar	180,639	— —	— —	— —	34,002,189	37,590,356	36,340,151
Orissa	83,392	— —	— —	— —	— —	— —	8,728,544
Bombay	324,122	18,901,123	18,530,000	19,672,642	19,348,219	21,102,126	25,384,848
Burma	444,002	7,605,560	N/A	12,115,217	13,212,192	14,652,272	— —
Central Provinces	224,037	10,784,294	11,971,000	13,916,308	13,912,760	15,472,628	16,813,584
Coorg	4,100	173,055	181,000	174,976	163,838	163,089	168,726
Delhi	1,536	— —	— —	— —	488,188	636,827	917,939 ➤

province	area-km	1891	1901	1911	1921	1931	1941
Madras	365,678	35,630,440	38,230,000	41,405,404	42,318,985	46,731,850	49,341,810
N.W. Frontier Prov.	34,755	— —	2,042,000	2,196,933	2,251,340	2,423,380	3,038,067
Punjab	286,626	20,866,847	19,942,000	19,974,956	20,685,024	23,580,520	28,418,819
United Provinces	278,431	46,905,085	47,313,000	47,182,044	45,375,787	48,423,264	55,020,617
major native states							
Baroda	21,305	2,415,000	1,953,000	2,033,000	2,126,522	2,442,924	2,855,010
Bhopal	18,000	952,486	N/A	N/A	N/A	N/A	785,322
Cochin	3,528	722,906	812,000	918,000	979,000	1,205,000	1,422,875
Travancore	17,431	2,557,736	2,952,000	3,429,000	4,006,000	5,096,000	6,070,018
Gwalior	66,964	3,378,774	3,066,000	3,228,000	3,195,475	3,520,708	4,006,159
Hyderabad	214,187	11,537,040	11,141,000	13,375,000	12,471,770	14,395,493	16,338,534
Kashmir	209,530	2,543,952	2,906,000	3,158,000	3,699,065	3,645,339	4,021,616
Manipur	22,326	N/A	284,000	346,000	384,000	626,000	512,069
Mysore	72,354	4,943,604	5,539,000	5,806,000	5,859,952	6,554,573	7,329,140
Rajputana	337,393	12,016,102	9,853,000	10,530,000	13,308,781	11,223,708	13,670,208
India		287,223,431	294,360,356	315,132,527	318,885,980	351,399,888	388,997,955

Notes: Areas listed are as of about 1900, except for states that were created later. Columns do not add up to the totals shown, because many native states are omitted. All Indian censuses were as of March 1.

Republic period

division	1951	1961	1971	1981	1991
Andaman and Nicobar Islands	30,963	63,548	115,133	188,741	280,661
Andhra Pradesh	31,260,000	35,983,447	43,502,708	53,549,763	66,508,008
Arunachal Pradesh	— —	336,558	467,511	631,839	864,558
Assam	9,603,707	11,872,772	14,625,152	19,896,843	22,414,322
Bihar	38,779,562	46,455,610	56,353,369	69,914,734	86,374,465
Chandigarh	— —	— —	257,251	451,610	642,015
Dadra and Nagar Haveli	— —	57,963	74,170	103,676	138,477
Daman and Diu	— —	— —	— —	— —	101,586
Delhi	1,744,072	2,658,612	4,065,698	6,220,406	9,420,644
Goa	— —	626,667	857,771	1,086,730	1,169,793
Gujarat	— —	20,633,350	26,697,475	34,085,799	41,309,582
Haryana	— —	— —	10,036,808	12,922,618	16,463,648
Himachal Pradesh	1,134,885	1,351,144	3,460,434	4,280,818	5,170,877
Jammu and Kashmir	4,370,000	3,560,976	4,616,632	5,987,389	7,718,700
Karnataka	19,401,193	23,586,772	29,299,014	37,135,714	44,977,201
Kerala	15,000,000	16,903,715	21,347,375	25,453,680	29,098,518
Lakshadweep	21,195	24,108	31,810	40,249	51,707
Madhya Pradesh	26,071,657	32,372,408	41,654,119	52,178,844	66,181,170
Maharashtra	48,300,000	39,553,718	50,412,235	62,784,171	78,937,187
Manipur	577,635	780,037	1,072,753	1,420,953	1,837,149
Meghalaya	— —	— —	1,011,699	1,335,819	1,774,778
Mizoram	— —	— —	332,390	439,757	689,756
Nagaland	— —	369,200	516,449	774,930	1,209,546
Orissa	14,645,946	17,548,846	21,944,615	26,370,271	31,659,736
Pondicherry	317,163	369,079	471,707	604,471	807,785
Punjab	16,134,890	20,306,812	13,551,060	16,788,915	20,281,969
Rajasthan	15,970,000	20,155,602	25,765,806	34,261,862	44,005,990
Sikkim	137,158	162,189	209,845	316,385	406,457
Tamil Nadu	29,970,000	33,686,953	41,199,168	48,408,007	55,858,946
Tripura	639,029	1,142,005	1,556,342	2,053,058	2,757,205
Uttar Pradesh	63,215,742	73,746,401	88,341,144	110,862,013	139,112,287
West Bengal	26,300,000	34,926,279	44,312,011	54,580,647	68,077,965
total	363,612,773	439,234,771	548,159,654	685,130,712	846,302,688

INDONESIA

ISO = ID/FIPS = ID   Language = Bahasa Indonesia   Time zone = (see table)   Capital = Jakarta

At the beginning of the 20th century, Indonesia was a newly coined name. It referred in a general way to the southern part of the Malay Archipelago. The modern country of Indonesia was then several Dutch colonies, known collectively as the Netherlands Indies or the East Indies. There was also one Portuguese colony (see the East Timor entry). During World War II, the area was almost completely occupied by Japanese forces. At the end of the war, the country declared its independence under the name of Indonesia. On 1949-12-27, the separation became official. Dutch New Guinea, however, remained a colony of the Netherlands until 1963-05-01. Indonesia unilaterally annexed Portuguese Timor in 1976. Portugal still contests the legality of the annexation, but the area is unquestionably under de facto Indonesian sovereignty, so it is listed as a province below.

   Other names of country: Dutch East Indies, East Indies, Netherlands Indies (obsolete); Indias Orientales Neerlandesas (obsolete–Spanish); Indonésia (Portuguese); Indónesía (Icelandic); Indonesië (Dutch); Indonésie (French); Indonesien (Danish, German, Swedish); Nederlandsch-Indië (Dutch-obsolete); Republic of Indonesia (formal–English); Republic of the United States of Indonesia (formal–obsolete); Republik Indonesia (formal).

   Origin of name: Indo- (combining form of India) + Greek *nes(os)*: islands + -ia (suffix for country).

   Spelling note: Names have been altered by spelling reforms. Older sources may show various obsolete spellings derived from Dutch phonetics, such as oe instead of u, tj for c, dj for j, or j for y.

division	ISO	FIPS	off	tz	population	area-km	area-mi	capital	reg
Aceh	AC	ID01	DIA	+7	3,416,156	55,392	21,387	Banda Aceh	SM
Bali	BA	ID02	BL	+8	2,777,811	5,561	2,147	Denpasar	NU
Bengkulu	BE	ID03	BK	+7	1,179,122	21,168	8,173	Bengkulu	SM
Irian Jaya	IJ	ID09	IJA	+9	1,648,708	421,981	162,928	Jayapura	IJ
Jakarta Raya	JK	ID04	DKIJ	+7	8,259,266	590	228	Jakarta	JW
Jambi	JA	ID05	JB	+7	2,020,568	44,924	17,345	Telanaipura	SM
Jawa Barat	JB	ID06	JWB	+7	35,384,352	46,300	17,877	Bandung	JW
Jawa Tengah	JT	ID07	JTG	+7	28,520,643	34,206	13,207	Semarang	JW
Jawa Timur	JI	ID08	JT	+7	32,503,991	47,922	18,503	Surabaya	JW
Kalimantan Barat	KB	ID11	KB	+7	3,229,153	146,760	56,664	Pontianak	KA
Kalimantan Selatan	KS	ID12	KS	+8	2,597,572	37,660	14,541	Banjarmasin	KA
Kalimantan Tengah	KT	ID13	KTG	+7	1,396,486	152,600	58,919	Palangkaraya	KA
Kalimantan Timur	KI	ID14	KT	+8	1,876,663	202,440	78,163	Samarinda	KA
Lampung	LA	ID15	LP	+7	6,017,573	33,307	12,860	Tanjungkarang	SM
Maluku	MA	ID16	ML	+9	1,857,790	74,505	28,767	Ambon	MA
Nusa Tenggara Barat	NB	ID17	NTB	+8	3,369,649	20,177	7,790	Mataram	NU
Nusa Tenggara Timur	NT	ID18	NTT	+8	3,268,644	47,876	18,485	Kupang	NU
Riau	RI	ID19	RI	+7	3,303,976	94,562	36,511	Pakanbaru	SM
Sulawesi Selatan	SN	ID20	SLS	+8	6,981,646	72,781	28,101	Ujung Pandang	SL
Sulawesi Tengah	ST	ID21	SLTG	+8	1,711,327	69,726	26,921	Palu	SL
Sulawesi Tenggara	SG	ID22	SLTA	+8	1,349,619	27,686	10,690	Kendari	SL
Sulawesi Utara	SA	ID23	SLU	+8	2,478,119	19,023	7,345	Manado	SL
Sumatera Barat	SB	ID24	SB	+7	4,000,207	49,778	19,219	Padang	SM
Sumatera Selatan	SS	ID25	SS	+7	6,313,074	103,688	40,034	Palembang	SM
Sumatera Utara	SU	ID26	SU	+7	10,256,027	70,787	27,331	Medan	SM
Timor Timur	TT	ID27	TT	+8	747,750	14,874	5,743	Dili	NU
Yogyakarta	YO	ID10	DIY	+7	2,913,054	3,169	1,224	Yogyakarta	JW
					179,378,946	1,919,443	741,103		

   Status: These divisions are propinsi (provinces), except for two daerah istimewa (special regions), Aceh and Yogyakarta, and one daerah khusus ibu kota (special district), Jakarta Raya.

   ISO: Codes from ISO 3166-2.

   FIPS: Codes from FIPS PUB 10-4.

   Off: Province abbreviations as found in some Indonesia government publications.

   Tz: Time zone for the province, in hours later (+) than UTC. No daylight saving time observed.

   Population: 1990 census.

   Area-km: Square kilometers.

Area-mi: Square miles.

Reg: Region containing the province, according to ISO 3166-2. The regions are Irian Jaya (IJ), Jawa (JW), Kalimantan (KA), Maluku (MA), Nusa Tenggara (NU), Sulawesi (SL), Sumatera (SM).

Postal codes: Indonesian postal codes are five digits. They are known as SKPI, for Sistem Kode Pos Indonesia.

Further subdivisions: The provinces are subdivided into kabupaten (districts) and kotamadya (municipalities). The districts are further subdivided into kecamtan (sub-districts).

Territorial extent: Indonesia is a nation of many islands. All of the islands are entirely contained in Indonesia except for Kalimantan and New Guinea. Kalimantan is shared with Brunei and Malaysia; New Guinea is shared with Papua New Guinea. (Sebatik Island is also in both Indonesia and Malaysia, but here the border is just an extension of the border on Kalimantan across a narrow strait.) The only islands that have more than one province on them are Jawa, Kalimantan, Sulawesi, Sumatera, and Timor. For each province, I have listed the main islands it occupies, roughly in descending order of size.

Aceh: Sumatera, Simeulue, Tuangku, We, Bangkaru

Bali: Bali, Penida, Lembongan, Ceningan, Menjangan

Bengkulu: Sumatera, Enggano

Irian Jaya: New Guinea, Yos Sudarso or Frederick Hendrik, Waigeo, Supiori Biak, Yapen, Misool, Salawati, Batanta, Numfoor, Kofiau, Adi, Rumberpon, Mioswaar, Roon, Gag

Jakarta Raya: Jawa

Jambi: Sumatera

Jawa Barat: Jawa, Panaitan

Jawa Tengah: Jawa, Karimun Archipelago

Jawa Timur: Jawa, Madura, Kangean Archipelago, Bawean, Sapudi, Barung, Raas, Masalembu Besar

Kalimantan Barat: Kalimantan, Padangtikar, Maya, Karimata, Bawal, Gelam

Kalimantan Selatan: Kalimantan, Laut, Sebuku, Laut Kecil, Masalembu Kecil

Kalimantan Tengah: Kalimantan, Damar

Kalimantan Timur: Kalimantan, Mandul, Tarakan, Sebatik, Bunyu, Maratua, Kakaban

Lampung: Sumatera

Maluku: Halmahera or Gilolo, Seram or Ceram, Aru Islands, Tanimbar or Timor Laut Islands, Buru, Sula Islands, Wetar, Obi, Morotai, Kai Islands, Ambon, Babar Islands, Leti Islands

Nusa Tenggara Barat: Sumbawa, Lombok, Moyo, Sangeang, Banta

Nusa Tenggara Timur: Flores, Timor, Sumba, Alor, Lomblen, Roti, Pantar, Komodo, Savu, Adonara, Semau

Riau: Sumatera, Tebingtinggi, Rupat, Padang, Rangsan, Bengkalis, Riau Archipelago, Lingga Archipelago, Anambas Islands, North and South Natuna Archipelagos, Tembelan Archipelago

Sulawesi Selatan: Sulawesi, Selayar, Tanahjampea, Bonerate Islands, Kalaotoa, Tanakeke, Sabalana Islands

Sulawesi Tengah: Sulawesi, Peleng, Manui, Togian Islands, Banggai Islands

Sulawesi Tenggara: Sulawesi, Buton, Muna, Kabaena, Wowoni, Wangiwangi, Binongko, Kaledupa, Siumpu

Sulawesi Utara: Sulawesi; Talaud Islands, Sangihe Islands

Sumatera Barat: Sumatera, Siberut, Sipura, South Pagai, North Pagai

Sumatera Selatan: Sumatera, Bangka, Belitung, Lepar, Mendanau

Sumatera Utara: Sumatera, Nias, Tanahbala, Tanahmasa, Pini; also contains Samosir, a large island in Lake Toba on the island of Sumatera

Timor Timur: Timor (eastern part, and a separate enclave in the northwest called Oe-Cussi or Ocussi Ambeno), Atauro, Jako

Yogyakarta: Jawa

Origins of names:

Aceh: Malay *aci*: beech tree

Bali: possibly from Sanskrit *bali*: strong

Borneo: Portuguese corruption of Brunei

Irian Jaya: Malay *irian*: land covered with clouds, *jaya*: victory

Jakarta Raya: Malay *jaya*: victory, *karta*: prosperous (old name Jayakarta); Bahasa Indonesia *Raya*: great (i.e. Greater Jakarta)

Java: Sanskrit yavadvipa, from *yava*: barley, *dvipa*: island

Sumatra: possibly from Sanskrit *samudra*: ocean

Change history:

1900 Indonesia consisted of the Dutch colonies of Borneo, Celebes, Java, Moluccas, New Guinea, and Sumatra, and the Portuguese colony of Timor (actually occupying about half of the island of Timor, and some smaller nearby islands). Some of the colonies had divisions or residencies. Borneo's West Division was the same as Kalimantan Barat; the other three provinces on the island made up the South and East Division. Celebes was divided into Celebes, Menado, and Ternate divisions in this period. At the time of independence, Sumatra was divided into the residencies of Atjeh, Benkoelen, Djambi, Lampongs, Oostkust, Palembang, Tapanoeli, and Westkust.

1950-08-15	New provisional constitution changed the name of the country from United States of Indonesia to Republic of Indonesia, and divided it into ten provinces, whose English names were Borneo, Celebes, Central Java, Central Sumatra, East Java, Lesser Sunda Isles, Moluccas, North Sumatra, South Sumatra, and West Java. Capital renamed from Batavia to Jakarta.
~1955	Indonesia reorganized into eighteen provinces and three special areas.
1962-10-01	Netherlands New Guinea taken from Dutch administration by United Nations Temporary Executive Authority, renamed Irian Barat (West Irian). Its capital was renamed from Hollandia to Kotabaru.
1963-05-01	Irian Barat became a province of Indonesia.
~1966	Name of capital of Aceh changed from Kutaradja to Banda Atjeh; name of capital of Irian Barat changed from Kotabaru to Sukarnapura; name of capital of Jambi changed from Jambi to Telanaipura; capital of Riau moved from Tandjungpinang to Pakanbaru; capital of Sumatera Barat moved from Bukittinggi to Padang.
1969	Name of capital of Irian Jaya changed from Sukarnapura to Jayapura.
~1970	Name of capital of Sulawesi Selatan changed from Makassar to Ujung Pandang.
1973	Name of Irian Barat province changed to Irian Jaya.
~1974	Sulawesi Selatan province (capital Makassar) split into Sulawesi Selatan and Sulawesi Tenggara; Sulawesi Utara province (capital Manado) split into Sulawesi Tengah and Sulawesi Utara; Bengkulu and Lampung provinces split from Sumatera Selatan; territory transferred from Jambi to Sumatera Barat, depriving Jambi of access to the west coast.
1976-07	Indonesia occupied and annexed Portuguese Timor as Loro Sae province.
~1977	Capital of Kalimantan Tengah moved from Pahandut to Palangkaraya; name of Loro Sae province changed to Timor Timur (East Timor).

Other names of subdivisions: In most Western European languages, the names for the islands of Sumatera, Kalimantan, Jawa, and Sulawesi, respectively, are Sumatra, Borneo (French: Bornéo), Java, and Celebes (French: Célèbes, Portuguese: Célebes). Nusa Tenggara is sometimes translated as Lesser Sunda Islands (French: Îles de la Sonde). If province names are translated, it's usually only by translating the name of one of those islands and a compass point. Barat is West, Selatan is South, Tengah is Central, Tenggara is Southeast, Timur is East, and Utara is North. For example, German for Sumatera Barat is West-sumatra; Italian for Jawa Tengah is Java centrale; Portuguese for Sulawesi Utara is Célebes Setentrionais or Célebes do Norte. See the table of compass points in the introduction.

Aceh: Achin, Atjeh (obsolete)
Bengkulu: Bencoolen, Benkoelen, Benkulen (obsolete)
Irian Jaya: Irian Barat, West Irian (variants); Nederlands Nieuw Guinea (Dutch-obsolete); Netherlands New Guinea (obsolete); Nouvelle Guinée Occidentale (French-obsolete)

Maluku: Molucas (Portuguese, Spanish); Moluccas (obsolete); Molucche (Italian); Moluckerna (Swedish); Moluques (French); Molukken (Dutch, German); Molukkene (Norwegian)
Riau: Rhio, Riou, Riouw (obsolete)

IRAN

ISO = IR/FIPS = IR   Language = Farsi   Time zone = +3:30 [d]   Capital = Tehran

Iran began the century as an absolute monarchy. It has had major changes in government since then, but its borders have undergone only minor adjustments. The names Persia and Iran had both been used for the area since antiquity. Although Iran was a more correct name for the modern kingdom, westerners used Persia preferentially until 1935. Then the Iranian government requested a change, and standard usage in the West shifted to Iran.

Other names of country: Irã (Portuguese); Irán (Spanish); Íran (Icelandic); Islamic Republic of Iran (formal–English);

Jomhoori-e-Islami-e-Iran (formal); Persia (obsolete); República Islámica del Irán (formal–Spanish); République Islamique d'Iran (formal–French)

Origin of name: from Avestian *Ayryanem*: land of the Aryans.

Spelling note: Farsi (Persian) is spelled with a modified Arabic alphabet. Transliteration into the Roman alphabet can be done by various systems. As a result, there are many alternate spellings for these names. In particular, the letters o and u are often switched. So are a, e, and i. Some schemes use x instead of kh. Many schemes use diacritical marks for long vowels or aspirated consonants, but they seem to be inconsistent, so I haven't attempted to use diacriticals.

division	abv	ISO	FIPS	population	area-km	area-mi	capital
Ardabil	AR	03	IR32	— —	— —	— —	Ardabil
Bakhtaran	BK	17	IR13	1,462,965	23,667	9,138	Bakhtaran
Bushehr	BS	06	IR22	612,183	27,653	10,677	Bushehr
Chahar Mahall and Bakhtiari	CM	08	IR03	631,179	14,870	5,741	Shahr-e-Kord
East Azarbaijan	EA	01	IR33	4,114,084	67,102	25,908	Tabriz
Esfahan	ES	04	IR28	3,294,916	104,650	40,406	Esfahan
Fars	FA	14	IR07	3,193,769	133,298	51,467	Shiraz
Gilan	GI	19	IR08	2,081,037	14,709	5,679	Rasht
Hamadan	HD	24	IR09	1,505,826	19,784	7,639	Hamadan
Hormozgan	HG	23	IR11	762,206	66,870	25,819	Bandar-e-Abbas
Ilam	IL	05	IR10	382,091	19,044	7,353	Ilam
Kerman	KE	15	IR29	1,622,958	179,916	69,466	Kerman
Khorasan	KR	09	IR30	5,280,605	313,337	120,980	Mashhad
Khuzestan	KZ	10	IR15	2,681,978	67,282	25,978	Ahvaz
Kohkiluyeh and Buyer Ahmadi	KB	18	IR05	411,828	14,261	5,506	Yasuj
Kordestan	KD	16	IR16	1,078,415	24,998	9,652	Sanandaj
Lorestan	LO	20	IR23	1,367,029	28,803	11,121	Khorramabad
Markazi	MK	22	IR24	1,082,109	29,080	11,228	Arak
Mazandaran	MD	21	IR17	3,419,346	46,456	17,937	Sari
Semnan	SM	12	IR25	417,035	90,905	35,099	Semnan
Sistan and Baluchestan	SB	13	IR04	1,197,059	181,578	70,108	Zahedan
Tehran	TE	07	IR26	8,712,087	29,993	11,580	Tehran
West Azarbaijan	WA	02	IR01	1,971,677	38,850	15,000	Orumiyeh
Yazd	YA	25	IR31	574,028	70,011	27,031	Yazd
Zanjan	ZA	11	IR27	1,588,600	36,398	14,053	Zanjan
				49,445,010	1,643,515	634,566	

Status: These divisions are ostanha (sing. ostan: provinces).

Abv: Two-letter code for international compatibility (defined by the author).

ISO: Codes from ISO 3166-2.

FIPS: Codes from FIPS PUB 10-4.

Population: 1991 census.

Area-km: Square kilometers.

Area-mi: Square miles.

Note: Ardabil province was created so recently that most data are not available for it.

Further subdivisions: The provinces are subdivided into shahrestan (counties), which are in turn subdivided into bakhsh (districts).

Territorial extent: Hormozgan includes most of the larger islands off Iran's south coast: Qeshm, Lavan, Qeys, Kish, Larak, Hormoz, Hengam, Forur, Sirri. It also includes Abu Musa, an island which is administered jointly by Iran and the United Arab Emirates.

Origins of names:

Azarbaijan: see the country listing for Azerbaijan

Baluchestan: land of the Baluchi (ethnic name; see Balochistan in Pakistan)

Esfahan: Avesti *espahan*: armies

Fars: from Old Persian *parsi*: pure

Gilan: from Farsi *gil*: a medicinal plant

Hamadan: Old Persian *hangmatana*, probably meaning place of assembly

Kordestan: land of the Kurds

Khuzestan: Middle Persian for the land of Husa (the city known in ancient times as Susa)

Markazi: Farsi for central

Tehran: possibly meaning "flat land"

Change history: In 1900, the provinces of Iran were Ardelan, Azarbaijan, Baluchestan, Farsistan, Gilan, Irakajemi, Khorasan, Khoristan, Kerman, Larestan, Lorestan, and Mazandaran. There were a number of splits and boundary changes in the first half of the century.

~1958	Iran reorganized into 10 numbered provinces: 1 (Gilan), 2 (Mazandaran), 3 (East Azarbaijan), 4 (West Azarbaijan), 5 (Kermanshahan), 6 (Khuzestan), 7 (Fars), 8 (Kerman), 9 (Khorasan), 10 (Esfahan).
~1960–1981	Governorates, which had hitherto been subordinate to provinces, were promoted one by one to province status. In this way, Chahar Mahall and Bakhtiari province (formerly Bakhtiari governorate) and Yazd split from Esfahan; Khalij-e Fars (Persian Gulf) split from Fars; Banader va Jazayer-e Bahr-e Oman (Ports and Islands of the Sea of Oman) split from Kerman; Kordestan and Zenjan split from Gilan; Hamadan and Ilam split from Kermanshahan; Bovir Ahmadi and Kohkiluyeh province and Lorestan split from Khuzestan; Markazi and Semnan split from Mazandaran.
~1977	Name of Khalij-e Fars changed to Bushehr; name of Banader va Jazayer-e Bahr-e Oman changed to Hormozgan. The two provinces appear to have been united for a period around 1970.
~1979	In the aftermath of the Islamic Revolution, all names reminiscent of Shah Reza Pahlavi were changed. Name of Kermanshahan, and its capital, Kermanshah, both changed to Bakhtaran. (There are indications that the name Kermanshahan is back in use since ~1995.) Name of capital of West Azarbaijan changed from Rezaiyeh to Orumiyeh. (The city had been renamed from Orumiyeh — then spelled Urmia — to Rezaiyeh in 1926, before it was a capital.)
~1986	Markazi province (capital: Tehran, FIPS = IR19) split up into a smaller Markazi, a new Tehran province, and portions which were annexed to Esfahan (formerly FIPS = IR06), Semnan (IR18), and Zanjan (IR21); part of Kerman province (IR12) annexed to Yazd (IR20).
~1990	Name of Bovir Ahmadi and Kohkiluyeh province changed to Kohkiluyeh and Buyer Ahmadi; name of Baluchestan and Sistan province changed to Sistan and Baluchestan.
~1995	Ardabil province split from East Azarbaijan (capital: Tabriz, FIPS = IR02).

Other names of subdivisions:

Bakhtaran: Kermanshahan, Kermanshah (variant)

Bushehr: Banader va Jazayer-e Khalij-e Fars, Khalij-e Fars (obsolete–Farsi); Bushire (variant); Persian Gulf (obsolete)

Chahar Mahall and Bakhtiari: Bakhtiari, Chaharmahal va Bakhtiari (variant–Farsi)

East Azarbaijan: Azarbayjan-e Khavari (Farsi); Azarbaijan-e Sharghi (variant)

Hormozgan: Banader va Jazayer-e Bahr-e Oman, Ports and Islands of the Sea of Oman, Saheli (obsolete)

Kohkiluyeh and Buyer Ahmadi: Bovir Ahmadi and Kohkiluyeh, Boyer-Ahmad and Koh-Giluye, Boyer Ahmadi-ye Sardir va Kohkiluyeh, Kohgiloyeh va Boyerahmad, Kohgiluyeh and Boveir Ahmadi (variant)

Sistan and Baluchestan: Baluchestan va Sistan, Seistan and Baluchistan (variant)

Tehran: Teheran (obsolete); Téhéran (French)

West Azarbaijan: Azarbayjan-e Bakhtari (Farsi); Azarbaijan-e Gharbi (variant)

IRAQ

ISO = IQ/FIPS = IZ   Language = Arabic   Time zone = +3 [d]   Capital = Baghdad

In 1900, almost all of Iraq was part of the Ottoman Empire; its southern strip of mostly desert land was in Arabia. The Ottoman Empire was aligned with Germany in World War I. British forces occupied Mesopotamia, or Iraq-Arabi, in 1917. The

Treaty of Sèvres (1920) divided up the Ottoman Empire. Iraq was one of the pieces. It was created as a British mandate under the League of Nations. The mandate ended in 1932, whereupon Iraq became independent.

From ~1935 to 1991 there was a lozenge-shaped neutral zone between Iraq and Saudi Arabia. It was occupied only by nomads, and neither Iraq nor Saudi Arabia wanted to be put to the trouble of administering it. After the Persian Gulf War, it was divided evenly between the two countries.

Other names of country: al Jumhouriya al 'Iraqia (formal); Irak (Danish, Dutch, Finnish, German, Norwegian, Swedish); Írak (Icelandic); Iraque (Portuguese); Republic of Iraq (formal–English).

Origin of name: Arabic: well rooted, or lowland.

division	ISO	FIPS	population	area-km	area-mi	capital
Al-Anbar	AN	IZ01	820,690	138,501	53,476	Ar-Ramadi
Al-Basrah	BA	IZ02	872,176	19,070	7,363	Al-Basrah
Al-Muthanna	MU	IZ03	315,815	51,740	19,977	As-Samawah
Al-Qadisiyah	QA	IZ04	559,805	8,153	3,148	Ad-Diwaniyah
An-Najaf	NA	IZ17	590,078	28,824	11,129	An-Najaf
Arbil	AR	IZ11	770,493	14,471	5,587	Arbil
As-Sulaymaniyah	AS	IZ05	951,723	17,023	6,573	As-Sulaymaniyah
At-Ta'mim	AT	IZ13	601,219	10,282	3,970	Kirkuk
Babil	BB	IZ06	1,109,574	6,468	2,497	Al-Hillah
Baghdad	BG	IZ07	3,841,268	734	283	Baghdad
Dahuk	DA	IZ08	293,304	6,553	2,530	Dahuk
Dhi Qar	DQ	IZ09	921,066	12,900	4,981	An-Nasiriyah
Diyala	DI	IZ10	961,073	19,076	7,365	Ba'qubah
Karbala'	KA	IZ12	469,282	5,034	1,944	Karbala'
Maysan	MA	IZ14	487,448	16,072	6,205	Al-Amarah
Ninawa	NI	IZ15	1,479,430	37,323	14,410	Mosul
Salah ad-Din	SD	IZ18	726,138	24,751	9,556	Samarra
Wasit	WA	IZ16	564,670	17,153	6,623	Al-Kut
			16,335,252	434,128	167,617	

Status: These divisions are muhafazat (sing. muhafazah: provinces). They were called liwa until ~1970.

ISO: Codes from ISO 3166-2.

FIPS: Codes from FIPS PUB 10-4.

Population: 1991 census.

Area-km: Square kilometers.

Area-mi: Square miles.

Further subdivisions: The provinces are further subdivided into qadhas and nahiyas.

Territorial extent: Al-Muthanna includes the Iraqi half of the former Neutral Zone.

The Kurdish Autonomous Region consists of the provinces of Arbil, Dahuk, and As-Sulaymaniyah.

Origins of names:

Arbil: Akkadian, thought to be from *arba*: four, *ilan*: gods

Babil: ancient Babylon, from Akkadian *babu*: gate, *ilan*: gods, i.e., gate of the gods

Baghdad: possibly "the gift of God"

Ninawa: ancient Nineveh, possibly from a Semitic word for habitation

Change history: Modern Iraq comprised roughly the vilayets (governorates) of Bagdad, Bassora (or Busra), and Mosul, plus a small section of Zor, under the Ottoman Empire, as well as a northern section of Arabia. A good deal of the western and southern border lies in desert lands, and has remained indefinite until quite recently. All province boundaries, especially those in the desert, have been subject to frequent change.

1920-12-23	Boundary between British mandate (Iraq) and French mandate (Syria) agreed on.
~1962	Name of Dulaim province changed to Ramadi; name of Muntafiq province changed to Nasiriyah.
1971	Name of Hilla province changed to Babil.
1976-02	Name of 'Amara province changed to Maysan; name of Diwaniya province changed to Al-Qadisiyah; name of Kirkuk province changed to At-Ta'mim; name of Kut province changed to Wasit; name of Mosul province changed to Ninawa; name of Nasiriya province changed to Dhi Qar; name of Ramadi province changed to Al-Anbar; An-Najaf province split from Al-Muthanna; Salah ad-Din province split from Baghdad.

Other names of subdivisions:

Spelling note: the original place names are in Arabic. There are many different schemes for transliterating from the Arabic to the Roman alphabet. Many of the variant names are just alternate transliterations of the same name. The definite article "al-" is sometimes omitted or inserted. The l of "al-" is usually assimilated to the following consonant if that consonant is ch, d, n, s, sh, or t.

Al-Anbar: Dulaim, Ramadi (obsolete)
Al-Basrah: Basra, Bassora (variant)
Al-Qadisiyah: Diwaniyah (obsolete)
Arbil: Arbela (obsolete); Erbil, Irbil (variant)
At-Ta'mim: Kirkuk (obsolete); Tamin (variant)
Babil: Babylon (variant); Hilla (obsolete)
Baghdad: Bagdá (Portuguese); Bagdad (Dutch, French, German, Norwegian, Spanish, Swedish)

Dahuk: D'hok (variant)
Dhi Qar: Muntafiq, Nasiriyah (obsolete); Thi-Qar (variant)
Karbala': Kerbela (variant)
Maysan: 'Amara (obsolete)
Ninawa: Al-Mawsil, Mosul (obsolete); Ninive (French, German); Nínive (Portuguese); Niniveh (variant)
Wasit: Kut, Kut-al-Imara (obsolete)

IRELAND

ISO = IE/FIPS = EI   Languages = English, Gaelic   Time zone = 0 [d]   Capital = Dublin

At the beginning of the 20th century, the whole island of Ireland was part of the United Kingdom. Irish patriots repeatedly argued and fought for independence. Finally, on 1921-12-06, the Anglo-Irish Treaty was signed. By its terms, Ireland became an independent country with dominion status, although Northern Ireland was to be allowed to make a separate decision. The name of the new country was the Irish Free State (Gaelic: Saorstát Éireann). On 1922-12-12, six counties in the north voted to revert to the United Kingdom. On 1949-04-18, the Irish Free State broke off its remaining links with Britain under a new constitution, becoming the Irish Republic (Poblacht na hÉireann).

Other names of country: Éire (formal); Ierse Republiek (Dutch); Irish Free State (obsolete); Irland (Danish, German, Norwegian, Swedish); Írland (Icelandic); Irlanda (Italian, Portuguese, Spanish); Irlande (French); Irlanti (Finnish); Republic of Ireland (formal–English).

Origin of name: Éire + land. Éire may be from *iar*: west + *fonn*: country; or from *i*: isle + *iarunn*: iron.

division	abv	ISO	FIPS	pr	population	area-km	area-mi	Gaelic	capital
Carlow	CW	CW	EI01	L	40,946	896	346	Ceatharlach	Carlow
Cavan	CN	CN	EI02	U	52,756	1,891	730	An Cabhán	Cavan
Clare	CE	CE	EI03	M	90,826	3,188	1,231	An Clár	Ennis
Cork	CK	C	EI04	M	409,814	7,460	2,880	Corcaigh	Cork
Donegal	DL	DL	EI06	U	127,994	4,831	1,865	Dún na nGall	Lifford
Dublin	DN	D	EI07	L	1,024,429	922	356	Baile Átha Cliath	Dublin
Galway	GY	G	EI10	C	180,304	5,940	2,293	An Ghaillimh	Galway
Kerry	KY	KY	EI11	M	121,719	4,701	1,815	Ciarraighe	Tralee
Kildare	KE	KE	EI12	L	122,516	1,694	654	Cill Dara	Naas
Kilkenny	KK	KK	EI13	L	73,613	2,062	796	Cill Chainnigh	Kilkenny
Laoighis	LS	LS	EI15	L	52,325	1,720	664	Laoighis	Port Laoighis
Leitrim	LM	LM	EI14	C	25,297	1,525	589	Liathdroim	Carrick on Shannon
Limerick	LK	LK	EI16	M	161,856	2,686	1,037	Luimneach	Limerick
Longford	LD	LD	EI18	L	30,293	1,044	403	Longphort	Longford
Louth	LH	LH	EI19	L	90,707	823	318	Lughbhadh	Dundalk
Mayo	MO	MO	EI20	C	110,696	5,398	2,084	Muigheo	Castlebar
Meath	MH	MH	EI21	L	105,540	2,336	902	An Mhídhe	Trim
Monaghan	MN	MN	EI22	U	51,262	1,291	498	Muineachán	Monaghan
Offaly	OY	OY	EI23	L	58,448	1,998	771	Uíbh Fáilghe	Tullamore
Roscommon	RN	RN	EI24	C	51,876	2,463	951	Roscomáin	Roscommon
Sligo	SO	SO	EI25	C	54,736	1,796	693	Sligeach	Sligo
Tipperary	TY	TA	EI26	M	132,620	4,255	1,643	Tiobraid Aran	Clonmel
Waterford	WD	WD	EI27	M	91,608	1,838	710	Port Láirghe	Waterford
Westmeath	WH	WH	EI29	L	61,882	1,763	681	An Iar-Mhídhe	Mullingar ➤

division	abv	ISO	FIPS	pr	population	area-km	area-mi	Gaelic	capital
Wexford	WX	WX	EI30	L	102,045	2,351	908	Loch Garman	Wexford
Wicklow	WW	WW	EI31	L	97,293	2,025	782	Cill Mhanntáin	Wicklow
					3,523,401	68,897	26,600		

Status: These divisions are counties.

Abv: Two-letter code for international compatibility (defined by the author).

ISO: Codes from ISO 3166-2. Based on Ireland's Statutory County Codes, used on license plates, etc., with minor differences (e.g. TN and TS for Tipperary North and South).

FIPS: Codes from FIPS PUB 10-4.

Pr: Traditional provinces (see list below).

Population: 1991 census.

Area-km: Square kilometers.

Area-mi: Square miles.

Gaelic: Name of county in Gaelic.

ISO	province	Gaelic	population	area-km	ISO	province	Gaelic	population	area-km
C	Connaught	Connacht	422,909	17,122	M	Munster	An Mhumhain	1,008,443	24,128
L	Leinster	Laighean	1,860,037	19,634	U	Ulster	Ulaidh	232,012	8,013

The provinces date back to about the beginning of the Christian era, when there were five of them (with Meath). They now have no administrative function. The separation of Northern Ireland divided Ulster into two parts: the larger (six counties at the time of the split) is all of Northern Ireland, and the smaller (three counties) is now two disjoint parts of the Irish Republic.

Further subdivisions: Some of the cities of Ireland are organized as county boroughs, administratively separate in some ways from the counties in which they are located. Also, county Tipperary is subdivided into North Riding and South Riding. The most common practice is to include these subdivisions in their counties.

Territorial extent: All of the counties lie primarily on the main island, Ireland. Other islands occupied are listed for each county, roughly in order of decreasing size.

Clare: Mutton, and islands in the Shannon Estuary, especially at the mouth of River Fergus

Cork: Bear (Bere), Dursey, Great (in Cork Harbor), Clear, Sherkin, Whiddy, Long

Donegal: Aran, Tory, Cruit, Inishbofin, Inishtrahull, Gola

Dublin: Lambay, Dalkey, Irelands Eye, Shenicks

Galway: the Aran Islands, of which the largest are Inishmore, Inishmaan, and Inisheer; Gorumna, Inishbofin, Letter-more, Inishshark, Lettermullan, Mweenish, Tawin, Omey, High, Croaghnakeela

Kerry: Valentia (Valencia), the Blasket Islands (largest is Great Blasket), Carrig, Scariff, Beginish

Mayo: Achill, Clare, Inishturk, Inishkea North and South, Caher

Sligo: Inishmurray

Wexford: Saltee Islands, Tuskar Rock

Origins of names:

Cork: from Irish *corcach*: swamp

Donegal: Irish *Dun na nGall*: fort of foreigners (probably Danes)

Dublin: Irish *dubh*: black, *linn*: pool, referring to the Liffey estuary

Kildare: Irish *cill*: convent, *dara*: oak

Limerick: Irish *luimneach*: barren land

Tipperary: Irish *tipper*: spring or well, and Ara, the name of a river

Ulster: Irish *uladh*: cairn, tomb, and a suffix -ster for land

Change history:

1920   Names of Kings and Queens counties changed to Offaly and Laoighis, respectively.

Sources disagree about some capitals (county seats). The capital of Laoighis is Port Laoighis. The same city is known as Maryborough, and has been known by both names throughout the 20th century. The name Maryborough was more common in English-language sources up to ~1955; after that, Port Laoighis, or one of its variant spellings (Portlaoise, Portlaoighise, etc.), was preferred. The sources seem to be divided on the capital of Meath: some say it is Trim (Baile Átha Troim), while others say Navan (An Uaimh). Most sources say that the capital of Tipperary is Clonmel, but a few maintain that is is Tipperary, and some say that it is Nenagh. Probably Nenagh is only the capital of the North Riding. Finally, most sources say that the capital of Waterford is Waterford, but a few of them — generally recent, reliable ones — say that it is Dungarvan.

Other names of subdivisions:

Laoighis: Laois, Leix (variant); Queens (obsolete)   Offaly: Kings (obsolete)

Population history:

county	1901	1936	1946	1956	1966	1971	1981	1991
Carlow	37,723	34,452	34,081	33,888	34,000	34,237	39,820	40,946
Cavan	97,368	76,670	70,355	61,740	54,000	52,618	53,855	52,756
Clare	112,129	89,879	85,064	77,176	74,000	75,008	87,567	90,826
Cork	404,813	355,957	343,668	336,663	340,000	352,892	402,465	409,814
Donegal	173,625	142,310	136,317	122,059	109,000	108,344	125,112	127,994
Dublin	447,266	586,925	636,193	705,781	795,000	852,219	1,003,164	1,024,429
Galway	192,146	168,198	165,201	155,553	148,000	149,223	172,018	180,304
Kerry	165,331	139,834	133,893	122,072	113,000	112,772	122,770	121,719
Kildare	63,469	57,892	64,849	65,915	66,000	71,977	104,122	122,516
Kilkenny	78,821	68,614	66,712	64,089	60,000	61,473	70,806	73,613
Laoighis	57,226	50,109	49,697	47,087	45,000	45,259	51,171	52,325
Leitrim	69,201	50,908	44,591	37,056	31,000	28,360	27,609	25,297
Limerick	146,018	141,153	142,559	137,881	137,000	140,459	161,661	161,856
Longford	46,581	37,847	36,218	32,969	29,000	28,250	31,140	30,293
Louth	65,741	64,339	66,194	69,194	70,000	74,951	88,514	90,707
Mayo	202,627	161,349	148,120	133,052	116,000	109,525	114,766	110,696
Meath	67,463	61,405	66,232	66,762	67,000	71,729	95,419	105,540
Monaghan	74,505	61,289	57,215	52,064	46,000	46,242	51,192	51,262
Offaly	60,129	51,308	53,686	51,970	52,000	51,829	58,312	58,448
Roscommon	101,639	77,566	72,510	63,710	56,000	53,519	54,543	51,876
Sligo	84,022	67,447	62,375	56,850	51,000	50,275	55,474	54,736
Tipperary	159,754	137,835	136,014	129,415	123,000	124,565	135,261	132,620
Waterford	87,030	77,614	76,108	74,031	73,000	77,315	88,591	91,608
Westmeath	61,527	54,706	54,949	54,122	53,000	53,570	61,523	61,882
Wexford	103,860	94,245	91,855	87,259	83,000	85,351	99,081	102,045
Wicklow	60,679	58,569	60,451	59,906	60,000	66,295	87,449	97,293
	3,221,823	2,968,420	2,955,107	2,898,264	2,885,000	2,978,248	3,443,405	3,525,719

ISRAEL

ISO = IL/FIPS = IS   Language = Hebrew   Time zone = +2 [d]   Capital = Jerusalem

The Gaza Strip and the West Bank are included in Israel for this writing, merely because the international standard has no entry representing a Palestinian Arab state. No inference should be drawn about the actual or rightful status of these territories.

In 1900, the land now contained in Israel was part of the Ottoman Empire. At the end of World War I, as the Ottoman Empire shattered, Palestine was one of the pieces. It became a British mandate under the League of Nations on 1923-09-29. After World War II, the United Nations drew up plans to partition Palestine into a Jewish state and an Arab state. Israel, the Jewish state, was created on 1948-05-14, as the British withdrew from their mandate. Initially, its borders conformed to the U.N. plan. War broke out almost immediately between Arabs and Jews. When fighting stopped in 1949-01, the territory controlled by Israel had grown to approximately the size of the six modern districts. During the Six-Day War (1967-06-05 to 1967-06-10), Israel occupied the Sinai Peninsula (later restored to Egypt), the Golan Heights (eventually annexed), the Gaza Strip, and the West Bank.

Other names of country: Israël (Dutch, French); Ísrael (Icelandic); Israele (Italian); Medinat Israel (formal); State of Israel (formal–English).

Origin of name: inhabited by tribe of Israel, i.e., descendents of the Biblical patriarch Israel (about 18th cent. B.C.).

division	abv	ISO	FIPS	population	area-km	area-mi	capital	subdistricts
HaDarom	HD	D	IS01	573,700	14,107	5,447	Beersheba	Ashqelon, Beersheba
Haifa	HA	HA	IS04	656,200	854	330	Haifa	Hadera, Haifa
HaMerkaz	HM	M	IS02	1,031,800	1,242	480	Ramla	Sharon, Petah Tiqwa, Ramla, Rehoboth
HaZafon	HZ	Z	IS03	805,100	4,501	1,738	Nazareth	Acre, Golan, Kinneret, Jezreel, Zefat
Jerusalem	JM	JM	IS06	578,400	627	242	Jerusalem	Jerusalem
Tel Aviv	TA	TA	IS05	1,094,700	170	66	Tel Aviv	Tel Aviv
Gaza Strip	GZ		GZ	658,200	363	140	Gaza	
West Bank	WE		WE	973,500	5,879	2,270		
				6,371,600	27,743	10,713		

Status: These divisions are mehozot (sing. mehoz: districts).

Abv: Two-letter code for international compatibility (defined by the author).

ISO: Codes from ISO 3166-2. The Working Group has reserved the country code PS for any future Palestine state.

FIPS: Codes from FIPS PUB 10-4. The Gaza Strip and the West Bank are treated as two separate countries by the FIPS standard.

Population: 1991 census.

Area-km: Square kilometers.

Area-mi: Square miles.

Postal codes: Israel uses five-digit postal codes.

Further subdivisions: The districts are divided into subdistricts, as listed above.

Origins of names:

HaDarom: Hebrew for Southern

Haifa: from Hebrew *kef*: cliff

HaMerkaz: Hebrew for Central

HaZafon: Hebrew for Northern

Jerusalem: probably Sumerian *uru*: city, Hebrew *shalem*: peace

Tel Aviv: Hebrew *tel*: hill, *aviv*: spring (the season)

Change history: In 1900, the land now contained in Israel was part of the vilayets of Beirut, Hejaz, and Jerusalem.

In 1923, Palestine was created as a British mandate, with almost exactly the same borders as Israel, the Gaza Strip, and the West Bank combined. Palestine had several different administrative divisions during the mandate period. At the end, it consisted of the districts of Galilee and Acre, Gaza, Haifa, Jerusalem, Lydda, and Samaria.

1949-02-24	Gaza Strip placed under Egyptian administration.
1950-04-24	West Bank, consisting of most of Jerusalem and Samaria and a small part of Lydda, annexed to Jordan. Samaria became Nablus (Nabulus) district in Jordan. The southwestern part of Jerusalem became Hebron (Al-Khalil) district. The remainder of the area became Jerusalem (Al-Quds) district.
~1952	Israel reorganized into the present six districts. HaZafon formed from Galilee and Acre and small parts of Haifa and Samaria. Haifa formed from most of Haifa and a small part of Samaria. HaMerkaz formed from a large part of Lydda and small parts of Samaria and Gaza. Tel Aviv formed from part of Lydda. Jerusalem formed from parts of former Jerusalem and Lydda. HaDarom formed from most of Gaza and a small part of former Jerusalem.
~1962	Tel Aviv, capital of Tel Aviv district, merged with neighboring Jaffa, becoming Tel Aviv-Jaffa (Tel Aviv-Yafo).
1967-06-10	At the end of the Six-Day War, the Jordanian districts of Hebron, Jerusalem, and Nablus had become the Israeli-occupied territory of the West Bank. The Gaza Strip remained territorially intact, but was now administered by Israel rather than the U.A.R. (Egypt). Also, a formerly neutral zone around 'Auja el Hafir in the Negev was annexed to HaDarom.
1967-06-28	Old City of Jerusalem unilaterally annexed by Israel to the Jerusalem district.
1980-07-30	East Jerusalem area of the West Bank unilaterally annexed by Israel to the Jerusalem district.
1981-12-14	Golan Heights in Syria, occupied by Israel since the Six-Day War, unilaterally annexed to HaZafon.

Other names of subdivisions:

Gaza Strip: Bande de Gaza (French); Faja de Gaza (Spanish)
HaDarom: Southern (variant)
Haifa: Hefa (Hebrew)
HaMerkaz: Central (variant)
HaZafon: Northern (variant)
Jerusalem: Al-Quds (Arabic); Gerusalemme (Italian); Jéru-

salem (French); Jerusalém (Portuguese); Jerusalén (Spanish); Yerushalayim (Hebrew)
West Bank: Cisjordania, Judea and Samaria (variant); Giudea e Samaria (Italian); Zona de Jericó (Spanish); Zone de Jéricho (French)

ITALY

ISO = IT/FIPS = IT   Language = Italian   Time zone = +1 ᵈ   Capital = Rome

Italy struggled its way to national unification in the 19th century, except for some Italian-speaking borderlands called Italia irredenta (unredeemed Italy). In World War I, Italy chose the winning side. In reward, it achieved its main territorial ambitions: the incorporation of the South Tyrol and the area around Trieste. After World War II, as a defeated Axis power, it lost part of Trieste, and all of its colonies.

Other names of country: Italia (Finnish, Italian, Norwegian, Spanish); Itália (Portuguese); Ítalía (Icelandic); Italian Republic (formal–English); Italie (French); Italië (Dutch); Italien (Danish, German, Swedish); Repubblica Italiana (formal).

Origin of name: from Vituli, name of a tribe in Apulia.

division	abv	CAP	population	area-km	area-mi	reg	adjective
Agrigento	AG	92	492,701	3,042	1,175	SC	agrigentini
Alessandria	AL	15	445,139	3,560	1,375	PM	alessandrini
Ancona	AN	60	437,669	1,938	748	MH	anconetani
Aosta	AO	11	115,270	3,262	1,259	VD	aostani
Arezzo	AR	52	313,723	3,232	1,248	TC	aretini
Ascoli Piceno	AP	63	361,136	2,086	805	MH	ascolani
Asti	AT	14	209,420	1,511	583	PM	astigiani
Avellino	AV	83	452,673	2,801	1,081	CM	avellinesi
Bari	BA	70	1,538,195	5,130	1,981	PU	baresi
Belluno	BL	32	214,495	3,678	1,420	VN	bellunesi
Benevento	BN	82	299,876	2,061	796	CM	beneventani
Bergamo	BG	24	924,804	2,759	1,065	LM	bergamaschi
Biella	BI	13	——	——	——	PM	biellesi
Bologna	BO	40	911,715	3,702	1,429	ER	bolognesi
Bolzano	BZ	39	439,765	7,400	2,857	TT	bolzanini
Brescia	BS	25	1,039,548	4,761	1,838	LM	bresciani
Brindisi	BR	72	409,965	1,838	710	PU	brindisini
Cagliari	CA	09	767,728	9,298	3,590	SD	cagliaritani
Caltanissetta	CL	93	293,485	2,105	813	SC	nisseni
Campobasso	CB	86	241,202	2,909	1,123	ML	campobassani
Caserta	CE	81	824,623	2,639	1,019	CM	casertani
Catania	CT	95	1,080,336	3,552	1,371	SC	catanesi
Catanzaro	CZ	88	775,801	5,247	2,026	CI	catanzaresi
Chieti	CH	66	387,781	2,587	999	AB	teatini
Como	CO	22	790,789	2,067	798	LM	comaschi
Cosenza	CS	87	785,187	6,650	2,568	CI	cosentini
Cremona	CR	26	327,536	1,771	684	LM	cremonesi
Crotone	KR	88	——	——	——	CI	crotoniati
Cuneo	CN	12	546,396	6,903	2,665	PM	cuneesi
Enna	EN	94	197,077	2,562	989	SC	ennesi
Ferrara	FE	44	366,323	2,631	1,016	ER	ferraresi
Florence	FI	50	1,192,967	3,880	1,498	TC	fiorentini
Foggia	FG	71	703,734	7,184	2,774	PU	foggiani
Forli	FO	47	609,943	2,910	1,124	ER	forlivesi
Frosinone	FR	03	485,536	3,239	1,251	LZ	frusinati
Genoa	GE	16	984,733	1,831	707	LG	genovesi ➤

division	abv	CAP	population	area-km	area-mi	reg	adjective
Gorizia	GO	34	139,266	466	180	FV	goriziani
Grosseto	GR	58	219,808	4,496	1,736	TC	grossetani
Imperia	IM	18	219,918	1,155	446	LG	imperiesi
Isernia	IS	86	94,146	1,529	590	ML	isernini
L'Aquila	AQ	67	300,201	5,034	1,944	AB	aquilani
La Spezia	SP	19	232,174	882	341	LG	spezzini
Latina	LT	04	475,191	2,250	869	LZ	latinensi
Lecce	LE	73	815,599	2,759	1,065	PU	leccesi
Lecco	LC	22	——	——	——	LM	lecchesi
Livorno	LI	57	342,554	1,220	471	TC	livornesi
Lodi	LO	20	——	——	——	LM	lodigiani
Lucca	LU	55	381,276	1,773	685	TC	lucchesi
Macerata	MC	62	295,516	2,774	1,071	MH	maceratesi
Mantua	MN	46	370,460	2,339	903	LM	mantovani
Massa-Carrara	MS	54	204,552	1,156	446	TC	massesi
Matera	MT	75	209,880	3,447	1,331	BC	materani
Messina	ME	98	695,656	3,247	1,254	SC	messinesi
Milan	MI	20	3,986,838	2,762	1,066	LM	milanesi
Modena	MO	41	600,120	2,690	1,039	ER	modenesi
Naples	NA	80	3,160,907	1,171	452	CM	napoletani
Novara	NO	28	500,653	3,594	1,388	PM	novaresi
Nuoro	NU	08	276,820	7,272	2,808	SD	nuoresi
Oristano	OR	09	160,028	——	——	SD	oristanesi
Padua	PD	35	819,822	2,142	827	VN	padovani
Palermo	PA	90	1,268,047	5,016	1,937	SC	palermitani
Parma	PR	43	394,603	3,449	1,332	ER	parmigiani
Pavia	PV	27	496,753	2,965	1,145	LM	pavesi
Perugia	PG	06	595,089	6,334	2,446	UM	perugini
Pesaro e Urbino	PS	61	336,405	2,893	1,117	MH	pesaresi
Pescara	PE	65	296,185	1,225	473	AB	pescaresi
Piacenza	PC	29	270,147	2,589	1,000	ER	piacentini
Pisa	PI	56	387,724	2,448	945	TC	pisani
Pistoia	PT	51	266,103	965	373	TC	pistoiesi
Pordenone	PN	33	275,486	2,273	878	FV	pordenonesi
Potenza	PZ	85	413,295	6,545	2,527	BC	potentini
Prato	PO	50	——	——	——	TC	pratesi
Ragusa	RG	97	292,989	1,614	623	SC	ragusani
Ravenna	RA	48	351,530	1,859	718	ER	ravennati
Reggio di Calabria	RC	89	591,551	3,183	1,229	CI	reggini
Reggio nell'Emilia	RE	42	417,216	2,291	885	ER	reggiani
Rieti	RI	02	146,431	2,749	1,061	LZ	reatini
Rimini	RN	47	——	——	——	ER	riminesi
Rome	RM	00	3,784,001	5,352	2,066	LZ	romani
Rovigo	RO	45	248,670	1,802	696	VN	rodigini
Salerno	SA	84	1,070,626	4,923	1,901	CM	salernitani
Sassari	SS	07	452,986	7,520	2,903	SD	sassaresi
Savona	SV	17	290,387	1,545	597	LG	savonesi
Siena	SI	53	251,875	3,821	1,475	TC	senesi
Sondrio	SO	23	176,485	3,212	1,240	LM	sondriesi
Syracuse	SR	96	413,073	2,109	814	SC	siracusani
Taranto	TA	74	601,866	2,437	941	PU	tarantini
Teramo	TE	64	282,281	1,948	752	AB	teramani
Terni	TR	05	225,227	2,122	819	UM	ternani
Trapani	TP	91	439,421	2,462	951	SC	trapanesi
Trento	TN	38	446,914	6,213	2,399	TT	trentini
Treviso	TV	31	738,905	2,477	956	VN	trevigiani
Trieste	TS	34	263,908	212	82	FV	triestini
Turin	TO	10	2,275,390	6,830	2,637	PM	torinesi
Udine	UD	33	524,217	4,894	1,890	FV	udinesi
Varese	VA	21	798,782	1,199	463	LM	varesini
Venice	VE	30	831,645	2,460	950	VN	veneziani
Verbania	VB	28	——	——	——	PM	verbanesi
Vercelli	VC	13	380,561	3,001	1,159	PM	vercellesi
Verona	VR	37	787,722	3,097	1,196	VN	veronesi ➤

division	abv	CAP	population	area-km	area-mi	reg	adjective
Vibo Valentia	VV	88	— —	— —	— —	CI	vibonesi
Vicenza	VI	36	743,764	2,722	1,051	VN	vicentini
Viterbo	VT	01	279,513	3,612	1,395	LZ	viterbesi
			57,576,429	301,252	116,319		

Status: These divisions are province (sing. provincia: provinces).

Abv: Sigle automobilistiche: abbreviations used on license plates in Italy to show the car's provenance. These abbreviations are also widely used on Italian maps, etc. Officially, the sigla for Rome is usually listed as ROMA, but RM is also used.

CAP: Codici di Avviamento Postale (postal codes). Italy has a system of five-digit postal codes. The first two digits are constant within each province. (In a few cases, two or more provinces use the same first two digits.)

Population: 1989-12-31 estimated by Istituto Nazionale di Statistica.

Area-km: Square kilometers.

Area-mi: Square miles.

Population and area figures are not available for some of the most recently formed provinces.

Reg: Regione (pl. regioni: region) to which the province belongs (see list below). Officially, these are autonomous regions with ordinary statute, except for five autonomous regions with special statute (FV, SC, SD, TT, VD).

Capital: Capitals have the same names as provinces, except for Massa-Carrara (capital Massa) and Pesaro e Urbino (capital Pesaro).

Adjective: Masculine plural adjective for inhabitants of the provincial capital, or the province as a whole.

region	abv	ISO	FIPS	NUTS	population	area-km	area-mi	capital	adjective
Abruzzi	AB	65	IT01	IT71	1,249,388	10,794	4,168	L'Aquila	abruzzesi
Apulia	PU	75	IT13	IT91	3,970,525	19,348	7,470	Bari	pugliesi
Basilicata	BC	77	IT02	IT92	591,897	9,992	3,858	Potenza	
Calabria	CI	78	IT03	IT93	2,010,195	15,080	5,823	Catanzaro	calabresi
Campania	CM	72	IT04	IT8	5,625,575	13,595	5,249	Naples	campani
Emilia-Romagna	ER	45	IT05	IT4	3,984,055	22,123	8,542	Bologna	emiliani
Friuli-Venezia Giulia	FV	36	IT06	IT33	1,216,398	7,845	3,029	Trieste	
Lazio	LZ	62	IT07	IT6	5,145,763	17,203	6,642	Rome	laziali
Liguria	LG	42	IT08	IT13	1,701,788	5,418	2,092	Genoa	liguri
Lombardy	LM	25	IT09	IT2	8,940,594	23,859	9,212	Milan	lombardi
Marche	MH	57	IT10	IT53	1,446,751	9,693	3,743	Ancona	marchigiani
Molise	ML	67	IT11	IT72	320,916	4,438	1,713	Campobasso	
Piedmont	PM	21	IT12	IT11	4,338,262	25,399	9,807	Turin	piemontesi
Sardinia	SD	88	IT14	ITB	1,645,192	24,090	9,301	Cagliari	sardi
Sicily	SC	82	IT15	ITA	4,989,871	25,707	9,926	Palermo	siciliani
Trentino-Alto Adige	TT	32	IT17	IT31	934,731	13,618	5,258	Trento	trentini
Tuscany	TC	52	IT16	IT51	3,599,085	22,992	8,877	Florence	toscani
Umbria	UM	55	IT18	IT52	822,972	8,456	3,265	Perugia	umbri
Valle d'Aosta	VD	23	IT19	IT12	117,208	3,262	1,260	Aosta	
Veneto	VN	34	IT20	IT32	4,452,667	18,364	7,090	Venice	veneti
					57,103,833	301,276	116,325		

Abv: Two-letter code for international compatibility (defined by the author). None of these codes are the same as any province code, but it is always possible that Italy will assign province codes in the future that conflict with these region codes.

ISO: Codes from ISO 3166-2.

FIPS: Codes from FIPS PUB 10-4.

NUTS: Nomenclature for Statistical Territorial Units. The three regions whose NUTS codes begin with IT1 may be grouped as Nord Ovest (northwest). Similarly, IT3 is Nord Est; IT5 is Centro; IT7 is Abruzzo-Molise; and IT9 is Sud.

Population: 1991 census.

Area-km: Square kilometers.

Area-mi: Square miles.

Adjective: Masculine plural adjective for inhabitants of the region.

Further subdivisions: As shown, Italy is subdivided into regions, and the regions are subdivided into provinces. Both regions and provinces are frequently used in statistical lists, and to locate places. Regions were known as compartimenti (departments) until World War II. The provinces are further subdivided into comuni (communes). There are also some groups of communes that form an intermediate administrative level, the circondari (districts).

Territorial extent: The region of Sardinia corresponds to the island of Sardinia. Any province in Sardinia region lies mainly on the island of Sardinia, although it may include other nearby islands. The same is true of Sicily.

The regions of Venezia, Venezia Giulia e Zara, and Venezia Tridentina together were sometimes called Tre Venezie (the three Venetias), or Triveneto. They correspond to the modern regions of Friuli-Venezia Giulia, Trentino-Alto Adige, and Veneto, plus some territory in Croatia and Slovenia.

Agrigento includes the Pelagian Islands: Lampedusa, Linosa, and the tiny islet of Lampione.

Arezzo includes an enclave within Pesaro e Urbino, which consequently is also an enclave of Tuscany region within Marche. It's part of Badia Tedalda commune.

Benevento includes an enclave within Avellino, constituting the commune of Pannarano.

Cagliari includes the islands of Sant' Antíoco and San Pietro.

Caltanissetta includes an enclave within Palermo, constituting the commune of Resuttano.

Como includes a small enclave within the canton of Ticino, Switzerland, constituting the commune of Campione d'Italia.

Enna includes a tiny enclave within Caltanissetta.

Foggia includes the Tremiti islands: San Domino, San Nicola, Caprara, Pianosa, etc.

Gorizia includes islands in the Laguna di Grado, as far west as the inlet of Porto Buso.

Grosseto includes the islands of Giglio, Giannutri, and the Formiche di Grosseto.

Latina includes the islands of Ponza, Palmarola, Ventoténe, Zamone, and other nearby islands.

Livorno includes most of the Tuscan Archipelago, including the islands of Elba, Capraia, Montecristo, Pianosa, and Gorgona.

Matera includes an enclave within Potenza, part of Tricárico commune.

Messina includes the Aeolian (Lipari) Islands, of which the largest are Lipari, Salina, Vulcano, Stromboli, Filicudi, Alicudi, and Panarea.

Naples includes the islands of Ischia, Capri, Prócida, and other nearby islands.

Oristano includes the island of Mal di Ventre.

Palermo includes an enclave within Agrigento, part of Bisacquino commune.

Perugia includes an enclave within Pesaro e Urbino (which consequently is also an enclave of Umbria region within Marche), part of Città di Castello commune.

Rimini includes a tiny enclave within Pesaro e Urbino (and barely touching San Marino; consequently also an enclave of Emilia-Romagna region within Marche), part of Verucchio commune.

Sassari includes neighboring islands such as Asinara, Maddalena, Caprera, Spargi, Tavolara, Molara, Santo Stefano, Santa Maria, Rázzoli, and Budelli.

Terni includes an enclave on the border between Perugia and Siena, part of Fabro commune.

Trapani includes the islands of Pantelleria, Maréttimo, and the Égadi islands (Favignana, Lévanzo, etc.).

Udine includes islands in the Laguna di Marano, as far east as Santa Andrea.

Viterbo includes a small enclave on the border between Rieti and Terni, part of Gallese commune.

Origins of names:

Abruzzi: unknown, may be related to Latin *aper*: boar or *abruptus*: steep

Alessandria: after Pope Alexander III

Ancona: Ancient Greek *ankon*: bent arms, for the shape of two promontories

Avellino: Latin *Abellinum*: pertaining to Abella, a city in Campania

Bari: possibly from Ancient Greek *baris*: fortified house

Basilicata: Ancient Greek *basilikos*: royal; former name Lucania is from Latin *lucus*: woods

Benevento: named Maleventum prior to 268 B.C., when it was changed to Beneventum (Latin *bene*: good, *eventum*: fortune); however, Maleventum probably came from *mal*: height, not *malus*: bad

Bolzano: possibly from *Bautianum*: Bautius's plantation

Brindisi: *brention*: stag's head

Cagliari: Greek Karalis, from pre–Indo-European *kar*: rock

Calabria: from Calaber, ethnic name

Caltanissetta: diminutive of Caltanissa, said to be from Arabic *Kal'at*: castle, *an-Nisa'*: of women

Campania: Latin *campania*: countryside, fields

Campobasso: Italian for low field

Caserta: Italian *casa*: house, *erta*: elevated, for a castle overlooking it

Crotone: possibly from Ancient Greek *kroton*: castor-oil plant

Cuneo: Latin *cuneus*: corner (between the Gesso and Stura Rivers)

Emilia: from Latin Æmilia Regio, the destination of the Via Æmilia, whose construction began under consul Marcus Æmilius Lepidus

Ferrara: probably Latin *ferraria*: iron smithy

Florence: from Latin *Florentia*: flowering place

Foggia: Italian dialect for ditch

Forlì: Latin *forum Livii*: city of Livius (Roman consul Marcus Livius Salinator)

Friuli: Latin *Forum Julium*: city of Julius Caesar

Gorizia: Slovenian *Gorica*: little mountain

Grosseto: possibly place of the *grossi* (type of fig trees)

Imperia: after the river Impero; created in 1923 by the union of Porto Maurizio and Oneglia

L'Aquila: Italian for "the eagle"

Latina: renamed from Littoria in 1945 to avoid Fascist overtones; located in northern Latium

Lazio: Latin *Latium*: broad plain

Liguria: from Liguri, ethnic name

Lodi: Latin *Laude Pompeia*: mention of Pompey, after Cneius Pompeius Strabo

Lombardy: from ethnic name Langobardi, meaning men with long beards (or axes)

Macerata: Latin for pisé, or rammed earth, because that method of construction was used

Marche: Italian for march (buffer state)

Messina: after the Greek region of Messinia, because of colonists from there

Milan: Gallic *medio*: middle, *lanon*: inhabited place, through Latin Mediolanum

Modena: possibly from Etruscan *mutna*: tomb

Naples: Ancient Greek *nea*: new, *polis*: city

Padua: probably from Padus, the Latin name of the Po River

Palermo: Ancient Greek *pan*: all, *hormos*: anchorage (i.e. good harbor)

Pescara: Medieval Latin *piscaria*: fish market

Piacenza: Latin *placentia*: pleasure

Piedmont: piedmont, or foothills, of the Alps

Pisa: possibly pre–Indo-European *pisa*: wetland

Pistoia: from Latin *pistor*: grinder of grain

Ravenna: possibly pre–Indo-European *rava*: torrent

Romagna: land of the Romans, as it remained part of the Byzantine (Eastern Roman) Empire after the fall of Rome

Sicily: from ethnic name Sikeloi

Syracuse: named for a swamp

Trapani: Ancient Greek *drepanon*: scythe, for the shape of a promontory

Trentino-Alto Adige: Alto Adige means the upstream part of the Adige River

Trieste: probably from an Indo-European root meaning market

Turin: Latin Augusta Taurinorum, from the ethnic name Taurini

Tuscany: Latin *Tuscus*: having to do with the Etruscans

Valle d'Aosta: Valley of Aosta (city). Aosta comes from Latin Augusta prætoria Salassorum. It was a colony founded by emperor Augustus to house his pretorian guard, in the land of the Salassi.

Venetia, Venice: land of the Veneti (ethnic name)

Change history:

1920-07-16	Treaty of Saint-Germain took effect. Territory was transferred from several provinces of the Austro-Hungarian Empire to Italy. The southern part of Tyrol province (about half) and a small part of Carinthia became Venezia Tridentina region, consisting of Trento province. Most of Coastland (Küstenland) province and the enclave of Zara in Dalmatia were annexed to Venezia region, becoming the provinces of Gorizia, Pola, and Trieste.
1920-11-12	Treaty of Rapallo signed, by which Fiume (Rijeka) became a free state, and Italy received two groups of Adriatic islands: in the north, Cherso (Cres), Lussin (Lošinj), and some smaller islands; in the south, Lagosta (Lastovo), Pelagosa (Palagruža), and others.
1923	Name of city and province of Porto Maurizio changed to Imperia. Name of Udine province, but not its capital, changed to Friuli.
1924-01-27	City of Fiume, and most of the Free State, annexed to Italy by treaty with Yugoslavia, becoming the province of Fiume in the region of Venezia.
1927	Name of city and province of Girgenti changed to Agrigento. Name of city and province of Castrogiovanni changed to Enna.
~1927	Aosta province split from Turin. Bolzano province split from Trento. Brindisi and Taranto provinces split from Lecce. Castrogiovanni province formed from parts of Caltanissetta and Catania. Frosinone and Viterbo provinces split from Rome. La Spezia and Savona provinces split from Genoa. Matera province split from Potenza. Nuoro province formed from parts of Cagliari and Sassari. Pescara province formed from parts of Chieti and Teramo. Pistoia province split from Florence. Ragusa province split from Syracuse. Rieti and Terni provinces split from Perugia; Rieti province transferred from Umbria region to Lazio. Varese province split from Como. Vercelli province split from Novara.
1934	Littoria province split from Rome.
~1935	Venezia region split into Venezia Euganea and Venezia Giulia e Zara regions. The latter consisted of Fiume, Gorizia, Pola, and Trieste provinces.

~1937	Name of Taranto province, but not its capital, changed to Ionio.
1937	Name of Pola province, but not its capital, changed to Istria.
1938	Name of Massa-Carrara province, and its capital Massa, changed to Apuania.
~1939	Asti province split from Alessandria. Name of Fiume province, but not its capital, changed to Carnaro. Name of Basilicata region changed to Lucania.
~1945	Massa city, Massa-Carrara, Taranto, and Udine provinces, and Basilicata region restored to their pre-war names. Name of Littoria city and province changed to Latina.
1946-05-15	Sicily became an autonomous region with special statute.
1947-02-10	Peace treaty signed. Four small areas transferred from Piedmont and Liguria regions to France. An area around Trieste was made into the Free Territory of Trieste. It consisted of Zone A, containing Trieste itself, under U.S.-British allied military administration, and Zone B, under Yugoslavian military administration. Venezia Giulia e Zara region (except for small part of Gorizia province and the Free Territory of Trieste) transferred to Yugoslavia.
1947	Name of Venezia Tridentina region changed to Trentino-Alto Adige.
1948	Name of Emilia region changed to Emilia-Romagna.
1948-02-26	Valle d'Aosta region, consisting of the province of Aosta, split from Piedmont. It and Sardinia and Trentino-Alto Adige became autonomous regions with special statute.
1954-10-25	Zone A of Free Territory of Trieste annexed to Italy as the province of Trieste.
1963-01-31	Venezia Euganea region (capital Venice) split into Friuli-Venezia Giulia and Veneto. Friuli-Venezia Giulia, an autonomous region with special statute, consisted of the provinces of Gorizia, Trieste, and Udine.
~1965	Abruzzi and Molise region (capital L'Aquila) split into Abruzzi region and Molise region.
~1969	Pordenone province split from Udine.
~1979	Isernia province split from Campobasso. Oristano province split from Cagliari.
1996-01-01	New provinces created: Biella split from Vercelli; Crotone and Vibo Valentia split from Catanzaro; Lecco formed from part of Como and smaller part of Bergamo; Lodi split from Milan; Prato split from Florence; Rimini split from Forlì; Verbania split from Novara. Several of these had previously been circondari.

Other names of subdivisions:

Regions:

Abruzzi: Abruzos (Portuguese, Spanish); Abruzzen (German); Abruzzes (French); Abruzzo (variant)

Apulia: Apulien (German); Pouilles, Pouille (French); Puglia (Italian, Portuguese); Puglie (Italian-variant)

Basilicata: Basilicate (French); Lucania (obsolete)

Calabria: Calabre (French); Calabrie (Italian-variant); Kalabrien (German)

Campania: Campanha (Portuguese); Campanie (French); Kampanien (German)

Emilia-Romagna: Emilia (Italian-obsolete); Emilia-Romaña (Spanish); Émilie-Romagne (French)

Friuli-Venezia Giulia: Friaul-Venetien (German); Frioul-Vénétie Julienne (French); Friuli-Venecia Julia (Spanish)

Lazio: Lacio (Spanish); Lácio (Portuguese); Latium (French, German, variant)

Liguria: Ligurie (French); Ligurien (German)

Lombardy: Lombardei (German); Lombardie (French); Lombardia (Italian, Portuguese, Spanish)

Marche: Marca (Spanish); Marches (French); Marches, The Marches (variant); Marken (German)

Molise: Molisa (Spanish)

Piedmont: Piamonte (Spanish); Piemont (German); Piémont (French); Piemonte (Italian, Portuguese)

Sardinia: Cerdeña (Spanish); Sardaigne (French); Sardegna (Italian); Sardenha (Portuguese); Sardinië (Dutch); Sardinien (German)

Sicily: Sicile (French); Sicilia (Italian, Spanish); Sicilië (Dutch); Sizilien (German)

Trentino-Alto Adige: Trentin-Haut Adige (French); Trentino-Alto Adigio (Spanish); Trentino-South Tirol (variant); Trentino-Südtirol (German); Venezia Tridentina (obsolete)

Tuscany: Toscana (Italian, Portuguese, Spanish); Toscane (French); Toskana (German)

Umbria: Ombrie (French); Umbrien (German)

Valle d'Aosta: Aostatal (German); Aosta Valley (variant); Val d'Aoste, Vallée d'Aoste (French)

Veneto: Venecia (Spanish); Venetia (variant); Vénétie (French); Venetien (German); Venezia Euganea (obsolete)

Provinces:

Agrigento: Agrigente (French); Girgenti (obsolete)

Alessandria: Alejandría (Spanish); Alexandrie (French)

Ancona: Ancône (French)

Aosta: Aoste (French); Val d'Aosta, Valle d'Aosta (variant)

Benevento: Bénévent (French)

Bergamo: Bergame (French)

Bologna: Bologne (French); Bolonha (Portuguese); Bolonia (Spanish)

Bolzano: Bozen, Südtirol (German)

Caserta: Caserte (French)

Catania: Catane (French)

Como: Côme (French)

Cremona: Crémone (French)

Cuneo: Coni (French)

Ferrara: Ferrare (French)

Florence: Firenze (Italian); Florença (Portuguese); Florencia (Spanish); Florens (Swedish); Florenz (German)

Foggia: Capitanata (obsolete)

Forli: Forlì (Italian)

Imperia: Porto Maurizio (obsolete)

L'Aquila: Aquila (variant)

La Spezia: Spezia (variant)

Latina: Littoria (obsolete)

Livorno: Leghorn (obsolete); Liorna (Spanish); Livourne (French)

Lucca: Lucques (French)

Genoa: Gênes (French); Genova (Italian); Gênova (Portuguese); Génova (Spanish); Genua (German, Swedish)

Gorizia: Görz (German)

Mantua: Mantoue (French); Mantova (Italian, Spanish, Swedish)

Massa-Carrara: Apuania (obsolete); Massa-Carrare (French); Massa e Carrara (variant)

Messina: Messine (French)

Milan: Mailand (German); Milán (Spanish); Milano (Italian, Swedish); Milão (Portuguese)

Modena: Modène (French); Módena (Spanish)

Naples: Nápoles (Portuguese, Spanish); Napoli (Italian); Neapel (German, Swedish)

Novara: Novare (French)

Padua: Padoue (French); Padova (Italian, Swedish)

Palermo: Palerme (French)

Parma: Parme (French)

Pavia: Pavie (French)

Perugia: Pérouse (French); Perúgia (Portuguese)

Pesaro e Urbino: Pesaro-et-Urbino (French); Pesaro-Urbino (variant); Pésaro y Urbino (Spanish)

Piacenza: Plaisance (French)

Pisa: Pise (French)

Ragusa: Raguse (French)

Ravenna: Rávena (Spanish); Ravenne (French)

Reggio di Calabria: Reggio Calabria (variant); Reggio de Calabre (French)

Reggio nell'Emilia: Reggio d'Émilie (French)

Rome: Rom (Danish, German, Swedish); Roma (Italian, Portuguese, Spanish)

Salerno: Salerne (French)

Siena: Sienne (French)

Syracuse: Siracusa (Italian, Spanish, Swedish); Syrakus (German)

Taranto: Ionio (obsolete); Tarent (German); Tarente (French)

Trento: Trente (French); Trient (German)

Treviso: Trévise (French)

Trieste: Triest (German)

Turin: Torino (Italian); Turim (Portuguese)

Udine: Friuli (obsolete)

Venice: Venecia (Spanish); Venedig (German, Swedish); Veneza (Portuguese); Venezia (Italian); Venise (French)

Verbania: Verbano-Cùsio-Ossola (variant)

Vercelli: Verceil (French)

Verona: Vérone (French)

Vicenza: Vicence (French)

Viterbo: Viterbe (French)

Population history:

region	1895	1911	1936	1943	1951	1961	1971	1981	1991
Abruzzi	1,384,355	1,430,706	1,600,631	1,677,146	1,684,030	1,461,000	1,166,694	1,217,791	1,249,388
Apulia	1,854,180	2,130,151	2,637,022	2,886,570	3,220,485	3,312,000	3,582,787	3,871,617	3,970,525
Basilicata	546,600	474,021	543,262	584,240	627,586	603,000	603,064	610,186	591,897
Calabria	1,338,264	1,402,151	1,771,651	1,907,953	2,044,287	1,937,000	1,988,051	2,061,182	2,010,195
Campania	3,128,223	3,311,990	3,698,695	3,991,409	4,346,264	4,668,000	5,059,348	5,463,134	5,625,575
Emilia-R.	2,292,097	2,681,201	3,339,058	3,472,017	3,544,340	3,628,000	3,846,755	3,957,513	3,984,055
Friuli-V.G.	— —	— —	977,257	1,030,231	1,226,121	1,165,000	1,213,532	1,233,984	1,216,398
Lazio	1,019,198	1,302,423	2,647,088	3,063,203	3,340,798	4,000,000	4,689,482	5,001,684	5,145,763
Liguria	976,654	1,197,231	1,466,915	1,535,976	1,566,961	1,758,000	1,853,578	1,807,893	1,701,788
Lombardy	4,032,668	4,790,473	5,836,342	6,190,361	6,566,154	7,372,000	8,543,387	8,891,652	8,940,594
Marche	973,807	1,093,253	1,278,071	1,330,774	1,364,030	1,312,000	1,359,907	1,412,404	1,446,751
Molise	— —	— —	— —	— —	— —	— —	319,807	328,371	320,916
Piedmont	3,325,733	3,424,450	3,506,134	3,602,721	3,518,177	3,949,000	4,432,313	4,479,031	4,338,262
Sardinia	751,255	852,407	1,034,206	1,153,384	1,276,023	1,373,000	1,473,800	1,594,175	1,645,192
Sicily	3,484,125	3,672,258	4,000,078	4,256,077	4,486,749	4,634,000	4,680,715	4,906,878	4,989,871
Trentino-A.A.	— —	— —	669,029	660,825	728,604	783,000	841,886	873,413	934,731 ➤

region	1895	1911	1936	1943	1951	1961	1971	1981	1991
Tuscany	2,310,534	2,694,706	2,974,439	3,088,511	3,158,811	3,293,000	3,473,097	3,581,051	3,599,085
Umbria	604,987	686,596	725,918	765,711	803,918	780,000	775,783	807,552	822,972
Valle d'A.	——	——	——	——	94,140	102,000	109,150	112,353	117,208
Veneto	3,080,153	3,527,360	4,287,806	4,483,891	3,918,059	3,774,000	4,123,411	4,345,047	4,452,667
	31,102,833	34,671,377	42,993,602	45,681,000	47,515,537	49,904,000	54,136,547	56,556,911	57,103,833

JAMAICA

ISO = JM/FIPS = JM   Language = English   Time zone = -5   Capital = Kingston

At the beginning of the 20th century, Jamaica was a British colony. Administratively subordinate to it were several dependencies: Cayman Islands, Turks and Caicos Islands, Morant Cays, and Pedro Cays. The Cayman Islands separated from Jamaica on 1959-07-04. Jamaica became an independent country, and Turks and Caicos Islands separated from it, on 1962-08-06. The tiny and uninhabited Morant and Pedro Cays are still part of Jamaica.

Other names of country: Giamaica (Italian); Jamaika (Finnish, German); Jamaíka (Icelandic); Jamaïque (French).

Origin of name: (Speculative) From Arawak *xamac*: hammock, or *xaymaca*: rich in springs, or land of springs.

division	abv	ISO	FIPS	population	area-km	area-mi	cty	capital
Clarendon	CL	13	JM01	219,400	1,196	462	MX	May Pen
Hanover	HA	09	JM02	66,000	450	174	CW	Lucea
Kingston	KI	01	JM17	679,100	22	8	SY	Kingston
Manchester	MA	12	JM04	167,900	830	320	MX	Mandeville
Portland	PO	04	JM07	77,600	814	314	SY	Port Antonio
Saint Andrew	SD	02	JM08	——	431	166	SY	Half Way Tree
Saint Ann	SN	06	JM09	151,700	1,213	468	MX	Saint Anns Bay
Saint Catherine	SC	14	JM10	364,400	1,192	460	MX	Spanish Town
Saint Elizabeth	SE	11	JM11	145,300	1,212	468	CW	Black River
Saint James	SJ	08	JM12	161,000	595	230	CW	Montego Bay
Saint Mary	SM	05	JM13	113,000	611	236	MX	Port Maria
Saint Thomas	ST	03	JM14	87,500	743	287	SY	Morant Bay
Trelawny	TR	07	JM15	73,800	875	338	CW	Falmouth
Westmoreland	WE	10	JM16	128,800	807	312	CW	Savanna-la-Mar
				2,435,500	10,991	4,243		

Status: These divisions are parishes.

Abv: Two-letter code for international compatibility (defined by the author).

ISO: Codes from ISO 3166-2.

FIPS: Codes from FIPS PUB 10-4.

Population: 1992 estimate (Saint Andrew's population is included in Kingston).

Area-km: Square kilometers.

Area-mi: Square miles.

Cty: County to which the parish belongs, according to the codes shown below. The counties have no administrative function, but are traditional divisions.

abv	county
CW	Cornwall
MX	Middlesex
SY	Surrey

Origins of names:

Clarendon: after Edward Hude, Earl of Clarendon

Hanover: for the House of Hanover, ruling dynasty of Great Britain

Manchester: after William, Duke of Manchester, governor of

Jamaica when it was created in 1814

Portland: after the Duke of Portland, governor of Jamaica when it was created in 1723

Saint Ann: translation of Santa Ana, name given by Columbus

Saint Elizabeth: in honor of Lady Elizabeth Modyford, wife of the governor of Jamaica in 1670

Saint James: in honor of James, Duke of York, later King James II of England

Saint Mary: after the capital, Puerto Santa Maria under Spanish rule (now Port Maria)

Trelawny: after Sir William Trelawny, governer of Jamaica when it was created in 1771

Westmoreland: after the county in England, because this county contains the westernmost point in Jamaica

Change history:

~1930   Saint George parish (capital Annotta, now called Annotto Bay) split into two parts and annexed by Portland and Saint Mary.

Other names of subdivisions:

Kingston: Kingston and Port Royal (obsolete)

JAPAN

ISO = JP/FIPS = JA   Language = Japanese   Time zone = +9   Capital = Tokyo

In 1900, Japan consisted of its present territory plus two major components. Taiwan, then more often called Formosa, with the Pescadores Islands, had been conquered from China and made a Japanese colony in 1895. The Kuril Islands, known to the Japanese as Chishima, had been annexed from Russia in 1875. Japan acquired additional lands as a result of the Russo-Japanese war of 1905: the southern half of Sakhalin Island (Karafuto in Japanese), the Kwantung peninsula, and other strongholds in Manchuria. Korea became a Japanese protectorate in 1905-12, then a colony on 1910-08-22. In 1920, by the terms of the Treaty of Versailles, Japan picked up the former German islands of Micronesia, making them its territory of Nanyo. In 1931, it invaded Manchuria, and set up the puppet state of Manchukuo there the following year. As World War II drew near and broke out, Japan extended its military occupation to much of the Far East and the Pacific. When the war ended in 1945, all of these conquests were taken from Japan, and restored, as far as possible, to their former status. Some of the islands in the southern chains, notably Okinawa, were placed under U.S. military administration, but later reintegrated into Japan. Nanyo became a trust territory of the United States on 1947-04-02. Japan still asserts its claim to the southern Kuril Islands, including Etorofu, Kunashiri, Shikotan, Shibotsu, and Suisho, which have been administratively part of Russia since the war's end.

Spelling note: Although several different transliteration methods have been used to convert from Japanese characters to the Roman alphabet, there is a surprising degree of unanimity about the Romanized form of Japanese place names, even in the other languages covered here. In some references, macrons are used to indicate long vowels. ISO standard 3166-2 is an exception; it uses a different transliteration method (and uses circumflex accents instead of macrons). Names as shown by ISO will be found under "Other names of subdivisions." (ISO also appends the generic -Ken, -Do, -Fu, or -To to the prefecture name, as in Aichi-Ken or Osaka-Fu. This form often appears in postal addresses, too.)

Other names of country: Giappone (Italian); Japani (Finnish); Japão (Portuguese); Japon (French); Japón (Spanish); Nihon, Nippon (formal).

Origin of name: Chinese *ri*: sun, *ben*: origin (i.e. land of the rising sun).

division	abv	ISO	FIPS	population	area-km	area-mi	region	capital
Aichi	AI	23	JA01	6,690,440	5,105	1,971	Chubu	Nagoya
Akita	AK	05	JA02	1,227,491	11,609	4,482	Tohoku	Akita
Aomori	AO	02	JA03	1,482,935	9,614	3,712	Tohoku	Aomori
Chiba	CH	12	JA04	5,555,467	5,103	1,970	Kanto	Chiba
Ehime	EH	38	JA05	1,515,027	5,664	2,187	Shikoku	Matsuyama
Fukui	FI	18	JA06	823,595	4,188	1,617	Chubu	Fukui
Fukuoka	FO	40	JA07	4,811,179	4,934	1,905	Kyushu	Fukuoka
Fukushima	FS	07	JA08	2,104,119	13,781	5,321	Tohoku	Fukushima
Gifu	GF	21	JA09	2,066,579	10,596	4,091	Chubu	Gifu
Gumma	GM	10	JA10	1,966,287	6,356	2,454	Kanto	Maebashi ➤

division	abv	ISO	FIPS	population	area-km	area-mi	region	capital
Hiroshima	HS	34	JA11	2,849,822	8,453	3,264	Chugoku	Hiroshima
Hokkaido	HK	01	JA12	5,643,715	78,515	30,315	Hokkaido	Sapporo
Hyogo	HG	28	JA13	5,405,090	8,362	3,229	Kinki	Kobe
Ibaraki	IB	08	JA14	2,845,411	6,087	2,350	Kanto	Mito
Ishikawa	IS	17	JA15	1,164,627	4,196	1,620	Chubu	Kanazawa
Iwate	IW	03	JA16	1,416,960	15,277	5,898	Tohoku	Morioka
Kagawa	KG	37	JA17	1,023,434	1,877	725	Shikoku	Takamatsu
Kagoshima	KS	46	JA18	1,797,766	9,149	3,532	Kyushu	Kagoshima
Kanagawa	KN	14	JA19	7,980,421	2,384	920	Kanto	Yokohama
Kochi	KC	39	JA20	825,063	7,106	2,744	Shikoku	Kochi
Kumamoto	KM	43	JA21	1,840,383	7,383	2,851	Kyushu	Kumamoto
Kyoto	KY	26	JA22	2,602,520	4,612	1,781	Kinki	Kyoto
Mie	ME	24	JA23	1,792,542	5,774	2,229	Kinki	Tsu
Miyagi	MG	04	JA24	2,248,521	7,288	2,814	Tohoku	Sendai
Miyazaki	MZ	45	JA25	1,168,922	7,734	2,986	Kyushu	Miyazaki
Nagano	NN	20	JA26	2,156,656	13,585	5,245	Chubu	Nagano
Nagasaki	NS	42	JA27	1,563,015	4,098	1,582	Kyushu	Nagasaki
Nara	NR	29	JA28	1,375,478	3,692	1,425	Kinki	Nara
Niigata	NI	15	JA29	2,474,602	12,577	4,856	Chubu	Niigata
Oita	OT	44	JA30	1,236,924	6,331	2,444	Kyushu	Oita
Okayama	OY	33	JA31	1,925,913	7,079	2,733	Chugoku	Okayama
Okinawa	ON	47	JA47	1,222,458	2,244	866	Ryukyu	Naha
Osaka	OS	27	JA32	8,734,670	1,845	712	Kinki	Osaka
Saga	SG	41	JA33	877,865	2,416	933	Kyushu	Saga
Saitama	ST	11	JA34	6,405,319	3,799	1,467	Kanto	Urawa
Shiga	SH	25	JA35	1,222,401	4,016	1,551	Kinki	Otsu
Shimane	SM	32	JA36	781,005	6,627	2,559	Chugoku	Matsue
Shizuoka	SZ	22	JA37	3,670,891	7,770	3,000	Chubu	Shizuoka
Tochigi	TC	09	JA38	1,935,186	6,414	2,476	Kanto	Utsunomiya
Tokushima	TS	36	JA39	831,582	4,144	1,600	Shikoku	Tokushima
Tokyo	TK	13	JA40	11,854,987	2,145	828	Kanto	Tokyo
Tottori	TT	31	JA41	615,741	3,492	1,348	Chugoku	Tottori
Toyama	TY	16	JA42	1,120,182	4,252	1,642	Chubu	Toyama
Wakayama	WK	30	JA43	1,074,321	4,722	1,823	Kinki	Wakayama
Yamagata	YT	06	JA44	1,258,404	9,325	3,600	Tohoku	Yamagata
Yamaguchi	YC	35	JA45	1,572,645	6,090	2,351	Chugoku	Yamaguchi
Yamanashi	YN	19	JA46	852,980	4,463	1,723	Chubu	Kofu
				123,611,541	372,273	143,732		

Status: These divisions are ken (prefectures), with four exceptions: Tokyo is a to (metropolis); Hokkaido is a do (territory); Kyoto and Osaka are fu (urban prefectures). The four words are combined in one, todofuken, to denote a division of any type.

Abv: Two-letter code for international compatibility (from the English-language Japan Almanac).

ISO: Codes from ISO 3166-2. These codes are used in Japanese government publications, which list prefectures sequentially by code. They basically run from north to south.

FIPS: Codes from FIPS PUB 10-4.

Population: 1990 census.

Area-km: Square kilometers.

Area-mi: Square miles.

Region: The prefectures are grouped into the regions listed below. They have no administrative function. Hokkaido, Kyushu, and Shikoku correspond to three of the main islands of Japan. Ryukyu consists of smaller islands in the south. The other five regions correspond to the largest island, Honshu.

region	population	area-km	chief town	region	population	area-km	chief town
Chubu	21,020,552	66,732	Nagoya	Kyushu	13,296,054	42,045	Fukuoka
Chugoku	7,745,126	31,741	Hiroshima	Ryukyu	1,222,458	2,244	Naha
Hokkaido	5,643,715	78,515	Sapporo	Shikoku	4,195,106	18,791	Matsuyama
Kanto	38,543,078	32,288	Tokyo	Tohoku	9,738,430	66,894	Sendai
Kinki	22,207,022	33,023	Osaka		123,611,541	372,273	

Further subdivisions: The prefecture-level units are subdivided into shi (cities), machi and cho (towns), mura and son (villages), and ku (wards). Some maps show Hokkaido subdivided into shicho (branch administrations).

Territorial extent: Each prefecture except Okinawa lies mainly on one of the four large islands: Hokkaido, Honshu, Kyushu, and Shikoku. (The island locale of each prefecture can be deduced from the region column above.) Most prefectures also contain some smaller islands. This list shows these additional islands roughly in decreasing order of size. ('Island' may be represented by -shima, -jima, or -to.)

Aichi: Saku-shima, Shino-shima, Himaga-shima

Aomori: Kyuroku-jima

Ehime: Omi-shima, O-shima, Naka-jima, Hakata-jima, Nuwa-jima, Gogo-shima, Hiburi-shima, Uo-shima, Shisaka-jima

Fukuoka: O-shima, Jino-shima, Aino-shima

Hiroshima: Eta-jima, Kurahashi-jima, Osaki-kami-jima, Itsuku-shima, Inno-shima, Ikuchi-shima, Osaki-shimo-jima, Hashiri-jima

Hokkaido: Okushiri-shima, Rishiri-to, Rebun-to, O-shima, Ko-jima

Hyogo: Awaji-shima, Nu-shima, and the Ieshima-shoto group

Ishikawa: Noto-jima, Hekura-jima, and the Nanatsu-shima group

Kagawa: Shodo-shima, Te-shima, Hiro-shima, Hon-jima, Nao-shima (part), Awa-shima, Megi-jima, Ibuki-jima

Kagoshima: Amami-o-shima, Yaku-jima, Tanega-shima, Tokuno-shima, Koshikijima Retto (including Kami-koshiki-jima and Shimokoshiki-jima), Okino-erabu-shima, Naga-shima, Shishi-jima, Kikai-shima, Yoron-jima, and other islands of the Satsunan-shoto group

Kochi: Okino-shima, Uguru-shima

Kumamoto: Amakusa-shoto group

Mie: Toshi-jima, Suga-jima, Kami-shima

Miyagi: Kinkazan-to, Aji-shima, Miyato-shima, Tashiro-jima

Miyazaki: Shimaura-to

Nagasaki: Tsu-shima (actually two main islands), Fukue-jima, Nakadori-jima, Iki-shima, Hirado-shima, Azuchi-oshima, and other islands of the Goto Retto group

Niigata: Sado-shima, Awa-shima

Oita: Hime-shima, Onyu-jima, Muku-shima, Hoto-jima, Fuka-shima

Okayama: Kono-shima, Kitagi-shima, Kakui-shima, Naga-shima, Nao-shima (part)

Okinawa consists of the Okinawa-shoto group. It includes several smaller groups, such as Sakishima-shoto, Senkaku-shoto, and Daito-shoto (Borodino Islands). Some of the larger islands are Okinawa-jima, Miyako-jima, Iriomote-jima, Ishigaki-jima, Kume-jima, and Iheya-jima. The most remote are Yonaguni-jima in the west and Okidaito-jima in the southeast. The name Ryukyu Islands, or Nansei-shoto, encompasses both Okinawa and Satsunan-shoto, the islands of Kagoshima prefecture.

Saga: Madara-shima, Kakara-shima

Shimane: Okino-Shima (the Oki Islands), consisting of Dogo and Dozen, where Dozen in turn consists of Nishino-shima, Nakano-shima, and Chiburi-jima; also the islands of Yatsuka village, in the inlet of Nakano-umi

Tokushima: Oge-jima, O-shima, I-shima, Ao-shima

Tokyo includes a long string of islands stretching almost due south for about 800 km. Among the largest islands are O-shima, Hachijo-jima, Miyake-jima, Nii-jima, Io-jima (Iwo Jima), and Chichi-jima. Island groups in Tokyo prefecture include Izu-shoto, Ogasawara-gunto (Bonin Islands), and Kazan Retto (Volcano Islands). The most remote islands from the Japanese mainland are Okino-tori-shima (Parece Vela) to the southwest, Minami-iwo-jima to the south, and Minami-tori-shima (Marcus) to the southeast.

Wakayama: O-shima, Chino-shima, Okino-shima; Wakayama also has two enclaves on the border between Mie and Nara, containing the villages of Kitayama and Tamakiguchi.

Yamagata: Tobi-shima

Yamaguchi: Yashiro-jima, Heigun-to, Kasado-shima, Omi-shima, Naga-shima, Otsu-shima, Mi-shima, Muko-shima, Ya-shima, Iwai-shima, Tsuno-shima, Futai-jima, Hashira-jima, Aino-shima, O-shima

Origins of names:

Akita: Japanese for field of ripe rice

Aomori: Japanese for green forest

Chiba: Japanese for a thousand leaves

Ehime: Japanese *ai*: to love, *hime*: princess

Fujisawa: Japanese *fuji*: wisteria, *sawa*: valley

Fukui: Japanese *fuku*: luck, *i*: good

Fukuoka: Japanese *fuku*: luck, *oka*: hill

Fukushima: Japanese *fuku*: luck, *shima*: island

Fukuyama: Japanese *fuku*: luck, *yama*: mountain

Funabashi: Japanese *fune*: ship, *hashi*: bridge (i.e. floating bridge)

Gumma: Japanese *gun*: group, *ma*: horse

Hiroshima: Japanese *hiro*: broad, *shima*: island

Hokkaido: Japanese *hoku*: north, *kai*: sea, *do*: province

Hyogo: Japanese *hyo*: army, *ko*: storehouse

Ibaraki: Japanese *ibara*: thorn, *ki*: castle

Ishikawa: Japanese *ishi*: stone, *kawa*: river

Iwate: Japanese *iwa*: rock, *te*: hand

Kyoto: Japanese for capital

Nagasaki: Japanese *naga*: long, *saki*: cape

Tokyo: Japanese *to*: east, *kyo*: capital

Change history:

The division into prefectures dates from 1871, as the Meiji restoration eliminated fiefs.

1947-07-19   Nanyo became a trust territory of the United States.

1968   United States restored the Ogasawara (Bonin), Kazan Retto, Rosario, Parece Vela, and Minami-Tori (Marcus) Islands to Japan.

1972   Okinawa restored to Japan.

Other names of subdivisions:

Aichi: Aiti (variant)
Chiba: Tiba (variant)
Fukui: Hukui (variant)
Fukuoka: Hukuoka (variant)
Fukushima: Hukusima (variant)
Gifu: Gihu (variant)
Gumma: Gunma (variant)
Hiroshima: Hirosima (variant)
Hokkaido: Ezo, Yeso, Yezo (obsolete)
Hyogo: Hiogo (variant)
Ishikawa: Isikawa (variant)

Kochi: Koti (variant)
Kyoto: Kioto (variant)
Mie: Miye (variant)
Shiga: Siga (variant)
Shimane: Simane (variant)
Shizuoka: Sizuoka (variant)
Tochigi: Totigi (variant)
Tokushima: Tokusima (variant)
Tokyo: Edo, Yedo (obsolete); Tokio (variant)
Yamaguchi: Yamaguti (variant)
Yamanashi: Yamanasi (variant)

Population history:

division	1896	1920	1930	1940	1950	1960	1970	1980	1990
Aichi	1,557,000	2,090,000	2,567,000	3,166,592	3,391,000	4,206,000	5,386,000	6,222,000	6,690,440
Akita	755,000	899,000	988,000	1,052,275	1,309,000	1,336,000	1,241,000	1,257,000	1,227,491
Aomori	593,000	756,000	880,000	1,000,509	1,283,000	1,427,000	1,428,000	1,524,000	1,482,935
Chiba	1,247,000	1,336,000	1,470,000	1,588,425	2,139,000	2,306,000	3,367,000	4,735,000	5,555,467
Ehime	972,000	1,047,000	1,142,000	1,178,705	1,522,000	1,501,000	1,418,000	1,507,000	1,515,027
Fukui	632,000	599,000	618,000	643,904	752,000	753,000	744,000	794,000	823,595
Fukuoka	1,314,000	2,188,000	2,527,000	3,094,132	3,530,000	4,007,000	4,027,000	4,553,000	4,811,179
Fukushima	1,028,000	1,363,000	1,508,000	1,625,521	2,062,000	2,051,000	1,946,000	2,035,000	2,104,119
Gifu	981,000	1,070,000	1,178,000	1,265,024	1,545,000	1,638,000	1,759,000	1,960,000	2,066,579
Gumma	749,000	1,053,000	1,186,000	1,299,027	1,601,000	1,578,000	1,659,000	1,849,000	1,966,287
Hiroshima	1,400,000	1,542,000	1,692,000	1,869,504	2,082,000	2,184,000	2,436,000	2,739,000	2,849,822
Hokkaido	508,000	2,359,000	2,812,000	3,272,718	4,296,000	5,039,000	5,184,000	5,576,000	5,643,715
Hyogo	1,618,000	2,302,000	2,646,000	3,221,232	3,310,000	3,906,000	4,668,000	5,145,000	5,405,090
Ibaraki	1,101,000	1,350,000	1,487,000	1,620,000	2,039,000	2,047,000	2,144,000	2,558,000	2,845,411
Ishikawa	782,000	747,000	757,000	757,676	957,000	973,000	1,002,000	1,119,000	1,164,627
Iwate	701,000	846,000	976,000	1,095,793	1,347,000	1,449,000	1,371,000	1,422,000	1,416,960
Kagawa	685,000	678,000	733,000	730,394	946,000	919,000	908,000	1,000,000	1,023,434
Kagoshima	1,076,000	1,416,000	1,557,000	1,589,467	1,804,000	1,963,000	1,729,000	1,785,000	1,797,766
Kanagawa	754,000	1,323,000	1,620,000	2,188,974	2,488,000	3,443,000	5,472,000	6,924,000	7,980,421
Kochi	600,000	671,000	718,000	709,286	874,000	855,000	787,000	831,000	825,063
Kumamoto	1,112,000	1,233,000	1,354,000	1,368,179	1,828,000	1,856,000	1,700,000	1,790,000	1,840,383
Kyoto	914,000	1,287,000	1,553,000	1,729,993	1,833,000	1,993,000	2,250,000	2,527,000	2,602,520
Mie	976,000	1,069,000	1,157,000	1,198,783	1,461,000	1,485,000	1,543,000	1,687,000	1,792,542
Miyagi	817,000	962,000	1,143,000	1,271,238	1,663,000	1,743,000	1,819,000	2,082,000	2,248,521
Miyazaki	439,000	651,000	760,000	840,357	1,091,000	1,135,000	1,051,000	1,152,000	1,168,922
Nagano	1,212,000	1,563,000	1,717,000	1,710,729	2,061,000	1,982,000	1,957,000	2,084,000	2,156,656
Nagasaki	796,000	1,136,000	1,233,000	1,370,063	1,645,000	1,760,000	1,570,000	1,591,000	1,563,015
Nara	526,000	565,000	596,000	620,509	764,000	781,000	930,000	1,209,000	1,375,478
Niigata	1,797,000	1,776,000	1,933,000	2,064,402	2,461,000	2,442,000	2,361,000	2,451,000	2,474,602
Oita	822,000	860,000	946,000	972,975	1,253,000	1,240,000	1,156,000	1,229,000	1,236,924
Okayama	1,109,000	1,218,000	1,284,000	1,329,358	1,661,000	1,670,000	1,707,000	1,871,000	1,925,913
Okinawa	440,000	572,000	578,000	574,579	915,000	883,000	945,000	1,107,000	1,222,458
Osaka	1,280,000	2,588,000	3,540,000	4,792,966	3,857,000	5,505,000	7,620,000	8,473,000	8,734,670
Saga	602,000	674,000	692,000	701,517	945,000	943,000	838,000	866,000	877,865
Saitama	1,149,000	1,320,000	1,459,000	1,608,039	2,146,000	2,431,000	3,866,000	5,420,000	6,405,319
Shiga	702,000	651,000	692,000	703,679	861,000	843,000	890,000	1,080,000	1,222,401
Shimane	713,000	715,000	740,000	740,940	913,000	889,000	774,000	785,000	781,005
Shizuoka	1,173,000	1,550,000	1,798,000	2,017,860	2,471,000	2,756,000	3,090,000	3,447,000	3,670,891 ➤

division	1896	1920	1930	1940	1950	1960	1970	1980	1990
Tochigi	759,000	1,046,000	1,142,000	1,206,657	1,550,000	1,514,000	1,580,000	1,792,000	1,935,186
Tokushima	688,000	670,000	717,000	718,717	879,000	847,000	791,000	825,000	831,582
Tokyo	1,468,000	3,699,000	5,409,000	7,354,971	6,278,000	9,684,000	11,408,000	11,618,000	11,854,987
Tottori	414,000	455,000	489,000	484,390	600,000	599,000	569,000	604,000	615,741
Toyama	789,000	724,000	779,000	822,569	1,009,000	1,033,000	1,030,000	1,103,000	1,120,182
Wakayama	666,000	750,000	831,000	865,074	982,000	1,002,000	1,043,000	1,087,000	1,074,321
Yamagata	808,000	969,000	1,080,000	1,119,338	1,357,000	1,321,000	1,226,000	1,252,000	1,258,404
Yamaguchi	967,000	1,041,000	1,136,000	1,294,242	1,541,000	1,602,000	1,511,000	1,587,000	1,572,645
Yamanashi	491,000	583,000	631,000	663,026	811,000	782,000	762,000	804,000	852,980
	42,682,000	55,962,000	64,451,000	73,114,308	84,113,000	94,302,000	104,663,000	117,058,000	123,611,541

JORDAN

ISO = JO/FIPS = JO   Language = Arabic   Time zone = +2 d   Capital = Amman

The area now in Jordan was once part of the vilayet of Syria, in the Ottoman Empire. Some eastern desert parts of Jordan were in Nejd (Arabia), but the border between Syria and Nejd was indeterminate. During World War I, the British and French defeated the Turks and divided up the southern part of their empire. Britain created several colonies, including Transjordania, which was established on 1922-09-01. The name was changed to Transjordan ~1935. Transjordan became independent on 1946-06-17, changing its name to the Hashemite Kingdom of Jordan. The West Bank was annexed by Jordan on 1950-04-24. Iraq and Jordan joined together to form the Arab Federation for a few months in 1958. The West Bank was occupied by Israel during the Six-Day War (1967-06-05 to 1967-06-10). Since then, it has been mainly under Israeli administration, although its status is still being discussed.

Other names of country: al Mamlaka al Urduniya al Hashemiyah (formal); Giordania (Italian); Hashemite Kingdom of Jordan (formal–English); Jordania (Finnish, Spanish); Jordânia (Portuguese); Jórdanía (Icelandic); Jordanie (French); Jordanië (Dutch); Jordanien (German, Swedish); Reino Hachemita de Jordania (formal–Spanish).

Origin of name: Arabic for land of the Jordan River.

division	ISO	FIPS	population	area-km	area-mi	capital
'Ammān	AM	JO11	1,297,100	17,882	6,904	Amman
Al Balqā'	BA	JO02	214,700	1,069	413	As Salṭ
Irbid	IR	JO14	753,400	22,654	8,747	Irbid
Al Karak	KA	JO09	132,800	4,601	1,776	Al Karak
Ma'ān	MN	JO07	108,300	43,000	16,602	Ma'ān
Al Mafraq	MA	JO10	109,000	N/A	N/A	Al Mafraq
Aṭ Ṭafīlah	AT	JO12	45,800	N/A	N/A	Aṭ Ṭafīlah
Az Zarqā'	AZ	JO13	449,900	N/A	N/A	Az Zarqā'
			3,111,000	89,206	34,442	

Status: These divisions are muhafazat (sing. muhafazah: provinces).
ISO: Codes from ISO 3166-2.
FIPS: Codes from FIPS PUB 10-4.
Population: 1989 estimate.
Area-km: Square kilometers.
Area-mi: Square miles.
Note: ISO 3166-2 lists four additional provinces and their codes: 'Ajlun (AJ), Al 'Aqabah (AQ), Jarash (JA), and Mādabā (MD). No other information on these provinces is available as yet.
Origins of names:

Amman: from Ammon, patriarch of the Ammonites

Change history:

1946-06-17	Jordan was composed of the provinces of Al Balqā', Al Karak, 'Ajlun, and Ma'ān, plus unorganized land in the east known as Desert.
1950-04-24	Jordan annexed the area of former Palestine between Israeli-held territory and the Jordan River, dividing it into the provinces of Hebron (Al-Khalil), Jerusalem (Al-Quds), and Nablus (Nabulus).
~1955	Al 'Āṣimah province split from Al Balqā'.
1967-06-10	West Bank came under control of Israel.
~1968	Name of 'Ajlun province changed to Irbid.
~1988	Al Karak (JO03) split into three parts, which became Al Karak, Aṭ Ṭafīlah, and part of Ma'ān provinces; Irbid (JO06) split into Irbid and part of Al Mafraq province; Al 'Āṣimah (JO01) split into 'Ammān, Az Zarqā', and the other part of Al Mafraq.
~1995	If reasonable inferences from ISO 3166-2 are correct: 'Ajlun and Jarash provinces split from Irbid, Al 'Aqabah split from Ma'ān, Mādabā split from 'Ammān.

Other names of subdivisions: These names are written originally in the Arabic alphabet. There are many ways to transliterate from Arabic to Roman letters. The article may be omitted.

Al Balqā': Balka, Belqa (variant)
Al Karak: Kerak (variant)

Irbid: 'Ajlun (obsolete)
'Ammān: Amã (Portuguese)

KAZAKHSTAN

ISO = KZ/FIPS = KZ   Language = Kazakh   Time zone = (see table)   Capital = Astana

Kazakhstan is the northern part of the old governor-generalship of Turkestan under the Russian Empire. During the Russian Revolution, the status of the Central Asian lands was unresolved for a time. On 1920-08-26, the Kirghiz A.S.S.R. was formed, followed by the Turkestan A.S.S.R. on 1921-04-11. In the fall of 1924, the Central Asian republics were reorganized to match nationalities more closely. The northern part of Turkestan was annexed to Kirghiz. In 1925-04, its name was changed from Kirghiz to Kazakh, and on 1936-12-05, it became an S.S.R. (Kazakhskaya Sovyetskaya Sotsialisticheskaya Respublika), with very nearly its modern boundaries. It remained a republic of the Soviet Union until the Union broke up in 1991. (S.S.R. = Soviet Socialist Republic; A.S.S.R. = Autonomous S.S.R. The former was a top-level division of the Soviet Union. A.S.S.R.s were generally subordinate to S.S.R.s.)

Other names of country: Cazaquistão (Portuguese); Kasachstan (German); Kasakhstan (Danish, Norwegian); Kasakstan (Icelandic); Kazachstan (Dutch); Kazajstán, Kazakstán (Spanish); Kazakhie (variant-French); Kazakistan (Italian); Kazak Respublikasy (formal); Kazakstan (Finnish, Swedish); Republic of Kazakhstan (formal–English).

Origin of name: land of the Kazakhs, ethnic name from Turkish *kazak*: free.

division	abv	ISO	FIPS	tz	population	area-km	area-mi	capital	Russian
Almaty	AA	ALM	KZ01	+6 d	860,000	105,000	40,500	Almaty	Alma-Ata
Almaty [City]	AC	ALA	KZ02	+6 d	1,006,000	N/A	N/A	Almaty	Alma-Ata
Aqmola	AM	AKM	KZ03	+6 d	829,000	125,000	48,300	Astana	Tselinograd
Aqtöbe	AT	AKT	KZ04	+5 d	661,000	299,000	115,400	Aqtöbe	Aktyubinsk
Atyraū	AR	ATY	KZ05	+5 d	380,000	112,000	43,200	Atyraū	Gur'yev
East Kazakhstan	EK	VOS	KZ15	+6 d	897,000	97,000	37,500	Öskemen	Ust'-Kamenogorsk
Kökshetaū	KK	KOK	KZ07	+6 d	628,000	78,000	30,100	Kökshetaū	Kokshetav
Mangghystaū	MG	MAN	KZ08	+4 d	278,000	167,000	64,500	Aqtaū	Shevchenko
North Kazakhstan	NK	SEV	KZ16	+6 d	586,000	44,000	17,000	Petropavlovsk	Petropavlovsk
Pavlodar	PA	PAV	KZ10	+6 d	851,000	128,000	49,400	Pavlodar	Pavlodar
Qaraghandy	QG	KAR	KZ11	+6 d	1,287,000	85,000	32,800	Qaraghandy	Karaganda
Qostanay	QS	KUS	KZ12	+6 d	975,000	114,000	44,000	Qostanay	Kustanay
Qyzylorda	QO	KZY	KZ13	+5 d	590,000	228,000	88,000	Qyzylorda	Kzyl-Orda
Semey	SE	SEM	KZ14	+6 d	788,000	180,000	69,500	Semey	Semipalatinsk
South Kazakhstan	SK	YUZ	KZ09	+6 d	1,644,000	116,000	44,800	Shymkent	Chimkent ▶

division	abv	ISO	FIPS	tz	population	area-km	area-mi	capital	Russian
Taldyqorghan	TQ	TAL	KZ17	+6 [d]	681,000	118,000	45,600	Taldyqorghan	Taldy-Kurgan
Torghay	TG	TUR	KZ18	+6 [d]	293,000	112,000	43,200	Arqalyk	Arkalyk
West Kazakhstan	WK	ZAP	KZ06	+4 [d]	599,000	151,000	58,300	Oral	Ural'sk
Zhambyl	ZM	ZHA	KZ19	+6 [d]	962,000	145,000	56,000	Zhambyl	Dzhambul
Zhezqazghan	ZQ	ZHE	KZ20	+6 [d]	458,000	313,000	120,800	Zhezqazghan	Dzhezkazgan
					15,253,000	2,717,000	1,048,900		

[d] = indicates that daylight saving time is in use.

Status: These divisions are oblysy (oblasts under the Soviet Union: regions), except for Almaty [City], which is a galasy (city with regional status). ISO 3166-2 implies that Leninsk (formerly Tyuratam, ISO code = LEN) has been split from Qyzylorda and made into another city with regional status, but no confirmation is available.

Abv: Two-letter code for international compatibility (defined by the author).

ISO: Codes from ISO 3166-2.

FIPS: Codes from FIPS PUB 10-4.

Tz: Time zone (number of hours by which local time is ahead of GMT). There have been several changes in these zones recently.

Population: 1982-01-01 estimate.

Area-km: Square kilometers.

Area-mi: Square miles.

Russian: Russian name of capital.

Origins of names:

Almaty: Kazakh for "grown with apple trees," formerly Alma-Ata from *alma*: apple, *ata*: father

Aqmola: Kazakh for white grave

Dzhambul: named for Dzhambul Dzhabayev, Kazakh poet

Qyzylorda: Kazakh *kzyl*: red, *orda*: camp

Petropavlovsk: city of Peter and Paul, named for the church of Saints Peter and Paul there

Semirechensk: from Russian *syem*: seven, *ryeki*: rivers

Tselinograd: from Russian *tselina*: virgin soil, *gorod*: city

Change history:

1920-08-26	Kirghiz A.S.S.R. formed from Akmolinsk (Petropavlovsk), Semipalatinsk (Semipalatinsk), Turgay (Kustanay), and Ural'sk (Ural'sk) regions, and the northern part of Transcaspian territory (Ashkhabad) (capitals in parentheses).
1921-04-11	Turkestan A.S.S.R. formed from Amu-Darya (Petro-Alexandrovsk, modern Turtkul'), Ferghana (Skobelev), Pamir, Samarkand (Samarkand), Semirechensk (Verniy), and Syr Darya (Tashkent) regions, and the southern part of Transcaspian. Name of capital of Semirechensk changed from Verniy to Alma-Ata.
1924-10	Most of Semirechensk and Syr Darya merged with Kirghiz A.S.S.R.
1925-04	Name of Kirghiz A.S.S.R. changed to Kazakh.
1929	Capital of Kazakh moved from Kzyl-Orda to Alma-Ata.
1936-12-05	Status of Kazakh changed to S.S.R. The republic was divided into 16 regions. Name of capital of Dzhambul region changed from Auliye-Ata to Mirzoyan.
1938	Name of capital of Dzhambul region changed from Mirzoyan to Dzhambul.
~1957	Taldy-Kurgan region merged with Alma-Ata.
~1961	Name of Akmolinsk region and its capital changed to Tselinograd.
1962	Name of South Kazakhstan region changed to Chimkent.
~1973	Dzhezkazgan region split from Karaganda; Mangyshlak region split from Atyrau; Taldy-Kurgan region split from Alma-Ata; Turgay region split from Kustanay.
~1980	Alma-Ata [City] split from Alma-Ata region.
1991-12-08	Soviet Union ceased to exist. Kazakhstan became an independent country. Westerners began to use the Kazakh, rather than the Russian, version of place names. Name of Chimkent region restored to South Kazakhstan.
1997-12-10	Capital of country officially moved from Almaty to Aqmola.
1998-05-06	Capital of country renamed from Aqmola to Astana.

Other names of subdivisions: Before the dissolution of the Soviet Union, western sources normally used transliterations from Russian names rather than Kazakh names. The standard form of the Russian names of the regions invariably ends in -skaya Oblast'. This form is listed only when the suffix -skaya alters the root name. There are various methods for transliterating from the Cyrillic to the Roman alphabet. The most common variant uses h instead of kh, c for ts, j for consonantal y, č for ch, š for sh, and ž for zh. Where region names are the same as capital names, these are also variant names of the capitals.

Almaty: Alma-Ata, Alma-Atinskaya Oblast', Almatinskaya Oblast' (Russian)

Aqmola: Akmolin, Akmolinsk (Russian); Tselinograd (obsolete)

Aqtöbe: Aktyubinsk (Russian)

Atyraū: Ateraısk (Russian); Gur'yev (obsolete)

East Kazakhstan: Shyghys Qazaqstan (Kazakh); Vostochno-Kazakhstan (Russian)

Kökshetaū: Kokchetav, Kokshetav (Russian)

Mangghystaū: Mangistau, Mangyshlak (Russian)

North Kazakhstan: Severo-Kazakhstan (Russian); Soltustik Qazaqstan (Kazakh)

Qaraghandy: Karaganda, Karagandinskaya Oblast' (Russian)

Qostanay: Kustanai, Kustanay (Russian)

Qyzylorda: Kyzyl-Orda, Kzyl-Orda, Kzyl-Ordinskaya Oblast' (Russian)

Semey: Semipalatinsk (Russian)

South Kazakhstan: Chimkent, Yuzhno-Kazakstan (Russian); Ôngtüstık Qazaqstan (Kazakh)

Taldyqorghan: Taldy-Kurgan, Taldykorgan (Russian)

Torghay: Turgai, Turgay (Russian)

West Kazakhstan: Batys Qazaqstan (Kazakh); Ural'sk, Zapadno-Kazakstan (Russian)

Zhambyl: Dzhambul (Russian)

Zhezqazghan: Dzhezkazgan (Russian)

KENYA

ISO = KE/FIPS = KE   Language = English, Swahili   Time zone = +3   Capital = Nairobi

At the start of the 20th century, British East Africa included the territory of Kenya and Uganda, plus some parts of Congo, Ethiopia, and Somalia. Kenya was split off as a British colony on 1905-04-01, under the same administration as the Kenya Protectorate, a coastal strip about ten miles wide owned by the Sultan of Zanzibar and leased to the British. The tiny Witu Protectorate was also included. The name British East Africa continued in use as a geographical term. Kenya became independent on 1963-12-12.

Other names of country: Jamhuri ya Kenya (formal); Kenia (Finnish, German, Italian, Spanish); Kenía (Icelandic); Quênia (Portuguese); Republic of Kenya (formal–English).

Origin of name: after Mount Kenya.

division	abv	ISO	FIPS	population	area-km	area-mi	capital
Central	CE	200	KE01	2,345,833	13,191	5,093	Nyeri
Coast	CO	300	KE02	1,342,794	83,603	32,279	Mombasa
Eastern	EA	400	KE03	2,719,851	159,891	61,734	Embu
Nairobi Area	NA	110	KE05	827,775	684	264	Nairobi
North-Eastern	NE	500	KE06	373,787	126,902	48,997	Garissa
Nyanza	NY	600	KE07	2,643,956	16,162	6,240	Kisumu
Rift Valley	RV	700	KE08	3,240,402	173,854	67,125	Nakuru
Western	WE	900	KE09	1,832,663	8,361	3,228	Kakamega
				15,327,061	582,648	224,960	

Status: These divisions are provinces, except for Nairobi, which is an "area."

Abv: Two-letter code for international compatibility (defined by the author).

ISO: Codes from ISO 3166-2.

FIPS: Codes from FIPS PUB 10-4.

Population: 1991 census.

Area-km: Square kilometers.

Area-mi: Square miles.

Further subdivisions: The provinces are subdivided into 40 districts.

Territorial extent: Coast includes all the islands along Kenya's coast, such as Funzi, Wasini (Shimoni), and the Lamu Archipelago (Lamu, Pate, Manda, and others).

There are three sizable islands in Lake Turkana. North Island is entirely within Rift Valley, South Island is entirely within Eastern, and Central Island is split between the two.

Origins of names:

Nairobi: Masai for the cool place

Rift Valley: contains the Kenyan section of the Great Rift

Change history:

1925-06-29	Transjuba (everything west of the Juba River in modern Somalia) transferred from Kenya to Italian Somaliland.
~1933	Land west of Lake Rudolf (now Lake Turkana) transferred from Uganda to Kenya.
~1955	Name of Masai District changed to Nairobi District. Southern province formed.
~1965	Northern and Southern provinces replaced by Eastern and North-Eastern. Western province formed.

Other names of subdivisions:

Nairobi: Federal Area, Nairobi District (variant); Masai District (obsolete)

KIRIBATI

ISO = KI/FIPS = KR   Language = English, Gilbertese   Time zone = (see table)   Capital = Tarawa

The British Empire acquired the islands composing this country over the years, a few at a time, as protectorates. On 1915-11-12 a colony was created, under the name of Gilbert and Ellice Islands. As time went by, the colony was augmented by the Phoenix Islands, the Union Islands, and the Line Islands. The Union Islands were offered to New Zealand. On 1926-02-11, New Zealand took over their administration. On 1949-01-01 they became an overseas territory of New Zealand under the name of Tokelau Islands. Due to a territorial dispute, the United States and the United Kingdom agreed to form a condominium of Canton and Enderbury Islands on 1939-04-06. The Gilbert and Ellice Islands were occupied by Japan during World War II. On 1975-10-01, the Ellice Islands broke off as a separate country, Tuvalu. The remaining territory was renamed the Gilbert Islands. It became independent and took the name Kiribati on 1979-07-12. Shortly afterward, the United States renounced its claim to Canton, Enderbury, and other islands in the Phoenix and Line groups.

Other names of country: Gilbert Islands (obsolete); Kíribatí (Icelandic); Republic of Kiribati (formal–English).

Origin of name: Gilbertese form of Gilbert[Island]s, for Joseph Gilbert, ship captain.

division	abv	ISO	FIPS	tz	population	area-km	area-mi
Gilbert Islands	GI	G	KR01	+12	61,539	300	116
Line Islands	LI	L	KR02	+14	2,598	329	127
Phoenix Islands	PI	P	KR03	+13	24	55	21
					64,161	684	264

Status: These divisions are island groups. They have no administrative function, but serve as a convenient geographical subdivision of Kiribati.

Abv: Two-letter code for international compatibility (defined by the author).

ISO: Codes from ISO 3166-2.

FIPS: Codes from FIPS PUB 10-4.

Tz: Time zone (number of hours by which local time is ahead of GMT).

Population: 1985 census.

Area-km: Square kilometers.

Area-mi: Square miles.

Territorial extent: The sequence of groups from west to east and their approximate limits of longitude is Gilbert, 180°, Phoenix, 165° W., Line.

The Gilbert Islands include Tarawa, Tabiteuea, Abaiang, Butaritari, Abemama, Nonouti, Beru, Marakei, Nukunau (Nikunau), Maiana, Onotoa, Makin, Arorae, Tamana, Kuria, Aranuka, and Banaba (Ocean).

The Line Islands include Kiritimati (Christmas), Tabuaeran (Fanning), Teraina (Washington), Starbuck, Caroline, Vostok, Malden, and Flint.

The Phoenix Islands include Kanton (Canton, Abariringa), Enderbury, Rawaki (Phoenix), McKean, Nikumaroro (Gardner), Orona (Hull), Manra (Sydney), and Birnie.

KOREA, NORTH

ISO = KP/FIPS = KN   Language = Korean   Time zone = +9   Capital = P'yongyang

In 1900, Korea had only recently come out from under Chinese hegemony, and was soon to submit to that of Japan. It became a Japanese protectorate in 1905-12, then a colony on 1910-08-22. At the end of World War II, the Soviet Union and the United States agreed to partition Korea at the 38th parallel, with the Soviet Army occupying the north and the U.S. the south. This arrangement was intended to last only until a democratic government could be set up for a united Korea. Instead, the communist north invaded the south in 1950, and the Korean War ensued. It was fought to a standoff. On 1953-07-27, an armistice was signed. North and South Korea were to be separated by a demilitarized zone about a kilometer wide, running near the 38th parallel across the peninsula.

Other names of country: Chosun Minchu-chui Inmin Konghwa-guk (formal); Corea del Nord (Italian); Corea del Norte (Spanish); Corée du Nord (French); Coréia do Norte (Portuguese); Democratic People's Republic of Korea (formal–English); Demokratische Volksrepublik Korea (German); Noord Korea (Dutch); Nord-Korea (Norwegian); Nordkorea (Danish, Swedish); Norður-Kórea (Icelandic); Pohjois-Korea (Finnish); República Popular Democrática de Corea (formal–Spanish); République populaire démocratique de Corée (formal–French).

Origin of name: Korean *koryo*, dynastic name, meaning high serenity.

division	abv	ISO	FIPS	population	area-km	area-mi	capital
Chagang-do	CH	CHA	KN01	780,000	16,050	6,200	Kanggye
Hamgyŏng-bukto	HB	HAB	KN16	1,495,000	17,600	6,800	Ch'ŏngjin
Hamgyŏng-namdo	HN	HAN	KN03	1,845,000	19,800	7,600	Hamhŭng
Hwanghae-bukto	WB	HWB	KN07	1,060,000	8,550	3,300	Sariwŏn
Hwanghae-namdo	WN	HWN	KN06	1,340,000	7,500	2,900	Haeju
Kaesŏng-si	KS	KAE	KN08	289,000	1,200	500	Kaesŏng
Kangwŏn-do	KW	KAN	KN09	1,030,000	10,600	4,100	Wŏnsan
Namp'o-si	NP	NAM	KN14	—	—	—	Namp'o
P'yŏngan-bukto	PB	PYB	KN11	1,760,000	11,900	4,600	Sinŭiju
P'yŏngan-namdo	PN	PYN	KN15	2,250,000	12,200	4,700	P'yŏngsŏng
P'yŏngyang-si	PY	PYO	KN12	1,275,000	1,800	700	P'yŏngyang
Yanggang-do	YG	YAN	KN13	435,000	14,000	5,400	Hyesan
				13,559,000	121,200	46,800	

Status: These divisions are do (provinces) and si (special cities). The final syllable of the name tells which type each division is. After "buk" (north), the -do changes to -to by assimilation. (Nam = south.)

Abv: Two-letter code for international compatibility (defined by the author).

ISO: Codes from ISO 3166-2.

FIPS: Codes from FIPS PUB 10-4.

Population: 1968 estimate.

Area-km: Square kilometers.

Area-mi: Square miles.

Further subdivisions: The provinces are further subdivided into 152 gun (counties).

Territorial extent: (The included entities ending in -do or -to are all islands.)

Hamgyŏng-namdo includes Mayang-do
Hwanghae-bukto included Kaesŏng-si before it became a special city.
Hwanghae-namdo includes Ch'o-do, Sŏk-to, Sunwi-do, and some other small islands along the Kyonggi-man
Kangwŏn-do includes Yŏ-do
P'yŏngan-bukto includes Sinmi-do, Sin-do, and Ka-do
P'yŏngan-namdo included Namp'o-si and P'yŏngyang-si before they became special cities.
Origins of names:

Hwanghae: named for the Hwanghae (Yellow Sea)

Change history:

See South Korea for provinces of the Japanese colonial period.
- ~1980   Chongjin-si special city split from Hamgyŏng-bukto province.
- ~1981   Hamhŭng-si special city split from Hamgyŏng-namdo province for a short time, then merged with it again.
- ~1988   Namp'o-si special city split from P'yŏngan-namdo (KN10 changed to KN15 to reflect the partition).
- ~1990   Chongjin-si special city (KN02) merged with Hamgyŏng-bukto province (KN04 changed to KN17 to reflect the acquisition).

Other names of subdivisions: During the period of Japanese rule, Japanese names for the cities and provinces were in use. Some Korean phonemes are variously transliterated; for example, the Roman letters b and p are particularly likely to be interchanged. Therefore, -bukto is often spelled -pukto.

Chagang-do: Jagang (variant)
Hamgyŏng-bukto: Kankyo Hoku-do (Japanese); North Hamgyong (variant)
Hamgyŏng-namdo: Kankyo Nan-do (Japanese); South Hamgyong (variant)
Hwanghae-bukto: North Hwanghae, North Hwanghai (variant)
Hwanghae-namdo: South Hwanghae, South Hwanghai (variant)

Kaesŏng-si: Kaesŏng-chigu (variant)
Kangwŏn-do: Kogen-do (Japanese); North Kangwon (variant)
P'yŏngan-bukto: Heian Hoku-do (Japanese); North Pyongan (variant)
P'yŏngan-namdo: Heian Nan-do (Japanese); South Pyongan (variant)
P'yŏngyang-si: Pjöngjang (German); P'yŏngyang-tŭkpyŏlsi (variant)

KOREA, SOUTH

ISO = KR/FIPS = KS   Language = Korean   Time zone = +9   Capital = Seoul

See North Korea for a history of the Korean peninsula's territorial division during the 20th century.
Other names of country: Corea del Sud (Italian); Corea del Sur (Spanish); Corée du Sud (French); Coréia do Sul (Portuguese); Daehan Min-kuk (formal); Etelä-Korea (Finnish); República de Corea (formal–Spanish); Republic of Korea (formal–English); Republik Korea, Südkorea (German); République de Corée (formal–French); Sør-Korea (Norwegian); Suður-Kórea (Icelandic); Sydkorea (Danish, Swedish); Zuid Korea (Dutch).
Origin of name: Korean *koryo*, dynastic name, meaning high serenity.

division	abv	ISO	FIPS	population	area-km	area-mi	capital	post
Cheju-do	CJ	15	KS01	514,605	1,826	705	Cheju	6
Chŏlla-bukto	CB	12	KS03	2,069,960	8,044	3,106	Chŏnju	5
Chŏlla-namdo	CN	13	KS16	2,507,439	11,818	4,563	Kwangju	5
Ch'ungch'ŏng-bukto	GB	06	KS05	1,389,686	7,436	2,871	Ch'ŏngju	3
Ch'ungch'ŏng-namdo	GN	04	KS17	2,013,926	8,319	3,212	Taejŏn	3 ➤

division	abv	ISO	FIPS	population	area-km	area-mi	capital	post
Inch'ŏn-jikhalsi	IN	07	KS12	1,817,919	335	129	Inch'ŏn	4
Kangwŏn-do	KW	03	KS06	1,580,430	16,898	6,524	Ch'unch'ŏn	2
Kwangju-jikhalsi	KJ	14	KS18	1,139,003	501	193	Kwangju	5
Kyŏnggi-do	KG	02	KS13	6,155,632	10,773	4,159	Suwŏn	4
Kyŏngsang-bukto	KB	08	KS14	2,860,595	19,447	7,509	Taegu	7
Kyŏngsang-namdo	KN	10	KS08	3,672,396	11,776	4,547	Ch'angwŏn	6
Pusan-jikhalsi	PU	11	KS10	3,798,113	529	204	Pusan	6
Soul-t'ŭkpyŏlsi	SO	01	KS11	10,612,577	605	234	Seoul	1
Taegu-jikhalsi	TG	09	KS15	2,229,040	456	176	Taegu	7
Taejŏn-jikhalsi	TJ	05	KS19	1,049,578	537	207	Taejŏn	3
				43,410,899	99,300	38,339		

Status: These divisions are do (provinces) and si (special cities). The final syllable of the name tells which type each division is. After "buk" (north), the -do changes to -to by assimilation. (Nam = south.)

Abv: Two-letter code for international compatibility (defined by the author).

ISO: Codes from ISO 3166-2.

FIPS: Codes from FIPS PUB 10-4.

Population: 1990 census.

Area-km: Square kilometers.

Area-mi: Square miles.

Postal codes: Korea uses six-digit postal codes, with a hyphen separating the first three digits from the last three. The first digit is determined by the province or city, as shown.

Further subdivisions: The provinces are subdivided into over 200 gun (counties) and shi (cities).

Territorial extent: Cheju-do is an island, formerly known to westerners as Quelpart, off the southern tip of the Korean Peninsula. It also includes the Ch'uja-kundo island group, whose largest island is Hach'uja-do, and the islands of Kap'a-do and Mara-do.

Chŏlla-bukto includes the islands of Wi-do, Ŏch'ŏng-do, Sŏnyu-do, and many more.

Chŏlla-namdo included Kwangju, now an enclave, before it became a special city. It includes the Hŭksan-chedo island group, of which Taehŭksan-do, Sohŭksan-do, and Hongdo are the largest; and an archipelago of coastal islands. The largest is Chin-do, and there are many others of considerable size. They extend as far north as Anma-do, and as far east as the Kŭmo-yŏlto group, containing Kŭmo-do.

Ch'ungch'ŏng-namdo included Taejŏn before it became a special city. It includes the islands of Wonsan-do, Sapshi-do, Taenanji-do, and many islets; the westernmost is Sogyŏngnyŏlbi-do.

Inch'ŏn-jikhalsi includes the islands of Yŏngjong-do, Yongyu-do, Muŭi-do, and Sammok-to.

Kangwŏn-do includes the fairly remote island of Ullŭng-do, long ago called Dagelet Island.

Kyŏnggi-do included Inch'ŏn and Soul (Seoul), now an enclave, before they became special cities. It includes the Tŏkchŏk-kundo island group, some of whose largest islands are Tŏkchŏk-to, Mungap-to, Soya-do, Chawol-to, and Paega-do; Paengnyŏng-do, Taech'ŏng-do, and Soch'ŏng-do, known long ago as the Sir James Hall Group; the Yŏnp'yŏng-yŏlto group; and many other islands, such as Kanghwa-do, Kyodong-do, Sŏngmo-do, Taebu-do, Yŏnghŭng-do, Polŭm-do, Chumun-do, Changbong-do, and Shin-do.

Kyŏngsang-bukto included Taegu, now an enclave, before it became a special city.

Kyŏngsang-namdo included Pusan before it became a special city. It includes the large coastal islands of Kŏje-do, Namhae-do (the westernmost), Ch'angsŏn-do, and Mirŭk-to, and many smaller ones.

Pusan-jikhalsi includes the islands of Yong-do and Ulsuk-to.

Origins of names:

Cheju: Korean *che*: end, *chu*: province, *do*: island

Inch'on: Korean *in*: virtue, *ch'on*: river

Seoul: Korean for capital, prince's residence

Change history: Until its liberation from Japan in 1945, Korea was a single country, divided into these provinces:

province	Japanese name	population	area-km	now in	capital
North Cholla	Zenra Hoku-do	1,535,827	8,550	South	Zenshu (Chŏnju)
South Cholla	Zenra Nan-do	2,409,602	13,882	South	Koshu
North Chungchung	Chusei Hoku-do	913,407	7,415	South	Seishu
South Chungchung	Chusei Nan-do	1,469,640	8,104	South	Taiden ➤

province	Japanese name	population	area-km	now in	capital
North Hamgyong	Kankyo Hoku-do	792,293	20,342	North	Ranan
South Hamgyong	Kankyo Nan-do	1,603,335	31,971	North	Kanko (Hamhŭng)
Hwanghae	Kokai-do	1,619,718	16,739	North	Kaishu
Kangwon	Kogen-do	1,529,357	26,257	both	Shunsen (Ch'unch'ŏn)
Kyunggi	Keiki-do	2,330,570	12,818	South	Keijo (Seoul)
North Kyungsang	Keisho Hoku-do	2,469,103	18,985	South	Taikyu (Taegu)
South Kyungsang	Keisho Nan-do	2,191,512	12,302	South	Fusan (Pusan)
North Pyongan	Heian Hoku-do	1,617,785	28,433	North	Shingishu (Sinŭiju)
South Pyongan	Heian Nan-do	1,409,031	14,934	North	Heijo
		21,891,180	220,732		

Population: 1935 census.
Now in: Country (North or South Korea) containing the successor to this province.
Capital: Japanese names of capitals (followed by Korean names, where available).

- ~1952 Soul-t'ŭkpyŏlsi split from Kyŏnggi-do.
- ~1964 Pusan-jikhalsi split from Kyŏngsang-namdo.
- 1985 Inch'ŏn-jikhalsi split from Kyŏnggi-do (coded KS07 before change); Taegu-jikhalsi split from Kyŏngsang-bukto (KS09).
- ~1990 Kwangju-jikhalsi split from Cholla-namdo (KS02); Taejŏn-jikhalsi split from Ch'ungch'ŏng-namdo (KS04).
- ~1994 Capital of Kyongsang-namdo moved from Ch'angwon to Pusan.

Other names of subdivisions: During the period of Japanese rule, Japanese names for the cities and provinces were in use. Some Korean phonemes are variously transliterated; for example, the Roman letters b and p are particularly likely to be interchanged. Therefore, -bukto is often spelled -pukto.

Cheju-do: Quelpart (obsolete)
Chŏlla-bukto: North Cholla (variant); Zenra Hoku-do (Japanese)
Chŏlla-namdo: South Cholla (variant); Zenra Nan-do (Japanese)
Ch'ungch'ŏng-bukto: Chusei Hoku-do (Japanese); North Chungchung (variant)
Ch'ungch'ŏng-namdo: Chusei Nan-do (Japanese); South Chungchung (variant)
Kangwŏn-do: Kogen-do (Japanese); South Kangwon (variant)

Kyŏnggi-do: Keiki-do (Japanese); Kyunggi (variant)
Kyŏngsang-bukto: Keisho Hoku-do (Japanese); North Kyungsang (variant)
Kyŏngsang-namdo: Keisho Nan-do (Japanese); South Kyungsang (variant)
Pusan-jikhalsi: Busan-chikalsi (variant)
Soul-t'ŭkpyŏlsi: Seoul (variant); Séoul (French); Seul (Italian, Portuguese); Seúl (Spanish); Söul (variant-German, Norwegian)

KUWAIT

ISO = KW/FIPS = KU   Language = Arabic   Time zone = +3   Capital = Kuwait

Kuwait was under British protection from 1899 to 1961-06-19, when it became fully independent. It was invaded by Iraq on 1990-08-08, but the annexation was never internationally recognized, and it was liberated again on 1991-02-26.
Other names of country: Dowlat al-Kuwait (formal); Koeweit (Dutch); Koweït (French); Kúveit (Icelandic); State of Kuwait (formal-English).
Origin of name: Arabic al-Kuwait, a diminutive form of kut: fort.

division	ISO	FIPS	population	area-km	area-mi	capital
Al Aḥmadi	AH	KU04	304,662	4,665	1,801	Al Aḥmadi ➤

division	ISO	FIPS	population	area-km	area-mi	capital
Al Farwānīyah	FA	KU06	— —	— —	— —	Al Farwānīyah
Al Jahrah	JA	KU05	279,466	11,550	4,459	Al Jahrah
Al Kuwayt	KU	KU02	167,750	983	380	Kuwait
Ḥawallī	HA	KU03	943,250	620	239	Ḥawallī
			1,695,128	17,818	6,879	

Status: These divisions are muhafazat (sing. muhafazah: provinces).
ISO: Codes from ISO 3166-2.
FIPS: Codes from FIPS PUB 10-4.
Population: 1985 census.
Area-km: Square kilometers.
Area-mi: Square miles.
Territorial extent: Al Jahrah includes Bubiyan and Warbah Islands.
Al Kuwayt includes Faylakah, Maskan, and Awhah Islands.
Change history:

1969-12   Kuwait took over administration of the northern half of the Kuwait-Saudi Arabia Neutral Zone.
~1986   Al Jahrah province split from Al Kuwayt (formerly FIPS = KU01).
1988   Al Farwānīyah province split from Al Kuwayt.

Other names of subdivisions:

Al Farwānīyah: Farwaniya (variant)
Ḥawallī: Hawali, Howali (variant)

Al Jahrah: Jahra (variant)
Al Kuwayt: Al Asimah, Capital, Kuwait (variant)

KYRGYZSTAN

ISO = KG/FIPS = KG   Language = Kirghiz   Time zone = +5 [d]   Capital = Bishkek

Under the Russian Empire, Kyrgyzstan was in the eastern part of the governor-generalship of Turkestan. During the Russian Revolution, the status of the Central Asian lands was unresolved for a time. The Turkestan A.S.S.R. was formed in 1921. In 1924, the Central Asian part of the Soviet Union was reorganized to correspond to the distribution of nationalities. The Kara-Kirghizskaya Autonomous Oblast was created then, on 1924-10-14. In subsequent changes, it became the Kirghizskaya Associated Soviet Socialist Republic on 1926-02-01; the Kirghizskaya Soviet Socialist Republic, one of the fifteen constituent republics of the U.S.S.R., on 1936-12-05; and finally, Kyrgyzstan, an independent country, on 1991-08-31, with the collapse of the Soviet Union.

Other names of country: Kirghizie, Kirguizie, Kirguizistan (French); Khirghizistan (French, Italian); Kirgiezië (Dutch); Kirgisia (Finnish); Kirgisistan (Danish, German, Icelandic, Norwegian); Kirgizistan (Swedish); Kirguistán (Spanish); Kyrgyz Respublikasy (formal); Quirguízia (Portuguese); Republic of Kyrgyzstan (formal–English).

Origin of name: land of the Kirghiz, ethnic name from Turkish *kir*: steppe, *gis*: nomad.

division	abv	ISO	FIPS	population	area-km	area-mi	capital
Chüy	CH	C	KG02	790,600	18,684	7,214	Bishkek
Jalal-Abad	DA	D	KG03	800,200	33,648	12,991	Jalal-Abad
Naryn	NA	I	KG04	263,200	46,707	18,034	Naryn
Osh	OS	N	KG05	1,353,800	46,189	17,834	Osh
Talas	TL	O	KG06	201,800	11,446	4,419	Talas
Ysyk-Köl	YK	T	KG07	428,800	43,144	16,658	Karakol
				3,838,400	199,818	77,150	

Status: These divisions are oblasty (regions). Some sources say that Bishkek is also an independent city with oblast status. FIPS even assigns it the code KG01. My best information is that Bishkek is merely part of Chüy oblast.

Abv: Two-letter code for international compatibility (defined by the author).
ISO: Codes from ISO 3166-2.
FIPS: Codes from FIPS PUB 10-4.
Population: 1997 estimate.
Area-km: Square kilometers.
Area-mi: Square miles.
Further subdivisions: The regions are divided into rayony (districts). There were a total of 43 districts in 1994-08.
Origins of names:

Issyk-Kul: from Lake Issyk-Kul, from Kirghiz *ysyk*: hot, *köl*: lake

Change history:

1921-04-11	Turkestan A.S.S.R. formed from Amu-Darya, Ferghana, Pamir, Samarkand, Semi-rechensk, and Syr Darya regions, and the southern part of Transcaspian.
1924-10-14	Kara-Kirghizskaya autonomous region, consisting of parts of Ferghana, Semirechensk, and Syr Darya, separated from Turkestan and became part of the Russian S.F.S.R.
1925	Name of capital of region changed from Pishpek to Frunze.
1926-02-01	Status and name of Kara-Kirghizia changed to Kirghizskaya A.S.S.R.
1936-12-05	Status of Kirghizia changed to S.S.R.
1950	The regions of the Kirghizskaya Sovyetskaya Sotsialisticheskaya Respublika were Dzha-lal-Abad, Frunze (modern Chüy), Issyk-Kul', Osh, Talas, and Tien-Shan (modern Naryn). The borders were similar to the modern ones, differing only in sparsely inhabited regions.
~1953	Talas region merged with Frunze.
~1959	Dzhalal-Abad region merged with Osh; Frunze and Issyk-Kul' merged with Tien-Shan.
~1969	Frunze region, consisting approximately of modern Chüy, Talas, and Ysyk-Köl, split from Tien-Shan.
~1973	Tien-Shan region split into Naryn and Issyk-Kul'.
~1981	Talas region split from Frunze.
~1990	Dzhalal-Abad region formed from parts of Osh and Talas.
1991-02	Capital of Kyrgyzstan, and of Chüy region, renamed from Frunze to Bishkek.
1991-08-31	Kirghizstan became an independent country. Westerners began to use the Kirghiz, rather than the Russian, version of place names (e.g., Kyrgyzstan).

Other names of subdivisions: Before the dissolution of the Soviet Union, western sources normally used transliterations from Russian names rather than Kirghiz names. There are various methods for transliterating from the Cyrillic to the Roman alphabet. The most common variant uses h instead of kh, c for ts, j for consonantal y, č for ch, š for sh, and ž for zh.

Chüy: Chu (variant); Frunze (obsolete)
Jalal-Abad: Djalal-Abad, Dzhalal-Abadskaya Oblast' (Russian)

Naryn: Tien-Shanskaya Oblast', Tyan'-Shan' (Russian)
Ysyk-Köl: Issyk-Kul'skaya Oblast' (Russian)

LAOS

ISO = LA/FIPS = LA   Language = Lao, French   Time zone = +7   Capital = Luang Prabang

Laos was a French colony at the start of the 20th century. It was a union of two former kingdoms, Luang Prabang and Vientiane. The French administered it as a territory within the protectorate of French Indo-China. After World War II, French Indo-China was divided up into three independent countries within the French Union: Cambodia, Laos (independent on 1949-07-19), and Vietnam. See Cambodia for related information.

Other names of country: Demokratische Volksrepublik Laos (German); Lanxang (obsolete); Lao People's Democratic

Republic (formal–English); República Democrática Popular Lao (Spanish); République démocratique populaire Lao (French); Saathiaranarath Prachhathipatay Prachhachhon Lao (formal).

Origin of name: ethnic name Lao, applied by Portuguese explorers in the plural.

division	ISO	FIPS	population	area-km	area-mi	capital
Attapu	AT	LA01	99,000	11,900	4,600	Attapu
Bokeo	BK	LA22	142,000	12,900	5,000	Ban Houayxay
Bolikhamxai	BL	LA23	51,000	6,200	2,400	Muang Pakxan
Champasak	CH	LA02	316,000	14,500	5,600	Pakxé
Houaphan	HO	LA03	211,000	16,300	6,300	Xam Nua
Khammouan	KH	LA15	259,000	26,400	10,200	Muang Khammouan
Louang Namtha	LM	LA16	——	——	——	Louang Namtha
Louangphrabang	LP	LA06	450,000	37,200	14,400	Louangphrabang
Oudômxai	OU	LA07	——	——	——	Muang Xay
Phôngsali	PH	LA08	127,000	15,800	6,100	Phôngsali
Saravan	SL	LA09	288,000	21,600	8,300	Saravan
Savannakhét	SV	LA10	456,000	21,700	8,400	Savannakhét
Vientiane	VI	LA11	351,000	14,400	5,600	Muang Phôn-Hông
Vientiane [prefecture]	VT	LA24	——	——	——	Vientiane
Xaignabouri	XA	LA13	213,000	18,400	7,100	Muang Xaignabouri
Xékong	XE	LA26	——	——	——	Lamam
Xiangkhoang	XI	LA14	218,000	19,500	7,500	Xiangkhoang
			3,181,000	236,800	91,500	

Status: These divisions are khoueng (provinces), except for the second Vientiane, which is a kampeng nakhon (municipality or prefecture).

ISO: Codes from ISO 3166-2.

FIPS: Codes from FIPS PUB 10-4.

Population: 1973 estimate.

Area-km: Square kilometers.

Area-mi: Square miles.

Capitals: Muang = town and Ban = village are usually included as part of the capital names shown.

Further subdivisions: The provinces are further subdivided into muong (districts).

Origins of names:

Vientiane: Lao *vieng*: city, *chan*: sandalwood

Change history:

1904   Two Siamese (Thai) provinces, corresponding to modern Xaignabouri and parts of Louangphrabang and Vientiane, annexed to Laos. Stœng Trêng province transferred from Laos to Cambodge.

1941   The same provinces were restored to Thailand under pressure from Japan.

1947   The same provinces reverted to Laos as pre-war boundaries were restored.

1966   Name of Nam Tha province changed to Houakhong.

~1976   (Capitals in parentheses.) Name of Houakhong province changed back to Louang Namtha; Borikhan province (Muang Pakxan) merged with Vientiane; Xédôn (Pakxé) and Sithandon (Muang Khong) provinces merged with Champasak (Champasak); Vapikhamthong province (Muang Khôngxédôn) merged with Saravan; Oudômxai province split from Louangphrabang; name of capital of Khammouan province changed from Thakhek to Muang Khammouan. At about this time, Xaignabouri was temporarily split into three parts: Hôngxa (Muang Hôngxa), Paklay (Muang Paklay), and Xaignabouri; and Savannakhét was temporarily split into two parts: Champhon (Ban Kengkok) and Savannakhét.

1983   Bokeo province split from Louang Namtha (formerly FIPS = LA05); Bolikhamxai province formed from parts of Khammouan (LA04) and Vientiane (LA11) provinces; Xékong province split from Saravan (LA09).

~1987   Capital of Oudômxai province moved from Ban Nahin to Muang Xay.

~1989   Vientiane prefecture split from Vientiane province; capital of Vientiane province moved from
           Vientiane to Muang Phôn-Hông.
~1997   Recent FIPS list indicates that a khetphiset (special zone) named Xaisomboun was created.

Other names of subdivisions: In transcription from Lao, some sources break names at syllable endings (e.g. Boli Kham Xai).

Attapu: Atpu, Attapeu, Attopeu, Muang Mai (variant)
Bolikhamxai: Bolikhamsai (variant); Borikane, Borikhan (obsolete)
Champasak: Bassac, Champassak (variant); Champassac, Khong, Pakse (French)
Houaphan: Hua Phan (variant); Sam Neua, Xam Nua (obsolete)
Khammouan: Khammouane, Khammuan (variant)
Louang Namtha: Haut-Mekong (French-obsolete); Muong Luang Namtha, Namtha (variant); Hiuakhong, Houa Khong, Upper Mekong (obsolete)

Louangphrabang: Loang Prabang, Luang Phabang, Luang Prabang (variant)
Phôngsali: Fong Sali, Phong Saly (variant)
Saravan: Salavan, Saravane (variant)
Savannakhét: Svannakhet (variant)
Vientiane: Viangchan (variant)
Vientiane [prefecture]: Kamphaeng Nakhon Viang Chan (formal)
Xaignabouri: Sayaboury, Xaignabouli (variant)
Xékong: Sekong (variant)
Xiangkhoang: Xieng Khouang, Xieng Khwang (variant)

LATVIA

ISO = LV/FIPS = LG   Language = Latvian   Time zone = +2 [d]   Capital = Riga

Latvia in 1900 was part of the Russian Empire. On 1918-11-18, it declared its independence, with essentially its present borders. Latvia was occupied by the army of the Soviet Union in 1940, and became a constituent republic of the U.S.S.R., the Latvian Soviet Socialist Republic, on 1940-08-05. The United States never recognized the annexation. Latvia declared independence again, this time from a crumbling Soviet Union, on 1991-08-21.

Other names of country: Latvija (Latvian); Latvijas Republika (formal); Letland (Dutch); Letonia (Spanish); Letônia (Portuguese); Lettland (Danish, German, Icelandic, Swedish); Lettonia (Italian); Lettonie (French); Republic of Latvia (formal-English).

Origin of name: Old Lithuanian *latu*: muddy.

division	ISO	FIPS	post	province	division	ISO	FIPS	post	province
Aizkraukle	AI	LG01	51	Zemgale	Limbaži	LM	LG18	40	Vidzeme
Alūksne	AL	LG02	43	Vidzeme	Ludza	LU	LG19	57	Latgale
Balvi	BL	LG03	45	Latgale	Madona	MA	LG20	48	Vidzeme
Bauska	BU	LG04	39	Zemgale	Ogre	OG	LG21	50	Vidzeme
Cēsis	CE	LG05	41	Vidzeme	Preiļi	PR	LG22	53	Latgale
Daugavpils	DA	LG07	54	Zemgale	Rēzekne	RE	LG24	46	Latgale
Dobele	DO	LG08	37	Kurzeme	Rīga	RI	LG26	1x,2x	Riga, Vidzeme
Gulbene	GU	LG09	44	Vidzeme	Saldus	SA	LG27	38	Kurzeme
Jēkabpils	JL	LG10	52	Zemgale	Talsi	TA	LG28	32	Kurzeme
Jelgava	JK	LG12	30	Zemgale	Tukums	TU	LG29	31	Kurzeme
Krāslava	KR	LG14	56	Latgale	Valka	VK	LG30	47	Vidzeme
Kuldīga	KU	LG15	33	Kurzeme	Valmiera	VM	LG31	42	Vidzeme
Liepāja	LE	LG17	34	Kurzeme	Ventspils	VE	LG33	36	Kurzeme

Status: These divisions are rajoni (districts).
ISO: Codes from ISO 3166-2.
FIPS: Codes from FIPS PUB 10-4. Note: the lists in ISO 3166-2 and FIPS also mention seven cities. The cities are all located in the districts of the same name, except for Jūrmala, which is in Rīga district.

city	ISO	FIPS	city	ISO	FIPS
Daugavpils	DGV	LG06	Rēzekne	REZ	LG23
Jelgava	JEL	LG11	Rīga	RIX	LG25
Jūrmala	JUR	LG13	Ventspils	VEN	LG32
Liepāja	LPX	LG16			

Postal code: First two digits of postal code. Latvian postal codes have four digits. "LV-" is prefixed to the postal code on correspondence from other countries.

Province: Approximate location of district within pre-war provinces.

Origins of names:

Daugavpils: Latvian *Daugava*: Western Dvina (river), *pils*: palace

Riga: possibly Old Lithuanian *ringi*: curve (in the river)

Change history:

1900 Present-day Latvia was in three Russian governments (guberniy): the southern part of Livonia, almost all of Courland (Kurland, Kurzeme), and the western part of Vitebsk.

1918 Latvia was subdivided into provinces corresponding to its traditional regions.

province	population	area-km	province	population	area-km
Kurzeme	292,659	5,099	Vidzeme	406,247	8,905
Latgale	567,164	6,052	Zemgale	299,369	5,258
Riga	385,063	81		1,950,502	25,395

Population: 1935 census.

Other names of subdivisions:

Aizkraukle: Stuchka (Russian-obsolete)
Cēsis: Wenden (German)
Daugavpils: Dünaburg (German); Dvinsk (Russian-obsolete)
Jelgava: Mitau (German)
Jēkabpils: Jakobstadt (German)
Kuldīga: Goldingen (German)
Liepāja: Libau (German)

Ludza: Ludsen (German)
Rēzekne: Rositten (German); Ryezhitsa (Russian-obsolete)
Talsi: Talsen (German)
Tukums: Tukkum (German)
Valmiera: Wolmar (German)
Ventspils: Windau (German)

LEBANON

ISO = LB/FIPS = LE   Language = Arabic, French   Time zone = +2 ^{d} Capital = Beirut

In 1900, the present area of Lebanon was part of the Ottoman Empire. At the end of World War I, Britain and France partitioned the empire. Lebanon was created as a French mandate. Although it was referred to as the Republic of Lebanon, it was adminstratively subordinate to Syria. It became effectively independent from France on 1944-01-01.

Other names of country: al-Jumhouriya al-Lubnaniya (formal); Liban (French); Libano (Italian); Líbano (Portuguese, Spanish); Libanon (Danish, Dutch, Finnish, German, Norwegian, Swedish); Líbanon (Icelandic); República Libanesa (formal–Spanish); Republic of Lebanon (formal–English).

Origin of name: from Semitic word for white.

division	ISO	FIPS	population	area-km	area-mi	capital	Arabic name
An Nabaṭīyah	NA		203,607	1,058	408	An Nabaṭīyah at Tahtā	An Nabaṭīyah
Beirut	BA	LE04	298,129	18	7	Bayrūt (Beirut)	Bayrūt
Beqaa	BI	LE01	320,967	4,280	1,653	Zaḥlah	Al Biqaʿ ➤

division	ISO	FIPS	population	area-km	area-mi	capital	Arabic name
Mount Lebanon	JL	LE05	622,284	1,950	753	B'abdā	Jabal Lubnān
North Lebanon	AS	LE03	506,079	1,981	765	Ṭarābulus (Tripoli)	Ash Shamāl
South Lebanon	JA	LE02	200,818	943	364	Ṣaydā (Sidon)	Al Janūb
			2,151,884	10,230	3,950		

Status: These divisions are muhafazat (sing. muhafazah: provinces).
ISO: Codes from ISO 3166-2.
FIPS: Codes from FIPS PUB 10-4.
Population: 1991 census.
Area-km: Square kilometers.
Area-mi: Square miles.
Arabic name: Name of the province transliterated from Arabic.
Further subdivisions: The provinces are further subdivided into districts.
Origins of names:

Beqaa: Arabic *al-biqa'*: fields

Beirut: From Hebrew *be'erot*: the wells

Change history:

1920-09-01   Following the Treaty of Sèvres, where France was given a mandate over the area, the state of Great Lebanon was formed from parts of Beirut and Lebanon vilayets of the Ottoman Empire.

1975   An Nabaṭīyah province split from al-Janūb.

Other names of subdivisions:

Beirut: Beirute (Portuguese); Beyrouth (French)
Beqaa: Bekaa, El Begaa (variant)

South Lebanon: Sayda (variant)

LESOTHO

ISO = LS/FIPS = LT   Language = Sesotho, English   Time zone = +2   Capital = Maseru

Basutoland was a British protectorate for the first part of the 20th century. On 1966-10-04, it became independent under the name of Lesotho.

Other names of country: Basutoland (obsolete); Basutia, Basutolandia (obsolete–Spanish); Kingdom of Lesotho (formal–English); Lesoto (Portuguese); Lesótó (Icelandic).

Origin of name: Land of the Sothos.

division	abv	ISO	FIPS	population	area-km	area-mi
Berea	BE	D	LT10	194,600	2,222	858
Butha-Buthe	BB	B	LT11	100,600	1,767	682
Leribe	LE	C	LT12	258,000	2,828	1,092
Mafeteng	MF	E	LT13	195,600	2,119	818
Maseru	MS	A	LT14	311,100	4,279	1,652
Mohale's Hoek	MH	F	LT15	164,400	3,530	1,363
Mokhotlong	MK	J	LT16	74,700	4,075	1,573
Qacha's Nek	QN	H	LT17	64,000	2,349	907
Quthing	QT	G	LT18	110,400	2,916	1,126
Thaba-Tseka	TT	K	LT19	104,100	4,270	1,649
				1,577,500	30,355	11,720

Status: These divisions are districts.

Abv: Two-letter code for international compatibility (defined by the author).
ISO: Codes from ISO 3166-2.
FIPS: Codes from FIPS PUB 10-4.
Population: 1986 census.
Area-km: Square kilometers.
Area-mi: Square miles.

Capitals have the same names as their districts. Note, however, that Berea district has an alternate name, Teyateyaneng. The district is commonly called Berea, but the capital is almost always known as Teyateyaneng.

Further subdivisions: The districts are further subdivided into wards.
Territorial extent: Lesotho is entirely surrounded by South Africa.
Change history:

~1910   Basutoland reorganized. New Berea district formed from part of old Berea; new Leribe formed from parts of old Berea and Leribe; Mafeteng formed from part of Thaba Bosigo; Maseru formed from parts of Berea and Thaba Bosigo; Mohale's Hoek formed from Kornet Spruit; Qacha's Nek formed from parts of Berea, Leribe, and Quthing; new Quthing formed from part of old Quthing.

~1944   Leribe district split into Butha-Buthe and Leribe; Qacha's Nek district split into Mokhotlong and Qacha's Nek.

~1980   Thaba-Tseka district formed from parts of Leribe, Maseru, Mokhotlong, and Qacha's Nek. The other districts all had minor border changes. Prior to this change, the nine districts excluding Thaba-Tseka had FIPS codes from LT01 to LT09, each one nine lower than the current code.

Other names of subdivisions: The apostrophes are sometimes omitted. In older sources, hyphens are sometimes omitted or replaced by spaces.

Berea: Teyateyaneng (variant)

LIBERIA

ISO = LR/FIPS = LI   Language = English   Time zone = +0   Capital = Monrovia

Liberia has been an independent country during the entire 20th century.
Other names of country: Libéria (French, Portuguese); Líbería (Icelandic); Republic of Liberia (formal).
Origin of name: Latin *liber*: free + -ia (suffix for country); founded by freed American slaves.

division	ISO	FIPS	population	area-km	area-mi	capital
Bomi	BM	LI15	66,420	1,955	755	Tubmanburg
Bong	BG	LI01	255,813	8,099	3,127	Gbarnga
Grand Bassa	GB	LI11	159,648	8,759	3,382	Buchanan
Grand Cape Mount	CM	LI12	79,322	5,827	2,250	Robertsport
Grand Gedeh	GG	LI02	102,810	17,029	6,575	Zwedru
Grand Kru	GK	LI16	––	––	––	Barclayville
Lofa	LO	LI05	247,641	19,360	7,475	Voinjama
Margibi	MG	LI17	97,992	3,263	1,260	Kakata
Maryland	MY	LI13	132,058	5,351	2,066	Harper
Montserrado	MO	LI14	544,878	2,740	1,058	Bensonville
Nimba	NI	LI09	313,050	12,043	4,650	Sanniquellie
Rivercess	RI	LI18	37,849	4,385	1,693	Rivercess
Sinoe	SI	LI10	64,147	10,254	3,959	Greenville
			2,101,628	99,065	38,250	

Status: These divisions are counties.

ISO: Codes from ISO 3166-2.
FIPS: Codes from FIPS PUB 10-4.
Population: 1984 census.
Area-km: Square kilometers.
Area-mi: Square miles.
Change history:

From 1900 to ~1963, the coastal strip of Liberia was divided into the counties of Grand Bassa, Grand Cape Mount, Maryland, Montserrado, and Sinoe. The interior, at first unorganized, was later divided into the provinces of Central, Eastern, and Western.

1911   Liberia ceded Kailahun territory to Sierra Leone in exchange for a strip south of the Mano River, which was annexed to Grand Cape Mount county.

~1963   Interior of Liberia reorganized into the counties of Bong, Grand Gedeh, Lofa, and Nimba. Most county boundaries were adjusted.

~1980   Capital of Grand Gedeh county renamed from Tchien to Zwedru.

~1983   Bomi county split from Montserrado (former FIPS code LI08). Margibi county formed from part of Montserrado and a small part of Bong. Rivercess county formed from part of Sinoe and part of Grand Bassa (LI03).

1985   Grand Kru county split from Maryland (former FIPS code LI06).

Other names of subdivisions:

Bomi: Bomy (variant)
Grand Cape Mount: Cape Mount (variant)
Grand Gedeh: Grand Jide (variant)

Lofa: Loffa (variant)
Maryland: Cape Palmas (variant)
Sinoe: Sino, Sinu (variant)

LIBYA

ISO = LY/FIPS = LY   Language = Arabic   Time zone = +2   Capital = Tripoli

In 1900, the vilayet of Tripoli, a part of the Ottoman Empire, covered roughly the same territory as modern Libya. It was conquered by Italy, and became an Italian colony by the Treaty of Ouchy on 1912-10-18. In 1939, the four provinces of Libya became an integral part of Italy under the name Libia Italiana. After World War II, Great Britain held Tripolitania and Cyrenaica, and France held Fezzan, under temporary military administration. On 1951-12-24, Libya was reunited and became an independent country.

Other names of country: al-Jamahiriyah al-Arabiya al-Libiya al-Shabiya al-Ishtirakiya al-Uzma (formal); Jamahiriya arabe libyenne, Libye (French); la Jamahiria Árabe Libia Popular y Socialista (formal–Spanish); Libia (Italian, Spanish); Líbia (Portuguese); Libië (Dutch); Líbýa (Icelandic); Libyan Arab Jamahiriya (formal–English); Libyen (Danish, Swedish); Libyen, Libysch-Arabische Dschamahirija (German).

Origin of name: from an ethnic name.

division	ISO	FIPS	population	capital	division	ISO	FIPS	population	capital
Ajdābiyā	AJ	LY47	100,547	Ajdābiyā	Benghazi	BA	LY54	485,386	Banghāzī
Al ʿAzīzīyah	AZ	LY03	85,068	Al ʿAzīzīyah	Darnah	DA	LY55	105,031	Darnah
Al Fātih	FA	LY48	102,763	Al Marj	Ghadāmis	GD	LY56	52,247	Ghadāmis
Al Jabal al Akhḍar	JA	LY49	120,662	Al Baydā'	Gharyān	GR	LY57	117,073	Gharyān
Al Jufrah	JU	LY05	N/A	Waddān	Murzūq	MU	LY30	42,294	Murzūq
Al Khums	KH	LY50	149,642	Al Khums	Miṣrātah	MI	LY58	178,295	Miṣrātah
Al Kufrah	KU	LY08	25,139	Al Jawf	Sabhā	SB	LY34	76,171	Sabhā
An Nuqāṭ al Khams	NK	LY51	181,584	Zuwārah	Sawfajjīn	SF	LY59	45,195	Banī Walīd
Ash Shāṭi'	SH	LY13	46,749	Birāk	Surt	SU	LY60	110,996	Surt
Awbārī	AW	LY52	48,701	Awbārī	Tarhūnah	TH	LY41	84,640	Tarhūnah
Az Zāwiyah	ZA	LY53	220,075	Az Zāwiyah	Tobruk	TU	LY42	94,006	Ṭubruq ➤

division	ISO	FIPS	population	capital	division	ISO	FIPS	population	capital
Tripoli	TB	LY61	990,697	Ṭarābulus	Zlītan	ZL	LY45	101,107	Zlītan
Yafran	YA	LY62	73,420	Yafran				3,637,488	

Status: These divisions are baladiyah (municipalities).
ISO: Codes from ISO 3166-2.
FIPS: Codes from FIPS PUB 10-4.
Population: 1991 census.
Origins of names:

Benghazi: Arabic *bani*: sons, *gazi*: conqueror, i.e. sons of the conqueror

Tarabulus: Greek *tri*: three, *polis*: city (Tripoli was formed by merging three cities)

Change history: Libya has traditionally been divided geographically into three regions: Cyrenaica (or Barca) in the east, Fezzan in the southwest, and Tripolitania in the northwest.

1919-05-17	Libya divided into Cyrenaica and Tripolitania provinces.
1919-09-12	France ceded some territory from Algeria to Libya, where it was incorporated into Tripolitania province, straightening the border somewhat.
1919	Egypt and Anglo-Egyptian Sudan ceded territory to Libya. Both cessions were incorporated into Cyrenaica.
1926	Egypt ceded more territory to Cyrenaica, leaving the border in its modern position, which follows the meridian of 25° East quite closely.
1934	Cyrenaica province split into Benghazi and Derne provinces; Tripolitania split into Tripoli and Misurata. The largest parts of each of the provinces, in the south, were under military administration as the Libyan Sahara Territory.
~1943	Occupying British and French forces established provinces of Cyrenaica, Fezzan, and Tripolitania.
1963-04	Libya reorganized from three provinces into ten muḥāfaẓāt (districts, governorates), as listed here:

governorate	population	capital	prv	equivalent
Al Jabal al Akhḍar	131,940	Al Bayḍā'	C	Al Fātiḥ, Al Jabal al Akhḍar
Al Khums	162,126	Al Khums	T	Al Khums, Sawfajjīn, Tarhūnah
Awbārī	106,647	Awbārī	F	Awbārī, Murzūq
Az Zāwiyah	247,628	Az Zāwiyah	T	An Nuqāṭ al Khams, Az Zāwiyah
Benghazi	337,423	Banghāzī	C	Ajdābiyā, Benghazi, Al Kufrah
Darnah	122,984	Darnah	C	Darnah, Tobruk
Gharyān	155,958	Gharyān	F,T	Ghadāmis, Gharyān, Yafran
Miṣrātah	177,939	Miṣrātah	T	Miṣrātah, Surt, Zlītan
Sabhah	113,006	Sabhā	F	Al Jufrah, Sabhā, Ash Shāṭi'
Ṭarābulus	735,083	Tripoli	T	Al 'Azīzīyah, Tripoli
	2,290,734			

Population: 1973 census.
Prv: Former province containing most of this territory (C = Cyrenaica, F = Fezzan, T = Tripolitania).
Equivalent: Present-day municipalities approximately equivalent to this territory.

~1973	It appears that there was a temporary reorganization. Benghazi governorate was reduced to a small northern stub, containing the city of Banghāzī. Al Khalīj governorate was formed from the remainder of Benghazi and the eastern part of Miṣrātah. Miṣrātah, in return, was augmented by the eastern parts of Gharyān and Sabhah. Awbārī merged with the remainder of Sabhah. The net effect on the list of governorates was that Awbārī was replaced by Al Khalīj.
~1983	Libya reorganized into 46 municipalities, as listed below:

municipality	FIPS	capital	municipality	FIPS	capital
Ajdābiyā	LY01	Ajdābiyā	Al Abyār	LY02	Al Abyār ➤

municipality	FIPS	capital	municipality	FIPS	capital
Al 'Azīzīyah	LY03	Al 'Azīzīyah	Jālū	LY25	Jālū
Al Bayḍā'	LY04	Al Bayḍā'	Janzūr	LY26	Janzūr
Al Jufrah	LY05	Waddān	Masallātah	LY27	Masallātah
Al Jumayl	LY06	Al Jumayl	Miṣrātah	LY28	Miṣrātah
Al Khums	LY07	Al Khums	Mizdah	LY29	Mizdah
Al Kufrah	LY08	Al Kufrah	Murzuq	LY30	Murzuq
Al Marj	LY09	Al Marj	Nālūt	LY31	Nālūt
Al Qarābūllī	LY10	Al Qarābūllī	Qamīnis	LY32	Qamīnis
Al Qubbah	LY11	Al Qubbah	Qaṣr Bin Ghashīr	LY33	Bin Ghashīr
Al 'Ujaylāt	LY12	Al 'Ujaylāt	Sabhā	LY34	Sabhā
Ash Shāṭi'	LY13	Birāk	Ṣabrātah	LY35	Ṣabrātah
Awbārī	LY14	Awbārī	Shaḥḥāt	LY36	Shaḥḥāt
Az Zahrā'	LY15	Az Zahrā'	Ṣurmān	LY37	Ṣurmān
Az Zāwiyah	LY16	Az Zāwiyah	Surt	LY38	Surt
Banī Walīd	LY18	Banī Walīd	Tājūrā'	LY39	Tājūrā'
Benghazi	LY17	Banghāzī	Tarhūnah	LY41	Tarhūnah
Bin Jawwād	LY19	Bin Jawwād	Tobruk	LY42	Ṭubruq
Darnah	LY20	Darnah	Tripoli	LY40	Ṭarābulus
Ghadāmis	LY21	Ghadāmis	Tūkrah	LY43	Tūkrah
Gharyān	LY22	Gharyān	Yafran	LY44	Yafran
Ghāt	LY23	Ghāt	Zlītan	LY45	Zlītan
Jādū	LY24	Jādū	Zuwārah	LY46	Zuwārah

~1987   Libya reorganized into 25 municipalities, as listed above.

Other names of subdivisions:

Al Fātiḥ: Fatah (variant)

Al Jabal al Akhḍar: Al Bayḍā', Beida, Djebel Akhdar, Jebel el Akhdar (variant)

Al Khums: Homs, Khoms (variant)

An Nuqāṭ al Khams: Nigat al Khums (variant)

Ash Shāṭi': Shati (variant)

Awbārī: Ubari (variant)

Az Zāwiyah: Zavia, Zawia (variant)

Benghazi: Banghāzī (Arabic), Bengasi (German, Italian, Spanish)

Darnah: Darna, Derna (variant)

Ghadāmis: Ghadames (variant)

Gharyān: Al Jabal al Gharbī, Gharian, Jabal al Gharb, Jebel el Gharb (variant)

Miṣrātah: Misurata (variant)

Sabhā: Sabhah, Sebha (variant)

Tobruk: Ṭubruq (Arabic)

Tripoli: Ṭarābulus (Arabic); Tripolis (German)

Provinces:

Cyrenaica: Barca, Barka (variant); Barqah (Arabic); Cirenaica (Italian, Portuguese, Spanish); Cyrenaika (German, Norwegian); Cyrénaïque (French)

Fezzan: Fazzān (Arabic)

Tripolitania: Tripolitaine (French); Tripolitan, Tripolitanien (German); Tripolitânia (Portuguese)

LIECHTENSTEIN

ISO = LI/FIPS = LS   Language = German   Time zone = +1 [d]   Capital = Vaduz

Liechtenstein is a principality, a feudal remnant that has remained independent to the present. It was a kind of client state of Austria until 1919; in 1924, it joined the Swiss customs union, and has been under the Swiss aegis ever since.

Other names of country: Fürstentum Liechtenstein (formal); Principado de Liechtenstein (formal–Spanish); Principality of Liechtenstein (formal–English).

Origin of name: after the ruling family, which was named for its castle near Vienna, from German *lichten*: light-colored, *Stein*: stone.

division	ISO	FIPS	population	area-km	area-mi	county
Balzers	BA	LS01	3,282	20	8	V
Eschen	ES	LS02	2,665	10	4	S
Gamprin	GA	LS03	825	6	2	S
Mauren	MA	LS04	2,575	7	3	S
Planken	PL	LS05	285	5	2	V
Ruggell	RU	LS06	1,200	7	3	S
Schaan	SN	LS07	4,534	27	10	V
Schellenberg	SB	LS08	577	4	1	S
Triesen	TN	LS09	3,021	26	10	V
Triesenberg	TB	LS10	2,186	30	11	V
Vaduz	VA	LS11	4,980	17	7	V
			26,130	159	61	

Status: These divisions are Gemeinden (communes).
ISO: Codes from ISO 3166-2.
FIPS: Codes from FIPS PUB 10-4.
Population: 1991 census.
Area-km: Square kilometers.
Area-mi: Square miles.
county: Old county to which the commune belongs (S = Schellenberg, V = Vaduz).
capital: Capital always has the same name as its commune.
Origins of names:

Vaduz: Latin *vallis*: valley, *dulcis*: sweet

Change history: Historically, Liechtenstein consists of the Reichsherrschaften (roughly, counties) of Schellenberg and Vaduz, also called the Unterland and Oberland (Lower and Upper Land), respectively. In the 1930s, their status was Verwaltungsbezirke (administrative districts). As they no longer have any administrative function, the significant division now is the commune.

LITHUANIA

ISO = LT/FIPS = LH   Language = Lithuanian   Time zone = +2 ^{d} Capital = Vilnius

The territory constituting modern Lithuania was almost entirely contained in the Russian Empire in 1900. On 1918-02-16, Lithuania declared its independence. It was occupied by the army of the Soviet Union in 1940, and became a constituent republic of the U.S.S.R., the Lithuanian Soviet Socialist Republic, on 1940-08-03. This annexation was never recognized by the United States. The Soviet Union acknowledged Lithuania's independence on 1991-09-06.

Other names of country: Liettua (Finnish); Lietuva (Lithuanian); Lietuvos Respublika (formal); Litauen (Danish, German, Norwegian, Swedish); Litháen (Icelandic); Litouwen (Dutch); Lituania (Italian, Spanish); Lituânia (Portuguese); Lituanie (French); Republic of Lithuania (formal–English).

Origin of name: Lithuanian *Lietuva*: land abundant with water.

division	abv	FIPS	type	population	district
Akmenė	AK	LH01	r	39,131	Šiauliai
Alytus	AL	LH02	r	33,540	Alytus
Alytus [town]	AT	LH03	t	77,211	Alytus
Anykščiai	AN	LH04	r	37,858	Utena
Birštonas	BS	LH05	t	3,821	Kaunas
Biržai	BZ	LH06	r	38,314	Panevėžys
Druskininkai	DR	LH07	t	21,753	Alytus
Ignalina	IG	LH08	r	25,014	Utena
Jonava	JV	LH09	r	54,947	Kaunas ➤

division	abv	FIPS	type	population	district
Joniškis	JS	LH10	r	34,465	Šiauliai
Jurbarkas	JR	LH11	r	40,757	Tauragė
Kaišiadoriai	KA	LH12	r	40,282	Kaunas
Kaunas	KU	LH14	r	83,489	Kaunas
Kaunas [town]	KN	LH13	t	415,801	Kaunas
Kėdainiai	KD	LH15	r	70,462	Kaunas
Kelmė	KM	LH16	r	43,213	Šiauliai
Klaipėda	KL	LH18	r	45,839	Klaipėda
Klaipėda [town]	KC	LH17	t	202,346	Klaipėda
Kretinga	KG	LH19	r	46,669	Klaipėda
Kupiškis	KK	LH20	r	26,142	Panevėžys
Ladzijai	LA	LH21	r	32,786	Alytus
Marijampolė	MR	LH23	r	51,123	Marijampolė
Marijampolė [town]	MP	LH22	t	52,067	Marijampolė
Mažeikiai	MZ	LH24	r	64,150	Telšiai
Molėtai	ML	LH25	r	26,442	Utena
Neringa	NE	LH26	t	2,648	Klaipėda
Pakruojas	PK	LH27	r	30,900	Šiauliai
Palanga	PG	LH28	t	19,623	Klaipėda
Panevėžys	PN	LH29	r	41,704	Panevėžys
Panevėžys [town]	PV	LH30	t	133,596	Panevėžys
Pasvalias	PS	LH31	r	36,841	Panevėžys
Plungė	PL	LH32	r	57,113	Telšiai
Prienai	PR	LH33	r	39,088	Kaunas
Radviliškis	RD	LH34	r	54,936	Šiauliai
Raseiniai	RN	LH35	r	46,556	Kaunas
Rokiškis	RK	LH36	r	45,976	Panevėžys
Šakiai	SK	LH37	r	42,361	Marijampolė
Šalčininkai	SC	LH38	r	40,009	Vilnius
Šiauliai	SA	LH40	r	52,401	Šiauliai
Šiauliai [town]	SL	LH39	t	147,086	Šiauliai
Šilalė	SI	LH41	r	33,280	Tauragė
Šilutė	SU	LH42	r	70,725	Klaipėda
Širvintai	ST	LH43	r	21,652	Vilnius
Skuodas	SD	LH44	r	27,739	Klaipėda
Švenčionys	SV	LH45	r	35,778	Vilnius
Tauragė	TA	LH42	r	56,041	Tauragė
Telšiai	TE	LH47	r	61,321	Telšiai
Trakai	TR	LH48	r	79,875	Vilnius
Ukmergė	UK	LH49	r	51,369	Vilnius
Utena	UT	LH50	r	53,714	Utena
Varėna	VR	LH51	r	37,014	Alytus
Vilkaviškis	VK	LH52	r	53,077	Marijampolė
Vilnius	VL	LH53	r	87,609	Vilnius
Vilnius [town]	VN	LH54	t	578,603	Vilnius
Visaginas	VG		t	33,780	Utena
Zarasai	ZA	LH55	r	24,793	Utena
				3,704,830	

Status: These divisions are miestai (towns, t) and rajonai (regions, r).

Abv: Two-letter code for international compatibility (defined by the author).

Population: 1998-01-01 estimate.

District: District to which the town or region belongs.

Capitals have the same name as their divisions.

Territorial extent: Neringa occupies the Lithuanian part of Kurshskaya Kosa, a long peninsula which is connected to the mainland in the Kaliningrad oblast of Russia.

Origins of names:

Klaipėda: Lithuanian *klai*: open, *pėda*: plain

Change history:

    1900   Present-day Lithuania consisted of Kovno (Kaunas), northwestern Vilna (Vilnius), northern

Suwalki (Suwalki), and a small part of southern Courland (Mitava) (all Russian guberniy, shown with capitals), plus the Memelgebiet in Prussia.

1920-10-07   Poland occupied the southeastern part of Vilna, including the city of Vilnius.

1923-01   Memel territory, which had been administered by France since the Treaty of Versailles (1919-06-28), occupied by Lithuania, and given the Lithuanian name Klaipėda.

1924-05-08   Memel territory became an autonomous part of Lithuania under the Memel Statute. It consisted of the districts of Memel, Pagegiai, and Šilutė. The divisions of Lithuania at this time were as follows:

district	population	area-km	area-mi	capital
Alytus	139,562	2,771	1,070	Alytus
Biržai-Pasvalys	110,426	2,722	1,051	Biržai
Kaunas	233,057	2,608	1,007	Kaunas
Kėdainiai	101,656	2,406	929	Kėdainiai
Kretinga	114,892	2,634	1,017	Kretinga
Marijampolė	118,964	2,279	880	Marijampolė
Mažeikiai	83,590	1,961	757	Mažeikiai
Memel	73,079	852	329	Memel
Pagegiai	42,138	938	362	Pagegiai
Panevėžys	178,058	4,387	1,694	Panevėžys
Raseiniai	129,275	3,077	1,188	Raseiniai
Rokiškis	95,459	2,165	836	Rokiškis
Šakiai	76,484	1,730	668	Šakiai
Seinai	48,029	1,248	482	Lazdijai
Šiauliai	238,892	6,048	2,335	Šiauliai
Šilutė	38,576	650	251	Šilutė
Tauragė	136,279	3,279	1,266	Tauragė
Telšiai	96,631	2,626	1,014	Telšiai
Trakai	99,388	2,145	828	Kaišiadorys
Ukmergė	148,540	3,069	1,185	Ukmergė
Utena	127,955	3,017	1,165	Utena
Vilkaviškis	93,578	1,321	510	Vilkaviškis
Zarasai	50,855	1,311	506	Zarasai
	2,575,363	55,244	21,330	

Population: 1938 estimate.

1939-10-10   Over half of the Polish territory in Vilna guberniya restored to Lithuania. Capital of Lithuania moved from Kaunas to Vilnius.

1990   Lithuania reorganized into 10 apskritis (districts, shown with their ISO 3166-2 codes): Alytus (AL), Kaunas (KU), Klaipėda (KL), Marijampolė (MR), Panevėžys (PN), Šiauliai (SA), Tauragė (TA), Telšiai (TE), Utena (UT), and Vilnius (VL).

1994   Lithuania reorganized into 56 towns and regions, as shown above. They ostensibly supersede the districts, but the Statistics Department still reports data at both levels.

Other names of subdivisions: In transcribing place names, č is often replaced by ch or tsch; š by sh or sch; ž by zh; and ė by ie or ye. Lithuanian is an inflected language, and names of divisions may have different endings depending on context. Most of the variants listed here are rather outdated.

Alytus: Olita (German); Alitus (Spanish)
Biržai: Birschi (German)
Jonava: Janowo (German); Ianova (variant)
Joniškis: Janischki (German)
Jurbarkas: Jurburg (German); Yurburg (variant)
Kaunas: Kowno (German); Kovno (variant)
Kėdainiai: Keidany (German)
Klaipėda: Memel (German, obsolete)
Kretinga: Krottingen (German)
Marijampolė: Mariampol (German)

Mažeikiai: Moscheiki (German)
Neringa: Nida (variant); Nidden (German)
Palanga: Polangen (German)
Panevėžys: Ponewiesch, Ponewjesh (German); Poneviezli (variant)
Prienai: Preny (German)
Radviliškis: Radsiwilischki (German)
Raseiniai: Rossieny (German)
Šiauliai: Schaulen (German); Shavli (variant)
Šilalė: Schileli (German)

Šilutė: Heydekrug (German)
Skuodas: Shkudy (variant)
Švenčionys: Schwentschionys, Swenzjany (German); Sven-
tziany (variant)
Tauragė: Tauroggen (German)
Telšiai: Telsche, Telschi (German); Telshe (variant)

Trakai: Troki (German)
Ukmergė: Wilkomir (German); Vilkomir (variant)
Vilkaviškis: Wilkowischki (German)
Vilnius: Wilna (German); Vilna (Italian, Portuguese, Span-
ish); Vilnious (French)

LUXEMBOURG

ISO = LU/FIPS = LU   Language = Luxemburgish, French, German   Time zone = +1 [d]   Capital = Luxembourg

Luxembourg has been an independent country for the whole of the 20th century.

Other names of country: Grand-Duché de Luxembourg (formal); Grand Duchy of Luxembourg (formal–English); Gran Ducado de Luxemburgo (formal–Spanish); Großherzogtum Luxemburg (formal–German); Lussemburgo (Italian); Lúxemborg (Icelandic); Luxemburg (Dutch, Finnish, German, Swedish); Luxemburgo (Portuguese, Spanish).

Origin of name: Old High German *Lützelburg*: little fort.

division	abv	ISO	FIPS	population	area-km	area-mi	cantons
Diekirch	DI	D	LU01	53,363	1,157	447	Clervaux, Diekirch, Redange, Vianden, Wiltz
Grevenmacher	GR	G	LU02	38,836	525	203	Echternach, Grevenmacher, Remich
Luxembourg	LU	L	LU03	272,407	904	349	Capellen, Esch, Luxembourg, Mersch
				364,606	2,586	999	

Status: These divisions are districts.
Abv: Two-letter code for international compatibility (defined by the author).
ISO: Codes from ISO 3166-2.
FIPS: Codes from FIPS PUB 10-4.
Population: 1979 census.
Area-km: Square kilometers.
Area-mi: Square miles.
Cantons: Cantons in the district.
Capitals: Capitals have the same names as their districts.
Postal codes: Luxembourg uses four-digit postal codes. Note: postal codes for addresses in Luxembourg can be identified by prefixing them with "L-".
Further subdivisions: The districts are subdivided into cantons (Kantone in German), which are further subdivided into municipalities (communes in French, Gemeinden in German)
Origins of names:

Diekirch: probably from Old High German *diot*: people, *kirch*: church (the people's church)
Grevenmacher: from Latin *maceria*: enclosing wall, with the
later addition of Luxemburgish *Greven*: count, i.e., the Count's Macher (by way of distinction from other towns named Macher)

MACAU

ISO = MO/FIPS = MC   Language = Portuguese   Time zone = +8   Capital = Macau

Macau has been a Portuguese colony since the age of exploration. After a Sino-Portuguese treaty of 1887-12-01, its status became that of a Portuguese territory. In 1961 it was made an overseas province of Portugal. A statute of 1976-02-17 redefined it as a collective entity. On 1987-04-13, Portugal agreed that Macau would be ceded to China on 1999-12-20.

Other names of country: Macao (Dutch, French, Italian, Norwegian, Spanish, Swedish).

Origin of name: Chinese *A-mangao*: bay of A-ma (patron goddess of sailors).

division	abv	ISO	FIPS	population	area-km	area-mi	capital
Ilhas	IL	I	MC01	9,795	10	4	Macau
Macau	MA	M	MC02	238,413	5	2	Macau
				248,208	15	6	

Status: These divisions are concelhos (districts).

Abv: Two letter code for international compatibility (defined by the author).

ISO: Codes from ISO 3166-2.

FIPS: Codes from FIPS PUB 10-4.

Population: 1981 census.

Area-km: Square kilometers.

Area-mi: Square miles.

Further subdivisions: Macau district is subdivided into five freguesias (parishes): Nossa Senhora de Fátima, Santo António, Santo Lázaro, Santo Lourenço, and Sé.

Territorial extent: Ilhas consists of the islands of Coloane and Taipa.

Macau occupies a peninsula off the Chinese mainland.

Origins of names:

Ilhas: Portuguese for islands

MACEDONIA

ISO = MK/FIPS = MK   Language = Macedonian   Time zone = +1 ^{d} Capital = Skopje

The territory now constituting "the Former Yugoslav Republic of Macedonia" was part of the Ottoman Empire in 1900. By the Bucharest Peace Treaty of 1913-08-10, Serbia acquired the territory (except for a small area around Strumica, which was part of Bulgaria until World War I). Serbia, with Macedonia, became part of the Kingdom of Serbs, Croats, and Slovenes on 1918-12-04. This kingdom was soon being called Yugoslavia, although the name didn't become official until 1929. Macedonia became one of the six constituent republics of Yugoslavia under the constitution of 1945. It declared independence from Yugoslavia on 1991-01-25. International recognition came slowly, primarily because Greece objected to its use of the name Macedonia. On 1995-09-13, Greece and Macedonia agreed to normalize relations.

Other names of country: Ehemalige jugoslawische Republik Mazedonien (German); la ex República Yugoslava de Macedonia (Spanish); Macédoine (French); Macedônia (Portuguese); Makedonia (Finnish, Norwegian); Makedónía (Icelandic); Makedonien (Danish, Swedish); Republika Makedonija (formal); the Former Yugoslav Republic of Macedonia (English-formal).

Origin of name: from ethnic name Makedon, probably related to Ancient Greek *makednos*: extended, broad.

division	abv	population	area-km	area-mi	division	abv	population	area-km	area-mi
Berovo	BV	20,048	807	312	Kočani	KO	38,136	571	220
Bitola	BT	111,581	1,699	656	Kratovo	KT	15,912	376	145
Brod	BD	18,034	924	357	Kriva Palanka	KP	31,536	720	278
Debar	DB	15,729	264	102	Kruševo	KR	13,367	201	78
Delčevo	DC	18,913	585	226	Kumanovo	KU	100,616	1,190	459
Demir Hisar	DH	17,218	431	166	Negotino	NE	15,682	736	284
Gevgelija	GG	24,419	757	292	Ohrid	OH	47,295	1,031	398
Gostivar	GS	69,602	1,356	524	Prilep	PL	93,216	1,824	704
Kavadarci	KA	30,981	1,134	438	Probištip	PS	15,283	326	126
Kičevo	KI	39,883	852	329	Radoviš	RA	22,358	736	284 ➤

division	abv	population	area-km	area-mi	division	abv	population	area-km	area-mi
Resen	RE	23,730	739	285	Tetovo	TE	104,224	1,080	417
Skopje	SK	270,299	1,840	710	Titov Veles	TV	57,877	1,536	593
Štip	SP	36,444	810	313	Valandovo	VA	8,784	331	128
Struga	SG	42,417	541	209	Vinica	VI	14,455	438	169
Strumica	SM	65,491	953	368			1,406,003	25,433	9,819
Sveti Nikole	SN	22,473	645	249					

Status: These divisions are municipalities.

Abv: Two-letter code for international compatibility (defined by the author).

Population: 1967 estimate.

Area-km: Square kilometers.

Area-mi: Square miles.

Capitals have the same name as their municipalities.

Further subdivisions: In 1968, Skopje commune is shown divided into three parts: Idadija, Kale, and Kisela Voda. In 1994, Skopje municipality is shown divided into five parts: Čair, Centar, Gazi Baba, Karpoš, and Kisela Voda.

Change history:

	The territory of Macedonia was parts of the Turkish provinces of Kosovo, Monastir, and Saloniki before 1913. From 1918 to 1945 it was part of Serbia within Yugoslavia.
1945	Macedonia became a republic of Yugoslavia, subdivided into the kotari (regions) of Bitola, Kumanovo, Ohrid, Skopje, Štip, Tetovo, and Titov Veles.
1952–1955	Regions abolished and replaced by opštini (communes).
1991-11-20	New constitution specified a division into municipalities, equivalent to the former communes, with the City of Skopje as a special unit.
1996-09	Macedonia reorganized into 123 communities by a Law on Territorial Division (details not available).

Other names of subdivisions: The Macedonian language is written in the Cyrillic alphabet, so the usual vagaries of transliteration are found. For example, č and š may be transliterated as c and s, or as ch and sh.

Bitola: Bitolia, Monastir (obsolete)
Brod: Makedonska Brod (variant)
Demir Hisar: Murgaševo (variant)
Gevgelija: Djevdjelija (variant)

Gostivar: Kostovo (obsolete)
Ohrid: Ochrida, Okhrida (obsolete)
Skopje: Skoplie, Skoplje, Üskub, Uskup (obsolete)
Štip: Ishtip, Istib (obsolete)

MADAGASCAR

ISO = MG/FIPS = MA   Language = French,Malagasy   Time zone = +3   Capital = Antananarivo

Madagascar became a French colony in 1896. It obtained its independence on 1958-10-14. After independence it used the name Malagasy Republic, but reverted to Madagascar in 1975.

Other names of country: Madagasikara (Malagasy); Madagaskar (Danish, Dutch, Finnish, German, Icelandic, Norwegian, Swedish); Malagasy Republic (English-obsolete); Repoblika Malagasy (obsolete); Repoblika n'i Madagasikara (formal); Republic of Madagascar (formal–English); République Malgache (French-obsolete).

Origin of name: incorrect application of the name of a different island, reported by Marco Polo.

division	abv	ISO	FIPS	population	area-km	area-mi	old name
Antananarivo	AV	T	MA05	3,811,000	58,283	22,503	Tananarive
Antsiranana	AS	D	MA01	715,000	43,046	16,620	Diégo-Suarez
Fianarantsoa	FI	F	MA02	2,420,000	102,373	39,526	Fianarantsoa
Mahajanga	MA	M	MA03	1,253,000	150,023	57,924	Majunga ➤

division	abv	ISO	FIPS	population	area-km	area-mi	old name
Toamasina	TM	A	MA04	1,585,000	71,911	27,765	Tamatave
Toliara	TL	U	MA06	1,659,000	161,405	62,319	Tuléar
				11,443,000	587,041	226,657	

Status: These divisions are faritanin' (provinces).
Abv: Two-letter code for international compatibility (defined by the author).
ISO: Codes from ISO 3166-2.
FIPS: Codes from FIPS PUB 10-4.
Population: 1990 estimate.
Area-km: Square kilometers.
Area-mi: Square miles.
Capitals have the same names as their provinces.
Further subdivisions: The provinces are subdivided into fivondronana (sub-prefectures), which are further subdivided into firaisana (cantons), which are further subdivided into fokontany (communes).
Territorial extent: The Comoro Islands, including Mayotte, have been administered from Madagascar in the early years of the 20th century. The same is true of the uninhabited islands of Bassas da India, Europa, Îles Glorieuses (Glorioso Islands), Juan de Nova, and Tromelin, in the Mozambique Channel, which have been administered from Réunion since 1960. The islands of Nosy Be and Sainte Marie (Nosy Boraha) were originally dependencies, but have become integral parts of Madagascar.
Antsiranana includes Nosy Be, Nosy Faly, and Nosy Mitsio.
Mahajanga includes the Barren Islands (Nosy Barren), Île Chesterfield, and Nosy Lava.
Toamasinia includes Nosy Boraha.
Origins of names:

Antananarivo: Malagasy for the city of a thousand
Antsiranana: Malagasy for the port
Diego-Suarez: From early explorers Diego Dias and Hernán Suárez (separate voyages)

Fianarantsoa: Malagasy for school of the good (i.e. ethics)
Toamasina: Malagasy, possibly meaning "as if holy"
Toliara: Malagasy for the anchorage over there

Change history:

1914-02-23	The Comoro Islands (including Mayotte) became a dependency of Madagascar.
1954	Tromelin Island transferred from the Seychelles to Madagascar.
1958-10-14	Madagascar became independent from France, but its dependencies (the Comoro Islands, Mayotte, and the islands in the Mozambique Channel) remained French possessions.
1976	Name of province of Tananarive and its capital changed to Antananarivo.
~1980	Names of provinces of Diégo-Suarez, Majunga, Tamatave, and Tuléar and their capitals changed to Antsiranana, Mahajanga, Toamasina, and Toliara, respectively.

Other names of subdivisions:

Antananarivo: Tananarive (obsolete)
Antsiranana: Antseranana (variant); Diégo-Suarez (obsolete)
Mahajanga: Majunga (obsolete)

Toamasina: Tamatave (obsolete)
Toliara: Toleary, Toliary (variant); Tuléar (obsolete)

MALAWI

ISO = MW/FIPS = MI   Language = English, Chichewa   Time zone = +2   Capital = Lilongwe

In 1900, modern Malawi was the protectorate of British Central Africa. In 1907, the name was changed to Nyasaland Protectorate. On 1953-07-14, Nyasaland joined with Northern Rhodesia (Zambia) and Southern Rhodesia (Zimbabwe) to form the Federation of Rhodesia and Nyasaland. The federation was dissolved when Nyasaland withdrew in 1963. When it became independent on 1964-07-06, it changed its name to Malawi.

Other names of country: Dziko la Malawi (formal); Malaui (Portuguese); Malaví (Icelandic); Nyasaland (obsolete); Republic of Malaŵi (formal–English).

Origin of name: after the Chewa name for the lake.

division	ISO	FIPS	population	area-km	area-mi	reg
Blantyre	BL	MI24	589,525	2,012	777	S
Chikwawa	CK	MI02	316,733	4,755	1,836	S
Chiradzulu	CR	MI03	210,912	767	296	S
Chitipa	CT	MI04	96,794	4,289	1,656	N
Dedza	DE	MI06	411,787	3,623	1,399	C
Dowa	DO	MI07	322,432	3,041	1,174	C
Karonga	KR	MI08	148,014	3,354	1,295	N
Kasungu	KS	MI09	323,453	7,879	3,042	C
Lilongwe	LI	MI11	976,627	6,159	2,378	C
Machinga	MH	MI10	515,265	5,965	2,303	S
Mangochi	MG	MI12	496,578	6,273	2,422	S
Mchinji	MC	MI13	249,843	3,357	1,296	C
Mulanje	MU	MI14	638,062	3,450	1,332	S
Mwanza	MW	MI25	121,513	2,295	886	S
Mzimba	MZ	MI15	433,696	10,430	4,027	N
Nkhata Bay	NB	MI17	138,381	4,090	1,579	N
Nkhotakota	NK	MI18	158,044	4,258	1,644	C
Nsanje	NS	MI19	204,374	1,942	750	S
Ntcheu	NU	MI16	358,767	3,424	1,322	C
Ntchisi	NI	MI20	120,860	1,655	639	C
Rumphi	RU	MI21	94,902	4,768	1,841	N
Salima	SA	MI22	189,173	2,196	848	C
Thyolo	TH	MI05	431,157	1,715	662	S
Zomba	ZO	MI23	441,615	2,580	996	S
			7,988,507	94,277	36,400	

Status: These divisions are districts.

ISO: Codes from ISO 3166-2.

FIPS: Codes from FIPS PUB 10-4.

Population: 1987 census.

Area-km: Square kilometers.

Area-mi: Square miles.

Reg: Region to which the district belongs (as coded in this table):

region	ISO	capital	area-km
Central	C	Lilongwe	35,592
Northern	N	Mzuzu	26,931
Southern	S	Blantyre	31,754

Capitals have the same name as their districts.

Territorial extent: Northern region contains the islands of Likoma and Chisamula in Lake Malawi. These islands are surrounded by Mozambican waters, making them enclaves.

Origins of names:

Blantyre: named by Livingstone for his birthplace, Blantyre, Scotland

Change history:

~1958   Name and capital of Chinteche district changed to Nkhata Bay; Chitipa district split from Karonga; Fort Manning-Lilongwe district split into Fort Manning (later Mchinji) and Lilongwe; Liwonde-Zomba district split into Liwonde (later Kasupe) and Zomba; Neno district merged with Blantyre; Ntchisi district split from Dowa; Rumphi district split from Mzimba; Salima district split from Kota Kota (later Nkhotakota).

1975-01-01   Capital of Malawi moved from Zomba to Lilongwe.
~1982   Mwanza district split from Blantyre (formerly FIPS MI01).

Other names of subdivisions:

Machinga: Kasupe, Kasupi, Liwonde (obsolete)
Mangochi: Fort Johnston (obsolete)
Mchinji: Fort Manning (obsolete)
Mulanje: Mlange, Mlanje (variant)
Nkhata Bay: Chinteche (obsolete)
Nkhotakota: Kota Kota (obsolete)

Nsanje: Port Herald (obsolete)
Ntcheu: Ncheu (obsolete)
Ntchisi: Nchisi (variant)
Rumphi: Rumpi (variant)
Thyolo: Cholo (obsolete)

Population history:

region	1945	1966	1977	1987
Central	751,390	1,474,952	2,143,716	3,110,986
Northern	290,859	497,491	648,853	911,787
Southern	1,007,802	2,067,140	2,754,891	3,965,734
	2,050,051	4,039,583	5,547,460	7,988,507

MALAYSIA

ISO = MY/FIPS = MY   Language = Malay, English   Time zone = +8   Capital = Kuala Lumpur, Putrajaya

In 1900, the term Malaysia referred to the Malay Archipelago, roughly equivalent to Indonesia and the Philippines. The area which we now call Malaysia was a motley collection of British-dominated entities. On the Malay Peninsula, there were the Straits Settlements, the Federated States of Malaya, other native states (unfederated states), and dependencies. On and near the island of Borneo, North Borneo was administered by the British North Borneo Company under charter, and Sarawak was a British colony. Japan occupied the whole area during World War II. After Japan's defeat, a series of proposals for union were considered and tried. On 1957-08-31, Malaya became independent. Malaysia was formed six years later. The capital is in the early stages of moving from Kuala Lumpur to a new city, Putrajaya.

Other names of country: Federation of Malaysia (formal–English); Malaísia (Portuguese); Malaisie (French); Malasia (Spanish); Malasía (Icelandic); Maleisië (Dutch); Malesia (Finnish); Persekutuan Tanah Malaysia (formal).

Origin of name: French malais: Malay (ethnic name) + -ia territorial suffix.

division	abv	ISO	FIPS	population	area-km	area-mi	capital
Johor	JH	J	MY01	2,074,297	18,985	7,330	Johor Baharu
Kedah	KH	K	MY02	1,304,800	9,425	3,639	Alor Setar
Kelantan	KN	D	MY03	1,181,680	14,931	5,765	Kota Baharu
Kuala Lumpur	KL	W	MY14	1,145,075	244	94	Kuala Lumpur
Labuan	LA	L	MY15	54,307	98	38	Victoria
Melaka	ME	M	MY04	504,502	1,650	637	Melaka
Negeri Sembilan	NS	N	MY05	691,200	6,643	2,565	Seremban
Pahang	PH	C	MY06	1,036,724	35,965	13,886	Kuantan
Perak	PK	A	MY07	1,880,016	21,005	8,110	Ipoh
Perlis	PL	R	MY08	184,070	795	307	Kangar
Pinang	PG	P	MY09	1,065,075	1,033	399	Georgetown
Sabah	SA	SA	MY16	1,736,902	73,711	28,460	Kota Kinabalu
Sarawak	SK	SK	MY11	1,648,217	124,449	48,050	Kuching
Selangor	SL	B	MY12	2,289,236	7,956	3,072	Shah Alam
Terengganu	TE	T	MY13	770,931	12,955	5,002	Kuala Terengganu
				17,567,032	329,845	127,354	

Status: These divisions are negeri (states), except for Kuala Lumpur and Labuan, which are wilayah persekutuan (federal territories).

Abv: Two-letter code for international compatibility (defined by the author).
ISO: Codes from ISO 3166-2.
FIPS: Codes from FIPS PUB 10-4.
Population: 1991 census (preliminary).
Area-km: Square kilometers.
Area-mi: Square miles.
Postal codes: Malaysia uses five-digit postal codes.
Further subdivisions: The states are subdivided into districts.
Territorial extent: (Island names are usually preceded by Pulau, the Malay word for island.)
Johor includes Tinggi, Sibu, Aur, Pemanggil, and Babi Besar on the east, and Kukub on the west.
Kedah includes Langkawi and adjacent small islands (Dayang Bunting, Singa Besar, Langgon, etc.).
Labuan is an island in the Gulf of Brunei, off the coast of Borneo.
Pahang includes Tioman and Seriburat.
Perak includes Pangkor and the Sembilan Islands (of which Rumbia is the largest).
Pinang consists mainly of the island of Pinang and a slightly larger coastal region called Province Wellesley.
Sabah includes Banggi, Jembongan, Balembangan, the northern half of Sebatik, Timbun Mata, Bum Bum, Malawali, Kanawi, Timbang, Sakar, Gaja, Mengalum, Tabawan, Tambisan, Tiga, and Mantanani Besar.
Sarawak includes Bruit, Patok, Satang Besar, Talang Talang Besar, and Lakei.
Selangor includes Kelang, Lumut, Pintu Gedong, and Ketam.
Terengganu includes Redang, Tenngol, Kapas, Perhentian Kecil, and Perhentian Besar.
Wilayah Persekutuan Kuala Lumpur is an enclave within Selangor.
Malaysia claims part of the Spratly Islands, south of about 8° N. latitude in the South China Sea. The group as a whole has been given the FIPS 10-4 country code PG.

Origins of names:

Johor: local word meaning "to tie," referring to the strait
Kuala Lumpur: Malay *kuala*: river mouth, *lumpur*: muddy, referring to the Klang River
Melaka: Malay for refuge
Negeri Sembilan: Malay for nine states

Perak: after the Perak River, from Malay *perak*: silver
Pinang: from the island Pulau Pinang, from Malay *pulau*: island, *pinang*: areca nut
Sarawak: corruption of Malay *sarakaw*: small harbor

Change history:

In 1900, the Straits Settlements consisted of Malacca, Penang, and Singapore. The Federated Malay States consisted of Negri Sembilan, Pahang, Perak, and Selangor. Johore was an unfederated state (British dependency). Kedah, Perlis, Kelantan, and Trengganu were dependencies of Siam (Thailand). Labuan was a dependency of North Borneo; Christmas Island and Cocos (Keeling) Islands were dependencies of Singapore; and Dindings and Province Wellesley were dependencies of Penang.

1900	Christmas Island became part of Singapore settlement.
1903	Cocos (Keeling) Islands became part of Singapore.
1905	Labuan transferred from North Borneo to Straits Settlements.
1907	Labuan merged with Singapore.
1909	Kedah, Kelantan, Perlis, and Trengganu became unfederated states.
1912	Labuan became a separate settlement in the Straits Settlements.
1935	Dindings dependency (Pulau Pangkor and adjacent mainland) merged with Perak state.
1946-04-01	Singapore split from Straits Settlements to become a British colony. The Federated States, the unfederated states, and the other Straits Settlements (Malacca and Penang) joined to form the Malayan Union.
1946-07-15	British North Borneo Company ceded to Britain its sovereign rights to North Borneo. Labuan merged with this area to form the British colony of North Borneo.
1947	Capital of North Borneo moved from Sandakan to Jesselton.
1948-02-01	Malayan Union became Federation of Malaya.
1955-11-23	Cocos (Keeling) Islands transferred from Singapore to Australia.
1958-10-01	Christmas Island transferred from Singapore to Australia.
~1960	Capital of Pahang state moved from Kuala Lipis to Kuantan.

1963-09-16   Federation of Malaysia formed by the union of Federation of Malaya, Singapore,
              Sarawak, and North Borneo. Name of North Borneo changed to Sabah.
1965-08-09   Singapore split from Federation of Malaysia.
1974-02-01   Kuala Lumpur federal territory split from Selangor. Capital of Selangor moved from
              Kuala Lumpur to Shah Alam.
~1980   Spelling of some state names and capitals changed. Johore state became Johor, Malacca
              became Melaka, Negri Sembilan became Negeri Sembilan, Penang became Pinang,
              Trengganu became Terengganu. Johore Bahru became Johor Baharu, Alor Star
              became Alor Setar, etc.
1984-04-16   Labuan federal territory split from Sabah state.

Other names of subdivisions:

Johor: Johor Darul Takzim (formal); Johore (variant)
Kedah: Kedah Darul Aman (formal)
Kuala Lumpur: Federal Territory, Wilayah Persekutuan Kuala
  Lumpur (variant); Territoire Fédéral (French); Território
  Federal (Portuguese)
Labuan: Labouan (French-variant); Pulau Labuan, Wilayah
  Persekutuan Labuan (variant)
Melaka: Malacca, Malaka (variant)
Negeri Sembilan: Negeri Sembilan Darul Khusus (formal);
  Negri Sembilan (variant)

Pahang: Pahang Darul Makmur (formal)
Perak: Perak Darul Ridzuan (formal)
Perlis: Perlis Indra Kayangan (formal)
Pinang: Penang and Province Wellesley, Penang, Pulau Pinang
  (variant)
Sabah: North Borneo (obsolete)
Selangor: Selangor Darul Ehsan (formal)
Terengganu: Terengganu Darul Iman (formal); Trengganu
  (variant)

Note: When it was the only federal territory, Kuala Lumpur was often called Wilayah Persekutuan. When Labuan became
a second federal territory, that name became ambiguous. The correct name now is Wilayah Persekutuan Kuala Lumpur. The
less cumbersome and more familiar Kuala Lumpur is used here.

Population history:

state	1931	1941	1957	1970	1980	1991
Johor	505,311	644,472	927,565	1,277,180	1,638,229	2,074,297
Kedah	429,691	520,719	701,643	954,947	1,116,140	1,304,800
Kelantan	362,517	404,470	505,585	684,738	893,753	1,181,680
Kuala Lumpur	— —	— —	— —	451,728	977,102	1,145,075
Labuan	7,507	8,963	— —	— —	12,219	54,307
Melaka	186,711	236,087	291,246	404,125	464,754	504,502
Negeri Sembilan	233,799	296,009	364,331	481,563	573,578	691,200
Pahang	180,111	221,800	312,949	504,945	798,782	1,036,724
Perak	785,581	992,691	1,221,390	1,569,139	1,805,198	1,880,016
Perlis	49,296	57,289	90,866	121,062	148,276	184,070
Pinang	340,259	419,047	572,132	776,124	954,638	1,065,075
Sabah	270,233	331,361	334,141	653,604	998,827	1,736,902
Sarawak	600,000	546,385	631,431	976,269	1,307,582	1,648,217
Selangor	533,197	701,552	1,012,891	1,630,366	1,515,536	2,289,236
Terengganu	179,789	203,253	278,165	405,368	540,627	770,931
	4,664,002	5,584,098	7,244,335	10,891,158	13,745,241	17,567,032

Notes:

1931: Dindings included in Perak; Sarawak population is estimate.
1941: estimated; Sabah and Sarawak populations are 1947 estimate.

1957: census; Sabah is 1951 census; Sarawak is 1956 estimate.

MALDIVES

ISO = MV/FIPS = MV   Language = Dhivehi   Time zone = +5   Capital = Male

The Maldive Islands were a British protectorate and a dependency of Ceylon (Sri Lanka) until 1948. Then the territory was separated from Ceylon and administered directly by Britain. It became independent on 1965-07-26.

Other names of country: Dhivehi Raajjeyge Jumhooriyyaa (formal); Maldivane (Norwegian nynorsk); Maldivas (Portuguese, Spanish); Maldive (Italian); Maldiven (Dutch); Maldivene (Norwegian bokmål); Maldiverna (Swedish); Maldiverne (Danish); Maldíveyjar (Icelandic); Malediivit (Finnish); Malediven (German); Republic of the Maldives (formal–English).

Origin of name: Arabic *al-Mahal*: palace + Sanskrit *dvipa*: island.

division	abv	ISO	FIPS	division	abv	ISO	FIPS
Aliff	AL	02	MV30	Laviyani	LV	03	MV39
Baa	BA	20	MV31	Male	MA	MLE	MV40
Daalu	DA	17	MV32	Meemu	ME	12	MV41
Faafu	FA	14	MV33	Naviyani	NA	29	MV42
Gaafu Aliff	GA	27	MV34	Noonu	NO	25	MV43
Gaafu Daalu	GD	28	MV35	Raa	RA	13	MV44
Haa Aliff	HA	07	MV36	Seenu	SE	01	MV01
Haa Daalu	HD	23	MV37	Shaviyani	SH	24	MV45
Kaafu	KA	26	MV38	Thaa	TH	08	MV46
Laamu	LM	05	MV05	Waavu	WA	04	MV47

Status: These divisions are atolls, except for Male, which is a city.
Abv: Two-letter code for international compatibility (defined by the author).
ISO: Codes from ISO 3166-2.
FIPS: Codes from FIPS PUB 10-4.
Capitals: The atolls have no adminstrative centers. If necessary, each atoll could be considered its own capital.
Territorial extent: The atolls in the Maldives form the middle link in a chain between British Indian Ocean Territory to the south and Lakshadweep union territory, India, to the north. They are separated from Lakshadweep by the Eight Degree Channel, at about eight degrees North latitude, and from B.I.O.T. by a broader channel centered at about three degrees South.

Origin of names:

Male: Arabic *al-Mahal*: palace

Change history:

~1987   Male city split from Kaafu atoll.

Other names of subdivisions:
Note: (Admiralty) refers to atoll names on the British Admiralty charts. Aliff may be transcribed instead as Alifu; Daalu may be Dhaal or Dhaalu. Names ending in "North" or "South" may equally well appear inverted (e.g. North Male instead of Male North). Names may be followed by "Atoll."

Aliff: Ari and Rasdu (Admiralty); Ari (variant)
Baa: Malosmadulu South (Admiralty); Maalhosmadulu South (variant)
Daalu: Nilandu South (Admiralty)
Faafu: Nilandu North (Admiralty); Faaf, Faafa (variant)
Gaafu Aliff: Suvadiva North (Admiralty); Huvadhoo North, Huvadu North (variant)
Gaafu Daalu: Suvadiva South (Admiralty); Huvadhoo South, Huvadu South (variant)
Haa Aliff: Tiladummati North (Admiralty); Ihavandiffulu,
Ihavandhippolhu (variant)
Haa Daalu: Tiladummati South (Admiralty)
Kaafu: North and South Male (Admiralty); Male (variant)
Laamu: Haddummati (Admiralty)
Laviyani: Fadiffolu (Admiralty); Lhaviyani (variant)
Meemu: Mulaku (Admiralty)
Naviyani: Fua Mulaku (Admiralty); Gnaviyani (variant)
Noonu: Miladummadulu South (Admiralty)
Raa: Malosmadulu North (Admiralty); Maalhosmadulu North (variant)

Seenu: Addu (Admiralty); Addoo (variant)
Shaviyani: Miladummadulu North (Admiralty); Shaviyan (variant)

Thaa: Kolumadulu (Admiralty)
Waavu: Felidu (Admiralty); Vaavu (variant)

MALI

ISO = ML/FIPS = ML   Language = French   Time zone = +0   Capital = Bamako

In 1900, the French possessions in West Africa as a whole were called French Sudan. In 1904, the French administration created the gouvernement général of French West Africa (Afrique Occidentale Française, or A.O.F.; the name had already been in use for some time). A.O.F. initially comprised the French colonies of Ivory Coast, Dahomey, French Guinea, Senegal, and Upper Senegal and Niger. Upper Senegal and Niger contained most of the older territory of Senegambia and Niger. Its name was changed to French Sudan on 1920-12-04. French Sudan and Senegal formed the Federation of Mali on 1959-04-04. On 1960-06-20, the Federation of Mali became independent. It split up into its two original components, Sudan and Senegal, on 1960-08-22. One month later (1960-09-22), Sudan changed its name to the Republic of Mali.

Other names of country: French Sudan, Upper Senegal and Niger (obsolete); Haut-Sénégal-Niger, Soudan Français (obsolete–French); Malí (Icelandic, Spanish); Republic of Mali (formal–English); République du Mali (formal); Sudán Francés (obsolete–Spanish).

Origin of name: named for an ancient Islamic empire in the same area.

division	abv	ISO	FIPS	population	area-km	area-mi
Bamako	BA	BKO	ML01	646,153	267	103
Gao	GA	7	ML02	383,734	321,996	124,323
Kayes	KY	1	ML03	1,058,575	197,760	76,356
Kidal	KD	8		— —	— —	— —
Koulikoro	KK	2	ML07	1,180,260	89,833	34,685
Mopti	MO	5	ML04	1,261,383	88,752	34,267
Ségou	SG	4	ML05	1,328,250	56,127	21,671
Sikasso	SK	3	ML06	1,308,828	76,480	29,529
Timbuktu	TB	6	ML08	453,032	408,977	157,907
				7,620,215	1,240,192	478,841

Status: These divisions are régions, except for Bamako, which is a district.
Abv: Two-letter code for international compatibility (defined by the author).
ISO: Codes from ISO 3166-2.
FIPS: Codes from FIPS PUB 10-4.
Population: 1991 census.
Area-km: Square kilometers.
Area-mi: Square miles.
Capitals have the same name as their divisions.
Further subdivisions: The regions are subdivided into cercles (circles), which are further subdivided into arrondissements.
Origins of names:

Bamako: from the capital, which is Mandingo for behind Bama (name of a tribal chief)

Ségou: Mandingo for walled city
Timbuktu: Tamashek *ti-n-butu*: the one in the hollow

Change history:

1932-09-06   Part of Upper Volta annexed to French Sudan.
1947-09-04   Districts of Ouahigouya and Tougan restored to Upper Volta.
1954-01-01   Hodh district of French Sudan annexed to Mauritania.
1959-04-04   Before independence, French Sudan was divided into 19 districts, including Bamako, Koutiala, Mopti, San, Ségou, and Sikasso. Afterwards, it was reorganized into the districts of Bamako, Gao, Kayes, Mopti, Ségou, and Sikasso.

~1980   Timbuktu district split from Gao.
~1984   Bamako district split from Bamako region, which was renamed to Koulikoro.
 1991   Kidal region split from Gao.

Other names of subdivisions:

Bamako: Capital District (variant)
Koulikoro: Bamako (obsolete)
Timbuktu: Timbouctou, Tombouctou (French); Timbuctù

(Italian); Timbuctu, Tombuktu (Portuguese); Tombuctú
(Spanish)

MALTA

ISO = MT/FIPS = MT   Language = Maltese, English   Time zone = +1 ^{d} Capital = Valletta

Malta was part of the British Empire until its independence on 1964-09-21.
Other names of country: Malte (French); Repubblika ta' Malta (formal); Republic of Malta (formal–English).
Origin of name: from Phoenician for refuge.

division	abv	population	area-km	area-mi	capital
Malta	MT	369,609	316	122	Valletta

Status: This division is the whole of the country, treated as a division for compatibility.
Abv: Two-letter code for international compatibility (defined by the author).
Population: 1996 estimate.
Area-km: Square kilometers.
Area-mi: Square miles.
Further subdivisions: Malta has no administrative divisions, but some sources list the following regions used in the census. All but the first are on the island of Malta.

region	population	area-km	region	population	area-km
Gozo and Comino	23,114	70	South Eastern	36,407	53
Inner Harbour	117,238	15	Western	36,784	69
Northern	24,699	78		319,936	316
Outer Harbour	81,694	32			

Territorial extent: Malta consists of the islands of Malta, Gozo (Ghawdex), Comino (Kemmuna), Cominotto, Selmunett, and Filfla, and a few tiny islets.

MARSHALL ISLANDS

ISO = MH/FIPS = RM   Language = Marshallese, English   Time zone = +12   Capital = Majuro

Micronesia, including the Marshall Islands, was a German possession at the start of the 20th century. The islands were mandated to Japan in 1920 by the League of Nations. The Trust Territory of the Pacific Islands was created on 1947-04-02 and granted in trust to the United States. This territory was divided into districts, one of which was the Marshall Islands. The Marshall Islands became a freely associated state of the United States on 1986-10-21. It became fully independent on 1991-09-17.
Other names of country: Îles Marshall (French); Islas Marshall (Spanish); Isole Marshall (Italian); Marshalleilanden

(Dutch); Marshalleyjar (Icelandic); Marshallinsaaret (Finnish); Marshallinseln (German); Marshallöarna (Swedish); Marshalløerne (Danish); Marshalløyane (Norwegian nynorsk); Marshalløyene (Norwegian bokmål); Republic of the Marshall Islands (formal–English).

Origin of name: Named for explorer Capt. Marshall.

division	abv	population	area-km	area-mi	capital
Marshall Islands	MH	56,167	181	70	Majuro

Status: This division is the whole of the country, treated as a division for compatibility.

Abv: Two-letter code for international compatibility (defined by the author). This is also the alphabetic state code from FIPS PUB 5-2; its numeric code in that standard is 68.

Area-km: Square kilometers

Area-mi: Square miles.

Further subdivisions: FIPS PUB 6-4 divides the Marshall Islands into atolls and islands. It assigns a three-digit code to each of them. When the FIPS 5-2 and 6-4 codes are concatenated, as in 68140 for Kili, the result is a code that uniquely identifies a county-equivalent unit in the United States.

code	name	code	name
007	Ailinginae	170	Lib
010	Ailinglapalap	180	Likiep
030	Ailuk	190	Majuro
040	Arno	300	Maloelap
050	Aur	310	Mejit
060	Bika	320	Mili
070	Bikini	330	Namorik
073	Bokak	340	Namu
080	Ebon	350	Rongelap
090	Enewetak	360	Rongrik
100	Erikub	385	Toke
110	Jabat	390	Ujae
120	Jaluit	400	Ujelang
130	Jemo	410	Utrik
140	Kili	420	Wotho
150	Kwajalein	430	Wotje
160	Lae		

Territorial extent: The Marshall Islands include numerous small islands and atolls. For convenience, they are grouped into two chains: the Ratak Chain on the east, and the Ralik chain on the west. The Ratak (Sunrise) chain stretches from Mili to Taongi, and includes Majuro. The Ralik (Sunset) chain stretches from Ebon to Enewetak (Eniwetok). Some sources specify that the capital is Dalap-Uliga-Darrit, on Majuro Atoll.

MARTINIQUE

ISO = MQ/FIPS = MB   Language = French   Time zone = -4   Capital = Fort-de-France

Martinique was a French colony until 1946, when it became an overseas department, and thus in theory a peer of any of the European departments of France. In 1974, when French regions were established, it became a one-department region as well. Martinique has a NUTS code of FR92, a department code of 972, and postal codes of the form 972xx, all of which are extensions of the French system.

Other names of country: Department of Martinique (formal–English); Martinica (Italian, Portuguese, Spanish).

Origin of name: named by Columbus, probably from native name Madinina: island of lush vegetation.

division	abv	population	area-km	area-mi
Fort-de-France	FF	243,000	782	302 ➤

division	abv	population	area-km	area-mi
Marin	MA	— —	— —	— —
Saint-Pierre	SP	— —	— —	— —
Trinité	TR	76,000	334	129
		319,000	1,116	431

Status: These divisions are arrondissements.
Abv: Two-letter code for international compatibility (defined by the author).
Population: 1967 census.
Area-km: Square kilometers.
Area-mi: Square miles.
Capitals have the same name as their arrondissements.
Further subdivisions: The arrondissements are subdivided into communes.
Territorial extent: Martinique includes the island of Martinique and a few adjacent islets, such as Îlet Ramville, Îlet Long, and Îlet Cabri.

Origins of names:

Fort-de-France: originally Fort Royal, name changed for
patriotic reasons after the French Revolution

Change history:

1946-03-19	Martinique became a département d'outre-mer (overseas department) of France. It had one arrondissement, Fort-de-France.
1965-09-15	Trinité arrondissement split from Fort-de-France.
1974-04-26	Marin arrondissement split from Fort-de-France.
~1996	Saint-Pierre arrondissement created.

Other names of subdivisions:

Marin: Le Marin (variant)   Trinité: La Trinité (variant)

MAURITANIA

ISO = MR/FIPS = MR   Language = Arabic, French   Time zone = +0   Capital = Nouakchott

Mauritania was an indigenous state within the French sphere of influence in 1900. It became a French protectorate in 1903-05. In ~1920 it became a colony within the gouvernement général of French West Africa (Afrique Occidentale Française). It became independent on 1960-11-28.

Other names of country: Islamic Arab and African Republic of Mauritania (formal–English); Máritanía (Icelandic); Mauretanien (Danish, German, Swedish); Mauritânia (Portuguese); Mauritanie (French); Mauritanië (Dutch); República Islámica de Mauritania (formal–Spanish); République Islamique Arabe et Africaine de Mauritanie (formal).

Origin of name: Latin name, derived from *Maurus*: Moor (ethnic name).

division	abv	ISO	FIPS	roman	spelled	population	area-km	area-mi	capital
Adrar	AD	07	MR07	VII	Septième	61,043	215,300	83,100	Atar
Assaba	AS	03	MR03	III	Troisième	167,123	36,600	14,100	Kiffa
Brakna	BR	05	MR05	V	Cinquième	192,157	33,000	12,700	Aleg
Dakhlet Nouadhibou	DN	08	MR08	VIII	Huitième	63,030	22,300	8,600	Nouadhibou (Port-Étienne)
Gorgol	GO	04	MR04	IV	Quatrième	184,359	13,600	5,300	Kaédi
Guidimaka	GD	10	MR10	X	Dixième	116,436	10,300	4,000	Sélibaby
Hodh ech Chargui	HC	01	MR01	I	Première	212,203	182,700	70,500	Néma
Hodh el Gharbi	HG	02	MR02	II	Deuxième	159,296	53,400	20,600	Aioun el Atrouss
Inchiri	IN	12	MR12	XII	Douzième	14,613	46,800	18,100	Akjoujt ▶

division	abv	ISO	FIPS	roman	spelled	population	area-km	area-mi	capital
Nouakchott	NO	NKC				393,325	1,000	400	Nouakchott
Tagant	TG	09	MR09	IX	Neuvième	64,908	95,200	36,800	Tidjikdja
Tiris Zemmour	TZ	11	MR11	XI	Onzième	33,147	252,900	97,600	Fdérik (Fort-Gouraud)
Trarza	TR	06	MR06	VI	Sixième	202,596	67,800	26,200	Rosso
						1,864,236	1,030,900	398,000	

Status: These divisions are régions, except for Nouakchott, which is a district.
Abv: Two-letter code for international compatibility (defined by the author).
ISO: Codes from ISO 3166-2.
FIPS: Codes from FIPS PUB 10-4.
Roman: Each region is given a Roman numeral to identify it in reports, etc.
Spelled: French ordinal corresponding to the Roman numeral.
Population: 1988 census.
Area-km: Square kilometers.
Area-mi: Square miles.
Capital: Old colonial name of capital in parentheses, where different.
Further subdivisions: The regions are further subdivided into départements.
Territorial extent: Dakhlet Nouadhibou includes Île Tidra, just off shore.
Origins of names:

Adrar: Touareg for mountain

Nouakchott: from Berber *in*: place of, *akchuz*: shell

Change history:

Before independence, the divisions were called cercles (circles).
- 1954-01-01   Hodh district of French Sudan annexed to Mauritania.
- ~1962   Tiris Zemmour region split from Adrar.
- 1976-02-28   Mauritania annexed the southern part of Spanish Sahara as Tiris el Gharbia region.
- 1979-08-14   Mauritania withdrew from Tiris el Gharbia, which was annexed to Western Sahara by Morocco.
- ~1979   Name of Lévrier Bay region changed to Dakhlet Nouadhibou.

Other names of subdivisions:

Assaba: el-'Açâba (variant)
Dakhlet Nouâdhibou: Baie du Lévrier (French-obsolete); Lévrier Bay (obsolete)
Hodh ech Chargui: Eastern Hodh (variant); Hodh Oriental (French)

Hodh el Gharbi: Hodh Occidental (French); Western Hodh (variant)

MAURITIUS

ISO = MU/FIPS = MP   Language = English   Time zone = +4   Capital = Port Louis

Although Mauritius was a British colony from 1814 until it gained independence on 1968-03-12, its place names retain a strong flavor of older times when it was the French colony of Île de France.

Other names of country: Máritíus (Icelandic); Maurice (French); Mauricio (Spanish); Maurício (Portuguese); Maurizio (Italian); Republic of Mauritius (formal–English).

Origin of name: named by early explorers after Maurice of Nassau (1567–1625).

division	ISO	FIPS	population	area-km	area-mi	capital
Agalega Islands	AG	MP21	366	70	27	Port Louis ➤

division	ISO	FIPS	population	area-km	area-mi	capital
Black River	BL	MP12	26,818	259	100	Tamarin
Cargados Carajos	CC	MP22	— —	1	0	Port Louis
Flacq	FL	MP13	92,226	298	115	Centre de Flacq
Grand Port	GP	MP14	82,744	259	100	Mahebourg
Moka	MO	MP15	49,865	231	89	Moka
Pamplemousses	PA	MP16	71,011	179	69	Pamplemousses
Plaines Wilhems	PW	MP17	262,820	205	79	Beau Bassin-Rose Hill
Port Louis	PL	MP18	136,802	44	17	Port Louis
Rivière du Rempart	RR	MP19	69,299	148	57	Poudre d'Or
Rodrigues	RO	MP23	24,769	104	40	Port Louis
Savanne	SA	MP20	54,170	243	94	Souillac
			878,451	2,041	787	

Status: These divisions are districts, except for Agalega Islands, Cargados Carajos, and Rodrigues, which are dependencies.

ISO: Codes from ISO 3166-2.

FIPS: Codes from FIPS PUB 10-4.

Population: 1974 estimate (1972 for dependencies).

Area-km: Square kilometers.

Area-mi: Square miles.

Territorial extent: The districts (as opposed to the dependencies) are all mainly located on Mauritius Island.

In addition to the districts and dependencies, ISO 3166-2 lists the following five cities. The FIPS standard also listed them, calling them "urban councils," until 1991. They are all located within Plaines Wilhems district, except Port Louis, which is in Port Louis district.

	ISO	FIPS
Beau Bassin-Rose Hill	BR	MP02
Curepipe	CU	MP04
Port Louis	PL	MP07
Quatre Bornes	QB	MP08
Vacoas-Phoenix	VP	MP11

Agalega Islands is an island group north of Mauritius.

Black River includes Île aux Bénitiers (Île Morne).

Cargados Carajos consists of a set of islets north of Mauritius, called the Cargados Carajos Shoals (Saint Brandon Rocks).

Flacq includes Île aux Cerfs.

Rivière du Rempart includes Flat Island, Gabriel Island, Gunner's Quoin, Île d'Ambre, and Round Island.

Rodrigues is an island east of Mauritius, with a few adjacent islets and shoals.

Origins of names:

Pamplemousses: French for grapefruit (plural)

Change history:

1965-11-08   Chagos Archipelago dependency split from Mauritius to form British Indian Ocean Territory.

~1976   Moka-Flacq district council (capital Quartier Militaire, FIPS code MP05) split into Flacq and Moka districts. North district council (capital Triolet, FIPS code MP06) split into Pamplemousses and Rivière du Rempart districts. South district council (capital Rose Belle, FIPS code MP10) split into Black River, Grand Port, Plaines Wilhems, and Savanne districts. The five urban councils were apparently absorbed into their respective districts.

Other names of subdivisions:

Cargados Carajos: Saint-Brandon (variant)   Rodrigues: Rodriguez (obsolete)

MAYOTTE

ISO = YT/FIPS = MF   Language = Mahorian, French   Time zone = +3   Capital = Mamoutsou

Mayotte was part of the French protectorate of the Comoro Islands at the start of the 20th century. On 1912-07-25, the Comoros became a French colony. When they gained full independence on 1975-07-06, the inhabitants of Mayotte voted to remain tied to France. Mayotte has a department code of 976, which is an extension of the French system.

Other names of country: Territorial Collectivity of Mayotte (formal–English).

division	abv	population	area-km	area mi	capital
Mayotte	YT	94,410	373	144	Mamoutsou

Status: This division is the whole of the country, treated as a division for compatibility.
Abv: Two-letter code for international compatibility (defined by the author).
Population: 1991 census.
Area-km: Square kilometers.
Area-mi: Square miles.
Further subdivisions: The collectivité territoriale (territorial collectivity) is subdivided into communes.
Territorial extent: Mayotte consists of the islands of Mayotte, Pamandzi, M'Bouini, Bouzi, and M'Zambora.
Change history:

1976-12-24   Status of Mayotte changed from French dependency to territorial collectivity.
~1986   Capital of Mayotte moved from Dzaoudzi to Mamoutsou.

MEXICO

ISO = MX/FIPS = MX   Language = Spanish   Time zone = (see table)   Capital = Mexico City

Mexico has been independent during the whole of the 20th century.

Other names of country: Estados Unidos Mexicanos (formal); Méjico, México (Spanish); Meksiko (Finnish); Messico (Italian); México (Portuguese); Mexiko (German); Mexíkó (Icelandic); Mexique (French); United Mexican States (formal–English).

Origin of name: from ethnic name, Mexic; said to mean "moon-navel-place" in Aztec.

division	abv	ISO	FIPS	conv	population	area-km	area-mi	tz	capital
Aguascalientes	AG	AGU	MX01	Ags	719,650	5,471	2,112	-6^d	Aguascalientes
Baja California Norte	BN	BCN	MX02	BCN	1,657,927	69,921	26,997	-8^d	Mexicali
Baja California Sur	BS	BCS	MX03	BCS	317,326	73,475	28,369	-7^d	La Paz
Campeche	CM	CAM	MX04	Camp	528,824	50,812	19,619	-6^d	Campeche
Chiapas	CP	CHP	MX05	Chis	3,203,915	74,211	28,653	-6^d	Tuxtla Gutiérrez
Chihuahua	CH	CHH	MX06	Chih	2,439,954	244,938	94,571	-6^d	Chihuahua
Coahuila	CA	COA	MX07	Coah	1,971,344	149,982	57,908	-6^d	Saltillo
Colima	CL	COL	MX08	Col	424,656	5,191	2,004	-6^d	Colima
Distrito Federal	DF	D.F	MX09	DF	8,236,960	1,479	571	-6^d	(Ciudad de) México
Durango	DU	DUR	MX10	Dgo	1,352,156	123,181	47,560	-6^d	(Victoria de) Durango
Guanajuato	GJ	GUA	MX11	Gto	3,980,204	30,491	11,773	-6^d	Guanajuato
Guerrero	GR	GRO	MX12	Gro	2,622,067	64,281	24,819	-6^d	Chilpancingo (de los Bravos)
Hidalgo	HI	HID	MX13	Hgo	1,880,632	20,813	8,036	-6^d	Pachuca (de Soto)
Jalisco	JA	JAL	MX14	Jal	5,278,987	80,836	31,211	-6^d	Guadalajara
México	MX	MEX	MX15	Méx	9,815,901	21,355	8,245	-6^d	Toluca (de Lerdo)
Michoacán	MC	MIC	MX16	Mich	3,534,042	59,928	23,138	-6^d	Morelia
Morelos	MR	MOR	MX17	Mor	1,195,381	4,950	1,911	-6^d	Cuernavaca ➤

division	abv	ISO	FIPS	conv	population	area-km	area-mi	tz	capital
Nayarit	NA	NAY	MX18	Nay	816,112	26,979	10,417	-7^d	Tepic
Nuevo León	NL	NLE	MX19	NL	3,086,466	64,924	25,067	-6^d	Monterrey
Oaxaca	OA	OAX	MX20	Oax	3,021,513	93,952	36,275	-6^d	Oaxaca (de Juárez)
Puebla	PU	PUE	MX21	Pue	4,118,059	33,902	13,090	-6^d	(Heroica) Puebla (de Zaragoza)
Querétaro	QE	QUE	MX22	Qro	1,044,227	11,449	4,420	-6^d	Querétaro
Quintana Roo	QR	ROO	MX23	QR	493,605	50,212	19,387	-6^d	(Ciudad) Chetumal
San Luis Potosí	SL	SLP	MX24	SLP	2,001,966	63,068	24,351	-6^d	San Luis Potosí
Sinaloa	SI	SIN	MX25	Sin	2,210,766	58,328	22,521	-7^d	Culiacán (Rosales)
Sonora	SO	SON	MX26	Son	1,822,247	182,052	70,291	-7^d	Hermosillo
Tabasco	TB	TAB	MX27	Tab	1,501,183	25,267	9,756	-6^d	Villahermosa
Tamaulipas	TM	TAM	MX28	Tamps	2,244,208	79,384	30,650	-6^d	Ciudad Victoria
Tlaxcala	TL	TLA	MX29	Tlax	763,683	4,016	1,551	-6^d	Tlaxcala (de Xicohténcatl)
Veracruz	VE	VER	MX30	Ver	6,215,142	71,699	27,683	-6^d	Jalapa (Enríquez)
Yucatán	YU	YUC	MX31	Yuc	1,363,540	38,402	14,827	-6^d	Mérida
Zacatecas	ZA	ZAC	MX32	Zac	1,278,279	73,252	28,283	-6^d	Zacatecas
					81,140,922	1,958,201	756,066		

^{d} = *daylight saving time observed.*

Status: These divisions are estados (states), except for Distrito Federal, which is a federal district.

Abv: Two-letter code for international compatibility (defined by the author).

ISO: Codes from ISO 3166-2.

FIPS: Codes from FIPS PUB 10-4.

Conv: Conventional abbreviation.

Population: 1990 census.

Area-km: Square kilometers.

Area-mi: Square miles.

Tz: Time zone (hours offset from Greenwich).

Capital: Common name is not in parentheses; adding parenthetical parts gives formal name.

Postal codes: Mexico uses five-digit postal codes.

Further subdivisions: The states are divided into municipios (municipalities), and the federal district is divided into delegaciones (delegations). There are also uninhabited islands (about 5,073 sq. km.) that are directly owned by the federal government.

Territorial extent: The states of Coahuila, Nuevo León, San Luis Potosí, and Zacatecas meet at a single point.

Baja California Norte includes Islas Angel de la Guarda, Montague, San Lorenzo, Salsipuedes, Smith, and other islands in the Gulf of California; and Cedros and Guadalupe in the Pacific Ocean.

Baja California Sur includes Islas El Carmen, San José, Cerralvo, Espíritu Santo, San Marcos, and other islands in the Gulf of California; and Santa Margarita and Magdalena in the Pacific Ocean.

Campeche includes Isla del Carmen, and some isolated cays up to Cayo Arcas.

Colima includes the Revillagigedo Islands (Socorro, Clarión, San Benedicto, and Roca Partida).

Jalisco broke into two separate parts, the smaller one containing Colotlán, when Nayarit split off in 1917. A few years later, some territory was annexed to form a corridor between the two.

Nayarit includes the Islas Marías, or Tres Marías Islands, consisting of Isla María Madre, Isla María Magdalena, and Isla María Cleofas, named for the three women who stood by the cross in the Gospel of John; as well as Islas San Juanito, Isabela, and the Marietas.

Quintana Roo includes Islas Cozumel, Mujeres, Holbox, Contoy, Tamalcas, Cayo Chelén, and the Banco Chinchorro (a ring of islands, including Cayos Lobos and Norte, around Cayo Centro).

Sinaloa includes a number of barrier islands, of which the largest are Islas Talchichilte, de Altamura, Santa Maria, and San Ignacio.

Sonora includes Islas Tiburon, San Esteban, Pelicano, Lobos, and other islands in the Gulf of California.

Tamaulipas includes a series of barrier islands, such as Barras Soto la Marina and Los Americanos.

Veracruz includes some small barrier islands and reefs. Isla El Idolo is behind a sandspit.

Yucatán includes the Arrecife Alacran, a group of islands of which Isla Pérez is the largest; and Cayo Arenas.

Origins of names:

Aguascalientes: Spanish *aguas*: waters, *calientes*: hot, for thermal springs near the city

Baja California: the 1824 Constitution created the territories of Alta and Baja California (Spanish for Upper and Lower

California). Alta California was later acquired by the United States. See the United States entry for the derivation of California.

Campeche: after the Mayan domain of Ah Kin Pech

Chiapas: from Nahuatl for "in the Chía River"

Chihuahua: native word for dry or sandy spot

Coahuila: after the ethnic name Coahuiltec

Colima: from native name Colliman, meaning that which our ancestors conquered

Distrito Federal: Spanish for federal district

Durango: native word for beyond the river

Guadalajara: named for its capital, which was named for the birthplace in Spain of its founder, Nuñez de Guzman, in 1531.

Guerrero: after Vicente Guerrero (1783–1831), fighter for independence

Hidalgo: after Miguel Hidalgo y Costilla (1753-1811), Mexican founding father

Jalisco: native word for "over the sand"

Mexico: see country name

Morelos: after José Maria Morelos y Pavón (1765–1815), fighter for independence

Nayarit: named for Nayar, a Cora chief and priest

Nuevo León: after the kingdom of León in Spain

Oaxaca: from Aztec *huaxyacac*: at the point of the robinia trees

Puebla: for the city, originally Ciudad de Puebla de los Angeles

Querétaro: from Tarasco for "place where they play ball"

Quintana Roo: after Andrés Quintana Roo, a Yucatec fighter for Mexican independence

San Luis Potosí: after Potosí in Bolivia, in the hope that it, too, would have rich mines

Sonora: Spanish for sonorous, to note the sound made by local marble when struck

Tabasco: probably named for Tabscoob, native chief

Tamaulipas: native word for "high mountains"

Tlaxcala: after the ethnic name Tlaxcaltec

Veracruz: for the city, originally Villa Rica de la Vera Cruz (rich city of the true cross). Formal name appends -Llave in honor of the governor, General Ignacio de la Llave.

Zacatecas: Nahuatl for "where zacate grass grows"

Change history:

1902-11-25	Quintana Roo territory split from Yucatán state.
1915	Name of capital of Tabasco state changed from San Juan Bautista to Villa Hermosa (later Villahermosa).
1917-05-01	Tepic territory changed name and status to Nayarit state. It had formerly been subordinate to Jalisco.
1931-02-07	Baja California territory (capital La Paz) split into Baja California Norte and Baja California Sur territories. They had previously been districts of the one territory.
1935	Name of capital of Quintana Roo territory changed from Payo Obispo to Chetumal.
1953-08-16	Status of Baja California Norte changed from territory to state.
1974-10-07	Status of Baja California Sul and Quintana Roo changed from territories to states.

Other names of subdivisions: There are two Baja Californias. If the name Baja California is used without either Norte or Sul, Norte is usually meant. There are three Méxicos: the country, the state, and the city. When it's necessary to distinguish the latter two, Estado de México and Ciudad de México are used.

Baja California Norte: Baixa Califórnia Norte (Portuguese); Baja California (variant); Bassa California del Nord (Italian); Basse-Californie du Nord (French); Lower California (variant); Niederkalifornien (German); Territorio Norte (obsolete)

Baja California Sur: Baixa Califórnia Sul (Portuguese); Bassa California del Sud (Italian); Basse-Californie du Sud (French); Territorio Sur (obsolete)

Campeche: Campeachy (obsolete); Campêche (French-variant)

Coahuila: Coahuila de Saragoza (variant); Coahuila de Zaragoza (formal)

Distrito Federal: Federal District (variant); Distretto Federale (Italian)

México: Edo. de Mexico, Estado de México (variant)

Michoacán: Michoacán de Ocampo (formal)

Nayarit: Tepic (obsolete)

Nuevo León: Neu-Leon (German)

Querétaro: Querétaro de Arteaga (formal)

Veracruz: Veracruz-Llave (formal)

Population history:

division	1900	1930	1940	1950	1960	1970	1980	1990
Aguascalientes	102,416	132,900	161,693	188,075	243,363	338,142	519,439	719,650
Baja California N	47,624	48,327	78,907	226,965	520,165	870,421	1,177,886	1,657,927
Baja California S	——	47,089	51,471	60,864	81,594	128,019	215,139	317,326
Campeche	86,542	84,630	90,460	122,098	168,219	251,556	420,553	528,824 ➤

division	1900	1930	1940	1950	1960	1970	1980	1990
Chiapas	360,799	529,983	679,885	907,026	1,210,870	1,569,053	2,084,717	3,203,915
Chihuahua	327,784	491,792	623,944	846,414	1,226,793	1,612,525	2,005,477	2,439,954
Coahuila	296,938	436,425	550,717	720,619	907,734	1,114,956	1,557,265	1,971,344
Colima	65,115	61,923	78,806	112,321	164,450	241,153	346,293	424,656
Distrito Federal	541,516	1,229,576	1,757,530	3,050,442	4,870,876	6,874,165	8,831,079	8,236,960
Durango	370,294	404,364	483,829	629,874	760,836	939,208	1,182,320	1,352,156
Guanajuato	1,061,724	987,801	1,046,490	1,328,712	1,735,490	2,270,370	3,006,110	3,980,204
Guerrero	479,205	641,690	732,910	919,386	1,186,716	1,597,360	2,109,513	2,622,067
Hidalgo	605,051	677,772	771,818	850,394	994,598	1,193,845	1,547,493	1,880,632
Jalisco	1,153,891	1,255,346	1,418,310	1,746,777	2,443,261	3,296,586	4,371,998	5,278,987
México	934,463	990,112	1,146,034	1,392,623	1,897,851	3,833,185	7,564,335	9,815,901
Michoacán	935,808	1,048,381	1,182,003	1,422,717	1,851,876	2,324,226	2,868,824	3,534,042
Morelos	160,115	132,068	182,711	272,842	387,264	616,119	947,089	1,195,381
Nayarit	150,098	167,724	216,698	290,124	389,929	544,031	726,120	816,112
Nuevo León	327,937	417,491	541,147	740,191	1,078,848	1,694,689	2,513,044	3,086,466
Oaxaca	948,633	1,084,549	1,192,794	1,421,313	1,727,266	2,015,424	2,369,076	3,021,513
Puebla	1,021,133	1,150,425	1,294,620	1,625,830	1,973,837	2,508,226	3,347,685	4,118,059
Querétaro	232,389	234,058	244,737	286,238	355,045	485,523	739,605	1,044,227
Quintana Roo	— —	10,620	18,752	26,967	50,169	88,150	225,985	493,605
San Luis Potosí	575,432	579,831	678,779	856,066	1,048,297	1,281,996	1,673,893	2,001,966
Sinaloa	296,701	395,618	492,821	635,681	838,404	1,266,528	1,849,879	2,210,766
Sonora	221,682	316,271	364,176	510,607	783,378	1,098,720	1,513,731	1,822,247
Tabasco	159,834	224,023	285,630	362,716	496,340	768,327	1,062,961	1,501,183
Tamaulipas	218,948	344,039	458,832	718,167	1,024,182	1,456,858	1,924,484	2,244,208
Tlaxcala	172,315	205,458	224,063	284,551	346,699	420,638	556,597	763,683
Veracruz	981,030	1,377,293	1,619,338	2,040,231	2,727,899	3,815,422	5,387,680	6,215,142
Yucatán	309,652	386,096	418,210	516,899	614,049	758,355	1,063,733	1,363,540
Zacatecas	462,190	459,047	565,437	665,524	817,831	951,462	1,136,830	1,278,279
	13,607,259	16,552,722	19,653,552	25,779,254	34,924,129	48,225,238	66,846,833	81,140,922

MICRONESIA, FEDERATED STATES OF

ISO = FM/FIPS = FM   Language = English   Time zones = see table   Capital = Palikir

Germany bought almost all of Micronesia — the Caroline, Mariana (excluding Guam), and Marshall Islands — from Spain in the 1890s. The islands were taken by Japan during World War I, and mandated to Japan in 1920 by the League of Nations. The Trust Territory of the Pacific Islands was created on 1947-04-02 and granted in trust to the United States. It contained the islands which are now in the Federated States of Micronesia, the Republic of Palau, the Commonwealth of the Northern Mariana Islands, and the Marshall Islands. On 1979-05-10, following a vote on self-government, the F.S.M. was formed. It contained most of the Caroline Island group. The four states of the F.S.M. had previously been four of the seven districts of the T.T.P.I. On 1986-11-03, it became a freely associated state of the United States, a status which falls somewhere between a protectorate and an independent country.

Note: Oceania is said to consist of Melanesia, Micronesia, and Polynesia. All of these names are unofficial, so their extent is determined just by convention. The three divisions are based on the ethnicity of the native inhabitants. In some people's usage Oceania also includes the Malay Archipelago (Indonesia), and even (rarely) Australia and New Zealand.

Other names of country: Estados Federados de Micronesia (Spanish); États fédérés de Micronésie (French); Föderierte Staaten von Mikronesien (German); Micronésia (Portuguese); Micronesië (Dutch); Mikronesia (Finnish); Míkrónesía (Icelandic); Mikronesiaføderasjonen (Norwegian); Mikronesien (Danish, Swedish).

Origin of name: Descriptive: union of island groups in Micronesia (Greek *mikros nesos*: small island).

division	abv	ISO	FIPS	F-6	tz	population	area-km	area-mi	capital
Chuuk	CH	TRK	FM03	002	+10	31,000	127	49	Moen (Wenn)
Kosrae	KO	KSA	FM01	005	+11	16,500	109	42	Lelu (Lele)
Pohnpei	PO	PNI	FM02	040	+11	52,000	344	133	Palikir ▶

division	abv	ISO	FIPS	F-6	tz	population	area-km	area-mi	capital
Yap	YA	YAP	FM04	060	+10	12,000 111,500	122 702	47 271	Colonia (Yap)

Status: These divisions are states.

Abv: Two-letter code for international compatibility (defined by the author).

ISO: Codes from ISO 3166-2.

FIPS: Codes from FIPS PUB 10-4.

F-6: Codes from FIPS PUB 6-4, representing second-level administrative divisions of the United States. The codes for Federated States of Micronesia in FIPS PUB 5-2 are FM (alpha) and 64 (numeric). When the FIPS 5-2 and 6-4 codes are concatenated, as in 64040 for Pohnpei, the result is a code that uniquely identifies a county-equivalent unit in the United States.

Tz: Time zone.

Population: 1990 estimate.

Area-km: Square kilometers.

Area-mi: Square miles.

Capital: Names in parentheses are newer, more indigenous forms.

Territorial extent: Chuuk consists of the Chuuk Islands, which are surrounded by barrier reefs and grouped into the Shichiyo Islands (Tol, the largest, Udot, Ulalu) and the Shiki Islands (Moen, the largest, Dublon, Fefan, Uman); the Mortlock Islands, including the Etal, Lukunor, and Satawan Atolls; the Hall Islands, including the East Fayu, Murilo, and Nomwin Atolls; the Magur Islands, including the Namonuito, Pisaras, and Ulul Atolls; and Kuop, Losap, Nama, Namoluk, Pulap, Pulusak, and Puluwat Atolls.

Kosrae consists of just the island of Kosrae.

Pohnpei consists of the Senyavin Islands (Pohnpei Island and the nearby atolls of Ant and Pakin) and other atolls, including Kapingamarangi, Mokil, Ngatik, Nukuoro, Oroluk, and Pingelap.

Yap consists of the Yap Islands (Gagil-Tamil, Maap, Rumung, and Yap), and Eauripik, Elato, Fais, Faraulep, Gaferut, Ifalik, Lamotrek, Ngulu, Olimarao, Piagailoe (West Fayu), Pikelot, Sorol, Ulithi, and Woleai Atolls.

The approximate boundaries of the states, from west to east, are the following longitudes in degrees East: Yap—148°—Chuuk—154°—Pohnpei—162°—Kosrae.

Origins of names:

Chuuk: Chuukese for mountain

Pohnpei: native word for "upon a stone altar" (refers to a creation legend)

Change history:

~1980	Name of the city of Ponape changed to Kolonia; name of the city of Colonia changed to Yap.
1984-11-08	Name of the state and island of Ponape changed to Pohnpei.
1989	Capital moved from Kolonia to Palikir (both on the island of Pohnpei).
1989-10-01	Name of the state of Truk changed to Chuuk; FIPS 6-4 code changed from 050 to 002.

Other names of subdivisions:

Chuuk: Truk (obsolete)

Kosrae: Kusaie (variant)

Pohnpei: Ponape (obsolete)

MOLDOVA

ISO = MD/FIPS = MD   Language = Romanian   Time zone = +2 [d]   Capital = Chişinau

Russia acquired the eastern part of the principality of Moldavia from the Ottoman Empire in the 19th century. It became the guberniya of Bessarabia, consisting of all the territory between the Prum and Dniestr Rivers east of about 26°45' East.

Bessarabia proclaimed its independence on 1918-01-24, in the chaos of World War I. It united with Romania two months later. The merger was ratified by the Paris Peace Conference in 1920. The Soviet Union asserted a claim to the territory. Unable to prevail, it established a Moldavian Autonomous Soviet Socialist Republic (capital Balta from 1924 to 1929, then Tiraspol) on the eastern side of the Dniestr. After the Molotov-Ribbentrop Pact, the Soviet Union and Germany carved up the intervening territory. In 1940, the Soviet Union moved in and annexed Bessarabia and Northern Bukovina from Romania. On 1940-08-02, the Moldavian Soviet Socialist Republic was created. It contained about 28,000 sq. km. of Bessarabian territory and 3,400 sq. km. of the Moldavian A.S.S.R. The remaining pieces — Northern Bukovina, 4,900 sq. km. of the Moldavian A.S.S.R., and 17,600 sq. km. of Bessarabia, including the districts of Belgorod Dniestrovskiy, Hertza, Hotin, and Izmail — became part of the Ukraine. Although Romania re-occupied this area during the war, the Soviet Union prevailed in 1944. Moldavia once again declared independence on 1991-08-27, taking the name Moldova. More recently, the part of Moldova east of the Dniestr has formed a breakaway government, Transdniestria, which has not been recognized by any other country.

    Other names of country: Moldavia (Italian, obsolete); Moldavía (Icelandic); Moldávia (Portuguese); Moldavie (French); Moldavië (Dutch); Republic of Moldova (formal–English); Republica Moldoveneasca (formal).

    Origin of name: from Molda River (not to be confused with the Moldau).

division	abv	ISO	Russian	division	abv	ISO	Russian
Anenii Noi	AN	ANE	Novyye Aneny	Grigoriopol	GR	GRI	Grigoriopol'
Basarabeasca	BA	BAS	Bessarabka	Hîncești	HI	HIN	Gincheshty
Briceni	BR	BRI	Brichany	Ialoveni	IA	IAL	Yaloveny
Cahul	CH	CHL	Kagul	Leova	LE	LEO	Leovo
Cainari	CI	CAI	Kaynary	Nisporeni	NI	NIS	Nisporeny
Calarași	CA	CAL	Kalarash	Ocnița	OC	OCN	Oknitsa
Camenca	CM	CAM	Kamenka	Orhei	OH	OHI	Orgeyev
Cantemir	CN	CAN	Kantemir	Rezina	RZ	REZ	Rezina
Causeni	CU	CAS	Kaushany	Rîbnița	RT	RIT	Rybnitsa
Ciadîr-Lunga	CL	CIA	Chadyr-Lunga	Rîșcani	RS	RIS	Ryshkany
Cimișlia	CS	CIM	Chimishliya	Sîngerei	SI	SIN	Synzhereya
Comrat	CO	COM	Komrat	Slobodzia	SB	SLO	Slobodzeya
Criuleni	CR	CRI	Kriulyany	Șoldanești	SD	SOL	Sholdaneshty
Dondușeni	DO	DON	Dondyushany	Soroca	SO	SOA	Soroki
Drochia	DR	DRO	Drokiya	Ștefan Voda	SV	STE	Shtefan Voda
Dubasari	DB	DBI	Dubossary	Strașeni	ST	STR	Strasheny
Edineț	ED	EDI	Yedintsy	Taraclia	TA	TAR	Tarakliya
Falești	FA	FAL	Faleshty	Telenești	TE	TEL	Teleneshty
Florești	FL	FLO	Floreshty	Ungheni	UG	UGI	Ungeny
Glodeni	GL	GLO	Glodyany	Vulcanești	VU	VUL	Vulkaneshty

    Status: These divisions are districts.

    Abv: Two-letter code for international compatibility (defined by the author).

    ISO: Codes from ISO 3166-2.

    Russian: Transliteration from Cyrillic of the name used under Soviet rule.

Statistics for the districts are not yet available.

    Further subdivisions: ISO 3166-2 also lists these cities as divisions:

city	ISO	Russian	city	ISO	Russian
Balti	BAL	Bel'tsy	Rîbnița	RIB	Rybnitsa
Cahul	CAH	Kagul	Soroca	SOC	Soroki
Chișinau	CHI	Kishinev	Tighina	TIG	Bendery
Dubasari	DUB	Dubossary	Tiraspol	TIR	Tiraspol'
Orhei	ORH	Orgeyev	Ungheni	UNG	Ungeny

    Other names of subdivisions: During the existence of the Moldavian S.S.R., the Soviet Union imposed the use of the Cyrillic alphabet for the Romanian language spoken in Moldavia. Names transliterated from Cyrillic are different from the native forms now used by Moldova, as shown in the tables above.

Tighina: Bender (obsolete)

MONACO

ISO = MC/FIPS = MN   Language = French   Time zone = +1 ^{d} Capital = Monaco

Monaco has been independent for the entire 20th century.

Other names of country: Mónaco (Spanish); Mônaco (Portuguese); Mónakó (Icelandic); Principado de Mónaco (formal–Spanish); Principality of Monaco (formal–English); Principauté de Monaco (formal).

Origin of name: Italian *monaco*: monk.

division	abv	population	area-km	area-mi	capital
Monaco	MC	31,515	2	1	Monaco

Status: This division is the whole of the country, treated as a division for compatibility.

Abv: Two-letter code for international compatibility (defined by the author).

Population: 1996 estimate.

Area-km: Square kilometers.

Area-mi: Square miles.

Further subdivisions: Monaco is divided into four quartiers (districts; the fact that there are four of them is coincidental, because quartiers does not translate as "fourths"). They are Fontvieille, La Condamine (FIPS code MN01), Monaco-Ville (MN02), and Monte-Carlo (MN03). I have chosen not to regard them as primary administrative divisions, because it seems absurd to list divisions of a principality occupying less than one square mile.

Change history:

~1979   Fontvieille district created, in part from built land.

MONGOLIA

ISO = MN/FIPS = MG   Language = Halh Mongol   Time zone = +8 ^{d} Capital = Ulaanbaatar

Mongolia in 1900 was under Chinese rule. The area then called Mongolia is now Mongolia, parts of several Chinese provinces, and Tannu Tuva. It acquired independence from China by stages, losing Inner Mongolia and Tannu Tuva in the process. During this period, it was sometimes called Outer Mongolia, to help distinguish it from Inner Mongolia. Mongolia became independent from China on 1921-07-11.

Other names of country: Äussere Mongolei (German-obsolete); Mongolei (German); Mongólia (Portuguese); Mongólía (Icelandic); Mongólia Exterior (Portuguese-obsolete); Mongolie (French); Mongolië (Dutch); Mongolie-Extérieure (French-obsolete); Mongoliet (Danish, Swedish); Outer Mongolia (obsolete); State of Mongolia (formal–English).

Origin of name: from ethnic name Mongol, said to mean brave.

division	abv	ISO	FIPS	population	area-km	area-mi	capital
Arhangay	AR	073	MG01	89,200	55,000	21,200	Tsetserleg
Bayanhongor	BH	069	MG02	78,700	116,000	44,800	Bayanhongor
Bayan-Ölgiy	BO	071	MG03	99,300	46,000	17,800	Ölgiy
Bulgan	BU	067	MG21	56,700	49,000	18,900	Bulgan
Darhan	DA	037	MG05	88,600	200	100	Darhan
Dornod	DD	061	MG06	82,600	122,000	47,100	Choybalsan (Bayan Tumen)
Dornogovĭ	DG	063	MG07	58,600	111,000	42,900	Buyant-Uhaa (Saynshand)
Dundgovĭ	DU	059	MG08	51,900	78,000	30,100	Mandalgovĭ
Dzavhan	DZ	057	MG09	93,600	82,000	31,700	Uliastay (Džavchlant)
Erdenet	ER		MG22	58,200	——	——	Erdenet
Govĭ-Altay	GA	065	MG10	65,100	142,000	54,800	Altay (Yösönbulag)
Hentiy	HN	039	MG11	76,700	82,000	31,700	Öndörhaan
Hovd	HD	043	MG12	81,100	76,000	29,300	Dund-Us (Hovd, Jirgalanta)
Hövsgöl	HG	041	MG13	106,900	101,000	39,000	Mörön ➤

division	abv	ISO	FIPS	population	area-km	area-mi	capital
Ömnögovĭ	OG	053	MG14	43,500	165,000	63,700	Dalandzadgad
Övörhangay	OH	055	MG15	100,400	63,000	24,300	Arvayheer
Selenge	SL	049	MG16	92,000	42,800	16,500	Sühbaatar
Sühbaatar	SB	051	MG17	44,600	82,000	31,700	Baruun-Urt
Töv	TO	047	MG18	105,900	81,000	31,300	Dzuunmod
Ulaanbaatar	UB	1	MG20	575,000	2,000	800	Ulaanbaatar
Uvs	UV	046	MG19	91,800	69,000	26,600	Ulaangom
				2,140,400	1,565,000	604,300	

Status: These divisions are aymguud (provinces; sing. aymag), except for Darhan, Erdenet, and Ulaanbaatar, which are hotuud (municipalities; sing. hot).

Abv: Two-letter code for international compatibility (defined by the author).

ISO: Codes from ISO 3166-2. The standard lists two additional provinces, Govĭ-Sümber (064) and Orhon (035), which can't be confirmed from other sources.

FIPS: Codes from FIPS PUB 10-4.

Population: 1990 estimate.

Area-km: Square kilometers.

Area-mi: Square miles.

Capitals: Names in parentheses are older names, sometimes still in use.

Further subdivisions: The provinces are subdivided into somon (districts) and horin (urban districts).

Origins of names:

Choybalsan: after Khorloghiyin Choybalsan, revolutionary leader

Gobi: Halh Mongol *gov'*: desert steppe

Sühbaatar: after Damdiny Sühbaatar, revolutionary leader

Ulaanbaatar: Halh Mongol *ulaan*: red, *baatar*: hero, knight, also named in honor of Sühbaatar.

Change history:

The area of present-day Mongolia was divided into khanates in 1900. From west to east, they were Kobdo, Jassaktu, Sain-Noin, Tushetu, and Tsetsen. (Many variant spellings exist.)

1911	Name of country's capital changed from Urga to Niislel Khureheh (meaning "capital of Mongolia").
1921-07-11	Outer Mongolia became independent from China. The Mongolian provinces of Ala-Shan, Ordos, Silin Gol, and Chearim remained part of China. Tannu Tuva split from Kobdo and became an independent country, called the Urjanchai Republic.
1924-11-26	Mongolian People's Republic proclaimed. Name of country's capital changed from Niislel Khureheh to Ulaanbaatar (then usually transliterated Ulan Bator).
~1941	Mongolia reorganized into the provinces of Arhangay, Choybalsan, Dornogovĭ, Dzavhan, Hentiy, Kobdo (Hovd), Hövsgöl, Ömnögovĭ, Övörhangay, Selenge, Töv, and Uvs.
1941	Name of capital of Choybalsan province changed from Bayan Tumen to Choybalsan.
1954-02	A long strip of southern Mongolia was annexed to Nei Mongol province of China.
~1958	Bayanhongor, Bayan-Ölgiy, Bulgan, Dundgovĭ, Govĭ-Altay, and Sühbaatar provinces formed.
~1965	Darhan city split from Selenge; Ulaanbaatar city split from Töv.
~1967	Name of Choybalsan province changed to Dornod.
~1979	Erdenet city split from Bulgan.
~1994	Name of capital of Dornogovĭ province changed from Saynshand to Buyant-Uhaa; name of capital of Hovd province changed from Hovd to Dund-Us.

Other names of subdivisions: There are many ways to transliterate from Mongolian. This list shows some that have appeared in print.

Arhangay: Alahangai, Ara-Khangai, Archangaj, North Hangay, North Khangai (variant)

Bayanhongor: Bajanchongor, Bayan Khongor (variant)

Bayan-Ölgiy: Bajan-Ölgij, Bayan-Ulegei (variant)

Bulgan: Bulagan (variant)

Darhan: Darchan, Darhan uul, Darkhan (variant)

Dornod: Choibalsan, Choybalsan, Eastern (variant)

Dornogovĭ: Dornogov', East Gobi (variant); Góbi Oriental (Portuguese)

Dundgovĭ: Central Gobi, Dundgov', Middle Gobi (variant), Góbi Central (Portuguese)

Dzavhan: Dzabkhan, Dzavchan, Psapchyn (variant)

Govĭ-Altay: Gobi-Altai, Gov'altaj, Gov'altay, Govyaltaj (variant)

Hentiy: Chentij, Kentai, Kentei, Khentei (variant)

Hovd: Chovd, Khobdo, Kobdo (variant)

Hövsgöl: Chövsgöl, Khubsugud, Khubsugul, Kossogol (variant)

Ömnögovĭ: Góbi do Sul (Portuguese); Ömnögov', South Gobi (variant)

Övörhangay: Övörchangaj, South Hangay, South Khangai, Ublhangai, Ubur-Khangai (variant)

Selenge: Selenga (variant)

Sühbaatar: Süchbaatar, Suhe-Bator, Sukh-Batar, Sukhe-Bator (variant)

Töv: Central (variant)

Ulaanbaatar: Oulan-Bator (French); Ulan Bator, Ulan Bator Choto (variant)

Uvs: Ubsa Nor, Upsanol (variant)

MONTSERRAT

ISO = MS/FIPS = MH   Language = English   Time zone = -4   Capital = Plymouth

At the beginning of the 20th century, Montserrat was one of five presidencies of the Leeward Islands, a British colony. On 1956-06-30, each presidency became a separate colony. From 1958-01-03 to 1962-05-24, Montserrat was the smallest member (in area) of the Federation of the West Indies.

Origin of name: named for a similarly-shaped mountain in northern Spain.

division	abv	ISO	FIPS	division	abv	ISO	FIPS
Saint Anthony	SA	A	MH01	Saint Peter	SP	P	MH03
Saint Georges	SG	G	MH02				

Status: These divisions are parishes.

Abv: Two-letter code for international compatibility (defined by the author).

ISO: Codes from ISO 3166-2.

FIPS: Codes from FIPS PUB 10-4.

Territorial extent: Montserrat includes the island of Montserrat and a neighboring islet, Little Redonda.

MOROCCO

ISO = MA/FIPS = MO   Language = Arabic   Time zone = +0   Capital = Rabat

In 1900, Morocco was an independent sultanate, although several European countries had sought varying degrees of influence. Spain, in particular, had possessed enclaves on the Mediterranean coast for many years. Spain also claimed, and later occupied, the coastal enclave of Ifni in the south. The French and Germans agreed on 1911-11-04 to respect French pretensions to Morocco in exchange for a French cession in the Cameroons. In the Treaty of Fez (1912-03-30), the sultan agreed to a Spanish protectorate over two strips of territory at the north and south ends, and a French protectorate over the rest of the country. From 1925 to 1956, Tangier, with its environs, was administered jointly by the European powers. In 1956, the sultanate once again became independent, first in the French protectorate, then the Spanish, and finally Tangier. In 1976, Spain relinquished Spanish Sahara. Mauritania and Morocco promptly divided it between them. However, Mauritania ceded its portion to Morocco three years later. Morocco has administered the region since then. The United Nations intends to hold a referendum to determine the future of this territory, now known as Western Sahara. Pending the decision, other governments have withheld recognition of Morocco's sovereignty over Western Sahara.

Other names of country: al-Mamlaka al-Maghrebia (formal); Kingdom of Morocco (formal–English); Maroc (French); Marocco (Italian); Marocko (Swedish); Marokko (Danish, Dutch, Finnish, German, Norwegian); Marokkó (Icelandic); Marrocos (Portuguese); Marruecos, Reino de Marruecos (Spanish).

Origin of name: Arabic *al-Maghreb*: the west, *al-aksa*: farthest.

division	abv	ISO	FIPS	typ	reg	population	area-km	area-mi
Agadir-Ida-Tanane	AG	AGD	MO01	f	SU	365,965	5,910	2,282
Aïn Chock-Hay Hassani	AC	——	——	f	CE	516,261	——	——
Aïn Sebaâ-Hay Mohammedi	AS	——	——	f	CE	520,993	——	——
Al Fida-Derb-Sultan	FS	——	——	f	CE	386,700	——	——
Al Haouz	HZ	HAO	——	v	TS	435,090	——	——
Al Hoceïma	HC	HOC	MO02	v	CN	382,972	3,550	1,371
Al Ismaïlia	IS	——	——	f	CS	314,916	——	——
Assa-Zag	AZ	ASZ	MO43	v	SU	21,848	——	——
Azilal	AL	AZI	MO03	v	CE	454,914	10,050	3,880
Béni-Mellal	BM	BEM	MO05	v	CE	869,748	7,075	2,732
Ben M'sick-Sidi Othmane	BO	——	——	f	CE	704,365	——	——
Ben Slimane	BS	BES	MO04	v	CE	213,398	2,760	1,066
Berkane-Taourirt	BT	BER	——	v	ES	399,017	——	——
Boulemane	BU	BOM	MO06	v	CN	161,622	14,395	5,558
Casablanca-Anfa	CA	CAS	MO07	f	CE	523,279	1,615	624
Chefchaouen	CF	CHE	MO08	v	NO	439,303	4,350	1,680
Chichaoua	CI	CHI	——	v	TS	311,800	——	——
Chtouka-Aït Baha	CB	BAH	——	v	SU	240,092	——	——
El Hajeb	HJ	HAJ	——	v	CS	180,494	——	——
El Jadida	JD	JDI	MO09	v	CE	970,894	6,000	2,317
El Kelâa des Sraghna	KS	KES	MO10	v	TS	682,428	10,070	3,888
Errachidia	RD	ERR	MO11	v	CS	522,117	59,585	23,006
Essaouira	ES	ESI	MO12	v	TS	433,681	6,335	2,446
Fès el Jadid-Dar Dbibagh	FD	——	——	f	CN	256,340	——	——
Fès-Médina	FM	FES	MO13	f	CN	284,822	5,400	2,085
Figuig	FG	FIG	MO14	v	ES	117,011	55,990	21,618
Guelmim	GU	GUE	MO42	v	SU	147,124	28,750	11,100
Ifrane	IF	IFR	MO34	v	CS	127,677	3,310	1,278
Inezgane-Aït Melloul	IA	MEL	——	f	SU	292,799	——	——
Jerada	JR	IRA	——	v	ES	149,686	——	——
Kénitra	KT	KEN	MO15	v	NO	979,210	4,745	1,832
Khémisset	KM	KHE	MO16	v	NO	485,541	8,305	3,207
Khénifra	KF	KHN	MO17	v	CS	465,061	12,320	4,757
Khouribga	KB	KHO	MO18	v	CE	480,839	4,250	1,641
Laâyoune	LY	——	MO35	v	SU	153,978	39,360	15,197
Larache	LR	LAR	MO41	v	NO	431,476	——	——
Marrakech-Ménara	MR	——	——	f	TS	432,547	——	——
Marrakech-Médina	MM	MAR	MO19	f	TS	189,367	14,755	5,697
Méchouar de Casablanca	MC	——	——	f	CE	3,956	——	——
Meknès-El Menzeh	ME	MEK	MO20	f	CS	293,525	3,995	1,542
Mohammedia	MO	——	——	f	CE	170,063	——	——
Nador	NA	NAD	MO21	v	ES	683,914	6,130	2,367
Ouarzazate	OZ	OUA	MO22	v	SU	694,884	41,550	16,043
Oujda-Angad	OA	OUJ	MO23	v	ES	419,063	20,700	7,992
Rabat	RA	RBA	MO24	f	NO	623,457	1,275	492
Safi	SA	SAF	MO25	v	TS	822,564	7,285	2,813
Salé	SL	——	——	f	NO	631,803	——	——
Sefrou	SF	SEF	——	v	CN	237,095	——	——
Settat	SE	SET	MO26	v	CE	847,422	9,750	3,764
Sidi Bernoussi-Zenata	SZ	——	——	f	CE	268,586	——	——
Sidi Kacem	SK	SIK	MO38	v	NO	645,872	4,060	1,568
Sidi-Youssef-Ben-Ali	SY	——	——	f	TS	239,291	——	——
Skhirate-Témara	ST	——	——	f	NO	244,801	——	——
Tanger	TG	TNG	MO27	v	NO	627,963	1,195	461
Tan-Tan	TT	TNT	MO36	v	SU	58,079	17,295	6,678
Taounate	TN	TAO	MO37	v	CN	628,840	5,585	2,156
Taroudannt	TR	TAR	MO39	v	SU	693,968	16,460	6,355
Tata	TA	TAT	MO29	v	SU	119,298	25,925	10,010 ►

division	abv	ISO	FIPS	typ	reg	population	area-km	area-mi
Taza	TZ	TAZ	MO30	v	CN	708,025	15,020	5,799
Tétouan	TE	TET	MO40	v	NO	537,290	6,025	2,326
Tiznit	TI	TIZ	MO32	v	SU	347,821	6,960	2,687
Zouagha-Moulay Yacoub	ZM	——	——	f	CN	382,594	——	——
						25,975,549	498,090	192,315

Status: These divisions are wilaya (provinces: v) and prefectures or municipalities (f).

Abv: Two-letter code for international compatibility (defined by the author).

ISO: Codes from ISO 3166-2.

FIPS: Codes from FIPS PUB 10-4.

Reg: The provinces and prefectures are grouped into seven economic regions, which have no administrative function. The codes in this column are also from ISO 3166-2, and derive from the French names of the regions, as follows:

region	ISO	French	region	ISO	French
Center	CE	Centre	North-West	NO	Nord-Ouest
North Center	CN	Centre-Nord	South	SU	Sud
South Center	CS	Centre-Sud	Tensift	TS	Tensift
East	ES	Est (Oriental)			

Population: 1994 census.

Area-km: Square kilometers (some prefecture areas are combined with the central city).

Area-mi: Square miles.

Capitals have the same names as the divisions themselves.

Further subdivisions: The provinces and prefectures are subdivided into communes.

Territorial extent: Morocco does not include the Spanish places of sovereignty in Africa, namely, the coastal cities of Ceuta and Melilla with small surrounding enclaves, and the islands of Peñón de Vélez de la Gomera, Peñón de Alhucemas, its nearby neighbors Isla de Mar and Isla de Tierra, and the Islas Chafarinas (Isabel II, Congreso, and del Rey).

Origins of names:

Agadir: Touareg for wall, possibly from Semitic *gadir*: walled place

Casablanca: Spanish *casa*: house, *blanca*: white, a calque of the city's Arabic name, Dar el Beida

El Jadida: Arabic for the new one, so named when the city was rebuilt

Essaouira: from Arabic for the beautiful

Fès-Médina: from a Berber word for springs + Arabic *madinat*: city

Marrakech: Classic Arabic *marrukuch*: the well adorned one

Rabat: after the city, originally *ar-Ribat al-fath*: the stronghold of victory

Tétouan: Berber *titawin*: little wells

Change history:

Note: The situation in Morocco is unusually complex. Since its independence, Morocco has been divided into provinces and prefectures. They are supposed to be at the same administrative level. However, the prefectures are much smaller in area, as each one contains only one or two cities and their suburbs. Many sources do not even list the prefectures. The numbers of provinces and prefectures have grown fairly steadily over the years. This history is only an approximation to the changes that have occurred. The treatment of prefectures is incomplete.

1912-03-30	Morocco divided into a French protectorate and a Spanish protectorate.
1925-06-01	Tangier established as an international zone (effective date).
~1946	French protectorate consisted of the regions of Agadir, Casablanca, Fès, Marrakech, Meknès, Oujda, and Rabat. Spanish protectorate consisted of the regions of Gomara, Kert, Lucus, Rif, and Yebala (northern area) and the Southern Protectorate of Morocco.
1956-04-07	Morocco became independent.
1956-10-29	Status of Tangier changed from international zone to province of Morocco.
~1957	Morocco divided into provinces. The provinces of Agadir, Beni-Mellal, Casablanca, Fès, Marrakech, Mazagan, Meknès, Ouarzazate, Oujda, Rabat, Safi, Tafilalet, and Taza corresponded to French Morocco. The provinces of Chauen, Larache, Nador,

Rif, Tangier, and Tetuan corresponded to Spanish Morocco (the northern protectorate). Southern Protectorate of Morocco became the province of Tarfaya.

1962-07-09	Name of Kenitra (the city) officially changed to Mina Hassan Tani (Port Hassan II, in honor of the king); however, the new name has not been in use.
~1967	Name of Tafilalet province and its capital changed to Ksar es Souk. Name of Rif province and its capital changed to Al Hoceïma. Chauen, Larache, and Tetuan provinces merged to form Tétouan. Mazagan province merged with Casablanca.
1969-06-30	Ifni restored to Morocco by Spain, becoming part of Agadir province.
~1973	El Jadida (formerly Mazagan), Khouribga, and Settat provinces split from Casablanca; Kenitra province split from Rabat; name of Rabat province changed to Rabat-Salé.
~1978	Azilal province formed from parts of Beni-Mellal and Marrakech. Ben Slimane province split from Casablanca. Boulemane province formed from parts of Fès and Taza. Chefchaouen (formerly Chauen) province split from Tétouan. Essaouira province split from Safi. Figuig province formed from parts of Ksar es Souk and Oujda. El Kelâa des Sraghna province split from Marrakech. Khémisset province split from Rabat. Khénifra province formed from parts of Ksar es Souk and Meknès. Taounate province split from Fès. Tata province formed from parts of Agadir and Ouarzazate. Tiznit province split from Agadir.
~1980	Tarfaya province split into three parts. Two of the parts became Guelmim and Tan-Tan provinces. The third part merged with Laayoune province in Western Sahara. Since Morocco's sovereignty over Western Sahara is not internationally recognized, we must regard this third part as a separate Laayoune province in Morocco.
1981	Casablanca divided into five prefectures: Aïn Chock-Hay Hassani, Aïn Sebâa-Hay Mohammedi, Ben M'sick-Sidi Othmane, Casablanca-Anfa, and Mohammedia-Zenata.
~1982	Ifrane province split from Meknès. Name of Ksar es Souk province and its capital changed to Errachidia.
~1986	Sidi Kacem province split from Kenitra. Taroudannt province split from Agadir.
~1990	Larache province split from Tétouan. Rabat-Salé province split into three prefectures: Rabat, Salé, and Skhirate-Témara.
~1993	Agadir province split into Chtouka-Aït Baha province and Agadir-Ida-Tenane and Inezgane-Aït Melloul prefectures. Meknès province split into El Hajeb province and Meknès-El Menzeh prefecture. Oujda province split into Berkane-Taourirt, Jerada, and Taourirt provinces and Oujda-Angad prefecture. Assa-Zag province split from Guelmim. Chichaoua and Al Haouz provinces split from Marrakech. Sefrou province split from Fès.
~1994	Mohammedia-Zenata prefecture split into Al Fida-Derb-Sultan, Méchouar de Casablanca, Mohammedia, and Sidi Bernoussi-Zenata (possibly with annexations from other prefectures). Marrakech split into Marrakech-Ménara province and Marrakech-Médina and Sidi-Youssef-Ben-Ali prefectures. Fès province split into Fès el Jadid-Dar Dbibagh, Fès-Médina, and Zouagha-Moulay Yacoub prefectures. Al Ismaïlia prefecture split from Meknès-El Menzeh, El Hajeb, or parts of both.
~1997	Berkane-Taourirt province split into Berkane and Taourirt.

Other names of subdivisions: Native names are written in the Arabic alphabet. There are many ways to transliterate from Arabic to the Roman alphabet. For example, the definite article can be transliterated el or al. Sources also disagree on the use of diacritical marks. Obsolete names may be for the city rather than the province.

Al Hoceïma: Alhucemas (Spanish); El Hoceïma, El Hosseïma (variant); Rif, Villa Sanjurjo (obsolete)

Ben Slimane: Boulhaut (obsolete)

Boulemane: Boulmane (variant)

Casablanca: Dar el Beida, Ed Dar el Baida (variant)

Chefchaouen: Chaouen, Chauen, Xauen (obsolete); Chechaouene, Chefchaouene (variant); Xexauen (Spanish)

El Jadida: Ej Jdida (variant); Mazagan (obsolete)

El Kelâa des Sraghna: El Kelâa des Srarhna, El Kelâa-Sraghna, Qel'at es Sraghna, Qel'at Sraghna (variant)

Errachidia: Rachidia, Rachidiya (variant); Ksar es Souk, Tafilalet (obsolete)

Essaouira: Mogador (obsolete); Eç Çaouira, Saouira (variant); Essauira (Italian)

Fès: Fâs, Fez (variant)
Guelmim: Aouguelmim (obsolete); Goulimim, Goulimime, Goulimine (variant)
Jerada: Irada (variant)
Kénitra: Port-Lyautey (obsolete); Qenitra (variant)
Laayoune: La'youn (variant)
Larache: El-Araïch, Laarach (variant)
Marrakech: Maroc (French-obsolete); Marrakesch (German); Marrakesh (variant); Morocco (obsolete)
Meknès: Mekinez (obsolete); Mequinez (Spanish)
Nador: Villa Nador (Spanish-obsolete)

Ouarzazate: Ouarzazat, Warzazat (variant)
Oujda: Oudjda (variant)
Rabat-Salé: Er Ribat, Rabat (variant)
Safi: Asfi (variant); Saffi (obsolete)
Sidi Kacem: Petitjean (French-obsolete); Sidi Qassem (variant)
Tangier: Tanger (French); Tânger (Portuguese); Tangeri (Italian); Tanja (variant)
Tan-Tan: Tantane (variant)
Taroudannt: Taroudant (variant)
Tétouan: Tetouane, Tetuan (variant); Tetuán (Spanish)

MOZAMBIQUE

ISO = MZ/FIPS = MZ   Language = Portuguese   Time zone = +2   Capital = Maputo

At the beginning of the 20th century, the Portuguese held a colony called Estado de Africa Oriental (literally, State of East Africa, but usually called Portuguese East Africa). Some parts of it had been chartered to Companhia de Moçambique (the Mozambique Company) and Companhia do Nyassa (the Nyassa Company). As the colony became better organized, it came to be called Mozambique as a whole. Mozambique attained full independence on 1975-06-25.

Other names of country: Mocambique (Danish); Moçambique (Portuguese, Swedish); Mosambik (Finnish, German, Norwegian); Mósambík (Icelandic); Mozambico (Italian); Republic of Mozambique (formal–English); República de Moçambique (formal).

Origin of name: after the city of that name.

division	abv	ISO	FIPS	population	area-km	area-mi	capital
Cabo Delgado	CD	P	MZ01	1,109,921	82,625	31,902	Pemba (Porto Amélia)
Gaza	GA	G	MZ02	1,138,724	75,709	29,231	Xai-Xai (Vila de João Belo)
Inhambane	IN	I	MZ03	1,167,022	68,615	26,492	Inhambane
Manica	MN	B	MZ10	756,886	61,661	23,807	Chimoio (Vila Pery)
Maputo	MP	L	MZ04	544,692	25,756	9,944	Maputo (Lourenço Marques)
Maputo [city]	MC	MPM		1,006,765	602	232	Maputo (Lourenço Marques)
Nampula	NM	N	MZ06	2,837,856	81,606	31,508	Nampula
Niassa	NS	A	MZ07	607,670	129,056	49,829	Lichinga (Vila Cabral)
Sofala	SO	S	MZ05	1,257,710	68,018	26,262	Beira
Tete	TE	T	MZ08	981,319	100,724	38,890	Tete
Zambezia	ZA	Q	MZ09	2,952,251	105,008	40,544	Quelimane
				14,360,816	799,380	308,641	

Status: These divisions are provincias (provinces), except for Maputo [city], which is a city.
Abv: Two-letter code for international compatibility (defined by the author).
ISO: Codes from ISO 3166-2.
FIPS: Codes from FIPS PUB 10-4.
Population: 1987 estimate.
Area-km: Square kilometers.
Area-mi: Square miles.
Capital: Present name and (colonial name, where different).
Further subdivisions: The provinces are subdivided into distritos (districts). The districts are further subdivided into town and city districts and localidades (localities).
Territorial extent: Cabo Delgado includes Ilhas do Ibo, Vamizi, Matemo, Metudo, and some other small coastal islands.
Inhambane includes Ilhas do Bazaruto and Benguérua.
Maputo includes Ilha Inhaca.

Nampula includes Ilhas Angoche, Njoro, and Moçambique.
Sofala includes Ilhas Chiloane, Macau, and Buene.
Origins of names:

Lourenço Marques: for the Portuguese trader who established
a post there in 1544.
Maputo: after the Maputo River.
Niassa: after Lake Nyasa, which comes from a Kitumbuka
word for lake.

Sofala: from Arabic for low, flat region.
Zambezia: after the Zambezi River.

Change history: In 1900, the part of modern Mozambique northwest of the Zambezi and Shire Rivers was called Moçambique; the rest of it was Lourenço Marques. Various districts existed, and even issued stamps, during the first part of the century, including Inhambane, Lourenço Marques, Mozambique Colony, Mozambique Company, Nyassa Company, Quelimane, Tete, and Zambesia. The Nyassa Company territory is now Cabo Delgado and Niassa.

1919-06-28	Kiongo Triangle (over 1,000 sq. km., south of the Rovuma River) transferred from German East Africa to Mozambique by the Versailles Treaty.
1942-07-19	Charter of the Mozambique Company expired; its territory, known as Manica and Sofala, became a district of Mozambique.
1943-01-01	Mozambique constituted as four districts: Manica and Sofala, Niassa, Sul do Save (South of the Save River), and Zambezia.
1954-10-20	Cabo Delgado and Mozambique districts split from Niassa. Sul do Save district divided into Gaza, Inhambane, and Lourenço Marques. Tete district split from Manica and Sofala.
1975-06-25	Mozambique became independent.
1976	Name of Lourenço Marques district changed to Maputo. Names of five district capitals changed, as listed in table above.
~1977	Name of Mozambique district changed to Nampula.
~1978	Status of divisions changed from districts to provinces. Manica and Sofala district divided into Manica province and Sofala province.

Other names of subdivisions:
Provinces are sometimes called by the names of their capitals.

Maputo [city]: Lourenço Marques (obsolete)
Nampula: Moçambique (Portuguese-obsolete); Mozambique

(obsolete)

MYANMAR

ISO = MM/FIPS = BM   Language = Burmese   Time zone = +6:30   Capital = Yangon

In 1900, Burma was one of the provinces of India. It was detached from India as a separate crown colony on 1937-04-01. It was occupied by Japan during World War II. It became independent on 1948-01-04. The government requested the use of the name Union of Myanmar in English as of 1989-06-19. Most western organizations have complied, with the exception, so far, of the U.S. Government.
Other names of country: Birma (German-obsolete); Birmania (Italian-obsolete, Spanish-obsolete); Birmanie (French-obsolete); Burma (Swedish, obsolete); Mianmá (Portuguese); Mjanmar (Icelandic); Myanmar Naingngandaw (formal); Union of Myanmar (formal–English).
Origin of name: Burmese *myamma naygan*: strong.

division	abv	ISO	FIPS	type	population	area-km	area-mi	capital
Ayeyarwaddy	AY	07	BM03	dv	4,991,057	35,167	13,578	Bassein ➤

division	abv	ISO	FIPS	type	population	area-km	area-mi	capital
Bago	BA	02	BM16	dv	3,800,240	49,787	19,223	Pegu
Chin	CH	14	BM02	st	368,985	36,009	13,903	Haka
Kachin	KC	11	BM04	st	903,982	87,808	33,903	Myitkyina
Kayah	KH	12	BM06	st	168,355	11,670	4,506	Loi-kaw
Kayin	KN	13	BM05	st	1,057,505	28,726	11,091	Pa-an
Magwe	MG	03	BM15	dv	3,241,103	44,799	17,297	Magwe
Mandalay	MD	04	BM08	dv	4,580,923	34,253	13,225	Mandalay
Mon	MO	15	BM13	st	1,682,041	11,831	4,568	Moulmein
Rakhine	RA	16	BM01	st	2,045,891	36,762	14,194	Akyab (Sittwe)
Sagaing	SA	01	BM10	dv	3,855,991	99,150	38,282	Sagaing
Shan	SH	17	BM11	st	3,718,706	158,222	61,090	Taunggyi
Tanintharyi	TN	05	BM12	dv	917,628	43,328	16,729	Tavoy
Yangon	YA	06	BM17	dv	3,973,782	521	201	Yangon
					35,306,189	678,033	261,790	

Status: These divisions are taing (dv: divisions) or states (st). Generally speaking, states are semi-autonomous areas allocated to particular ethnic groups.

Abv: Two-letter code for international compatibility (defined by the author).

ISO: Codes from ISO 3166-2.

FIPS: Codes from FIPS PUB 10-4.

Population: 1991 census.

Area-km: Square kilometers.

Area-mi: Square miles.

Capital: The capital of Rakhine has been known as Akyab or Sittwe interchangeably for many years. During the 1960s, the capital of Magwe temporarily moved from Magwe to Yenangyaung.

Further subdivisions: The divisions and states are subdivided into kayaing (districts) and substates. These are further subdivided into townships and villages. Here are the names of the districts and substates:

Ayeyarwaddy: Bassein, Henzada, Ma-ubin, Myaungmya, Pyapon

Bago: Hanthawaddy, Insein, Pegu, Prome, Tharrawaddy

Chin: Northern Chin Hills, Pakokku Hill Tracts, Southern Chin Hills

Kachin: Bhamo, Myitkyina, Putao

Kayah: Bawlake, Kantarawaddy, Kyebogyi, Mong Pai

Kayin: Salween

Magwe: Magwe, Minbu, Pakokku, Thayetmyo

Mandalay: Kyaukse, Mandalay, Meiktila, Myingyan, Yamethin

Mon: Mon

Rakhine: Kyaukpyu, Sandoway, Sittwe

Sagaing: Katha, Lower Chindwin, Sagaing, Shwebo, Upper Chindwin

Shan: Eastern, Northern, Southern

Tanintharyi: Amherst, Mergui, Tavoy, Thaton, Toungoo

Yangon: Yangon

Territorial extent: Ayeyarwaddy includes the islands in the Preparis Channel: Great Coco, Little Coco, Preparis, and Table Islands, as well as the islands in the delta of the Ayeyarwaddy (Irrawaddy) River.

Mon includes Bilugyun Island in the mouth of the Salween River, and some small coastal islands.

Rakhine includes Ramree and Cheduba Islands, Ye Kyun, and the Boronga Islands.

Tanintharyi includes the Mergui Archipelago, from Christie, Auriol, and Graham Islands in the south to Mali Kyun in the north; and the Moscos Islands off Tavoy. The largest islands in the Merguis are Kadan Kyun (King), Kanmaw Kyun (Kissaraing), Letsok-aw Kyun (Dome), and Lanbi Kyun (Sullivan).

Origins of names:

Ayeyarwaddy: from the river name, which comes from Sanskrit for refreshing

Kawthule: Karen for flowery land

Tanintharyi: from Malay for land of delight

Yangon: Burmese for armistice, named by King Alompra after conquering the area

Change history:

In 1900, Burma was a province of India, and was divided into Lower Burma (capital Rangoon) and Upper Burma (Mandalay). Upper Burma contained the divisions of Mandalay, Meiktila, Minbu, Sagaing, and the Federated Shan States (North and South). Lower Burma consisted of Arakan, Irrawaddy, Pegu, and Tenasserim. These divisions were further subdivided into districts.

1922-10-10	Karenni States (Bawlake, Kantarawaddy, and Kyebogyi) placed under the administration of the Federated Shan States.
~1940	Name of Minbu division changed to Magwe; Meiktila division merged with Mandalay.
1948-01-04	Burmese independence. Chin Hills special division split from Arakan division. Kachin state formed by taking Myitkyina and Bhamo districts from Mandalay; Karen state formed by taking parts of Amherst, Thaton, and Toungoo districts from Tenasserim; Karenni state split from Federated Shan States; Shan state formed by merging the Federated Shan States and the Wa States.
1952-01-14	Name of Karenni state changed to Kayah.
1964	Rangoon division, formerly a district of Pegu division, split from Pegu. Capital of Pegu division changed from Rangoon to Pegu. Name of Karen state changed to Kawthule.
1974-01-04	New constitution enters in force. Status and name of Chin Hills special division changed to Chin state. Capital of Chin moved from Falam to Haka. Name of Kawthule state changed back to Karen. Mon state split from Tenasserim division. Capital of Tenasserim moved from Moulmein to Tavoy.
1989-06-19	Name of country changed from Burma to Myanmar. Names of Irrawaddy, Pegu, Rangoon, and Tenasserim divisions and Karen state changed to Ayeyarwaddy, Bago, Yangon, Tanintharyi, and Kayin, respectively. Name of national capital changed from Rangoon to Yangon.

Other names of subdivisions: Names of the states often include the generic (e.g., Chin State; État Mon).

Ayeyarwaddy: Irawadi (German); Irraouaddi (French); Irrauaddy (Portuguese); Irrawaddy (obsolete)

Bago: Pégou (French); Pegu (obsolete)

Chin: Chin Hills (obsolete)

Kayah: Karenni (obsolete)

Kayin: Karen, Kawthule (obsolete); Karin, Kawthoolei, Kawthulay (variant)

Magwe: Magway (variant); Minbu (obsolete)

Mon: Mun (variant)

Rakhine: Arakan (obsolete)

Tanintharyi: Tenasserim (obsolete); Thanintharyi (variant)

Yangon: Rangoon (obsolete); Rangum (Portuguese); Rangun (German); Rangún (Spanish)

NAMIBIA

ISO = NA/FIPS = WA   Language = English, Afrikaans   Time zone = +1 [d]   Capital = Windhoek

South-West Africa was a German protectorate at the beginning of the 20th century. After World War I, when Germany was divested of all its colonies, South-West Africa was made a Class C mandated territory of South Africa (Treaty of Versailles, effective 1920-12-17). After World War II, there was a prolonged dispute in which South Africa continued to exercise its mandate, while the United Nations ineffectually revoked it. The United Nations renamed it from South-West Africa to Namibia on 1968-06-12. Namibia finally gained its independence from South Africa on 1990-03-21.

Other names of country: Namibía (Icelandic); Namíbia (Portuguese); Namibie (French); Namibië (Dutch); Republic of Namibia (formal–English); South West Africa (obsolete); Suidwes-Afrika (Afrikaans-obsolete).

Origin of name: after the Namib Desert, from a Nama word variously translated as bare place, vast arid plain, area where there is nothing.

division	ISO	FIPS	capital	division	ISO	FIPS	capital
Caprivi	CA	WA28	Katima Mulilo	Okavango	OK	WA34	Rundu
Erongo	ER	WA29	Omaruru	Omaheke	OH	WA35	Gobabis
Hardap	HA	WA30	Mariental	Omusati	OS	WA36	Ongandjera
Karas	KA	WA31	Keetmanshoop	Oshana	ON	WA37	Oshakati
Khomas	KH	WA21	Windhoek	Oshikoto	OT	WA38	Tsumeb
Kunene	KU	WA32	Opuwo	Otjozondjupa	OD	WA39	Grootfontein
Ohangwena	OW	WA33	Oshikango				

Status: These divisions are regions.

ISO: Codes from ISO 3166-2.

FIPS: Codes from FIPS PUB 10-4.

Population, area: The division into regions is so recent that figures are not yet available.

Territorial extent: In the division into districts prevailing before 1990, Hereroland East was split into two disjoint parts, separated by Gobabis. The Caprivi Strip (Afrikaans: Caprivi Zipfel), a panhandle in the northeast, consisted of Caprivi East and part of Kavango.

Origins of names:

Bethanien: German for Bethany, after the Biblical city   Damaraland: Land of the Damaras (Hottentot tribe)

Change history:

1922 Walvis Bay (then called Walfisch Bay) transferred from Cape Province of the Union of South Africa to Namibia (then called South West Africa).

1948 South Africa reclaimed sovereignty over Walvis Bay.

~1977 Divisions of Namibia reorganized. Kavango and Bushmanland split from Grootfontein. Part of Outjo and all of Walvis Bay (a district adjacent to the enclave of Walvis Bay) annexed to Swakopmund. Damaraland formed from parts of Outjo, Omaruru, and Swakopmund. Owambo formed from Ovamboland and a small part of Grootfontein. Hereroland West formed from parts of Grootfontein, Gobabis, and Otjiwarongo. Part of Rehoboth transferred to Windhoek. Hereroland East split from Gobabis. Gibeon (capital Mariental) split into Mariental (with the addition of part of Rehoboth) and Namaland (with the addition of parts of Bethanien and Keetmanshoop). Other, lesser boundary adjustments occurred. Names of Kaokoveld and Warmbad changed to Kaokoland and Karasburg, respectively. The resulting divisions were:

division	FIPS	population	area-km	area-mi	typ	capital	became
Bethanien	WA01	2,911	18,004	6,951	m	Bethanien	Karas
Bushmanland	WA03	3,828	18,468	7,131	r	Tsumkwe	Otjozondjupa
Caprivi East	WA02	70,782	11,533	4,453	r	Katima Mulilo	Caprivi
Damaraland	WA22	32,938	46,560	17,977	r	Khorixas	Erongo, Kunene
Gobabis	WA04	27,844	41,447	16,003	m	Gobabis	Omaheke
Grootfontein	WA05	34,905	26,520	10,239	m	Grootfontein	Otjozondjupa
Hereroland East	WA23	25,255	51,949	20,058	r	Otjinene	Omaheke, Otjozondjupa
Hereroland West	WA24	18,824	16,500	6,371	r	Okakarara	Otjozondjupa
Kaokoland	WA06	26,313	58,190	22,467	r	Opuwo	Kunene
Karasburg	WA20	11,284	38,116	14,717	m	Karasburg	Karas
Karibib	WA07	12,147	13,230	5,108	m	Karibib	Erongo
Kavango	WA25	136,592	50,955	19,674	r	Rundu	Caprivi, Okavango
Keetmanshoop	WA08	20,804	38,302	14,788	m	Keetmanshoop	Karas
Lüderitz	WA09	17,475	53,063	20,488	m	Lüderitz	Karas
Maltahöhe	WA10	4,110	25,573	9,874	m	Maltahöhe	Hardap
Mariental	WA26	24,892	47,689	18,413	m	Mariental	Hardap
Namaland	WA27	16,234	21,120	8,154	r	Gibeon	Hardap, Karas
Okahandja	WA11	20,118	17,640	6,811	m	Okahandja	Otjozondjupa
Omaruru	WA12	7,446	8,425	3,253	m	Omaruru	Erongo
Otjiwarongo	WA13	23,326	20,550	7,934	m	Otjiwarongo	Otjozondjupa
Outjo	WA14	12,377	38,722	14,951	m	Outjo	Kunene
Owambo	WA15	615,057	51,800	20,000	r	Ondangwa	Ohangwena,Omusati,Oshana,Oshikoto
Rehoboth	WA16	34,372	14,182	5,476	r	Rehoboth	Hardap, Khomas
Swakopmund	WA17	20,757	44,697	17,258	m	Swakopmund	Erongo, Hardap, Kunene
Tsumeb	WA18	22,511	16,420	6,340	m	Tsumeb	Kunene, Oshikoto
Windhoek	WA21	158,609	33,489	12,930	m	Windhoek	Khomas
		1,401,711	824,268	318,253			

FIPS: Codes from FIPS PUB 10-4.

Population: 1991 census.

Area-km: Square kilometers.

Area-mi: Square miles.

Typ: Created as magisterial districts (m) or reserves (r).
Became: Present-day region(s) occupying the same territory.

~1991	Namibia reorganized from 26 districts into 13 regions.
1992-08	Walvis Bay placed under joint Namibian and South African administration.
1994-03-01	Walvis Bay fully incorporated into Namibia as part of Erongo region.

Other names of subdivisions:

Caprivi: Liambezi (variant)

Ohangwena: Ohanguena (variant)

Former divisions:

Bushmanland: Boesmanland (Afrikaans)

Caprivi East: Caprivi Oos (Afrikaans); East Caprivi (variant)

Hereroland East: Hereroland Oos (Afrikaans)

Hereroland West: Hereroland Wes (Afrikaans)

Kaokoland: Kaokoveld (obsolete)

Karasburg: Warmbad (obsolete)

Walvis Bay: Walfisch Bay (obsolete); Walvisbaai (Afrikaans)

Windhoek: Windhuk (German)

NAURU

ISO = NR/FIPS = NR   Language = Nauruan, English   Time zone = +12   Capital = Yaren

Initially a German possession, Nauru was occupied by Australia in 1914-11. The League of Nations mandated it to the British Empire on 1920-12-17. Nauru was occupied by Japan during World War II. The United Nations extended the League of Nations mandate as a trusteeship of Australia, New Zealand, and the United Kingdom on 1947-11-01. Nauru became independent in 1968.

Other names of country: Naoero (formal); Nárú (Icelandic); Republic of Nauru (formal–English).

division	ISO	FIPS	division	ISO	FIPS
Aiwo	AI	NR01	Denigomodu	DE	NR08
Anabar	AB	NR02	Ewa	EW	NR09
Anetan	AT	NR03	Ijuw	IJ	NR10
Anibare	AR	NR04	Meneng	ME	NR11
Baiti	BA	NR05	Nibok	NI	NR12
Boe	BO	NR06	Uaboe	UA	NR13
Buada	BU	NR07	Yaren	YA	NR14

Status: These divisions are districts.
ISO: Codes from ISO 3166-2.
FIPS: Codes from FIPS PUB 10-4.
Capitals: The districts, which average only 1.5 sq. km., can be considered as the Nauruan equivalent of cities; therefore, each district is its own capital.
Territorial extent: Nauru consists of just a single island.

NEPAL

ISO = NP/FIPS = NP   Language = Nepali   Time zone = +5:45   Capital = Kathmandu

Nepal has been independent during the entire 20th century.
Other names of country: Kingdom of Nepal (formal–English); Népal (French); Nepal Adhirajya (formal).

division	ISO	FIPS	population	area-km	area-mi	reg	capitals
Bagmati	BA	NP01	2,250,805	9,428	3,640	1	Kathmandu
Bheri	BH	NP02	1,103,043	10,545	4,071	2	Nepalganj, Surkhet
Dhawalagiri	DH	NP03	490,877	8,148	3,146	3	Baglun
Gandaki	GA	NP04	1,266,128	12,275	4,739	3	Pokhara
Janakpur	JA	NP05	2,061,816	9,669	3,733	1	Sindhulimadi, Ramechhap
Karnali	KA	NP06	260,529	21,351	8,244	2	Jumla
Kosi	KO	NP07	1,728,247	9,669	3,733	4	Biratnagar, Dharan
Lumbini	LU	NP08	2,013,673	8,975	3,465	3	Butawal, Bhairawa
Mahakali	MA	NP09	664,952	6,989	2,698	5	Dadeldhura, Patan
Mechi	ME	NP10	1,118,210	8,196	3,164	4	Ilam
Narayani	NA	NP11	1,871,334	8,313	3,210	1	Hetauda (Bhimphedi), Birgunj
Rapti	RA	NP12	1,046,842	10,482	4,047	2	Tulsipur, Sallyana
Sagarmatha	SA	NP13	1,600,292	10,591	4,089	4	Rajbiraj
Seti	SE	NP14	1,014,349	12,550	4,846	5	Dhangarhi, Silgadhi
			18,491,097	147,181	56,825		

Status: These divisions are aanchal (zones).
ISO: Codes from ISO 3166-2.
FIPS: Codes from FIPS PUB 10-4.
Population: 1991 census.
Area-km: Square kilometers.
Area-mi: Square miles.
Capitals: Sources disagree about the identities of the district capitals. The author could not resolve the discrepancies as to moves from one city to another, so all the capitals named by more than one independent source are shown, with the most frequently cited capital appearing first. Some of the discrepancies may reflect summer and winter capitals.
Reg: The zones are grouped into vikas kshetra (development regions), as follows:

name	abv	ISO	population	area-km	Nepali name	capital
Central	MM	1	6,183,955	27,410	Madhyamanchal	Kathmandu
Mid-Western	MP	2	2,410,414	42,378	Madhya Pashchimanchal	Surkhet
Western	PM	3	3,770,678	29,398	Pashchimanchal	
Eastern	PW	4	4,446,749	28,456	Purwanchal	Dhankuta
Far-Western	SP	5	1,679,301	19,539	Sudur Pashchimanchal	Kaski

Further subdivisions: The zones are subdivided into districts, which are further subdivided into villages. Note: recent publications of the Central Bureau of Statistics of Nepal list development region and district names, but not zone names. The zones are probably less significant than the districts.
Origins of names:

Dhawalagiri: Nepalese *dhaval*: white, *giri*: mountain

Change history:

~1964   Nepal reorganized from 34 districts into 14 zones.

Other names of subdivisions: In some transcriptions from Nepali, long vowels are marked, but not always consistently.

Dhawalagiri: Dhaulagiri (variant)   Kosi: Koshi (variant)

NETHERLANDS

ISO = NL/FIPS = NL   Language = Dutch   Time zone = +1 [d]   Capitals = Amsterdam, The Hague

The Netherlands have been independent for the whole of the 20th century. They have extended their territory by reclaiming land from the sea.

Other names of country: Alankomaat (Finnish); Holland (Danish, Icelandic); Kingdom of the Netherlands (formal–English); Koninkrijk der Nederlanden (formal); Nederland (Dutch, Norwegian); Nederländerna (Swedish); Niederlande (German); Paesi Bassi, Olanda (Italian); Países Baixos (Portuguese); Países Bajos (Spanish); Pays-Bas (French).

Origin of name: Descriptive: Land at low elevation.

Spelling note: the diphthong 'ij' is treated as a single letter in Dutch. At the beginning of a proper name, both the I and J are capitalized. The letter y is sometimes substituted for ij.

division	ISO	FIPS	conv	NUTS	population	area-km	area-mi	gem	capital
Drenthe	DR	NL01	D.	NL13	461,000	2,655	1,025	34	Assen
Flevoland	FL	NL16	Fle.	NL23	281,000	1,412	545	6	Dronten
Friesland	FR	NL02	F.	NL12	615,000	3,359	1,297	31	Leeuwarden
Gelderland	GE	NL03	Gld.	NL22	1,887,000	5,015	1,936	86	Arnhem
Groningen	GR	NL04	Gr.	NL11	558,000	2,346	906	25	Groningen
Limburg	LI	NL05	L.	NL42	1,137,000	2,169	838	56	Maastricht
Noord-Brabant	NB	NL06	NB.	NL41	2,307,000	4,943	1,908	71	's-Hertogenbosch
Noord-Holland	NH	NL07	NH.	NL32	2,475,000	2,663	1,028	70	Haarlem
Overijssel	OV	NL15	O.	NL21	1,058,000	3,340	1,289	45	Zwolle
Utrecht	UT	NL09	U.	NL31	1,081,000	1,363	526	36	Utrecht
Zeeland	ZE	NL10	Z.	NL34	369,000	1,793	692	17	Middelburg
Zuid-Holland	ZH	NL11	ZH.	NL33	3,346,000	2,877	1,111	95	The Hague
					15,575,000	33,935	13,101	572	

Status: These divisions are provincies (provinces).

ISO: Codes from ISO 3166-2.

FIPS: Codes from FIPS PUB 10-4.

Conv: Conventional abbreviations used in the Netherlands.

NUTS: Nomenclature of Territorial Units for Statistics. Note: by taking the first three characters of the NUTS codes, the provinces can be grouped into four regions: NL1 Noord-Nederland, NL2 Oost-Nederland, NL3 West-Nederland, and NL4 Zuid-Nederland.

Population: 1997 estimate.

Area-km: Square kilometers (land area).

Area-mi: Square miles.

Gem: Number of gemeenten in each province as of 1997-01-01.

Postal codes: Netherlands uses a system of postal codes consisting of four digits, one space, and two letters. Unlike other European countries, Netherlands discourages the use of a country prefix. The borders of postal code areas do not match well with province borders.

Further subdivisions: The provinces are subdivided into gemeenten (municipalities or parishes; sing. gemeente). The number of municipalities has decreased from 1,014 in 1948 to 840 in 1976 and 572 in 1997.

Territorial extent: Flevoland consists of three polders. Noord-Oost Polder is connected to the mainland; East and South Flevoland form an island in the IJsselmeer, except for some dikes which link them to shore.

Friesland includes part of the Dutch mainland and the West Frisian Islands (Waddeneilanden) from Vlieland in the west to Schiermonnikoog in the east.

Groningen includes a few small islands in the Frisian chain: Rottumerplaat, Rottumeroog, Zuiderstrand, and Simonszand.

Noord-Holland includes the islands of Texel and Noorderhaaks, at the southwest end of the Frisian chain.

Zeeland includes a mainland part, the islands of Schouwen Duiveland, Tholen, Noord-Beveland and Sint Philipsland, and the peninsula of Walcheren and Zuid-Beveland. Note that the many dikes and canals make it hard to define what is and is not an island.

Zuid-Holland includes the islands of Goeree-Overflakkee, Voorne-Putten, Beijerland-Hoekse Waard, IJsselmonde, and Dordrecht (same comment as for Zeeland).

Aruba and Netherlands Antilles are overseas dependencies of the Netherlands. The Netherlands Antilles have a status which is nominally the same as that of the provinces. Since ISO 3166 assigns them separate country codes, they are listed here as individual countries.

Origins of names:

Drenthe: Germanic *þrija*: three, *hantja*: countries

Friesland: Land of the Frisii, from ethnic name

Groningen: Germanic Groningja, from *groni*: green

Gelderland: Germanic *gelwa*: yellow, *haru*: mountain

Limburg: Germanic *lindo*: linden, *burg*: fort.

Noord-Brabant: Dutch *Noord*: north, Old High German *bracha*: new country, *bant*: region

Noord-Holland: Dutch *Noord*: north + Old Dutch, either *holt*: woods or *hol*: hollow, *land*: land

Oberijssel: German *ober*: upper, province on the upper IJssel River

Utrecht: corruption of Latin *Trajectum*: ford (*ad Rhenum*: on the Rhine)

Zeeland: Dutch *zee*: sea (land in the sea)

Zuid-Holland: Dutch Zuid: south + Holland

Change history: The Netherlands have repeatedly reclaimed land from the sea by building polders. There have been four major polders (and some smaller ones) in the 20th century. In 1932, the Wieringen-Friesland Barrage (dike) enclosed the Zuider Zee (South Sea), whereupon its name was changed to IJsselmeer (Yssel Lake).

1930	Wieringermeer Polder completed, adding 195 sq. km. to Noord-Holland.
1942	Noord-Oost Polder completed (504 sq. km.) as a municipality not belonging to any province.
~1954	Noord-Oost Polder annexed to Overijssel.
1957-06	East Flevoland completed.
1969	South Flevoland completed.
1986-01-01	Flevoland province formed from the municipalities of Dronten and Lelystad (East Flevoland), the administrative area of Zuidelijke IJsselmeerpolders (South Flevoland), and Noord-Oost Polder (taken from Overijssel). The ISO draft standard doesn't show this change. ISO and FIPS codes for the entities as they stood before the change were Dronten (DT, NL12), Lelystad (LE, NL14), Overijssel (OV, NL08), and Zuidelijke IJsselmeerpolders (ZI, NL13).

Other names of subdivisions:

Friesland: Frise (French); Frisia (Italian, Spanish); Frísia (Portuguese)

Gelderland: Geldern (German); Gheldria (Portuguese); Guelders (obsolete); Gueldre (French)

Groningen: Groninga (Italian, Portuguese); Groningue (French)

Limburg: Limbourg (French); Limburgo (Italian, Portuguese, Spanish)

Noord-Brabant: Brabante del Norte (Spanish); Brabante do Norte (Portuguese); Brabante settentrionale (Italian); Brabant-septentrional (French); Nord-Brabant (German); North Brabant (variant)

Noord-Holland: Holanda do Norte (Portuguese); Hollande-septentrionale (French); North Holland (variant)

Zeeland: Zelanda (Italian); Zélande (French); Zelândia (Portuguese)

Zuid-Holland: Hollande-méridionale (French); South Holland (variant)

Population history:

province	1895	1910	1930	1947	1960	1972	1987	1997
Drenthe	141,225	176,043	222,432	273,800	312,176	380,000	434,038	461,000
Flevoland	——	——	——	2,369	——	20,000	185,365	281,000
Friesland	338,911	362,293	399,659	460,519	478,931	533,000	599,061	615,000
Gelderland	540,937	647,567	829,293	1,039,025	1,274,042	1,558,000	1,771,972	1,887,000
Groningen	288,885	331,248	392,436	453,057	475,462	527,000	558,378	558,000
Limburg	272,044	340,053	550,840	691,493	886,026	1,022,000	1,091,553	1,137,000
Noord-Brabant	533,477	633,155	898,386	1,192,640	1,495,559	1,850,000	2,139,626	2,307,000
Noord-Holland	912,511	1,122,996	1,509,587	1,794,070	2,057,322	2,274,000	2,334,209	2,475,000
Overijssel	314,805	387,381	520,788	644,492	775,759	946,000	1,003,915	1,058,000
Utrecht	238,282	292,131	406,960	556,391	680,678	827,000	953,957	1,081,000
Zeeland	209,546	234,191	247,606	262,589	283,465	316,000	355,434	369,000
Zuid-Holland	1,061,828	1,418,097	1,957,578	2,308,382	2,706,810	3,013,000	3,186,249	3,346,000
	4,852,451	5,945,155	7,935,565	9,678,827	11,426,230	13,266,000	14,613,757	15,575,000

Census data in 1910, 1930, 1947, and 1960; the others are official estimates. Figures for Flevoland refer to the IJsselmeer polders before Flevoland was established.

NETHERLANDS ANTILLES

ISO = AN/FIPS = NT   Language = Dutch   Time zone = -4   Capital = Willemstad

In 1900, Curaçao was a Dutch colony, comprising the present-day Netherlands Antilles and Aruba. In 1948 its name was changed to the Netherlands Antilles. On 1954-12-29, Surinam and the Netherlands Antilles both changed their status from colonies to integral parts of the Kingdom of the Netherlands. Aruba split from Netherlands Antilles on 1986-01-01 to become a separate colony. The name Netherlands West Indies has been applied sometimes to the Netherlands Antilles alone, and sometimes to Surinam as well.

Other names of country: Antilhas Holandesas (Portuguese); Antillas Holandesas, Antillas Neerlandesas (Spanish); Antille olandesi (Italian); Antilles néerlandaises (French); Curaçao (obsolete); Nederlandse Antillen (Dutch); Nederlandske Antiller (Norwegian); Niederländische Antillen (German).

Origin of name: Possessions of the Netherlands in the Antilles Islands, which were named for a legendary western island of Antillia.

division	abv	population	area-km	area-mi	capital
Bonaire	BO	11,139	288	111	Kralendijk
Curaçao	CU	143,816	444	171	Willemstad
Saba	SB	1,116	13	5	Bottom
Sint Eustatius	SE	1,781	21	8	Oranjestad
Sint Maarten	SM	33,459	34	13	Philipsburg
		191,311	800	308	

Status: These divisions are eilandgebieden (island regions).
Abv: Two-letter code for international compatibility (defined by the author).
Population: 1991 estimate.
Area-km: Square kilometers.
Area-mi: Square miles.
Territorial extent: Each of the island regions is primarily composed of an island of the same name, except Sint Maarten, which is the southern part of an island shared with Guadeloupe. Bonaire and Curaçao also have much smaller neighboring islands, named Klein Bonaire and Klein Curaçao respectively. Within the Netherlands Antilles, Bonaire and Curaçao together constitute the Benedenwindse Eilanden (Windward Islands), and the other three, the Bovenwindse Eilanden (Leeward Islands).

Origins of names:

Sint Maarten: island discovered by Columbus on 1493-11-11, Saint Martin's Day

Change history:

1951   Netherlands Antilles organized into the insular communities of Aruba, Bonaire, Curaçao, and the Windward Islands.
1977   Windward Islands split into Saba, Sint Eustatius, and Sint Maarten.

Other names of subdivisions:

Curaçao: Curazao (Spanish)
Sint Eustatius: San Eustaquio (Spanish), Santo Eustáquio (Portuguese)

Sint Maarten: Saint Martin (French), San Martín (Spanish)

NEW CALEDONIA

ISO = NC/FIPS = NC   Language = French   Time zone = +11   Capital = Nouméa

New Caledonia has been a French possession for the whole 20th century. In 1958 its status changed to territoire d'outre-mer (overseas territory). On 1959-12-27, its dependencies, the Wallis and Futuna Islands, were split from New Caledonia to become a separate overseas territory.

Other names of country: Neukaledonien (German); Nieuw Caledonië (Dutch); Nouvelle-Calédonie (French); Nouvelle-Calédonie et Dépendances (formal); Nova Caledônia (Portuguese); Nueva Caledonia (Spanish); Nuova Caledonia (Italian); Ny Caledonia (Norwegian); Territory of New Caledonia and Dependencies (formal–English).

Origin of name: Caledonia is a poetic name for Scotland.

division	abv	population	capital
Îles Loyauté	IL	20,877	Wé
Nord	NO	41,413	Koné
Sud	SU	134,546	Nouméa
		196,836	

Status: These divisions are provinces.

Abv: Two-letter code for international compatibility (defined by the author). ISO and FIPS don't list divisions for New Caledonia.

Population: 1996 census.

Further subdivisions: The provinces are subdivided into 32 communes.

Territorial extent: New Caledonia consists of the large island of New Caledonia, some nearby smaller islands, and some remote tiny islands.

Îles Loyauté includes Lifou, Maré, Ouvéa, Tiga, and some nearby islets.

Nord includes the northern end of New Caledonia with the adjacent islands of Balabio, Baaba, Yandé, etc.; the Bélep Islands (Art, Pott, and some smaller ones); and probably the remote dependencies of Chesterfield Islands and Huon Islands.

Sud includes the southern end of New Caledonia with the adjacent islands of Ouen, Hugon, Ducos, Toupéti, etc.; Île des Pins and neighboring islets; and probably the remote dependency of Walpole Island.

Change history:

1988-11-09   New Caledonia reorganized into three provinces following a referendum. Before this date it had been divided into four provinces, formerly circonscriptions: Centre-Sud-Est (capital La Foa), Îles Loyauté, Nord, and Nouméa.

Other names of subdivisions:

Îles Loyauté: Loyalty Islands (variant); Islas de la Lealtad (Spanish)

NEW ZEALAND

ISO = NZ/FIPS = NZ   Language = English, Maori   Time zone (see note)   Capital = Wellington

New Zealand was a British colony at the beginning of the century. On 1907-09-26 it became a dominion of the British Empire. Since then it has gained or lost some small island dependencies, but the territory of New Zealand itself has remained unchanged. The Ross Dependency in Antarctica has been administered by New Zealand since 1923-07-30.

Other names of country: Aotearoa (Maori); Neuseeland (German); Nieuw Zeeland (Dutch); Nouvelle-Zélande (French); Nova Zelândia (Portuguese); Nueva Zelandia (Spanish); Nuova Zelanda (Italian); Nya Zeeland (Swedish); Nýja-Sjáland (Icelandic); Uusi-Seelanti (Finnish).

Origin of name: after the province of Zeeland (Sea-land) in the Netherlands.

divison	abv	ISO	population	area-km	area-mi	isl	capital
Auckland	AU	AUK	1,068,645	5,580	2,154	N	Auckland
Bay of Plenty	BP	BOP	224,365	36,899	14,247	N	Hamilton
Canterbury	CA	CAN	468,040	43,579	16,826	S	Christchurch
Chatham Islands	CI	––	730	963	372	–	––
Gisborne	GI	GIS	45,787	10,914	4,214	N	Gisborne ➤

divison	abv	ISO	population	area-km	area-mi	isl	capital
Hawke's Bay	HB	HKB	142,789	11,289	4,359	N	Napier, Hastings
Manawatu-Wanganui	MW	MWT	228,770	——	——	N	Palmerston North
Marlborough	MA	——	38,397	11,080	4,278	S	Blenheim
Nelson	NE	NSB	40,279	17,675	6,824	S	Nelson
Northland	NO	NTL	137,052	12,653	4,885	N	Whangarei
Otago	OT	OTA	185,083	37,105	14,326	S	Dunedin
Southland	SO	STL	97,100	29,124	11,245	S	Invercargill
Taranaki	TK	TKI	106,589	9,729	3,756	N	New Plymouth
Tasman	TS	——	37,973	——	——	S	——
Waikato	WK	WKO	350,125	——	——	N	Hamilton
Wellington	WG	WGN	414,048	27,766	10,721	N	Wellington
West Coast	WC	WTC	32,512	15,415	5,952	S	Greymouth
			3,618,284	269,771	104,159		

Status: These divisions are regions, regional authorities, or regional councils, except for Chatham Islands, which is a county not in any region.

Abv: Two-letter code for international compatibility (defined by the author).

ISO: Codes from ISO 3166-2.

Population: 1996 census.

Area-km: Square kilometers.

Area-mi: Square miles.

Isl: Island containing most of the region (using codes from ISO 3166-2: N = North, S = South)

Time zones: New Zealand lies in the +12 [d] time zone, except for the Chatham Islands, which are +12:45 [d].

Postal codes: New Zealand uses four-digit postal codes.

Further subdivisions: A complete explanation of New Zealand's territorial structures would fill a book. North Island and South Island have always been recognized as a partition, although they don't correspond to any of the usual administrative structures. The divisions shown above represent the present state of an evolutionary process. They began as provinces (prior to 1876), became provincial districts, lost their administrative functions, became statistical areas in 1961, local government regions in ~1982, and regions in 1989. The regions are responsible for certain environmental issues, transportation, and civil defense. The New Zealand Department of Statistics also tracks population in statistical divisions and main urban areas, but some parts of New Zealand are not in any statistical division or main urban area; some main urban areas are within a statistical division, and some are not. Since 1876, the administrative divisions have had various statuses: initially counties and cities, currently districts and cities. The overall phrase for divisions at this level is territorial authorities. On the average, the counties/districts have been much smaller than the provinces/regions. However, especially in the North Island, there are overlaps: not every district is entirely contained in one region. There are other local governments, called special purpose authorities. On the level below the counties, there are 159 community boards (only serving some areas of the country), whose function is simply to advise the district councils. There are also wards, some of which coincide with community boards. This table shows the relationship between the territorial authorities and the regions.

division	abv	type	population	region(s)
Ashburton	AB	ds	25,177	Canterbury
Auckland	AL	cy	345,768	Auckland
Banks Peninsula	BK	ds	7,581	Canterbury
Buller	BU	ds	10,513	West Coast
Carterton	CR	ds	6,812	Wellington
Central Hawke's Bay	CH	ds	13,037	Hawke's Bay
Central Otago	CO	ds	14,954	Otago, Canterbury
Chatham Islands	CT	co	730	Chatham Islands
Christchurch	CC	cy	309,028	Canterbury
Clutha	CL	ds	18,006	Otago
Dunedin	DU	cy	118,143	Otago
Far North	FN	ds	52,935	Northland
Franklin	FK	ds	47,826	Waikato, Auckland
Gisborne	GB	ds	45,780	Gisborne
Gore	GO	ds	13,279	Southland
Grey	GR	ds	13,700	West Coast
Hamilton	HM	cy	108,428	Waikato
Hastings	HS	ds	66,280	Hawke's Bay ▶

division	abv	type	population	region(s)
Hauraki	HK	ds	17,320	Waikato
Horowhenua	HW	ds	30,148	Manawatu-Wanganui
Hurunui	HN	ds	9,403	Canterbury
Invercargill	IC	cy	53,209	Southland
Kaikoura	KK	ds	3,516	Canterbury
Kaipara	KP	ds	17,369	Northland
Kapiti Coast	KC	ds	38,584	Wellington
Kawerau	KW	ds	7,829	Bay of Plenty
Lower Hutt	LH	cy	95,872	Wellington
Mackenzie	MZ	ds	4,077	Canterbury
Manawatu	MN	ds	28,078	Manawatu-Wanganui
Manukau	MK	cy	254,278	Auckland
Marlborough	MB	ds	38,397	Marlborough
Masterton	MT	ds	22,756	Wellington
Matamata-Piako	MP	ds	29,663	Waikato
Napier	NR	cy	53,462	Hawke's Bay
Nelson	NL	cy	40,240	Nelson
New Plymouth	NP	ds	68,111	Taranaki
North Shore	NS	cy	172,164	Auckland
Opotiki	OP	ds	9,375	Bay of Plenty
Otorohanga	OH	ds	9,662	Waikato
Palmerston North	PN	cy	73,095	Manawatu-Wanganui
Papakura	PP	ds	39,627	Auckland
Porirua	PR	cy	46,626	Wellington
Queenstown-Lakes	QL	ds	14,285	Otago
Rangitikei	RT	ds	16,356	Manawatu-Wanganui, Hawke's Bay
Rodney	RD	ds	66,485	Auckland
Rotorua	RR	ds	64,509	Waikato, Bay of Plenty
Ruapehu	RP	ds	16,742	Manawatu-Wanganui
Selwyn	SY	ds	24,783	Canterbury
South Taranaki	ST	ds	29,135	Taranaki
South Waikato	SW	ds	25,010	Waikato
South Wairarapa	SP	ds	8,938	Wellington
Southland	SL	ds	30,562	Southland
Stratford	SF	ds	9,544	Taranaki, Manawatu-Wanganui
Tararua	TR	ds	19,068	Manawatu-Wanganui, Wellington
Tasman	TM	ds	37,973	Tasman
Taupo	TP	ds	30,691	Waikato, Bay of Plenty, Hawke's Bay, Manawatu-Wanganui
Tauranga	TG	ds	77,775	Bay of Plenty
Thames-Coromandel	TC	ds	24,820	Waikato
Timaru	TU	ds	42,631	Canterbury
Upper Hutt	UH	cy	36,716	Wellington
Waikato	WT	ds	39,139	Waikato
Waimakariri	WR	ds	32,347	Canterbury
Waimate	WM	ds	7,619	Canterbury
Waipa	WP	ds	38,853	Waikato
Wairoa	WW	ds	9,900	Hawke's Bay
Waitakere	WA	cy	155,565	Auckland
Waitaki	WI	ds	21,573	Otago
Waitomo	WO	ds	9,731	Waikato, Manawatu-Wanganui
Wanganui	WU	ds	45,042	Manawatu-Wanganui
Wellington	WE	cy	157,646	Wellington
Western Bay of Plenty	WB	ds	34,971	Bay of Plenty
Westland	WL	ds	8,280	West Coast
Whakatane	WH	ds	33,125	Bay of Plenty
Whangarei	WN	ds	66,748	Northland

Abv: Two-letter code for international compatibility (defined by the author).

Type: These divisions are districts (ds), cities (cy), and one county (co).

ISO: Codes from ISO 3166-2.

Population: 1996 census.

Region(s): Regions containing part of the division, in decreasing order of their share of area.

Territorial extent: The bulk of each region lies on either the North or South Island, as shown in the table above.

Auckland includes most of the islands in Hauraki Gulf, such as Great Barrier, Waiheke, Little Barrier, Rangitoto, Motutapu, Ponui, and Kawau.

Bay of Plenty includes Motiti, White, and Whale Islands.

Chatham Islands includes Chatham Island (Rekohua), Pitt Island (Rangiauria), and some smaller islets.

Marlborough includes many small islands in the Cook Strait, such as D'Urville and Arapawa Islands.

Northland includes the Hen and Chickens Group, Poor Knights Islands, and some other coastal islets.

Southland includes Steward, Ruapuke, Resolution, Codfish, and many smaller islands.

Tasman includes Rabbit and Adele Islands.

Waikato includes the Mercury Islands and Cuvier Island.

Wellington includes Kapiti and Mana Islands.

New Zealand includes some remote island groups which are not part of any region. The Kermadec Islands are grouped with North Island for statistical purposes. The Antipodes Islands, Campbell Island, the Auckland Islands, Three Kings, Snares, Solander, and Bounty Islands are grouped with South Island.

New Zealand administers Tokelau as a territory overseas. It maintains a claim to Ross Dependency in Antarctica. It also has relationships of free association with its former territories of Cook Islands and Niue. In this book, following the ISO standard, these all have separate listings (see Antarctica, Cook Islands, Niue, and Tokelau). Samoa is a former trust territory.

Origins of names:

Auckland: named by Captain William Hobson in gratitude to Lord Auckland, former First Lord of the Admiralty

Bay of Plenty: named by Captain Cook to mark the Maori inhabitants' successful cultivation of the adjoining land

Canterbury: named for Canterbury Cathedral by colonists sponsored in part by the Archbishop of Canterbury

Chatham Islands: discovered by Lieutenant W. R. Broughton, commanding the vessel Chatham

Hawke's Bay: named by Captain Cook in honor of Edward Hawke, First Lord of the Admiralty

Marlborough: after John Churchill, Duke of Marlborough (1650–1722), British commander at Blenheim (whence the name of the capital of this region)

Nelson: after Horatio Nelson (1758–1805), British commander at Trafalgar

Taranaki: the Maori name for Mount Egmont

Tasman: after the Tasman Sea, the Tasman Bay, and Dutch explorer Abel Janszoon Tasman

Waikato: Maori *wai*: water, *kato*: strong

Wanganui: from Maori *wanga*: harbor, *nui*: big

Wellington: after Arthur Wellesley, Duke of Wellington (1769–1852), British commander at Waterloo

Change history:
Regions and their analogues:

1900   New Zealand consisted of nine provincial districts, as shown here. Otago was further subdivided into Otago portion and Southland portion.

region	population	area-km	region	population	area-km
Auckland	264,520	66,682	Otago	191,130	66,011
Canterbury	173,185	36,363	Taranaki	51,569	8,568
Hawke's Bay	48,546	11,422	Wellington	199,094	28,498
Marlborough	15,985	12,310	Westland	15,714	12,020
Nelson	48,463	26,597		1,008,206	268,471

Population: 1911 census.

1961   Status of provincial districts changed to statistical areas. Auckland split into Central Auckland, East Coast, Northland, and South Auckland-Bay of Plenty. Parts of Nelson transferred to Canterbury and Westland.

~1984   New Zealand reorganized from 13 statistical areas into 22 local government regions, as shown in this table.

region	population	area-km	isl	capital
Aorangi	84,772	19,910	S	Timaru
Auckland	827,408	5,201	N	Auckland
Bay of Plenty	172,480	9,126	N	Tauranga
Canterbury	336,846	17,465	S	Christchurch
Clutha-Central Otago	45,402	28,982	S	Balclutha ➤

region	population	area-km	isl	capital
Coastal-North Otago	138,164	10,590	S	Dunedin
East Cape	53,295	11,461	N	Gisborne
Hawke's Bay	137,840	12,396	N	Napier, Hastings
Horowhenua	49,296	1,614	N	Levin
Manawatu	113,238	6,669	N	Palmerston North
Marlborough	37,557	12,882	S	Blenheim
Nelson Bays	65,934	10,197	S	Nelson
Northland	113,994	12,604	N	Whangarei
Southland	107,905	27,716	S	Invercargill
Taranaki	103,798	7,876	N	New Plymouth
Thames Valley	54,343	4,666	N	Thames-Coromandel
Tongariro	40,089	12,085	N	Taupo
Waikato	221,850	13,241	N	Hamilton
Wairarapa	39,689	6,894	N	Masterton
Wanganui	68,702	9,171	N	Wanganui
Wellington	323,162	1,379	N	Wellington
West Coast	34,178	22,893	S	Greymouth
	3,169,942	265,018		

Population: 1981 census.
Isl: (N)orth or (S)outh Island.

1989-11-01   New Zealand reorganized from 22 local government regions into 14 regional councils. By comparison with the older statistical areas, Nelson was split, its southern part merging with Westland, its northern part with Marlborough to form Nelson-Marlborough; Manawatu-Wanganui split from Wellington; South Auckland-Bay of Plenty split into Bay of Plenty and Waikato; name of Central Auckland changed to Auckland; name of East Coast changed to Gisborne; and almost all borders were adjusted to conform to major watersheds, since the new regions had environmental responsibilities.

~1996   Marlborough district, Nelson city, and Tasman district became regions. At the same time, Nelson-Marlborough region was abolished; its orphaned areas in Hurunui and Kaikoura districts were transferred to Canterbury region; and West Coast region lost its part of Tasman district.

Territorial authorities: In 1876, New Zealand was divided into 63 counties and 45 municipalities. By 1950, it had 125 counties and 134 municipalities. The FIPS standard hasn't changed since 1984, when it listed 93 counties, nine districts, and three town districts. On 1987-03-31, New Zealand consisted of 87 counties, 118 boroughs, 18 districts, and three town districts. The reform of 1989-11-01 converted it to 59 districts, 14 cities, and one county (Chatham Islands). It has remained stable since then, except that in ~1990 the status of Invercargill changed from district to city.

Other names of subdivisions:

Gisborne: East Coast (obsolete)
Hawke's Bay: Hawkes Bay (variant)

Horowhenua: Horohenua (variant)

NICARAGUA

ISO = NI/FIPS = NU   Language = Spanish   Time zone = -6   Capital = Managua

Nicaragua has been independent for the whole 20th century.
Other names of country: Nicarágua (Portuguese); Nikaragúa (Icelandic); Republic of Nicaragua (formal–English); República de Nicaragua (formal).
Origin of name: Named for Nicarao, chief of the tribe of Nicaraos.

division	ISO	FIPS	population	area-km	area-mi	zone	capital
Boaco	BO	NU01	117,900	4,982	1,924	NC	Boaco
Carazo	CA	NU02	150,000	1,032	398	Pa	Jinotepe
Chinandega	CI	NU03	330,500	4,662	1,800	Pa	Chinandega
Chontales	CO	NU04	129,600	4,947	1,910	NC	Juigalpa
Estelí	ES	NU05	169,100	2,199	849	NC	Estelí
Granada	GR	NU06	162,600	964	372	Pa	Granada
Jinotega	JI	NU07	175,600	9,576	3,697	NC	Jinotega
León	LE	NU08	344,500	5,234	2,021	Pa	León
Madriz	MD	NU09	88,700	1,758	679	NC	Somoto
Managua	MN	NU10	1,026,100	3,635	1,403	Pa	Managua
Masaya	MS	NU11	230,800	543	210	Pa	Masaya
Matagalpa	MT	NU12	322,300	6,794	2,623	NC	Matagalpa
Nueva Segovia	NS	NU13	122,100	3,341	1,290	NC	Ocotal
Río San Juan	SJ	NU14	52,200	7,448	2,876	At	San Carlos
Rivas	RI	NU15	149,800	2,149	830	Pa	Rivas
Zelaya	ZE	NU16	298,900	59,094	22,816	At	Bluefields
			3,870,700	118,358	45,698		

Status: These divisions are departamentos (departments).
ISO: Codes from ISO 3166-2.
FIPS: Codes from FIPS PUB 10-4.
Population: 1991 census.
Area-km: Square kilometers.
Area-mi: Square miles.
Zone: Nicaragua is unofficially divided into three zones: Atlantic (At), North Central (NC), and Pacific (Pa).
Further subdivisions: The departments are subdivided into municipios (municipalities). Since 1982-07-26, there has also been a subdivision into six regions and three special zones. However, the departments are still the divisions most often referenced. The regions are:

name	capital	departments
Región I	Estelí	Estelí, Madriz, Nueva Segovia
Región II	León	Chinandega, León
Región III	Managua	Managua
Región IV	Jinotepe	Carazo, Granada, Masaya, Rivas
Región V	Juigalpa	Boaco, Chontales
Región VI	Matagalpa	Jinotega, Matagalpa
Región Autónoma del Atlántico Norte	Rosita	Zelaya (part)
Región Autónoma del Atlántico Sur	Bluefields	Zelaya (part)
Zona Especial III	San Carlos	Río San Juan

The parts of Zelaya are also known by their acronyms, RAAN and RAAS; or as Zelaya Norte and Zelaya Sul. In the latest FIPS list, they have separate codes of NU17 and NU18, respectively, superseding Zelaya.
Territorial extent: Granada includes Zapatera Island in Lake Nicaragua.
Río San Juan includes the Solentiname Archipelago in Lake Nicaragua.
Rivas includes Ometepe Island in Lake Nicaragua.
Zelaya includes Nicaragua's Caribbean islands: the Corn Islands (Isla Grande del Maíz and Isla Pequeña del Maíz), the Cayos Miskitos, and some islets.
Origins of names: Granada, León, and Segovia were named for cities in Spain.

Gracias a Dios: Spanish for thanks to God, name bestowed on the cape by Columbus in 1502 after finding refuge from a storm in its lee
Managua: possibly from ethnic name

Nueva Segovia: Spanish *nueva*: new, named when the department was split from Segovia
Zelaya: after general and president José Santos Zelaya

Change history:

1900	Nicaragua consisted of the departments of Chinandega, Chontales, Granada, Leon, Managua, Masaya, Matagalpa, Segovia, Rivas, and Zelaya (also known as Mosquito Reservation).

~1902	Districts of Cabo Gracias a Dios, Prinzapolka, Rio Grande, and Siquia formed from the eastern parts of Chontales, Matagalpa, and Segovia; Estelí and Jinotega also split from Segovia; Carazo split from Granada.
~1915	District of San Juan del Norte split from Chontales.
~1938	Status of Cabo Gracias a Dios changed from district to comarca; Boaco split from Chontales; Segovia split into Madriz and Nueva Segovia; Zelaya merged with the four districts.
~1957	Río San Juan formed from parts of Chontales and Zelaya.
~1977	Cabo Gracias a Dios merged with Zelaya.
1982-07-26	Six regions and three special zones formed as a higher-level subdivision of Nicaragua.

NIGER

ISO = NE/FIPS = NG   Language = French   Time zone = +1   Capital = Niamey

The area now known as Niger was part of French Sudan at the beginning of the 20th century. As the French administration got better organized, the area became a military territory, separate from the colony of Upper Senegal and Niger to its west. Niger became a territory within French West Africa on 1922-10-13. It obtained full independence on 1960-08-03.

Other names of country: Níger (Icelandic, Spanish); Republic of Niger (formal–English); République du Niger (formal).

Origin of name: Named for the Niger River, from Tamashek *gher n-gheren*: river among rivers.

division	abv	ISO	FIPS	population	area-km	area-mi
Agadez	AG	1	NG01	203,959	634,209	244,869
Diffa	DF	2	NG02	189,316	140,216	54,138
Dosso	DS	3	NG03	1,019,997	31,002	11,970
Maradi	MA	4	NG04	1,388,999	38,581	14,896
Niamey	NI	8	NG08	398,265	670	259
Tahoua	TH	5	NG06	1,306,652	106,677	41,188
Tillabéry	TL	6	NG09	1,332,398	89,623	34,604
Zinder	ZI	7	NG07	1,410,797	145,430	56,151
				7,250,383	1,186,408	458,075

Status: These divisions are départements (departments), except Niamey, which is a capital district.

Abv: Two-letter code for international compatibility (defined by the author).

ISO: Codes from ISO 3166-2.

FIPS: Codes from FIPS PUB 10-4.

Population: 1988 census.

Area-km: Square kilometers.

Area-mi: Square miles.

Capitals: Have the same name as their departments.

Further subdivisions: The departments are subdivided into arrondissements, which are further subdivided into communes.

Change history:

1932-09-06	Part of Upper Volta transferred to Niger.
1947-09-04	Districts of Dori and Fada N'Gourma restored to Upper Volta.
1964-07-17	Niger reorganized from sixteen districts (Agadez, Birni N'Konni, Dogondoutchi, Dosso, Filingué, Gouré, Madaoua, Magaria, Maradi, N'Guigmi, Niamey, Tahoua, Téra, Tessaoua, Tillabéry, and Zinder; capitals had same names as their districts) into seven departments.
~1992	Tillabéry department split from Niamey (whose FIPS code was NG05 before the change).

Other names of subdivisions:

Agadez: Agadès (obsolete)   Tillabéry: Tillaberi (variant)

NIGERIA

ISO = NG/FIPS = NI   Language = English   Time zone = +1   Capital = Abuja

In 1899, the Royal Niger Company surrendered its charter to the British Crown. On 1900-01-01, Great Britain created two protectorates: Northern Nigeria (most of the Company land), and Southern Nigeria (the rest of the Company land, merged with the Niger Coast Protectorate). The Colony and Protectorate of Lagos was a separate entity at that time. The parts became a single "colony and protectorate" on 1914-01-01. France and England seized Kamerun (Cameroon) from Germany during World War I. On 1922-07-20, part of Kamerun was mandated to Britain, which administered the mandate as part of Nigeria. Nigeria became independent on 1960-10-01. A plebiscite was held in the Cameroons, now a trust territory. The northern part chose to unite with Nigeria, effective 1962-06-01, while the southern part joined with the recently independent Cameroon Republic, effective 1961-10-01. On 1967-05-30, the Republic of Biafra (consisting of the Eastern and Mid-Western regions, recently reorganized) announced its secession from Nigeria, but the revolt was defeated by 1970, and Biafra never attained international recognition.

Other names of country: Nigéria (French, Portuguese); Nígería (Icelandic); Federal Republic of Nigeria (formal–English).

Origin of name: Named for the Niger River, from Tamashek *gher n-gheren*: river among rivers.

division	ISO	FIPS	population	area-km	area-mi	capital
Abia	AB	NI34	2,297,978	6,320	2,440	Umuahia
Abuja Capital Territory	FC	NI11	378,671	7,315	2,824	Abuja
Adamawa	AD	NI35	2,124,049	36,917	14,254	Yola
Akwa Ibom	AK	NI21	2,359,736	7,081	2,734	Uyo
Anambra	AN	NI25	2,767,903	4,844	1,870	Awka
Bauchi	BA	NI06	4,294,413	64,605	24,944	Bauchi
Benue	BE	NI26	2,780,398	34,059	13,150	Makurdi
Borno	BO	NI27	2,596,589	70,898	27,374	Maiduguri
Cross River	CR	NI22	1,865,604	20,156	7,782	Calabar
Delta	DE	NI36	2,570,181	17,698	6,833	Asaba
Edo	ED	NI37	2,159,848	17,802	6,873	Benin City
Enugu	EN	NI38	3,161,295	12,831	4,954	Enugu
Imo	IM	NI28	2,485,499	5,530	2,135	Owerri
Jigawa	JI	NI39	2,829,929	23,154	8,940	Dutse
Kaduna	KD	NI23	3,969,252	46,053	17,781	Kaduna
Kano	KN	NI29	5,632,040	20,131	7,773	Kano
Katsina	KT	NI24	3,878,344	24,192	9,341	Katsina
Kebbi	KE	NI40	2,062,226	36,800	14,209	Birnin-Kebbi
Kogi	KO	NI41	2,099,046	29,833	11,519	Lokoja
Kwara	KW	NI30	1,566,469	36,825	14,218	Ilorin
Lagos	LA	NI05	5,685,781	3,345	1,292	Ikeja
Niger	NI	NI31	2,482,367	76,363	29,484	Minna
Ogun	OG	NI16	2,338,570	16,762	6,472	Abeokuta
Ondo	ON	NI17	3,884,485	20,959	8,092	Akure
Osun	OS	NI42	2,203,016	9,251	3,572	Oshogbo
Oyo	OY	NI32	3,488,789	28,454	10,986	Ibadan
Plateau	PL	NI19	3,283,704	58,030	22,406	Jos
Rivers	RI	NI10	3,983,857	21,850	8,436	Port-Harcourt
Sokoto	SO	NI33	4,392,391	65,735	25,380	Sokoto
Taraba	TA	NI43	1,480,590	54,473	21,032	Jalingo
Yobe	YO	NI44	1,411,481	45,502	17,568	Damaturu
			88,514,501	923,768	356,668	

Status: These divisions are states, except for the capital territory.

ISO: Codes from ISO 3166-2.

FIPS: Codes from FIPS PUB 10-4.
Population: 1991 census.
Area-km: Square kilometers (areas after the 1991 reorganization not yet available).
Area-mi: Square miles.
Further subdivisions: The states are subdivided into local authorities.
Origins of names:

Adamawa: conquered by Moddibo (King) Adama in the early
   19th century
Bendel: from first syllables of the constituent provinces, Benin
   and Delta.
Benue: name of a river, means mother of waters.

Cross River: the Cross River flows through it.
Delta: located in the delta of the Niger River.
Plateau: contains the Jos Plateau.
Rivers: riddled with rivers, mostly in the delta of the Niger
   River.

Change history:

1903	Sultanate of Sokoto merged with protectorate of Northern Nigeria.
1906-02	The "colony and protectorate of Lagos" and the "protectorate of Southern Nigeria" merged to form the "colony and protectorate of Southern Nigeria."
~1938	Southern Nigeria split into Eastern and Western regions. Northern Nigeria became a region. The regions were further subdivided into provinces: Eastern contained Calabar, Cameroons, Ogoja, Onitsha, and Owerri provinces; Northern contained Adamawa, Bauchi, Benue, Bornu, Ilorin, Kabba, Kano, Niger, Plateau, Sokoto, and Zaria provinces; and Western contained Abeokuta, Benin, Colony, Ijebu, Ondo, Oyo, and Warri provinces.
1960-10-01	Constitution of the Federation of Nigeria came into force. The divisions of the country were the three regions (with capitals): Eastern (Enugu), Northern (Kaduna), and Western (Ibadan). Note: the federal territory around Lagos was an entity both before and after independence, but it's not clear whether it was ranked equally with the regions, or was simply part of Western region.
1962-06-01	Northern Cameroons merged with Northern region.
1963-06	Benin and Delta provinces split from Western region to form Mid-Western region (capital, Benin City).
1966-05-24	Following a coup, the military government changed the status of Nigeria to a republic, its regions to provinces, and Lagos federal territory to a capital territory; however, these changes were reversed after another coup later in the year.
1967-05-27	Eastern region split into East-Central (Enugu), Rivers (Port Harcourt), and South-Eastern (Calabar) states; Northern region split into Benue-Plateau (Jos), Kano (Kano), Kwara (Ilorin), North-Central (Kaduna), North-Eastern (Maiduguri), and North-Western (Sokoto) states; Western region split into Lagos (Lagos) and Western (Ibadan) states. Lagos state consisted of Colony province and Lagos federal territory. Status of Mid-Western region changed to state.
1976-02-03	Benue-Plateau state divided into Benue (Makurdi) and Plateau states; East-Central state divided into Anambra and Imo (Owerri) states; Federal Capital Territory (Abuja) formed from parts of Niger and Plateau states; North-Eastern state divided into Bauchi (Bauchi), Borno, and Gongola (Yola) states; Niger (Minna) state split from Sokoto; Western state divided into Ogun (Abeokuta), Ondo (Akure), and Oyo states. Capital of Lagos state moved from Lagos to Ikeja. Also, state boundaries were adjusted: Igala (east of the Niger River) transferred from Kwara to Benue state; Ughelli transferred from Mid-Western to Rivers state; Opobo transferred from South-Eastern to Rivers state. Also, name of Mid-Western state changed to Bendel; name of South-Eastern state changed to Cross River.
~1989	Akwa Ibom state (FIPS code NI21) split from Cross River (NI22, formerly NI09); Katsina state (NI24) split from Kaduna (NI23, formerly NI14); name of Federal Capital Territory changed to Abuja Capital Territory.
1991-12-12	Abia state split from Imo; Bendel state divided into Delta and Edo; Enugu state split from Anambra; Gongola state divided into Adamawa and Taraba; Jigawa state split

from Kano; Kebbi state split from Sokoto; Kogi state formed from parts of Benue and Kwara; Osun state split from Oyo; Yobe state split from Borno. National capital moved from Lagos to Abuja. FIPS codes changed to their present values.

Other names of subdivisions:

Abuja Capital Territory: Federal Capital Territory (variant);   Rivers: Rivières (French)
    Territoire de la capitale fédérale (French)

NIUE

ISO = NU/FIPS = NE   Language = English, Niuean   Time zone = -11   Capital = Alofi

Niue was part of the Cook Islands protectorate in 1900. Along with the Cook Islands, it became an integral part of New Zealand on 1901-06-11. A separate administration for Niue was established in 1903. It became a self-governing state in free association with New Zealand on 1974-10-19.
    Other names of country: Nioué (French); Savage Island (obsolete).
    Origin of name: Niuean *niu*: coconuts + *e*: there are (i.e., There are coconuts).

division	abv	population	area-km	area-mi
Niue	NU	1,751	260	101

Status: This division is the whole of the country, treated as a division for compatibility.
Abv: Two-letter code for international compatibility (defined by the author).
Population: 1992 estimate.
Area-km: Square kilometers.
Area-mi: Square miles.
Territorial extent: The country consists of the island of Niue and isolated reefs named Antiope and Beveridge.

NORFOLK ISLAND

ISO = NF/FIPS = NF   Language = English   Time zone = +11:30   Capital = Kingston

Norfolk Island is a territory of Australia, but it is remote enough from the Australian continent to be given a separate code by the international standards. It was administered by New South Wales until 1901-01-01, when the Commonwealth of Australia was formed, and thenceforth by Australia.
    Other names of country: Île Norfolk (French); Ilha Norfolk (Portuguese); Isla Norfolk (Spanish); Norfolk (Dutch); Norfolkinsel (German); Territory of Norfolk Island (formal–English).
    Origin of name: named by Captain Cook after the duchess of Norfolk.

division	abv	population	area-km	area-mi
Norfolk Island	NF	2,620	35	13

Status: This division is the whole of the country, treated as a division for compatibility.
Abv: Two-letter code for international compatibility (defined by the author).
Population: 1992 estimate.

Area-km: Square kilometers
Area-mi: Square miles
Territorial extent: The territory consists of Norfolk Island and its smaller neighbors, Philip and Nepean Islands.

NORTHERN MARIANA ISLANDS

ISO = MP/FIPS = CQ   Language = English   Time zone = +10   Capital = Garapan

Guam is geographically one of the Mariana Islands (the southernmost), but has been politically separate during the 20th century. Germany bought almost all of Micronesia, including the Marianas but excluding Guam, from Spain in the 1890s. The islands were mandated to Japan in 1920 by the League of Nations. The Trust Territory of the Pacific Islands was created on 1947-04-02 and granted in trust to the United States. This territory was divided into districts, one of which was the Northern Mariana Islands. Eventually a referendum was held on its status. As a result, on 1978-01-01, the Northern Mariana Islands became a commonwealth of the United States.

Other names of country: Commonwealth of the Northern Mariana Islands (formal–English); Îles Mariannes du Nord (French); Isole Marianne del Nord (Italian); Nördliche Marianen (German).

Origin of name: named in honor of Archduchess Maria Anna of Austria (called Mariana in Spanish), regent of Spain vice her son, Charles II.

division	abv	FIPS	population	area-km	area-mi
Northern Islands	NI	085	36	171	60
Rota	RO	100	2,295	83	33
Saipan	SA	110	38,896	122	47
Tinian	TI	120	2,118	101	39
			43,345	471	182

Status: These divisions are municipalities.

Abv: Two-letter code for international compatibility (defined by the author).

FIPS: Codes from FIPS PUB 6-4, representing second-level administrative divisions of the United States. The codes for the Northern Mariana Islands in FIPS PUB 5-2 are MP (alpha) and 69 (numeric). When the FIPS 5-2 and 6-4 codes are concatenated, as in 69100 for Rota, the result is a code that uniquely identifies a county-equivalent unit in the United States.

Population: 1990 census.

Area-km: Square kilometers.

Area-mi: Square miles.

Territorial extent: The commonwealth is divided approximately as follows, from south to north: 14° N., Rota, 14°30' N., Tinian, 15°5' N., Saipan, 15°20' N., Northern Islands, 21° N.

Other names of subdivisions:

Rota: Luta (variant)

NORWAY

ISO = NO/FIPS = NO   Language = Norwegian   Time zone = +1   Capital = Oslo

Norway was united with Sweden through most of the 19th century. The united kingdom was called Sweden and Norway. Norway proclaimed its independence on 1905-06-07.

Other names of country: Kingdom of Norway (formal–English); Kongeriket Norge (formal); Noorwegen (Dutch); Noreg (Norwegian nynorsk); Noregur (Icelandic); Norge (Danish, Norwegian bokmål, Swedish); Norja (Finnish); Noruega (Portuguese, Spanish); Norvège (French); Norvegia (Italian); Norwegen (German).

Origin of name: Old Norwegian *Norvegr*: Northern way, referring to the sea route.

division	abv	ISO	FIPS	conv	population	area-km	area-mi	capital
Akershus	AK	02	NO01	Ak	238,296	4,917	1,898	Oslo
Aust-Agder	AA	09	NO02	AA	97,333	9,212	3,557	Arendal
Buskerud	BU	06	NO04	Bu	225,172	14,927	5,763	Drammen
Finnmark	FI	20	NO05	Fi	74,524	48,637	18,779	Vadsø
Hedmark	HE	04	NO06	He	187,275	27,388	10,575	Hamar
Hordaland	HO	12	NO07	Ho	410,568	15,634	6,036	Bergen
Møre og Romsdal	MR	15	NO08	MR	238,408	15,104	5,832	Molde
Nordland	NO	18	NO09	No	239,311	38,327	14,798	Bodø
Nord-Trøndelag	NT	17	NO10	NT	127,157	22,463	8,673	Steinkjer
Oppland	OP	05	NO11	Op	182,578	25,260	9,753	Lillehammer
Oslo	OS	03	NO12	Os	459,299	454	175	Oslo
Østfold	OF	01	NO13	Øf	417,653	4,183	1,615	Moss
Rogaland	RO	11	NO14	Ro	337,504	9,141	3,529	Stavanger
Sogn og Fjordane	SF	14	NO15	SF	106,659	18,634	7,194	Hermansverk
Sør-Trøndelag	ST	16	NO16	ST	250,978	18,831	7,271	Trondheim
Telemark	TE	08	NO17	Te	162,907	15,315	5,913	Skien
Troms	TR	19	NO18	Tr	146,716	25,954	10,021	Tromsø
Vest-Agder	VA	10	NO19	VA	144,917	7,280	2,811	Kristiansand
Vestfold	VF	07	NO20	Vf	198,399	2,216	856	Tønsberg
					4,245,654	323,877	125,049	

Status: These divisions are fylker (counties, sometimes translated provinces).

Abv: Two-letter code for international compatibility (defined by the author).

ISO: Codes from ISO 3166-2. They are based on numbers used officially in Norway. Bergen was 13 before it merged with Hordaland. Statistical lists are often ordered by these numbers.

FIPS: Codes from FIPS PUB 10-4.

Conv: Conventional abbreviations commonly used in Norway. Occasional variations will be found, such as Øs for Østfold and Ve for Vestfold.

Population: 1990 census.

Area-km: Square kilometers.

Area-mi: Square miles.

Capitals: Some references disagree about these capitals. Some atlases even show different capitals on different pages. The inference is that administrative offices are in more than one city.

Further subdivisions: The provinces are subdivided into kommuner (municipalities), which were of two types: bykommuner (urban) and herredskommuner (rural). On 1992-09-25, the legal distinction between these two types was abolished.

Territorial extent: Most of the counties have coastlines, and include many islands, mostly quite near shore. Some of the larger or outermost islands are mentioned here.

Akershus includes Ilåøya, Ostøya, Brønnøya, and Nesøya, all in Oslo Fjord.

Aust-Agder includes Tromøy, Justøya, and Sandøya.

Finnmark includes the islands of Sørøya, Magerøy, Seiland, Skogerøy, Rolvsøy, Silda, and Ingøy.

Hedmark includes Kelgøya in Lake Mjøsa.

Hordaland includes Stord, Osterøya, Store Sotra, Askøy, Holsnøy, Radøy, Fosnøy, Huftarøy, and Hellisøy.

Møre og Romsdal includes Smøla, Gurskøy, Averøy, Tustna, Ertvågøy, Nerlandsøy, and Harøy.

Nord-Trøndelag includes most of the island of Austra, as well as Vikna, Leka, and the fjord island of Ytterøy.

Nordland includes about half of the island of Hinnøy in the north, a share of Austra in the south, and many other islands in the Lofoten and Vesterålen groups and along the shore. Some of the largest are Andøya, Langøy, Austvågøy, Vestvågøy, Moskenesøy, and Vega.

Østfold includes Jeløy, Kirkeøy, Vesterøy, Spjær, Asmaløy, and Rauer.

Rogaland includes Karmøy, Bokn, Ombo, Rennesøy, Finnøy, and Utsira.

Sogn og Fjordane includes Bremanger, Sula, Vågsøy, and Hovden.

Sør-Trøndelag includes Hitra and Frøya.

Telemark includes Skatøy and Jomfruland.

Troms includes about half of the island of Hinnøy, and Soenja, Kvaløy, Ringvassøy, Arnøy, and Vanna.

Vest-Agder includes Kråka and Flekkerøy.

Vestfold includes Nøtterøy, Tjøme, and Bastøy.

Norway also includes several external territories. Svalbard is a large Arctic island group. It became part of Norway on 1925-08-14. Jan Mayen is an island east of Greenland, incorporated on 1930-02-27. Bouvet Island is an island in the South Atlantic, which became a Norwegian dependency on 1930-02-27. These are treated as two separate countries by ISO 3166 (and this book): Svalbard and Jan Mayen Islands, and Bouvet Island. However, ISO 3166-2 assigns Jan Mayen the alternative Norwegian code NO-22, and Svalbard, NO-21. Peter I Island, near Antarctica, became a Norwegian dependency on 1933-03-24. Norway has also claimed part of Antarctica, Queen Maud Land, since 1939-01-14. In view of the Antarctic Treaty, both Peter I Island and Queen Maud Land are listed under Antarctica.

Origins of names:

Bergen: Old Norse *Björgvin*, from björg: mountain, vin: pas-   Finnmark: Norwegian for field of the Finns
turage

Change history: There have been many minor boundary changes. Probably the most people were affected ~1955 when Oslo annexed many of its suburbs from Akershus.

~1922   Name of Nedenes county changed to Aust-Agder; Finmarken changed to Finnmark; Hede-
        marken changed to Hedmark; Søndre Bergenhus changed to Hordaland; Romsdal changed
        to Møre; Nordre Trondhjem changed to Nord-Trøndelag; Kristian changed to Opland;
        Smaalenene changed to Østfold; Stavanger changed to Rogaland; Nordre Bergenhus changed
        to Sogn og Fjordane; Søndre Trondhjem changed to Sør-Trøndelag; Bratsberg changed to
        Telemark; Tromsø changed to Troms; Lister og Mandal changed to Vest-Agder; Jarlsberg
        og Larvik changed to Vestfold.
1925   Name of capital of country changed from Kristiania to Oslo.
~1950   Name of Møre changed to Møre og Romsdal.
~1955   Name of Opland changed to Oppland.
1973   Bergen county merged with Hordaland. Before the merger, Bergen was the capital of both.
        Bergen's county number was 13, and its FIPS code, NO03.

Other names of subdivisions: The letters Ö ö sometimes appear instead of Ø ø, even in Norwegian sources. The word 'og' means 'and', and is sometimes translated.

Aust-Agder: Austur-Agðir (Icelandic); Nedenes (obsolete)
Finnmark: Finmarken (obsolete); Finnmörk (Icelandic)
Hedmark: Hedemarken (obsolete); Heiðmörk (Icelandic)
Hordaland: Hörðaland (Icelandic); Søndre Bergenhus (obso-
lete)
Møre og Romsdal: Møre, Romsdal (obsolete)
Nord-Trøndelag: Nordre Trondhjem (obsolete); Norður-
Þrændalög (Icelandic)
Oppland: Kristian, Opland (obsolete); Upplönd (Icelandic)
Oslo: Kristiania (obsolete)
Østfold: Austfold (Icelandic); Smaalenene (obsolete)

Rogaland: Stavanger (obsolete)
Sogn og Fjordane: Nordre Bergenhus (obsolete); Sogn og
Firða-Fylki (Icelandic)
Sør-Trøndelag: Søndre Trondhjem (obsolete); Suður-Þræn-
dalög (Icelandic)
Telemark: Bratsberg (obsolete); Þelamörk (Icelandic)
Troms: Tromsø (obsolete); Troms-Fylki (Icelandic)
Vest-Agder: Lister og Mandal (obsolete); Vestur-Agðir (Ice-
landic)
Vestfold: Jarlsberg og Larvik (obsolete)

Population history:

county	1900	1930	1946	1960	1970	1980	1990
Akershus	116,228	490,000	306,884	233,747	322,321	369,193	238,296
Aust-Agder	79,935	73,800	71,790	77,061	80,575	90,629	97,333
Bergen	72,251	— —	107,293	115,689	— —	— —	— —
Buskerud	112,676	151,800	150,032	168,328	198,225	214,571	225,172
Finnmark	32,952	53,300	54,800	71,982	75,791	78,331	74,524
Hedmark	126,182	157,400	166,384	177,195	178,923	187,223	187,275
Hordaland	135,752	262,700	180,254	225,296	372,172	391,463	410,568
Møre og Romsdal	136,137	165,100	175,364	213,027	223,360	236,062	238,408
Nord-Trøndelag	83,433	96,000	104,541	116,635	117,718	125,835	127,157
Nordland	152,144	186,900	205,566	237,193	240,461	244,493	239,311
Oppland	116,280	137,700	152,102	166,109	172,163	180,765	182,578
Oslo	227,626	— —	285,884	475,562	477,898	452,023	459,299 ➤

county	1900	1930	1946	1960	1970	1980	1990
Østfold	136,886	167,000	173,795	202,641	220,892	233,301	417,653
Rogaland	127,592	173,300	196,572	238,662	268,171	305,490	337,504
Sogn og Fjordane	89,041	91,800	92,326	99,844	100,761	105,924	106,659
Sør-Trøndelag	135,382	175,500	189,502	211,648	233,420	244,760	250,978
Telemark	99,052	127,800	127,933	149,848	156,405	162,050	162,907
Troms	74,362	97,500	109,289	127,549	136,224	146,818	146,716
Vest-Agder	81,567	81,200	91,621	108,876	124,013	136,718	144,917
Vestfold	104,554	125,400	139,292	174,362	174,640	186,691	198,399
	2,240,032	2,814,200	3,081,224	3,591,254	3,874,133	4,092,340	4,247,553

Census dates, where known: 1900-12-03, 1930-12-01, 1970-11-01, 1980-11-01, 1990-11-03
Where no figures are listed, Bergen is combined with Hordaland; Oslo is combined with Akershus.

OMAN

ISO = OM/FIPS = MU   Language = Arabic   Time zone = +4   Capital = Muscat

In 1900, Oman was an independent country. It was officially called the Sultanate of Muscat and Oman. The name Oman was used to refer to what is now Qatar and the United Arab Emirates, as well as Muscat and Oman. However, the territory was in reality a collection of sheikhdoms and emirates. The inland boundaries with Arabia were indefinite. By 1916, Britain had concluded treaties with Qatar and the seven emirates that in effect made them protectorates. Oil discoveries made it increasingly important to settle questions of sovereignty. By 1950, maps were showing boundaries between Qatar, Trucial Oman (now the United Arab Emirates), and the sultanate. In 1970, Sultan Qaboos ibn Said overthrew his father and changed the country's name to Oman. Oman's boundaries with Saudi Arabia and Yemen were finally delimited in the early 1990s.

Other names of country: Mascat y Omán (obsolete–Spanish); Muscat and Oman (obsolete); Omā (Portuguese); Óman (Icelandic); Omán (Spanish); Saltanat 'Uman (formal); Sultanate of Oman (formal–English); Sultanía de Omán (formal–Spanish).

division	ISO	FIPS	type	population	capital
Ad Dakhliyah	DA	MU01	r	229,791	Nizwa
Adh Dhahirah	AZ	MU05	r	181,224	Ibri
Al Batinah	BA	MU02	r	564,677	Sohar, Rustaq
Al Wusta	WU	MU03	r	17,067	Haima
Ash Sharqiyah	AS	MU04	r	258,344	Sur
Dhofar	ZU	MU08	p	189,094	Salalah
Musandam	MU	MU07	p	28,727	Khasab
Muscat	MA	MU06	p	549,150	Muscat
				2,018,074	

Status: These divisions are mintaqat (r; sing. mintaqah: regions) or muhafazat (p; sing. muhafazah: provinces).
ISO: Codes from ISO 3166-2.
FIPS: Codes from FIPS PUB 10-4.
Population: 1993 census.
Further subdivisions: Below the regions and provinces, Oman is divided into wilayat (governorates). There were 37 in 1977, 41 in 1988, and 59 in 1996.
Territorial extent: Ash Sharqiyah includes the islands of Masirah and Mahawt.
Dhofar includes the Kuria Muria Islands, also known as the Halaniyat after their largest member.
Musandam is a discontiguous part of Oman, at the northern tip of the Musandam Peninsula.
Origins of names:

Adh Dhahirah: = back (rear or inland side of the Western Hajar (Stone) Mountains)
Al Batinah: = belly (front or seaward side of the Western Hajar (Stone) Mountains)
Al Wusta: = central
Ash Sharqiyah: = eastern

Change history: The administrative divisions of Oman had little significance or definition until very recently. Between ~1960 and ~1990, the number of primary divisions has varied from eight to ten, and their status was liwa (province). Most of the divisions have kept approximately the same territory.

1958-09-08   Gwadar (a coastal enclave in Baluchistan) ceded to Pakistan.
1967-11-30   Kuriya Muriya Islands transferred from British control to Dhofar province.

Other names of subdivisions:

Ad Dakhliyah: A'Dakhliya, Ad Dakhiliyah, Al Jauf, Al Joof, Dakhlia, Interior (variant); Al Goof (German)

Adh Dhahirah: A'Dhahirah, Az Zahirah (variant)

Al Wusta: Central Oman, Oman Proper, Rub al Khali, 'Umān al-Wusṭā (variant)

Ash Sharqiyah: Al Hajar, A'Shariqiyah, Eastern (variant)

Dhofar: Dhufar, Al Janubiyah, Southern Region, Zufar (variant)

Musandam: Mussandam, Ru'us al-Jibal (variant)

Muscat: Mascat (Spanish); Mascate (French, Italian, Portuguese); Maskat (German, Norwegian); Masqat, Muscat and Matrah (variant)

PAKISTAN

ISO = PK/FIPS = PK   Language = Urdu, English   Time zone = +5   Capital = Islamabad

In 1900, the name Pakistan did not exist. The land was part of India, which was a collection of British provinces under the direct sovereignty of the British crown, along with small states ruled by Indian princes under British hegemony. When India obtained its independence on 1947-08-15, the area hitherto known as India was divided into two countries along religious lines. Majority-Muslim areas were to go to Pakistan, majority-Hindu areas to India. As it worked out, Pakistan was created as two pieces on opposite sides of the Indian subcontinent. Pakistan became a Dominion of the British Commonwealth on 1947-08-14. Pakistan's eastern and western sections had conflicting interests. On 1971-03-26, East Pakistan declared its independence from Pakistan. A war ensued between India and Pakistan. On 1971-12-15, Pakistan accepted defeat, and East Pakistan became a separate country.

Other names of country: Islami Jamhuriya e Pakistan (formal); Islamic Republic of Pakistan (formal–English); Pakistán (Spanish); Paquistão (Portuguese).

Origin of name: Land of the spiritually pure: coined in 1933. It has been widely reported that the name was also chosen as an acrostic on Punjab, Afghan (borderlands), Kashmir, Sind, and BaluchISTAN.

division	ISO	FIPS	type	population	area-km	area-mi	capital
Azad Kashmir	JK	PK06	a	2,800,000	84,160	32,494	Muzaffarabad
Balochistan	BA	PK02	p	4,332,000	347,190	134,051	Quetta
Federally Administered Tribal Areas	TA	PK01	t	2,199,000	27,220	10,510	Islamabad
Islamabad	IS	PK08	c	340,000	906	350	Islamabad
Northern Areas	NA	PK07	a	(included in Azad Kashmir)			
North-West Frontier	NW	PK03	p	11,061,000	74,521	28,773	Peshawar
Punjab	PB	PK04	p	47,292,000	205,344	79,284	Lahore
Sindh	SD	PK05	p	19,029,000	140,914	54,407	Karachi
				87,053,000	880,255	339,869	

Status: These divisions are provinces (p), centrally administered areas (a), a territory (t), and a capital territory (c).

ISO: Codes from ISO 3166-2.

FIPS: Codes from FIPS PUB 10-4. (Codes PK06-PK08 were added as recently as 1991.)

Population: 1981 census (Kashmir: estimate).

Area-km: Square kilometers.

Area-mi: Square miles.

Note: Some sources include Federally Administered Tribal Areas in North-West Frontier province, and combine Northern Areas and Azad Kashmir into a single unit (Kashmir).

Further subdivisions: The four provinces are each subdivided into divisions. Federally Administered Tribal Areas is equivalent to a single division. The divisions (including the territory) are subdivided into districts. The districts are further subdivided into tahsils.

Territorial extent: The modern divisions are fairly close counterparts of the pre-independence divisions listed here.

Azad Kashmir: part of Kashmir state

Balochistan: Baluchistan province, Kalat, Kharan, Las Bela, and Mekran states

Federally Administered Tribal Areas: Khyber, Kurram, Malakand, North Waziristan, and South Waziristan agencies

Islamabad: part of Punjab province

Northern Areas: Baltistan and Gilgit states

North-West Frontier: North-West Frontier province, Amb, Chitral, Dir, Nagir Phulra, and Swat states

Punjab: part of Punjab province, Bahawalpur state

Sindh: Sind province, Khairpur state

Origins of names:

Azad Kashmir: Urdu *azad*: free

Balochistan: Land of the Baluch people

Punjab: Persian *panj*: five, *ab*: river (the area is drained by five tributaries of the Indus)

Sindh: from Sanskrit *sindhu*: river, district of the lower Indus River

Change history: In 1900, India included over 500 native states (also called princely states); the British provinces of Assam, Bengal, Berar, Bihar, Burma, Central Provinces, Orissa, Punjab, and North Western Provinces and Oudh; and the presidencies of Bombay and Madras. The presidency of Bombay contained the provinces of Bombay, Sind, and Aden. Burma was divided into Lower Burma and Upper Burma. The United Provinces of Agra and Oudh contained Oudh province and North Western Provinces.

1901	North-West Frontier Area split from Punjab by taking parts of the districts of Bannu, Dera Ismail Khan, Hazara, Kohat, and Peshawar.
1936-04-01	Status of Sind division of Bombay presidency changed to province.
1947-08-14	Pakistan created. It consisted of East Bengal province (formed from part of Bengal province and most of Sylhet district of Assam); West Punjab province (part of Punjab province); and the entire provinces of Beluchistan, North-West Frontier, and Sind. The capital was Karachi. The native states and agencies became effectively independent. They were allowed to decide whether to accede to (merge with) India or Pakistan.
1948-07-23	Federal Capital territory formed from Karachi and surrounding areas, totaling 2,103 sq. km.
~1948	Baluchistan States Union formed as a part of Pakistan from the native states of Kalat, Kharan, Las Bela, and Mekran.
1950	Native states of Amb and Nagir Phulra merged with North-West Frontier province. Name of West Punjab province changed to Punjab.
1955-10-14	West Pakistan province of Pakistan formed by merging Bahawalpur state, Baluchistan province, Baluchistan States Union, Chitral state, Dir state, Hunza state, Karachi province, Khairpur state, Northwest Frontier province, Punjab province, Sind province, Swat state; i.e., all of Pakistan west of India except the Federal Capital territory. Its capital was Lahore.
1958-09-08	Gwadar annexed to West Pakistan (Baluchistan) from Oman.
1960-08-01	Capital of Pakistan moved from Karachi to Rawalpindi (provisional capital).
1961	Federal Capital territory merged with West Pakistan province.
1967	Capital of Pakistan moved from Rawalpindi to Islamabad.
1970-07-01	West Pakistan split into the provinces of Baluchistan, Northwest Frontier, Punjab, and Sind, and the centrally administered area of Islamabad.
1971-12-15	Secession of East Pakistan recognized by West Pakistan.
1981	Status of Islamabad administered area changed to capital territory.
~1990	Spelling of Baluchistan changed to Balochistan; Sind changed to Sindh.

Other names of subdivisions:

Azad Kashmir: Cachemira (Portuguese); Cachemire libre (French); Kaschmir (German)

Balochistan: Baloutchistan, Béloutchistan (French); Baluchistan, Beluchistan (variant); Baluchistão (Portuguese); Belucistan (Italian); Belutschistan (German)

Federally Administered Tribal Areas: Áreas tribais sob administração federal (Portuguese); F A T A (variant); Zones tribales sous administration fédérale (French)

Islamabad: Federal Capital Territory, Federal Capital Territory

Islamabad (variant); Territoire de la Capitale fédérale (French); Território da Capital Federal (Portuguese)

Northern Areas: Zones du Nord (French)

North-West Frontier: Fronteira Noroeste (Portuguese); Frontière du Nord-Ouest (French); Nordwestlich-Grenzprovinz (German); N.W.F.P. (variant); Provincia Fronteriza del Noroeste (Spanish)

Punjab: Panjab (German); Pendjab, Penjab (French)

Sindh: Sind (French, German, obsolete)

Population history (see India for earlier years):

division	1951	1961	1972	1981
Azad Kashmir	— —	— —	1,300,000	2,800,000
Balochistan	1,174,036	1,353,000	2,409,000	4,332,000
Federally Administered Tribal Areas	1,126,417	1,847,000	2,507,000	2,199,000
Islamabad	— —	94,000	235,000	340,000
North-West Frontier	5,899,905	5,731,000	8,402,000	11,061,000
Punjab	20,651,110	25,488,000	37,374,000	47,292,000
Sindh	4,928,057	8,367,000	13,965,000	19,029,000
	33,779,525	42,880,000	66,192,000	87,053,000

PALAU

ISO = PW/FIPS = PS   Language = English   Time zone = +9   Capital = Koror

Palau consists of some of the westernmost of the Caroline Islands, in Micronesia. Germany bought almost all of Micronesia from Spain in the 1890s. The islands were conquered by Japan, and mandated to it in 1920 by the League of Nations. The Trust Territory of the Pacific Islands was created on 1947-04-02 and granted in trust to the United States. This territory was divided into districts, one of which was Palau. On 1995-10-01, Palau became a freely associated state of the United States, a status somewhere between protectorate and independent country.

Other names of country: Belau (variant); Republic of Palau (formal).

division	abv	population	area-km	area-mi	capital
Palau	PW	15,122	461	178	Koror

Status: This division is the whole of the country, treated as a division for compatibility.

Abv: Two-letter code for international compatibility (defined by the author). This is also the alphabetic state code from FIPS PUB 5-2; its numeric code in that standard is 68.

Population: 1990 census.

Area-km: Square kilometers.

Area-mi: Square miles.

Further subdivisions: FIPS PUB 6-4 divides Pelau into states (formerly designated as municipalities). It assigns a three-digit code to each of them. When the FIPS 5-2 and 6-4 codes are concatenated, as in 70004 for Airai, the result is a code that uniquely identifies a county-equivalent unit in the United States.

code	name	code	name
002	Aimeliik	150	Koror
004	Airai	212	Melekeok
010	Angaur	214	Ngaraard
050	Hatobohei	218	Ngarchelong
100	Kayangel	222	Ngardmau ▶

code	name	code	name
224	Ngatpang	228	Ngiwal
226	Ngchesar	350	Peleliu
227	Ngeremlengui	370	Sonsorol

Territorial extent: Palau includes a chain of islands running from Tobi in the southwest to Kayangel Atoll in the northeast. The largest is Babelthaup Island. The capital is on nearby Koror Island.

Change history:

~1994   Status of the divisions of Palau changed from municipalities to states; spelling of Melekeiok changed to Melekeok; spelling of Ngaremlengui changed to Ngeremlengui, and its code changed from 223 to 227; name of Tobi changed to Hatobohei, and its code changed from 380 to 050; Palau Islands Unorganized Territory (code 300) annexed to Koror and Peleliu.

PANAMA

ISO = PA/FIPS = PM   Language = Spanish   Time zone = -5   Capital = Panama City

Panama was a department of Colombia in 1900. With the encouragement of the United States, Panama declared its independence from Colombia on 1903-11-03. The United States then acquired control of the Canal Zone from it. In 1979, the Canal Zone was restored to Panama.

Other names of country: Panamá (German, Italian, Portuguese, Spanish); República de Panamá (formal); Republic of Panama (formal–English).

Origin of name: named for a village, whose name meant "place where many fish are taken."

division	abv	ISO	FIPS	population	area-km	area-mi	capital
Bocas del Toro	BT	1	PM01	92,731	8,945	3,454	Bocas del Toro
Chiriquí	CQ	4	PM02	368,023	8,653	3,341	David
Coclé	CC	2	PM03	172,165	4,927	1,902	Penonomé
Colón	CL	3	PM04	167,873	4,890	1,888	Colón
Darién	DA	5	PM05	43,032	16,671	6,437	La Palma
Herrera	HE	6	PM06	93,360	2,341	904	Chitré
Los Santos	LS	7	PM07	76,604	3,806	1,469	Las Tablas
Panamá	PA	8	PM08	1,064,221	11,887	4,590	Panama City
San Blas	SB	0	PM09	34,134	2,357	910	El Porvenir
Veraguas	VE	9	PM10	202,904	11,239	4,340	Santiago
				2,315,047	75,716	29,235	

Status: These divisions are provincias (provinces), except for San Blas, which is a comarca or intendencia (intendency).

Abv: Two-letter code for international compatibility (defined by the author).

ISO: Codes from ISO 3166-2.

FIPS: Codes from FIPS PUB 10-4.

Population: 1990 census.

Area-km: Square kilometers.

Area-mi: Square miles.

Further subdivisions: The provinces of Panama are divided into municipal districts, which are further subdivided into corregimientos.

Territorial extent: The city of Colón formed an enclave within the Canal Zone while it existed.

Origins of names:

Colón: named for Christopher Columbus

Change history: There have been numerous minor boundary adjustments.

1904-02-26 Treaty of Hay and Bunau-Varilla took effect, by which the United States acquired the "use, occupation, and control" of the Canal Zone.

~1925 Capital of Canal Zone moved from Ancón to Balboa Heights (a district in the city of Balboa).

~1930 Herrera province split from Los Santos; Darién province split from Panamá; San Blas intendency formed from parts of Colón and Panamá.

1979-10-01 By the Panama Canal Treaty, the United States relinquished the Canal Zone. The zone (1,432 sq. km.) was split and annexed to Colón and Panamá.

PAPUA NEW GUINEA

ISO = PG/FIPS = PP   Language = English   Time zone = +10   Capital = Port Moresby

In 1900, the island of New Guinea was divided into a Dutch colony in the west, a German colony in the northeast, and a British protectorate in the southeast. In 1905-11, the Commonwealth of Australia took over the administration of British New Guinea. On 1906-09-01, British New Guinea was renamed the Territory of Papua. German New Guinea was mandated to Great Britain by the League of Nations on 1920-12-17. On 1946-12-13, the mandate became a Trust Territory of Australia under the United Nations. The two territories were jointly administered beginning on 1949-07-01, under the name Papua New Guinea. They became a single independent country on 1975-09-16.

Other names of country: Papouasie-Nouvelle-Guinée (French); Papúa (Icelandic); Papua Neuguinea (German); Papua Nieuw Guinea (Dutch); Papua-Nova Guiné (Portuguese); Papua Nueva Guinea (Spanish); Papua Nuova Guinea (Italian); Papua Nya Guinea (Swedish); Papua Ny Guinea (Danish); Papua Ny-Guinea (Norwegian); Papua-Uusi-Guinea (Finnish).

Origin of name: union of Papua and Australian New Guinea. Papua is Malay for frizzled, referring to natives' hair. The island of New Guinea was named by Spanish explorer Ortiz de Rez, from natives' resemblance to those of Guinea in Africa.

division	abv	ISO	FIPS	population	area-km	area-mi	capital
Central	CE	CPM	PP01	140,584	29,500	11,390	Port Moresby
Chimbu	CH	CPK	PP08	183,801	6,100	2,360	Kundiawa
Eastern Highlands	EH	EHG	PP09	299,619	11,200	4,320	Goroka
East New Britain	EN	EBR	PP10	184,408	15,500	5,980	Rabaul
East Sepik	ES	ESW	PP11	248,308	42,800	16,530	Wewak
Enga	EG	EPW	PP19	238,357	12,800	4,940	Wabag
Gulf	GU	GPK	PP02	68,060	34,500	13,320	Kerema
Madang	MD	MPM	PP12	270,299	29,000	11,200	Madang
Manus	MN	MRL	PP13	32,830	2,100	810	Lorengau
Milne Bay	MB	MBA	PP03	157,288	14,000	5,410	Alotau
Morobe	MR	MPL	PP14	363,535	34,500	13,320	Lae
National Capital District	NC	NCD	PP20	193,242	240	90	Port Moresby
New Ireland	NI	NIK	PP15	87,194	9,600	3,710	Kavieng
Northern	NO	NPP	PP04	96,762	22,800	8,800	Popondetta
North Solomons	NS	NSA	PP07	159,500	9,300	3,590	Arawa
Sandaun	SA	SAN	PP18	135,185	36,300	14,020	Vanimo
Southern Highlands	SH	SHM	PP05	302,724	23,800	9,190	Mendi
Western	WE	WPD	PP06	108,705	99,300	38,340	Daru
Western Highlands	WH	WHM	PP16	291,090	8,500	3,280	Mount Hagen
West New Britain	WN	WBK	PP17	127,547	21,000	8,110	Kimbe
				3,689,038	462,840	178,710	

Status: These divisions are provinces, except for National Capital District, which is a district.

Abv: Two-letter code for international compatibility (defined by the author).

ISO: Codes from ISO 3166-2.

FIPS: Codes from FIPS PUB 10-4.

Population: 1990 census.

Area-km: Square kilometers.

Area-mi: Square miles.

Further subdivisions: Before independence, the districts were divided into subdistricts.

Territorial extent: Papua New Guinea shares the island of New Guinea with Indonesia. Chimbu, Eastern Highlands, Enga, Northern, Sandaun, Southern Highlands, and Western Highlands provinces and the National Capital District are almost entirely on New Guinea. For each of the other provinces, the main islands it occupies are listed, roughly in descending order of size.

Central: New Guinea, Yule

East New Britain: New Britain, Duke of York, Watom

East Sepik: New Guinea, Kairiru, Mushu, Vokeo, Walis, Blup Blup

Gulf: New Guinea, Morigio

Madang: New Guinea, Long, Karkar, Manam, Bagbag

Manus: Admiralty Islands (Manus, Rambutyo, Lou, etc.), Ninigo Islands, Hermit Islands, etc.

Milne Bay: New Guinea, D'Entrecasteaux Islands (Fergusson, Normanby, Goodenough), Louisiade Archipelago (Sudest or Tagula, Yela or Rossel, Misima, Panatinane), Marshall Bennett Islands (Woodlark, Madau), Trobriand Islands (Kiriwina, Kaduaga), Engineer Group (Sideia, Basilaki)

Morobe: New Guinea, Umbo, Sakar, Tolokiwa

New Ireland: New Ireland, New Hanover, Saint Matthias Group (Mussau, Emirau), Tabar Group (Tabar, Tatau, Simberi), Lihir Group (Lihir), Tanga Group (Malendok, Boang), Feni Islands (Ambitle, Babase)

North Solomons: Bougainville, Buka, Green Islands (Nissan, Pinipel)

Western: New Guinea, Kiwai, Purutu, Wabuda, Naviu, and other islands in the deltas of the Fly and Bumu Rivers

West New Britain: New Britain, Lolobau, Witu Islands (Garove, Unea)

Origins of names:

Bougainville: named for French explorer Louis Antoine, Count of Bougainville

Change history:

1904	Bougainville and Buka Islands transferred from British Solomon Islands to German New Guinea.
1950-03-01	Umbo, Sakar, and Tolokiwa Islands transferred from New Britain district to Morobe district; East Central district merged with Central; Eastern and South Eastern districts merged to form Milne Bay.
1950-11-20	Name of Kieta district changed to Bougainville.
1951-09-06	Status of the units of Papua changed from divisions to districts; Central Highlands split up to form the new districts of Eastern Highlands, Southern Highlands, and Western Highlands, with other parts annexed to Sepik, Western, and Madang; Delta district merged with Gulf. Note: Central Highlands district had straddled the border between Papua and New Guinea territories. After this reorganization, each district was entirely within one or the other.
1966-06-21	Chimbu district formed from parts of Eastern Highlands, Gulf, Southern Highlands, and Western Highlands; Sepik split into East Sepik and West Sepik; New Britain split into East New Britain and West New Britain.
1975-09-16	Upon independence, status of the units of Papua New Guinea changed from districts to provinces.
1973	Enga province formed from parts of Southern Highlands and Western Highlands.
1974	National Capital district split from Central province.
1975	Name of Bougainville province changed to North Solomons.
~1978	Capital of Milne Bay moved from Samarai to Alotau; capital of North Solomons moved from Sohano to Arawa.
~1989	Name of West Sepik province changed to Sandaun.

Other names of subdivisions:

Chimbu: Simbu (variant)

Eastern Highlands: Planalto Oriental (Portuguese)

East New Britain: Nova Bretanha Oriental (Portuguese); Nuova Britannia Orientale (Italian)

New Ireland: Neuirland (German); Nouvelle-Irlande (French); Nova Irlanda (Portuguese); Nuova Irlanda (Italian)
Northern: Oro (variant)
North Solomons: Bougainville (obsolete)
Sandaun: West Sepik (obsolete)

Western: Fly (variant)
Western Highlands: Planalto Ocidental (Portuguese)
West New Britain: Nova Bretanha Ocidental (Portuguese); Nuova Britannia Occidentale (Italian)

PARAGUAY

ISO = PY/FIPS = PA   Language = Spanish   Time zone = -4 ᵈ   Capital = Asunción

The Gran Chaco was disputed between Paraguay and Bolivia for many years. Until 1932, it was divided along a line roughly from the split of the Pilcomayo River to Fuerte Olimpo. Then oil was discovered, and the Chaco War (1932–1935) broke out. In 1938-07, with the signing of a peace treaty, Paraguay expanded to its present limits.

Other names of country: Paraguai (Portuguese); Paragvæ (Icelandic); Republic of Paraguay (formal–English); República del Paraguay (formal).

Origin of name: Theory 1: Guaraní *para*: river + *guaso*: big; theory 2: Paragua (chief's name) + *y*: river.

division	abv	ISO	FIPS	population	area-km	area-mi	capital
Alto Paraguay	AP	16	PA18	10,100	45,982	17,754	Fuerte Olimpo
Alto Paraná	AA	10	PA01	373,300	14,895	5,751	Ciudad del Este
Amambay	AM	13	PA02	97,700	12,933	4,993	Pedro Juan Caballero
Asunción	AS	ASU	— —	607,700	117	45	Asunción
Boquerón	BO	19	PA03	16,900	46,708	18,034	Doctor Pedro P. Peña
Caaguazú	CG	5	PA04	462,500	11,474	4,430	Coronel Oviedo
Caazapá	CZ	6	PA05	132,000	9,496	3,666	Caazapá
Canendiyú	CY	14	PA19	120,800	14,667	5,663	Salto del Guairá
Central	CE	11	PA06	769,100	2,465	952	Asunción
Chaco	CH	17	PA20	300	36,367	14,041	Mayor Pablo Lagerenza
Concepción	CN	1	PA07	181,051	18,051	6,970	Concepción
Cordillera	CR	3	PA08	222,200	4,948	1,910	Caacupé
Guairá	GU	4	PA10	179,800	3,846	1,485	Villarrica
Itapúa	IT	7	PA11	371,600	16,525	6,380	Encarnación
Misiones	MI	8	PA12	97,500	9,556	3,690	San Juan Bautista (de las Misiones)
Ñeembucú	NE	12	PA13	83,300	12,147	4,690	Pilar
Nueva Asunción	NA	18	PA21	300	44,961	17,360	General Eugenio A. Garay
Paraguarí	PG	9	PA15	230,700	8,705	3,361	Paraguarí
Presidente Hayes	PH	15	PA16	38,200	72,907	28,150	Pozo Colorado
San Pedro	SP	2	PA17	284,000	20,002	7,723	San Pedro
				4,279,051	406,752	157,048	

Status: These divisions are departamentos (departments), except for Asunción, which is a capital district.

Abv: Two-letter code for international compatibility (defined by the author).

ISO: Codes from ISO 3166-2. Except for ASU, these are the same as the department numbers officially used by Paraguay.

FIPS: Codes from FIPS PUB 10-4. For FIPS, Asunción is presumably part of Central.

Population: 1990 estimate.

Area-km: Square kilometers.

Area-mi: Square miles.

Capital: The capital of Central is also reported to be Areguá, Limpio, or Ypacaraí. The capital of Misiones is commonly called San Juan Bautista; its full name is San Juan Bautista de las Misiones.

Further subdivisions: The Paraguay River divides Paraguay into two provincias (provinces), named Occidente and Oriente (West and East, respectively). The provinces are further divided into the departments listed above. The only departments in Occidente are Alto Paraguay, Boquerón, Chaco, Nueva Asunción, and Presidente Hayes. The departments are subdivided into partidos, which are subdivided into compañías and municipios.

Origins of names: Alto Paraguay, Alto Paraná: Spanish *alto*: high, along the upper course of the Paraguay (respectively, Paraná) River in Paraguay.

Asunción: Originally Spanish *Nuestra Señora de la Asunción*: Our Lady of the Assumption. Founded on 1536-08-15, Assumption Day

Chaco: from Guaraní *chako*: hunting ground

Misiones: = Missions, for Jesuit missions to the natives

Ñeembucú: local word for endless

Nueva Asunción: Spanish *nueva*: new, named after the capital Asunción

Presidente Hayes: named after U.S. President Rutherford B. Hayes in gratitude for his favorable decision in arbitration of a border conflict

Change history:

The division of Paraguay at the end of the Chaco War was:

department	no.	population	area-km	capital	approximate equivalent
Caazapá	6	74,267	10,790	Caazapá	Caazapá
Caraguatay	3	146,479	5,625	Caraguatay	Cordillera
Concepción	1	43,953	32,569	Concepción	Concepción; Amambay (part)
Encarnación	7	71,685	27,363	Encarnación	Itapúa
Federal District	—	154,923	632	Asunción	Asunción
Paraguarí	10	88,769	2,836	Paraguarí	Paraguarí (part)
Pilar	12	31,144	8,632	Pilar	Ñeembucú (part)
Quyyndy	9	48,139	6,768	Quyyndy	Paraguarí (part)
Región Occidental	—	45,860	230,000	Villa Hayes	Boquerón, Olimpo, Presidente Hayes
San Ignacio	8	50,351	7,648	San Ignacio	Misiones
San Pedro	2	35,907	35,633	San Pedro	San Pedro; Amambay, Caaguazú, Alto Paraná (parts)
Villarrica	4	46,740	1,958	Villarrica	Guairá
Villeta	11	57,341	4,496	Villeta	Central; Ñeembucú (part)
Yhú	5	55,783	14,882	Yhú	Caaguazú, Alto Paraná (parts)
		951,341	389,832		

Population: 1936 incomplete census results (include some duplicate counts).

Approximate equivalent: departments covering this area after the reorganization.

~1949　Paraguay reorganized into sixteen departments and one capital district, as shown in table.

~1975　Capital of Alto Paraná department moved from Hernandarias (alternatively called Tacurupucú) to Puerto Presidente Stroessner.

~1978　Canendiyú department formed from the northern parts of Alto Paraná and Caaguazú. Occidental province reorganized. Olimpo (capital Fuerte Olimpo) was split into two parts, which became part of the new Alto Paraguay and Chaco departments. Four parts of Boquerón (Mariscal Estigarribia) were split off from it, leaving a much smaller Boquerón; one became the new department of Nueva Asunción; the others were annexed to Alto Paraguay, Chaco, and Presidente Hayes (Villa Hayes).

~1989　Name of capital of Alto Paraná department changed from Puerto Presidente Stroessner to Ciudad del Este.

Other names of subdivisions:

Asunción: Assunção (Portuguese); Distrito Capital, Distrito Federal (variant)

Canendiyú: Canindeyú (frequent mistake, found even in some official Paraguayan sources)

Cordillera: Caraguatay (obsolete); Las Cordilleras, La Cordillera (variant)

Guairá: Villarrica (obsolete)

Itapúa: Encarnación (obsolete); Itapua, Itapuá (variant)

Misiones: Las Misiones (variant); San Ignacio (obsolete)

Ñeembucú: Neembucú (variant)

Nueva Asunción: Nova Assunção (Portuguese)

PERU

ISO = PE/FIPS = PE   Language = Spanish, Quechua   Time zone = -5   Capital = Lima

Ecuador and Peru have fought repeatedly over disputed territories in the Amazon basin. Ecuador's territorial claim extended as far as the Marañón River before 1942. In that year, the Protocol of Rio de Janeiro drew the border between Ecuador and Peru shown on most modern maps. However, Ecuador still claims some of the region adjudicated to Peru. Most of this area is now part of Loreto department.

Other names of country: Pérou (French); Perú (Icelandic, Spanish); Perù (Italian); Republic of Peru (formal–English); República del Perú (formal).

Origin of name: Corruption of village name Biruquete, possibly meaning "granary."

division	abv	ISO	FIPS	reg	population	area-km	area-mi	capital
Amazonas	AM	AMA	PE01	NM	354,171	39,249	15,154	Chachapoyas
Ancash	AN	ANC	PE02	GC	983,677	35,041	13,530	Huaraz
Apurímac	AP	APU	PE03	IN	396,098	20,896	8,068	Abancay
Arequipa	AR	ARE	PE04	AQ	939,062	65,345	25,230	Arequipa
Ayacucho	AY	AYA	PE05	LW	512,438	43,815	16,917	Ayacucho
Cajamarca	CJ	CAJ	PE06	NM	1,297,835	34,023	13,136	Cajamarca
Callao	CL	CAL	PE07	LC	647,565	147	57	Callao
Cusco	CS	CUS	PE08	IN	1,066,495	71,892	27,758	Cuzco
Huancavelica	HV	HUV	PE09	LW	400,376	22,131	8,545	Huancavelica
Huánuco	HC	HUC	PE10	AC	677,910	37,722	14,565	Huánuco
Ica	IC	ICA	PE11	LW	578,766	21,328	8,235	Ica
Junín	JU	JUN	PE12	AC	1,092,993	44,410	17,147	Huancayo
La Libertad	LL	LAL	PE13	SL	1,287,383	24,795	9,573	Trujillo
Lambayeque	LB	LAM	PE14	NM	950,842	14,231	5,495	Chiclayo
Lima	LI	LIM	PE15	LC	6,478,957	34,802	13,437	Lima
Loreto	LO	LOR	PE16	AZ	736,161	368,852	142,415	Iquitos
Madre de Dios	MD	MDD	PE17	IN	69,854	85,183	32,889	Puerto Maldonado
Moquegua	MQ	MOQ	PE18	JM	130,192	15,813	6,106	Moquegua
Pasco	PA	PAS	PE19	AC	239,191	25,320	9,776	Cerro de Pasco
Piura	PI	PIU	PE20	GU	1,409,262	35,892	13,858	Piura
Puno	PU	PUN	PE21	JM	1,103,689	72,012	27,804	Puno
San Martín	SM	SAM	PE22	SL	572,352	51,253	19,789	Moyobamba
Tacna	TA	TAC	PE23	JM	223,768	15,983	6,171	Tacna
Tumbes	TU	TUM	PE24	GU	158,582	4,669	1,803	Tumbes
Ucayali	UC	UCA	PE25	UY	331,824	102,411	39,541	Pucallpa
					22,639,443	1,287,215	496,999	

Status: These divisions are departamentos (departments), except for Callao, which is a provincia constitucional (constitutional province).

Abv: Two-letter code for international compatibility (defined by the author).

ISO: Codes from ISO 3166-2.

FIPS: Codes from FIPS PUB 10-4.

Reg: Region code, keyed to the list below.

Population: 1993 census.

Area-km: Square kilometers.

Area-mi: Square miles.

region	abv	date created	region	abv	date created
Amazonas	AZ	1988-03-03	José Carlos Mariátegui	JM	1989-04-14
Andrés Avelino Cáceres	AC	1989-04-14	Lima y Callao	LC	1821-08-04
Arequipa	AQ	1989-04-14	Los Libertadores-Wari	LW	1989-02-16
Gran Chavín	GC	1989-04-14	Nor Oriental del Marañón	NM	1982-07-11
Grau	GU	1988-03-01	San Martín-La Libertad	SL	1989-01-20
Inka	IN	1989-01-19	Ucayali	UY	1988-11-24

Abv: Also defined by the author.

Further subdivisions: Peru embarked on a regionalization program in 1988. The government intends the regions to be the top-level administrative divisions. There has been some delay in setting up administrative structures for them. The regions are subdivided into departments, which are subdivided into provincias (provinces), which are further subdivided into partidos.

Origins of names:

Departments:

Amazonas: Spanish name for the Amazon River (see Brazil for its derivation)

Apurimac: probably Quechua *apu rimak*: the lord who speaks

Cusco: Inca for navel (city considered the center of the world)

Huanuco: native word for dry

La Libertad: = liberty, named shortly after Peru gained its independence from Spain in 1821

Lima: Corruption of Rimaco (river name, meaning "speaking")

Madre de Dios: = Mother of God, an epithet of the Virgin Mary

San Martín: named for the revolutionary hero José de San Martín (1778–1850)

Regions:

Andrés Avelino Cáceres: named for a former president of Peru and military leader (~1836–1923)

Gran Chavín: Spanish *gran*: great; Chavín is the name of a prehistoric Indian culture

Grau: named for Admiral Miguel Grau (1838–1879), naval hero of the Pacific War

Inka: name of the empire which dominated Peru immediately before the Spanish conquest

José Carlos Mariátegui: named for a Peruvian Marxist theorist and revolutionary (1894–1930)

Nor Oriental del Marañón: = Northeastern [region] of the Marañón [River]

Change history:

1901-12-20	Tumbes department split from Piura.
1906-09-14	San Martín department split from Loreto.
1912-12-26	Madre de Dios department created from parts of Cuzco and Puno.
~1925	Status of Moquegua changed from province to department.
1929-06-03	Tacna restored to Peru by Chile, which had seized it in 1882.
~1940	Name of Ancachs department changed to Ancash.
1944-11	Pasco province split from Junín (former capital: Cerro de Pasco).
~1983	Ucayali province split from Loreto.

Other names of subdivisions:

Ancash: Ancachs (obsolete)
Cajamarca: Caxamarca (obsolete)
Callao: El Callao (variant)

Cusco: Cuzco (variant)
La Libertad: Libertad (variant)
Tumbes: Tumbez (obsolete)

Population history:

department	1876	1940	1961	1972	1981	1993
Amazonas	34,245	89,560	129,003	196,469	268,121	354,171
Ancash	284,091	465,135	605,548	726,665	862,495	983,677
Apurímac	119,246	280,213	303,648	307,805	342,964	396,098
Arequipa	160,282	270,996	407,163	530,528	738,482	939,062
Ayacucho	142,205	414,208	430,289	459,747	523,821	512,438
Cajamarca	213,391	568,118	786,599	916,331	1,063,474	1,297,835
Callao	34,492	84,438	219,420	315,605	454,313	647,565
Cuzco	238,445	565,458	648,168	708,719	874,463	1,066,495
Huancavelica	104,155	265,557	315,730	331,155	361,548	400,376
Huánuco	78,856	276,833	355,003	420,764	498,417	677,910
Ica	60,111	144,547	261,126	357,973	446,902	578,766
Junín	209,871	500,161	548,662	691,216	896,962	1,092,993
La Libertad	147,541	404,024	609,105	806,368	1,011,631	1,287,383
Lambayeque	85,984	199,660	353,657	515,363	708,820	950,842
Lima	226,922	849,171	2,093,435	3,485,411	4,993,032	6,478,957
Loreto	61,125	321,341	411,340	494,895	516,371	736,161
Madre de Dios	— —	25,212	25,269	21,968	35,788	69,854
Moquegua	28,786	35,709	53,260	74,573	103,283	130,192 ➤

department	1876	1940	1961	1972	1981	1993
Pasco	— —	— —	150,575	176,750	229,701	239,191
Piura	135,502	431,487	692,414	854,668	1,155,682	1,409,262
Puno	256,594	646,385	727,309	779,594	910,377	1,103,689
San Martín	— —	120,913	170,456	224,310	331,692	572,352
Tacna	— —	37,512	67,800	95,623	147,693	223,768
Tumbes	— —	26,473	57,378	75,399	108,064	158,582
Ucayali	— —	— —	— —	— —	178,135	331,824
	2,621,844	7,023,111	10,422,357	13,567,899	17,762,231	22,639,443

Census dates, where available:
1940-06-09
1961-06-02
1972-06-02

PHILIPPINES

ISO = PH/FIPS = RP   Language = English, Pilipino   Time zone = +8   Capital = Manila

In 1900, the United States had recently acquired the Philippines from Spain by conquest and purchase. Rebels against Spain had declared a Philippine Republic upon Spain's defeat. U.S. forces overcame the nationalists as well. The archipelago was invaded by Japan during World War II. After the war, the United States granted independence on 1946-07-04.

Other names of country: Filipijnen (Dutch); Filipinas (Portuguese, Spanish); Filippiinit (Finnish); Filippine (Italian); Filippinene (Norwegian); Filippinerna (Swedish); Filippinerne (Danish); Filippseyjar (Icelandic); Philippinen (German); Republic of the Philippines (formal–English); Republika ng Pilipinas (formal).

Origin of name: Named after King Philip II of Spain (1527–1598).

division	abv	ISO	FIPS	reg	population	area-km	area-mi	capital
Abra	AB	ABR	RP01	CAR	195,964	3,976	1,535	Bangued
Agusan del Norte	AN	AGN	RP02	13	514,485	2,590	1,000	Butuan
Agusan del Sur	AS	AGS	RP03	13	514,736	8,966	3,462	Prosperidad
Aklan	AK	AKL	RP04	6	410,539	1,818	702	Kalibo
Albay	AL	ALB	RP05	5	1,005,315	2,553	986	Legaspi
Antique	AQ	ANT	RP06	6	431,713	2,522	974	San Jose (de Buenavista)
Apayao	AP			CAR	83,660	— —	— —	Kabugao
Aurora	AU	AUR	RPG8	4	159,621	3,240	1,251	Baler
Basilan	BS	BAS	RP22	9	295,565	1,372	530	Isabela
Bataan	BA	BAN	RP07	3	491,459	1,373	530	Balanga
Batanes	BN	BTN	RP08	2	14,180	209	81	(Santo Domingo de) Basco
Batangas	BT	BTG	RP09	4	1,658,567	3,166	1,222	Batangas
Benguet	BG	BEN	RP10	CAR	540,716	2,655	1,025	La Trinidad
Biliran	BI			8	132,209	555	214	Naval
Bohol	BO	BOH	RP11	7	994,440	4,117	1,590	Tagbilaran
Bukidnon	BK	BUK	RP12	10	940,403	8,294	3,202	Malaybalay
Bulacan	BU	BUL	RP13	3	1,784,441	2,625	1,014	Malolos
Cagayan	CG	CAG	RP14	2	895,050	9,003	3,476	Tuguegarao
Camarines Norte	CN	CAN	RP15	5	439,151	2,113	816	Daet
Camarines Sur	CS	CAS	RP16	5	1,432,598	5,267	2,034	Pili
Camiguin	CM	CAM	RP17	10	68,039	230	89	Mambajao
Capiz	CP	CAP	RP18	6	624,469	2,633	1,017	Roxas
Catanduanes	CT	CAT	RP19	5	202,464	1,512	584	Virac
Cavite	CV	CAV	RP20	4	1,610,324	1,288	497	Trece Martires
Cebu	CB	CEB	RP21	7	2,921,145	5,088	1,964	Cebu
Cotabato	NC	NCO	RP57	12	862,666	6,566	2,535	Kidapawan
Davao	DV	DAV	RP24	11	1,191,443	8,130	3,139	Tagum
Davao del Sur	DS	DAS	RP25	11	1,683,909	6,378	2,463	Digos
Davao Oriental	DO	DAO	RP26	11	413,472	5,165	1,994	Mati ➤

division	abv	ISO	FIPS	reg	population	area-km	area-mi	capital
Eastern Samar	ES	EAS	RP23	8	362,324	4,340	1,676	Borongan
Guimaras	GU			6	126,470	604	233	Jordan
Ifugao	IF	IFU	RP27	CAR	149,598	2,518	972	Lagawe
Ilocos Norte	IN	ILN	RP28	1	482,651	3,399	1,312	Laoag
Ilocos Sur	IS	ILS	RP29	1	545,385	2,580	996	Vigan
Iloilo	II	ILI	RP30	6	1,749,561	4,720	1,822	Iloilo
Isabela	IB	ISA	RP31	2	1,160,721	10,665	4,118	Ilagan
Kalinga	KA	KAL	RP32	CAR	154,145	7,048	2,721	Tabuk
Laguna	LG	LAG	RP33	4	1,631,082	1,760	680	Santa Cruz
Lanao del Norte	LN	LAN	RP34	12	713,787	3,092	1,194	Tubod
Lanao del Sur	LS	LAS	RP35	ARMM	686,193	3,873	1,495	Marawi
La Union	LU	LUN	RP36	1	597,442	1,493	576	San Fernando
Leyte	LE	LEY	RP37	8	1,511,251	5,713	2,206	Tacloban
Maguindanao	MG	MAG	RP56	ARMM	808,959	5,078	1,961	Sultan Kudarat
Marinduque	MQ	MAD	RP38	4	199,910	959	370	Boac
Masbate	MB	MAS	RP39	5	653,852	4,048	1,563	Masbate
Metropolitan Manila	MM	MNL	RPD9	NCR	9,454,040	636	246	Manila
Mindoro Occidental	MC	MDC	RP40	4	337,231	5,880	2,270	Mamburao
Mindoro Oriental	MR	MDR	RP41	4	608,616	4,365	1,685	Calapan
Misamis Occidental	MD	MSC	RP42	10	458,965	1,939	749	Oroquieta
Misamis Oriental	MN	MSR	RP43	10	1,015,865	3,570	1,378	Cagayan de Oro
Mountain	MT	MOU	RP44	CAR	130,755	2,097	810	Bontoc
Negros Occidental	ND	NEC	RPH3	6	2,434,186	7,926	3,060	Bacolod
Negros Oriental	NR	NER	RP46	7	1,025,247	5,402	2,086	Dumaguete
Northern Samar	NS	NSA	RP67	8	454,195	3,499	1,351	Catarman
Nueva Ecija	NE	NUE	RP47	3	1,505,827	5,284	2,040	Palayan
Nueva Vizcaya	NV	NUV	RP48	2	334,965	3,904	1,507	Bayombong
Palawan	PL	PLW	RP49	4	640,486	14,896	5,751	Puerto Princesa
Pampanga	PM	PAM	RP50	3	1,635,767	2,181	842	San Fernando
Pangasinan	PN	PAN	RP51	1	2,178,412	5,368	2,073	Lingayen
Quezon	QZ	QUE	RPH2	4	1,537,742	8,707	3,362	Lucena
Quirino	QR	QUI	RP68	2	131,119	3,057	1,180	Cabarroguis
Rizal	RI	RIZ	RP53	4	1,312,489	1,309	505	Pasig, MM
Romblon	RO	ROM	RP54	4	244,654	1,356	524	Romblon
Samar	SM	SAM	RP55	8	588,373	5,591	2,159	Catbalogan
Sarangani	SG			11	367,006	2,980	1,151	Alabel
Siquijor	SQ	SIG	RP69	7	73,756	344	133	Siquijor
Sorsogon	SR	SOR	RP58	5	591,927	2,141	827	Sorsogon
South Cotabato	SC	SCO	RP70	11	948,328	4,489	1,733	Koronadal
Southern Leyte	SL	SLE	RP59	8	317,565	1,735	670	Maasin
Sultan Kudarat	SK	SUK	RP71	12	522,187	4,715	1,820	Isulan
Sulu	SU	SLU	RP60	ARMM	536,201	1,600	618	Jolo
Surigao del Norte	SN	SUN	RP61	13	442,203	2,739	1,058	Surigao
Surigao del Sur	SS	SUR	RP62	13	471,263	4,552	1,758	Tandag
Tarlac	TR	TAR	RP63	3	945,810	3,053	1,179	Tarlac
Tawi-Tawi	TT	TAW	RP72	ARMM	250,718	1,087	420	Balimbing
Zambales	ZM	ZMB	RP64	3	569,266	3,714	1,434	Iba
Zamboanga del Norte	ZN	ZAN	RP65	9	770,697	6,618	2,555	Dipolog
Zamboanga del Sur	ZS	ZAS	RP66	9	1,728,397	8,052	3,109	Pagadian
					68,610,332	300,080	115,864	

Status: These divisions are provinces, except for Metropolitan Manila, which is a region.

Abv: Two-letter code for international compatibility (defined by the author).

ISO: Codes from ISO 3166-2.

FIPS: Codes from FIPS PUB 10-4.

Reg: Region (keyed to list below).

Population: 1995 census.

Area-km: Square kilometers.

Area-mi: Square miles.

Capitals: Note that the capitals of La Union and Pampanga are two different cities with the same name.

Note: Unconfirmed Internet sources say that Isabela province was divided into Isabela del Norte (capital Ilagan) and Isabela del Sur (capital Cauayan) on 1995-02-20; and that Compostela Valley province will be split from Davao.

Further subdivisions: The Philippines have been divided into provinces since they were a Spanish colony, although there have been many changes in the division. Since 1975, the provinces have been grouped into regions. More recently, some new regions have been created with autonomous status. In addition, over the years, certain cities have been designated as chartered cities. Technically, the chartered cities are no longer part of the province within which they are located. Most of the provinces are further subdivided into numbered districts. There are also sub-provinces, which generally split off and form separate provinces in due course. All provinces are subdivided into municipalities. The municipalities are similar in size to the chartered cities, but generally lower in population. Municipalities and chartered cities are subdivided into barangays. The divisions shown are the provinces, each one combined with the chartered cities located within its limits, because it is easiest to get statistics or maps for those units.

The Philippines identifies each ordinary region with a name and a number. The number is often presented as a Roman numeral. The autonomous regions and the capital region have long names, so they are often identified by their initials. In some sources, the capital region is given the number IV-A, and region 4 is designated IV-B. The current list of regions is as follows:

reg	name	population	area-km	capital
1	Ilocos Region	3,803,890	12,840	San Fernando
2	Cagayan Valley	2,536,035	26,838	Tuguegarao
3	Central Luzon	6,932,570	18,231	San Fernando
4	Southern Tagalog	9,940,722	46,601	Quezon
5	Bicol Region	4,325,307	14,544	Legaspi
6	Western Visayas	5,776,938	20,223	Iloilo
7	Central Visayas	5,014,588	14,951	Cebu
8	Eastern Visayas	3,366,917	21,433	Tacloban
9	Western Mindanao	2,794,659	16,042	Zamboanga
10	Northern Mindanao	2,483,272	14,033	Cagayan de Oro
11	Southern Mindanao	4,604,158	27,141	Davao
12	Central Mindanao	2,359,808	14,373	Cotabato
13	Caraga	1,942,687	18,847	
NCR	National Capital Region	9,454,040	4,048	Manila
CAR	Cordillera Autonomous Region	1,254,838	18,294	
ARMM	Autonomous Region in Muslim Mindanao	2,020,903	11,638	Sultan Kudarat
		68,616,536	300,077	

Reg: region number or abbreviation.

Population: 1995 census.

Capitals: Note that the capitals of regions 1 and 3 are two different cities with the same name.

The chartered cities have ISO and FIPS codes that are on a par with the province codes. The following list shows those codes, and the province in which each city is situated.

city	ISO	FIPS	province	city	ISO	FIPS	province
Angeles	ANG	RPA1	Pampanga	Dumaguete	DGT	RPC5	Negros Oriental
Bacolod	BCD	RPA2	Negros Occidental	General Santos	GES	RPC6	South Cotabato
Bago	BGO	RPA3	Negros Occidental	Gingoog	GIN	RPC7	Misamis Oriental
Baguio	BAG	RPA4	Benguet	Iligan	IGN	RPC8	Lanao del Norte
Bais	BAI	RPA5	Negros Oriental	Iloilo	ILO	RPC9	Iloilo
Basilan	BAS	RPA6	Basilan	Iriga	IRI	RPD1	Camarines Sur
Batangas	BAT	RPA7	Batangas	La Carlota	LCA	RPD2	Negros Occidental
Butuan	BXU	RPA8	Agusan del Norte	Laoag	LAO	RPD3	Ilocos Norte
Cabanatuan	CAB	RPA9	Nueva Ecija	Lapu-Lapu	LAP	RPD4	Cebu
Cadiz	CAD	RPB1	Negros Occidental	Legaspi	LGP	RPD5	Albay
Cagayan de Oro	CGY	RPB2	Misamis Oriental	Lipa	LIP	RPD6	Batangas
Calbayog	CYP	RPB3	Samar	Lucena	LUC	RPD7	Quezon
Caloocan	COO	RPB4	Metropolitan Manila	Mandaue	MDE	RPD8	Cebu
Canlaon	CAN	RPB5	Negros Oriental	Marawi	MAR	RPE1	Lanao del Sur
Cavite	CAV	RPB6	Cavite	Naga	NAG	RPE2	Camarines Sur
Cebu	CEB	RPB7	Cebu	Olongapo	OLO	RPE3	Zambales
Cotabato	CBO	RPB8	Maguindanao	Ormoc	OMC	RPE4	Leyte
Dagupan	DAG	RPB9	Pangasinan	Oroquieta	ORO	RPE5	Misamis Occidental
Danao	DAN	RPC1	Cebu	Ozamis	OCZ	RPE6	Misamis Occidental
Dapitan	DAP	RPC2	Zamboanga del Norte	Pagadian	PAG	RPE7	Zamboanga del Sur
Davao	DVO	RPC3	Davao del Sur	Palayan	PAL	RPE8	Nueva Ecija
Dipolog	DPL	RPC4	Zamboanga del Norte	Pasay	PAS	RPE9	Metropolitan Manila ➤

city	ISO	FIPS	province	city	ISO	FIPS	province
Puerto Princesa	PPS	RPF1	Palawan	Surigao	SUG	RPF9	Surigao del Norte
Quezon City	QUE	RPF2	Metropolitan Manila	Tacloban	TAC	RPG1	Leyte
Roxas	RXS	RPF3	Capiz	Tagaytay	TGT	RPG2	Cavite
San Carlos	SCN	RPF4	Negros Occidental	Tagbilaran	TAG	RPG3	Bohol
San Carlos	SCP	RPF5	Pangasinan	Tangub	TAN	RPG4	Misamis Occidental
San Jose	SJI	RPF6	Nueva Ecija	Toledo	TOL	RPG5	Cebu
San Pablo	SPA	RPF7	Laguna	Trece Martires	TRM	RPG6	Cavite
Silay	SIL	RPF8	Negros Occidental	Zamboanga	ZAM	RPG7	Zamboanga del Sur

Territorial extent: The Philippines claims part of the Spratly Islands, north of about 7.5° N. latitude in the South China Sea. The group as a whole has been given the FIPS 10-4 country code PG.

There is a single point in Mindanao where four provinces (Bukidnon, Davao, Davao del Sur, and North Cotabato) meet.

As a rule, Philippine provinces are either part or all of a large island, along with some number of entire smaller nearby islands. In the following list, the large island is mentioned first. A star (☆) before its name indicates that the province only covers part of this island.

Abra: ☆Luzon

Agusan del Norte: ☆Mindanao

Agusan del Sur: ☆Mindanao

Aklan: ☆Panay, Borocay

Albay: ☆Luzon, Batan, Cagraray, Rapu Rapu, San Miguel

Antique: ☆Panay, Semirara Islands (Semirara, Sibay, Caluya), Batbatan, Maniquin, Seco

Apayao: ☆Luzon

Aurora: ☆Luzon

Basilan: Basilan, Pilas Group, Tapiantana Group

Bataan: ☆Luzon, Corregidor

Batanes: Batan, Itbayat, Sabtang, Y'ami (northernmost point in Philippines)

Batangas: ☆Luzon, Maricaban, Verde

Benguet: ☆Luzon

Biliran: Biliran, Maripipi

Bohol: Bohol, Panglao, Lapinin, Mahanay

Bukidnon: ☆Mindanao

Bulacan: ☆Luzon

Cagayan: ☆Luzon, Babuyan Islands (Camiguin, Calayan, Babuyan, Fuga, Dalupiri), Palaui

Camarines Norte: ☆Luzon, Calagua Islands (Tinaga, Maculabo, Guintinua)

Camarines Sur: ☆Luzon, Quinasalag, Lahuy, Butauanan

Camiguin: Camiguin

Capiz: ☆Panay, Olutayan

Catanduanes: Catanduanes, Panay, Palumbanes, Parongpong, Calbagio

Cavite: ☆Luzon

Cebu: Cebu, Camotes Islands (Pacijan, Poro, Ponson), Bantayan, Mactan, Guintacan, Olango

Davao: ☆Mindanao, Samal, Talicud

Davao del Sur: ☆Mindanao, Sarangani Islands (Balut, Sarangani)

Davao Oriental: ☆Mindanao

Eastern Samar: ☆Samar, Homonhon, Hilaban, Manicani, Calicoan, Suluan

Guimaras: Guimaras, Inampulugan

Ifugao: ☆Luzon

Ilocos Norte: ☆Luzon

Ilocos Sur: ☆Luzon

Iloilo: ☆Panay, Calagnaan, Tagubanhan, Sicogon, Pan de Azucar, Gigante Islands

Isabela: ☆Luzon

Kalinga: ☆Luzon

La Union: ☆Luzon

Laguna: ☆Luzon, Talim Island in Laguna de Bay (lake)

Lanao del Norte: ☆Mindanao

Lanao del Sur: ☆Mindanao

Leyte: ☆Leyte

Maguindanao: ☆Mindanao

Marinduque: Marinduque, Mompog, Tres Reyes Islands

Masbate: Masbate, Burias, Ticao, Naro, Jintotolo, Deagan

Metropolitan Manila: ☆Luzon

Mindoro Occidental: ☆Mindoro, Lubang Islands (Lubang, Ambil, Cabra, Golo), Ilin, Ambulong

Mindoro Oriental: ☆Mindoro

Misamis Occidental: ☆Mindanao

Misamis Oriental: ☆Mindanao

Mountain: ☆Luzon

Negros Occidental: ☆Negros, Molocaboc

Negros Oriental: ☆Negros

North Cotabato: ☆Mindanao

Northern Samar: ☆Samar, Balicuatro Islands, Batag, Laoang, Capul, Dalupiri, Destacado, Cabaun

Nueva Ecija: ☆Luzon

Nueva Vizcaya: ☆Luzon

Palawan: Palawan, Calamian Group (Busuanga, Culion, Coron, Calauit), Dumaran, Balabac, Linapacan, Bugsuk, Pandanan, Maytiguid, Batas, Boayan, Cuyo Islands (Cuyo, Agutaya, Canipo), Cagayan Islands (Cagayan, Calusa), Quiniluban Islands, San Miguel Islands, and the Philippines' claim to the Spratly Islands

Pampanga: ☆Luzon

Pangasinan: ☆Luzon, Cabarruyan, Santiago

Quezon: ☆Luzon, Polillo Islands (Polillo, Patnanongan, Jomalig), Alabat, Cabalete, Pagbilao Grande

Quirino: ☆Luzon

Rizal: ☆Luzon

Romblon: Tablas, Sibuyan, Romblon, Carabao, Banton, Maestre de Campo, Simara

Samar: ☆Samar, Daram, Buad, Santo Niño, Almagro, Tagapula, Camandag, Libucan

Sarangani: ☆Mindanao

Siquijor: Siquijor

Sorsogon: ☆Luzon

South Cotabato: ☆Mindanao

Southern Leyte: ☆Leyte, Panaon, Limasawa

Sultan Kudarat: ☆Mindanao

Sulu: Jolo Group (Jolo, Pata, Capual), Tapul Group (Siasi, Lugus, Tapul, Lapac), Pangutaran Group (Pangutaran,

Kulassein, North Ubian), Samales Group (Tungkil, Balanguingui), Laparan

Surigao del Norte: ☆Mindanao, Dinagat, Siargao, Bucas Grande, Nonoc, East Bucas, Hibuson, Poneas, Hikdop, Zaragosa, Sumilon, Basul, San Jose, Nasapilid

Surigao del Sur: ☆Mindanao, General

Tarlac: ☆Luzon

Tawitawi: Tawi Tawi, Sibutu Group (southernmost point in Philippines), Tandubatu, Sanga Sanga

Zambales: ☆Luzon, Salvador

Zamboanga del Norte: ☆Mindanao

Zamboanga del Sur: ☆Mindanao, Olutanga, Sacol, Great Santa Cruz, Malanipa, Lanhil, Sibago

Origins of names: Most place names in the Philippines are native words that were sometimes misapplied, and always corrupted in transmission from the natives to the Spanish explorers and colonists. There are also some Spanish names bestowed by the colonists, and a few that have been translated into English. Usually the compass points are identified as del Norte (Northern), del Sur (Southern), Occidental (Western), and Oriental (Eastern), but the nomenclature is not consistent.

Agusan: Malay *agasan*: where the water flows, originally a river name

Albay: from former name of its capital, Albaybay, which means "by the bay"

Antique: from *hantic-hantic*, native name of a species of ant

Aurora: named for Doña Maria Aurora Quezon, wife of President Manuel Quezon

Basilan: = iron trail

Bohol: named after Bool, a village on the island

Bukidnon: natives were called *bukidnon*: mountain people

Bulacan: native word *bulaklakan*, freely translated "many flowers," or from Tagalog *bulak*: cotton

Cagayan: Ilocano *carayan*: big river, or *catagayan*: where the tagay trees grow

Camarines: Spanish translation of a native place name *Kamalig*: granaries

Camiguin: from kamagong, a tree in the ebony family

Capiz: from *kapid*: twins, named by Spanish conquistadores when the local chief's wife had twins

Caraga: Calagan, from Bisayan *calag*: soul, people + *an*: land

Catanduanes: from *catanduan*: where the tando trees grow

Cavite: Tagalog *kawit*: hook, after the shape of the city's peninsula

Cotabato: Maguindanao *kota wato*: stone fort

Davao: from *Daba-o Daba-o*: justice to the Bagobos, an epithet of ancient chieftain Datu Duli

Ifugao: from *pugo*: hills

Iloilo: from *ilong-ilong*, which means nose-shaped, referring to promontory between two rivers

Isabela: named for Queen Isabela II of Spain

Kalinga: Ibanag *kalinga*: headhunters

Laguna: province contains part of Laguna de Bay (Spanish *laguna*: lake; Bay is a city name)

La Union: Spanish; province was formed by the union of towns from Ilocos Sur and Pangasinan

Lanao: from *ranao*: lake, because of Lake Lanao

Maguindanao: means "people of the flooded plains" (*danao*: flood)

Manila: contraction of Maynilad, place of the nilad plant

Masbate: supposedly, an explorer asked a local woman what the place was called. She thought he asked what she was doing, and replied, "*Masa bati*": mix and beat more

Mindanao: native name for "that which has been flooded"

Mindoro: Spanish *mina de oro*: gold mine

Misamis: from kuyamis, a variety of coconut found there

Mountain: Spanish *la montañosa*: the mountainous [province]

Negros: Spanish *negros*: blacks, referring to Negrito natives

Nueva Ecija: = New Ecija, named by Governor Cruzar after Ecija, Spain, where he was born

Nueva Vizcaya: = New Biscay, named by Governor Luis Lardizabal after his home province in Spain

Palawan: Chinese *pa-lao-yu*: "land of beautiful harbors"

Pampanga: from *pangpang*: river banks; explorers found natives mostly living by rivers

Panay: Spanish *pan*: bread + *hay*: there is ("there is bread")

Pangasinan: = the place where salt is made

Quezon: named for Manuel Quezon (1878–1944), President of the Philippine Commonwealth

Quirino: named for President Elpidio Quirino (1890–1956)

Rizal: named for independence hero Dr. José P. Rizal (1861–1896)

Siquijor: supposedly, an explorer asked a native for the name of the island. He replied *quipjod*: the tide is ebbing.

Sorsogon: supposedly, an explorer asked a native where they were. He directed them to proceed upstream, saying the Bicol word *solsogon*: "follow the river upstream."

Sultan Kudarat: named after Sultan Mohammed Dipatuan Kudarat, 17th-century ruler of Mindanao and Sulu

Sulu: from *sug*: water current (inhabitants were good navigators)

Surigao: said to be named for an inhabitant named Saliagao

Tawitawi: from Malay *jaui-jaui*: far away, referring to the trip from the Asian mainland

Zambales: from Malay *sambali*: worshippers, *samba*: to wor-

ship; natives worshipped a spirit called Anitos

Zamboanga: Malay *jambanga*: place of flowers

Change history: When the United States defeated Spain in 1898, the Philippine Islands were divided into four gobiernos (governments): Bisayas, Islas Adjacentes (present-day Palawan), Luzon, and Mindanao. These were further subdivided into provinces and districts. The American administration initially inherited the Spanish divisions, placing them under military government. As the rebels were pacified, civil government was established in the provinces, one by one.

1901-06-11	Morong district (capital Tanay) merged with part of Manila province to form Rizal province.
1902	Mindoro province merged with Marinduque; Amburayan province split from La Union; Mindoro province, including Lubang Island, merged with Marinduque province; later, Marinduque province merged with Tayabas.
1903	Moro province formed, consisting of the districts of Cotabato, Davao, Lanao, Sulu, and Zamboanga. Its capital was Zamboanga.
1905	Name of Paragua province changed to Palawan, and capital moved from Cuyo to Puerto Princesa; Masbate province merged with Sorsogon.
1907	Romblon province merged with Capiz; split from it again in 1917.
1907-08-20	Agusan province split from Surigao.
1908	Abra province merged with Ilocos Sur; split from it again on 1917-03-09.
1908-08-13	Mountain province formed by merging Amburayan, Apayao, Benguet, Bontoc, Ifugao, Kalinga, and Lepanto province, which became its sub-provinces.
1909	Batanes province split from Cagayan.
1912	Capital of Nueva Ecija moved from San Isidro to Cabanatuan.
~1914	Capital of Bulacan moved from Bulacan to Malolos.
1916-08-29	Name and status of Moro province changed to Mindanao and Sulu department. Status of its districts (Bukidnon, Cotabato, Davao, Lanao, Misamis, Sulu, and Zamboanga) changed to provinces.
1917-03-10	Ambos Camarines province divided into Camarines Norte and Camarines Sur provinces. (Spanish *ambos*: both. They had also been divided at various times in the 19th century, most recently 1857–1893.)
1920-02-21	Marinduque province split from Tayabas.
1920-12-15	Masbate province split from Sorsogon.
1921-02-20	Mindoro province split from Marinduque.
1925	Name of capital of Albay province changed from Albay to Legaspi (sometimes spelled Legazpi).
1929-11-02	Misamis province divided into Misamis Occidental and Misamis Oriental provinces (implemented 1939-11-28).
1945-09-26	Catanduanes province split from Albay.
1946	Romblon province merged with Capiz; split from it again on 1947-01-01.
1946-09-07	Name of Tayabas province changed to Quezon.
1948	Capital of country moved from Manila to Quezon City.
~1950	Name of capital of Capiz changed from Capiz to Roxas, in honor of President Manuel Roxas.
1950-06-13	Mindoro province (capital Calapan) split into Mindoro Occidental and Mindoro Oriental.
1952-06-06	Zamboanga province (capital Zamboanga) split into Zamboanga del Norte and Zamboanga del Sur.
1954	Capital of Cavite province moved from Cavite to Trece Martires.
1955-06-16	Capital of Camarines Sur province moved provisionally from Naga (formerly Nueva Caceres) to Pili; change made permanent ~1962.
1956	Name of capital of Lanao changed from Dansalan to Marawi.
1956-04-25	Aklan province split from Capiz (implemented 1956-11-08).
1959-05-22	Lanao province (capital Marawi) divided into Lanao del Norte and Lanao del Sur; Southern Leyte province split from Leyte.

1960-06-19	Surigao province (Surigao) divided into Surigao del Norte and Surigao del Sur provinces.
1965-06-19	Samar province (capital Catbalogan) divided into Eastern Samar, Northern Samar, and Western Samar.
1966-06-18	South Cotabato province (capital Koronadal) split from Cotabato (capital Cotabato, moved to Pagalungan after the split); Benguet, Ifugao, and Kalinga-Apayao provinces split from Mountain; Camiguin province split from Misamis Oriental.
1967-05-08	Davao province (capital Davao) divided into Davao del Norte, Davao del Sur, and Davao Oriental provinces (implemented 1967-07-01).
1967-06-17	Agusan province divided into Agusan del Norte and Agusan del Sur provinces (implemented 1970-01-01).
~1968	Capital of Nueva Ecija moved from Cabanatuan to Palayan.
1969-06-21	Name of Western Samar province changed to Samar.
1971-09-10	Quirino province split from Nueva Vizcaya.
1972	Creation of the initial twelve regions begun under Integrated Reorganization Plan.
1972-01-08	Siquijor province split from Negros Oriental, following a referendum.
1972-06-17	Name of Davao del Norte province changed to Davao.
1973-09-11	Tawi-Tawi province split from Sulu.
1973-11-22	Cotabato province divided into Maguindanao, North Cotabato, and Sultan Kudarat provinces.
1973-12-27	Status of Basilan (formerly within Zamboanga del Sur province) changed from chartered city to province.
1975-11-08	Metropolitan Manila area split from Rizal province.
1976	Capital of country returned from Quezon City to Manila.
~1978	Capital of Maguindanao moved from Maganoy to Sultan Kudarat.
1979-08-13	Aurora province split from Quezon, following a referendum.
1982-06-24	Capital of Lanao del Norte moved from Iligan to Tubod.
1983-12-19	Name of North Cotabato province changed to Cotabato.
1986-01-03	Negros del Norte province (capital Cadiz) split from Negros Occidental, following a referendum. This action was found unconstitutional by the Supreme Court. Negros Occidental reverted to its original status on 1986-08-18.
1987-07-15	Cordillera Administrative Region created by taking Abra, Benguet, Ifugao, Kalinga-Apayao, and Mountain provinces and Baguio chartered city from regions 1 and 2, by order of President Corazon Aquino. It was intended to become Cordillera Autonomous Region, but that move required a favorable vote by the inhabitants, which has not yet been obtained.
1989-11-26	Autonomous Region in Muslim Mindanao (ARMM) created by taking Lanao del Sur, Maguindanao, Sulu, and Tawi-Tawi provinces from regions 9 and 12, following a referendum. However, the chartered cities of Cotabato and Marawi, although they lie within Maguindanao and Lanao del Sur, respectively, voted not to become part of ARMM, and so remained in region 12.
1990-10-12	Marawi chartered city transferred from region 12 to region 9.
1992-03-16	Sarangani province split from South Cotabato.
1992-05-11	Biliran province split from Leyte, following a referendum; Guimaras province split from Iloilo, following a referendum.
1995-02-14	Kalinga-Apayao province split into Kalinga and Apayao provinces.
1995-02-23	Caraga region (region 13) created by taking Agusan del Norte, Agusan del Sur, Surigao del Norte, and Surigao del Sur provinces, and Butuan and Surigao chartered cities from regions 10 and 11. Sultan Kudarat province moved from region 12 to region 11.

Other names of subdivisions: The names ending with Occidental and Oriental have variants with the words interchanged, such as Occidental Mindoro for Mindoro Occidental.

Cotabato: North Cotabato (obsolete)   Eastern Samar: Samar Oriental (variant)
Davao: Davao del Norte (obsolete)   Manila: Manilha (Portuguese); Manille (French)

Mountain: Mountain Province (variant)
Nueva Vizcaya: Nueva Viscaya (variant)

Samar: Western Samar (obsolete)
Sulu: Jolo (obsolete)

PITCAIRN

ISO = PN/FIPS = PC   Language = English   Time zone = -8:30   Capital = Adamstown

Pitcairn Island was a British possession at the beginning of the 20th century. In 1902, it annexed Ducie, Henderson, and Oeno Islands.

Other names of country: Île Pitcairn (French); Pitcairn, Henderson, Ducie, and Oeno Islands (formal–English); Pitcairn-Insel (German); Pitcairneilanden (Dutch).

Origin of name: Named for Robert Pitcairn (1747?–1770?), helmsman.

division	abv	population	area-km	area-mi	capital
Pitcairn Islands	PN	66	49	19	Adamstown

Status: This division is the whole of the country, treated as a division for compatibility.
Abv: Two-letter code for international compatibility (defined by the author).
Population: 1991-31-12 estimate.
Area-km: Square kilometers.
Area-mi: Square miles.
Territorial extent: The country includes the South Pacific islands of Pitcairn, Ducie, Henderson, and Oeno.

POLAND

ISO = PL/FIPS = PL   Language = Polish   Time zone = +1 [d]   Capital = Warsaw

In 1900, historical Poland was entirely subjected to other nations. The area that is now Poland was split among the German, Russian, and Austro-Hungarian Empires. At the end of World War I, the Poles proclaimed a republic which was then validated by the Versailles Treaty. As World War II began, Germany and the Soviet Union overran the country from opposite sides to the middle. In the settlements ending the war, Poland was reconstituted. As compared to the interbellum period, it gained territory in the west from Germany, but lost territory in the east to the Soviet Union. It remained independent, but under the hegemony of the Soviet Union, until the Iron Curtain fell in 1989.

Other names of country: Polen (Danish, Dutch, German, Norwegian, Swedish); Polish Republic (formal–English); Pólland (Icelandic); Pologne (French); Polonia (Italian, Spanish); Polônia (Portuguese); Puola (Finnish); Rzeczpospolita Polska (formal).

Origin of name: from ethnic name Polane, from Slavic *pole*: field.

division	abv	capital	old
dolnośląskie	DS	Wrocław	Jelenia Góra, Legnica, Wałbrzych, Wrocław
kujawsko-pomorskie	KP	Bydgoszcz, Toruń	Bydgoszcz, Toruń, Włocławek
łódzkie	LD	Łódź	Łódź, Piotrków, Sieradz, Skierniewice
lubelskie	LU	Lublin	Biała Podlaska, Chełm, Lublin, Zamość
lubuskie	LB	Gorzów, Zielona Góra	Gorzów, Zielona Góra
małopolskie	MP	Kraków	Kraków, Nowy Sącz, Tarnów
mazowieckie	MA	Warszawa	Ciechanów, Ostrołęka, Płock, Radom, Siedlce, Warszawa
opolskie	OP	Opole	Opole ➤

division	abv	capital	old
podkarpackie	PK	Rzeszów	Krosno, Przemyśl, Rzeszów, Tarnobrzeg
podlaskie	PD	Białystok	Białystok, Łomża
pomorskie	PM	Gdańsk	Elbląg, Gdańsk, Słupsk
śląskie	SL	Katowice	Bielsko-Biała, Częstochowa, Katowice
świętokrzyskie	SW	Kielce	Kielce
warmińsko-mazurskie	WM	Olsztyn	Olsztyn, Suwałki
wielkopolskie	WP	Poznań	Kalisz, Konin, Leszno, Piła, Poznań
zachodniopomorskie	ZP	Szczecin	Koszalin, Szczecin

Status: These divisions are województwa (sing. województwo: voivodships or provinces). Poland was reorganized as this book was being prepared, and few details are available yet.

Abv: Abbreviations found on a Web page <http://hum.amu.edu.pl/~zbzw/ph/pro/plpro.html>

Old: Former provinces included in the new province. In most cases, provincial boundaries have changed. I listed each old province under the new province that contains its capital and the greater part of its territory, as far as I could determine.

Further subdivisions: The voivodships are divided into 308 powiaty (sing. powiat: districts, counties) and 65 cities of county right. These are subdivided into miasta (towns), which are further subdivided into gminy (sing. gmina: communes, wards). The powiaty were abolished in 1975, but reinstated in 1998.

Territorial extent: Zachodniopomorskie contains the Polish part of Uznam Island (German name, Usedom).

Origins of names of former provinces:

Bialystok: Polish *biały*: white, *stok*: river
Bydgoszcz: Indo-European *bredahe*: swampy water
Elblag: from Old Norwegian *elf*: river
Gdansk: from Gothic *Gutisk-andja*: end of the Goths
Gdynia: from Gothic *Gutisk-andja*: end of the Goths

Jelenia Gora: Polish *jelen*: stag, *gora*: mountain (cf. German name, from *Hirsch*: stag, *Berg*: mountain)
Krakow: man's name Krak, legendary founder of city
Zielona Góra: Polish *zielona*: green, *gora*: mountain (cf. German name, from *grün*: green, *Berg*: mountain)

Change history:

1900 — The Russian Empire included the Kingdom of Poland, which was divided into Kalish, Kel'tsy, Lomzha, Lyublin, Petrokov, Plotsk, Radom, Sedlets, Suvalki, and Varshava guberniy. (Present-day Poland also contains part of the Russian guberniya of Grodno.) The Austro-Hungarian Empire consisted of Austria (Cisleithania) and Hungary (Transleithania); Austria, in turn, was divided into provinces, parts of two of which (Galicia and Silesia) are now in Poland. The German-owned section of modern Poland lay within two states of the German Empire: the Kingdom of Prussia (Brandenburg, East Prussia, Pomerania, Posen, Silesia, and West Prussia provinces) and the Kingdom of Saxony (Bautzen province).

1919-06-28 — Treaty of Versailles signed. Poland's independence, which it had proclaimed on 1918-11-09, was recognized. Poland comprised most of Posen and West Prussia provinces from Germany, the Kingdom of Poland from Russia, and Galicia from Austria. Galicia was in fact divided into East and West Galicia. West Galicia became fully part of Poland; East Galicia was mandated to Poland but a plebiscite was planned for it. Germany retained East Prussia and a small section of West Prussia, an enclave separated from the rest of Germany by the "Polish Corridor." A 1893-sq. km. section on the West Prussian Baltic shore around Danzig (Gdańsk) became the Free City of Danzig (Freie Stadt Danzig). The provisional border between Poland and Russia was the Curzon Line, soon wiped from the map in the Russo-Polish War (1919–20), which also gave Poland full sovereignty in East Galicia.

1920-10-07 — Poland occupied the southeastern part of Vilna, including the city of Vilnius.

1921-03-18 — Poland and Russia signed the Riga Treaty, dividing Byelorussia between them. Poland gained Grodno, most of Vilna, the western part of Volhynia, and a western fringe of Minsk. Brest-Litovsk was renamed to Brześč nad Bugiem.

1921-05-21 — Plebiscite held in most of Upper Silesia (part of Silesia province, Prussia). A few eastern cantons voted for union with Poland, which took place in 1922. The divisions of Poland at this time were the former Prussian Bezirke (districts) of Bydgoszcz (Bromberg), Gdansk (Danzig), Kwidzyn (Marienwerder), and Poznan (Posen); the guberniy of Russian Poland, Kalisz (Kalish), Kielce (Kel'tsy), Łomża (Lomzha), Lublin

(Lyublin), Piotrkow (Petrokov), Płock (Plotsk), Radom, Siedlce (Sedlets), Suwalki (Suvalki), and Warszawa (Varshava); the conquered sections of the West Russian guberniy of Grodno, Minsk, Vilna, and Wołyń (Volhynia); and Kraków (West Galicia) and Lwów (East Galicia). Names in parentheses are the prewar names of these divisions.

1939-09-01 Germany invaded Poland, igniting World War II. The Soviet Union invaded Poland on 1939-09-17. By 1939-09-21, Poland had been divided between Germany and the Soviet Union. Germany also annexed the Free City of Danzig, which it renamed Hanseatic City of Danzig (Hansestadt Danzig) in 1940.

1939-10-10 Over half of the Polish territory in Vilna guberniya restored to Lithuania.

1945-07-16 Potsdam Conference began. It transferred large parts of the German provinces of Pomerania, Brandenburg, Silesia, East and West Prussia to Poland, except that the northern part of East Prussia became Kaliningrad Oblast of Russia. The new western border of Poland was called the Oder-Neisse Line, as it generally followed the course of the Oder and Neisse Rivers. A small area east of Ostrava was transferred from Poland to Czechoslovakia, splitting in two the city known as Cieszyn in Polish, Těšín in Czech, and Teschen in German. The Soviet Union recovered territory lost in the Russo-Polish War up to approximately the Curzon Line, annexing it to the republics of Byelorussia, Lithuania, and Ukraine. By 1946, Poland was organized into fourteen voivodships and two independent cities on the same administrative level as a voivodship. Boundaries were redrawn, so the correspondence is only fair, but Mazury is roughly East Prussia; Śląsk Dabrowski and Śląsk Dolny roughly match Silesia; Pomorze Zachodnie roughly matches Pomerania; and the Free City of Danzig merged with the new Gdańsk voivodship.

voivodship	population	area-km	capital
Białystok	917,600	22,551	Białystok
Gdańsk	732,100	10,725	Sopot
Kielce	1,717,300	18,052	Kielce
Kraków	2,133,400	15,918	Kraków
Łódź	1,772,400	20,233	Łódź
Łódź [City]	496,900	212	Łódź
Lublin	1,889,700	27,741	Lublin
Mazury	351,800	19,319	Olsztyn
Pomorze	1,406,500	20,028	Bydgoszcz
Pomorze Zachodnie	892,600	30,251	Szczecin
Poznań	2,422,100	39,243	Poznań
Rzeszów	1,535,400	18,200	Rzeszów
Śląsk Dabrowski	2,823,400	15,369	Katowice
Śląsk Dolny	1,941,100	24,740	Wrocław
Warszawa	2,114,400	29,000	Pruszków
Warszawa [City]	478,800	140	Warszawa
	23,929,800	311,722	

Population: 1946 census.

~1949 Name of Mazury changed to Olsztyn; name of Pomorze changed to Bydgoszcz; name of Pomorze Zachodnie changed to Szczecin; name of Śląsk Dabrowski changed to Śląsk; name of Śląsk Dolny changed to Wrocław.

~1955 Koszalin voivodship formed from parts of Bydgoszcz, Gdańsk, and Szczecin; Śląsk voivodship split into Katowice and Opole (with small annexations from Kielce and Wrocław); Zielona Góra voivodship formed from parts of Poznań and Wrocław; Kraków, Poznań, and Wrocław independent cities split from the voivodships of the same names; other border adjustments made; capital of Warszawa voivodship moved from Pruszków to Warszawa (Warsaw). After these changes, the list of voivodships was:

division	population	area-km	after 1975
Białystok	1,177,000	23,167	Białystok, Łomża, Suwałki ➤

division	population	area-km	is now
Bydgoszcz	1,871,000	20,973	Bydgoszcz, Piła, Toruń, Włocławek
Gdańsk	1,393,000	10,924	Elbląg, Gdańsk, Słupsk
Katowice	3,585,000	9,389	Bielsko-Biała, Częstochowa, Katowice
Kielce	1,910,000	19,258	Częstochowa, Kielce, Piotrków, Radom, Tarnobrzeg
Koszalin	774,000	17,774	Koszalin, Piła, Słupsk
Kraków	2,159,000	15,408	Bielsko-Biała, Katowice, Kielce, Kraków, Nowy Sącz, Tarnów
Kraków City	540,200	230	Kraków
Łódź	1,675,000	16,710	Łódź, Piotrków, Płock, Sieradz, Skierniewice
Łódź City	750,400	212	Łódź
Lublin	1,920,000	25,047	Biała Podlaska, Chełm, Lublin, Siedlce, Tarnobrzeg, Zamość
Olsztyn	973,000	21,020	Elbląg, Olsztyn, Suwałki, Toruń
Opole	1,027,000	9,532	Katowice, Opole
Poznań	2,159,000	27,224	Kalisz, Konin, Leszno, Piła, Poznań
Poznań City	446,700	219	Poznań
Rzeszów	1,720,000	18,639	Krosno, Przemyśl, Rzeszów, Tarnobrzeg, Tarnów
Szczecin	872,000	12,744	Gorzów, Szczecin
Warszawa	2,483,000	29,080	Ciechanów, Ostrołęka, Płock, Radom, Siedlce, Skierniewice, Warszawa
Warszawa City	1,282,600	427	Warszawa
Wrocław	1,994,000	18,808	Jelenia Góra, Legnica, Leszno, Wrocław, Wałbrzych
Wrocław City	487,000	225	Wrocław
Zielona Góra	866,000	14,720	Gorzów, Legnica, Leszno, Zielona Góra
	32,064,900	311,730	

Status: Divisions are voivodships except for those whose name says "City," which are independent cities.

Population: 1972 estimate.

Capital: Name of capital is the same as that of voivodship.

After 1975: List of post–1975 voivodships having significant territory in common with this division.

1975-06-01   Administrative reform changed the seventeen voivodships into the forty-nine listed below, and elminated the districts. There were also three cities with voivodship status (Kraków, Łódź, and Warszawa), which for most purposes were included with the voivodships of the same names.

division	ISO	FIPS	population	area-km	area-mi	adjectival	German
Biała Podlaska	BP	PL23	304,500	5,348	2,065	Bialskopodlaskie	
Białystok	BK	PL24	690,300	10,055	3,882	Białostockie	
Bielsko-Biała	BB	PL25	895,300	3,704	1,430	Bielskie	Bielitz
Bydgoszcz	BY	PL26	1,106,600	10,349	3,996	Bydgoskie	Bromberg
Chełm	CH	PL27	246,200	3,866	1,493	Chełmskie	Cholm
Ciechanów	CI	PL28	427,000	6,362	2,456	Ciechanowskie	
Częstochowa	CZ	PL29	776,100	6,182	2,387	Częstochowskie	Tschenstochau
Elbląg	EL	PL30	476,600	6,103	2,356	Elbląskie	Elbing
Gdańsk	GD	PL31	1,423,300	7,394	2,855	Gdańskie	Danzig
Gorzów	GO	PL32	498,300	8,484	3,276	Gorzowskie	Landsberg
Jelenia Góra	JG	PL33	517,000	4,378	1,690	Jeleniogórskie	Hirschberg
Kalisz	KL	PL34	708,300	6,512	2,514	Kaliskie	Kalisch
Katowice	KA	PL35	3,968,300	6,650	2,568	Katowickie	Kattowitz
Kielce	KI	PL36	1,126,000	9,211	3,556	Kieleckie	
Konin	KN	PL37	467,600	5,139	1,984	Konińskie	
Koszalin	KO	PL38	504,200	8,470	3,270	Koszalińskie	Köslin
Kraków	KR	PL39	1,227,800	3,254	1,256	Krakowskie	Krakau
Krosno	KS	PL40	491,800	5,702	2,202	Krośnieńskie	
Legnica	LG	PL41	512,000	4,037	1,559	Legnickie	Liegnitz
Leszno	LE	PL42	384,500	4,154	1,604	Leszczyńskie	Lissa
Łódź	LD	PL43	1,142,700	1,523	588	Łódzkie	
Łomża	LO	PL44	345,600	6,684	2,581	Łomżyńskie	
Lublin	LU	PL45	1,013,400	6,792	2,622	Lubelskie	
Nowy Sącz	NS	PL46	692,200	5,576	2,153	Nowosądeckie	Neusandez
Olsztyn	OL	PL47	748,500	12,327	4,759	Olsztyńskie	Allenstein
Opole	OP	PL48	1,014,900	8,535	3,295	Opolskie	Oppeln
Ostrołęka	OS	PL49	395,000	6,498	2,509	Ostrołęckie	
Piła	PI	PL50	478,000	8,205	3,168	Pilskie	Schneidemühl ➤

division	ISO	FIPS	population	area-km	area-mi	adjectival	German
Piotrków	PT	PL51	642,000	6,266	2,419	Piotrkowskie	Petrikau
Płock	PL	PL52	515,400	5,117	1,976	Płockie	
Poznań	PO	PL53	1,327,900	8,151	3,147	Poznańskie	Posen
Przemyśl	PR	PL54	405,100	4,437	1,713	Przemyskie	
Radom	RA	PL55	748,300	7,294	2,816	Radomskie	
Rzeszów	RZ	PL56	717,400	4,397	1,698	Rzeszowskie	
Siedlce	SE	PL57	649,300	8,499	3,281	Siedleckie	
Sieradz	SI	PL58	408,000	4,869	1,880	Sieradzkie	
Skierniewice	SK	PL59	418,200	3,960	1,529	Skierniewickie	
Słupsk	SL	PL60	410,400	7,453	2,878	Słupskie	Stolp
Suwałki	SU	PL61	466,300	10,490	4,050	Suwalskie	
Szczecin	SZ	PL62	967,300	9,981	3,854	Szczecińskie	Stettin
Tarnobrzeg	TG	PL63	596,400	6,283	2,426	Tarnobrzeskie	
Tarnów	TA	PL64	666,000	4,151	1,603	Tarnowskie	
Toruń	TO	PL65	655,700	5,348	2,065	Toruńskie	Thorn
Wałbrzych	WB	PL66	741,200	4,168	1,609	Wałbrzyskie	Waldenburg
Warszawa	WA	PL67	2,419,100	3,788	1,463	Warszawskie	Warschau
Włocławek	WL	PL68	428,900	4,402	1,700	Włocławskie	
Wrocław	WR	PL69	1,126,300	6,287	2,427	Wrocławskie	Breslau
Zamość	ZA	PL70	489,800	6,980	2,695	Zamojskie	
Zielona Góra	ZG	PL71	657,400	8,868	3,424	Zielonogórskie	Grünberg
			38,038,400	312,683	120,727		

ISO: Codes from ISO 3166-2.

FIPS: Codes from FIPS PUB 10-4.

Population: 1989 census.

Area-km: Square kilometers.

Area-mi: Square miles.

Adjectival: In Polish text, the voivodship name will often appear in this adjectival form.

German: German name of capital; used officially for province during periods of German occupation.

Capitals: Voivodships had the same names as their capitals, except for Gorzów (capital, Gorzów Wielkopolski) and Piotrków (Piotrków Trybunalski).

1998-07-27   President Kwaśniewski signed a bill reorganizing Poland from 49 voivodships to sixteen. Subsequently, on 1998-08-07, the subdivision of the country into 308 countries (powiaty), plus 65 cities with county rights, was decided.

Other names of subdivisions:

Gdańsk: Dantzig (French); Danzica (Italian); Danzig (obsolete)

Krakow: Cracovia (Italian, Spanish); Cracóvia (Portuguese); Cracovie (French); Cracow (variant)

Lublin: Lublino (Italian); Lyublin (Russian)

Szczecin: Stettino (Italian)

Warszawa: Stołeczne Warszawskie (formal); Varsavia (Italian); Varshava (Russian); Varsovia (Spanish); Varsóvia (Portuguese); Varsovie (French); Warsaw (variant)

Wroclaw: Breslavia (Italian)

PORTUGAL

ISO = PT/FIPS = PO   Language = Portuguese   Time zone = (see table)   Capital = Lisbon

Portugal has been an independent country throughout the 20th century.

Other names of country: Portogallo (Italian); Portúgal (Icelandic); Portugali (Finnish); Portuguese Republic (formal–English); República Portuguesa (formal).

Origin of name: possibly from Latin *portus*: port + Arabic *cala*: castle.

division	abv	ISO	FIPS	tz	population	area-km	area-mi	region
Aveiro	AV	01	PO02	+1 [d]	657,600	2,708	1,046	Centro (Norte)
Azores	AC	20	PO23	-1 [d]	236,500	2,335	902	Açores
Beja	BE	02	PO03	+1 [d]	166,300	10,240	3,954	Alentejo
Braga	BR	03	PO04	+1 [d]	748,300	2,730	1,054	Norte
Bragança	BA	04	PO05	+1 [d]	156,500	6,545	2,527	Norte
Castelo Branco	CB	05	PO06	+1 [d]	213,300	6,704	2,588	Centro
Coimbra	CO	06	PO07	+1 [d]	426,400	3,956	1,527	Centro
Évora	EV	07	PO08	+1 [d]	172,900	7,393	2,854	Alentejo
Faro	FA	08	PO09	+1 [d]	340,600	5,072	1,958	Algarve
Guarda	GU	09	PO11	+1 [d]	186,400	5,496	2,122	Centro (Norte)
Leiria	LE	10	PO13	+1 [d]	427,700	3,516	1,358	Centro (Lisboa e Vale do Tejo)
Lisboa	LI	11	PO14	+1 [d]	2,062,300	2,762	1,066	Lisboa e Vale do Tejo
Madeira	MA	30	PO10	0 [d]	253,000	796	307	Madeira
Portalegre	PA	12	PO16	+1 [d]	133,400	5,882	2,271	Alentejo (Lisboa e Vale do Tejo)
Porto	PO	13	PO17	+1 [d]	1,626,200	2,282	881	Norte
Santarém	SA	14	PO18	+1 [d]	441,100	6,689	2,583	Lisboa e Vale do Tejo (Centro)
Setúbal	SE	15	PO19	+1 [d]	715,300	5,152	1,989	Lisboa e Vale do Tejo
Viana do Castelo	VC	16	PO20	+1 [d]	247,800	2,108	814	Norte
Vila Real	VR	17	PO21	+1 [d]	235,300	4,239	1,637	Norte
Viseu	VI	18	PO22	+1 [d]	399,100	5,019	1,938	Centro (Norte)
					9,846,000	91,624	35,376	

[d] = *areas where daylight saving time is in effect during summer.*

Status: These divisions are distritos (districts), except for Azores and Madeira, which are regiões autônomas (autonomous regions).

Abv: Two-letter code for international compatibility (defined by the author).

ISO: Codes from ISO 3166-2.

FIPS: Codes from FIPS PUB 10-4.

Tz: Time zones. Convert from UTC to local time by adding this number of hours.

Population: 1992 estimate.

Area-km: Square kilometers.

Area-mi: Square miles.

Capitals: Capitals have the same names as their districts. Capital of Azores is Ponta Delgada; of Madeira, Funchal.

Region: Planning region containing the district. When a district is partly in two regions, the lesser portion is shown in parentheses. Here are more details on the regions:

region	NUTS	population	region	NUTS	population
Açores	PT2	243,640	Lisboa e Vale do Tejo	PT13	3,319,590
Alentejo	PT14	514,790	Madeira	PT3	259,090
Algarve	PT15	347,280	Norte	PT11	3,561,130
Centro	PT12	1,709,890			9,955,410

NUTS: Codes from Nomenclature for Statistical Territorial Units (European standard). Note: the code PT1 is designated "Continente," and represents the five regions PT11-PT15 together.

Population: 1997-12-31 provisional estimate.

Further subdivisions: The districts of Portugal have been recognized since 1835, with only minor changes, although at certain periods they were nearly powerless. The districts are divided into concelhos (municipalities), sometimes called municípios. They, in turn, are subdivided into freguesias (parishes). Various schemes for províncias (provinces), on a level above the districts, have been proposed over the years; one such subdivision was implemented from 1933 to 1959. The Constitution of 1976-04-25 calls for the creation of regiões administrativas (administrative regions). The country is still debating how this is to be done. The regions listed above, except for Azores and Madeira, are planning regions, and are not considered to meet the constitutional requirement. The islands constitute two autonomous regions. For various specialized purposes, there are also NUTS III divisions, sub-regions, and "groupings of concelhos." The units of each of these types are subordinate to regions, above concelhos, and overlap with districts.

Territorial extent: Azores has nine inhabited islands and their neighboring islets. Before 1976, it was divided into three districts (shown with their islands): Angra do Heroísmo (Terceira, São Jorge, Graciosa); Horta (Pico, Faial, Flores, Corvo); and Ponta Delgada (São Miguel, Santa Maria). The capitals had the same names as the districts.

Faro includes some barrier islands (Tavira, Armona, Culatra, Barreta). It is coextensive with the planning region and former province of Algarve.

Lisboa includes some islands in the Tagus estuary. Note: the Portuguese call this river Tejo, the Spaniards, Tajo. To avoid favoritism, English speakers use its Latin name, Tagus.

Madeira consists of the islands of Madeira, Porto Santo, the Ilhas Selvagens, and a number of smaller islets. It is coextensive with the old district of Funchal, and with the old province of Madeira.

Origins of names:

Alentejo: Portuguese: *alem Tejo*: beyond the Tagus River (from viewpoint of Lisbon)

Algarve: Arabic *al-gharb*: the west

Azores: Portuguese *açor*: goshawk

Beira: = riverbank

Braga: from Latin Augusta Bracarum

Bragança: Celtic *briga*: height

Castelo Branco: = white castle

Coimbra: ancient Conimbriga from Celtic *cun*: high place, *briga*: fort

Estremadura: Latin *Extrema Durii*: end of the Douro (River)

Lisboa: Latin Olisippo, possibly from Phoenician *hippo*: fort

Madeira: = wood (island was forested when discovered)

Ribatejo: = bank of the Tagus

Setúbal: corruption of Sant' Ubel = Saint Ives

Trás-os-Montes: = behind the mountains

Vale do Tejo: = Tagus valley

Vila Real: = royal villa

Change history:

1900   Portugal consisted of continental Portugal (on the Iberian peninsula), Azores, and Madeira. Its colonies are treated separately. Portugal was administratively divided into distritos, which were subdivided into concelhos, which were further subdivided into paróquias (parishes). The term paróquia was changed to freguesia in 1916. Maps from this period often show six provinces: Alentejo, Algarve, Beira, Entre Minho e Douro, Estremadura, and Tras os Montes. These were not official units of government, but represented one of several proposals over the years; the division even passed the Senate, but not Parliament, in 1914.

1926-12-22   Setúbal district split from Lisboa.

1933-02-22   Continental Portugal divided into eleven provinces. The districts and lower-level divisions remained unchanged.

province	population	area-km	capital	districts
Algarve	325,971	5,072	Faro	Faro
Alto Alentejo	394,789	12,516	Évora	Évora, Portalegre
Azores	266,990	797	Ponta Delgada	Angra do Heroísmo, Horta, Ponta Delgada
Baixo Alentejo	375,147	13,785	Beja	Beja, Setúbal
Beira Alta	691,713	9,536	Viseu	Guarda, Viseu
Beira Baixa	355,806	7,504	Castelo Branco	Castelo Branco
Beira Litoral	969,166	7,596	Coimbra	Aveiro, Coimbra, Leiria
Douro Litoral	1,237,170	3,285	Porto	Aveiro, Porto
Estremadura	1,595,067	5,333	Lisbon	Leiria, Lisboa, Setúbal
Madeira	317,409	2,305	Funchal	Funchal
Minho	815,909	4,839	Braga	Braga, Viana do Castelo
Ribatejo	459,853	7,237	Santarém	Santarém
Trás-os-Montes e Alto Douro	636,322	11,848	Vila Real	Bragança, Vila Real
	8,441,312	91,653		

Population: 1950 census.

Districts: Lists the districts which had a significant fraction of their area in each region. In many places the district and province boundaries did not match.

1959-09-21   Provinces abolished.

1976-04-02   New Constitution adopted. It called for the replacement of the administrative hierarchy by administrative regions, municipalities, and parishes. The autonomous regions of Azores (Angra do Heroísmo, Horta, and Ponta Delgada districts) and Madeira (Funchal district) were formed. However, it proved difficult to settle on a regional division for continental Portugal, and a law of 1977-10-25 allowed the districts to continue to function.

~1988　　　Continental Portugal divided into five planning regions, each one with its regional coordination commission (Comissão de Coordenação Regional). These may or may not become the regions required by the constitution.

Other names of subdivisions:

Alentejo: Alemtejo (obsolete)
Azores: Açores (Portuguese); Azoren (Dutch, German); Azorene (Norwegian); Azzorre (Italian)
Bragança: Braganza (obsolete)
Castelo Branco: Castello Branco (obsolete)
Lisboa: Lisbon (variant); Lisbona (Italian); Lisbonne (French); Lissabon (German, Swedish)

Madeira: Funchal (obsolete); Madère (French)
Porto: Oporto, Pôrto (variant)
Viana do Castelo: Vianna do Castello (obsolete)
Vila Real: Villa Real (obsolete)
Viseu: Vizeu (obsolete)

Population history:

district	1911	1940	1950	1960	1970	1981	1992
Angra do Heroísmo	——	78,109	86,577	96,174	86,458	——	——
Aveiro	336,243	429,870	477,191	524,592	548,039	622,988	657,600
Beja	192,499	275,441	286,803	276,895	204,816	188,420	166,300
Braga	382,461	482,914	541,377	596,768	612,710	708,924	748,300
Bragança	192,133	213,233	227,125	233,441	179,763	184,252	156,500
Castelo Branco	241,509	299,670	320,279	316,536	255,575	234,230	213,300
Coimbra	360,056	411,677	432,044	433,656	401,160	436,324	426,400
Évora	144,307	207,952	219,638	219,916	178,538	180,277	172,900
Faro	274,122	317,628	325,971	314,841	268,440	323,534	340,600
Guarda	271,816	294,166	304,368	282,606	213,538	205,631	186,400
Horta	——	52,731	54,823	49,382	41,422	——	——
Leiria	262,558	353,675	389,182	404,500	379,429	420,229	427,700
Lisboa	853,415	1,070,103	1,226,815	1,382,959	1,577,390	2,069,467	2,062,300
Madeira	169,777	250,124	266,990	268,937	251,059	252,844	253,000
Ponta Delgada	242,613	156,045	176,009	181,924	161,216	243,410	236,500
Portalegre	141,778	186,373	196,993	188,482	145,929	142,905	133,400
Porto	679,978	938,288	1,052,663	1,193,368	1,312,392	1,562,287	1,626,200
Santarém	322,753	421,996	453,192	461,707	430,885	454,123	441,100
Setúbal	——	268,884	324,186	377,186	467,946	658,326	715,300
Viana do Castelo	227,420	258,596	274,532	277,748	251,219	256,814	247,800
Vila Real	245,687	289,114	317,372	325,358	267,079	264,381	235,300
Viseu	416,860	465,563	487,182	482,416	413,366	423,648	399,100
	5,957,985	7,722,152	8,441,312	8,889,392	8,648,369	9,833,014	9,846,000

1911 and 1992 are estimates; others are censuses. Azores population listed under Ponta Delgada for 1911, 1981, and 1992. For 1911, Setúbal population is combined with Lisboa.

PUERTO RICO

ISO = PR/FIPS = RQ　　Language = Spanish, English　　Time zone = -4　　Capital = San Juan

The United States acquired Puerto Rico from Spain in the Spanish-American War (1898), calling it Porto Rico. Its name was changed back to Puerto Rico on 1932-05-17. It became a commonwealth in free association with the United States on 1952-07-25.

Other names of country: Commonwealth of Puerto Rico (formal–English); Porto Rico (French, Portuguese, obsolete); Portorico (Italian).

Origin of name: Spanish *puerto*: port, *rico*: rich.

division	abv	F-6	population	area-km	area-mi	division	abv	F-6	population	area-km	area-mi
Adjuntas	AJ	001	19,451	173	67	Lajas	LJ	079	23,271	157	61
Aguada	AD	003	35,911	78	30	Lares	LR	081	29,015	161	62
Aguadilla	AL	005	59,335	94	36	Las Marías	LM	083	9,306	119	46
Aguas Buenas	AB	007	25,424	78	30	Las Piedras	LP	085	27,896	86	33
Aibonito	AI	009	24,971	80	31	Loíza	LZ	087	29,307	62	24
Añasco	AN	011	25,234	104	40	Luquillo	LQ	089	18,100	67	26
Arecibo	AC	013	93,385	329	127	Manatí	MT	091	38,692	118	46
Arroyo	AR	015	18,910	39	15	Maricao	MR	093	6,206	96	37
Barceloneta	BC	017	20,947	62	24	Maunabo	MB	095	12,347	54	21
Barranquitas	BQ	019	25,605	88	34	Mayagüez	MG	097	100,371	198	76
Bayamón	BY	021	220,262	115	44	Moca	MC	099	32,926	130	50
Cabo Rojo	CR	023	38,521	185	71	Morovis	MV	101	25,288	101	39
Caguas	CG	025	133,447	152	59	Naguabo	NG	103	22,620	136	53
Camuy	CA	027	28,917	121	47	Naranjito	NR	105	27,914	73	28
Canovanas	CV	029	36,816	76	29	Orocovis	OR	107	21,158	164	63
Carolina	CN	031	177,806	120	46	Patillas	PT	109	19,633	123	47
Cataño	CT	033	34,587	14	5	Peñuelas	PN	111	22,515	116	45
Cayey	CY	035	46,553	131	51	Ponce	PO	113	187,749	301	116
Ceiba	CB	037	17,145	70	27	Quebradillas	QB	115	21,425	60	23
Ciales	CL	039	18,084	172	66	Rincón	RC	117	12,213	36	14
Cidra	CD	041	35,601	93	36	Río Grande	RG	119	45,648	159	61
Coamo	CO	043	33,837	202	78	Sabana Grande	SB	121	22,843	93	36
Comerío	CM	045	20,265	73	28	Salinas	SA	123	28,335	180	69
Corozal	CZ	047	33,095	110	42	San Germán	SG	125	34,962	140	54
Culebra	CU	049	1,542	28	11	San Juan	SJ	127	437,745	122	47
Dorado	DO	051	30,759	60	23	San Lorenzo	SL	129	35,163	139	54
Fajardo	FJ	053	36,882	80	31	San Sebastián	SS	131	38,799	184	71
Florida	FL	054	8,689	26	10	Santa Isabel	SI	133	19,318	89	34
Guánica	GC	055	19,984	93	36	Toa Alta	TA	135	44,101	71	27
Guayama	GM	057	41,588	170	66	Toa Baja	TB	137	89,454	62	24
Guayanilla	GL	059	21,581	109	42	Trujillo Alto	TJ	139	61,120	54	21
Guaynabo	GB	061	92,886	70	27	Utuado	UT	141	34,980	298	115
Gurabo	GR	063	28,737	73	28	Vega Alta	VA	143	34,559	73	28
Hatillo	HA	065	32,703	109	42	Vega Baja	VB	145	55,997	121	47
Hormigueros	HO	067	15,212	28	11	Vieques	VQ	147	8,602	135	52
Humacao	HU	069	55,203	117	45	Villalba	VL	149	23,559	96	37
Isabela	IS	071	39,147	145	56	Yabucoa	YB	151	36,483	142	55
Jayuya	JY	073	15,527	104	40	Yauco	YU	153	42,058	178	69
Juana Díaz	JD	075	45,198	158	61				3,522,037	8,891	3,429
Juncos	JC	077	30,612	68	26						

Status: These divisions are municipios (municipalities).

Abv: Two-letter code for international compatibility (defined by the author).

F-6: Codes from FIPS PUB 6-4, representing second-level administrative divisions of the United States. The codes for Puerto Rico in FIPS PUB 5-2 are PR (alpha) and 72 (numeric). When the FIPS 5-2 and 6-4 codes are concatenated, as in 72033 for Cataño, the result is a code that uniquely identifies a county-equivalent unit in the United States.

Population: 1990 census.

Area-km: Square kilometers.

Area-mi: Square miles.

Capital: All municipalities have the same name as their capitals.

Further subdivisions: Puerto Rico is also divided into eight senatorial districts, which are often shown on medium-scale maps of Puerto Rico, the number of municipalities being too great for convenient depiction. The senatorial districts change whenever the island gets redistricted, but their number and names have been fairly stable. Their names are Aguadilla, Arecibo, Bayamón, Guayama, Humacao, Mayagüez, Ponce, and San Juan; all but San Juan date back to Spanish colonial days. The capitals have the same names as the districts. The municipalities are subdivided into barrios.

Territorial extent: Puerto Rico consists of the islands of Puerto Rico, Vieques, Culebra, Mona, and many small neighboring islets. All of the municipalities except Culebra and Vieques (which occupy those respective islands) are mainly located on Puerto Rico island. Mona Island belongs to Mayagüez district; Culebra and Vieques, to Humacao district.

Change history:

- ~1915   Ceiba municipality split from Fajardo; Guánica split from Yauco; Guaynabo formed from parts of Bayamón and Río Piedras; Hormigueros split from Mayagüez; Jayuya split from Utuado; Las Piedras split from Humacao; Luquillo formed from parts of Fajardo and Río Grande; Villalba split from Juana Díaz.
- ~1925   Cataño municipality split from Bayamón; name of Barros changed to Orocovis.
- ~1956   San Juan senatorial district split from Bayamón. Río Piedras municipality merged with San Juan.
- ~1975   Canovanas municipality split from Loíza; Florida split from Barceloneta.

Population history:

division	1910	1920	1930	1940	1950	1970	1980	1990
Adjuntas	16,954	17,988	18,075	22,556	22,415	18,691	18,786	19,451
Aguada	11,587	12,981	14,670	17,923	20,727	25,658	31,567	35,911
Aguadilla	21,419	24,287	28,319	34,956	43,748	51,355	54,606	59,335
Aguas Buenas	8,292	10,741	12,885	14,671	15,546	18,600	22,429	25,424
Aibonito	10,815	13,264	16,361	16,819	18,206	20,044	22,167	24,971
Añasco	14,407	13,834	14,276	15,701	17,173	19,416	23,274	25,234
Arecibo	42,429	46,578	56,525	69,192	75,058	73,468	86,766	93,385
Arroyo	6,940	7,074	8,199	10,746	12,899	13,033	17,014	18,910
Barceloneta	11,644	13,442	15,751	18,545	19,899	20,792	18,942	20,947
Barranquitas	10,503	11,600	14,901	17,096	17,590	20,118	21,639	25,605
Bayamón	29,986	30,739	29,524	37,190	48,179	156,192	196,206	220,262
Cabo Rojo	19,562	22,412	23,792	28,586	29,488	26,060	34,045	38,521
Caguas	27,160	35,920	47,728	53,356	60,132	95,661	117,959	133,447
Camuy	11,342	14,228	16,149	18,922	20,865	19,922	24,884	28,917
Canovanas	——	——	——	——	——	——	31,880	36,816
Carolina	15,327	15,563	18,751	24,046	29,143	107,643	165,954	177,806
Cataño	——	——	8,504	9,719	19,856	26,459	26,243	34,587
Cayey	17,711	23,618	28,797	31,391	36,634	38,432	41,099	46,553
Ceiba	——	5,973	7,275	7,021	9,192	10,312	14,944	17,145
Ciales	18,398	20,730	20,492	22,906	19,423	15,595	16,211	18,084
Cidra	10,595	14,789	19,662	20,392	20,518	23,892	28,365	35,601
Coamo	17,129	17,749	18,125	22,772	26,463	26,468	30,822	33,837
Comerío	11,170	14,708	16,715	18,539	17,969	18,819	18,212	20,265
Corozal	12,978	14,369	16,454	20,458	23,080	24,545	28,221	33,095
Culebra	1,315	839	847	860	877	732	1,265	1,542
Dorado	4,885	5,842	7,579	9,481	11,752	17,388	25,511	30,759
Fajardo	21,135	14,302	16,321	20,405	22,036	23,032	32,087	36,882
Florida	——	——	——	——	——	——	7,232	8,689
Guánica	——	9,948	10,238	12,685	15,575	14,889	18,799	19,984
Guayama	17,379	19,192	23,624	30,511	32,713	36,249	40,183	41,588
Guayanilla	10,354	12,083	13,121	15,577	17,373	18,144	21,050	21,581
Guaynabo	——	10,800	13,502	18,319	29,075	67,042	80,742	92,886
Gurabo	11,139	12,882	15,095	15,870	16,274	18,289	23,574	28,737
Hatillo	10,630	13,979	16,168	18,322	20,857	21,913	28,958	32,703
Hormigueros	——	4,584	4,872	6,098	6,907	10,827	14,030	15,212
Humacao	26,678	20,229	25,466	29,833	34,965	36,023	46,134	55,203
Isabela	16,852	19,809	23,068	25,842	29,061	30,430	37,435	39,147
Jayuya	——	12,463	12,223	14,589	15,062	13,588	14,722	15,527
Juana Díaz	29,157	18,529	19,516	23,396	27,660	36,270	43,505	45,198
Juncos	11,692	13,151	17,469	19,464	21,668	21,814	25,397	30,612
Lajas	11,071	11,908	12,454	14,736	16,275	16,545	21,236	23,271
Lares	22,650	25,197	27,351	29,914	29,921	25,263	26,743	29,015
Las Marías	10,046	10,736	8,881	9,626	10,806	7,841	8,747	9,306
Las Piedras	——	10,620	12,907	15,389	16,235	18,112	22,412	27,896
Loíza	13,317	15,804	18,762	22,145	24,313	39,062	20,867	29,307
Luquillo	——	6,251	7,799	8,851	9,979	10,390	14,895	18,100
Manatí	17,240	20,100	24,838	29,366	30,427	30,559	36,562	38,692 ▶

division	1910	1920	1930	1940	1950	1970	1980	1990
Maricao	7,158	8,291	6,463	7,724	7,353	5,991	6,737	6,206
Maunabo	7,106	7,973	9,084	10,792	11,742	10,792	11,813	12,347
Mayagüez	42,429	41,612	58,270	76,487	87,038	85,857	96,193	100,371
Moca	13,640	15,791	17,089	19,716	21,622	22,361	29,185	32,926
Morovis	12,446	14,660	17,332	19,167	19,294	19,059	21,142	25,288
Naguabo	14,365	15,788	18,212	19,180	20,991	17,996	20,617	22,620
Naranjito	8,876	10,503	11,645	13,954	15,949	19,913	23,633	27,914
Orocovis	15,028	15,758	16,115	19,770	21,085	20,201	19,332	21,158
Patillas	14,448	14,284	14,178	17,319	18,789	17,828	17,774	19,633
Peñuelas	11,991	13,598	13,278	14,789	14,867	15,973	19,116	22,515
Ponce	63,444	71,426	87,604	105,116	126,451	158,981	189,046	187,749
Quebradillas	8,152	9,404	10,190	11,494	13,720	15,582	19,728	21,425
Rincón	7,275	8,476	8,178	9,256	9,862	9,094	11,788	12,213
Río Grande	13,948	13,247	14,085	16,116	16,640	22,032	34,283	45,648
Río Piedras	18,880	23,035	40,853	68,290	143,897	— —	— —	— —
Sabana Grande	11,523	12,305	11,881	14,146	16,080	16,343	20,207	22,843
Salinas	11,403	12,971	15,446	19,400	23,412	21,837	26,438	28,335
San Germán	22,143	23,848	23,768	26,473	29,514	27,990	32,922	34,962
San Juan	48,716	71,443	114,715	169,247	223,949	463,242	434,849	437,745
San Lorenzo	14,278	18,136	23,479	26,627	29,209	27,755	32,428	35,163
San Sebastián	18,904	22,049	25,691	30,266	34,439	30,157	35,690	38,799
Santa Isabel	6,959	7,257	8,886	11,468	13,462	16,056	19,854	19,318
Toa Alta	9,127	10,505	11,696	13,371	14,170	18,964	31,910	44,101
Toa Baja	6,254	7,121	9,865	11,410	15,795	46,384	78,246	89,454
Trujillo Alto	6,345	7,470	9,576	11,726	13,588	30,669	51,389	61,120
Utuado	41,054	35,135	37,434	42,531	46,615	35,494	34,505	34,980
Vega Alta	8,134	9,970	12,333	14,329	16,510	22,810	28,696	34,559
Vega Baja	12,831	15,756	20,406	23,105	28,896	35,327	47,115	55,997
Vieques	10,425	11,651	10,582	10,362	9,211	7,767	7,662	8,602
Villalba	— —	13,040	11,847	12,871	14,903	18,733	20,734	23,559
Yabucoa	17,338	19,623	21,914	27,438	28,674	30,165	31,425	36,483
Yauco	31,504	25,848	27,787	30,533	33,657	35,103	37,742	42,058
	1,118,012	1,299,809	1,543,913	1,869,255	2,205,398	2,712,033	3,196,520	3,522,037

Census dates are all April 1.

QATAR

ISO = QA/FIPS = QA   Language = Arabic   Time zone = +3   Capital = Doha

The emirate of Qatar became a British protectorate on 1916-11-03. It became fully independent on 1971-09-03.
Other names of country: Dawlat Qatar (formal); Katar (German, Icelandic, obsolete); State of Qatar (formal–English).

division	ISO	FIPS	division	ISO	FIPS
Ad Dawhah	DA	QA01	Ar Rayyan	RA	QA06
Al Ghuwariyah	GH	QA02	Jariyan al Batnah	JB	QA07
Al Jumaliyah	JU	QA03	Madinat ach Shamal	MS	QA08
Al Khawr	KH	QA04	Umm Salal	US	QA09
Al Wakrah	WA	QA05			

Status: These divisions are baladiyat (sing: baladiyah; municipalities).
ISO: Codes from ISO 3166-2.
FIPS: Codes from FIPS PUB 10-4.
Territorial extent: Qatar occupies a peninsula in the Persian Gulf, and neighboring reefs and islets. It disputes the Hawar Islands with Bahrain. If Qatar's claim is valid, the Hawar Islands are in Al Jumaliyah municipality.

Origins of names:

Ad-Dawhah: Arabic *ad-dawha*: the big tree

Other names of subdivisions: There are various systems in use for transliterating from the Arabic to the Latin alphabet. The variant names listed here are just a sampling.

Ad Dawhah: Doha (variant)
Al Jumaliyah: Al Gummaylah, Al Jumaylīyah (variant)
Al Khawr: Al Khor (variant)

Jariyan al Batnah: Jarayān al Baṭnah, Jerian al Batna (variant)
Madinat ach Shamal: Ash Shamāl (variant)
Umm Salal: Um Salal, Umm Ṣalāl (variant)

REUNION

ISO = RE/FIPS = RE   Language = French   Time zone = +4   Capital = Saint-Denis

Reunion was a French possession until 1946, when it was made an overseas department of France. Reunion has a NUTS code of FR94, a department code of 974, and postal codes of the form 974xx, all of which are extensions of the French system.

Other names of country: Department of Reunion (formal–English); Reunião (Portuguese); Reunión (Spanish); Réunion (French, German, Norwegian).

Origin of name: French *réunion*: meeting, in commemoration of the meeting on 1792-08-10 of forces which stormed the Tuileries Palace.

division	abv	population	area-km	area-mi	division	abv	population	area-km	area-mi
Îles Éparses	IE	0	38	15	Saint-Paul	PL	113,072	466	180
Saint-Benoît	BN	85,132	738	285	Saint-Pierre	PR	192,462	883	341
Saint-Denis	DN	207,158	421	163			597,824	2,546	984

Status: These divisions are arrondissements, except for the Îles Éparses, which are French possessions administered by Reunion.

Abv: Two-letter code for international compatibility (defined by the author).

Population: 1990 census.

Area-km: Square kilometers.

Area-mi: Square miles.

Capitals: Capitals of arrondissements have the same names as the arrondissements.

Further subdivisions: The arrondissements are subdivided into 24 communes.

Territorial extent: The Îles Éparses (scattered islands) are five remote Indian Ocean islands or island groups that belong to France and are administered by Reunion. They are not part of any arrondissement. Oddly, FIPS 10-4 has assigned each of them a separate country code.

name	FIPS	area-km	name	FIPS	area-km
Bassas da India	BS	~0	Juan de Nova Island	JU	4
Europa Island	EU	28	Tromelin Island	TE	1
Glorioso Islands	GO	5			

Origins of names:

Juan de Nova Island: named for the ship captain who discovered it

Saint-Denis: named for the patron saint of France

Change history:

1946-03-19   Reunion became a département d'outre-mer (overseas department) of France, a status nominally equivalent to a European department of France. It had one arrondissement, Saint-Denis.

1964-09-05   Saint-Pierre arrondissement split from Saint-Denis. Saint-Denis was also called Arrondissement-du-Vent (Windward), and Saint-Pierre was Arrondissement-sous-le-Vent (Leeward).

1968-10-02   Saint-Benoît arrondissement split from Saint-Denis.

1969-09-24   Saint-Paul arrondissement split from Saint-Pierre.

Other names of subdivisions:

Glorioso Islands: Îles Glorieuses (French)

ROMANIA

ISO = RO/FIPS = RO   Language = Romanian   Time zone = +2 [d]   Capital = Bucharest

In 1900, Romania was a young kingdom (since 1881). In comparison with today's map, it contained most of Moldova, but the Austro-Hungarian Empire owned Transylvania, which now forms its northwest section. It acquired additional territory, including Transylvania, during the Balkan Wars and World War I. World War II caused a net loss of territory, establishing the present-day boundaries.

Other names of country: Roemenie (Dutch); România (formal); Romênia (Portuguese); Roumania (obsolete); Roumanie (French); Rumænien (Danish); Rumania (Spanish, variant); Rumänien (German, Swedish); Rúmenía (Icelandic).

Origin of name: Roman + country suffix -ia, adopted in the 19th century to reflect political and linguistic heritage from Roman Empire.

division	ISO	FIPS	population	area-km	area-mi	capital	German
Alba	AB	RO01	408,457	6,231	2,406	Alba Iulia	Karlsburg
Arad	AR	RO02	482,144	7,652	2,954	Arad	
Argeş	AG	RO03	679,868	6,801	2,626	Piteşti	Piteschti
Bacău	BC	RO04	742,901	6,606	2,551	Bacău	
Bihor	BH	RO05	633,629	7,535	2,909	Oradea	Großwardein
Bistriţa-Năsăud	BN	RO06	328,786	5,305	2,048	Bistriţa	Bistritz
Botoşani	BT	RO07	462,370	4,965	1,917	Botoşani	Botoschani
Brăila	BR	RO08	391,923	4,724	1,824	Brăila	
Braşov	BV	RO09	642,764	5,351	2,066	Braşov	Kronstadt
Bucharest	B *	RO10	2,339,156	1,820	703	Bucharest	Bukarest
Buzău	BZ	RO11	515,202	6,072	2,344	Buzău	
Călăraşi	CL	RO41	336,657	5,074	1,959	Călăraşi	Kalarasch
Caraş-Severin	CS	RO12	370,058	8,503	3,283	Reşiţa	Reschitza
Cluj	CJ	RO13	727,033	6,650	2,568	Cluj-Napoca	Klausenburg
Constanţa	CT	RO14	747,441	7,055	2,724	Constanţa	Konstanza
Covasna	CV	RO15	232,951	3,705	1,431	Sfîntu Gheorghe	
Dîmboviţa	DB	RO16	558,518	4,036	1,558	Tîrgovişte	Türgowischte
Dolj	DJ	RO17	758,895	7,413	2,862	Craiova	Krajowa
Galaţi	GL	RO18	642,983	4,425	1,709	Galaţi	Galatz
Giurgiu	GR	RO42	305,661	3,511	1,356	Giurgiu	
Gorj	GJ	RO19	397,927	5,641	2,178	Tîrgu Jiu	Türgschi
Harghita	HR	RO20	347,145	6,610	2,552	Miercurea-Ciuc	
Hunedoara	HD	RO21	547,180	7,016	2,709	Deva	
Ialomiţa	IL	RO22	305,454	4,449	1,718	Slobozia	
Iaşi	IS	RO23	815,368	5,469	2,112	Iaşi	Jassy
Maramureş	MM	RO25	539,718	6,215	2,400	Baia Mare	
Mehedinţi	MH	RO26	330,017	4,900	1,892	Drobeta-Turnu Severin	
Mureş	MS	RO27	607,355	6,696	2,585	Tîrgu Mureş	Neumarkt
Neamţ	NT	RO28	584,364	5,890	2,274	Piatra-Neamţ ➤	

division	ISO	FIPS	population	area-km	area-mi	capital	German
Olt	OT	RO29	520,871	5,507	2,126	Slatina	
Prahova	PH	RO30	874,219	4,694	1,812	Ploieşti	Plojeschti
Sălaj	SJ	RO31	264,448	3,850	1,486	Zalău	
Satu Mare	SM	RO32	398,401	4,405	1,701	Satu Mare	
Sibiu	SB	RO33	448,474	5,422	2,093	Sibiu	Hermannstadt
Suceava	SV	RO34	708,571	8,555	3,303	Suceava	
Teleorman	TR	RO35	477,527	5,760	2,224	Alexandria	
Timiş	TM	RO36	691,797	8,692	3,356	Timişoara	Temeschburg
Tulcea	TL	RO37	269,311	8,430	3,255	Tulcea	Tultscha
Vaslui	VS	RO38	463,832	5,297	2,045	Vaslui	
Vîlcea	VL	RO39	436,989	5,705	2,203	Rîmnicu Vîlcea	
Vrancea	VN	RO40	394,257	4,863	1,878	Focşani	Fokschani
			22,730,622	237,500	91,700		

* = *To get a uniform two-letter code, I recommend using BU for Bucharest.*

Status: These divisions are judeţe (sing. judeţ: counties), except for Bucharest, which is a municipiu (city).
ISO: Codes from ISO 3166-2.
FIPS: Codes from FIPS PUB 10-4.
Population: 1992-01-07 census.
Area-km: Square kilometers.
Area-mi: Square miles.
German: German names of capitals generally date from the Austro-Hungarian Empire. They are included here because some are still in common use.
Further subdivisions: The counties are divided into oraşe (towns), municipii (municipalities), and comune (communes).
Origins of names:

Banat: brief form of Banat of Temesvar; banat is a generic for the territory governed by a ban
Bistriţa: Slavic for running brook
Braşov: Slavic for city of Braso (man's name)
Bucharest: attributed to founding by a shepherd named Bucur

Cluj: from Medieval Latin *castrum clus*: enclosed camp
Constanţa: named for a sister of Roman emperor Constantine the Great
Galaţi: possibly from an early settlement of Galatians
Timişoara: Hungarian *Temes*: name of a county, *var*: fort

Change history:

1900   Romania consisted of three provinces: Dobruja, Moldavia, and Wallachia. Wallachia was split by the Olt River into Little Wallachia (or Lesser Wallachia, or Oltenia, to the west) and Great Wallachia (or Greater Wallachia, or Muntenia). Provinces were further subdivided into districts or departments, as follows (using modern spelling where possible):

district	population	area-km	province	capital
Argeş	242,946	4,430	Muntenia	Piteşti
Bacău	232,146	3,990	Moldavia	Bacău
Botoşani	197,118	3,160	Moldavia	Botoşani
Brăila	181,033	4,350	Muntenia	Brăila
Buzău	277,598	4,870	Muntenia	Buzău
Constanţa	217,740	6,920	Dobruja	Constanţa
Covurlui	171,710	2,950	Moldavia	Galaţi
Dîmboviţa	258,367	3,470	Muntenia	Tîrgovişte
Dolj	437,517	6,580	Oltenia	Craiova
Dorohoi	184,357	2,820	Moldavia	Dorohoi
Falciu	108,324	2,200	Moldavia	Huşi
Gorj	200,859	4,690	Oltenia	Tîrgu Jiu
Ialomiţa	242,611	6,790	Muntenia	Călăraşi
Iaşi	213,196	3,130	Moldavia	Iaşi
Ilfov	678,769	5,780	Muntenia	Bucharest
Mehedinţi	295,548	4,950	Oltenia	Turnu Severin
Muscel	135,616	2,950	Muntenia	Cîmpulung
Neamţ	169,794	3,990	Moldavia	Piatra ➤

district	population	area-km	province	capital
Olt	171,262	2,820	Muntenia	Slatina
Prahova	389,785	4,660	Muntenia	Plocşti
Putna	181,103	3,240	Moldavia	Focşani
Roman	128,190	2,100	Moldavia	Roman
Rîmnicu-Sărat	164,166	3,260	Muntenia	Rîmnicu-Sărat
Rumanaţi	248,401	4,580	Oltenia	Caracal
Suceava	158,971	3,420	Moldavia	Fălticeni
Tecuci	142,993	2,540	Moldavia	Tecuci
Teleorman	296,759	4,690	Muntenia	Turnu-Măgurele
Tulcea	172,566	8,620	Dobruja	Tulcea
Tutova	129,858	2,380	Moldavia	Barlad
Vaslui	127,704	2,180	Moldavia	Vaslui
Vîlcea	231,572	4,250	Oltenia	Rîmnicu Vîlcea
Vlaşka	259,482	4,480	Muntenia	Giurgiu
	7,248,061	131,240		

Population: 1912-12-19 census.

1913-08-10	Southern Dobruja transferred from Bulgaria to Romania by the Treaty of Bucharest. This territory is now part of Razgrad and Varna regions in Bulgaria.
1918-04-09	Romania annexed Bessarabia from Russia.
1920-06-04	Treaty of Trianon redistributed more than half of Hungary's land. Romania received all of Transylvania, part of Banat, and Crişana-Maramureş. For details, see Hungary.
1920-07-16	Bukovina transferred from Austria to Romania by the Treaty of Saint-Germain. Romania now contained nine provinces (Banat, Bessarabia, Bukovina, Crişana-Maramureş, Dobruja, Moldavia, Muntenia, Oltenia, and Transylvania), subdivided into about 73 counties or parts of counties.
1940-06	Northern Bukovina ceded to Soviet Union by treaty.
1940-08-20	Northern Transylvania ceded to Hungary.
1940-09-07	Southern Dobruja ceded to Bulgaria.
1947-02-10	Transylvanian territory restored to Romania from Hungary. Bessarabia, which had changed hands repeatedly during World War II, formally restored to Russia.
1950	Romania reorganized into rayons (districts), with groups of districts designated as provinces.
1950	Names of Braşov province and its capital changed to Stalin.
1960	Names of Stalin province and its capital changed back to Braşov.
~1960	Constanţa town split from Dobrogea province. The resulting division was:

division	population	area-km	capital	division	population	area-km	capital
Argeş	1,189,395	15,800	Piteşti	Galaţi	1,065,646	14,800	Galaţi
Bacău	1,103,964	13,400	Bacău	Hunedoara	656,452	11,000	Deva
Banat	1,241,832	21,800	Timişoara	Iaşi	1,052,378	11,100	Iaşi
Braşov	1,062,481	12,450	Braşov	Maramureş	782,127	10,500	Baia Mare
Bucharest	1,681,599	18,700	Bucharest	Mureş-Magyar	814,632	13,500	Tîrgu Mureş
Bucharest [city]	1,366,794	550	Bucharest	Oltenia	1,570,574	20,300	Craiova
Cluj	1,217,401	18,000	Cluj	Ploieşti	1,460,693	13,100	Ploieşti
Constanţa [town]	153,871	— —	Constanţa	Suceava	1,002,883	13,750	Suceava
Crişana	873,393	12,450	Oradea		18,813,131	237,500	
Dobrogea	517,016	16,300	Constanţa				

Population: 1966 estimate.

1968	Rayons and provinces abolished, replaced by 39 counties and the city of Bucharest.
~1982	Ilfov county (capital Bucharest, FIPS code RO24) split into Călăraşi county, Giurgiu county, and a portion that was annexed to Bucharest municipality.

Other names of subdivisions:

Bucharest: Bucarest (French, Italian, Spanish); Bucareste (Portuguese); Bucureşti (Romanian); Bukarest (German, Swedish)

Bukovina: Bucovina (Italian, Portuguese, Spanish); Bucovine (French); Bukowina (German)

Dobruja: Dobrogea (Romanian); Dobroudja (French); Dobrudja (variant); Dobrudscha (German); Dobrugia (Italian)

Transylvania: Siebenbürgen (German); Transilvania (Italian, Spanish); Transilvânia (Portuguese); Transylvanie (French)

Wallachia: Valacchia (Italian); Valachie (French); Valaquia (Spanish); Valáquia (Portuguese); Walachei (German); Walachia (variant)

RUSSIA

ISO = RU/FIPS = RS   Language = Russian   Time zone = (see table)   Capital = Moscow

Russia is the largest country in the world in area. Fittingly, it requires a long article. At the beginning of the 20th century, the Russian Empire embraced almost all of what later became the Soviet Union, as well as Finland and much of Poland. On 1917-03-15, Czar Nicholas II abdicated, and a provisional government was installed. On 1917-11-07, Bolsheviks led by Lenin overthrew this government, replacing it with a Communist one. (Russians call this the October Revolution because Russia still observed the Julian calendar at the time.) Many of the peripheral territories of the empire became independent or were conquered and alienated from Russia by peace settlements. A civil war ensued. It ended with the Red faction victorious in 1920. In 1922, a new constitution created the Union of Soviet Socialist Republics (U.S.S.R., or Soviet Union). The U.S.S.R. gained territory as a result of World War II. The Communist system eventually proved unviable. On 1991-12-25, the Soviet Union was officially dissolved, breaking into 15 countries corresponding to its constituent republics (some of them had already unilaterally declared independence). The Commonwealth of Independent States (C.I.S.) was formed to replace it on 1991-12-21. The members at its foundation were Armenia, Azerbaijan, Byelorussia, Kazakhstan, Kirghizstan, Moldavia, Russia, Tadzhikistan, Turkmenistan, Ukraine, and Uzbekistan. The C.I.S. still endures as a very loose federation.

Note: this entry uses the abbreviations G. for Government (Guberniya), S.S.R. for Soviet Socialist Republic (Sovyetskaya Sotsialisticheskaya Respublika), S.F.S.R. for Soviet Federated Socialist Republic (Sovyetskaya Federativnaya Sotsialisticheskaya Respublika), A.S.S.R. for Autonomous S.S.R. (Avtonomnaya S.S.R.), Obl. for Region (Oblast'), A.Obl. for Autonomous Region (Avtonomnaya Oblast'), and A.Okr. for Autonomous Province (Avtonomnyy Okrug, formerly called Natsional'niy Okrug). The Russian names in context may be inflected, as in Soyuz Sovyetskikh Sotsialisticheskikh Respublik (Union of Soviet Socialist Republics), where S.S.R. is in the genitive plural. "Constituent republics" refers to S.S.R.s and the S.F.S.R.

Other names of country: Federação Russa (Portuguese); Federación de Rusia (Spanish); Fédération Russe (French-formal); Rossiiskaya Federatsiya (formal); Rusland (Danish); Russian Federation (English-formal); Russie (French); Russische Föderation (German-formal); Russland (Norwegian); Rußland (German); Rússland (Icelandic); Ryssland (Swedish); Venäjä (Finnish).

Other names of Union of Soviet Socialist Republics: Soviet Union, U.S.S.R. (variant); Unión de Repúblicas Socialistas Soviéticas, U.R.S.S., Unión Soviética (Spanish); Unione delle Repubbliche Socialiste Sovietiche, U.R.S.S. (Italian); Union des républiques socialistes soviétiques, U.R.S.S., Union soviétique (French); União das Repúblicas Socialistas Soviéticas, União Soviética (Portuguese); Union der sozialistischen Sowjetrepubliken, U.d.S.S.R., Sowjetunion (German); Sovjet-Unionen (Norwegian, Swedish).

Origin of name: land of the Rus (possibly a group of Vikings).

division	abv	ISO	FIPS	typ	tz	population	area-km	area-mi	capital
Adygey	AD	AD	RS01	r	+4 d	* 451,000	7,600	2,900	Maykop
Aga Buryat	AB	AGB	RS02	a	+9 d	* 79,000	19,000	7,300	Aginskoye
Altay	AL	AL	RS04	k	+7 d	2,523,000	169,000	65,300	Barnaul
Amur	AM	AMU	RS05	o	+9 d	990,000	364,000	140,500	Blagoveshchensk
Arkhangel'sk	AR	ARK	RS06	o	+3 d	1,440,000	410,000	158,300	Archangel
Astrakhan'	AS	AST	RS07	o	+4 d	931,000	44,000	17,000	Astrakhan'
Bashkortostan	BK	BA	RS08	r	+5 d	* 4,080,000	143,600	55,400	Ufa
Belgorod	BL	BEK	RS09	o	+3 d	1,316,000	27,000	10,400	Belgorod
Bryansk	BR	BRY	RS10	o	+3 d	1,485,000	35,000	13,500	Bryansk ➤

division	abv	ISO	FIPS	typ	tz	population	area-km	area-mi	capital
Buryat	BU	BU	RS11	r	+8 [d]	* 1,053,000	351,300	135,600	Ulan-Ude
Chechnya	CN	CE	RS12	r	+4 [d]	* 624,000	19,300	7,500	Groznyy
Chelyabinsk	CL	CHE	RS13	o	+5 [d]	3,493,000	88,000	34,000	Chelyabinsk
Chita	CT	CHI	RS14	o	+9 [d]	1,208,000	413,000	159,500	Chita
Chukot	CK	CHU	RS15	a	+12 [d]	* 100,000	737,700	284,800	Anadyr'
Chuvash	CV	CU	RS16	r	+4 [d]	* 1,361,000	18,300	7,100	Cheboksary
Dagestan	DA	DA	RS17	r	+4 [d]	* 2,067,000	50,300	19,400	Makhachkala
Evenk	EN	EVE	RS18	a	+7 [d]	* 21,000	767,600	296,400	Tura
Gorno-Altay	GA	ALT	RS03	r	+9 [d]	* 200,000	92,600	35,800	Gorno-Altaysk
Ingush	IN	IN	RS19	r	+4 [d]	* 280,000	——	——	Nazran'
Irkutsk	IR	IRK	RS20	o	+8 [d]	2,517,000	746,000	288,000	Irkutsk
Ivanovo	IV	IVA	RS21	o	+4 [d]	1,314,000	24,000	9,300	Ivanovo
Kabardin-Balkar	KB	KB	RS22	r	+4 [d]	* 790,000	12,500	4,800	Nal'chik
Kaliningrad	KN	KGD	RS23	o	+2 [d]	822,000	15,000	5,800	Kaliningrad
Kalmyk	KL	KL	RS24	r	+4 [d]	* 320,000	76,100	29,400	Elista
Kaluga	KG	KLS	RS25	o	+3 [d]	1,017,000	30,000	11,600	Kaluga
Kamchatka	KA	KAM	RS26	o	+12 [d]	369,000	170,000	65,600	Petropavlovsk-Kamchatskiy
Karachay-Cherkess	KC	KC	RS27	r	+4 [d]	* 436,000	14,100	5,400	Cherkessk
Karelia	KI	KR	RS28	r	+3 [d]	* 789,000	172,400	66,600	Petrozavodsk
Kemerovo	KE	KEM	RS29	o	+7 [d]	3,014,000	96,000	37,100	Kemerovo
Khabarovsk	KH	KHA	RS30	k	+10 [d]	1,439,000	789,000	304,600	Khabarovsk
Khakass	KK	KK	RS31	r	+7 [d]	* 584,000	61,900	23,900	Abakan
Khanty-Mansiy	KM	KHM	RS32	a	+5 [d]	* 1,326,000	523,100	202,000	Khanty-Mansiysk
Kirov	KV	KIR	RS33	o	+4 [d]	1,659,000	121,000	46,700	Kirov
Komi	KO	KO	RS34	r	+3 [d]	* 1,202,000	415,900	160,600	Syktyvkar
Komi-Permyak	KP	KOP	RS35	a	+5 [d]	* 159,000	32,900	12,700	Kudymkar
Koryak	KR	KOR	RS36	a	+12 [d]	* 34,000	301,500	116,400	Palana
Kostroma	KT	KOS	RS37	o	+4 [d]	794,000	60,000	23,200	Kostroma
Krasnodar	KD	KDY	RS38	k	+4 [d]	4,493,000	76,000	29,300	Krasnodar
Krasnoyarsk	KY	KYY	RS39	k	+7 [d]	2,739,000	1,478,000	570,700	Krasnoyarsk
Kurgan	KU	KGK	RS40	o	+5 [d]	1,089,000	71,000	27,400	Kurgan
Kursk	KS	KRS	RS41	o	+3 [d]	1,326,000	30,000	11,600	Kursk
Leningrad	LN	LEN	RS42	o	+3 [d]	6,294,000	86,000	33,200	Saint Petersburg
Lipetsk	LP	LIP	RS43	o	+4 [d]	1,219,000	24,000	9,300	Lipetsk
Magadan	MG	MAG	RS44	o	+11 [d]	357,000	461,000	178,000	Magadan
Mariy-El	ME	ME	RS45	r	+3 [d]	* 766,000	23,200	9,000	Yoshkar-Ola
Mordovia	MR	MO	RS46	r	+3 [d]	* 959,000	26,200	10,100	Saransk
Moscow City	MC	MOW	RS48	g	+3 [d]	——	——	——	Moscow
Moskva	MS	MOS	RS47	o	+3 [d]	14,790,000	47,000	18,100	Moscow
Murmansk	MM	MUR	RS49	o	+3 [d]	1,025,000	145,000	56,000	Murmansk
Nenets	NN	NEN	RS50	a	+3 [d]	* 49,000	176,700	68,200	Nar'yan-Mar
Nizhegorod	NZ	NIZ	RS51	o	+4 [d]	3,680,000	75,000	29,000	Nizhniy Novgorod
North Ossetia	NO	SE	RS68	r	+3 [d]	* 659,000	8,000	3,100	Vladikavkaz
Novgorod	NG	NGR	RS52	o	+6 [d]	731,000	55,000	21,200	Novgorod
Novosibirsk	NS	NVS	RS53	o	+6 [d]	2,676,000	178,000	68,700	Novosibirsk
Omsk	OM	OMS	RS54	o	+6 [d]	1,984,000	140,000	54,100	Omsk
Orel	OL	ORL	RS56	o	+4 [d]	876,000	25,000	9,700	Orel
Orenburg	OB	ORE	RS55	o	+5 [d]	2,119,000	124,000	47,900	Orenburg
Penza	PZ	PNZ	RS57	o	+5 [d]	1,495,000	43,000	16,600	Penza
Perm'	PM	PER	RS58	o	+5 [d]	2,835,000	128,000	49,400	Perm'
Primor'ye	PR	PRI	RS59	k	+10 [d]	2,046,000	166,000	64,100	Vladivostok
Pskov	PS	PSK	RS60	o	+4 [d]	841,000	55,000	21,200	Pskov
Rostov	RO	ROS	RS61	o	+4 [d]	4,168,000	101,000	39,000	Rostov-na-Donu
Ryazan'	RZ	RYA	RS62	o	+11 [d]	1,334,000	40,000	15,400	Ryazan'
Saint Petersburg City	SP	SPE	RS66	g	+3 [d]	——	——	——	Saint Petersburg
Sakha	SK	SA	RS63	r	+9 [d]	* 1,036,000	3,103,200	1,198,200	Yakutsk
Sakhalin	SL	SAK	RS64	o	+11 [d]	676,000	87,000	33,600	Yuzhno-Sakhalinsk
Samara	SA	SAM	RS65	o	+4 [d]	3,149,000	54,000	20,800	Samara
Saratov	SR	SAR	RS67	o	+4 [d]	2,587,000	100,000	38,600	Saratov
Smolensk	SM	SMO	RS69	o	+4 [d]	1,129,000	50,000	19,300	Smolensk
Stavropol'	ST	STA	RS70	k	+5 [d]	2,245,000	67,000	25,900	Stavropol'
Sverdlovsk	SV	SVE	RS71	o	+5 [d]	4,522,000	195,000	75,300	Yekaterinburg
Tambov	TB	TAM	RS72	o	+7 [d]	1,344,000	34,000	13,100	Tambov ➤

division	abv	ISO	FIPS	typ	tz	population	area-km	area-mi	capital
Tatarstan	TT	TA	RS73	r	+3 [d]	* 3,755,000	68,000	26,300	Kazan'
Taymyr	TM	TAY	RS74	a	+7 [d]	* 47,000	862,100	332,900	Dudinka
Tomsk	TO	TOM	RS75	o	+3 [d]	904,000	317,000	122,400	Tomsk
Tula	TL	TUL	RS76	o	+6 [d]	1,884,000	26,000	10,000	Tula
Tuva	TU	TY	RS79	r	+7 [d]	* 308,000	170,500	65,800	Kyzyl
Tver'	TV	TVE	RS77	o	+4 [d]	1,643,000	84,000	32,400	Tver'
Tyumen'	TY	TYU	RS78	o	+6 [d]	1,171,000	162,000	62,500	Tyumen'
Udmurt	UD	UD	RS80	r	+4 [d]	* 1,641,000	42,100	16,300	Izhevsk
Ul'yanovsk	UL	ULY	RS81	o	+4 [d]	1,281,000	37,000	14,300	Simbirsk
Ust-Orda Buryat	UB	UOB	RS82	a	+8 [d]	* 143,000	22,400	8,600	Ust'-Ordynskiy
Vladimir	VL	VLA	RS83	o	+4 [d]	1,597,000	29,000	11,200	Vladimir
Vologda	VO	VLG	RS85	o	+9 [d]	1,317,000	146,000	56,400	Vologda
Volgograd	VG	VGG	RS84	o	+4 [d]	2,494,000	114,000	44,000	Volgograd
Voronezh	VR	VOR	RS86	o	+4 [d]	2,465,000	52,000	20,100	Voronezh
Yamal-Nenets	YN	YAN	RS87	a	+5 [d]	* 480,000	750,300	289,700	Salekhard
Yaroslavl'	YS	YAR	RS88	o	+4 [d]	1,436,000	36,000	13,900	Yaroslavl'
Yevrey	YV	YEV	RS89	b	+10 [d]	* 212,000	36,000	13,900	Birobidzhan
						142,303,000	17,845,400	6,890,200	

* = 1995-01 estimate; [d] = DST is observed

Typ: These divisions are avtonomnaya oblast' (b, autonomous region); avtonomnyy okrug (a, autonomous province); gorod (g, [federal] city); kray (k, territory); oblast' (o, region); or respublika (r, republic).

Abv: Two-letter code for international compatibility (defined by the author).

ISO: Codes from ISO 3166-2.

FIPS: Codes from FIPS PUB 10-4.

Tz: Time zone (hours offset from GMT during standard time; [d] indicates that DST is observed). Some divisions are in more than one time zone. Time zones have been somewhat unstable recently, and do not always coincide with division borders.

Population: 1982-01-01 estimate, except figures marked with *, which are 1995-01 estimate.

Area-km: Square kilometers.

Area-mi: Square miles.

Notes: Population and area of Moscow and Saint Petersburg cities are combined with the regions containing them (respectively Moscow and Leningrad). Area of Ingush is combined with Chechnya because the border between them is still indefinite. Some of these divisions are subordinate to others; in those cases, the population and area of each part is shown separately. For example, although Komi-Permyak is part of Perm', the figures given for Perm' refer to that part of Perm' that is not in Komi-Permyak.

Subordinate subdivisions: Altay contains Gorno-Altay; Arkhangel'sk contains Nenets; Chita contains Aga Buryat; Irkutsk contains Ust-Orda Buryat; Kamchatka contains Koryak; Khabarovsk contains Yevrey; Krasnodar contains Adygey; Krasnoyarsk contains Evenk, Khakass, and Taymyr; Magadan contains Chukot; Perm' contains Komi-Permyak; Stavropol' contains Karachay-Cherkess; Tyumen' contains Khanty-Mansiy and Yamal-Nenets. In each case, the containing entity has some territory that is not in any of the contained entities.

Territorial extent: Adygey is entirely surrounded by Krasnodar.

Aga Buryat is entirely surrounded by Chita.

Arkhangel'sk includes the White Sea islands of Morzhovets, Solovetskiye, and Anzerskiy.

Astrakhan' includes Caspian Sea islands in the Volga River delta, such as Zyudev.

Chukot includes Ostrov Vrangelya (Wrangel Island) and Ayon Island in the Arctic Ocean.

Dagestan includes the Caspian Sea islands of Chechen and Tyuleniy.

Irkutsk includes Ol'khon Island in Lake Baykal.

Kaliningrad contains the northern end of the Baltiyskaya Kosa, a spit of land attached to the mainland in Poland.

Kamchatka includes the Commander Islands.

Khabarovsk includes the Shantarskiye Ostrova (Shantar Islands), the biggest of which is Bol'shoy Shantar.

Koryak includes Karaginskiy Island.

Leningrad includes islands in the Gulf of Finland: Bol'shoy Berezovyy, Gogland, Kotlin, Moshchnyy, etc.

Moscow City is entirely surrounded by Moskva region. It also has three small enclaves within Moskva region, one each containing the towns of Elino and Rasskazovka, and one north of Reutov.

Murmansk includes Kil'din Island.

Nenets includes the Arctic islands and groups of Novaya Zemlya (New Land), Zemlya Frantsa-Iosifa (Franz Joseph Land), Kolguyev, and Vaygach.

Primor'ye includes Ostrov Russkiy (Russian Island).

Sakha includes the Arctic islands and groups of Novosibirskiye Ostrova (New Siberian Islands), Lyakhovskiye Ostrova, and Bol'shoy Begichev.

Sakhalin consists of Sakhalin Island, the Kuril'skiye Ostrova (Kuril Islands), and adjacent islets.

Samara has a tiny enclave inside Orenburg containing a village called Dal'niy, north of Buzuluk.

Taymyr includes the islands of Severnaya Zemlya (North Land): October Revolution Island, Komsomolets Island, Bolshevik Island, Pioneer Island, etc., and other islands along the Arctic coast as far west as Sibiryakova.

Ust-Orda Buryat is entirely surrounded by Irkutsk.

Yamal-Nenets includes the Arctic islands of Belyy, Oleniy, and others.

Origins of names:

Adygey: people of the sea, from Abkhazian *adi*: water

Altay: after the Altay Mountains, originally Turkic *Altun*: gold, *Tagh*: mountain

Amurskaya: after the Amur River, from Tungus *amor*: big river

Arkhangel'sk: named for a convent there, dedicated to the archangel Michael

Astrakhan: from Turkish *haci*: hajji (pilgrim to Mecca), *tarhan*: free from taxes

Belgorod: Russian *byelo*: white, *gorod*: city

Buryat: Mongol *buriad*: forest-dwelling people

Chuvash: ethnic name, from Turkic *dzhyvash*: peaceful

Dagestan: Turkish *dag*: mountain, Iranian *ostan*: land (land of mountains)

Ivanovo: named for Tsar Ivan IV of Russia (Ivan the Terrible = Ivan Groznyy)

Kaliningrad: city of (communist leader Mikhail Ivanovich) Kalinin, renamed from Königsberg in 1946

Kalmyk: after the ethnic name Kalmuk, from Mongolian *kalimak*: beyond the shore

Kamchatka: named by Semyon Dechnev in 1648 from Russian *kamtsatka*: a type of patterned cloth

Karelia: possibly from Finnish *karja*: herds

Khabarovsk: after Zherofey Pavlovich Khabarov, explorer of the area

Kirov: renamed from Vyatka in 1934 on the assassination of Kirov (Sergey Mironovich Kostrikov), communist leader

Komi: ethnic name, from Zyrian *komi*: men

Krasnodar: Russian *krasniy*: red, *dar*: gift, renamed from Yekaterinodar in 1920, as the Red Army displaced the tsars

Krasnoyarsk: shortened from Krasnoyarskiy Ostrov, from Russian *krasniy*: red, *yar*: bank, *-skiy*: adjectival suffix, *ostrov*: island (island with red clay banks)

Kurgan: Turkic for walled city

Leningrad: renamed in 1924, along with the city, in honor of Lenin (Vladimir Ilyich Ulyanov, 1870–1924)

Mari: ethnic name, from Iranian word for men

Mordovia: from the ethnic name Mordvin

Moscow/Moskva: after the Moscow River (Moskva in Russian)

Murmansk: corruption of the Russian adjective for Normans or Norsemen

Nizhniy-Novgorod: Russian for lower Novgorod; Novgorod means new city (called Gorkiy 1932–1992)

Novgorod: Russian *noviy*: new, *gorod*: city

Omsk: Om (River) + *-sk*: adjectival suffix

Orenburg: Or (River) + German *burg*: fort, originally planned as a fort on the Or, but actually built elsewhere

Perm': probably from Finnish *perä*: back, *maa*: land (considered back country by the Finns) (called Molotov 1940-1957)

Primor'ye: Russian *pri*: by, *morye*: sea (seaside, maritime)

Rostov: after the capital, Rostov-na-Donu (Rostov on the Don), which was originally called Krepost Dmitriya Rostovskovo (fortress of Dmitri of Rostov), after the patron saint of its church, a native of a different city named Rostov

Sakhalin: the Manchus called the island *Sakhalin anga hata*, the island at the mouth of the Black River (meaning the Amur), simplified to Sakhalin (Black River)

North Ossetia: Northern part of Ossetia, from Georgian *osi*: ethnic name

Smolensk: adjectival form of Russian *smola*: pitch (area was a source of pitch for boats)

Stavropol: Byzantine Greek *stavros*: cross, *polis*: city (city of the cross)

Sverdlovsk: after revolutionary hero Yakov Mikhailovich Sverdlov (Yekaterinburg before 1924 and after 1991)

Tatarstan: land of the Tatars (ethnic name used by the Mongols)

Tomsk: Tom (River) + *-sk*: adjectival suffix

Udmurt: after an ethnic name

Ul'yanovsk: after Lenin (nom de guerre of Vladimir Ilyich Ul'yanov [1870–1924])

Volgogradskaya: after the city, from Volga (River) + *grad*: city

Voronezhskaya: after the Voronezh River, from Russian *voron*: crow

Yakutsk: inhabitants are Yakuts, from Yakut *yeko*: stranger

Yaroslavl': named for Iaroslav Vladimirovich the Wise, Prince of Kiev

Birobidzhan city was Tikhonkaya -1928

Change history:

For additional information about the divisions of the Russian Empire/Soviet Union that are not included in the Russian Federation, see individual country listings.

1905   Japan acquired the southern half of Sakhalin Island and the Kwantung peninsula (now part of Liaoning province, China) from Russia in the Russo-Japanese War.

The divisions of Russia before World War I were as follows:

name	Russian name	country/division now	population	area-km	capital
Åbo-Björneborg	Abo-B'yorneborgskaya G.	Finland/Turku ja Pori			Åbo
Akmolinsk	Akmolinskaya Obl.	Kazakhstan/Aqmola	1,064,000	225,074	Omsk
Amur	Amurskaya Obl.	Russia/Amur	230,200	154,795	Blagoveshchensk
Archangel	Arkhangel'skaya G.	Russia/Arkhangel'sk	449,400	326,063	Arkhangel'sk
Astrakhan	Astrakhanskaya G.	Russia/Astrakhan'	1,262,000	91,042	Astrakhan'
Baku	Bakinskaya G.	Azerbaijan	1,033,700	15,061	Baku
Batum	Batumskaya Obl.	Georgia/Adjaria	166,300	2,693	Batum
Bessarabia	Bessarabskaya G.	Moldova	2,490,200	17,143	Kishinev
Bokhara Khanate	Bukhara	Uzbekistan/Bukhara			Bokhara
Chernigov	Chernigovskaya G.	Ukraine/Chernigov	3,031,100	20,232	Chernigov
Courland	Kurlyandskaya G.	Latvia	749,100	10,435	Mitava
Dagestan	Dagestanskaya Obl.	Russia/Dagestan	689,300	11,471	Temir-Khan-Shura
Don Cossacks	Voyska Donskovo Obl.	Russia/Rostov	3,591,900	63,532	Novocherkassk
Elizabethpol	Yelisavetpol'skaya G.	Azerbaijan	1,021,900	16,991	Yelisavetpol'
Erivan	Erivanskaya G.	Armenia	971,200	10,725	Erivan'
Estonia	Estlyandskaya G.	Estonia	471,400	7,605	Revel'
Fergana	Ferganskaya Obl.	Uzbekistan/Ferghana	2,069,000	55,483	Skobelev
Grodno	Grodnenskaya G.	Belarus/Hrodna	1,974,400	14,896	Grodno
Irkutsk	Irkutskaya G.	Russia/Irkutsk	696,200	280,429	Irkutsk
Kalisz	Kalishskaya G.	Poland/Kalisz	1,183,800	4,377	Kalish
Kaluga	Kaluzhskaya G.	Russia/Kaluga	1,412,900	11,942	Kaluga
Kamchatka	Kamchatskaya Obl.	Russia/Kamchatka	37,300	502,424	Petropavlovsk
Kars	Karskaya Obl.	Turkey/Kars	377,200	7,239	Kars
Kazan	Kazanskaya G.	Russia/Tatarstan	2,749,200	24,587	Kazan'
Kharkov	Khar'kovskaya G.	Ukraine/Khar'kov	3,288,500	21,041	Khar'kov
Kherson	Khersonskaya G.	Ukraine/Nikolayev	3,495,600	27,337	Kherson
Khiva Khanate	Khiva	Uzbekistan/Kara-Kalpak			Khiva
Kielce	Keletskaya G.	Poland/Kielce	973,200	3,897	Kel'tsy
Kiev	Kievskaya G.	Ukraine/Kiyev	4,604,200	19,676	Kiev
Kostroma	Kostromskaya G.	Russia/Kostroma	1,723,700	32,432	Kostroma
Kovno	Kovenskaya G.	Lithuania	1,796,700	15,518	Kovno
Kuban	Kubanskaya Obl.	Russia/Krasnodar	2,731,100	36,645	Yekaterinodar
Kuopio	Kuopioskaya G.	Finland/Kuopio			Kuopio
Kursk	Kurskaya G.	Russia/Kursk	3,074,700	17,937	Kursk
Kutais	Kutaisskaya G.	Georgia	1,008,500	8,145	Kutais
Livonia	Liflyandskaya G.	Estonia,Latvia	1,466,900	17,574	Riga
Lomzha	Lomzhinskaya G.	Poland/Łomża	688,500	4,072	Lomzha
Lublin	Lyublinskaya G.	Poland/Lublin	1,556,600	6,499	Lyublin
Maritime	Primorskaya Obl.	Russia/Primor'ye	547,200	281,154	Khabarovsk
Minsk	Minskaya G.	Belarus/Minsk	2,868,900	35,220	Minsk
Mogilev	Mogilevskaya G.	Belarus/Mahilyow	2,261,500	18,514	Mogilev
Moscow	Moskovskaya G.	Russia/Moskva	3,257,200	12,847	Moskva
Nizhnii-Novgorod	Nizhegorodskaya G.	Russia/Nizhegorod	2,017,000	19,789	Nizhniy-Novgorod
Novgorod	Novgorodskaya G.	Russia/Novgorod	1,642,200	45,770	Novgorod
Nyland	Nyulandskaya G.	Finland/Uusimaa	3,084,000	125,689	Gel'singfors
Olonets	Olonetskaya G.	Russia/Karelia	448,700	49,355	Petrozavodsk
Orel	Orlovskaya G.	Russia/Orel	2,629,000	18,042	Orel
Orenburg	Orenburgskaya G.	Russia/Orenburg	2,093,200	73,254	Orenburg
Penza	Penzenskaya G.	Russia/Penza	1,829,700	14,997	Penza
Perm	Permskaya G.	Russia/Perm'	3,792,800	127,502	Perm'
Piotrkow	Pyotrokovskaya G.	Poland/Piotrków	1,981,300	4,730	Pyotrokov
Plotsk	Plotskaya G.	Poland/Płock	739,900	3,641	Plotsk
Podolia	Podol'skaya G.	Ukraine/Khmel'nits	3,812,000	16,224	Kamenets-Podol'sk
Poltava	Poltavskaya G.	Ukraine/Poltava	3,626,300	19,265	Poltava ▶

name	Russian name	country/division now	population	area-km	capital
Pskov	Pskovskaya G.	Russia/Pskov	1,373,300	16,678	Pskov
Radom	Radomskaya G.	Poland/Radom	1,112,200	4,769	Radom
Ryazan	Ryazanskaya G.	Russia/Ryazan'	2,510,200	16,190	Ryazan'
Saint Michel	Sankt-Mikhel'skaya G.	Finland/Mikkeli			Sankt-Mikhel'
Saint Petersburg	Sankt-Peterburgskaya G.	Russia/Leningrad	2,903,000	17,226	Sankt-Peterburg
Samara	Samarskaya G.	Russia/Samara	3,600,900	58,320	Samara
Samarkand	Samarkandskaya Obl.	Uzbekistan/Samarkand	1,183,600	26,627	Samarkand
Saratov	Saratovskaya G.	Russia/Saratov	3,125,400	32,624	Saratov
Semipalatinsk	Semipalatinskaya Obl.	Kazakhstan/Semey	848,900	178,320	Semipalatinsk
Semirechensk	Semirechenskaya Obl.	Kazakhstan/Almaty	1,210,100	144,550	Verniy
Siedlce	Sedletskaya G.	Poland/Siedlce	1,003,400	5,528	Siedlce
Simbirsk	Simbirskaya G.	Russia/Ul'yanovsk	1,961,500	19,110	Simbirsk
Smolensk	Smolenskaya G.	Russia/Smolensk	1,988,700	21,624	Smolensk
Stavropol	Stavropol'skaya G.	Russia/Stavropol'	1,273,400	20,970	Stavropol'
Sukhum	Sukhumskiy Okrug	Georgia/Abkhazia	271,500	5,765	Sukhum
Suwalki	Suvalkskaya G.	Poland/Suwałki	681,300	4,756	Suvalki
Syr Daria	Syr-Darinskaya Obl.	Kazakhstan/S. Kazakhstan	1,874,100	194,147	Tashkent
Tambov	Tambovskaya G.	Russia/Tambov	3,442,700	25,710	Tambov
Taurida	Tavricheskaya G.	Ukraine/Crimea	1,921,000	23,312	Simferopol'
Tavastehus	Tavastgusskaya G.	Finland/Häme			Tavastgus
Terek	Terskaya Obl.	Russia/Kalmyk	1,214,700	28,153	Vladikavkaz
Tiflis	Tiflisskaya G.	Georgia	1,183,300	15,776	Tiflis
Tobolsk	Tobol'skaya G.	Russia/Tyumen'	1,842,400	535,739	Tobol'sk
Tomsk	Tomskaya G.	Russia/Tomsk	3,228,300	327,173	Tomsk
Transbaikalia	Zabaykal'skaya Obl.	Russia/Chita	853,400	238,308	Chita
Transcaspian	Zakaspiyskaya Obl.	Turkmenistan	451,300	235,120	Askhabad
Tula	Tul'skaya G.	Russia/Tula	1,801,800	11,954	Tula
Turgay	Turgayskaya Obl.	Kazakhstan/Aqtöbe	624,000	169,832	Kustanay
Tver	Tverskaya G.	Russia/Tver'	2,213,800	24,975	Tver'
Ufa	Ufimskaya G.	Russia/Bashkortostan	2,942,900	47,109	Ufa
Uleåborg	Uleaborgskaya G.	Finland/Oulu			Uleaborg
Uralsk	Ural'skaya Obl.	Kazakhstan/W. Kazakhstan	782,300	137,679	Ural'sk
Vasa	Vazaskaya G.	Finland/Vaasa			Nikolaystad
Viborg	Vyborgskaya G.	Russia/Leningrad			Vyborg
Vilna	Vilenskaya G.	Lithu.,Belarus	1,957,000	16,181	Vil'no
Vitebsk	Vitebskaya G.	Latvia,Belarus/Vitsyebsk	1,850,700	16,983	Vitebsk
Vladimir	Vladimirskaya G.	Russia/Vladimir	1,918,200	18,821	Vladimir
Volhynia	Volynskaya G.	Ukraine/Volyn	3,920,400	27,699	Zhitomir
Vologda	Vologodskaya G.	Russia/Vologda	1,651,200	155,265	Vologda
Voronezh	Voronezhskaya G.	Russia/Voronezh	3,421,000	25,443	Voronezh
Vyatka	Vyatskaya G.	Russia/Kirov	3,806,800	59,329	Vyatka
Warsaw	Varshavskaya G.	Poland/Warszawa	2,547,100	6,749	Varshava
Yakutsk	Yakutskaya Obl.	Russia/Sakha	322,600	1,530,253	Yakutsk
Yaroslavl	Yaroslavskaya G.	Russia/Yaroslavl'	1,228,900	13,723	Yaroslavl'
Yekaterinoslav	Yekaterinoslavskaya G.	Ukraine/Dnepropetrovsk	3,138,200	24,477	Yekaterinoslav
Yeniseisk	Yeniseyskaya G.	Russia/Krasnoyarsk	961,600	981,607	Krasnoyarsk
Zakataly	Zakatal'skiy Okr.	Azerbaijan	95,100	1,539	Zakataly
			167,003,000	8,417,118	

Country/division now: the present-day country and division that best approximate the territory under the Russian Empire. In many cases the old division has been cut into several pieces since 1900.

Population: 1911 estimate. Entire population and area of Finland is listed under Nyland.

There were also larger divisions called general-guberniy (general governments, or governor-generalships), comprising several oblasts or guberniyas. They included Caucasus, Finland, Kiev, and Warsaw (Poland).

1914	Name of capital of Russia changed from Saint Petersburg to Petrograd.
1917-07-20	Finland declared independence from the Russian Empire.
1917	Erivan government became independent and took the name Armenia.
1918	Capital of Russia moved from Petrograd to Moscow.
1918-01-24	Bessarabia government declared independence.
1918-02-16	Lithuania, consisting mainly of the governments of Kovno and parts of Vilna and Suwalki, declared independence.

1918-02	Estonia, consisting of the government of Estonia and part of Livonia, declared independence.
1918-03-03	Treaty of Brest-Litovsk allowed Germany to occupy Byelorussia, consisting of the governments of Minsk, Mogilev, most of Grodno, part of Vitebsk, and part of Vilna. Both Germany and Russia later renounced this treaty.
1918-03	Capital of Russia moved from Petrograd to Moscow.
1918-05-26	Georgia, consisting of the governments of Kars, Kutais, and Tiflis, declared independence.
1918-05-28	Democratic Republic of Azerbaijan, consisting of the governments of Baku, Elizabethpol, and Zakataly, declared independence.
1918-07-10	Under a new constitution, Russia became the Russian (Rossiyskaya) S.F.S.R.
1918-11-09	Poland, consisting of the Kingdom of Poland (a part of Russia, divided into the governments of Kalish, Kel'tsy, Lomzha, Lyublin, Petrokov, Plotsk, Radom, Sedlets, Suvalki, and Varshava) and parts of Germany and Austria, declared independence.
1918-11-18	Latvia, consisting of the governments of Courland and parts of Livonia and Vitebsk, declared independence.
1919-01-01	Byelorussian (Byelorusskaya) S.S.R. was declared. Its territory remained in dispute.
1919-06-28	Treaty of Versailles signed. Poland's independence confirmed.
1920-04-06	Far Eastern Republic (Dal'nye-Vostochnoy Respublika; capital Chita) formed from Amur, Kamchatka, Maritime, and Transbaikalia. It was nominally independent, although coastal areas were occupied by Japan.
1920-08-26	Kirghiz A.S.S.R. formed from Akmolinsk, Semipalatinsk, Turgay, and Ural'sk regions, and the northern part of Transcaspian territory.
1920-10-07	Poland occupied the southeastern part of Vilna, including the city of Vilnius.
1921-03-18	Treaty of Riga between Poland and Russia divided Byelorussia into a western section, annexed to Poland, and an eastern section, the Byelorussian S.S.R. The latter contained almost all of Minsk and parts of Gomel', Mogilev, and Vitebsk.
1921-04-11	Turkestan A.S.S.R. formed from Amu-Darya, Ferghana, Pamir, Samarkand, Semirechensk, and Syr Darya regions, and the southern part of Transcaspian.
1922	Russia annexed the Transcaucasian Federation, which became the Transcaucasian S.S.R. (Armenia 1922-03-12, Azerbaijan 1922-12-30, Georgia 1922-12-15).
1922-11-15	Far Eastern Republic merged with Russian S.F.S.R., becoming Far Eastern Obl.
1922-12-30	Treaty of Union adopted, creating the Union of Soviet Socialist Republics (Soviet Union) (capital Moscow). The constituent republics were Byelorussian S.S.R., Russian Soviet Federated Socialist Republic (R.S.F.S.R.), Ukrainian S.S.R., and Transcaucasian S.S.R.
1924-03-03	Byelorussian S.S.R. annexed the remainder of Mogilev and Vitebsk, and part of Gomel'.
1924	Central Asian republics reorganized in the autumn to match nationalities more closely. The northern part of Turkestan was annexed to Kirghiz.
1924	Kazakh A.S.S.R. formed by merging Kirghiz A.S.S.R. with most of Semirechensk and Syr Darya.
1924	Moldavian A.S.S.R. split from Ukraine, consisting of Bessarabian territory on the left bank of the Dniestr River.
1924	Name of Petrograd oblast and city changed to Leningrad.
1924-10	Turkmen A.S.S.R. and Uzbek A.S.S.R. formed.
1924-10-14	Kara-Kirghizskaya autonomous region, consisting of parts of Ferghana, Semirechensk, and Syr Darya, separated from Turkestan and became part of the Russian S.F.S.R.
1925	Name of capital of Kara-Kirghizia changed from Pishpek to Frunze.
1925-05	Status of Uzbek and Turkmen changed from A.S.S.R.s to S.S.R.s.
1926-02-01	Status and name of Kara-Kirghizia changed to Kirghizskaya A.S.S.R.
1926-12-06	Remaining part of Gomel' transferred from Russia to Byelorussia.
1929	Capital of Kirghiz moved from Kzyl-Orda to Alma-Ata.
1929-12	Status of Tadzhik changed from A.S.S.R. to S.S.R.
1936-12-05	Under a new constitution, Transcaucasian S.S.R. split into Armenian S.S.R., Azerbaijan S.S.R., and Georgian S.S.R.; status of Kazakh and Kirghiz changed from A.S.S.R. to S.S.R.

1936-12-05	Name and status of Kirghiz changed to Kazakh (Kazakhskaya) S.S.R.
1938	Far Eastern territory split into Khabarovsk and Maritime territories.
1939-09-17	The Soviet Union invaded Poland. By November, Poland had been divided between Germany and the Soviet Union. West Byelorussia (from Poland) merged with the Byelorussian S.S.R. The territory changed hands back and forth during the war. By 1946, Byelorussia had essentially the territory that is now Belarus.
1940-03-12	Soviet Union gained about half of Kymen province (with the port of Viborg) and part of Kuopio from Finland.
1940-03-31	Karelian A.S.S.R. merged with territory ceded by Finland to form Karelo-Finnish S.S.R.
1940-06	Northern Bukovina ceded to Soviet Union by treaty.
1940-08-02	Moldavian S.S.R. created by merging most of the conquered Bessarabian territory with half of the Moldavian A.S.S.R. Northern Bukovina, the other half of the Moldavian A.S.S.R., and part of Bessarabia, merged with Ukraine.
1940-08	Soviet Union annexed the three Baltic republics: Lithuania (1940-08-03), Latvia (1940-08-05), and Estonia (1940-08-06). All three became S.S.R.s.
1944	Tannu Tuva, independent from Mongolia since 1921-07-11 as the Urjanchai Republic, became an autonomous oblast of the Soviet Union.
1945-06-29	Soviet Union acquired Ruthenia from Czechoslovakia by treaty. It became the region of Transcarpathia within the Ukrainian S.S.R.
1945-07-16	Potsdam Conference began. As a result, the northern part of East Prussia became Kaliningrad region of the Russian S.F.S.R. (1946-04-07). The Soviet Union recovered territory lost in the Russo-Polish War, annexing it to the republics of Byelorussia, Lithuania, and Ukraine.
1945-09-02	Former Russian territories reverted to the Soviet Union by Japan's surrender. They included the southern half of Sakhalin Island, Kwantung peninsula, and all of the Kuril Islands.
1946	Crimean A.S.S.R. became an oblast (Krymskaya Oblast') of the Russian S.F.S.R.
1946-07	Name of capital of Kaliningrad changed from Königsberg to Kaliningrad.
1947-02-10	By Paris Peace Treaty, Finland ceded territory to the Soviet Union, including the strip of Lappi that had connected Finland to the Arctic Ocean around Petsamo. Bessarabia formally restored to the Soviet Union.
1954-02-19	Crimea transferred from Russian S.F.S.R. to Ukrainian S.S.R.
1955	Kwantung territory returned to China by the Soviet Union.
1956-07-16	Karelo-Finnish S.S.R. became Karelian A.S.S.R., part of the Russian S.F.S.R.
1958-07-07	Name of Buryat-Mongol A.S.S.R. changed to Buryat.
1991-12-08	Commonwealth of Independent States formed.
1991-12-25	Soviet Union officially dissolved. Its 15 constituent republics became independent countries. Many of them had already unilaterally declared independence in the preceding few months. The Russian S.F.S.R. became the Russian Federation. Its internal divisions were unchanged, except that A.S.S.R.s became simply republics.
~1994	Chechen-Ingush republic split into Chechnya and Ingushetia. Both have been fighting for independence, but are still considered part of Russia.
~1994	Moscow City split from Moscow region; Saint Petersburg City split from Leningrad region.

Other names of subdivisions:

Note: There are many ways of transliterating from the Cyrillic alphabet to the Roman. The methods used tend to be specific to a target language. For example, English speakers normally transliterate the Russian word for emperor as tsar; German speakers render it czar. Both transliterations are intended to transcribe the sounds of Russian so that the reader will be able to approximate them. Here are some consistent patterns that you will observe in alternative transliterations. The letter or cluster of letters used by the present book appears first, followed by some other possibilities, tagged with cues to the context in which these alternatives might be used. The tag "(Slavic)" refers to Eastern European languages written in the Roman alphabet. Serbo-Croatian is essentially a single language that is written with Cyrillic letters by Serbs and Roman letters by Croats. There is a direct substitution of letters used for converting between Serb and Croatian that defines the Slavic transliteration. The Slavic seems to be gaining acceptance as a language-neutral Romanization.

v: f, ff (older); w (German)
y: i, no letter; j (German, Slavic)
': y, no letter
zh: ž (Slavic); j (French, Portuguese)
dzh: j; g (Italian, before e or i)
kh: x; j; ch (German); h (Slavic)

sh: ch (French); š (Slavic); sch (German); sj (Norwegian)
ch: tch (French); tsch (German); c or ci (Italian); č (Slavic); tsj (Norwegian)
ts: c, z, tz, or cz (German); c (Slavic)
z: s (German)

Ordinarily, Russian sources use the adjectival form of the name, followed by the type of division. Several of the capital names were changed to honor heroes of the Soviet Union, and then changed back to their original names when the heroes fell from favor, or when the Soviet Union shut down.

Adygey: Adygea, Adygeya, Republic of Adygeya (variant); Adygeyskaya A.Obl. (obsolete); Respublika Adygeya (Russian)

Aga Buryat: Aga-Buryatiya, Agin-Buryat, Agino-Buryatiya, Aginsk A.Okr. (variant); Aginskiy Buryatskiy A.Okr. (Russian)

Altay: Altayskiy Kray (Russian)

Amur: Amurskaya Obl. (Russian)

Arkhangel'sk: Arcangelo (Italian); Archangel, Archangelsk (variant); Arkhangel'skaya Obl. (Russian)

Astrakhan': Astrachan (variant); Astrakhanskaya Obl. (Russian)

Bashkortostan: Bashkir, Bashkirskaya A.S.S.R., Republic of Bashkortostan (variant); Respublika Bashkortostan (Russian); Ufa, Ufimskaya G. (obsolete)

Belgorod: Belgorodskaya Obl. (Russian)

Bryansk: Bryanskaya Obl. (Russian)

Buryat: Buryatiya, Buryat-Mongol A.S.S.R., Republic of Buryatia (variant); Buryatskaya A.S.S.R. (obsolete); Respublika Buryatiya (Russian)

Chechnya: Chechen-Ingush A.S.S.R., Checheno-Ingushetia, Checheno-Ingushskaya A.S.S.R. (obsolete); Chechen Republic, Chechnya-Ichkeria (variant); Chechenskaya Respublika (Russian)

Chelyabinsk: Chelyabinskaya Obl. (Russian)

Chita: Chitinskaya Obl. (Russian); Transbaikalia, Zabaykal'skaya Obl. (obsolete); Transbaikalien (German-obsolete)

Chukot: Chukchi A.Okr. (variant); Chukotskiy A.Okr. (Russian)

Chuvash: Chuvashskaya A.S.S.R. (Russian); Chuvashskaya Respublika, Chuvashiya, Chuvash Republic

Dagestan: Dagestanskaya A.S.S.R. (obsolete); Daghestan, Republic of Dagestan (variant); Respublika Dagestan (Russian)

Evenk: Evenki (variant); Evenkiyskiy A.Okr. (Russian)

Gorno-Altay: Gorno-Altayskaya A.Obl. (Russian); Oirot (obsolete); Republic of Altai (variant)

Ingush: Ingushetiya, Ingush Republic (variant); Ingushskaya Respublika (Russian)

Irkutsk: Irkutskaya Obl. (Russian)

Ivanovo: Ivanovskaya Obl. (Russian)

Kabardin-Balkar: Kabardin A.S.S.R., Kabardino-Balkarskaya A.S.S.R. (obsolete); Kabardino-Balkariya, Kabardino-Balkarsk (variant); Kabardino-Balkarskaya Respublika (Russian)

Kaliningrad: Kaliningradskaya Obl. (Russian)

Kalmyk: Kalmykiya, Khalmg Tangch, Republic of Kalmykia (variant); Kalmytskaya A.S.S.R. (obsolete); Respublika Kalmykiya (Russian)

Kaluga: Kaluzhskaya Obl. (Russian)

Kamchatka: Kamchatskaya Obl. (Russian)

Karachay-Cherkess: Karachay-Cherkessiya, Karachayevo-Cherkesskaya Respublika (Russian); Karachayevo-Cherkessiya, Karachayevo-Cherkess Republic (variant)

Karelia: Karelian A.S.S.R., Karelo-Finnish A.S.S.R., Karel'skaya A.S.S.R., Olonets, Olonetskaya G. (obsolete); Kareliya, Republic of Karelia (variant); Respublika Kareliya (Russian)

Kemerovo: Kemerovskaya Obl. (Russian)

Khabarovsk: Khabarovskiy Kray (Russian)

Khakass: Khakassiya, Republic of Khakasia (variant); Khakasskaya A.Obl. (obsolete); Respublika Khakasiya (Russian)

Khanty-Mansiy: Khanty-Mansiysk (variant); Khanty-Mansiyskiy A.Okr. (Russian)

Kirov: Vyatka, Vyatskaya G. (obsolete); Kirovskaya Obl. (Russian)

Komi: Komi A.S.S.R., Republic of Komi (variant); Respublika Komi (Russian)

Komi-Permyak: Komi-Permyatskiy A.Okr. (Russian)

Koryak: Koryakskiy A.Okr. (Russian)

Kostroma: Kostromskaya Obl. (Russian)

Krasnodar: Cossacks of the Black Sea, Kuban, Kubanskaya Obl., Yekaterinodar (obsolete); Krasnodarskiy Kray (Russian)

Krasnoyarsk: Krasnoyarskiy Kray (Russian); Yeniseisk, Yeniseyskaya G. (variant)

Kurgan: Kurganskaya Obl. (Russian)

Kursk: Kurskaya Obl. (Russian)

Leningrad: Saint Petersburg, Sankt-Peterburgskaya G. (obsolete); Leningradskaya Obl. (Russian)

Lipetsk: Lipetskaya Obl. (Russian)

Magadan: Magadanskaya Obl. (Russian)

Mariy-El: Mari, Mari-El, Republic of Mari El (variant); Mariyskaya A.S.S.R. (obsolete); Respublika Mariy El (Russian)

Mordovia: Mordov, Mordvian Autonomous Republic, Mordvinia, Republic of Mordovia (variant); Mordovian

A.S.S.R., Mordovskaya A.S.S.R., Mordva A.S.S.R. (obsolete); Respublika Mordoviya (Russian)

Moskva: Mosca (Italian); Moscou (French); Moscow (variant); Moscú (Spanish); Moskau (German); Moskovskaya Obl. (Russian)

Murmansk: Murmanskaya Obl. (Russian)

Nenets: Nenetskiy A.Okr. (Russian)

Nizhegorod: Gor'kiy, Gor'kovskaya Obl., Gorky (obsolete); Nizhegorodskaya Obl. (Russian); Nizhniy-Novgorod (variant)

North Ossetia: Respublika Severnaya Osetiya, Severnaya Osetiya-Alaniya (Russian); North Ossetian A.S.S.R., Severo-Osetinskaya A.S.S.R. (obsolete); North Osetiya-Alaniya, Republic of North Ossetia (variant)

Novgorod: Novgorodskaya Obl. (Russian)

Novosibirsk: Novosibirskaya Obl. (Russian)

Omsk: Omskaya Obl. (Russian)

Orel: Orlovskaya Obl. (Russian); Or'ol, Oryol (variant)

Orenburg: Chkalov (obsolete); Orenburgskaya Obl. (Russian)

Penza: Penzenskaya Obl. (Russian)

Perm': Molotov (obsolete); Permskaya Obl. (Russian)

Primor'ye: Küsten-Gebiet (German); Maritime Territory, Primorsk (variant); Primorskiy Kray (Russian)

Pskov: Pskovskaya Obl. (Russian)

Rostov: Province of the Don Cossacks, Provinz des Donischen Heeres, Voyska Donskovo Obl. (obsolete); Rostovskaya Obl. (Russian)

Ryazan': Ryazanskaya Obl. (Russian)

Saint Petersburg City: Saint-Pétersbourg (French); Sankt-Peterburg (Russian); Sankt Petersburg (German); San Pietroburgo (Italian)

Sakha: Republic of Sakha, Yakutia-Sakha, Yakutsk (variant); Yakut A.S.S.R., Yakutskaya A.S.S.R. (obsolete); Respublika Sakha (Russian)

Sakhalin: Sakhalinskaya Obl. (Russian)

Samara: Kuybyshev, Kuybyshevskaya Obl. (obsolete); Samarskaya Obl. (Russian)

Saratov: Saratovskaya Obl. (Russian)

Smolensk: Smolenskaya Obl. (Russian)

Stavropol': Stavropol'skiy Kray (Russian)

Sverdlovsk: Sverdlovskaya Obl. (Russian); Yekaterinburg (obsolete)

Tambov: Tambovskaya Obl. (Russian)

Tatarstan: Kazan, Kazanskaya G., Tatar A.S.S.R., Tatarskaya A.S.S.R. (obsolete); Republic of Tatarstan (variant); Respublika Tatarstan (Russian)

Taymyr: Dolgan-Nenets, Dolgano-Nenetskiy A.Okr. (variant); Taymyrskiy A.Okr. (Russian)

Tomsk: Tomskaya Obl. (Russian)

Tula: Tul'skaya Obl. (Russian)

Tuva: Respublika Tyva (Russian), Republic of Tuva, Tyva (variant); Tuvinskaya A.S.S.R. (obsolete)

Tver': Kalinin, Kalininskaya Obl. (obsolete); Tverskaya Obl. (Russian)

Tyumen': Tobol'sk, Tobol'skaya G. (obsolete); Tyumenskaya Obl. (Russian)

Udmurt: Udmurtiya, Udmurt Republic (variant); Udmurtskaya A.S.S.R. (obsolete); Udmurtskaya Respublika (Russian)

Ul'yanovsk: Simbirsk, Simbirskaya G. (obsolete); Ul'yanovskaya Obl. (Russian)

Ust-Orda Buryat: Ust'-Ordynsk Buryat A.Okr. (variant); Ust'-Ordynskiy Buryatskiy A.Okr. (Russian)

Vladimir: Vladimirskaya Obl. (Russian)

Vologda: Vologodskaya Obl. (Russian)

Volgograd: Stalingrad (obsolete); Volgogradskaya Obl. (Russian)

Voronezh: Voronezhskaya Obl. (Russian)

Yamal-Nenets: Yamalo-Nenetskiy A.Okr. (Russian)

Yaroslavl': Yaroslavskaya Obl. (Russian)

Yevrey: Den jødiske autonome oblasten (Norwegian); Evrey, Jewish A.Obl. (variant); Provincia autônoma dos Judeus (Portuguese); Yevreyskaya A.Obl. (Russian)

Population history of the U.S.S.R.:

name	1926	1939	1959	1970	1989	area-km	capital
Armenia	870,700	1,282,000	1,768,000	2,492,000	3,283,000	29,800	Yerevan
Azerbaidzhan	2,312,000	3,205,000	3,700,000	5,117,000	7,029,000	86,600	Baku
Byelorussia	4,983,900	8,910,000	8,060,000	9,002,000	10,200,000	207,600	Minsk
Estonia	— —	— —	1,196,000	1,356,000	1,573,000	45,100	Tallinn
Georgia	2,668,000	3,540,000	4,049,000	4,686,000	5,449,000	69,700	Tbilisi
Kazakhstan	— —	6,094,000	9,301,000	12,849,000	16,538,000	2,717,300	Alma-Ata
Kirghizia	— —	1,458,000	2,063,000	2,933,000	4,291,000	198,500	Frunze
Latvia	— —	— —	2,094,000	2,364,000	2,681,000	63,700	Riga
Lithuania	— —	— —	2,713,000	3,128,000	3,690,000	65,200	Vilnius
Moldavia	— —	— —	2,880,000	3,569,000	4,341,000	33,700	Kishinev
Russia	100,858,000	108,379,000	117,494,000	130,079,000	147,386,000	17,075,400	Moscow
Tadzhikistan	822,600	1,484,000	1,982,000	2,900,000	5,112,000	143,100	Dushanbe
Turkmenistan	1,030,500	1,252,000	1,520,000	2,159,000	3,534,000	488,100	Ashkhabad
Ukraine	29,020,300	40,469,000	41,893,000	47,126,000	51,704,000	603,700	Kiev ➤

name	1926	1939	1959	1970	1989	area-km	capital
Uzbekistan	4,447,600	6,336,000	8,113,000	11,960,000	19,906,000	447,400	Tashkent
	147,013,600	182,409,000	208,826,000	241,720,000	286,717,000	22,274,900	

Populations are by census except for 1939, which are estimated.

RWANDA

ISO = RW/FIPS = RW   Language = Kinyarwanda, French   Time zone = +2   Capital = Kigali

Rwanda was part of German East Africa in 1900. In 1919, as Germany's colonies were being divided up, Ruanda-Urundi was mandated to Belgium. It consisted of the counties of Ruanda and Urundi. It came under the administration of the Belgian Congo on 1925-08-21. In 1960, the Belgian Congo became independent; Ruanda-Urundi remained a colony until 1962-07-01. On that date, the two counties became the countries of Rwanda and Burundi.

Other names of country: Republic of Rwanda (formal–English); Republika y'u Rwanda (formal); Ruanda (Finnish, German, Italian, Portuguese); Rúanda (Icelandic); República Rwandesa (Spanish-formal).

division	abv	ISO	FIPS	population	area-km	area-mi
Butare	BT	C	RW01	601,165	1,830	707
Byumba	BM	I	RW02	519,968	4,987	1,925
Cyangugu	CY	E	RW03	331,380	2,226	859
Gikongoro	GK	D	RW04	369,891	2,192	846
Gisenyi	GS	G	RW05	468,786	2,395	925
Gitarama	GT	B	RW06	602,752	2,241	865
Kibungo	KN	J	RW07	360,934	4,134	1,596
Kibuye	KY	F	RW08	337,729	1,320	510
Kigali	KL	K	RW09	698,063	3,251	1,255
Ruhengeri	RU	H	RW10	528,649	1,762	680
				4,819,317	26,338	10,168

Status: These divisions are préfectures (Kinyarwanda: prefegitura).
Abv: Two-letter code for international compatibility (defined by the author).
ISO: Codes from ISO 3166-2.
FIPS: Codes from FIPS PUB 10-4.
Population: 1978 census.
Area-km: Square kilometers.
Area-mi: Square miles.
Capitals: Capitals have the same names as their prefectures.
Further subdivisions: The prefectures are subdivided into communes. The constitution allows the formation of sub-prefectures on a level between the prefecture and the commune, but this may not have been done yet.
Origins of names:

Kigali: Kinyarwanda for big mountain

Change history:

~1996   There is evidence that Kigali has split into two prefectures, Kigali-Ville (ISO code L) and Kigali-Rural (K), and that a new prefecture, Mutara (M) has been formed from part of Byumba, Kibungo, or both. No details are yet available.

Other names of subdivisions:

Butare: Astrida (obsolete)
Cyangugu: Shangugu (obsolete)

Gisenyi: Kisenyi (obsolete)

SAINT HELENA

ISO = SH/FIPS = SH   Language = English   Time zone = +0   Capital = Jamestown

Saint Helena has been a British possession for the entire 20th century.

Other names of country: Sainte-Hélène (French); Sankt Helena (German); Santa Elena (Spanish); Santa Helena (Portuguese); Sant'Elena (Italian); Sint Helena (Dutch).

Origin of name: named after Saint Helena (248?-328?), mother of Eastern Roman Emperor Constantine; discovered by João da Nova on Saint Helena's Day, 1502-08-18.

division	ISO	FIPS	population	area-km	area-mi	capital
Ascension	AC	SH01	1,007	88	34	Georgetown
Saint Helena	SH	SH02	5,564	122	47	Jamestown
Tristan da Cunha	TA	SH03	313	98	38	Edinburgh
			6,884	308	119	

Status: These divisions are an administrative area (Ascension) and two dependencies.
ISO: Codes from ISO 3166-2.
FIPS: Codes from FIPS PUB 10-4.
Population: 1988 estimates.
Area-km: Square kilometers.
Area-mi: Square miles.
Capitals: These are not formally so designated; they are the only significant population centers.
Territorial extent: Tristan da Cunha includes Inaccessible Island, Gough Island, and the Nightingale Islands.
Origins of names:

Ascension Island: discovered by João da Nova on 1501-06-01, Ascension Day

Tristan da Cunha: discovered by Portuguese navigator Tristão da Cunha in 1506

Change history:

1922	Ascension transferred from direct rule by the Admiralty Board to Saint Helena.
1938-01-12	Tristan da Cunha became a dependency of Saint Helena.

Other names of subdivisions:

Ascension: Ascensão (Portuguese)

Tristan da Cunha: Tristão da Cunha (Portuguese)

SAINT KITTS-NEVIS

ISO = KN/FIPS = SC   Language = English   Time zone = -4   Capital = Basseterre

At the beginning of the 20th century, Saint Kitts-Nevis was part of the Leeward Islands, a British colony which consisted of five presidencies. On 1956-06-30, each presidency became a separate colony. Saint Kitts became part of the colony of Saint Kitts-Nevis-Anguilla. Anguilla seceded unilaterally in 1967. Saint Kitts-Nevis became fully independent on 1983-09-19. The names Saint Kitts and Saint Christopher are used interchangeably.

Other names of country: Federation of Saint Kitts and Nevis (formal–English); Saint Christopher and Nevis (variant); Saint Christopher och Nevis (Swedish); Saint Christopher og Nevis (Danish, Norwegian); Saint Kitts ja Nevis (Finnish); Saint-Christophe et Niévès (French); San Cristóbal-Nevis, San Cristóbal y Nieves, Saint Kitts y Nevis (Spanish); Sankt Kitts und Nevis (German); Sankti Kristófer og Nevis (Icelandic); São Cristóvão-Neves (Portuguese); Sint Christopher en Nevis (Dutch).

Origin of name: Saint Kitts named by Christopher Columbus in 1493 after his patron saint, Saint Christopher (3rd cent.);

Kitts is a diminutive of Christopher. Nevis originally named Nuestra Señora de las Nieves (Our Lady of the Snows) by the Spanish, as the clouds formed at the mountain top resembled snow.

division	abv	ISO	FIPS	population	st	capital
Christ Church Nichola Town	CC	CCN	SC01	1,989	K	Mansion
Saint Anne Sandy Point	AS	ASP	SC02	3,145	K	Sandy Point
Saint George Basseterre	GB	GBA	SC03	14,283	K	Basseterre
Saint George Gingerland	GG	GGI	SC04	2,295	N	Gingerland
Saint James Windward	JW	JWI	SC05	1,691	N	Newcastle
Saint John Capisterre	JC	JCA	SC06	3,163	K	Sadlers
Saint John Figtree	JF	JFI	SC07	2,224	N	Fig Tree
Saint Mary Cayon	MC	MCA	SC08	3,308	K	Cayon
Saint Paul Capisterre	PP	PCA	SC09	2,080	K	Saint Paul's
Saint Paul Charlestown	PL	PCH	SC10	1,700	N	Charlestown
Saint Peter Basseterre	PB	OBS	SC11	2,497	K	Monkey Hill Village
Saint Thomas Lowland	TL	TLO	SC12	1,975	N	Cotton Ground
Saint Thomas Middle Island	TM	TMI	SC13	2,255	K	Middle Island
Trinity Palmetto Point	TP	TPP	SC15	1,161	K	Boyd's
				43,766		

Status: These divisions are parishes.
Abv: Two-letter code for international compatibility (defined by the author).
ISO: Codes from ISO 3166-2.
FIPS: Codes from FIPS PUB 10-4.
Population: 1980 census.
St: The two islands of Saint Kitts (ISO code K, chief town Basseterre) and Nevis (N, Charlestown) are states.
Capital: Not official. This column shows a chief town in each parish.
Territorial extent: Includes tiny Booby Island between the two main islands.

Change history:

1967-06-16   Anguilla seceded unilaterally from Saint Kitts-Nevis-Anguilla.

SAINT LUCIA

ISO = LC/FIPS = ST   Language = English   Time zone = -4   Capital = Castries

Saint Lucia was a British possession until granted independence on 1979-02-22.
Other names of country: Sainte-Lucie (French); Sankti Lúsía (Icelandic); Santa Lucia (Italian); Santa Lucía (Spanish); Santa Lúcia (Portuguese); Sint Lucia (Dutch).
Origin of name: after Saint Lucy (3rd cent.).

division	abv	ISO	FIPS	population	division	abv	ISO	FIPS	population
Anse-la-Raye	AR	AR	ST01	5,564	Laborie	LB		ST07	8,271
Canaries	CN			1,987	Micoud	MI	MI	ST08	16,660
Castries	CS	CA	ST03	57,401	Soufrière	CO	SO	ST09	8,478
Choiseul	CH		ST04	7,065	Vieux Fort	VF	VF	ST10	14,512
Dennery	DE	DE	ST05	12,333					147,180
Gros Islet	GI	GI	ST06	14,909					

Status: These divisions are districts.
Abv: Two-letter code for international compatibility (defined by the author).
ISO: Codes from ISO 3166-2. ISO also lists Babonneau (BA) and calls the districts "administrative regions."
FIPS: Codes from FIPS PUB 10-4. FIPS also lists Dauphin (ST02) and Praslin (ST11), and calls the districts "quarters."

Population: 1996-07-01 estimate.
Capital: Capitals have the same name as their district.
Territorial extent: Vieux Fort includes the small Maria Islands.

SAINT PIERRE AND MIQUELON

ISO = PM/FIPS = SB   Language = French   Time zone = -3 [d]   Capital = Saint-Pierre

Saint Pierre and Miquelon was a colony of France. It became a territoire d'outre-mer (overseas territory) in 1946, a département d'outre-mer (overseas department) on 1976-07-19, and then a collectivité territoriale (territorial collectivity) on 1985-06-11. Saint Pierre and Miquelon has a department code of 975, which is an extension of the French system.

Other names of country: Saint-Pierre-et-Miquelon (French); Saint-Pierre og Miquelon (Norwegian); Saint-Pierre und Miquelon (German); San Pedro y Miquelón (Spanish); São Pedro e Miquelon (Portuguese); Sint Pierre en Miquelon (Dutch); Territorial Collectivity of Saint Pierre and Miquelon (formal–English).

Origin of name: after the two main islands constituting the territory.

division	abv	population	area-km	area-mi	capital
Miquelon-Langlade	ML	710	216	83	Miquelon
Saint-Pierre	SP	5,682	26	10	Saint-Pierre
		6,392	242	93	

Status: These divisions are communes.
Abv: Two-letter code for international compatibility (defined by the author).
Population: 1990 estimate.
Area-km: Square kilometers.
Area-mi: Square miles.
Territorial extent: The island of Miquelon consists of two masses, called Grande Miquelon and Langlade (Petite Miquelon), connected by a narrow strip of land.
Origins of names:

Saint-Pierre: after Saint Peter (1st cent.)   Miquelon: Norman diminutive for the male surname, Michel

SAINT VINCENT AND THE GRENADINES

ISO = VC/FIPS = VC   Language = English   Time zone = -4   Capital = Kingstown

Saint Vincent was a British colony until it became independent on 1979-10-27, taking its present name.

Other names of country: Saint-Vincent-et-Grenadines (French); Saint Vincent ja Grenadiinit (Finnish); Saint Vincent och Grenadinerna (Swedish); Saint Vincent og Grenadinene (Norwegian); Saint Vincent og Grenadinerne (Danish); Sankti Vinsent og Grenadíneyjar (Icelandic); Sankt Vincent und die Grenadinen (German); San Vicente y las Granadinas (Spanish); São Vincente e Granadinas (Portuguese); Sint Vincent (Dutch).

Origin of name: Saint Vincent; Grenadines is the name of the island group of which the largest is Grenada.

division	ISO	FIPS	capital	division	ISO	FIPS	capital
Charlotte	CH	VC01	Georgetown	Saint David	DA	VC03	Chateaubelair
Grenadines	GT	VC06	Port Elizabeth	Saint George	GE	VC04	Kingstown
Saint Andrew	AN	VC02	Layou	Saint Patrick	PA	VC05	Barrouallie

Status: These divisions are parishes.

ISO: Codes from ISO 3166-2.

FIPS: Codes from FIPS PUB 10-4.

Capital: Not official. This column shows a chief town in each parish.

Territorial extent: All of the parishes except Grenadines are mostly or entirely on Saint Vincent island.

Charlotte includes the Cow and Calves, rocks off the north shore of Saint Vincent.

Grenadines includes the northern Grenadine Islands, from Petit Saint Vincent in the south to Bequia in the north. The largest islands are Bequia, Mustique, Canouan, and Union.

Saint George includes the offshore islets Milligan Cay and Young Island.

SAMOA

ISO = WS/FIPS = WS   Language = Samoan, English   Time zone = -11   Capital = Apia

By 1900, the islands of Samoa had recently been divided between Germany and the United States. The line between them fell at about 171° W., with Germany getting the islands to the west. German Samoa was occupied by New Zealand and Britain on 1914-08-29, and mandated to New Zealand by the League of Nations in 1920. The mandate was converted to a United Nations trusteeship in 1946. It voted for independence, which was granted on 1962-01-01. Although the ISO standard gives Samoa as the short name, the country is still generally called Western Samoa to distinguish it from American Samoa.

Other names of country: Estado Independiente de Samoa Occidental, Samoa Occidental (Spanish); Independent State of Western Samoa (formal–English); Länsi-Samoa (Finnish); Malotuto'atasi o Samoa i Sisifo (formal); Samoa occidentales (French); Samoa Occidentali (Italian); Samoa Ocidental (Portuguese); Västsamoa (Swedish); Vest-Samoa (Norwegian); Vestsamoa (Danish); Vestur-Samóa (Icelandic); Western Samoa (English-obsolete); West Samoa (Dutch); Westsamoa (German).

Origin of name: may be from a chief's name, or may mean "place of the moa."

division	ISO	FIPS	population	island	division	ISO	FIPS	population	island
A'ana	AA	WS01	18,000	Upolu	Palauli	PA	WS08	8,000	Savai'i
Aiga-i-le-Tai	AL	WS02	4,000	Upolu	Satupa'itea	SA	WS09	4,000	Savai'i
Atua	AT	WS03	18,000	Upolu	Tuamasaga	TU	WS10	51,000	Upolu
Fa'asaleleaga	FA	WS04	10,000	Savai'i	Va'a-o-Fonoti	VF	WS06	2,000	Upolu
Gaga'emauga	GE	WS05	6,000	Savai'i, Upolu	Vaisigano	VS	WS11	6,000	Savai'i
Gagaifomauga	GI	WS07	5,000	Savai'i				132,000	

Status: These divisions are districts.

ISO: Codes from ISO 3166-2.

FIPS: Codes from FIPS PUB 10-4.

Population: 1966 census.

Island: Which of the main islands contains each district.

Capitals: The districts do not have capitals.

Territorial extent: Aiga-i-le-Tai district contains the small islands of Apolima and Manono.

Atua district contains the uninhabited islands of Namu'a, Nu'utele, and Nu'ulua.

A'ana district has an enclave on the coast of Upolu, surrounded on three sides by Aiga-i-le-Tai.

Gaga'emauga district, which lies primarily on Savai'i island, has two enclaves on Upolu. One is on the north shore and is surrounded by Tuamasaga; the other on the south shore, between Tuamasaga and A'ana.

Satupa'itea and Palauli each consist of two separate sections with part of the other in between.

The country's capital, Apia, is in Tuamasaga district.

SAN MARINO

ISO = SM/FIPS = SM   Language = Italian   Time zone = +1 ^{d} Capital = San Marino

San Marino has been an independent republic for the whole of the 20th century.

Other names of country: Most Serene Republic of San Marino (formal–English); Saint-Marin (French); San Marínó (Icelandic); Serenissima Repubblica di San Marino (formal).

Origin of name: after Saint Marinus (4th cent.), a stonecutter of Rimini who founded San Marino as a refuge from persecution.

division	ISO	FIPS	population	division	ISO	FIPS	population
Acquaviva	AC	SM01	1,240	Fiorentino	FI	SM05	1,716
Borgo Maggiore	BM	SM06	5,127	Monte Giardino	MG	SM08	672
Chiesanuova	CH	SM02	812	San Marino	SM	SM07	4,385
Domagnano	DO	SM03	2,146	Serravalle	SE	SM09	7,706
Faetano	FA	SM04	795				24,599

Status: These divisions are castelli (sing. castello: municipalities).
ISO: Codes from ISO 3166-2.
FIPS: Codes from FIPS PUB 10-4.
Population: 1993-12-31 estimate.
Capital: Capitals have same names as their municipalities.
Origins of names:

Acquaviva: = living water (after a spring in a rock face)   Chiesanuova: = new church

SÃO TOMÉ AND PRÍNCIPE

ISO = ST/FIPS = TP   Language = Portuguese   Time zone = +0   Capital = São Tomé

São Tomé and Príncipe was a Portuguese colony at the beginning of the 20th century. In 1951 it was made an overseas province of Portugal. It became independent on 1975-07-12.

Other names of country: Democratic Republic of Sao Tome and Principe (formal–English); República Democrática de São Tomé e Príncipe (formal); Santo Tomé y Príncipe (Spanish); São Tomé e Príncipe (Italian, Portuguese); Sao Tomé-et-Principe (French); São Tomé ja Príncipe (Finnish); São Tomé och Príncipe (Swedish); São Tomé og Príncipe (Danish, Norwegian); Saó Tóme og Prinsípe (Icelandic); São Tomé und Principe (German); Sint Tome en Principe (Dutch).

Origin of name: São Tomé after Saint Thomas.

division	abv	ISO	FIPS	population	area-km	area-mi	capital
Príncipe	PR	P	TP01	5,255	142	55	Santo António
São Tomé	ST	S	TP02	91,356	859	332	São Tomé
				96,611	1,001	387	

Status: These divisions are concelhos (municipalities).
Abv: Two-letter code for international compatibility (defined by the author).
ISO: Codes from ISO 3166-2.
FIPS: Codes from FIPS PUB 10-4.
Population: 1991 census.
Area-km: Square kilometers.
Area-mi: Square miles.

Further subdivisions: The municipalities are further subdivided into distritos (districts). Príncipe is coextensive with its district, but São Tomé has six districts.

Territorial extent: Príncipe consists of the islands of Príncipe, Caroço, Bombom, and the Pedras Tinhosas. São Tomé consists of São Tomé and Rôlas islands.

SAUDI ARABIA

ISO = SA/FIPS = SA Language = Arabic Time zone = +3 Capital = Riyadh

In 1900, Arabia occupied the interior and south coast of the Arabian peninsula. It consisted of the regions of Jebel Shammar (El Shammar), Hadramaut, and Nejd. The eastern and western shores of the peninsula belonged to the Ottoman Empire. The western shore included the vilayets (districts) of Hejaz, Asir, and Yemen; the eastern shore was El Hasa. The borders of these regions were ill-defined, running through deserts. King Abdul-Aziz ibn Sa'ud, King of Nejd, conquered El Hasa, Jebel Shammar, Hejaz, and Asir successively between 1913 and 1926. He proclaimed the Kingdom of Hejaz and Nejd in 1927, and renamed it to Sa'udi Arabia effective 1932-09-23. Two lozenge-shaped neutral zones were created on the northern border in 1922, one with Iraq and the other with Kuwait, but both have been partitioned and annexed since then.

Other names of country: al-Mamlaka al-'Arabiya as-Sa'udiya (formal); Arabia Saudita (Italian, Spanish); Arábia Saudita (Portuguese); Arabie Saoudite (French); Kingdom of Saudi Arabia (formal–English); Sádi-Arabía (Icelandic); Saoedi Arabië (Dutch); Saudi-Arabia (Finnish, Norwegian); Saudi-Arabien (Danish, German); Saudiarabien (Swedish).

Origin of name: named by ibn Sa'ud (~1880–1953) for himself or his family. Arabia means land of the Arabs; Arab comes from a Semitic word for desert.

division	abv	ISO	FIPS	capital	division	abv	ISO	FIPS	capital
Al Bāhah	BA	11	SA02	Baha	'Asīr	AS	14	SA11	Abha
Al Ḥudūd ash Shamāliyah	HS	08	SA15	Ar'ar	Ḥā'il	HA	06	SA13	Ha'il
Al Jawf	JF	12	SA03	Sakaka	Jīzan	JZ	09	SA17	Jizan
Al Madīnah	MD	03	SA05	Medina	Makkah	MK	02	SA14	Mecca
Al Qaṣīm	QS	05	SA08	Buraidah	Najrān	NJ	10	SA16	Najran
Ar Riyāḍ	RI	01	SA10	Riyadh	Tabūk	TB	07	SA19	Tabuk
Ash Sharqīyah	SH	04	SA06	Dammam					

Status: These divisions are manaṭiq (sing. minṭaqah: regions or emirates).

Abv: Two-letter code for international compatibility (defined by the author).

ISO: Codes from ISO 3166-2.

FIPS: Codes from FIPS PUB 10-4.

Capital: Not official capitals, but emirs (governors) have their offices there.

Further subdivisions: There is a division into four provinces, on a historical basis. Their boundaries do not necessarily coincide with emirate boundaries. The larger emirates are subdivided into districts and subdistricts.

Territorial extent: Ash Sharqīyah contains all of Saudi Arabia's islands in the Persian Gulf: Al 'Arabiyah, Abu 'Ali, Al Batinah, Tarut, Harqus, Karan, Kurayn, Al Jurayd, and others.

Jīzan includes the Farasan Islands in the Red Sea.

Makkah includes Qishran, Sirrayn, Abu Latt, and other Red Sea islands.

Tabūk includes the islands of Tiran, Sanafir, Al Hasani, Shaybara, Mashabih, and others along the Red Sea coast.

Origins of names:

Al Madīnah: Arabic for city; full name is *al-Madinat an-Nabi*: the city of the prophet

Ar Riyāḍ: Arabic for the gardens

'Asīr: = inaccessible

Hejaz: = boundary (between 'Asīr and Nejd)

Nejd: = plateau

Change history:

1914 El Hasa conquered by Nejd.

1921	Jebel Shammar conquered by Nejd and merged with Nejd region.
1922	By the Al Uqair Convention, two lozenge-shaped neutral zones were created: Iraq-Saudi Arabia (~7,000 sq. km.) and Kuwait-Saudi Arabia (5,790 sq. km.).
1924	Hejaz conquered by Nejd.
1926	Asir conquered by Nejd.
1927	Name of Nejd and its possessions changed to the Kingdom of Hejaz and Nejd.
1932-09-23	Name of country changed to Sa'udi Arabia. Provinces were now as follows:

division	capital	area-km	alt. name	division	capital	area-km	alt. name
Asir	Abha	103,936	Southern	Nejd	Riyadh	1,685,527	Central
El Hasa	Dammam	106,731	Eastern			2,244,808	
Hejaz	Mecca	348,614	Western				

1969-12	Saudi Arabia-Kuwait neutral zone divided between its two neighbors.
~1980	Northern province formed from parts of Western and Central.
1991-02	Iraq-Saudi Arabia neutral zone (ISO = NT/FIPS = NT) divided between Saudi Arabia and Iraq.
1993-11	Al Qurayyāt (ISO = SA-13/FIPS = SA09, capital Qurayat) merged with Al Jawf.

Other names of subdivisions:

Al Ḥudūd ash Shamāliyah: Northern, Northern Border, Northern Frontier (variant)

Al Jawf: Al-Jouf (variant)

Al Madīnah: Al Madinah al Munawwarah, Medina (variant)

Ar Riyāḍ: Riad (German); Riyadh (variant)

Ash Sharqiyah: Eastern (variant)

El Hasa: Al Hasa, El Hassa, Hasa (variant)

Hejaz: Al Hijaz (variant); Hedjaz (Swedish, variant); Hedjas (German); Hedsjas (Norwegian); Héyaz (Spanish); Higiaz (Italian, Portuguese)

Jīzan: Qīzān (variant)

Makkah: La Meca (Spanish); La Mecca (Italian); La Mecque (French); Meca (Portuguese); Mecca (variant); Mecka (Swedish); Mekka (German, Norwegian)

Nejd: Najd, Nedjed (variant); Nedjd (German); Negged (Italian); Néyed (Spanish)

SENEGAL

ISO = SN/FIPS = SG   Language = French   Time zone = +0   Capital = Dakar

In 1900, present-day Senegal was part of French Sudan. In 1904, it became part of the gouvernement général of French West Africa (Afrique Occidentale Française, or A.O.F.). A.O.F. initially comprised the French colonies of Ivory Coast, Dahomey, French Guinea, Senegal, and Upper Senegal and Niger. The name of Upper Senegal and Niger was changed to French Sudan on 1920-12-04. French Sudan and Senegal formed the Federation of Mali on 1959-04-04. On 1960-06-20, the Federation of Mali became independent. It split up into its two original components, Sudan and Senegal, on 1960-08-22. Senegal and The Gambia formed a federation called Senegambia from 1982-02-01 to 1989-09-21.

Other names of country: Republic of Senegal (formal–English); République du Sénégal (formal); Sénégal (French).

Origin of name: from ethnic name.

division	ISO	FIPS	population	area-km	area-mi
Dakar	DK	SG01	1,380,700	550	212
Diourbel	DB	SG03	501,000	4,359	1,683
Fatick	FK	SG09	506,500	7,935	3,064
Kaolack	KL	SG10	741,600	16,010	6,181
Kolda	KD	SG11	517,600	21,011	8,112
Louga	LG	SG08	493,900	29,188	11,270
Saint-Louis	SL	SG04	612,100	44,127	17,038
Tambacounda	TC	SG05	355,000	57,602	22,240
Thiès	TH	SG07	837,900	6,601	2,549 ➤

division	ISO	FIPS	population	area-km	area-mi
Ziguinchor	ZG	SG12	361,000	7,339	2,834
			6,307,300	194,722	75,183

Status: These divisions are régions.
ISO: Codes from ISO 3166-2.
FIPS: Codes from FIPS PUB 10-4.
Population: 1984 estimate.
Area-km: Square kilometers.
Area-mi: Square miles.
Capital: Capitals have the same names as their regions.
Further subdivisions: The regions are divided into 28 départements, which are further subdivided into arrondissements.
Origins of names:

Dakar: Wolof *n'dakar*: tamarind tree (answer to a misunderstood inquiry)

Change history:

~1980	Louga region split from Diourbel.
1984-03-24	Casamance region (FIPS code SG02, capital Ziguinchor) split into Kolda and Ziguinchor; Sine-Saloum region (FIPS code SG06, capital Kaolack) split into Fatick and Kaolack; name of Cap Vert region changed to Dakar; name of Fleuve changed to Saint-Louis; name of Sénégal Oriental changed to Tambacounda.

Other names of subdivisions:

Dakar: Cap Vert (obsolete); Dacar (Portuguese)
Saint-Louis: Fleuve, Vallée du Fleuve (obsolete)

Tambacounda: Sénégal Oriental (obsolete)

SEYCHELLES

ISO = SC/FIPS = SE   Language = English, French   Time zone = +4   Capital = Victoria

Initially a dependency of Mauritius, the Seychelles became a separate British colony in 1903-11. It gained independence on 1976-06-29.

Other names of country: Republic of Seychelles (formal–English); Seicelle (Italian); Seychellen (Dutch, German); Seychellene (Norwegian); Seychellerna (Swedish); Seychellerne (Danish); Seychelleseyjar (Icelandic); Seychellit (Finnish).

Origin of name: named in honor of Marie Jean Hérault de Séchelles, French comptroller at the time of discovery.

division	ISO	FIPS	division	ISO	FIPS
Anse aux Pins	PI	SE01	Grand' Anse (Mahé)	GM	SE13
Anse Boileau	AB*	SE02	Grand' Anse (Praslin)	GP	SE14
Anse Étoile	ET	SE03	La Digue	DI	SE15
Anse Louis	LO	SE04	La Rivière Anglaise	RA	SE16
Anse Royale	RO	SE05	Mont Buxton	MB	SE17
Baie Lazare	BL	SE06	Mont Fleuri	MF	SE18
Baie Sainte Anne	BS	SE07	Plaisance	PL	SE19
Beau Vallon	BV	SE08	Pointe la Rue	PR	SE20
Bel Air	BA	SE09	Port Glaud	PG	SE21
Bel Ombre	BO	SE10	Saint Louis	SL	SE22
Cascade	CA	SE11	Takamaka	TA	SE23
Glacis	GL	SE12			

* = The draft standard lists BO for both Anse Boileau and Bel Ombre; I changed the code for Anse Boileau to make them distinct.

Status: These divisions are districts.
ISO: Codes from ISO 3166-2.
FIPS: Codes from FIPS PUB 10-4.
Territorial extent: The main island of the Seychelles is Mahé, where the capital, Victoria, is located. Within 100 km. of it, there are Praslin, Silhouette, La Digue, North, Curieuse, and some smaller islands. More remote are the Cosmoledo Group, including Aldabra, Assumption, and Astove; the Farquhar Group, including Cerf, Saint Pierre, and Providence; and other scattered islands like Desroches.
Origins of names:

Mahé: named by Capt. Lazare Picault in honor of Bertrand-
    François Mahé, governor of Mauritius.

Change history: The divisions of the Seychelles before World War II were five districts: Central, North, Outlying Islands, Praslin, and South.

1965-11-08	Islands of Aldabra, Desroches, and Farquhar taken from Seychelles to form part of the new British Indian Ocean Territory.
1976-06-29	Aldabra, Desroches, and Farquhar Islands restored to Seychelles.

SIERRA LEONE

ISO = SL/FIPS = SL   Language = English   Time zone = +0   Capital = Freetown

In 1900, Sierra Leone consisted of a British colony occupying two coastal areas, and a British protectorate in the hinterland. Britain granted independence on 1961-04-27.
Other names of country: Republic of Sierra Leone (formal–English); Serra Leoa (Portuguese); Sierra Leona (Spanish); Síerra Leóne (Icelandic).
Origin of name: Hispanicized from Portuguese *Serra Leão*: lion mountain.

division	abv	ISO	FIPS	population	area-km	area-mi	capital
Eastern	EA	E	SL01	960,551	15,553	6,005	Kenema
Northern	NO	N	SL02	1,262,226	35,936	13,875	Makeni
Southern	SO	S	SL03	740,510	19,694	7,604	Bo
Western	WE	W	SL04	554,243	557	215	Freetown
				3,517,530	71,740	27,699	

Status: These divisions are provinces, except for Western, which is an "area."
Abv: Two-letter code for international compatibility (defined by the author).
ISO: Codes from ISO 3166-2.
FIPS: Codes from FIPS PUB 10-4.
Population: 1985 census.
Area-km: Square kilometers.
Area-mi: Square miles.
Further subdivisions: The provinces are subdivided into districts. The districts are further subdivided into chiefdoms.
Territorial extent: Eastern contains the districts of Kailahun, Kenema, and Kono.
Northern is divided into Bombali, Kambia, Koinadugu, Port Loko, and Tonkolili districts.
Southern includes Sherbro Island and the Turtle Islands. Its districts are Bo, Bonthe, Moyamba, Pujehun, and Sherbro urban district council.
Western includes the Sierra Leone peninsula, Tasso Island in the Rokel River estuary, and the Banana Islands.
Change history:

1900	Sierra Leone colony consisted of Sherbro Island and adjacent islets, and a disjoint area

	on the Sierra Leone peninsula around Freetown. Sierra Leone protectorate was divided into the districts of Bandajuma (capital Bandajuma), Karene (Karene), Koinadugu (Falaba), Panguma (Panguma), and Ronietta (Kwelu).
~1901	Capital of Karene moved to Batkanu; capital of Koinadugu moved to Kabala; capital of Ronietta moved to Moyamba.
1904	Îles de Los transferred from Sierra Leone to French Guinea by cession.
1907	Districts reorganized. Bandajuma and Panguma districts were replaced by Central, North Sherbro, and Railway. Other borders realigned.
1909	Central district split between Railway and Ronietta. Headquarters district formed from coastal sections of Karene and Ronietta.
1912	The Karene section of Headquarters was restored to Karene.
1920	Sierra Leone reorganized into three provinces: Northern (capital Makump), Central (Kenema), and Southern (Pujehun). The Freetown section of the colony remained separate, but the Sherbro Island part merged with Southern. The provinces were subdivided into 13 districts.
1931	Central province merged with Southern; capital of Northern moved from Makump to Makeni; capital of Southern moved to Bo; districts rearranged.
1932	Freetown became capital of Northern province.
1939	Capital of Northern returned to Makeni.
1945	Eastern province (capital Kenema) split from Southern.
1961-04-27	Sierra Leone became independent. Colony of Sierra Leone became Western area.

SINGAPORE

ISO = SG/FIPS = SN   Language = Chinese, Malay, Tamil, English   Time zone = +8   Capital = Singapore

In 1900, Singapore was one of the Straits Settlements. It had two dependencies: Christmas Island and Cocos (Keeling) Islands. See the history of Malaysia for the context of Singapore's changes. Singapore gained independence on 1965-08-09.

Other names of country: Cingapura (Portuguese); Republic of Singapore (formal–English); Singapour (French); Singapur (German, Spanish); Singapúr (Icelandic); Singapura (formal).

Origin of name: Hindi *singh*: lion, *pur*: city.

division	abv	population	area-km	area-mi
Singapore	SG	2,690,200	639	244

Status: This division is the whole of the country, treated as a division for compatibility.

Abv: Two-letter code for international compatibility (defined by the author).

Population: 1990 census.

Area-km: Square kilometers.

Area-mi: Square miles.

Further subdivisions: Singapore has six districts with no administrative function: Bukit Panjang, Jurong, Katong, Serangoon, Singapore City, and Southern Islands.

Territorial extent: Singapore consists entirely of islands off the southern tip of the Malay peninsula. By far the largest is Singapore Island. Some others are Pulau Tekong, Pulau Ubin, Sentosa, and Pulau Senang.

Change history:

1900	Christmas Island became part of Singapore settlement.
1903	Cocos (Keeling) Islands became part of Singapore.
1907	Labuan, an island off the coast of Borneo, merged with Singapore.
1912	Labuan split from Singapore to become a separate settlement in the Straits Settlements.
1946-04-01	Singapore split from Straits Settlements to become a British colony.

1955-11-23 Cocos (Keeling) Islands transferred from Singapore to Australia.
1958-10-01 Christmas Island transferred from Singapore to Australia.
1963-09-16 Singapore merged with other entities to form Federation of Malaysia.
1965-08-09 Singapore split from Federation of Malaysia to become an independent country.

SLOVAKIA

ISO = SK/FIPS = LO   Language = Slovak   Time zone = +1^d Capital = Bratislava

At the beginning of the 20th century, Slovakia was a region in the north of Hungary, which was one of two kingdoms linked together as the Austro-Hungarian Empire. At the end of World War I, shortly before the Armistice, the Slovaks organized a new government in northern Hungary. They merged with the Czechs to form Czechoslovakia on 1918-11-14. The Treaty of Saint-Germain (1919-09-10) confirmed the new country. During World War II, Slovakia was invaded and became a German protectorate. At the end of the war, Czechoslovakia was restored almost to its pre-war borders. The Soviet Union annexed Transcarpathian Ukraine, also known as Ruthenia, at the eastern end. By its constitution of 1948-06-09, Czechoslovakia became a "people's democratic republic." Its primary divisions were the Czech and the Slovak Socialist Republic. On 1993-01-01, the two republics became separate countries. What had been the second-level subdivisions of Czechoslovakia were now first-level subdivisions of the Czech Republic and of Slovakia.

Other names of country: Eslováquia (Portuguese); Eslovaquia, República Eslovaca (Spanish); Repubblica Slovacca, Slovacchia (Italian); République Slovaque, Slovaquie (French); Slóvakía (Icelandic); Slovakien (Swedish); Slovakiet (Danish); Slovak Republic (formal–English); Slovenská Republika, Slovensko (formal); Slowakei, Slowakische Republik (German); Slowakije (Dutch).

Origin of name: from ethnic name Slovak, a variant of Slav.

division	abv	ISO	population	area-km	area-mi	capital
Bratislava	BR		444,482	368	142	Bratislava
Central Slovakia	CS	SSS	1,622,380	17,982	6,943	Banská Bystrica
East Slovakia	ES	SVS	1,512,506	16,193	6,252	Košice
West Slovakia	WS	SZS	1,730,786	14,492	5,595	Bratislava
			5,310,154	49,035	18,932	

Status: These divisions are kraje (regions), except for Bratislava, which is a hlavné mesto (city).
Abv: Two-letter code for international compatibility (defined by the author).
ISO: Codes from ISO 3166-2.
Population: 1990-12-31 estimate.
Area-km: Square kilometers.
Area-mi: Square miles.
Further subdivisions: Bratislava is subdivided into obvodi (4 in 1978). The regions are subdivided into 38 okresi. The regions have fallen into disuse since 1993.
Origins of names:

Bratislava: Slovak Brecislava, name of an old Slav colony

Change history:

1918 Slovakia formed. It consisted of two provinces: Slovakia proper and Carpathian Ruthenia. Slovakia proper consisted of the former Hungarian counties of Árva, Bars, Lipto, Nyitra, Pozsony, Saros, Szepes, Trencsen, Turocz, Zólyom, and parts of Abauj-Torna, Gömör, Györ, Hont, Komárom, Mozsony, Nógrád, Ung, and Zemplen. Carpathian Ruthenia consisted of Bereg, Máramaros, Ugocsa, and the rest of Ung. For more details about the Hungarian counties, see Hungary listing.
1918-11-14 Slovakia merged with a Czech government in formation, creating Czechoslovakia.

1920	Poland took two small pieces of land from Slovakia near Nowy Targ.
1945-06-29	Soviet Union acquired Carpathian Ruthenia from Czechoslovakia by treaty.
1949-01-01	The země (provinces) of Slovakia were replaced by six regions. This table shows populations as of 1957-01-01. The capitals have the same names as their regions. The German names of the capitals, used during the occupation, are also shown.

region	population	area-km	German name	region	population	area-km	German name
Bratislava	970,285	7,519	Preßburg	Prešov	448,319	8,495	Preschau
Banská Bystrica	587,215	9,266	Neusohl	Nitra	747,787	7,968	Neutra
Žilina	525,072	8,269	Sillein		3,820,037	48,957	
Košice	541,359	7,440	Kaschau				

1960	Banská Bystrica and Žilina merged to form Central Slovakia; Košice and Prešov merged to form East Slovakia; Bratislava and Nitra merged to form West Slovakia.
~1970	Bratislava city split from West Slovakia.
1993-01-01	Czechoslovakia split into Slovakia and the Czech Republic. Slovakia consisted of the four divisions listed above. They had all been secondary divisions of Czechoslovakia, using the same boundaries.

The current FIPS list shows eight kraje: Banskobystricky (LO01, CS), Bratislavsky (LO02, BR), Kosicky (LO03, ES), Nitrinsky (LO04, WS), Presovsky (LO05, ES), Treciansky (LO06, WS), Trnavsky (LO07, WS), and Zilinsky (LO08, CS). The first code in parentheses is the FIPS code. The second one shows the likely correspondence between these and the kraje listed above.

Other names of subdivisions:

Bratislava: Preßburg (German)
Central Slovakia: Eslováquia Central (Portuguese); Slovacchia Centrale (Italian); Stredné Slovensko (Slovak); Středoslovenský (Czech)
East Slovakia: Eslováquia Oriental (Portuguese); Slovacchia Orientale (Italian); Východné Slovensko (Slovak); Východoslovenský (Czech)
West Slovakia: Eslováquia Ocidental (Portuguese); Slovacchia Occidentale (Italian); Západné Slovensko (Slovak); Západoslovenský (Czech)

Population history:

division	1900	1921	1930	1950	1961	1970	1982	1990
Bratislava						284,000	394,644	444,482
Central Slovakia	885,000	949,000	1,030,000	1,053,000	1,301,000	1,403,000	1,549,112	1,622,380
East Slovakia	779,000	797,000	889,000	899,000	1,113,000	1,256,000	1,428,558	1,512,506
West Slovakia	1,119,000	1,248,000	1,405,000	1,490,000	1,761,000	1,599,000	1,701,547	1,730,786
	2,783,000	2,994,000	3,324,000	3,442,000	4,175,000	4,542,000	5,073,861	5,310,154

(Populations for 1900–1950 correspond to regional boundaries as of 1961.)

SLOVENIA

ISO = SI/FIPS = SI   Language = Slovenian   Time zone = +1 [d]   Capital = Ljubljana

Before World War I, Slovenia was part of the Austro-Hungarian Empire. It consisted of Carniola and parts of Carinthia, Coastland, and Styria provinces of Austria, as well as small parts of Vasvár and Zala counties of Hungary. In the aftermath of World War I, this area was divided between the Kingdom of Serbs, Croats, and Slovenes (later Yugoslavia) and Italy. The border between Italy and Yugoslavia was settled only in 1924. In the settlement, Italy received Istria. Yugoslavia was occupied by the axis powers in World War II. After the war, Istria was joined to Yugoslavia. Part of it went to Croatia; the rest eventually became Južna Primorska and Severna Primorska in Slovenia. Meanwhile, Trieste became an independent city in 1947. Its territory was divided into the A Zone (north) and the B Zone (south). In 1954, the B Zone was annexed to Yugoslavia. Slovenia received part of it. On 1991-10-08, Slovenia declared independence from Yugoslavia.

Other names of country: Eslovenia (Spanish); Eslovênia (Portuguese); Republic of Slovenia (formal–English); Republika Slovenija (formal); Slóvenía (Icelandic); Slovenië (Dutch); Slovénie (French); Slovenien (Danish, Swedish); Slowenien (German).

Origin of name: from ethnic name Slovene, a variant of Slav.

division	abv	population	area-km	area-mi	capital
Dolenjska	DO	115,460	2,683	1,036	Nove Mesto
Gorenjska	GO	136,176	2,092	808	Kranj
Južna Primorska	JP	73,992	1,045	403	Koper
Koroška	KO	62,507	1,041	402	Slovenj Gradec
Ljubljana	LJ	316,237	2,566	991	Ljubljana
Notranjska	NO	48,682	1,455	562	Postojna
Podravska	PD	283,391	2,085	805	Maribor
Pomurska	PM	127,329	1,334	515	Murska Sobota
Posavska	PS	70,561	906	350	Krško
Savinjska	SA	185,334	2,071	800	Celje
Severna Primorska	SP	109,336	2,321	896	Nova Gorica
Zasavska	ZS	62,502	513	198	Zagorje ob Savi
		1,591,507	20,112	7,766	

Status: These divisions are upravne enote (administrative areas).

Abv: Two-letter code for international compatibility (defined by the author).

Population: 1967 estimate.

Area-km: Square kilometers.

Area-mi: Square miles.

Capitals: Actually chief towns; no official capitals.

Further subdivisions: It appears that after Slovenia became independent in 1991, it had 62 občine (communes, although the CIA World Factbook described them as pokajine [provinces]). In 1995, they were reorganized into 146 communes. A referendum in 1998 created 37 more communes. There are also several unofficial sets of higher-level divisions, which are defined as groups of communes. I felt that almost 200 divisions was too long a listing for such a small country, especially when most useful information (such as area and population) is unavailable. The international standards don't list any divisions for Slovenia. I chose a set of divisions which seem to be in current use, although they may not have a legal basis.

Territorial extent: These are the communes in each administrative area as of 1997.

Dolenjska: Novo Mesto (urban), Črnomelj, Dobrepolje, Kočevje, Loški Potok, Metlika, Osilnica, Ribnica, Semič, Šentjernej, Škocjan, Trebnje

Gorenjska: Kranj (urban), Bled, Bohinj, Cerklje na Gorenjskem, Gorenja Vas-Poljane, Jesenice, Kranjska Gora, Naklo, Prcddvor, Radovljica, Šenčur, Škofja Loka, Tržič, Železniki, Žiri

Južna Primorska: Koper (urban), Divača, Hrpelje-Kozina, Izola, Komen, Piran, Sežana

Koroška: Slovenj Gradec (urban), Črna na Koroškem, Dravograd, Mežica, Mislinja, Muta, Podvelka-Ribnica, Radlje ob Dravi, Ravne-Prevalje, Vuzenica

Ljubljana: Ljubljana (urban), Borovnica, Brezovica, Dobrova-Horjul-Polhov Gradec, Dol pri Ljubljani, Domžale, Grosuplje, Ig, Ivančna Gorica, Kamnik, Litija, Logatec, Lukovica, Medvode, Mengeš, Moravče, Škofljica, Velike Lašče, Vodice, Vrhnika

Notranjska: Cerknica, Ilirska Bistrica, Loška Dolina, Pivka, Postojna

Podravska: Maribor (urban), Ptuj (urban), Destrnik-Trnovska Vas, Dornava, Duplek, Gorišnica, Juršinci, Kidričevo, Kungota, Lenart, Majšperk, Ormož, Pesnica, Rače-Fram, Ruše, Slovenska Bistrica, Starše, Šentilj, Videm, Zavrč

Pomurska: Murska Sobota (urban), Beltinci, Cankova-Tišina, Črenšovci, Gornja Radgona, Gornji Petrovci, Hodoš-Šalovci, Kobilje, Kuzma, Lendava, Ljutomer, Moravske Toplice, Odranci, Puconci, Radenci, Rogaševci, Sveti Jurij

Posavska: Brežice, Krško, Sevnica

Savinjska: Celje (urban), Velenje (urban), Gornji Grad, Kozje, Laško, Ljubno, Luče, Mozirje, Nazarje, Podčetrtek, Radeče, Rogaška Slatina, Rogatec, Slovenske Konjice, Šentjur pri Celju, Šmarje pri Jelšah, Šmartno ob Paki, Šoštanj, Štore, Turnišče, Vitanje, Vojnik, Zreče, Žalec

Severna Primorska: Nova Gorica (urban), Ajdovščina, Bovec, Brda, Cerkno, Idrija, Kanal, Kobarid, Miren-Kostanjevica, Tolmin, Vipava

Zasavska: Hrastnik, Trbovlje, Zagorje ob Savi

Change history:

1920-07-16   Treaty of Saint-Germain took effect. Most of Coastland province annexed to Venezia region of Italy. Kingdom of Serbs, Croats, and Slovenes created.

1946	Yugoslavia organized as federal republic, with Slovenia as one of its constituent republics.
1947-02-10	Peace treaty signed. Trieste and a surrounding area were made into the Free Territory of Trieste. The rest of Venezia Giulia e Zara region transferred from Italy to Yugoslavia.
1954	Yugoslavia received Zone B of Trieste, part of which (including the port cities of Izola, Koper, and Piran) merged with Slovenia republic. During the 1950s and early '60s, Slovenia was divided into the following counties (population is 1959 estimate):

county	population	area-km		county	population	area-km
Celje	197,000	2,314		Maribor	345,000	3,208
Gorica	113,000	2,324		Murska Sobota	133,000	1,336
Koper	106,000	2,031		Novo Mesto	159,000	2,567
Kranj	135,000	2,132			1,577,000	20,251
Ljubljana	389,000	4,339				

| 1995-01-01 | Slovenia reorganized. The 62 communes were replaced with 146 communes. The latest FIPS list available shows these communes. |
| 1998-03-20 | Referendum created 37 new communes. |

Other names of subdivisions:

Ljubljana: Laibach (German)

SOLOMON ISLANDS

ISO = SB/FIPS = BP   Language = Pidgin, English   Time zone = +11   Capital = Honiara

By the end of 1900, all of the Solomon Islands were a British protectorate (except Bougainville and neighboring islands, which are geographically part of the Solomons but have been politically associated with New Guinea). The formal name was British Solomon Islands Protectorate. Most of the Solomons were occupied by Japan in World War II. The country became independent on 1978-07-07.

Other names of country: British Solomon Islands Protectorate (obsolete); Îles Salomon (French); Ilhas Salomão (Portuguese); Islas Salomón (Spanish); Isole Salomone (Italian); Salomoneilanden (Dutch); Salomonen, Salomon-Inseln (German); Salomonöarna (Swedish); Salomonøerne (Danish); Salomonøyene (Norwegian); Salomonsaaret (Finnish); Salómonseyjar (Icelandic).

Origin of name: discovered 1568 by Álvaro de Mendaña de Neira and named Islas de Solomon in the hope that they were the legendary islands of King Solomon (king of Israel 961-922 B.C.).

division	ISO	FIPS	population	area-km	area-mi	capital
Capital Territory	CT		34,900	22	8	Honiara
Central	CE	BP05	19,600	1,286	497	Tulagi
Guadalcanal	GU	BP06	50,400	5,336	2,060	Honiara
Isabel	IS	BP07	15,300	4,136	1,597	Buala
Makira and Ulawa	MK	BP08	22,300	3,188	1,231	Kirakira
Malaita	ML	BP03	85,900	4,225	1,631	Auki
Temotu	TE	BP09	16,800	895	346	Lata
Western	WE	BP04	73,100	9,312	3,595	Gizo
			318,300	28,400	10,965	

Status: These divisions are provinces, except for Capital Territory, which is a capital territory.
ISO: Codes from ISO 3166-2.
FIPS: Codes from FIPS PUB 10-4.
Population: 1990 estimate.
Area-km: Square kilometers.

Area-mi: Square miles.

Territorial extent: Capital Territory occupies part of the island of Guadalcanal.

Central includes the Florida Islands (Nggela Sule and Nggela Pile are the largest), Rennell Island, Bellona Island, Savo Island, and the Russell Islands.

Guadalcanal includes Guadalcanal Island (except Capital Territory) and adjacent islets.

Isabel includes Santa Isabel, San Jorge, Barora Fa, Barora Ite, the Ghizunabeana Islands, and others.

Makira and Ulawa includes San Cristobal, Ulawa, Uki Ni Masi, Santa Ana, and others.

Malaita includes Malaita, Maramasike, Manaoba, Ndai, and the islets and reefs of Stewart Islands (Sikaiana), Ontong Java (Lord Howe), Roncador, etc.

Temotu includes the Santa Cruz Islands (Vanikoro and Ndeni are largest).

Western includes Choiseul, Vaghena, Rob Roy, the New Georgia Islands (New Georgia, Kolombangara, Vella Lavella, Rendova, Ranongga, Gizo, etc.), and the Shortland Islands (Alu, Treasury Islands, Fauro).

Origins of names:

Guadalcanal: named by the discoverer, Álvaro de Mendaña de
    Neira, after his home town in Spain

Change history: Before World War II, the Solomon Islands were divided into the administrative districts of Choiseul, Eastern Solomons, Gizo, Guadalcanal, Lord Howe (Ontong Java), Malaita, Nggela and Savo, Rennell and Bellona Islands, Santa Cruz, Shortlands, Sikaiana (Stewart), and Ysabel (Isabel) and Cape Marsh. There were also some small islands not contained in any of these districts.

~1945   Capital of country moved from Tulagi to Honiara.

Postwar division of Solomon Islands was as follows. These districts were further subdivided into councils (in some cases one council was one district), which matched the present-day districts.

district	FIPS	population	area-km	district	FIPS	population	area-km
Central	BP01	113,317	10,780	Western	BP04	55,250	9,312
Eastern	BP02	36,577	4,083			285,176	28,400
Malaita	BP03	80,032	4,225				

Population: 1986 census.

~1988   Eastern district split into Makira and Temotu districts; Central district split into Central,
            Guadalcanal, and Isabel districts; Malaita and Western districts became provinces.
~1991   All districts became provinces.
~1992   Capital Territory split from Guadalcanal.

Other names of subdivisions:

Capital Territory: Honiara (variant)   Temotu: Eastern Islands (variant)
Makira and Ulawa: Makira (variant)

SOMALIA

ISO = SO/FIPS = SO   Language = Somali   Time zone = +3   Capital = Mogadishu

Italian Somaliland was chartered to a company until 1905, when it became a simple Italian colony. It acquired a strip of land beyond the Juba River (Italian Jubaland; Oltre Giuba [Italian]) from Kenya in 1925. In 1936-06, it merged with Eritrea and Ethiopia to form Italian East Africa (Africa Orientale Italiana), in which it was a state. After the British took it in World War II, it remained under British military government until 1950-04-01, when it was restored to Italy as a U.N. trust territory.

Meanwhile, British Somaliland was a British protectorate (except for a brief Italian occupation) until it became independent on 1960-06-26. Less than a week later, on 1960-07-01, Italian Somaliland also became independent, and the two states merged to form the Somali Republic. The border with Ethiopia has never been finally established.

Other names of country: Jamhuriyadda Dimugradiga ee Soomaaliya (formal); Somália (Portuguese); Sómalía (Icelandic); Somali Democratic Republic (formal–English); Somalie (French).

Origin of name: from local word *somal*: black, used to describe the natives.

division	ISO	FIPS	area-km	area-mi	capital	former
Awdal	AW	——	——	——	Baki	Hargeisa
Bakool	BK	SO01	27,000	10,000	Oddur	Alto Giuba
Banaadir	BN	SO02	1,657	640	Mogadishu	Banaadir
Bari	BR	SO03	70,000	27,000	Boosaaso	Migiurtinia
Bay	BY	SO04	39,000	15,000	Baidoa	Alto Giuba
Galguduud	GA	SO05	43,000	17,000	Dusa Marreb	Mudug
Gedo	GE	SO06	32,000	12,000	Garbahaarrey	Alto Giuba
Hiiraan	HI	SO07	34,000	13,000	Beled Weyne	Hiiraan
Jubbada Dhexe	JD	SO08	23,000	9,000	Bu'aale	Basso Giuba, Alto Giuba
Jubbada Hoose	JH	SO09	61,000	24,000	Kismayu	Basso Giuba
Mudug	MU	SO10	70,000	27,000	Galka'yo	Mudug, Migiurtinia
Nugaal	NU	SO11	50,000	19,000	Garoe	Migiurtinia
Sanaag	SA	SO12	54,000	21,000	Erigavo	Burao
Shabeellaha Dhexe	SD	SO13	22,000	8,000	Giohar	Banaadir
Shabeellaha Hoose	SH	SO14	25,000	10,000	Marka	Banaadir
Sool	SO	——	——	——	Laascaanood	Burao
Togdheer	TO	SO15	41,000	16,000	Burao	Burao, Hargeisa
Woqooyi Galbeed	WO	SO16	45,000	17,000	Hargeisa	Hargeisa, Burao
			637,657	245,640		

Status: These divisions are gobolka (regions).

ISO: Codes from ISO 3166-2.

FIPS: Codes from FIPS PUB 10-4.

Area-km: Square kilometers.

Area-mi: Square miles.

Former: Province(s) from ~1968 covering approximately the same area.

Further subdivisions: The regions are subdivided into 84 districts.

Change history:

1925-06-29	Transjuba (everything in modern Somalia west of the Juba River) transferred from Kenya to Italian Somaliland.
1931	Italian Somaliland at this time consisted of seven commissariats. Their names and populations in the 1931 census were Alto Giuba (292,263), Alto Uebi-Scebeli (257,219), Basso Giuba (173,994), Basso Uebi-Scebeli (109,644), Migiurtinia (48,863), Mogadiscio (20,288), and Mudugh (119,301).
1960-07-01	British Somaliland and Italian Somaliland (Somalia) merged to form the Somali Republic. Its divisions were the six districts of British Somaliland: Berbera, Borama, Burao, Erigavo, Hargeisa, and Las Anod; and the six districts of Italian Somaliland: Alto Giuba, Basso Giuba, Benadir, Hiran, Migiurtinia, and Mudugh.
~1964	North-Eastern (Burao) Province formed by merging Burao, Erigavo, and Las Anod districts; North-Western (Hargeisa) Province formed by merging Berbera, Borama, and Hargeisa districts.
~1968	Capital of Basso Giuba moved from Kismayu (Italian: Chisimaio) to Jamame. After this change, the provinces, with some of the variant names of their capitals, were:

province	population	area-km	capital
Alto Giuba	362,397	131,492	Baidoa; Baydhabo (variant); Iscia Baidoa, Isha Baidoa (obsolete)
Basso Giuba	113,774	49,917	Jamame; Margherita (Italian)
Banaadir	392,189	45,004	Mogadishu; Mogadiscio (Italian); Muqdisho (Somali)
Burao		128,000	Burao; Burco (variant)
Hargeisa		48,000	Hargeisa; Hargeysa, Harghessa (variant) ▶

province	population	area-km	capital
Hiiraan	176,603	25,647	Beled Weyne; Belet Uen, Belet Wein (variant)
Migiurtinia	82,710	90,744	Boosaaso; Bender Cassim, Bender Kassim (obsolete); Bosaso (variant)
Mudug	141,197	118,737	Galka'yo; Gaalkacyo (variant); Gallacaio, Rocca Littorio (Italian)
		637,541	

~1984   Somalia reorganized from eight provinces into sixteen regions.
~1991   Awdal region split from Woqooyi Galbeed; Sool region split from Nugaal.

Other names of subdivisions:

Alto Giuba: Alto Juba, Upper Juba (variant)
Banaadir: Benadir (variant)
Bari: East (variant)
Basso Giuba: Basso Juba, Lower Juba (variant)
Burao: Burro, Eastern, North-East (variant)
Galguduud: Galgudug (variant)
Hargeisa: Hargeysa, Harghessa, North-West, Western (variant)
Hiiraan: Hiran (variant)
Jubbada Dhexe: Central Juba (variant)

Jubbada Hoose: Lower Juba (variant)
Migiurtinia: Mijertein, Mijirtein, Mijurtein (variant)
Mudug: Madugh, Mudugh (variant)
Nugaal: Nogal (variant)
Shabeellaha Dhexe: Central Shabele (variant)
Shabeellaha Hoose: Lower Shabele (variant)
Sool: Sol (variant)
Togdheer: Togder (variant)
Woqooyi Galbeed: North-West, Woqooyi Gelbeed (variant)

SOUTH AFRICA

ISO = ZA/FIPS = SF   Language = Afrikaans, English   Time zone = +2   Capital = Pretoria, Cape Town, Bloemfontein

In 1900, the Boer republics of Orange Free State and Transvaal were fighting Great Britain and the British colonies of Cape of Good Hope and Natal in the Boer War. The British won, and the peace treaty signed on 1902-05-31 made British colonies of all four lands. On 1910-05-31, they united to form the Union of South Africa (Afrikaans: Unie van Zuid-Afrika, but the Afrikaans spelling was changed from Zuid to Suid a few years later). The country voted on independence in 1960, and on 1961-05-31 it became independent under the name Republic of South Africa. Even before independence, the South African government was planning to address its racial problems by creating homelands, or Bantustans: black-majority enclaves within its territory. The first of the Bantustans was Transkei, delimited in 1963 and granted nominal independence in 1976. There were eventually ten homelands, of which four became nominally independent. None of them ever received international recognition. In 1994, the segregationist apartheid policy came to an end, and the homelands were re-incorporated into the country. South Africa held a mandate over South-West Africa for many years (see Namibia).

Other names of country: Africa del Sud (Italian); Africa do Sul (Portuguese); Afrique du Sud (French); Etelä-Afrikka (Finnish); Repubblica Sudafricana (Italian); Republic of South Africa (formal–English); Republiek van Suid-Afrika (formal); Sør-Afrika (Norwegian); Sudáfrica (Spanish); Südafrika (German); Suður-Afríka (Icelandic); Sydafrika (Danish, Swedish); Zuid Afrika (Dutch).

Origin of name: descriptive: Southern part of African continent.

division	ISO	FIPS	CSS	population	area-km	area-mi	capital	former
Eastern Cape	EP	SF05	02	5,865,000	170,571	65,858	Bisho	Cape of Good Hope
Free State	FS	SF03	04	2,470,000	129,404	49,963	Bloemfontein	Orange Free State
Gauteng	GT	SF06	07	7,171,000	18,754	7,241	Johannesburg	Transvaal
KwaZulu-Natal	NL	SF02	05	7,672,000	91,458	35,312	Pietermaritzburg	Natal, Cape of Good Hope
Mpumalanga	ET	SF07	08	2,646,000	81,794	31,581	Nelspruit	Transvaal
North-West	NW	SF10	06	4,128,000	118,678	46,168	Mmabatho	Transvaal, Cape of Good Hope
Northern Cape	NC	SF08	03	746,000	363,292	140,268	Kimberley	Cape of Good Hope
Northern Province	NT	SF09	09	3,043,000	119,575	45,822	Pietersburg	Transvaal
Western Cape	WP	SF11	01	4,118,000	129,352	49,943	Cape Town	Cape of Good Hope
				37,859,000	1,222,878	472,156		

Status: These divisions are provinces.

ISO: Codes from ISO 3166-2.

FIPS: Codes from FIPS PUB 10-4.

CSS: Province codes used by the Central Statistical Service of South Africa.

Population: 1996 census preliminary figures (with large margins of error).

Area-km: Square kilometers.

Area-mi: Square miles.

Former: Former provinces from which these provinces were formed (there are a few small slivers of land that don't appear in this column).

Postal codes: South Africa uses four-digit postal codes. The numbers are not aligned with province boundaries.

Further subdivisions: The provinces are subdivided into magisterial districts and administrative districts.

Territorial extent: Eastern Cape has an enclave within KwaZulu-Natal, around the town of Umzimkulu. It coincides with the part of Transkei that used to lie within Natal.

The Bantustans were generally composed of many scattered enclaves. The four Bantustans that were granted independence by South Africa, called the TBVC countries for short, were Transkei, Bophuthatswana, Venda, and Ciskei. Here are the capitals and approximate locations, relative to the old provinces, of all ten Bantustans. (The actual number of enclaves changed as boundaries were redrawn.)

Bophuthatswana (capital Mmabatho) was seven enclaves in northern Cape of Good Hope, western Transvaal, and Orange Free State.

Ciskei (Bisho) was one enclave in eastern Cape of Good Hope.

Gazankulu (Giyani) was four enclaves (two of them quite small) in northeastern Transvaal.

KaNgwane (Louieville) was two enclaves in eastern Transvaal.

KwaNdebele (Siyabuswa) was one enclave in central Transvaal.

KwaZulu (Ulundi) was eight enclaves (one quite small) in Natal.

Lebowa (Lebowakgomo) was eight enclaves (two or three very small) in northern Transvaal.

Qwaqwa (Phuthaditjhaba) was a small area in Orange Free State, in its corner with Natal and Lesotho.

Transkei (Umtata) was two enclaves in Cape of Good Hope and one in Natal.

Venda (Thohoyandou) was two enclaves in northern Transvaal.

Origins of names:

Gauteng: Sotho for place of gold

Mpumalanga: = where the sun rises

Natal: Portuguese for Christmas, named by Captain Manuel Mascaranhas when he established it on 1597-12-25

Orange Free State: after the Orange River, which was named for the ruling Dutch family of Orange-Nassau

Transvaal: Latin *trans*: beyond + Vaal River (from Afrikaans *vaal*: yellowish), land beyond the Vaal from viewpoint of Capetown

Change history:

1902-05-31	Orange Free State became the British colony of Orange River Colony.
1903-01-27	Northern Districts (Babanango, Paulpietersburg, Utrecht, Vryheid) transferred from Transvaal to Natal.
1910-05-31	Union of South Africa formed. Name of Orange River Colony restored to Orange Free State.
1922	Walvis Bay (then called Walfisch Bay) transferred from Cape Province of the Union of South Africa to Namibia (then called South West Africa).
1947-12-25	Prince Edward Islands annexed to Cape Province, followed by Marion Island on 1947-12-30.
1948	South Africa reclaimed sovereignty over Walvis Bay, making it again part of Cape Province.
1976-10-25	Transkei called independent.
1977-12-06	Bophuthatswana called independent.
1979-09-13	Venda called independent.
1981-12-04	Ciskei called independent.
1992-08	Walvis Bay placed under joint Namibian and South African administration.
1994-03-01	Walvis Bay fully transferred to Namibia.

1994-04-27　South Africa reorganized into nine provinces. Before the reorganization, it was divided into the following four provinces, which had endured since 1910 with only minor changes. On this date, the Bantustans ceased to exist, even as a legal fiction.

division	FIPS	conv	population	area-km	capital
Cape of Good Hope	SF01	C.P.	5,514,413	721,001	Cape Town
Natal	SF02	Natal	2,074,513	86,967	Pietermaritzburg
Orange Free State	SF03	O.F.S.	1,929,369	129,152	Bloemfontein
Transvaal	SF04	Tvl.	8,630,016	283,917	Pretoria
			18,148,311	1,221,037	

FIPS: Codes from FIPS PUB 10-4.
Conv: conventional abbreviation in use among English speakers in South Africa.
Population: 1991 census.

~1995　Name of Pretoria/Witwatersrand/Vaal province changed to Gauteng; name of Eastern Transvaal changed to Mpumalanga; name of Orange Free State changed to Free State; name of Northern Transvaal changed to Northern Province.

Other names of subdivisions:

Eastern Cape: Oos-Kaap (Afrikaans)
Free State: Orange Free State (obsolete); Vrystaat (Afrikaans)
Gauteng: Pretoria/Witwatersrand/Vaal (obsolete); PWV (informal)
Mpumalanga: Eastern Transvaal (obsolete)

North-West: Noordwes (Afrikaans)
Northern Cape: Noord-Kaap (Afrikaans)
Northern Province: Limpopo (variant); Noordelike Provinsie (Afrikaans); Northern Transvaal (obsolete)
Western Cape: Wes-Kaap (Afrikaans)

Old provinces:

Cape of Good Hope: Cape Colony (obsolete); Cape Province (variant); Kaapland (Dutch); Kaapprovinsie, Provinsie die Kaap die Goeie Hoop (Afrikaans); Kapland (German); Kapplande (Norwegian); Province du Cap (French); Provincia del Capo (Italian); Província do Cabo (Portuguese)

Natal: Natal and Zululand (obsolete)
Orange Free State: Estado Livre de Orange (Portuguese); État libre d'Orange (French); Orange (Italian); Orange River Colony (obsolete); Oranje-Fristaten (Norwegian); Oranje-Vrijstaat (Dutch); Oranje-Vrystaat (Afrikaans); Oranjefreistaat (German)

Population history:

province	1911	1921	1936	1946	1951	1961	1970	1980	1991
Cape	2,564,965	2,781,542	3,529,900	4,053,848	4,426,726	5,342,720	6,731,820	5,091,360	5,514,413
Natal	1,194,043	1,429,398	1,946,468	2,202,392	2,415,318	2,979,920	4,236,770	2,676,340	2,074,513
Orange	528,174	628,827	772,060	879,071	1,016,570	1,386,547	1,716,350	1,931,860	1,929,369
Transvaal	1,686,212	2,087,636	3,341,470	4,283,038	4,812,838	6,273,477	6,478,904	8,717,530	8,630,016
	5,973,394	6,927,403	9,589,898	11,418,349	12,671,452	15,982,664	19,163,844	18,417,090	18,148,311

Note: after 1970, these figures exclude population of Bantustans.

SOUTH GEORGIA AND THE SOUTH SANDWICH ISLANDS

ISO = GS/FIPS = SX　Language = English　Time zone = -2　Capital = Grytviken

These islands have belonged to the United Kingdom throughout the 20th century. From 1908 to 1962, they were dependencies of the Falkland Islands. On 1985-10-03, South Georgia and the South Sandwich Islands came under the direct administration of the United Kingdom. Argentina claims the islands along with the Falklands, and occupied South Georgia briefly in 1982.

Other names of country: Géorgie du Sud et les Îles Sandwich du Sud (French); Islas Georgias del Sur y Sandwich del Sur (Spanish); Isole della Georgia Australe e dalle Sandwich Australi (Italian); Südgeorgien und Südliche Sandwichinseln (German).

Origin of name: South Georgia was named in honor of King George III of England by Captain James Cook. South Sandwich Islands were named Sandwich Islands by Captain Cook in honor of his patron, John Montague, Lord Sandwich, then First Lord of the Admiralty.

division	abv	population	area-km	area-mi
South Georgia and the South Sandwich Islands	GS	0	4,090	1,580

Status: This divisions is the whole of the country, treated as a division for compatibility.

Abv: Two-letter code for international compatibility (defined by the author).

Population: Islands have no permanent residents.

Area-km: Square kilometers.

Area-mi: Square miles.

Territorial extent: This territory consists of South Georgia Island and nearby small islands, and the South Sandwich Islands, of which the largest are Montagu, Saunders, Bristol, and Visokoi.

SPAIN

ISO = ES/FIPS = SP   Language = Spanish   Time zone = +1[d]   Capital = Madrid

Spain has been an independent country during the entire 20th century.

Other names of country: Espagne (French); España (Spanish); Espanha (Portuguese); Espanja (Finnish); Kingdom of Spain (formal–English); Reino de España (formal); Spagna (Italian); Spania (Norwegian); Spanien (Danish, German, Swedish); Spanje (Dutch); Spánn (Icelandic).

Origin of name: possibly from a Phoenician word for mine, digging; or Phoenician for coast of the rabbits.

division	abv	ISO	NUTS	FIPS	rs	population	area-km	area-mi	prov	capital
Andalusia	AN	AN	ES61	SP51	h	7,234,873	87,268	33,694	8	Seville
Aragon	AR	AR	ES24	SP52	l	1,187,546	47,669	18,405	3	Zaragoza
Asturias	AS	O	ES12	SP34	l	1,087,885	10,565	4,079	1	Oviedo
Balearic Islands	PM	PM	ES53	SP07	l	760,379	5,014	1,936	1	Palma de Mallorca
Basque Country	PV	PV	ES21	SP59	h	2,098,055	7,261	2,803	3	Vitoria-Gasteiz
Canary Islands	CN	CN	ES7	SP53	h	1,606,534	7,273	2,808	2	Santa Cruz de Tenerife
Cantabria	CB	S	ES13	SP39	l	527,437	5,289	2,042	1	Santander
Castile and Leon	CL	CL	ES41	SP55	l	2,508,496	94,147	36,350	9	Valladolid
Castile-La Mancha	CM	CM	ES42	SP54	l	1,712,529	79,226	30,589	5	Toledo
Catalonia	CT	CT	ES51	SP56	h	6,090,040	31,930	12,328	4	Barcelona
Ceuta	CE	CE	ES631	——	-	68,796	18	7	-	Ceuta
Extremadura	EX	EX	ES43	SP57	l	1,070,244	41,602	16,063	2	Mérida
Galicia	GA	GA	ES11	SP58	h	2,742,622	29,434	11,365	4	Santiago de Compostela
La Rioja	LO	LO	ES23	SP27	l	264,941	5,034	1,944	1	Logroño
Madrid	MD	M	ES3	SP29	l	5,022,289	7,995	3,087	1	Madrid
Melilla	ML	ML	ES632	——	-	59,576	14	5	-	Melilla
Murcia	MU	MU	ES62	SP31	l	1,097,249	11,317	4,370	1	Murcia
Navarra	NA	NA	ES22	SP32	h	520,574	10,421	4,024	1	Pamplona
Valencia	VC	VC	ES52	SP60	h	4,009,329	23,305	8,998	3	Valencia
						39,669,394	504,782	194,897	50	

Status: These divisions are comunidades autónomas (autonomous communities), except for Ceuta and Melilla (see below).

Abv: Two-letter code for international compatibility (defined by the author).

ISO: Codes from ISO 3166-2.

NUTS: Nomenclature of Territorial Units for Statistics. Note: the first three characters of the NUTS code identify still larger regions, described as Noroeste (ES1), Noreste (ES2), Madrid (ES3), Centro (ES4), Este (ES5), Sur (ES6), and Canarias (ES7).

FIPS: Codes from FIPS PUB 10-4.

Rs: Autonomous communities are classified as having high (h) or low (l) responsibility.

Population: 1996-05-01 census.

Area-km: Square kilometers.

Area-mi: Square miles.

Prov: Number of provinces in each region.

Further subdivisions: The division of Spain into provinces has endured, essentially unchanged, since 1833. The constitution of 1978 mandated the creation of autonomous communities. They were implemented by statute, and created by stages from 1979 to 1983, each consisting of one or more provinces. The smallest administrative divisions of Spain are the municipios (municipalities). There are various groupings of municipalities below the provincial level, varying by autonomous community: comarcas (counties), cabildo insular or consell insular (island council), and others. Ceuta and Melilla are special cases. Officially, they are plazas de soberanía del norte de Africa (places of sovereignty in the north of Africa; Spanish Africa for short). The ISO standard lists them as two separate entities, although it might make more sense to list them as one. Ceuta and Melilla are each municipalities. Formerly, Ceuta was administered as part of Cádiz province, and Melilla as part of Málaga.

The fifty provinces are listed here because of their historical and continuing significance.

province	post	FIPS	NUTS	ac	population	area-km	capital
Álava	01	SP01	ES211	PV	281,821	3,047	Vitoria-Gasteiz (see note)
Albacete	02	SP02	ES421	CM	359,010	14,858	Albacete
Alicante	03	SP03	ES521	VC	1,379,762	5,863	Alicante
Almería	04	SP04	ES611	AN	501,761	8,774	Almería
Ávila	05	SP05	ES411	CL	169,342	8,048	Ávila
Badajoz	06	SP06	ES431	EX	656,848	21,657	Badajoz
Baleares	07	SP07	ES53	PM	760,379	5,014	Palma
Barcelona	08	SP08	ES511	CT	4,628,277	7,733	Barcelona
Burgos	09	SP09	ES412	CL	350,074	14,269	Burgos
Cáceres	10	SP10	ES432	EX	413,396	19,945	Cáceres
Cádiz	11	SP11	ES612	AN	1,105,762	7,385	Cádiz
Castellón	12	SP12	ES522	VC	456,727	6,679	Castellón de la Plana
Ciudad Real	13	SP13	ES422	CM	478,672	19,749	Ciudad Real
Córdoba	14	SP14	ES613	AN	761,401	13,718	Córdoba
Cuenca	16	SP15	ES423	CM	201,712	17,061	Cuenca
Gerona	17	SP16	ES512	CT	530,631	5,886	Gerona
Granada	18	SP17	ES614	AN	808,053	12,531	Granada
Guadalajara	19	SP18	ES424	CM	157,255	12,190	Guadalajara
Guipúzcoa	20	SP19	ES212	PV	676,208	1,997	Donostia-San Sebastián (see note)
Huelva	21	SP20	ES615	AN	454,735	10,085	Huelva
Huesca	22	SP21	ES241	AR	206,916	15,671	Huesca
Jaén	23	SP22	ES616	AN	648,551	13,498	Jaén
La Coruña	15	SP23	ES111	GA	1,110,302	7,876	La Coruña
Las Palmas	35	SP24	ES701	CN	834,085	4,065	Las Palmas de Gran Canaria
León	24	SP25	ES413	CL	517,191	15,468	León
Lérida	25	SP26	ES513	CT	356,456	12,028	Lérida
Logroño	26	SP27	ES23	LO	264,941	5,034	Logroño
Lugo	27	SP28	ES112	GA	370,303	9,803	Lugo
Madrid	28	SP29	ES3	M	5,022,289	7,995	Madrid
Málaga	29	SP30	ES617	AN	1,249,290	7,276	Málaga
Murcia	30	SP31	ES62	MU	1,097,249	11,317	Murcia
Navarra	31	SP32	ES22	NA	520,574	10,421	Pamplona
Orense	32	SP33	ES113	GA	346,913	7,278	Orense
Oviedo	33	SP34	ES12	O	1,087,885	10,565	Oviedo
Palencia	34	SP35	ES414	CL	180,571	8,029	Palencia
Pontevedra	36	SP36	ES114	GA	915,104	4,477	Pontevedra
Salamanca	37	SP37	ES415	CL	353,020	12,336	Salamanca
Santa Cruz de Tenerife	38	SP38	ES702	CN	772,449	3,208	Santa Cruz de Tenerife
Santander	39	SP39	ES13	S	527,437	5,289	Santander ➤

province	post	FIPS	NUTS	ac	population	area-km	capital
Segovia	40	SP40	ES416	CL	147,770	6,949	Segovia
Sevilla	41	SP41	ES618	AN	1,705,320	14,001	Sevilla
Soria	42	SP42	ES417	CL	92,848	10,287	Soria
Tarragona	43	SP43	ES514	CT	574,676	6,283	Tarragona
Teruel	44	SP44	ES242	AR	138,211	14,804	Teruel
Toledo	45	SP45	ES425	CM	515,880	15,368	Toledo
Valencia	46	SP46	ES523	VC	2,172,840	10,763	Valencia
Valladolid	47	SP47	ES418	CL	490,205	8,202	Valladolid
Vizcaya	48	SP48	ES213	PV	1,140,026	2,217	Bilbao
Zamora	49	SP49	ES419	CL	207,475	10,559	Zamora
Zaragoza	50	SP50	ES243	AR	842,419	17,194	Saragossa

Province: Spanish name of province.

Postal code: Spain uses a five-digit código postal (postal code). The first two digits determine the province, as shown. Ceuta = 51, Melilla = 52.

FIPS: Old codes from FIPS PUB 10-4. These were superseded by the FIPS codes for autonomous communities in ~1990.

NUTS: Nomenclature of Territorial Units for Statistics.

Ac: ISO code for the autonomous community containing this province.

Population: 1996-05-01 census.

Capitals: Vitoria and San Sebastián are the Spanish names of these cities, and Gasteiz and Donostia, the Basque names. They are often given in this hyphenated form.

Up until ~1970, there was a well-established grouping of provinces into historical regions. Many of the regions could be traced back to kingdoms of the Age of Exploration. In modern times, the historical regions had no administrative functions. Andalusia, Aragon, Asturias, Basque Country, Catalonia, Extremadura, Galicia, Navarra, and Valencia contained the same provinces as the autonomous communities of the same names. (However, Basque Country and Navarra were often grouped together as "Provincia Vascongadas y Navarra.") Murcia included the provinces of Albacete (now in Castile-La Mancha) and Murcia. The other three historical regions were Leon, New Castile, and Old Castile (Spanish: León, Castilla la Nueva, and Castilla la Vieja). Leon comprised the provinces of León, Salamanca, and Zamora, all now in Castile and Leon. New Castile consisted of Madrid and all the provinces that are now in Castile-La Mancha except Albacete. Old Castile consisted of Castile and Leon, minus the three provinces of Leon, plus the autonomous communities of Cantabria and La Rioja. The Balearic Islands, Canary Islands, Ceuta, and Melilla were not included among the historical regions.

Territorial extent: Almería includes Alborán Island.

Baleares consists of the islands of Mallorca, Menorca, Ibiza, Formentera, Cabrera, and nearby islets.

Burgos includes a large enclave called Condado de Treviño, surrounded by Álava province, as well as three tiny enclaves: two within Logroño, and one within Palencia province. It follows that Treviño is an enclave of Castile and Leon autonomous community within Basque Country, and the two in Logroño are enclaves of Castile and Leon within La Rioja.

Castellón includes the tiny Islas Columbretes.

Ceuta lies on a peninsula on the coast of Morocco, across the Strait of Gibraltar.

Ciudad Real includes an enclave called Rincón de Anchuras, on the border between Badajoz and Toledo provinces.

Córdoba includes a small enclave around Villar, contained within Sevilla province.

Gerona includes the enclave of Llivia, surrounded by Pyrénées-Orientales department of France, as well as a small enclave within Barcelona province.

Guipúzcoa contains the Spanish share of Isla de los Faisanes, a condominium of France and Spain.

La Coruña includes some small coastal islands: Sálvora, the Islas Sisargas, etc.

Las Palmas consists of the islands of Gran Canaria, Fuerteventura, Lanzarote, Graciosa, Alegranza, Lobos, and Montaña Clara.

Madrid includes the small enclave of La Cepeda, lying on the border between Ávila and Segovia provinces. This is therefore also an enclave of Madrid autonomous community within Castile and Leon.

Melilla consists of a small coastal enclave in Morocco around the city of Melilla, and several small islands off the coast of Morocco: Islas Chafarinas (Isabel II, Congreso, Isla del Rey), Peñón de Alhucemas and its neighbors Isla de Mar and Isla de Tierra, and Peñón de Vélez de la Gomera.

Navarra includes two small enclaves within Zaragoza province, around Petilla de Aragón and Bastanes. Consequently, these are also enclaves of Navarra autonomous community within Aragon.

Palencia includes five small enclaves: two within Burgos province, two within Santander, and one on the border between Burgos and Santander. The two within Santander are also enclaves of Castile and Leon autonomous community within Cantabria.

Pontevedra includes some coastal islands: Arosa, Ons, and the Islas Cíes (Monte Agudo and San Martín).

Santa Cruz de Tenerife consists of the islands of Tenerife, La Palma, Gomera, and Hierro.

Santander includes an enclave around La Matanza, within Vizcaya province. Consequently, this is also an enclave of Cantabria autonomous community within Basque Country.

Valencia includes an enclave called Rincón de Ademuz, on the border between Cuenca and Teruel provinces (Castile-La Mancha and Aragón autonomous communities, respectively).

Valladolid includes two enclaves, one within León province, and a larger one on the border between León and Zamora.

Vizcaya includes an enclave around Orduña, on the border between Álava and Burgos.

Origins of names:

Álava: possibly from Basque *araiiar*: land between mountains, or *ara ba*: low plain

Albacete: Arabic *al-Basit*: the plain

Alicante: from Greek *leuke akte*: white cape, through Latin Lucentum and Arabic Alicante, as a city name

Almería: Arabic *al-Meriya*: the watchtower

Andalusia: through Arabic from Low Latin *Vandalusia*: land of the Vandals

Aragon: from the river Aragón

Asturias: from Basque *asta*: rock, *ur*: water

Badajoz: from city name, from Latin *Pax Augusti*: peace of Augustus

Baleares: the ancients explained it as a Semitic name meaning "slingers' islands"

Barcelona: from Hamilcar Barca, Carthaginian general

Burgos: Spanish for cities. Burgos, the city, was formed by uniting several smaller cities

Cádiz: from Semitic *gadir*: walled place

Canary Islands: from Latin *canis*: dog

Cantabria: for the Cantabrian Mountains, named for Cantabri (ethnic name)

Castile: Latin *castella*: castle

Catalonia: probably from Catalauni, name of Celtic tribe

Ceuta: Latin *Castellum ad Septem Fratres*: castle of the seven brothers, referring to seven mountains, through Arabic *Sebta*

Ciudad Real: Spanish for royal city; founded by King Alfonso X of Castille in 1252.

Córdoba: possibly from Phoenician *qorteb*: oil press

Cuenca: Spanish *cuenca*, from Latin *concha*: basin; the city is situated in a deep river valley

Extremadura: Latin *Extrema Durii*: end of the Douro (River)

Galicia: possibly from Latin *Gallus*: man from Gaul

Granada: Latin *granatum*: fruit

Guadalajara: Arabic *wadi al-hajara*: stony river

Guipúzcoa: Basque for the place of Ipuz (person or tribe)

La Coruña: possibly from Latin *columna*: column, referring to an ancient lighthouse

La Mancha: from Arabic for the high plain

León: from Latin *Legionis*, genitive case of *Legio*: legion; headquarters of the Seventh Legion

Madrid: possibly from Celtic *mago*: big + *ritu*: ford

Málaga: possibly from Phoenician *malaka*: refuge

Murcia: from Arabic for the firmly founded

Navarra: possibly from Basque *naba*: mountain pass or valley, *Nabarra*: tribe from mountain valleys

Santa Cruz de Tenerife: = Holy Cross of Tenerife; Tenerife is the name of the island, from native words *tener*: island, *ife*: white, referring to snowy mountain peaks

Santander: probably a corruption of Sant Andres: Saint Andrew

Sevilla: from a Semitic name meaning plain

Valencia: from city name, from Latin *Valentia Edetanorum*, probably meaning "strong city of the Edetani tribe"

Valladolid: Arabic *vali*: governor + Walid; the city was the governorate of Walid Abul Abbas

Vizcaya: from Basque *bizkar*: mountain pass

Zaragoza: city renamed Cæsaria Augusta when it became a military colony in 25 B.C., shortened to Cæsaraugusta, then to Sarakusta by the Moors

Change history:

1927-09-21	Canary Islands split into Las Palmas de Gran Canaria and Santa Cruz de Tenerife provinces.
1979	Basque Country and Catalonia autonomous communities formed.
1981	Andalusia, Asturias, Cantabria, and Galicia autonomous communities formed.
1982	Aragon, Canary Islands, Castile-La Mancha, La Rioja, Murcia, Navarra, and Valencia autonomous communities formed.
1983	Balearic Islands, Castile and Leon, Extremadura, and Madrid autonomous communities formed.

Other names of subdivisions:

autonomous communities:

Andalusia: Andalousie (French); Andalucía (Spanish); Andalusien (German); Andaluzia (Portuguese)

Aragon: Aragão (Portuguese); Aragón (Spanish); Aragona (Italian); Aragonien (German)

Asturias: Astúrias (Portuguese); Asturie (Italian); Asturien

(German); Asturies (French); Principado de Asturias (formal)

Balearic Islands: Balearen (German); Balearene (Norwegian); Baleares, Islas Baleares (Spanish); Baleari (Italian); Îles Baléares (French); Illes Balears (Catalan)

Basque Country: Baskenland, Baskische Provinzen (German); Basque Provinces (variant); CAV, Comunidad Autonoma Vasca (formal); EKE, Euskadi, Euskal Autonomia Erkidegoa (Basque); País Basco (Portuguese); País Vasco (Spanish); Pays Basque, Provinces Basques (French); Province Basche (Italian); Vascongadas (Spanish-obsolete)

Canary Islands. Canarias, Islas Canarias (Spanish); Canárias (Portuguese); Canarie (Italian); Îles Canaries (French); Kanariøyene (Norwegian); Kanarische Inseln (German)

Cantabria: Cantábria (Portuguese); Cantabrie (French); Kantabrien (German)

Castile and Leon: Castile-Leon (variant); Castilha-León (Portuguese); Castilla y León (Spanish); Castille et Léon (French); Kastilien-León (German)

Castile-La Mancha: Castilha-La Mancha (Portuguese); Castilla-La Mancha (Spanish); Castille-La Manche (French); Kastilien-La Mancha (German)

Catalonia: Catalogna (Italian); Catalogne (French); Cataluña (Spanish); Catalunha (Portuguese); Catalunya (Catalan); Katalonien (German)

Extremadura: Estremadura (German, Italian, Portuguese); Estrémadure (French)

Galicia: Galice (French); Galícia (Portuguese); Galicien (German); Galizia (Galician, Italian)

La Rioja: Rioja (French, German, variant)

Madrid: Communauté de Madrid (French); Comunidad de Madrid (formal); Madri (Portuguese)

Murcia: Región de Murcia (formal); Région de Murcie (French)

Navarra: Communauté forale de Navarre (French); Comunidad Foral de Navarra (Spanish); Nafarroa (Basque); Navarre (variant)

Valencia: Communauté de Valence (French); Comunidade Valenciana (Portuguese); Comunidad Valenciana (Spanish)

provinces:

Álava: Araba (Basque)

Barcelona: Barcellona (Italian); Barcelone (French)

Cáceres: Cacerès (French)

Cádiz: Cádice (Italian); Cadix (French)

Castellón: Castellón de la Plana (variant)

Córdoba: Cordoue (French); Cordova (English, Italian)

Gerona: Gérone (French); Girona (Catalan)

Granada: Grenada (English); Grenade (French)

Guipúzcoa: Gipuzkoa (Basque)

La Coruña: A Coruña (Galician); Coruña (variant); Corunna (obsolete); La Corogne (French)

Lérida: Lleida (Catalan)

Logroño: La Rioja (variant)

Orense: Orenze (Portuguese); Ourense (Galician)

Oviedo: Asturias (variant)

Salamanca: Salamanque (French)

Santa Cruz de Tenerife: Santa Cruz de Santiago (variant)

Santander: Cantabria (variant)

Segovia: Ségovie (French)

Sevilla: Sevilha (Portuguese); Seville (English); Séville (French); Siviglia (Italian)

Tarragona: Tarragone (French)

Toledo: Tolède (French)

Vizcaya: Biscay (English); Biscaye (French); Bizkaia (Basque); Viscaya (Portuguese)

Zaragoza: Saragossa (English); Saragosse (French); Saragozza (Italian)

Population history:

province	1910	1930	1940	1956	1970	1986	1996
Álava	96,511	104,176	112,876	120,936	204,323	275,703	281,821
Albacete	259,074	332,619	374,472	410,123	335,026	342,278	359,010
Alicante	483,986	545,838	607,562	649,132	920,105	1,254,920	1,379,762
Almería	354,344	341,550	359,730	356,125	375,004	448,592	501,761
Ávila	209,022	221,386	234,671	260,508	203,798	179,207	169,342
Badajoz	561,897	702,418	742,547	859,094	687,599	664,516	656,848
Baleares	325,703	365,512	407,497	430,335	558,287	754,777	760,379
Barcelona	1,133,883	1,800,638	1,931,875	2,416,703	3,929,194	4,598,249	4,628,277
Burgos	395,710	355,299	378,580	407,588	358,075	363,530	350,074
Cáceres	395,082	449,756	511,377	570,982	457,777	424,027	413,396
Cádiz	467,836	507,972	600,440	762,296	885,433	1,054,503	1,105,762
Castellón	320,338	308,746	312,475	332,246	385,823	437,320	456,727
Ciudad Real	368,492	491,657	530,308	588,196	507,650	477,967	478,672
Córdoba	490,647	668,862	761,150	793,565	724,116	745,175	761,401
Cuenca	268,458	309,526	333,335	337,039	247,158	210,932	201,712
Gerona	318,622	325,551	322,360	330,082	414,397	490,667	530,631
Granada	503,898	643,705	737,690	809,023	733,375	796,857	808,053
Guadalajara	208,447	203,998	205,726	201,946	147,732	146,008	157,255
Guipúzcoa	225,271	302,329	331,753	399,533	631,003	688,894	676,208 ➤

province	1910	1930	1940	1956	1970	1986	1996
Huelva	309,744	354,963	366,526	368,838	397,683	430,918	454,735
Huesca	247,027	242,958	231,647	238,793	222,238	220,824	206,916
Jaén	514,368	674,415	753,308	772,597	661,146	633,612	648,551
La Coruña	658,201	767,608	883,090	998,267	1,004,188	1,102,376	1,110,302
Las Palmas	— —	250,991	320,524	409,196	579,710	855,494	834,085
León	393,888	441,908	493,258	575,375	548,721	528,502	517,191
Lérida	283,486	314,435	297,440	339,706	347,015	356,811	356,456
Logroño	188,285	203,789	221,160	234,681	235,713	262,611	264,941
Lugo	445,031	468,619	512,735	506,826	415,052	399,232	370,303
Madrid	871,308	1,383,951	1,579,793	2,148,303	3,792,561	4,854,616	5,022,289
Málaga	504,683	613,160	677,474	793,337	867,330	1,215,479	1,249,290
Murcia	600,744	645,449	719,701	777,888	832,313	1,014,285	1,097,249
Navarra	312,020	345,883	369,618	390,457	464,867	512,676	520,574
Orense	406,648	426,043	458,272	473,290	413,733	399,378	346,913
Oviedo	686,132	791,855	836,642	917,817	1,045,635	1,114,115	1,087,885
Palencia	195,476	207,546	217,108	242,698	198,763	188,472	180,571
Pontevedra	465,542	568,011	641,763	688,612	750,701	884,408	915,104
Salamanca	327,100	339,101	390,468	424,283	371,607	366,668	353,020
Santa Cruz de Tenerife	419,809	304,137	359,770	454,121	590,514	759,388	772,449
Santander	300,005	364,147	393,710	411,222	467,138	524,670	527,437
Segovia	167,759	174,158	189,190	208,497	162,770	151,520	147,770
Sevilla	587,186	805,252	963,044	1,182,416	1,327,190	1,550,492	1,705,320
Soria	156,555	156,207	159,824	161,930	114,956	97,565	92,848
Tarragona	339,042	350,668	339,299	366,826	431,961	531,281	574,676
Teruel	255,408	252,785	232,064	238,196	170,284	148,073	138,211
Toledo	392,307	489,396	480,008	555,551	468,925	487,844	515,880
Valencia	810,266	1,042,154	1,256,633	1,400,912	1,767,327	2,079,762	2,172,840
Valladolid	283,394	301,571	332,526	356,447	412,572	503,306	490,205
Vizcaya	349,706	485,205	511,135	603,881	1,043,310	1,168,405	1,140,026
Zamora	272,143	280,148	298,722	325,740	251,934	221,560	207,475
Zaragoza	448,198	535,816	595,095	636,943	760,186	845,832	842,419
	19,578,682	23,563,867	25,877,971	29,239,098	33,823,918	38,764,297	39,541,022

For 1910, Las Palmas is included under Santa Cruz de Tenerife. Figures for 1956 are estimated. Totals do not include Spanish Africa.

SRI LANKA

ISO = LK/FIPS = CE   Language = Sinhala, Tamil, English   Time zone = +5:30   Capital = Colombo

Ceylon was a British colony at the beginning of the 20th century. It became an independent member of the Commonwealth on 1948-02-04. On 1972-05-22, it became a republic and changed its English name to Sri Lanka.

Other names of country: Ceylon (obsolete); Democratic Socialist Republic of Sri Lanka (formal–English); Srilanka (Dutch); Srí Lanka (Icelandic); Sri Lanka Prajathanthrika Samajavadi Janarajaya (formal).

Origin of name: Sri is an honorific title; Lanka is the name of a mythical island country mentioned in the Ramayana.

division	abv	ISO	FIPS	pab	pc	population	area-km	area-mi	province
Ampara	AP	52	CE01	APR	32	388,786	2,984	1,152	Eastern
Anuradhapura	AD	71	CE02	AD	50	587,822	7,128	2,752	North Central
Badulla	BD	81	CE03	BD	90	642,893	2,818	1,088	Uva
Batticaloa	BC	51	CE04	BC	30	330,899	2,463	951	Eastern
Colombo	CO	11	CE23	CO	10	1,698,322	642	248	Western
Galle	GL	31	CE06	GL	80	814,579	1,673	646	Southern
Gampaha	GQ	12	CE24	GQ	11	1,389,490	1,393	538	Western
Hambantota	HB	33	CE07	HB	82	424,102	2,593	1,001	Southern
Jaffna	JA	41	CE25	JA	40	739,356	1,114	430	Northern ➤

division	abv	ISO	FIPS	pab	pc	population	area-km	area-mi	province
Kalutara	KT	13	CE09	KT	12	827,189	1,606	620	Western
Kandy	KY	21	CE10	KY	20	1,126,296	2,365	913	Central
Kegalle	KE	92	CE11	KE	71	682,411	1,663	642	Sabaragamuwa
Kilinochchi	KL	42	—	—	—	91,756	1,171	452	Northern
Kurunegala	KG	61	CE12	KG	60	1,212,755	4,771	1,842	North Western
Mannar	MB	43	CE26	MB	41	106,940	1,963	758	Northern
Matale	MT	22	CE14	MT	21	357,441	1,987	767	Central
Matara	MH	32	CE15	MH	81	644,231	1,246	481	Southern
Moneragala	MJ	82	CE16	MJ	91	279,743	7,133	2,754	Uva
Mullaitivu	MP	45	CE27	MP	42	77,512	1,580	610	Northern
Nuwara Eliya	NW	23	CE17	NW	22	522,219	1,228	474	Central
Polonnaruwa	PR	72	CE18	PR	51	262,753	3,403	1,314	North Central
Puttalam	PX	62	CE19	PX	61	493,344	2,976	1,149	North Western
Ratnapura	RN	91	CE20	RN	70	796,468	3,237	1,250	Sabaragamuwa
Trincomalee	TC	53	CE21	TC	31	256,790	2,616	1,010	Eastern
Vavuniya	VA	44	CE28	VA	43	95,904	2,642	1,020	Northern
						14,850,001	64,395	24,862	

Status: These divisions are distrikkaya (districts).

Abv: Two-letter code for international compatibility (defined by the author).

ISO: Codes from ISO 3166-2.

FIPS: Codes from FIPS PUB 10-4.

Pab: Abbreviations used by the Sri Lanka Post Office.

Postal code: Sri Lanka uses five-digit postal codes. The first two digits usually indicate the district, as shown here, although there are some deviations.

Population: 1981 census.

Area-km: Square kilometers.

Area-mi: Square miles.

Province: Province to which this district belongs.

Capitals: All district capitals have the same names as their districts.

Further subdivisions: Subordinate to the districts, there are the pradeshiya mandalaya (divisional council) and gramodaya mandalaya (village council). Since the late 19th century, both palata (provinces) and districts have coexisted, with each province being a group of districts. The provinces had no administrative function until 1988. The Northern and Eastern provinces have been temporarily merged into a North Eastern province, intended to placate Tamil demands for greater self-rule. The merger will become permanent after a referendum which has been repeatedly postponed. Some lists now show eight provinces, and some nine. The nine provinces are:

province	abv	ISO	population	area-km	capital
Central	CE	29	2,311,000	5,584	Kandy
Eastern	EA	—	1,310,000	9,951	Trincomali
North Central	NC	30	1,110,000	10,724	Anuradhapura
Northern	NO	31	1,383,000	8,882	Jaffna
North Western	NS	32	2,148,000	7,812	Puttalam
Sabaragamuwa	SA	33	1,765,000	4,902	Ratnapura
Southern	SO	34	2,366,000	5,559	Galle
Uva	UV	35	1,128,000	8,488	Badulla
Western	WE	36	4,687,000	3,709	Colombo
			18,208,000	65,611	

Abv: Two-letter code for international compatibility (defined by the author).

ISO: Codes from ISO 3166-2. (31 represents North Eastern.) Recent FIPS lists show the same eight provinces; the FIPS codes are CE followed by the two-digit ISO code.

Population: 1996 estimate.

Territorial extent: All districts are situated mostly on the island of Sri Lanka.

Jaffna is located on the Jaffna peninsula, which is nearly separated from the rest of Sri Lanka. It also contains some islands in Palk Strait, such as Delft, Velanai, Karaitivu, and Punkudutivu.

Mannar includes Mannar Island, part of the chain of islands and peninsulas called Adam's Bridge.

Origins of names:

Colombo: possibly Sinhala *kolamba*: port, ferry; assimilated
   to Columbus's name by Portuguese colonists

Change history:

~1958	Chilaw district merged with Puttalam district, both in North-Western province; Amparai district split from Batticaloa; Moneragala district split from Badulla; Polonnaruwa district split from Anuradhapura.
1974-06-28	Kachchativu island transferred from India to Sri Lanka.
1978-08-31	New constitution adopted. Gampaha district split from Colombo. Mullaitivu district formed from parts of Jaffna, Mannar, and Vavuniya.
1982	Some governmental functions moved from Colombo to Sri Jayawardenapura (formerly Kotto).
1983-10-04	Jaffna district split into Jaffna and Kilinochchi by the seventh amendment to the constitution.
1987-11-14	Thirteenth amendment to the constitution passed, authorizing the establishment of provincial councils to govern the nine provinces.

Other names of subdivisions:

districts:
Ampara: Amparai (variant)
Kegalle: Kegalla (variant)
Moneragala: Monaragala (variant)

provinces:
Central: Madhyama (Sinhala)

North Central: Uturumeda (Sinhala)
North Western: Wayamba (Sinhala)
Southern: Dakunu (Sinhala)
Western: Basnahira (Sinhala)

Population history:

province	1901	1911	1921	1931	1946	1953	1963	1971	1981	1996
Central	622,800	672,300	717,739	953,395	1,135,200	1,481,000	1,698,000	1,956,755	2,005,956	2,311,000
Eastern	173,600	183,700	192,821	213,980	279,100	400,000	547,000	722,883	976,475	1,310,000
N. Central	79,100	86,300	96,525	97,365	139,500	270,000	394,000	553,065	850,575	1,110,000
Northern	341,000	369,600	374,829	399,094	479,500	625,000	742,000	877,768	1,111,468	1,383,000
N. Western	353,600	434,100	492,181	546,988	667,900	962,000	1,156,000	1,407,894	1,706,099	2,148,000
Sabaragamuwa	321,800	408,500	471,814	578,368	745,400	978,000	1,125,000	1,313,804	1,478,879	1,765,000
Southern	566,800	628,800	671,234	771,283	961,400	1,257,000	1,430,000	1,666,710	1,882,912	2,366,000
Uva	186,700	216,700	233,864	303,419	372,200	517,000	654,000	807,820	922,636	1,128,000
Western	920,700	1,106,300	1,246,847	1,448,648	1,876,900	2,439,000	2,838,000	3,404,444	3,915,001	4,687,000
	3,566,100	4,106,300	4,497,854	5,312,540	6,657,100	8,929,000	10,584,000	12,711,143	14,850,001	18,208,000

All figures are from censuses except 1996. Some census dates: 1953-03-20, 1971-10-09, and 1981-03-17.

SUDAN

ISO = SD/FIPS = SU   Language = Arabic   Time zone = +2   Capital = Khartoum

From just before 1900 until its independence on 1956-01-01, Sudan was a condominium of Egypt and the United Kingdom.

Other names of country: Anglo-Egyptian Sudan (obsolete); Jamhuryat es-Sudan (formal); Republic of the Sudan (formal–English); Soudan (French); Sudán (Spanish); Súdan (Icelandic); Sudão (Portuguese).

Origin of name: from a native word for black (people).

division	abv	ISO	FIPS	capital	region
Bahr el Gabel	BG	17	SU44	Juba	Equatoria
Blue Nile	BN	24	SU42	Ed Damazin	Central
Eastern Equatoria	EE	19	SU57	Kaboita	Equatoria
El Buhayrat	EB	18	SU37	Rumbek	Bahr el Ghazal
Gedaref	GD	06	SU39	El Gedaref	Eastern
Gezira	GZ	07	SU38	Wad Medani	Central
Jonglei	JG	20	SU51	Bor	Upper Nile
Kassala	KA	05	SU52	Kassala	Eastern
Khartoum	KH	03	SU29	Khartoum	Khartoum
Northern	NO	01	SU43	Dongola	Northern
Northern Bahr el Ghazal	NB	15	SU54	Aweel	Bahr el Ghazal
Northern Darfur	ND	02	SU55	El Fashir	Darfur
Northern Kordofan	NK	09	SU56	El Obeid	Kordofan
Red Sea	RS	26	SU36	Port Sudan	Eastern
River Nile	RN	04	SU53	Ed Damer	Northern
Sinnar	SI	25	SU58	Singa	Central
Southern Darfur	SD	11	SU49	Nyala	Darfur
Southern Kordofan	SK	13	SU50	Kadogli	Kordofan
Upper Nile	UN	23	SU35	Malakal	Upper Nile
Wahda	WH	22	SU40	Bantio	Upper Nile
Warab	WR	21	SU59	Warap	Bahr el Ghazal
Western Bahr el Ghazal	WB	14	SU46	Waw	Bahr el Ghazal
Western Darfur	WD	12	SU47	El Geneina	Darfur
Western Equatoria	WE	16	SU45	Yambio	Equatoria
Western Kordofan	WK	10	SU48	El Fula	Kordofan
White Nile	WN	08	SU41	Rabak	Central

Status: These divisions are wilayat (states).

Abv: Two-letter code for international compatibility (defined by the author).

ISO: Codes from ISO 3166-2.

FIPS: Codes from FIPS PUB 10-4.

Region: Approximate equivalent area before 1994.

Population and area of states not yet available.

Further subdivisions: The states are subdivided into districts.

Territorial extent: Red Sea includes Sudan's Red Sea islands, such as Mukawwar and the Suakin Archipelago.

The administrative boundary between Sudan and Egypt deviates from the legal boundary. There is a small region in Sudan, south of 22°, administered by Egypt, and a larger triangle in Egypt, north of the parallel, administered by Sudan (in Red Sea state).

Similarly, there is a triangle adjacent to the Kenya border that is administered by Kenya but part of Sudan (Eastern Equatoria state).

Origins of names:

Bahr el Ghazal: Arabic "river of the gazelles"

Darfur: Arabic *dar fur*: home of the Fur (ethnic name)

Equatoria: area closest to the Equator, although nowhere farther south than 3° N. latitude

Gezira: Arabic *al-gazira*: the island, referring to area between the White Nile and Blue Nile

Khartoum: means "the snout," from shape of land where the White and Blue Nile meet

Change history:

1919 Anglo-Egyptian Sudan ceded a roughly triangular area in the northwest to Libya. The division of Anglo-Egyptian Sudan into eight mudiriyas (provinces) was poorly defined at first, but by the time World War II began, they were well established.

1948 Bahr el Ghazal province split from Equatoria. The division of Sudan into provinces was now:

province	FIPS	population	area-km	capital	region
Bahr el Ghazal	SU32	2,265,510	201,048	Waw	S
Central	SU27	4,012,543	139,124	Wad Medani	N
Darfur	SU33	3,093,699	509,075	El Fashir	N
Eastern	SU31	2,208,209	334,331	Kassala	N ➤

province	FIPS	population	area-km	capital	region
Equatoria	SU28	1,406,181	198,121	Juba	S
Khartoum	SU29	1,802,299	28,187	Khartoum	N
Kordofan	SU34	3,093,294	380,552	El Obeid	N
Northern	SU30	1,083,024	476,405	Ed Damer	N
Upper Nile	SU26	1,599,605	238,976	Malakal	S
		20,564,364	2,505,819		

Population: 1983 census.

Region: the Northern (N) and Southern (S) regions have sometimes been called divisions of Sudan.

~1976   Sudan reorganized from nine provinces into eighteen districts, as follows:

district	population	area-km	capital	district	population	area-km	capital
Bahr el Ghazal	1,492,597	134,576	Waw	Northern	433,391	348,697	Dongola
Blue Nile	1,056,313	62,135	Ed Damazin	Northern Darfur	1,327,947	346,155	El Fashir
Eastern Equatoria	359,056	119,237	Juba	Northern Kordofan	1,805,769	221,900	El Obeid
El Buheyrat	772,913	66,318	Rumbek	Red Sea	695,874	21,990	Port Sudan
El Gezira	2,023,094	35,057	Wad Medani	Southern Darfur	1,765,752	162,529	Nyala
Junglei	797,251	121,644	Bor	Southern Kordofan	1,287,525	158,355	Kadogli
Kassala	1,512,335	114,154	Kassala	Upper Nile	802,354	117,148	Malakal
Khartoum	1,802,299	28,165	Khartoum	Western Equatoria	1,047,125	78,732	Yambio
Nile	649,633	127,343	Ed Damer	White Nile	933,136	41,825	Ed Dueim

~1990   The nine provinces were reinstated as the divisions of Sudan. (The reality may be that the districts were subdivisions of the provinces all along, but that sometimes one level of administration gets emphasized over the other.)

1994-02-14   Sudan reorganized from nine provinces into twenty-six states.

Other names of subdivisions: The article al is often transliterated el. Before certain consonants, it is usually assimilated, as in Ash Shamaliyah (instead of Al Shamaliyah).

provinces:
Central: Al Wusṭá (Arabic)
Darfur: Darfour (French); Dārfūr (Arabic)
Eastern: Ash Sharqī, Ash Sharqīyah (Arabic)
Equatoria: Al Istiwā'ī, Al Istiwā'īyah, Al Istiwā'īyahal (Arabic)
Khartoum: Al Kharṭūm, Al Khurṭūm (Arabic); Cartum (Portuguese); Jartum (Spanish); Khartum (German, Italian, Norwegian)
Kordofan: Kordofam (Portuguese); Kòrdofan (Italian); Kurdufān (Arabic)
Northern: Ash Shamālī, Ash Shamālīyah (Arabic)
Upper Nile: A'ālī an Nīl (Arabic)

states:
Bahr el Gabel: Bahr al-Jabal (variant)
Blue Nile: An Nīl al Azraq (Arabic)
Eastern Equatoria: Al Istiwā'īyah ash Sharqīyah, Sharq al Istiwā'īyah (Arabic)
El Buhayrat: Al Buhairat, Al Buḥayrah, Buheirat, El Boheirat, Lakes (variant)
Gedaref: Al Qadarif, Gadarif (variant)
Gezira: Al Jazīrah, El Gezira (variant)
Jonglei: Jonglie, Jonqley, Junglei, Junqalī (variant)
Kassala: Kessala (variant)
Northern Darfur: Dārfūr ash Shamālīyah, Shamāl Dārfūr (Arabic)

Northern Kordofan: Kurdufān ash Shamālīyah, Shamāl Kurdufān (Arabic)
Red Sea: Al Baḥr al Aḥmar (Arabic); Mar Rojo (Spanish); Mar Rosso (Italian); Mar Vermelho (Portuguese); Mer Rouge (French); Röda havet (Swedish); Rødehavet (Norwegian); Rotes Meer (German)
River Nile: an Nīl, Nahr an Nīl (Arabic); Nil (German); Nile, Nile River (variant); Nilen (Norwegian, Swedish); Nilo (Italian, Portuguese)
Sinnar: Sennar (variant)
Southern Darfur: Dārfūr al Janūbīyah, Janūb Dārfūr (Arabic)
Southern Kordofan: Kurdufān al Janūbīyah, Janūb Kurdufān (Arabic)
Upper Nile: a'Ālī an Nīl (Arabic)
Wahda: Al-Wahdah, Unity (variant)
Warab: Warap (variant)
Western Bahr el Ghazal: Bahr al-Ghazāl al Gharbīyah, Gharb Bahr al-Ghazāl (Arabic)
Western Darfur: Dārfūr al Gharbīyah, Gharb Dārfūr (Arabic)
Western Equatoria: Al Istiwā'īyah al Gharbīyah, Gharb al Istiwā'īyah (Arabic)
Western Kordofan: Kurdufān al Gharbīyah, Gharb Kurdufān (Arabic)
White Nile: An Baḥr al Abyad, An Nīl al-Abyad (Arabic)

SURINAME

ISO = SR/FIPS = NS   Language = Dutch   Time zone = -3   Capital = Paramaribo

Suriname began the 20th century as a colony of the Netherlands. It became an integral part of the Netherlands on 1954-12-29, and then an independent country on 1975-11-25.

Other names of country: Dutch Guiana, Netherlands Guiana, Surinam (obsolete); Republic of Suriname (formal–English); Sranan (local); Surinam (Danish, Norwegian, Swedish); Súrínam (Icelandic).

division	ISO	FIPS	capital	division	ISO	FIPS	capital
Brokopondo	BR	NS10	Brokopondo	Para	PR	NS15	Onverwacht
Commewijne	CM	NS11	Nieuw Amsterdam	Paramaribo	PM	NS16	Paramaribo
Coronie	CR	NS12	Totness	Saramacca	SA	NS17	Groningen
Marowijne	MA	NS13	Albina	Sipaliwini	SI	NS18	Paramaribo
Nickerie	NI	NS14	Nieuw Nickerie	Wanica	WA	NS19	Lelydorp

Status: These divisions are districts.
ISO: Codes from ISO 3166-2.
FIPS: Codes from FIPS PUB 10-4.
Population and area not yet available.
Further subdivisions: The districts are subdivided into departments.
Change history:

~1960   Brokopondo district formed.
1966-09-08   Para district split from Suriname district. The resulting division of Suriname was:

division	FIPS	population	area-km	capital
Brokopondo	NS01	20,249	21,440	Brokopondo
Commewijne	NS02	14,351	4,110	Nieuw Amsterdam
Coronie	NS03	2,777	1,620	Totness
Marowijne	NS04	23,402	45,980	Albina
Nickerie	NS05	34,480	64,610	Nieuw Nickerie
Para	NS06	14,867	980	Onverwacht
Paramaribo	NS07	67,905	32	Paramaribo
Saramacca	NS08	10,335	23,420	Groningen
Suriname	NS09	166,494	1,628	Paramaribo
		354,860	163,820	

Status: All divisions are districts except for Paramaribo, which is an urban district.
Population: 1980 census.

~1988   Suriname reorganized. Suriname district divided among Commewijne, Para, Saramacca, and the new Wanica district. Sipaliwini district formed from large parts of Brokopondo, Marowijne, Nickerie, and Saramacca districts, constituting about the southern two-thirds of the country. Other borders adjusted.

SVALBARD AND JAN MAYEN

ISO = SJ/FIPS = SV   Language = Russian, Norwegian   Time zone = (see table)   Capital = Longyearbyen

The question of sovereignty over Svalbard wasn't settled until 1920-02-09, when the Svalbard treaty assigned it to Norway.

Svalbard became a territory of Norway on 1925-08-14. Jan Mayen Island, already a possession, was made a Norwegian territory on 1929-05-08.

Other names of country: Ilhas Svalbard e Jan Mayen (Portuguese); Svalbard e Isla de Jan Mayen; Islas Svalbard y Jan Mayen (Spanish); Svalbard et île Jan Mayen (French); Svalbard und Jan Mayen (German).

Origin of name: Svalbard is Norse *sval*: cold, *bard*: coast. Captain Jan Mayen was based in Jan Mayen I. 1611–1635.

division	FIPS	tz	population	area-km	area-mi	capital
Jan Mayen	JN	-1 [d]	0	373	144	
Svalbard	SV	+1 [d]	3,181	62,049	23,957	Longyearbyen
			3,181	62,422	24,101	

[d] = *indicates daylight saving time observed.*

Status: These divisions are territories of Norway.

FIPS: Codes from FIPS PUB 10-4, which treats each of these territories as a separate country.

Tz: Time zone (hours offset from Greenwich).

Population: 1992-07 estimate. Jan Mayen has no permanent residents.

Area-km: Square kilometers.

Area-mi: Square miles.

Territorial extent: Jan Mayen is a single isolated island in the Arctic.

Svalbard includes all the islands between 74° and 81° N. latitude and between 10° and 35° E. longitude. The largest of the islands are Spitsbergen, Nordaustlandet, Edgeøya, Barentsøya, Prins Karls Forland, Kvitøya, and Bjørnøya (Bear Islands), which is isolated and south of the main group.

SWAZILAND

ISO = SZ/FIPS = WZ   Language = English, siSwati   Time zone = +2   Capital = Mbabane,Lobamba

Swaziland was a British protectorate from 1903 until 1968-09-06, when it became independent.

Other names of country: Kingdom of Swaziland (formal–English); Suazilândia (Portuguese); Svasíland (Icelandic); Swasiland (German); Swazilandia (Spanish); Swazimaa (Finnish); Umbuso weSwatini (formal).

Origin of name: after King Mswati I (mid–19th century).

division	ISO	FIPS	population	area-km	area-mi	capital
Hhohho	HH	WZ01	178,936	3,569	1,378	Mbabane
Lubombo	LU	WZ02	153,958	5,945	2,295	Sireki
Manzini	MA	WZ03	192,596	4,070	1,571	Manzini
Shiselweni	SH	WZ04	155,569	3,779	1,459	Hlatikulu
			681,059	17,363	6,703	

Status: These divisions are districts.

ISO: Codes from ISO 3166-2.

FIPS: Codes from FIPS PUB 10-4.

Population: 1986 census.

Area-km: Square kilometers.

Area-mi: Square miles.

Note: ISO 3166-2 also lists a district called Praslin, with a code of PR. I haven't been able to find any other mention of Praslin as a geographical name in Swaziland. I think what happened is that Praslin slipped into some versions of FIPS PUB 10-4 by mistake (code WZ05); ISO copied it from FIPS; and then the mistake was corrected in FIPS.

Change history: At independence, Swaziland was reorganized from six districts (Bremersdorp, Hlatikulu, Mankaiana, Mbabane, Pigg's Peak, and Stegi) into the present four.

Other names of subdivisions:

Shiselweni: Shiselwini (variant)

SWEDEN

ISO = SE/FIPS = SW   Language = Swedish   Time zone = +1^d Capital = Stockholm

Sweden was sovereign over Norway during most of the 19th century. The united kingdom was called Sweden and Norway. Norway became separate on 1905-06-07.

Other names of country: Kingdom of Sweden (formal–English); Konungariket Sverige (formal); Ruotsi (Finnish); Schweden (German); Suecia (Spanish); Suécia (Portuguese); Suède (French); Sverige (Danish, Norwegian, Swedish); Svezia (Italian); Svíþjóð (Icelandic); Zweden (Dutch).

Origin of name: from ethnic name variously transcribed Suethi, Svear, etc.

division	abv	ISO	lb	FIPS	NU	population	area-km	area-mi	Swedish	capital
Blekinge	BL	10	K	SW02	4	149,960	3,039	1,173	Blekinge län	Karlskrona
Gävleborg	GV	21	X	SW03	6	288,223	19,722	7,615	Gävleborgs län	Gävle
Gotland	GT	09	I	SW05	3	56,840	3,173	1,225	Gotlands län	Visby
Halland	HA	13	N	SW06	5	250,959	4,930	1,903	Hallands län	Halmstad
Jämtland	JA	23	Z	SW07	7	134,789	51,548	19,903	Jämtlands län	Östersund
Jönköping	JO	06	F	SW08	3	306,590	13,904	5,369	Jönköpings län	Jönköping
Kalmar	KA	08	H	SW09	3	239,564	11,622	4,487	Kalmar län	Kalmar
Dalarna	KO	20	W	SW10	6	286,667	30,362	11,723	Dalarnes län	Falun
Kronoberg	KR	07	G	SW12	3	176,589	9,913	3,827	Kronobergs län	Växjö
Norrbotten	NB	25	BD	SW14	8	262,838	105,877	40,879	Norrbottens län	Luleå
Örebro	OR	18	T	SW15	2	271,523	9,047	3,493	Örebro län	Örebro
Östergötland	OG	05	E	SW16	2	399,506	11,080	4,278	Östergötlands län	Linköping
Scania	SN	12	M	SW27	4	1,058,015	11,283	4,356	Skåne län	Malmö
Södermanland	SD	04	D	SW18	2	253,363	6,851	2,645	Södermanlands län	Nyköping
Stockholm	ST	01	AB	SW26	1	1,629,631	7,950	3,070	Stockholms län	Stockholm
Uppsala	UP	03	C	SW21	2	264,738	5,398	2,084	Uppsala län	Uppsala
Värmland	VR	17	S	SW22	6	282,375	19,416	7,497	Värmlands län	Karlstad
Västerbotten	VB	24	AC	SW23	8	250,134	59,140	22,834	Västerbottens län	Umeå
Västernorrland	VN	22	Y	SW24	7	260,488	25,704	9,924	Västernorrlands län	Härnösand
Västmanland	VM	19	U	SW25	2	256,510	6,772	2,615	Västmanlands län	Västerås
Västra Götaland	VG	—	O	SW28	5	1,447,734	23,941	9,244	Västra Götalands län	Göteborg
						8,527,036	440,672	170,144		

Status: These divisions are län (counties).

Abv: Two-letter code for international compatibility (defined by the author).

ISO: Codes from ISO 3166-2; identical to länskoder. The counties are often sorted by länskod.

Lb: Länsbokstäver (county letters), widely used in Sweden.

FIPS: Codes from FIPS PUB 10-4.

NU: Last digit of level-2 NUTS code (Nomenclature of Territorial Units for Statistics; see below for list of codes and their meanings).

Population: 1989 census.

Area-km: Square kilometers.

Area-mi: Square miles.

Swedish: Names of counties in Swedish.

NUTS codes: These areas have no administrative significance, but are used for statistical summaries.

NUTS	area	explanation
SE01	Stockholm	Stockholm city and county
SE02	Östra Mellansverige	East Central Sweden
SE03	Småland med Öarna	Småland with Islands (i.e., Gotland and Öland)
SE04	Sydsverige	South Sweden
SE05	Västsverige	West Sweden
SE06	Norra Mellansverige	North Central Sweden
SE07	Mellersta Norrland	Central Norrland
SE08	Övre Norrland	Upper Norrland

Some data are not yet available for the recently formed counties of Scania and Västra Götaland.

Further subdivisions: The counties are divided into kommuner (municipalities; 288 in 1998), which are further subdivided into församlingar (parishes). Sweden has a hierarchical system of numerical codes for these entities. The first two digits are a länskod, the first four are a kommunkod, and all six digits are a församlingskod.

There are also 25 traditional divisions called landskap (provinces). The counties and the provinces overlap, but rarely coincide. There are also three traditional regions: Götaland, Norrland, and Svealand, each consisting of several provinces.

Territorial extent: All of the counties except Gotland are predominantly on the Scandinavian mainland.

Gotland consists of the island of Gotland and its smaller neighbors, such as Fårö and Gotska Sandön. Gotland is the only county that consists of a single municipality.

Jönköping includes Visingsö in Lake Vättern.

Kalmar includes Öland.

Scania includes Ven island in Øresund sound.

Stockholm includes many islands, in both the Baltic Sea and Lake Mälaren. The Baltic islands extend from Torö and Mörkö in the south to Gräsö in the north. The lake islands include Svartsjölandet, Munsö, and Adelsö.

Västerbotten includes Ängesön and Holmön.

Västra Götaland includes Torsö, Källandsö, and Djurö in Lake Vänern.

Origins of names:

Älvsborg: Old Swedish Eluesborg, from *älv*: river, *ö*: mouth,   Gotland: Land of the Goths
    borg: fort   Jämtland: Land of Jämte (ethnic name)
Botten (Bothnia): Swedish *botten*: bottom

Change history:

1968-01	Stockholm City merged with Stockholm county. Before the change, Stockholm City had länskod 01, länsbokstav A, FIPS code SW20; Stockholm county had 02, B, and SW19, respectively. Stockholm was the capital of both. This was the first change in the number or identity of primary administrative divisions of Sweden since 1825.
1997-01-01	Kristianstad (ISO = 11, lb = L, FIPS = SW11, capital = Kristianstad) and Malmöhus (ISO = 12, lb = M, FIPS = SW13, capital = Malmö) counties merged to form Scania. Name of Kopparberg county changed to Dalarna.
1998-01-01	Älvsborg (ISO = 15, lb = P, FIPS = SW01, capital = Vänersborg), Göteborg och Bohus (ISO = 14, lb = O, FIPS = SW04, capital = Göteborg), and Skaraborg (ISO = 16, lb = R, FIPS = SW17, capital = Mariestad) counties merged to form Västra Götaland. Two municipalities (Habo and Mullsjö) transferred from Västra Götaland county to Jönköping.

More changes of this sort are planned in the near future.

Other names of subdivisions: In the early years of the 20th century, it was common to see e instead of ä, f instead of medial v, and w instead of initial v (Elfsborg, Gefleborg, Wermland, etc.).

Göteborg: Gothenburg (German)   Stockholm: Estocolmo (Portuguese, Spanish); Stoccolmo (Italian)
Gotland: Gothland, Gottland (obsolete)
Scania: Scanie (French)

Population history:

county	1895	1910	1945	1955	1965	1976	1989
Älvsborg	274,698	287,692	338,996	366,827	390,000	420,192	437,516
Blekinge	143,387	149,359	146,908	146,034	149,000	154,962	149,960
Gävleborg	218,864	253,792	275,436	290,676	293,000	294,627	288,223
Göteborg and Bohus	313,340	381,270	510,896	579,551	666,000	714,374	735,672
Gotland	51,855	55,217	59,505	57,526	54,000	54,621	56,840
Halland	139,356	147,224	155,257	165,865	180,000	219,780	250,959
Jämtland	104,259	118,115	143,213	144,880	131,000	133,752	134,789
Jönköping	195,856	214,454	253,794	277,949	296,000	302,142	306,590
Kalmar	229,176	228,129	231,336	776,462	236,000	240,969	239,564
Kopparberg	206,774	233,873	253,507	276,172	282,000	283,350	286,667 ▶

county	1895	1910	1945	1955	1965	1976	1989
Kristianstad	219,858	228,307	253,277	259,398	262,000	273,941	286,654
Kronoberg	158,838	157,965	153,572	159,112	164,000	170,319	176,589
Malmöhus	383,202	457,214	551,610	596,809	667,000	739,682	771,361
Norrbotten	115,500	161,132	229,568	250,521	260,000	266,113	262,838
Örebro	188,771	207,021	235,989	254,136	268,000	273,819	271,523
Östergötland	270,973	294,179	332,946	354,126	366,000	389,431	399,506
Skaraborg	244,514	241,284	244,737	249,389	255,000	264,286	274,546
Södermanland	161,722	178,568	201,051	219,501	241,000	251,996	253,363
Stockholm City	271,638	342,323	671,284	776,947	— —	— —	
Stockholm	157,457	229,181	321,989	386,489	1,382,000	1,500,868	1,629,631
Uppsala	123,015	128,171	146,415	159,752	185,000	233,115	264,738
Värmland	252,915	260,135	272,275	286,786	287,000	284,529	282,375
Västerbotten	133,336	161,366	228,135	236,434	234,000	237,705	250,134
Västernorrland	217,220	250,512	278,707	288,599	277,000	268,237	260,488
Västmanland	142,735	155,920	183,346	213,723	250,000	260,164	256,510
	4,919,259	5,522,403	6,673,749	7,773,664	7,775,000	8,232,974	8,527,036

Data for 1895, 1955, and 1976 are estimates.

SWITZERLAND

ISO = CH/FIPS = SZ   Language = German, French, Italian, Romansh   Time zone = +1^d Capital = Bern

Switzerland has been independent throughout the 20th century.

Other names of country: Confederación Suiza, Suiza (Spanish); Confédération Suisse (French); Confederazione Svizzera (Italian); Confoederatio Helvetica (Latin); Schweiz (Danish, German, Swedish); Schweizerische Eidtgenossenschaft (formal); Suiça (Portuguese); Sveits (Norwegian); Sveitsi (Finnish); Sviss (Icelandic); Swiss Confederation (formal–English); Zwitserland (Dutch).

Origin of name: name of Schwyz, one of the founding cantons, applied to the entire federation.

division	ISO	FIPS	population	area-km	area-mi	lang	capital
Aargau	AG	SZ01	531,700	1,405	542	g	Aarau
Appenzell Ausser-Rhoden	AR	SZ02	54,100	243	94	g	Herisau
Appenzell Inner-Rhoden	AI	SZ10	14,800	172	66	g	Appenzell
Basel-Landschaft	BL	SZ03	253,900	428	165	g	Liestal
Basel-Stadt	BS	SZ04	194,900	37	14	g	Basel
Bern	BE	SZ05	940,900	6,049	2,336	g	Bern
Fribourg	FR	SZ06	227,900	1,670	645	fg	Fribourg
Geneva	GE	SZ07	394,600	282	109	f	Geneva
Glarus	GL	SZ08	39,200	685	264	g	Glarus
Graubünden	GR	SZ09	186,000	7,106	2,744	gr	Chur; Coire (f); Coira (i)
Jura	JU	SZ26	68,900	838	323	f	Delémont; Delsberg (g)
Lucerne	LU	SZ11	341,800	1,492	576	g	Lucerne
Neuchâtel	NE	SZ12	165,200	797	308	f	Neuchâtel
Nidwalden	NW	SZ13	36,800	276	106	g	Stans
Obwalden	OW	SZ14	31,400	491	189	g	Sarnen
Sankt Gallen	SG	SZ15	443,800	2,014	778	g	Saint Gall
Schaffhausen	SH	SZ16	73,800	298	115	g	Schaffhausen
Schwyz	SZ	SZ17	123,800	908	351	g	Schwyz
Solothurn	SO	SZ18	240,800	791	305	g	Solothurn
Thurgau	TG	SZ19	224,800	1,013	391	g	Frauenfeld
Ticino	TI	SZ20	304,800	2,811	1,085	i	Bellinzona; Bellenz (g)
Uri	UR	SZ21	35,900	1,077	416	g	Altdorf
Valais	VS	SZ22	272,300	5,226	2,018	fg	Sion; Sitten (g)
Vaud	VD	SZ23	606,500	3,219	1,243	f	Lausanne
Zug	ZG	SZ24	93,700	239	92	g	Zug ▶

division	ISO	FIPS	population	area-km	area-mi	lang	capital
Zurich	ZH	SZ25	1,178,800	1,729	667	g	Zürich
			7,081,100	41,296	15,942		

Status: These divisions are cantons (French), kantone (German), cantoni (Italian): cantons.

ISO: Codes from ISO 3166-2. These have been the official Swiss abbreviations for years.

FIPS: Codes from FIPS PUB 10-4.

Population: 1996 estimate.

Area-km: Square kilometers.

Area-mi: Square miles.

Lang: Majority language(s): French (f), German (g), Italian (i), Romansh (r).

Postal code: Switzerland uses a four-digit postal code (Liechtenstein is also part of the system). The postal code areas are not directly correlated with canton boundaries. The prefix CH- is often used on international mail within Europe to designate Swiss postal codes.

Capital: English name of capital. Name is also given in French, German, or Italian, when different from English. Exception: when canton has same name as capital, look under "Other names of subdivisions," because the foreign names of the capital will be the same.

Further subdivisions: Technically, Switzerland is divided into 23 cantons, of which three are further divided into half-cantons (French, demi-cantons; German, halb-kantone): Appenzell into Ausser-Rhoden and Inner-Rhoden; Basel into Basel-Landschaft and Basel-Stadt; and Unterwalden into Nidwalden and Obwalden. The cantons are the territorial divisions. Switzerland is also divided into 26 states, of which 20 are coextensive with the 20 undivided cantons, and six are coextensive with the half-cantons. The states are the administrative divisions. On a lower level, the cantons are divided into districts, which are further subdivided into communes.

Territorial extent: Appenzell Inner-Rhoden consists of three separate areas, each of which lies on the border between Appenzell Ausser-Rhoden and Sankt Gallen. Appenzell as a whole is entirely surrounded by Sankt Gallen, although at one point Sankt Gallen is only a corridor less than one kilometer wide between Appenzell and Austria.

Bern has five enclaves. There are two tiny ones surrounded by Fribourg and containing Münchenwiler and Clavaleyres. There are also three that were created in 1979, when Jura was split from Bern.

Fribourg has four enclaves: one tiny one surrounded by Bern, two surrounded by Vaud, and the largest, around Estavayer-le-Lac, surrounded by Vaud on three sides and Lake Neuchâtel on the fourth.

Geneva has two enclaves. One tiny one is surrounded by Vaud. A larger one nearby is surrounded on three sides by Vaud and the fourth by Lac Léman (Lake Geneva), where it has a water border with France.

Obwalden consists of two separate sections separated by Nidwalden, and both bordering on Bern. The smaller one contains Engelberg.

Schaffhausen has three separate areas. They are all predominantly on the right bank of the Rhine. The first one, heading downstream from the Bodensee (Lake Constance), contains Ramsen and Stein am Rhein (and has a tiny extension on the left bank). The second, main section contains Schaffhausen city. The third and smallest contains Buchberg.

Solothurn has three enclaves. The ones containing Kleinlützel and Mariastein are on the French border, separated from the main part of Solothurn by part of Bern. The tiny one containing Steinhof is surrounded by Bern.

Thurgau has a small enclave containing the town of Horn, although if territorial waters in the Bodensee are taken into account, the enclave may be connected to the main section.

Vaud has one enclave around Avenches, separated from it by Fribourg, but also bordering on Bern and having a water boundary with Neuchâtel.

Origins of names:

Aargau: from the river Aar and German *gau*: district

Appenzell: from Latin *abbatis cella*: abbot's chamber

Basel-Landschaft: Rural Basel, from Ancient Greek *basileia*: royal (was fort of Emperor Valentinian I)

Basel-Stadt: Basel City

Bern: Indo-European *ber*: swampy place; or from Italian Verona (city name); cf. Berlin, Germany

Fribourg: German *frei*: free, *burg*: fort

Geneva: Indo-European *gen*: bend, *ava*: water

Glarus: Latin *claris*: clear, for a village in a clearing

Graubünden: German *graue bund*: gray league, a league devoted to resistance to the Hapsburg Empire

Jura: after the Jura Mountains, from Gallic *iuris*: wooded mountain

Lucerne: probably after Saint Leodegar, the city's patron, but possibly Latin *lucerna*: lantern

Neuchâtel: Latin *Novum Castellum*: new castle

Nidwalden: German *nieder*: lower, *Wald*: forest

Obwalden: German *ober*: upper, *Wald*: forest

Sankt Gallen: abbey founded by Saint Gall in 612

Schaffhausen: Old German *Sciphúsen*: ship houses, because boats in Lake Constance trade were sheltered there

Solothurn: Latin Salodurum, in which durum means fort

Ticino: after the Ticino River
Valais: Latin *Vallis Poenina*: pennine valley

Vaud: Latin Comitatus Valdensis, possibly from *valdum*: defensible spot

Change history:

1979-01-01   Jura canton split from Bern. It consisted of the majority French-speaking areas.

Other names of subdivisions:

Aargau: Argovia (Italian); Argóvia (Portuguese); Argovie (French)

Appenzell Ausser-Rhoden: Appenzell Rhodes Extérieures (French); Appenzell-Outer Rhodes (variant); Appenzello Esterno (Italian)

Appenzell Inner-Rhoden: Appenzell Rhodes Intérieures (French); Appenzell-Inner Rhodes (variant); Appenzello Interno (Italian)

Basel-Landschaft: Bâle-Campagne (French); Basel-Country, Baselland, Basel-Land (variant); Basilea campagna (Italian); Basiléia região (Portuguese)

Basel-Stadt: Bâle-Ville (French); Basel-City, Basel-Town (variant); Basilea (Spanish); Basilea città (Italian); Basiléia cidade (Portuguese)

Bern: Berna (Italian, Portuguese, Spanish); Berne (French)

Fribourg: Freiburg (German); Friburgo (Italian, Portuguese, Spanish)

Geneva: Genebra (Portuguese); Genève (French); Genf (German); Ginebra (Spanish); Ginevra (Italian)

Glarus: Glaris (French, Spanish); Glarona (Italian)

Graubünden: Grigioni (Italian); Grisons (French)

Jura: Giura (Italian)

Lucerne: Lucerna (Italian, Portuguese, Spanish); Luzern (German, Norwegian)

Neuchâtel: Neuenburg (German)

Nidwalden: Nidwald, Unterwalden-le-Bas (French); Nidwaldo (Italian)

Obwalden: Obwald, Unterwalden-le-Haut (French); Obwaldo (Italian)

Sankt Gallen: Saint-Gall (French); San Gallo (Italian)

Schaffhausen: Schaffhouse (French); Sciaffusa (Italian)

Schwyz: Svitto (Italian)

Solothurn: Soletta (Italian); Soleure (French); Soleuro (Spanish)

Thurgau: Thurgovie (French); Turgovia (Italian); Turgóvia (Portuguese)

Ticino: Tesino (Spanish); Tessin (French, German)

Valais: Vallese (Italian); Wallis (German)

Vaud: Waadt (German)

Zug: Zoug (French); Zugo (Italian)

Zurich: Zürich (German, Norwegian, Swedish); Zurigo (Italian); Zurique (Portuguese)

Population history:

	1900	1910	1930	1941	1950	1960	1970	1980	1989	1996
Aargau	206,498	229,850	259,644	270,463	300,782	360,940	433,284	453,442	489,567	531,700
Ausser-Rhoden	55,281	57,723	48,977	44,756	47,938	48,920	49,023	47,611	54,087	54,100
Inner-Rhoden	13,499	14,631	13,988	13,383	13,427	12,943	13,124	12,844	14,680	14,800
Basel-Land	68,497	76,241	92,541	94,459	107,549	148,282	204,889	219,822	234,910	253,900
Basel-Stadt	112,227	135,546	155,030	169,961	196,498	225,588	234,945	203,915	197,403	194,900
Bern	589,433	642,744	688,774	728,916	801,943	889,523	983,296	912,022	942,721	940,900
Fribourg	127,951	139,200	143,230	152,053	158,695	159,194	180,309	185,246	203,878	227,900
Geneva	132,609	154,159	171,366	174,855	202,918	259,234	331,599	349,040	377,108	394,600
Glarus	32,349	33,211	35,653	34,771	37,663	40,148	38,155	36,718	37,686	39,200
Graubünden	104,520	118,262	126,340	128,247	137,100	147,458	162,086	164,641	177,096	186,000
Jura	—	—	—	—	—	—	—	64,986	65,376	68,900
Lucerne	146,159	166,782	189,391	206,608	223,249	253,446	289,641	296,159	316,210	341,800
Neuchâtel	126,279	132,184	124,324	117,900	128,152	147,633	169,173	158,368	159,543	165,200
Nidwalden	13,070	13,796	15,055	17,348	19,389	22,188	25,634	28,617	35,393	36,800
Obwalden	15,260	17,118	19,401	20,340	22,125	23,135	24,509	25,865	30,837	31,400
Sankt Gallen	250,285	301,141	286,362	286,201	309,106	339,489	384,475	391,995	416,578	443,800
Schaffhausen	41,514	45,943	51,187	53,772	57,515	65,981	72,854	69,413	71,210	73,800
Schwyz	55,385	58,347	62,337	66,555	71,082	78,048	92,072	97,354	108,576	123,800
Solothurn	100,762	116,728	144,198	154,944	170,508	200,816	224,133	218,102	223,803	240,800
Thurgau	113,221	134,055	136,063	138,122	149,738	166,420	182,835	183,795	201,773	224,800
Ticino	138,638	158,556	159,223	161,882	175,055	195,566	245,458	265,899	286,537	304,800
Uri	19,700	22,055	22,968	27,302	28,556	32,021	34,091	33,883	34,042	35,900
Valais	114,438	129,579	136,394	148,319	159,178	177,783	206,563	218,707	249,473	272,300
Vaud	281,379	315,428	331,853	343,398	377,585	429,512	511,851	528,747	576,319	606,500 ▶

	1900	1910	1930	1941	1950	1960	1970	1980	1989	1996
Zug	25,093	28,013	34,395	36,643	42,239	52,489	67,996	75,930	84,742	93,700
Zurich	431,036	500,679	617,706	674,505	777,002	952,304	1,107,788	1,122,839	1,152,769	1,178,800
	3,315,083	3,741,971	4,066,400	4,265,703	4,714,992	5,429,061	6,269,783	6,365,960	6,742,317	7,081,100

All figures are census data as of December 1 of the given year. Jura included in Bern until 1980.

SYRIA

ISO = SY/FIPS = SY   Language = Arabic   Time zone = +2 ᵈ   Capital = Damascus

The Ottoman Empire had a Syria province, containing the vilayets of Aleppo, Beirut, Syria (or Damascus), and Zor. During World War I, the British and French seized the southern part of the Ottoman Empire and parceled it out between themselves. The Treaty of Sèvres (1920-08-10) mandated Syria and Lebanon to France. Syria and Lebanon became independent and separate countries on 1944-01-01. Syria formed a union with Egypt, the United Arab Republic (U.A.R.), on 1958-02-01. They both became regions of the U.A.R. Syria withdrew from the union on 1961-09-29.

Other names of country: al-Jumhuriya al-Arabiya as-Suriya (formal); Arabische Republik Syrien (German); República Árabe Siria, Siria (Spanish); République arabe syrienne, Syrie (French); Siria (Italian); Síria (Portuguese); Syrian Arab Republic (formal–English); Syrië (Dutch); Syrien (Danish, Swedish, Swiss German); Sýrland (Icelandic); Syyria (Finnish).

Origin of name: Syria is probably from Phoenician *tsur*: rock.

division	ISO	FIPS	population	area-km	area-mi
Aleppo	HL	SY09	1,878,701	16,142	6,232
Al Ḥasakah	HA	SY01	669,887	23,371	9,024
Al Qunayṭirah	QU	SY03	26,258	1,710	660
Ar Raqqah	RA	SY04	348,383	22,000	8,494
As Suwaydā'	SU	SY05	199,114	5,550	2,143
Damascus	DI	SY13	1,112,214	573	221
Darʻā	DR	SY06	362,969	3,790	1,463
Dayr az Zawr	DY	SY07	409,130	33,060	12,765
Ḥamāh	HM	SY10	736,412	8,844	3,415
Ḥimṣ	HI	SY11	812,517	42,226	16,304
Idlib	ID	SY12	579,581	5,933	2,291
Latakia	LA	SY02	554,384	2,437	941
Rif Dimashq	RD	SY08	917,364	17,654	6,816
Ṭarṭūs	TA	SY14	443,290	1,890	730
			9,050,204	185,180	71,499

Status: These divisions are muhafazah (provinces).
ISO: Codes from ISO 3166-2.
FIPS: Codes from FIPS PUB 10-4.
Population: 1991 census.
Area-km: Square kilometers.
Area-mi: Square miles.
Capitals: Capitals have the same names as their provinces, except that Damascus is the capital of both Damascus and Rif Dimashq.
Further subdivisions: The provinces are divided into mantika (districts), which are further divided into nahia (subdistricts).
Territorial extent: Syria claims the Turkish province of Hatay, which the Syrians call Iskenderun.
Origins of names:

Aleppo: said to derive from Arabic *Hala al-Shahbaa*: milking the fair cow, referring to a legend that the patriarch Abraham milked a cow there

Al Jazira: Arabic for the island, referring to the area between the Tigris and Euphrates rivers

Jabal Druze: Arabic *jabal*: mountain, named for Mount Druze in southern Syria

Change history:

1920	France organized its mandate of Syria. Beirut became the capital. There were six semi-autonomous areas: Aleppo, Alexandretta, Damascus, Jabal Druze, Alaouites (Alawiya, 'Alawite), and Lebanon (Great Lebanon; French: Grand Liban).
1923	Northern strip of Syria restored to Turkey by the Treaty of Lausanne.
1925	Syria state formed by merging Aleppo and Damascus provinces.
1926-05	Status of Lebanon changed from province to state, with its borders somewhat enlarged.
1930-05-14	The French imposed a new constitution, under which the French mandate consisted of the republics of Latakia (former Alaouites; French: Lattaquié), Lebanon, and Syria (including Alexandretta), and the semi-autonomous area of Jabal Druze.
1936	Latakia and Jabal Druze merged with Syria under new treaty with France.
1938-09-02	Alexandretta became independent as the Republic of Hatay (later merged with Turkey).
1944-01-01	Lebanon split from Syria.
~1946	Syria reorganized into the districts of Aleppo, Damascus, Euphrates (Al Furat), Ḥamāh, Hauran, Ḥimṣ, Jabal Druze, Al Jazira, and Latakia.
~1954	Name of Hauran changed to Darʻā; name of Jabal Druze changed to As Suwaydāʼ; name of Al Jazira changed to Al Ḥasakah.
~1961	Euphrates split into Al Rashid and Dayr az Zawr; Idlib split from Aleppo.
~1965	Damascus split into Dimashq (Damascus) province and Damascus city (Madīnat Dimashq).
~1966	Name of Al Rashid changed to Ar Raqqah.
~1967	Al Qunayṭirah province split from Dimashq.
1967	Israel occupied the Golan Heights. This represents most of Al Qunayṭirah and part of Darʻā.
~1972	Ṭarṭūs split from Latakia.
1987	Status of Damascus city changed from governorate to province; Dimashq province brought under the jurisdiction of Damascus and called Rif Dimashq rural area.

Other names of subdivisions:

Aleppo: Alep (French); Alepo (Spanish); Haleb, Ḥalab (variant)

Al Ḥasakah: El Haseke, Haseke, Hassakeh, Hazakieh (variant); Hassetché (French); Al Jezira, Jezireh (obsolete)

Al Qunayṭirah: Al Qunatirah, El Quneitra, El Kenitra, Kunaitra, Kuneitra, Quneitra (variant)

Ar Raqqah: Al Rashid, Rashid (obsolete); Al Rakka, Raqqa (variant)

As Suwaydāʼ: Djebel Druze, Jabal Druze, Jebel Druse, Jebel ed Druz, Al Jubal ad Duze (obsolete); Gebel Druso (Italian-obsolete); Al Sueida, Es Sueida, Es Suweida, Soueida, Suwaydá, Sweida (variant)

Damascus: Damas (French); Damasco (Italian, Portuguese, Spanish); Damaskus (German, Norwegian, Swedish); Dimashq, Dimishq (variant)

Darʻā: Dária, Deraʻa (variant); Hauran (obsolete)

Dayr az Zawr: Dayr az Zaur, Deir ez Zor (variant)

Ḥamāh: Hama (variant)

Ḥimṣ: Homs (variant)

Latakia: Al Lādhiqīyah, El Ladhiqiya, Lattakia, Lattakieh (variant)

Ṭarṭūs: Tartous (variant)

TAIWAN

ISO = TW/FIPS = TW   Language = Chinese   Time zone = +8   Capital = Taipei

Taiwan belonged to Japan in 1900, as a spoil of the Sino-Japanese War of 1895. When World War II ended, Taiwan returned to Chinese rule. As Communists extended their control throughout mainland China, the Nationalist government of Chiang Kai-Shek retreated to Taiwan. At present, all concerned parties agree that there is only one China. The open question is whether its legitimate government is the People's Republic of China (PRC) in Beijing, or the Republic of China (ROC) in

Taipei. According to the ROC government, the provinces of China still stand as they did in 1949. The province which the ROC calls Fukien is the same as the one which the PRC, using Pinyin transcription, calls Fujian. However, in the listing below, only the area and population under the control of the ROC are shown.

Other names of country: Chung-hua Min-kuo (formal); Formosa (obsolete); Formose (French-obsolete); Republic of China (formal–English); Taívan (Icelandic); Taiwán (Spanish); Taïwan Province de Chine (French); Taiwan Province of China (English).

Origin of name: Chinese *tai*: terrace, *wan*: bay, referring to a harbor on the western coast.

division	abv	ISO	FIPS	population	area-km	area-mi	capital
Fukien	FK	FUC	TW01	51,000	175	68	(Fuzhou)
Kaohsiung	KH	KHH	TW02	1,372,000	113	44	Kaohsiung
Taipei	TP	TPE	TW03	2,663,000	67	26	Taipei
Taiwan	TW	TAI	TW04	16,753,000	35,660	13,768	Chung-hsing-hsin-tsun (Chunghsing New Village)
				20,839,000	36,015	13,906	

Status: These divisions are sheng (provinces), except for Kaohsiung and Taipei, which are chuan-shih (special municipalities).

Abv: Two-letter code for international compatibility (defined by the author).

ISO: Codes from ISO 3166-2.

FIPS: Codes from FIPS PUB 10-4.

Population: 1995 estimate.

Area-km: Square kilometers.

Area-mi: Square miles.

Further subdivisions: The provinces are subdivided into hsien (counties) and shih (municipalities, cities), as follows.

county	ISO	type	pr	population	area-km	capital	postcodes
Changhwa	CHA	cn	TW	1,243,000	1,062	Changhua	500-530
Chiayi	CYI	cn	TW	540,000	1,951	Chiai	602-625
Chiayi City	CYI	mu	TW	255,000		Chiai	600
Hsinchu	HSZ	cn	TW	387,000	1,529	Hsinchu	302-315
Hsinchu City	HSZ	mu	TW	349,000		Hsinchu	300
Hualien	HUA	cn	TW	338,000	4,629	Hualien	970-983
Ilan	ILA	cn	TW	445,000	2,137	Ilan	260-272
Kaohsiung	KHH	cn	TW	1,154,000	2,833	Fengshan	814-852
Kaohsiung City	KHH	sm	KH	1,372,000	113	Kaohsiung	800-813
Keelung City	CHI	mu	TW	356,000	132	Chilung	200-206
Kinmen	FUC	cn	FK	45,000	148		890-896
Lienkiang	TAI	cn	FK	6,000	27		209-212
Miaoli	MIA	cn	TW	534,000	1,820	Miaoli	350-369
Nantou	NAN	cn	TW	524,000	4,106	Nantou	540-558
Penghu	PEN	cn	TW	88,000	127	Makung	880-885
Pingtung	PIF	cn	TW	879,000	2,776	Pingtung	900-947
Taichung	TXG	cn	TW	1,378,000	2,051	Fengyüan	411-439
Taichung City	TXG	mu	TW	842,000	163	Taichung	400-408
Tainan	TNN	cn	TW	1,049,000	2,004	Hsinying	710-745
Tainan City	TNN	mu	TW	689,000	175	Tainan	700-709
Taipei	TPE	cn	TW	3,266,000	2,138	Panchiao	207-208, 220-253
Taipei City	TPE	sm	TP	2,663,000	67	Taipei	100-116
Taitung	TTT	cn	TW	240,000	3,515	Taitung	950-966
Taoyuan	TAO	cn	TW	1,480,000	1,221	Taoyüan	320-338
Yunlin	YUN	cn	TW	718,000	1,291	Touliu	630-655
				20,840,000	36,015		

ISO: Codes from ISO 3166-2, which assigned codes to both levels of district, but used some codes twice.

Type: cn = county, mu = municipality, sm = special municipality.

Pr: province or special municipality containing this county, using codes from above.

Population: 1995 estimate

Postal code: Taiwan uses five-digit postal codes in nnn-nn format. The first three digits indicate the county.

Territorial extent: Fukien province consists of two island groups, each constituting a hsien. One of them is Kinmen (islands of Quemoy (Kinmen), Tatan Tao, Hsiaochinmen Tao, Tungting Tao). The other is Lienkiang (islands of Matsu, Changhsu Chan, Tungyin Tao, Tungchuan Tao).

Kaohsiung includes the area around Kaohsiung city on the main island, and the island of Liuch'iu Yü.

Taipei is completely surrounded by Taiwan province.

Taiwan province includes the Penghu island group, called the Pescadores (fisherman islands) by early Portuguese explorers, and some smaller islands: Pengchia Yü, Chihwei, Kueishan, Huoshao, and Hungfou Hsü (Lan Yü).

Taiwan, as a country, also claims the Spratly and Paracel Islands.

Origins of names:

Taipei means "Taiwan north."

Change history:

    1967   Taipei special municipality split from Taiwan province.

  ~1989   Capital of Taiwan province moved from Taichung to Chung-hsing-hsin-tsun.

Other names of subdivisions:

Fukien: Fuchien, Fujian (variant)
Kaohsiung: Gaoxiong (Pinyin)

Taipei: Taibei (Pinyin); Taipé (Portuguese); Taipeh (German, Italian)

TAJIKISTAN

ISO = TJ/FIPS = TI   Language = Tajik   Time zone = +5   Capital = Dushanbe

In 1900, the territory that now constitutes Tajikistan was partly in the Khanate of Bukhara, and partly in the Ferghana, Pamir, and Zarafshan regions of the Turkestan general government of the Russian Empire. During the Russian Revolution, the status of the Central Asian lands was unresolved for a time. The Turkestan A.S.S.R. was formed in 1921. In 1924, the Central Asian part of the Soviet Union was reorganized to correspond to the distribution of nationalities. The Tadzhikskaya Associated Soviet Socialist Republic was created then. It became a constituent republic of the Soviet Union in 1929. As the Soviet Union broke up, it became Tajikistan, an independent country, on 1991-09-09.

Other names of country: Republic of Tajikistan (formal–English); Jumhurii Tojikistan, Respublika i Tojikiston (formal); Tadjikistan (French); Tadjiquistão (Portuguese); Tadschikistan (German); Tadsjikistan (Danish, Icelandic, Norwegian); Tadžikistan (Finnish); Tadzjikistan (Dutch, Swedish); Tagikistan (Italian); Tayikistán (Spanish).

Origin of name: Land of the Tajiks.

division	abv	population	area-km	area-mi	capital
Badakhshoni Kuni	BK	136,000	64,000	25,000	Khorugh (Khorog)
Karotegin	KR	1,387,000	28,000	11,000	Dushanbe (Stalinabad)
Khatlon	KL	1,307,000	25,000	10,000	Qurghonteppa (Kurgan-Tyube)
Leninobod	LE	1,289,000	26,000	10,000	Khujand (Leninabad)
		4,119,000	143,000	56,000	

Status: Khatlon and Leninobod are viloyatho (sing. viloyat: regions); Badakhshoni Kuni is a viloyati avtonomii (autonomous region); and Karotegin refers to the rest of Tajikistan, which has only divisions at a lower level than regions.

Abv: Two-letter code for international compatibility (defined by the author).

Population: 1982 estimate.

Area-km: Square kilometers.

Area-mi: Square miles.

Capital: Modern name in Tajiki (old Soviet name in parentheses).

Territorial extent: Leninobod includes an enclave around the town of Vorukh, surrounded by Kyrgyzstan; and another enclave northwest of Kokand, in Uzbekistan.

Change history:

1920-10-05	Khanate of Bukhara became a Soviet Republic.
1921-04-11	Turkestan A.S.S.R. formed from Amu-Darya, Ferghana, Pamir, Samarkand, Semirechensk, and Syr Darya regions, and the southern part of Transcaspian.
1924-10	Turkestan A.S.S.R. and Bukhara reorganized into several units, one of which was the Uzbekskaya S.S.R. The Tadzhikskaya A.S.S.R., in turn, was part of the Uzbekskaya S.S.R.
1927	Gorno-Badakhshanskaya A.Obl. formed.
1929-10-15	Tadzhikskaya A.S.S.R. split from Uzbekskaya S.S.R., and its status changed to S.S.R. Name of country's capital changed from Dyushambe to Stalinabad.
1936	Name of Khodjent and its capital changed to Leninabad.
1950	Divisions were Gorno-Badakhshan A.Obl., Gharm Oblast, Kulyab Oblast, Leninabad Oblast, and the rest of Tadzhikskaya S.S.R. around Dushanbe. Gharm is now eastern Karotegin.
1961	Name of capital changed back to Dushanbe.
1990	Name of capital of Leninobod changed from Leninabad to Khujand.
~1995	Kulob and Qurghonteppa regions merged to form Khatlon. Before the change, the capitals had the same names as the regions. The old Russian names were Kulyab and Kurgan-Tyube.

Other names of subdivisions:

Badakhshoni Kuni: A.G. der Berg-Badachschanen (German-obsolete); Gorno-Badakhshan (Russian, obsolete)

Leninobod: Hodžent, Khodzhent, Khujand (variant); Leninabadskaya Oblast (Russian, obsolete)

TANZANIA

ISO = TZ/FIPS = TZ   Language = Swahili, English   Time zone = +3   Capital = Dar es Salaam, Dodoma

In 1900, Zanzibar (including Pemba) was a British protectorate, and Tanganyika was part of German East Africa. After Germany's defeat in World War I, Tanganyika was mandated to Great Britain by the League of Nations. Following World War II, the mandate became a United Nations trusteeship. Tanganyika became independent on 1961-12-09; Zanzibar did likewise on 1963-12-19. The two countries joined on 1964-04-26 to form the United Republic of Tanganyika and Zanzibar. The name was shortened to United Republic of Tanzania on 1964-10-29. Governmental functions are gradually being transferred from Dar es Salaam to Dodoma.

Other names of country: Jamhuri ya Muungano wa Tanzania (formal); República Unida de Tanzanía, Tanzanía (Spanish); République-Unie de Tanzanie (French); Tansania (Swiss-German); Tansanía (Icelandic); United Republic of Tanzania (formal–English); Vereinigte Republik Tansania (German).

Origin of name: Coined from Tan(ganyika) + Zan(zibar) + -ia (suffix for country).

division	abv	ISO	FIPS	population	area-km	area-mi	capital
Arusha	AR	01	TZ01	1,351,675	84,574	32,654	Arusha
Dar es Salaam	DS	02	TZ23	1,360,850	1,393	538	Dar es Salaam
Dodoma	DO	03	TZ03	1,237,819	41,310	15,950	Dodoma
Iringa	IR	04	TZ04	1,208,914	58,922	22,750	Iringa
Kagera	KR	05*	TZ19	1,326,183	28,388	10,961	Bukoba
Kigoma	KM	08	TZ05	854,817	45,066	17,400	Kigoma
Kilimanjaro	KL	09	TZ06	1,108,699	13,209	5,100	Moshi
Lindi	LI	12	TZ07	646,550	66,046	25,501	Lindi
Mara	MA	13	TZ08	970,942	29,526	11,400	Musoma
Mbeya	MB	14	TZ09	1,476,199	90,129	34,799	Mbeya
Morogoro	MO	16	TZ10	1,222,737	73,035	28,199	Morogoro ➤

division	abv	ISO	FIPS	population	area-km	area-mi	capital
Mtwara	MT	17	TZ11	889,494	16,707	6,451	Mtwara
Mwanza	MW	18	TZ12	1,878,271	35,872	13,850	Mwanza
Pemba North	PN	06	TZ13	137,399	574	222	Wete
Pemba South	PS	10	TZ20	127,640	332	128	Chake Chake
Pwani	PW	19	TZ02	638,015	32,407	12,512	Dar es Salaam
Rukwa	RK	20	TZ24	694,974	68,635	26,500	Sumbawanga
Ruvuma	RV	21	TZ14	783,327	64,232	24,800	Songea
Shinyanga	SH	22	TZ15	1,772,549	40,401	15,599	Shinyanga
Singida	SD	23	TZ16	791,814	50,508	19,501	Singida
Tabora	TB	24	TZ17	1,036,293	76,151	29,402	Tabora
Tanga	TN	25	TZ18	1,283,636	26,806	10,350	Tanga
Zanzibar North	ZN	07	TZ22	97,028	470	181	Mkokotoni
Zanzibar South and Central	ZS	11	TZ21	70,184	854	330	Koani
Zanzibar West	ZW	15	TZ25	208,327	230	89	Zanzibar
				23,174,336	945,777	365,167	

* = ISO lists Ziwa Magharibi as a separate region with code 26. Actually, it's an old name for Kagera.

Status: These divisions are regions.

Abv: Two-letter code for international compatibility (defined by the author).

ISO: Codes from ISO 3166-2.

FIPS: Codes from FIPS PUB 10-4.

Population: 1988 census.

Area-km: Square kilometers.

Area-mi: Square miles.

Territorial extent: Kagera includes Bumbiri, Ikusa, Bukerebe, Nabuyongo, and other islands in Lake Victoria.

Lindi includes Songa Manara Island in the Indian Ocean.

Mara includes Lukuba Island and a few other small islands in Lake Victoria.

Mwanza includes Ukerewe, Rubondo, Ukara, Maisome, Kome, Irugwa, and other islands in Lake Victoria.

Pemba North and Pemba South share Pemba Islands.

Pwani includes Mafia Island in the Indian Ocean.

Tanga includes Mwambawamba Island and other small islands in the Pemba Channel.

Zanzibar North, Zanzibar South and Central, and Zanzibar West share Zanzibar Island. Tumbatu Island is in Zanzibar North; Uzi and Pungume Islands are in Zanzibar South and Central.

Origins of names:

Dar es Salaam: Arabic *dar as-salam*: home of peace　　　　Zanzibar: from an Arabic word for blacks

Change history: Divisions of Tanganyika in 1922 were: Arusha, Bagamoyo, Bukoba, Daressalam, Dodoma, Iringa, Kilwa, Kondoa-Irangi, Lindi, Mahenge, Morogoro, Moshi, Mwanza, Pangani, Rufiji, Rungwe, Songea, Tabora, Tanga, Ufipa, Ujiji, and Usambara. Numerous changes occurred between then and independence.

~1961　　Dar es Salaam province split from Eastern; West Lake province split from Lake.

~1966　　Tanzania reorganized. It had formerly consisted of these provinces:

division	population	area-km	capital	regions
Central	886,962	94,301	Dodoma	Dodoma, Singida
Dar es Salaam	128,742	1,393	Dar es Salaam	Coast (part)
Eastern	955,828	107,630	Dar es Salaam	Coast (part), Morogoro
Lake	1,731,794	107,711	Mwanza	Mara, Mwanza, Shinyanga (part)
Northern	772,434	85,374	Arusha	Arusha, Kilimanjaro (part)
Pemba	133,858	984	Chake Chake	Pemba
Southern	1,014,265	143,027	Mtwara	Mtwara, Ruvuma
Southern Highlands	1,030,269	119,253	Mbeya	Iringa, Mbeya (part)
Tanga	688,290	35,750	Tanga	Kilimanjaro (part), Tanga
West Lake	514,431	28,388	Bukoba	West Lake
Western	1,062,598	203,068	Tabora	Kigoma, Mbeya (part), Shinyanga (part), Tabora
Zanzibar	165,253	1,658	Zanzibar	Zanzibar Rural, Zanzibar West
	9,084,724	928,537		

Population: 1958 census.

Regions: approximate equivalent regions after the reorganization.

~1978   Zanzibar Rural region split into Zanzibar North and Zanzibar South and Central.

~1979   Dar es Salaam region split from Coast; Lindi region split from Mtwara; Rukwa split from Mbeya.

~1982   Name of Coast region changed to Pwani; Pemba region split into Pemba North and Pemba South.

~1984   Name of West Lake region changed to Kagera.

Other names of subdivisions:

Dar es Salaam: Daressalam (German)

Kagera: West Lake (obsolete); Ziwa Magharibi (Swahili-obsolete)

Pemba North: Kaskazini Pemba (Swahili)

Pemba South: Kusini Pemba (Swahili)

Pwani: Coast (obsolete)

Zanzibar: Sansibar (German); Zanzíbar (Spanish)

Zanzibar North: Kaskazini Unguja (Swahili); Zanzibar Rural North, Zanzibar Shambani North (variant)

Zanzibar South and Central: Kusini Unguja (Swahili); Zanzibar Rural South, Zanzibar Shambani South (variant)

Zanzibar West: Mjini Magharibi (Swahili); Zanzibar Mjini, Zanzibar Urban, Zanzibar Urban/West (variant)

THAILAND

ISO = TH/FIPS = TH   Language = Thai   Time zone = +7   Capital = Bangkok

At the beginning of the 20th century, Siam was an independent country, but the British and French had "spheres of influence": the British in the west and south, the French in the east. Part of the French sphere was transferred to French Indo-China in 1907. In 1909, part of the British sphere became unfederated states of Malaya. On 1939-06-24 Siam proclaimed that its English name was to be Thailand. During World War II, Thailand annexed some of the territory back from Indo-China, but was forced to return it at the end of the war.

Other names of country: Kingdom of Thailand (formal–English); Muang Thai, Prathes Thai (formal); Siam (obsolete); Taíland (Icelandic); Tailândia (Portuguese); Tailandia (Spanish); Thaïlande (French); Thailandia (Italian); Thaimaa (Finnish).

Origin of name: Land of the Thais (an ethnic name meaning free people).

division	abv	ISO	FIPS	pc	reg	population	area-km	area-mi
Amnat Charoen	AC	—	TH77	37	NE	360,340	3,164	1,222
Ang Thong	AT	35	TH35	14	C	289,397	969	374
Bangkok Metropolis	BM	40	TH40	10	C	5,604,772	1,444	558
Buri Ram	BR	28	TH28	31	NE	1,494,836	10,352	3,997
Chachoengsao	CC	44	TH44	24	C	627,119	5,334	2,059
Chai Nat	CN	32	TH32	17	C	352,534	2,470	954
Chaiyaphum	CY	26	TH26	36	NE	1,115,519	12,785	4,936
Chanthaburi	CT	48	TH48	22	E	484,170	6,301	2,433
Chiang Mai	CM	02	TH02	50	N	1,573,757	20,185	7,793
Chiang Rai	CR	03	TH03	57	N	1,261,138	11,716	4,524
Chon Buri	CB	46	TH46	20	E	1,028,625	4,369	1,687
Chumphon	CP	58	TH58	86	S	448,087	6,009	2,320
Kalasin	KL	23	TH23	46	NE	974,460	6,973	2,692
Kamphaeng Phet	KP	11	TH11	62	N	766,048	8,589	3,316
Kanchanaburi	KN	50	TH50	71	C	766,352	19,586	7,562
Khon Kaen	KK	22	TH22	40	NE	1,726,594	10,914	4,214
Krabi	KR	63	TH63	81	S	344,610	4,696	1,813
Lampang	LG	06	TH06	52	N	807,362	12,466	4,813
Lamphun	LN	05	TH05	51	N	408,804	4,525	1,747
Loei	LE	18	TH18	42	NE	630,876	11,384	4,395
Lop Buri	LB	34	TH34	15	C	756,484	6,215	2,400 ➤

division	abv	ISO	FIPS	pc	reg	population	area-km	area-mi
Mae Hong Son	MH	01	TH01	58	N	229,284	13,077	5,049
Maha Sarakham	MS	24	TH24	44	NE	927,753	5,287	2,041
Mukdahan	MD	73	TH78	49	NE	326,188	4,343	1,677
Nakhon Nayok	NN	43	TH43	26	C	241,939	2,120	819
Nakhon Pathom	NP	53	TH53	73	C	753,599	2,166	836
Nakhon Phanom	NF	21	TH73	48	NE	703,935	5,498	2,123
Nakhon Ratchasima	NR	27	TH27	30	NE	2,510,839	20,433	7,889
Nakhon Sawan	NS	16	TH16	60	N	1,131,900	9,565	3,693
Nakhon Si Thammarat	NT	64	TH64	80	S	1,511,857	9,973	3,851
Nan	NA	04	TH04	55	N	484,116	11,499	4,440
Narathiwat	NW	31	TH31	96	S	646,871	4,470	1,726
Nong Bua Lam Phu	NB	—	TH79	39	NE	486,153	3,848	1,486
Nong Khai	NK	17	TH17	43	NE	888,702	7,360	2,842
Nonthaburi	NO	38	TH38	11	C	800,741	622	240
Pathum Thani	PT	39	TH39	12	C	592,328	1,525	589
Pattani	PI	69	TH69	94	S	590,735	1,937	748
Phangnga	PG	61	TH61	82	S	229,704	4,133	1,596
Phatthalung	PL	66	TH66	93	S	498,805	3,421	1,321
Phayao	PY	41	TH41	56	N	517,622	6,306	2,435
Phetchabun	PH	14	TH14	67	N	1,040,917	12,651	4,885
Phetchaburi	PE	56	TH56	76	C	453,391	6,211	2,398
Phichit	PC	13	TH13	66	N	601,117	4,538	1,752
Phitsanulok	PS	12	TH12	65	N	865,408	10,760	4,154
Phra Nakhon Si Ayutthaya	PA	36	TH36	13	C	721,496	2,561	989
Phrae	PR	07	TH07	54	N	494,637	6,549	2,529
Phuket	PU	62	TH62	83	S	221,835	542	209
Prachin Buri	PB	45	TH74	25	C	436,956	4,742	1,831
Prachuap Khiri Khan	PK	57	TH57	77	C	468,880	6,370	2,459
Ranong	RN	59	TH59	85	S	151,868	3,287	1,269
Ratchaburi	RT	52	TH52	70	C	813,293	5,187	2,003
Rayong	RY	47	TH47	21	E	504,631	3,540	1,367
Roi Et	RE	25	TH25	45	NE	1,310,095	8,311	3,209
Sa Kaeo	SK	—	TH80	27	C	521,432	7,168	2,768
Sakon Nakhon	SN	20	TH20	47	NE	1,077,208	9,633	3,719
Samut Prakan	SP	42	TH42	10	C	956,266	1,004	388
Samut Sakhon	SS	55	TH55	74	C	407,146	873	337
Samut Songkhram	SM	54	TH54	75	C	207,707	417	161
Saraburi	SR	37	TH37	18	C	596,533	3,577	1,381
Satun	SA	67	TH67	91	S	253,177	2,467	953
Si Sa Ket	SI	30	TH30	33	NE	1,422,527	8,865	3,423
Sing Buri	SB	33	TH33	16	C	225,080	823	318
Songkhla	SG	68	TH68	90	S	1,191,233	7,407	2,860
Sukhothai	SO	09	TH09	64	N	627,090	6,593	2,546
Suphan Buri	SH	51	TH51	72	C	853,313	5,363	2,071
Surat Thani	ST	60	TH60	84	S	861,233	12,937	4,995
Surin	SU	29	TH29	32	NE	1,367,685	8,128	3,138
Tak	TK	08	TH08	63	N	471,596	16,447	6,350
Trang	TG	65	TH65	92	S	576,060	4,906	1,894
Trat	TT	49	TH49	23	E	220,000	2,822	1,090
Ubon Ratchathani	UR	71	TH75	34	NE	1,731,105	15,811	6,105
Udon Thani	UN	19	TH76	41	NE	1,491,560	11,756	4,539
Uthai Thani	UT	15	TH15	61	N	328,978	6,789	2,621
Uttaradit	UD	10	TH10	53	N	481,563	7,785	3,006
Yala	YL	70	TH70	95	S	418,790	4,533	1,750
Yasothon	YS	72	TH72	35	NE	549,466	4,170	1,610
						60,816,227	513,552	198,287

Status: These divisions are changwats (provinces), except for Bangkok Metropolis, which is a municipality.

Abv: Two-letter code for international compatibility (defined by the author).

ISO: Codes from ISO 3166-2 (obviously based on the FIPS codes).

FIPS: Codes from FIPS PUB 10-4.

Postal code: Thailand uses five-digit postal codes. The first two digits imply a province, as shown.

Reg: Thailand has unofficial, but standardized, regions: Central (C), Eastern (E), Northern (N), Northeastern (NE), and Southern (S). Some sources make Eastern part of Central.

Population: 1997 estimate.

Area-km: Square kilometers.

Area-mi: Square miles.

Capitals: Capitals have the same names as their provinces, except for Bangkok Metropolis (Bangkok). Sometimes the capital name is given with the generic prefix "Muang."

Further subdivisions: The provinces are divided into amphoes (or amphurs: districts) and king amphoes (subdistricts). These are in turn subdivided into tambons (communes), which are further subdivided into moobans (villages). Above the provinces, there are regions (as shown above). In the early part of the 20th century, there were groupings of provinces called monthons (administrative circles).

Territorial extent: Chon Buri includes Ko Si Chang, Ko Khram, Ko Pai, and other islands.

Krabi includes Ko Lanta (actually two islands, Ko Lanta Yai and Ko Lanta Noi, constituting one district); and Phi Phi Don, Phi Phi Le, and other islands.

Phuket consists of one large island, Ko Phuket; and numerous smaller islands, such as Ko Yao Yai, Ko Yao Noi, Ko Sire, and Ko Kaeo Pitsadan.

Phangnga includes Ko Phra Thong, Ko Kho Kao, and other islands.

Ranong includes Ko Phayam, Ko Chang, and other islands.

Satun includes Ko Tarutao; the Butong Group, containing Ladang, Rawi, Tanga, and Bitsi; Ko Khao Yai, Ko Bulon Lae, Ko Laoling, and other small islands.

Songkhla includes Ko Yo, Ko Nu and Ko Maeo islands.

Surat Thani includes the islands Ko Samui, Ko Phangan, Ko Tao, Ko Nangyuan, Ko Ang Thong, etc.

Trang includes Ko Libong, Ko Muk, and other small islands.

Trat includes Ko Chang, Ko Kut, Ko Mak, and adjacent islands.

Origins of names:

Bangkok: region of plum-olive trees, also known as Krung Thep: city of angels; Phra Nakhon: lord city

Buri Ram: city of pleasantness

Chai Nat: place of victory

Phatthalung: town of the hollow hill

Phuket: Malayan *bukit*: hill

Sukhothai: dawn of happiness

Surat Thani: city of the good people

Change history:

1912-06	Isan province split into Roi Et and Ubon Ratchathani.
1915	Thailand had 83 provinces. There were some merges between then and 1950.
~1959	Kalasin province split from Maha Sarakham.
1972	Yasothon province split from Ubon Ratchathani.
1977-08-28	Phayao province split from Chiang Rai.
~1980	Phra Nakhon and Thon Buri provinces merged to form Bangkok Metropolis.
1981	Name of Prathum Thani province changed to Pathum Thani.
1982-09	Mukdahan province split from Nakhon Phanom (FIPS code TH21 before the split).
1993	Amnat Charoen province split from Ubon Ratchathani (formerly FIPS = TH71); Nong Bua Lam Phu split from Udon Thani (TH19); Sa Kaeo split from Prachin Buri (TH45). New ISO codes not yet available.

Other names of subdivisions: Although names have to be transliterated from the Thai alphabet, they have become fairly standardized by now. Some names often appear as one word, especially Buriram and Sisaket. In older sources, Nakhon often appears as Nakhorn. The following list shows some typical variants, as well as some odd ones.

Chachoengsao: Chaxerngsao, Pad Rew, Paed Riu, Petrieu, Sha-jeun Dhrao (variant)

Chanthaburi: Chantaburi, Muang Chan (variant)

Kamphaeng Phet: Gampheang Phet, Kambhengbhej (variant)

Kanchanaburi: Kan Buri, Park Prag (variant)

Bangkok Metropolis: Krung Thep, Krung Thep Maha Nakhon, Phra Nakhon-Thonburi (variant)

Lamphun: Hariphunchai, Lampoon (variant)

Nakhon Ratchasima: Khorat, Nagara Rajasima, Nakaun Rachasima (variant)

Nakhon Si Thammarat: Nagara Sridharmaraj, Nakhon Sri Thammarat, Nakhornsrithamrat, Nakornsrithamaraj (variant)

Phetchaburi: Bejraburi, Petchburi, Phet Buri, Tetchburit (variant)

Phitsanulok: Bisnulok, Phisanulauk, Phitsnulok, Pitsanuloke (variant)

Phra Nakhon Si Ayutthaya: Ayudhya, Ayutthaya, Phranakhornsri-ayuthaya (variant)

Prachuap Khiri Khan: Korh Luxk, Prachuab Girikhand, Prachuapkirikhan, Prachut Khirikhan (variant)

Samut Prakan: Pak Nam, Samudh Prakarn, Samudraprakar, Samut Phrakhan (variant)

Samut Sakhon: Krokkrak Maha Chai, Mahachai, Samudrasagara (variant)

Samut Songkhram: Mae Klong, Samudrasonggram (variant)

Si Sa Ket: Khukhan, Khukhandh, Srisaket (variant)

Sukhothai: Sawankhalokt, Sukhotai, Sukothai, Svargalok (variant)

Trang: Tab Tiang (variant)

Population history:

province	1947	1960	1970	1980	1990	1997
Amnat Charoen	—	—	—	—	—	360,340
Ang Thong	150,304	198,000	217,000	255,240	279,032	289,397
Bangkok Metropolis	827,290	—	2,132,000	5,153,902	5,546,937	5,604,772
Buri Ram	339,496	584,000	797,000	1,132,980	1,441,517	1,494,836
Chachoengsao	240,410	323,000	338,000	498,148	582,783	627,119
Chai Nat	171,918	245,000	256,000	330,385	356,297	352,534
Chaiyaphum	293,738	486,000	626,000	857,692	1,059,549	1,115,519
Chanthaburi	110,808	158,000	211,000	330,610	439,273	484,170
Chiang Mai	534,623	798,000	1,024,000	1,166,123	1,376,120	1,573,757
Chiang Rai	476,118	812,000	1,086,000	922,850	1,039,388	1,261,138
Chon Buri	210,329	392,000	542,000	725,407	910,570	1,028,625
Chumphon	118,427	175,000	235,000	330,455	397,679	448,087
Kalasin	—	427,000	573,000	755,274	894,985	974,460
Kamphaeng Phet	65,742	173,000	333,000	559,223	668,001	766,048
Kanchanaburi	140,164	233,000	321,000	518,927	697,750	766,352
Khon Kaen	590,664	844,000	1,025,000	1,354,855	1,681,479	1,726,594
Krabi	59,483	94,000	148,000	218,814	298,406	344,610
Lampang	332,276	472,000	616,000	659,433	772,635	807,362
Lamphun	180,781	250,000	318,000	353,607	417,565	408,804
Loei	134,202	211,000	326,000	449,535	551,892	630,876
Lop Buri	203,313	336,000	433,000	655,537	747,154	756,484
Mae Hong Son	66,280	81,000	104,000	132,391	172,825	229,284
Maha Sarakham	698,087	499,000	613,000	764,509	900,906	927,753
Mukdahan	—	—	—	—	288,151	326,188
Nakhon Nayok	117,547	154,000	161,000	201,230	228,981	241,939
Nakhon Pathom	268,958	370,000	411,000	561,346	657,182	753,599
Nakhon Phanom	307,172	436,000	561,000	760,319	634,966	703,935
Nakhon Ratchasima	723,237	1,095,000	1,547,000	1,916,681	2,384,252	2,510,839
Nakhon Sawan	373,006	648,000	758,000	976,971	1,088,213	1,131,900
Nakhon Si Thammarat	494,261	730,000	927,000	1,261,408	1,427,001	1,511,857
Nan	204,499	240,000	310,000	378,999	449,257	484,116
Narathiwat	166,487	266,000	326,000	441,803	565,456	646,871
Nong Bua Lam Phu	—	—	—	—	—	486,153
Nong Khai	144,201	257,000	442,000	673,884	879,215	888,702
Nonthaburi	135,537	196,000	254,000	386,741	668,760	800,741
Pathum Thani	139,339	190,000	233,000	324,468	452,693	592,328
Pattani	199,253	282,000	330,000	457,760	537,542	590,735
Phangnga	61,077	93,000	135,000	174,973	212,923	229,704
Phatthalung	149,431	234,000	298,000	412,265	460,626	498,805
Phayao	—	—	—	461,620	503,711	517,622
Phetchabun	162,730	320,000	513,000	785,238	955,467	1,040,917
Phetchaburi	180,509	238,000	278,000	366,612	427,985	453,391
Phichit	237,241	389,000	440,000	534,481	558,818	601,117
Phitsanulok	202,249	352,000	492,000	709,073	786,509	865,408
Phra Nakhon Si Ayutthaya	362,761	479,000	501,000	623,242	685,394	721,496
Phrae	213,351	299,000	365,000	446,431	493,530	494,637
Phuket	49,324	76,000	100,000	133,669	168,429	221,835
Prachin Buri	217,395	335,000	421,000	631,276	877,491	436,956
Prachuap Khiri Khan	72,343	152,000	249,000	377,212	424,766	468,880
Ranong	21,488	38,000	59,000	83,707	117,440	151,868
Ratchaburi	295,534	411,000	464,000	644,746	720,157	813,293 ▶

province	1947	1960	1970	1980	1990	1997
Rayong	84,197	148,000	250,000	358,896	453,850	504,631
Roi Et	535,662	668,000	780,000	1,061,085	1,228,834	1,310,095
Sa Kaeo	—	—	—	—	—	521,432
Sakon Nakhon	273,262	427,000	598,000	776,510	974,008	1,077,208
Samut Prakan	164,227	235,000	325,000	535,858	854,883	956,266
Samut Sakhon	111,479	166,000	158,000	265,464	358,155	407,146
Samut Songkhram	124,894	162,000	159,000	196,659	206,506	207,707
Saraburi	203,562	304,000	342,000	470,655	535,160	596,533
Satun	46,514	70,000	131,000	164,740	222,768	253,177
Si Sa Ket	451,576	601,000	790,000	1,082,121	1,336,161	1,422,527
Sing Buri	116,227	154,000	162,000	202,605	230,913	225,080
Songkhla	349,392	500,000	621,000	849,601	1,090,083	1,191,233
Sukhothai	193,696	316,000	394,000	531,624	592,658	627,090
Suphan Buri	340,872	491,000	561,000	709,364	827,951	853,313
Surat Thani	208,390	325,000	434,000	593,095	738,350	861,233
Surin	435,370	582,000	747,000	1,035,577	1,288,503	1,367,685
Tak	102,193	168,000	217,000	276,994	353,803	471,596
Thon Buri	289,352	2,136,000	919,000	—	—	—
Trang	148,591	240,000	326,000	427,055	519,155	576,060
Trat	44,819	66,000	94,000	138,185	197,155	220,000
Ubon Ratchathani	849,451	1,131,000	1,480,000	1,560,272	1,932,052	1,731,105
Udon Thani	382,564	744,000	1,118,000	1,448,066	1,825,337	1,491,560
Uthai Thani	104,852	146,000	177,000	259,464	304,776	328,978
Uttaradit	170,844	260,000	321,000	432,995	460,516	481,563
Yala	81,471	149,000	199,000	273,866	356,904	418,790
Yasothon	—	—	—	458,535	527,134	549,466
	17,256,840	26,260,000	34,152,000	46,961,338	56,303,273	60,816,227

Figures for Bangkok Metropolis represent only Phra Nakhon before 1980.

TOGO

ISO = TG/FIPS = TO   Language = French   Time zone = +0   Capital = Lomé

Togoland was a German protectorate in 1900. After World War I, the Allies split up Germany's African possessions. The League of Nations mandated Togoland to Great Britain and France. They split it longitudinally. On 1922-07-20, France received the broader eastern strip. The French mandate of Togo was administered under Dahomey (see Benin), and thus was part of French West Africa. After World War II, the mandate was extended as a U.N. trusteeship. Togo became independent on 1960-04-27.

Other names of country: Republic of Togo (formal–English); República Togolesa (formal–Spanish); République Togolaise (formal); Tógó (Icelandic).

Origin of name: from the name of a lake.

division	abv	population	area-km	area-mi	capital	formal
Centre	CE	269,174	13,182	5,090	Sokodé	Région Centrale, Région du Centre
Kara	KA	432,626	11,631	4,491	Kara	Région de la Kara
Maritime	MA	1,039,700	6,395	2,469	Lomé	Région Maritime
Plateaux	PL	561,656	16,974	6,554	Atakpamé	Région des Plateaux
Savanes	SA	326,826	8,603	3,322	Dapaong	Région des Savanes
		2,629,982	56,785	21,926		

Status: These divisions are régions.
Abv: Two-letter code for international compatibility (defined by the author).
Population: 1981 census.

Area-km: Square kilometers.

Area-mi: Square miles.

Formal: Full name of region.

Further subdivisions: Information available about the secondary administrative divisions of Togo is spotty and unreliable. It appears that there were 19 divisions from about 1970 to 1985. Since then, there have been 21. Their status has been given variously as circonscriptions (circumscriptions) and préfectures. The ISO and FIPS standards agree on the list below.

division	ISO	FIPS	reg	alternate
Amlamé	AM	TO01	PL	Amou
Aného	AN	TO02	MA	Anécho, Lacs
Atakpamé	AT	TO03	PL	Ogou
Badou	BD	TO15	PL	Wawa
Bafilo	BF	TO04	CE	Assoli
Bassar	BS	TO05	CE	Bassari
Dapaong	DA	TO06	SA	Dapango, Tôné
Kanté	KA	TO07	KA	Kandé, Kéran
Klouto	KL	TO08	PL	Kloto, Kpalimé, Palimé
Kpagouda	KP	TO14	KA	Binah, Pagouda
Lama-Kara	LK	TO09	KA	Kara, Kozah
Lomé	LO	TO10	MA	Golfe
Mango	MA	TO11	SA	Oti, Sansanne-Mango
Niamtougou	NI	TO12	KA	Doufelgou
Notsé	NI	TO13	PL	Haho, Nuatja
Sotouboua	SO	TO16	CE	
Tabligbo	TA	TO17	MA	Yoto
Tchamba	TB	TO19	CE	Nyala
Tchaoudjo	TO	TO20	CE	Sokodé
Tsévié	TS	TO18	MA	Zio
Vogan	VO	TO21	MA	Vo

ISO: Codes from ISO 3166-2. (Duplicated code NI is an error in the draft standard.)

FIPS: Codes from FIPS PUB 10-4.

Reg: Region in which the prefecture lies, keyed to the list of regions above.

Capital: Capitals have the same names as their prefectures, as shown in the first column.

Alternate: Alternate and variant names for the prefecture. Note: Klouto and Palimé are both cities in Klouto prefecture. The alternate names may be due to a change of capital.

Change history:

1914-08	Under French administration, capital moved from Sebbe to Aného.
1920	Capital moved from Aného to Lomé.
~1965	Togo reorganized from six cercles (Aného, Centre, Klouto, Lomé, Mango, and Sokodé) into four regions (Centre, Maritime, Plateaux, and Savanes).
~1980	Kara region formed from parts of Centre and Savanes.

TOKELAU

ISO = TK/FIPS = TL   Language = Tokelauan, English   Time zone = -11   Capital = none

The Union Islands, also known as the Tokelau Islands, became a British protectorate in 1911. They were joined with several other island groups to form the colony of Gilbert and Ellice Islands on 1915-11-12. On 1926-02-11, the Tokelau Islands were transferred to New Zealand as a dependency. On 1949-01-01 they became an overseas territory of New Zealand. The name was changed to Tokelau in 1976-12.

Other names of country: Ilhas Tokelau (Portuguese); Tokélaou (French); Tokelau eilanden (Dutch); Tokelau-Inseln (German).

division	abv	population	area-km	area-mi
Tokelau	TK	1,760	10	4

Status: This division is the whole of the country, treated as a division for compatibility.
Abv: Two-letter code for international compatibility (defined by the author).
Population: 1992 estimate.
Area-km: Square kilometers.
Area-mi: Square miles.
Territorial extent: Tokelau consists of three atolls: Atafu, Fakaofo, and Nukunonu.

TONGA

ISO = TO/FIPS = TN   Language = Tongan, English   Time zone = +13   Capital = Nuku'alofa

Tonga became a protectorate of Great Britain on 1900-05-18, formalizing a previous agreement. Great Britain abandoned the relationship on 1970-06-04, leaving Tonga completely independent.

Other names of country: Friendly Islands, Toga (obsolete); Kingdom of Tonga (formal–English); Pule 'anga Tonga (formal).

Origin of name: shortened form of Tongatabu, from *tonga*: island, *tabu*: sacred.

division	abv	ISO	FIPS	population	area-km	area-mi	capital
Ha'apai	HA	H	TN01	8,919	110	42	Pangai, Lifuka I.
Tongatapu	TO	T	TN02	70,555	420	162	Nuku'alofa, Tongatapu I.
Vava'u	VA	V	TN03	15,175	119	46	Neiafu, Vava'u I.
				94,649	649	250	

Status: These divisions are island groups.
Abv: Two-letter code for international compatibility (defined by the author).
ISO: Codes from ISO 3166-2.
FIPS: Codes from FIPS PUB 10-4.
Population: 1986 census.
Area-km: Square kilometers.
Area-mi: Square miles.
Further subdivisions: There are 23 districts, subordinate to the island groups. The Statesman's Year-Book also lists five "divisions," which I haven't been able to confirm from any other source.
Territorial extent: Ha'apai includes the islands of the Ha'apai group, from Hunga Ha'apai to Kelefesia to Ha'ano to Kao. The largest are Lifuka and Tofua.

Tongatapu includes the Tongatapu Group, consisting of Tongatapu, 'Eua, 'Euaiki, and smaller islands; 'Ata Island to the south; and, at the opposite end of Tonga, the Niuas: Niua Toputapu, Niua Fo'ou, and Tafahi.

Vava'u includes the islands of the Vava'u group, from Vava'u to Late to Fonualei.

TRINIDAD AND TOBAGO

ISO = TT/FIPS = TD   Language = English   Time zone = -4   Capital = Port of Spain

Trinidad and Tobago was a British colony for the first part of the 20th century. On 1962-08-31 it became an independent member of the British Commonwealth.

Other names of country: Republic of Trinidad and Tobago (formal–English); Trinidad e Tobago (Portuguese); Trinidad en Tobago (Dutch); Trinidad ja Tobago (Finnish); Trinidad och Tobago (Swedish); Trinidad og Tobago (Danish, Norwegian); Trínidad og Tóbagó (Icelandic); Trinidad und Tobago (German); Trinidad y Tabago (Spanish); Trinité-et-Tobago (French).

Origin of name: Spanish *Trinidad*: Trinity, named by Columbus on sighting three peaks; Carib *tavaco*: tobacco pipe.

division	abv	ISO	FIPS	typ	population	area-km	area-mi	capital
Arima	AR	ARI	TD01	mu	28,500	10	4	Arima
Caroni	CA	CAR	TD02	cn	167,300	554	214	Chaguanas
Mayaro	MA	MAY	TD03	cn	— —	378	146	Rio Claro, Nariva
Nariva	NA	NAR	TD04	cn	33,200	534	206	Rio Claro
Point Fortin	PF	PTF		mu	17,300	— —	— —	Point Fortin
Port of Spain	PS	POS	TD05	mu	58,300	6	3	Port-of-Spain
Saint Andrew	SA	SAN	TD06	cn	57,800	733	283	Sangre Grande
Saint David	SD	SDA	TD07	cn	— —	205	79	Sangre Grande, Saint Andrew
Saint George	SG	SGE	TD08	cn	435,800	917	354	Tunapuna
Saint Patrick	SP	SPA	TD09	cn	122,800	676	261	Siparia
San Fernando	SF	SFO	TD10	mu	33,100	2	1	San Fernando
Tobago	TO	TOB	TD11	wd	44,300	300	116	Scarborough
Victoria	VI	VIC	TD12	cn	218,700	813	314	Princes Town
					1,217,100	5,128	1,981	

Typ: These divisions are counties (cn), except for municipalities (mu), and a ward (wd).

Abv: Two-letter code for international compatibility (defined by the author).

ISO: Codes from ISO 3166-2.

FIPS: Codes from FIPS PUB 10-4.

Population: 1987 estimate. The Central Statistics Office reports Mayaro and Nariva as a unit, and Saint Andrew and Saint David as another unit.

Area-km: Square kilometers.

Area-mi: Square miles.

Territorial extent: Tobago consists of the islands of Tobago, Little Tobago, and Saint Giles' Islands.

The other divisions lie mainly on the island of Trinidad. In addition, Saint George includes the islands of Monos, Chacachacare, Gaspar Grande, and Huevos.

Change history:

      1980-04-30   Point Fortin municipality split from Saint Patrick county. FIPS 10-4 has not yet adjusted for this change.

      1991-10-01   According to a government Web page, Chaguanas municipality split from Caroni county. This change hasn't appeared in any standards or reference books yet.

Other names of subdivisions:

Port of Spain: Port-of-Spain (variant); Puerto España (Spanish)   Tobago: Tabago (Spanish)

TUNISIA

ISO = TN/FIPS = TS   Language = Arabic   Time zone = +1   Capital = Tunis

Tunisia (more commonly called Tunis, formally the Regency of Tunis, until about 1930) began the 20th century as a French protectorate. It gained full independence on 1956-03-20. Tunisia's desert boundaries were indistinct at first, and there is still a border dispute with Algeria.

Other names of country: al Jumhuriya at-Tunisiya (formal); Republic of Tunisia (formal–English); Tunesië (Dutch); Tunesien (Danish, German); Túnez (Spanish); Tunis (obsolete); Túnis (Icelandic); Tunísia (Portuguese); Tunisie (French); Tunisien (Swedish).

Origin of name: from the capital, Tunis + -ia (suffix for country).

division	abv	ISO	FIPS	population	area-km	area-mi
Ariana	AR	12	TS26	415,800	1,558	602
Béja	BJ	31	TS17	286,000	3,558	1,374
Ben Arous	BA	13	TS27	271,600	761	294
Bizerte	BZ	23	TS18	412,700	3,685	1,423
Gabès	GB	81	TS29	264,000	7,175	2,770
Gafsa	GF	71	TS10	253,300	8,990	3,471
Jendouba	JE	32	TS06	379,800	3,102	1,198
Kairouan	KR	41	TS03	451,000	6,712	2,592
Kassérine	KS	42	TS02	322,700	8,066	3,114
Kebili	KB	73	TS31	104,200	22,084	8,527
Le Kef	KF	33	TS14	256,000	4,965	1,917
Mahdia	MH	53	TS15	290,400	2,966	1,145
Médenine	ME	82	TS28	324,400	8,588	3,316
Monastir	MS	52	TS16	297,700	1,019	393
Nabeul	NB	21	TS19	489,600	2,788	1,076
Sfax	SF	61	TS32	627,000	7,545	2,913
Sidi Bou Zid	SZ	43	TS33	314,500	6,994	2,700
Siliana	SL	34	TS22	232,700	4,631	1,788
Sousse	SS	51	TS23	346,000	2,621	1,012
Tataouine	TA	83	TS34	109,600	38,889	15,015
Tozeur	TO	72	TS35	73,900	4,719	1,822
Tunis	TU	11	TS36	815,600	346	134
Zaghouan	ZA	22	TS37	126,400	2,768	1,069
				7,464,900	154,530	59,665

Status: These divisions are wilayat (governorates).
Abv: Two-letter code for international compatibility (defined by the author).
ISO: Codes from ISO 3166-2.
FIPS: Codes from FIPS PUB 10-4.
Population: 1986 estimate.
Area-km: Square kilometers.
Area-mi: Square miles.
Capitals: All governorates have the same name as their capitals.
Further subdivisions: The provinces are divided into mutamadiyat (delegations, districts), which are subdivided into shaykhats (municipalities).
Territorial extent: Bizerte includes the islands of La Galite.
Médenine includes the island of Djerba.
Nabeul includes the island of Zembra.
Sfax includes the Kerkenna Islands. The two main islands are Chergui and Gharbi, and nearby are the small and uninhabited Rhermedi, Roumedia, and Sefnou.
Origins of names:

Bizerte: originally Hippo Diarrhytos (Phoenician *hippo*: fort, Greek *diarrhytos*: split in two), rendered in Arabic as Hippo Zarytos, later Banzart.
Le Kef: Arabic *kef*: rock
Mahdia: named after Caliph Obaid Allah el Mahdi (early 10th cent.)

Monastir: from Greek *monasterion*: monastery
Nabeul: from Greek *nea*: new, *polis*: city
Tunis: possibly from Tanit, Phoenician moon goddess

Change history:

~1967   Name of Souk-El-Arba governorate changed to Jendouba; name of Sbeitla changed to Kassérine; name of Cap Bon changed to Nabeul.
~1979   Mahdia and Monastir governorates split from Susa; Sidi Bou Zid governorate split from Gafsa; Siliana governorate split from Le Kef; Tunis governorate (also known as Tunis et Banlieue, or Tunis and Suburbs) split into Tunis North and Tunis South.

1981   Tozeur governorate split from Gafsa; Tunis North and Tunis South reorganized into Zaghouan (mostly from Tunis South) and Tunis; Kebili governorate split from Gabès; Tataouine governorate split from Médenine.

~1986   Ariana and Ben Arous governorates split from Tunis.

Other names of subdivisions: There are numerous methods for transliterating from Arabic to the Roman alphabet. The names here labeled Arabic are not the only possible versions.

Ariana: Al Ariānah, L'Ariana, Tunis Ariana (variant); Al Aryānah (Arabic)

Béja: Bājah (Arabic); Béjah (variant)

Ben Arous: Bin 'Arūs (Arabic); Tunis Ben Arous (variant)

Bizerte: Banzart (Arabic); Bensert, Binzart (variant); Biserta (German, Italian); Bizerta (Portuguese, Spanish)

Gabès: Gābis (variant); Qābis (Arabic)

Gafsa: Gafşah (variant); Qafşah (Arabic)

Jendouba: Jendoûbah, Jenduba, Jondouba (variant); Jundūbah (Arabic); Souk-El-Arba (obsolete)

Kairouan: Al Qayrawān (Arabic); Al Qīrwān, Qairouân (variant); Kairuã (Portuguese)

Kassérine: Al Gaşrīn, Al Qasrin, Kasserim (variant); Al Qaşrayn (Arabic); Sbeitla (obsolete)

Kebili: Kebilli, Qbili (variant); Qibilī (Arabic)

Le Kef: Al Kāf (Arabic); El Kef, Kaf, Kef (variant)

Mahdia: Al Madīyah, Al Mahdiyya, Mahdiâh (variant); Al Mahdīyah (Arabic)

Médenine: Madanīn, Medenin (variant); Madanīyīn (Arabic)

Monastir: Al Munastīr (Arabic)

Nabeul: Cap Bon (obsolete); Nabil, Nābol (variant); Nābul (Arabic)

Sfax: Şafāqis (Arabic); Şfāqis (variant)

Sidi Bou Zid: Qamudah, Sidi Boû Sa'îd, Sidi Buzid, Sidi Bū Sa'îd (variant); Sīdī Bū Zayd (Arabic)

Siliana: Siliānah (variant); Silyānah (Arabic)

Sousse: Sousa, Sussa, Susse (variant); Susa (Italian, Spanish); Sūsah (Arabic)

Tataouine: Foum Tataouine, Tatahouine, Tatuine (variant); Taţāwīn (Arabic)

Tozeur: Tawzar (Arabic); Touzar, Tūzar (variant)

Tunis: Tounis, Tunis City, Tūnus (variant); Túnez (Spanish); Túnis (Portuguese); Tunisi (Italian); Tūnis (Arabic)

Zaghouan: Tunis South (obsolete); Zachouan, Zaguan (variant); Zaghwān (Arabic)

TURKEY

ISO = TR/FIPS = TU   Language = Turkish   Time zone = +2^d Capital = Ankara

In 1900, the Ottoman Empire (often informally called Turkey) was in decline. It controlled extensive territory, but had been losing ground at an accelerating pace. It had control in some degree over Albania, northern Greece, parts of Bulgaria and what later became Yugoslavia, Crete, Cyprus, the Archipelago (the eastern Aegean islands), Tripoli (Libya), Egypt, most of modern Turkey, the Fertile Crescent, and the east and west coasts of the Arabian peninsula. (Egypt and Cyprus were under British hegemony in actuality.) It lost Libya in the Italo-Turkish War of 1911–1912, followed by most of its European lands in the Balkan Wars of 1912–1913. It was defeated in World War I, and the empire was broken up into pieces. Turkey became its successor state.

Other names of country: Republic of Turkey (formal–English); Turchia (Italian); Türkei (German); Turkiet (Swedish); Turkije (Dutch); Türkiye Çumhuriyeti (formal); Turkki (Finnish); Turquia (Portuguese); Turquía (Spanish); Turquie (French); Tyrkia (Norwegian); Tyrkiet (Danish); Tyrkland (Icelandic).

Origin of name: land of the Turks.

division	abv	ISO	FIPS	population	area-km	area-mi	old capital
Adana	AA	01	TU01	1,693,332	17,253	6,661	Seyhan
Adıyaman	AD	02	TU02	684,339	7,614	2,940	
Afyon	AF	03	TU03	760,628	14,556	5,620	Afyon Karahisar
Ağri	AG	04	TU04	474,894	11,376	4,392	Karaköse
Aksaray	AK	68	TU75	351,998	7,738	2,988	
Amasya	AM	05	TU05	345,097	5,520	2,131	
Ankara	AN	06	TU68	3,627,098	25,960	10,023	Angora
Antalya	AL	07	TU07	1,419,551	20,591	7,950	Adalia ▶

division	abv	ISO	FIPS	population	area-km	area-mi	old capital
Ardahan	AR	75	——	138,397	5,576	2,153	
Artvin	AV	08	TU08	188,532	7,436	2,871	
Aydın	AY	09	TU09	895,973	8,011	3,093	
Balıkesir	BK	10	TU10	1,038,482	14,528	5,609	
Bartın	BR	74	——	191,167	151	58	
Batman	BM	72	TU76	406,055	4,682	1,808	
Bayburt	BB	69	TU77	101,591	3,582	1,383	
Bilecik	BC	11	TU11	187,832	4,308	1,663	
Bingöl	BG	12	TU12	232,273	8,138	3,142	Çapakçur
Bitlis	BT	13	TU13	341,586	8,587	3,315	
Bolu	BO	14	TU14	554,382	11,051	4,267	
Burdur	BD	15	TU15	251,231	7,056	2,724	
Bursa	BU	16	TU16	1,905,990	11,043	4,264	Brusa
Çanakkale	CK	17	TU17	440,373	9,737	3,759	
Çankırı	CI	18	TU18	254,290	8,451	3,263	
Çorum	CM	19	TU19	593,945	12,820	4,950	
Denizli	DN	20	TU20	808,400	11,908	4,598	
Diyarbakır	DY	21	TU21	1,280,201	15,354	5,928	
Edirne	ED	22	TU22	386,286	6,276	2,423	Adrianople
Elazığ	EG	23	TU23	519,941	9,151	3,533	
Erzincan	EN	24	TU24	279,680	11,903	4,596	
Erzurum	EM	25	TU25	888,103	25,066	9,678	
Eskişehir	ES	26	TU26	648,342	13,652	5,271	
Gaziantep	GA	27	TU27	1,130,982	7,642	2,950	
Giresun	GI	28	TU28	481,023	6,934	2,677	
Gümüşhane	GU	29	TU69	155,745	6,649	2,567	
Hakkari	HK	30	TU70	211,179	7,171	2,769	Çölemerik
Hatay	HT	31	TU31	1,202,009	5,403	2,086	Antioch (Antakya, Antioquia)
İçel	IC	33	TU32	1,513,956	15,853	6,121	Mersin
Iğdir	IG	76	——	144,833	3,539	1,366	
Isparta	IP	32	TU33	455,753	8,933	3,449	
İstanbul	IB	34	TU34	9,061,096	5,712	2,205	Constantinople
İzmir	IZ	35	TU35	3,076,928	11,973	4,623	Smyrna
Kahramanmaraş	KM	46	TU46	1,028,590	14,327	5,532	Maraş
Karabük	KB	78	——	228,592	——	——	
Karaman	KR	70	TU78	223,360	7,673	2,963	
Kars	KA	36	TU36	316,019	18,557	7,165	
Kastamonu	KS	37	TU37	371,964	13,108	5,061	Kostambul
Kayseri	KY	38	TU38	952,264	16,917	6,532	
Kilis	KI	79	——	110,043	——	——	
Kırıkkale	KK	71	TU79	363,446	4,292	1,657	
Kırklareli	KL	39	TU39	308,090	6,550	2,529	
Kırşehir	KH	40	TU40	246,933	6,570	2,537	
Kocaeli	KC	41	TU41	1,173,811	3,626	1,400	İzmit, Ismid
Konya	KO	42	TU71	1,937,814	40,255	15,543	
Kütahya	KU	43	TU43	645,077	11,875	4,585	
Malatya	ML	44	TU44	802,306	12,313	4,754	
Manisa	MN	45	TU45	1,226,307	13,810	5,332	
Mardin	MR	47	TU72	651,150	8,892	3,433	
Muğla	MG	48	TU48	625,776	13,338	5,150	
Muş	MS	49	TU49	428,914	8,196	3,164	
Nevşehir	NV	50	TU50	283,343	5,467	2,111	
Niğde	NG	51	TU73	321,543	7,794	3,009	
Ordu	OR	52	TU52	858,775	6,010	2,320	
Osmaniye	OS	—	——	438,110	——	——	
Rize	RI	53	TU53	334,285	3,920	1,514	Çoruh
Sakarya	SK	54	TU54	732,898	4,817	1,860	Adapazarı
Samsun	SS	55	TU55	1,170,275	9,570	3,695	
Şanlıurfa	SU	63	TU63	1,313,076	18,584	7,175	Urfa
Siirt	SI	56	TU74	264,503	5,609	2,166	
Sinop	SP	57	TU57	221,151	5,862	2,263	
Şırnak	SR	73	TU80	312,068	6,930	2,676	
Sivas	SV	58	TU58	705,719	28,488	10,999	
Tekirdağ	TG	59	TU59	545,266	6,218	2,401 ➤	

division	abv	ISO	FIPS	population	area-km	area-mi	old capital
Tokat	TT	60	TU60	712,081	9,958	3,845	
Trabzon	TB	61	TU61	862,358	4,685	1,809	
Tunceli	TC	62	TU62	82,535	7,761	2,997	Kalan
Uşak	US	64	TU64	317,692	5,341	2,062	
Van	VA	65	TU65	772,944	20,902	8,070	
Yalova	YL	77	——	161,466	——	——	
Yozgat	YZ	66	TU66	615,608	14,123	5,453	
Zonguldak	ZO	67	TU67	620,607	8,478	3,274	
				62,610,252	789,700	304,903	

Status: These divisions are iller (sing. il: provinces).

Abv: Two-letter code for international compatibility (defined by the author).

ISO: Codes from ISO 3166-2, also used as a standard in Turkey.

FIPS: Codes from FIPS PUB 10-4.

Population: 1997 estimate.

Area-km: Square kilometers.

Area-mi: Square miles.

Capital: Currently, the standard name of each provincial capital is the same as its province's name.

Old capital: Some capitals have other historical names, which in many cases are still in common use.

Further subdivisions: The provinces are divided into ilçe (districts) with limited function. The districts are subdivided into communes, or municipalities, and villages. There are widely recognized regions in Turkey (Thrace, or Turkey in Europe; Black Sea Coast; Central Anatolia, etc.), but their standing is unofficial.

Territorial extent: Antalya includes some tiny Mediterranean islands such as Kekova.

Balıkesir includes the islands of Marmara, Paşalimanı, Türkeli, and smaller islands in the Sea of Marmara; and Alibey and other small islands in the Aegean Sea.

Bursa includes İmrali island in the Sea of Marmara.

Çanakkale is partly in Asia and partly in Europe, straddling the Dardanelles. It includes the Aegean islands of Gökçeada (İmroz) and Bozcaada.

Erzincan and Elazığ are adjacent, but their boundary is entirely in water (Keban reservoir).

İstanbul is partly in Asia and partly in Europe, lying across the Bosporus.

İzmir includes Uzun and Kara islands in the Aegean Sea.

Muğla includes some tiny islands such as Salih, Kara, and Tersane.

Van includes the small islands of Adır and Carbanab in Lake Van.

Origins of names:

Antalya: from Attalus II, king of Pergamon, founder of city

Bursa: from founder Prusias I, king of Bithynia

Çanakkale: Turkish *çanak*: pottery, *kale*: fort

Edirne: Ancient Greek Hadrianopolis, after Roman emperor Hadrian.

Erzurum: Arabic *ard ar-rum*: the land of Rome (referring to Christian population)

Eskişehir: Turkish *eski*: ancient, *sehir*: city

İzmir: Turkish corruption of *eis Smyrne*: to Smyrna

İstanbul: Turkish corruption of Byzantine Greek *eis ten polin*: to the city; or, more likely, of Constantinople

Change history: In 1900, the Ottoman Empire was divided into vilayets (governorates), which were subdivided into sanjaks (provinces). The sanjaks were similar in size to the modern provinces, though different in detail. The vilayets which fell mainly within the area of modern Turkey were:

division	population	area-km	division	population	area-km
Adana	422,400	39,886	Ismid	222,700	8,107
Adrianople	1,028,200	38,389	Kastamuni	961,200	50,686
Angora	932,800	70,888	Konieh	1,069,000	102,071
Bigha	129,500	6,604	Mamuret-ul-Aziz	575,200	32,893
Bitlis	398,700	27,091	Sivas	1,057,500	62,082
Brusa	1,626,800	65,786	Smyrna	2,500,000	6,682
Chatalja	60,000	1,898	Trebizond	1,265,000	43,178
Constantinople	1,203,000	3,898	Van	379,800	39,290
Diarbekir	471,500	37,503		14,949,000	686,608
Erzurum	645,700	49,676			

Status: These divisions are vilayets, except for Bigha, Chatalja, and Ismid, which are mutessarifats.
Population: 1912 estimate (apparently based on much earlier figures).

1918-03	By the treaty of Brest-Litovsk, Russia ceded the Armenian districts of Ardahan, Batum, and Kars to Turkey.
1920-08-10	Treaty of Sèvres created an independent Armenia, boundaries not fixed. The proposed territory would have included most of Bitlis, Erzerum, Trebizond, and Van vilayets.
1920-12-02	Treaty of Alexandropol restored Turkish Armenia, including Ardahan and Kars, to Turkey.
1923	Northern strip of Syria restored to Turkey by the Treaty of Lausanne.
~1926	Turkey reorganized from 20 vilayets into 63 iller (also called vilayets at first).
1926	Name of capital of country officially changed from Constantinople to İstanbul (which had already been in widespread use for many years).
1939-06-23	The Republic of Hatay, previously part of Syria as the Sanjuk of Alexandretta, merged with Turkey as Hatay province.
~1946	Çoruh province split into Artvin and Rize; Bitlis province formed from parts of Muş and Sitlis; Çapakçur and Tunceli provinces formed from parts of Elazığ and Erzincan; Hakkari province split from Van; capital of Ağri province moved from Bayazit to Karaköse.
1953-07-11	Uşak province split from Kütahya.
~1954	Capital of Tunceli moved from Hozat to Kalan; name of Çapakçur province and its capital changed to Bingöl.
1954	Adıyaman province split from Malatya; Sakarya province split from Kocaeli.
1957	Nevşehir province formed from parts of Kirşehir and Niğde.
~1963	Name of Seyhan province changed to Adana.
~1991	Aksaray province split from Niğde; Batman and Şırnak formed from parts of Hakkari, Mardin, and Siirt; Bayburt split from Gümüşhane; Karaman split from Konya; Kırıkkale split from Ankara.
~1992	Ardahan and Iğdir provinces split from Kars; Bartın split from Zonguldak.
1995-06-06	Karabük province split from Zonguldak; Kilis split from Gaziantep; Yalova split from İstanbul.
~1997	Osmaniye province split from Adana.

Other names of subdivisions:

Note: the Turkish alphabet includes two forms of the letter I. The capital form of i is İ, and the capital form of ı is I. Some sources may transcribe Turkish letters phonetically, using ch for ç, j for ğ, or sh for ş.

Ankara: Ancara (Portuguese); Angora (obsolete)
Antalya: Anatolia (variant)
Bingöl: Çapakçur (obsolete)
Bursa: Burssa, Brusa, Brussa (obsolete); Brousse (French)
Edirne: Adrianople (obsolete); Adrianopel (German-obsolete)
İstanbul: Constantinople (obsolete); Estambul (Spanish); Istambul (Portuguese); Konstantinopel (German-obsolete); Stamboul (French-obsolete)

İzmir: Esmirna (Portuguese, Spanish); Smirne (Italian); Smyrna (obsolete)
Konya: Konieh (obsolete); Kunja (German-obsolete)
Trabzon: Trapezunt (German-obsolete); Trebizond (obsolete); Trebizonda (Portuguese); Trébizonde (French)

Population history:

division	1945	1955	1965	1975	1985	1997
Adana	418,740	633,225	903,000	1,234,735	1,725,940	1,693,332
Adıyaman	——	211,002	267,000	345,764	430,728	684,339
Afyon	335,609	407,126	502,000	576,860	666,978	760,628
Ağri	133,504	181,422	247,000	337,606	421,131	474,894
Aksaray	——	——	——	——	——	351,998
Amasya	147,870	227,479	286,000	318,082	358,289	345,097
Ankara	695,526	1,120,622	1,644,000	2,572,562	3,306,327	3,627,098
Antalya	278,178	357,919	487,000	669,913	891,149	1,419,551 ➤

division	1945	1955	1965	1975	1985	1997
Ardahan	— —	— —	— —	— —	— —	138,397
Artvin	159,328	176,888	210,000	227,107	226,338	188,532
Aydın	294,407	415,352	525,000	607,126	743,419	895,973
Balıkesir	524,748	613,447	708,000	788,576	910,282	1,038,482
Bartın	— —	— —	— —	— —	— —	191,167
Batman	— —	— —	— —	— —	— —	406,055
Bayburt	— —	— —	— —	— —	— —	101,591
Bilecik	136,053	139,532	139,000	136,011	160,909	187,832
Bingöl	75,510	114,957	151,000	209,107	241,548	232,273
Bitlis	71,950	111,789	154,000	218,997	300,843	341,586
Bolu	276,367	318,612	384,000	427,273	504,778	554,382
Burdur	125,792	158,302	195,000	222,375	248,002	251,231
Bursa	491,899	613,263	756,000	960,034	1,324,015	1,905,990
Çanakkale	317,254	312,679	350,000	367,121	417,121	440,373
Çankırı	197,356	228,777	251,000	266,450	263,964	254,290
Çorum	312,723	403,527	486,000	550,426	599,204	593,945
Denizli	315,934	368,853	463,000	556,173	667,478	808,400
Diyarbakır	249,949	345,247	476,000	649,796	934,505	1,280,201
Edirne	198,271	253,319	303,000	337,898	389,638	386,286
Elazığ	198,081	240,842	323,000	417,751	483,715	519,941
Erzincan	171,868	216,413	259,000	284,660	299,985	279,680
Erzurum	395,876	521,836	628,000	749,157	856,175	888,103
Eskişehir	244,251	324,614	415,000	492,902	597,397	648,342
Gaziantep	290,058	370,808	511,000	715,474	966,490	1,130,982
Giresun	283,626	334,701	428,000	462,449	502,151	481,023
Gümüşhane	190,130	212,376	263,000	286,922	283,753	155,745
Hakkari	35,124	54,604	84,000	126,241	182,645	211,179
Hatay	254,141	364,992	506,000	744,318	1,002,252	1,202,009
İçel	279,484	372,932	511,000	710,728	1,034,085	1,513,956
Iğdir	— —	— —	— —	— —	— —	144,833
Isparta	172,543	211,687	266,000	322,062	382,844	455,753
İstanbul	1,078,399	1,542,941	2,293,000	3,864,493	5,842,985	9,061,096
İzmir	673,581	898,480	1,235,000	1,660,529	2,317,829	3,076,928
Kahramanmaraş	261,550	337,735	438,000	620,246	840,472	1,028,590
Karabük	— —	— —	— —	— —	— —	228,592
Karaman	— —	— —	— —	— —	— —	223,360
Kars	381,176	488,406	606,000	701,772	722,431	316,019
Kastamonu	385,410	394,299	442,000	436,946	450,353	371,964
Kayseri	370,089	423,189	536,000	674,015	864,060	952,264
Kilis	— —	— —	— —	— —	— —	110,043
Kırıkkale	— —	— —	— —	— —	— —	363,446
Kırklareli	178,203	223,843	258,000	268,224	297,098	308,090
Kırşehir	157,565	— —	197,000	231,973	260,156	246,933
Kocaeli	416,058	254,263	336,000	478,468	742,245	1,173,811
Konya	661,877	849,771	1,123,000	1,423,910	1,769,050	1,937,814
Kütahya	384,625	330,906	398,000	480,442	543,384	645,077
Malatya	428,660	341,925	453,000	577,309	665,809	802,306
Manisa	472,789	564,457	749,000	870,841	1,050,130	1,226,307
Mardin	234,457	306,784	398,000	529,260	652,069	651,150
Muğla	220,678	266,789	335,000	401,413	486,290	625,776
Muş	82,699	136,248	199,000	252,135	339,492	428,914
Nevşehir	— —	239,608	203,000	248,971	278,129	283,343
Niğde	296,584	285,824	362,000	460,928	560,386	321,543
Ordu	333,008	409,891	544,000	661,679	763,857	858,775
Osmaniye	— —	— —	— —	— —	— —	438,110
Rize	171,929	213,075	281,000	334,952	374,206	334,285
Sakarya	— —	298,488	404,000	495,771	610,500	732,898
Samsun	407,541	551,125	756,000	904,774	1,108,710	1,170,275
Şanlıurfa	263,855	347,712	451,000	598,238	795,034	1,313,076
Siirt	133,627	191,657	265,000	389,347	524,741	264,503
Sinop	205,276	239,688	266,000	266,609	280,140	221,151
Şırnak	— —	— —	— —	— —	— —	312,068
Sivas	490,493	590,890	705,000	739,073	772,209	705,719
Tekirdağ	202,606	251,920	287,000	318,704	402,721	545,266 ➤

division	1945	1955	1965	1975	1985	1997
Tokat	340,749	388,724	495,000	592,612	679,071	712,081
Trabzon	395,384	463,918	596,000	716,168	786,194	862,358
Tunceli	90,446	121,907	154,000	163,273	151,906	82,535
Uşak	— —	166,271	191,000	228,715	271,261	317,692
Van	127,858	176,203	267,000	386,059	547,216	772,944
Yalova	— —	— —	— —	— —	— —	161,466
Yozgat	287,371	393,235	438,000	497,960	545,301	615,608
Zonguldak	383,481	492,422	650,000	829,204	1,044,945	620,607
	18,790,174	24,121,738	31,392,000	40,197,669	50,664,458	62,610,252

Census dates: 1945-10-21, 1955-10-23, 1965-10-24, 1975-10-26, 1985-10-20.

TURKMENISTAN

ISO = TM/FIPS = TX   Language = Turkmen   Time zone = +5   Capital = Ashkhabad

Turkmenistan corresponds to most of the Transcaspian (Zakaspiyskaya) oblast of the Turkestan general-government of the Russian Empire in 1900, plus a small part of the Khanate of Khiva. During most of the history of the Soviet Union, it was the Turkmenistan S.S.R., a constituent republic. It became independent on 1991-10-27.

Other names of country: Republic of Turkmenistan (formal–English); Toerkmenistan (Dutch); Turcomênia (Portuguese); Turkmenistán (Spanish); Turkménistan (French); Túrkmenistan (Icelandic); Turkmenostan Respublikasy (formal).

Origin of name: land of the Turkmens, possibly from *turk*: Turk, *men*: pure.

division	abv	ISO	population	area-km	area-mi	capital
Ahal	AH	A	764,000	95,000	37,000	Ashgabat
Balkan	BA	B	326,000	138,000	53,000	Nebitdag
Dashhowuz	DA	D	580,000	74,000	29,000	Dashhowuz
Lebap	LE	L	622,000	94,000	36,000	Chärjew
Mary	MA	M	678,000	87,000	34,000	Mary
			2,970,000	488,000	189,000	

Status: These divisions are welayah (sing. welayat: provinces).
Abv: Two-letter code for international compatibility (defined by the author).
ISO: Codes from ISO 3166-2.
FIPS: Codes from FIPS PUB 10-4.
Population: 1982 estimate.
Area-km: Square kilometers.
Area-mi: Square miles.
Origins of names:

Ashkhabad: Iranian *'esq abad*: city of love

Change history:

1919	Name of capital of Transcaspian province changed from Askhabad to Poltoratsk.
1921-04-11	Turkestan A.S.S.R. formed from Amu-Darya, Ferghana, Pamir, Samarkand, Semirechensk, and Syr Darya regions, and the southern part of Transcaspian.
1924-10	Turkestan A.S.S.R. and Bukhara reorganized into several units, one of which was the Turkmenskaya S.S.R.
1927	Name of capital of Turkmenskaya A.S.S.R. changed from Poltoratsk to Ashkhabad (note slight spelling change from 1919).
~1967	Krasnovodskaya oblast split from Ashkhabadskaya oblast.

~1988   Capital of Krasnovodskaya oblast moved from Krasnovodsk to Nebitdag.

1991-10-27   Turkmenistan became independent, and Turkmen names became official. Names of
               provinces changed from Ashkhabad to Ahal, Krasnovodsk to Balkan, Tashauz to
               Dashhowuz, and Chardzhou to Lebap. Name of capital of Lebap changed from
               Chardzhou to Chärjew.

Other names of subdivisions:

Ahal: Ashkhabad, Ashkhabadskaya Oblast (obsolete)   Lebap: Chardzhou, Chardzhouskaya Oblast (obsolete)
Balkan: Krasnovodsk, Krasnovodskaya Oblast (obsolete)   Mary: Maruy, Marysk, Maryyskaya Oblast (obsolete)
Dashhowuz: Tashauz, Tashauzskaya Oblast (obsolete)

TURKS AND CAICOS ISLANDS

ISO = TC/FIPS = TK   Language = English   Time zone = -5 ^{d} Capital = Cockburn Town

Turks and Caicos Islands was a dependency of Jamaica until Jamaica became independent, on 1962-08-06. Then it reverted to the status of territory of the United Kingdom.

Other names of country: Îles Turks et Caïques (French); Ilhas Turcas y Caicos (Portuguese); Islas Turcas y Caicos (Spanish); Turks- en Caicoseilanden (Dutch); Turks- und Caicos-Inseln (German).

division	abv	population	area-km	area-mi	capital
Turks and Caicos Islands	TC	11,696	430	166	Grand Turk

Status: This division is the whole of the country, treated as a division for compatibility.
Abv: Two-letter code for international compatibility (defined by the author).
Population: 1990 census.
Area-km: Square kilometers.
Area-mi: Square miles.
Territorial extent: Turks and Caicos islands consists of two island groups. The larger is Caicos Islands, including Grand Caicos, East Caicos, North Caicos, Providenciales, West Caicos, South Caicos, Ambergris Cays, Long Cay, Seal Cay, and French Cay. To the east, the Turks Islands include Grand Turk (site of the capital) and Salt Cay.

TUVALU

ISO = TV/FIPS = TV   Language = Tuvalu, English   Time zone = +12   Capital = Funafuti

The Gilbert and Ellice Islands were a British protectorate at the beginning of the 20th century. The colony of Gilbert and Ellice Islands was formed on 1915-11-12, by annexing some additional island possessions to the protectorate. The Ellice Islands separated on 1975-10-01, taking the name Tuvalu. The country became fully independent exactly three years later.

Other names of country: Túvalú (Icelandic).

division	abv	ISO	division	abv	ISO
Funafuti	FN	FUN	Nui	NU	NIU
Nanumanga	NG	NMG	Nukufetau	NF	NKF
Nanumea	NA	NMA	Nukulaelae	NL	NKL
Niutao	NT	NIT	Vaitupu	VI	VAI

Status: These divisions are island councils, except for Funafuti, which is a town council.
Abv: Two-letter code for international compatibility (defined by the author).
ISO: Codes from ISO 3166-2.
Population: 1992 estimate.
Area-km: Square kilometers.
Area-mi: Square miles.
Territorial extent: Niutao includes the island of Niulakita (Nurakita).

UGANDA

ISO = UG/FIPS = UG   Language = English   Time zone = +3   Capital = Kampala

Uganda was a British protectorate at the beginning of the 20th century. On 1962-10-09 it became an independent member of the British Commonwealth.

Other names of country: Ouganda (French); Republic of Uganda (formal–English); Úganda (Icelandic).

Origin of name: Swahili for land of the Ganda, ethnic name.

division	abv	ISO	FIPS	population	area-km	area-mi	reg	former
Apac	AP	APA	UG26	460,700	6,488	2,505	N	Northern
Arua	AR	ARU	UG27	624,600	7,830	3,023	N	Nile
Bundibugyo	BN	BUN	UG28	116,000	2,338	903	W	Western
Bushenyi	BS	BUS	UG29	734,800	5,396	2,083	W	Southern
Gulu	GU	GUL	UG30	338,700	11,735	4,531	N	Nile, Northern
Hoima	HO	HOI	UG31	197,800	5,492	2,120	W	Western
Iganga	IG	IGA	UG32	944,000	13,113	5,063	E	Busoga
Jinja	JI	JIN	UG33	284,900	734	283	E	Busoga
Kabale	KA	KBL	UG34	412,800	1,827	705	W	Southern
Kabarole	KB	KBR	UG35	741,400	8,361	3,228	W	Western
Kalangala	KN	KLG	UG36	16,400	5,716	2,207	C	South Buganda
Kampala	KM	KLA	UG37	773,500	238	92	C	Central
Kamuli	KL	KLI	UG38	480,700	4,348	1,679	E	Busoga
Kapchorwa	KC	KAP	UG39	116,300	1,738	671	E	Eastern
Kasese	KS	KAS	UG40	343,000	3,205	1,237	W	Western
Kibale	KI	KLE	UG41	219,300	4,718	1,822	W	Western
Kiboga	KG	KIB	UG42	140,800	3,774	1,457	C	North Buganda
Kisoro	KR	KIS	UG43	184,900	662	256	W	Southern
Kitgum	KT	KIT	UG44	350,300	16,136	6,230	N	Northern
Kotido	KO	KOT	UG45	190,700	13,208	5,100	N	Karamoja
Kumi	KU	KUM	UG46	237,000	2,861	1,105	E	Eastern
Lira	LI	LIR	UG47	498,300	7,251	2,800	N	Northern
Luwero	LU	LUW	UG48	449,200	9,198	3,551	C	North Buganda
Masaka	MA	MSK	UG49	831,300	10,611	4,097	C	South Buganda
Masindi	MS	MSI	UG50	253,500	9,326	3,601	W	Western
Mbale	ML	MBL	UG51	706,600	2,546	983	E	Eastern
Mbarara	MR	MBR	UG52	929,600	10,839	4,185	W	Southern
Moroto	MO	MOR	UG53	171,500	14,113	5,449	N	Karamoja
Moyo	MY	MOY	UG54	178,500	5,006	1,933	N	Nile
Mpigi	MP	MPI	UG55	915,400	6,222	2,402	C	Central
Mubende	MU	MUB	UG56	497,500	6,536	2,524	C	North Buganda
Mukono	MK	MUK	UG57	816,200	14,242	5,499	C	North Buganda
Nebbi	NE	NEB	UG58	315,900	2,891	1,116	N	Nile
Ntungamo	NT	NTU	UG59	——	——	——	W	Southern
Pallisa	PA	PAL	UG60	356,000	1,919	741	E	Eastern
Rakai	RA	RAK	UG61	382,000	4,973	1,920	C	South Buganda
Rukungiri	RU	RUK	UG62	388,000	2,753	1,063	W	Southern
Soroti	SO	SOR	UG63	430,900	10,060	3,884	E	Eastern
Tororo	TO	TOR	UG64	554,000	2,634	1,017	E	Eastern
				16,583,000	241,038	93,065		

Status: These divisions are districts.

Abv: Two-letter code for international compatibility (defined by the author).

ISO: Codes from ISO 3166-2.

FIPS: Codes from FIPS PUB 10-4.

Population: 1991 census.

Area-km: Square kilometers.

Area-mi: Square miles.

Reg: Region (C = Central, E = Eastern, N = Northern, W = Western).

Capitals: Capitals have the same names as their districts, except Kabarole (capital Fort Portal).

Former: Pre–1990 province from which the district was formed.

Further subdivisions: The districts are divided into counties, which are subdivided into sub-counties. The old regions are still referred to, but no longer have any administrative status.

Territorial extent: Iganga includes the islands of Sigulu, Lolui, Dagusi, Sagitu, and others in Lake Victoria. Kalangala consists of the Sese Islands in Lake Victoria. The largest ones are Bugala and Bukasa. Mukono includes the islands of Buvuma, Kome, Damba, Bugaia, and others in Lake Victoria.

Change history: From 1945 or earlier until after independence, Uganda was divided into four provinces:

division	1948	1959	1969	area-km	capital
Buganda	1,317,705	1,881,149	2,667,332	61,609	Kampala
Eastern	1,514,428	1,902,697	2,817,066	63,018	Jinja
Northern	945,104	1,249,310	1,631,899	57,320	Gulu
Western	1,177,939	1,503,375	2,432,550	54,913	Masindi
	4,955,176	6,536,531	9,548,847	236,860	

Population: 1948 census, 1959 census, 1969 census.

These provinces were subdivided into districts. In the 1960s and 1970s, the districts became the primary division, and the provinces were redesignated as regions. This is how the districts stood at the time of the 1969 census:

district	FIPS	population	area-km	reg	capital
Acholi	— —	463,844	27,853	Northern	Gulu
Ankole	UG01	861,145	16,182	Western	Mbarara
Bugisu	UG02	421,433	2,546	Eastern	Mbale
Bukedi	UG03	527,090	4,553	Eastern	Tororo
Bunyoro	UG04	351,903	19,609	Western	Hoima
Busoga	UG05	949,384	14,047	Eastern	Jinja
East Mengo	UG07	851,583	23,440	Buganda	Bombo
Karamoja	UG08	284,067	27,213	Eastern	Moroto
Kigezi	UG09	647,988	5,218	Western	Kabale
Lango	UG10	504,315	13,740	Northern	Lira
Madi	UG11	89,978	5,006	Northern	Moyo
Masaka	UG12	640,596	21,300	Buganda	Masaka
Mubende	UG13	330,955	10,310	Buganda	Mubende
Sebei	UG14	64,464	1,738	Eastern	Kapchorua
Teso	UG15	570,628	12,921	Eastern	Soroti
Toro	UG16	571,514	13,904	Western	Fort Portal
West Mengo	UG18	844,198	6,559	Buganda	Mpigi
West Nile	UG19	573,762	10,721	Northern	Arua
		9,548,847	236,860		

FIPS: Codes from FIPS PUB 10-4.

| 1971-04 | Acholi district split into East Acholi (FIPS code UG06) and West Acholi (UG17); Karamoja district split into North Karamoja and South Karamoja. |
| ~1976 | Uganda reorganized from districts into provinces, as listed: |

province	FIPS	population	area-km	capital	former
Busoga	UG05	1,221,872	13,340	Jinja	Busoga
Central	UG18	1,117,648	6,270	Kampala	West Mengo
Eastern	UG20	2,015,530	22,260	Mbale	Bugisu, Bukedi, Sebei, Teso ➤

province	FIPS	population	area-km	capital	former
Karamoja	UG08	350,908	26,960	Moroto	Karamoja (North and South)
Nile	UG21	811,755	15,730	Arua	Madi, West Acholi (part), West Nile
North Buganda	UG22	1,554,371	27,010	Bombo	East Mengo, Mubende
Northern	UG23	1,261,364	41,520	Gulu	Acholi (East and part of West), Lango
South Buganda	UG12	905,754	15,970	Masaka	Masaka
Southern	UG24	1,963,428	21,280	Mbarara	Ankole, Kigezi
Western	UG25	1,427,446	30,980	Fort Portal	Bunyoro, Toro
		12,630,076	221,320		

FIPS: Codes from FIPS PUB 10-4.
Population: 1980 census.
Former: Pre–1976 districts forming this province.

~1990   Name of Buganda region changed to Central. Uganda reorganized from 10 provinces into 33 districts.
~1992   Kalangala, Kibale, Kiboga, Kisoro, and Pallisa districts created.
~1994   Ntungamo district created, probably by splitting from Mbarara.

Other names of subdivisions:

East Mengo: East Buganda (variant)   West Mengo: West Buganda (variant)
Kibale: Kibaale (variant)

UKRAINE

ISO = UA/FIPS = UP   Language = Ukrainian   Time zone = +2 ^{d} Capital = Kiev

At the beginning of the 20th century, the bulk of modern Ukraine was in the Russian Empire; the rest was in the Austro-Hungarian Empire. In the chaos of World War I and the Russian Revolution, the Russian part of Ukraine declared itself an independent republic. In 1922, it joined the U.S.S.R. as one of its constituent republics. In World War II, the Soviet Union made significant territorial gains, some of which were annexed to the Ukrainian S.S.R. Ukraine became independent once again in 1991 when the Soviet Union dissolved.

Other names of country: Oekraine (Dutch); Ucraina (Italian); Ucrania (Spanish); Ucrânia (Portuguese); Ukraina (Finnish, Norwegian, Swedish); Ukrayina (formal); Úkraína (Icelandic).

Origin of name: Russian u: near, krai: border, named when the Mongol invasion had reached that area.

division	abv	ISO	FIPS	typ	population	area-km	area-mi	capital
Cherkasy	CK	71	UP01	o	1,538,000	21,000	8,000	Cherkasy
Chernihiv	CH	74	UP02	o	1,472,000	32,000	12,000	Chernihiv
Chernivtsi	CV	77	UP03	o	904,000	8,000	3,000	Chernivtsi
Crimea	KR	43	UP11	r	2,247,000	27,000	10,000	Simferopol'
Dnipropetrovs'k	DP	12	UP04	o	3,718,000	32,000	12,000	Dnipropetrovs'k
Donets'k	DT	14	UP05	o	5,234,000	26,000	10,000	Donets'k
Ivano-Frankivs'k	IF	26	UP06	o	1,353,000	14,000	5,000	Ivano-Frankivs'k
Kharkiv	KK	63	UP07	o	3,100,000	31,000	12,000	Kharkiv
Kherson	KS	65	UP08	o	1,185,000	28,000	11,000	Kherson
Khmel'nyts'kyy	KM	68	UP09	o	1,546,000	21,000	8,000	Khmel'nyts'kyy
Kiev	KV	32	UP13	o	1,925,000	29,000	11,000	Kiev
Kiev City	KC	30	UP12	m	2,304,000	— —	— —	Kiev
Kirovohrad	KH	35	UP10	o	1,242,000	25,000	10,000	Kirovohrad
Luhans'k	LH	09	UP14	o	2,803,000	27,000	10,000	Luhans'k
L'viv	LV	46	UP15	o	2,609,000	22,000	8,000	L'viv
Mykolayiv	MY	48	UP16	o	1,263,000	25,000	10,000	Mykolayiv
Odessa	OD	51	UP17	o	2,579,000	33,000	13,000	Odessa ➤

division	abv	ISO	FIPS	typ	population	area-km	area-mi	capital
Poltava	PL	53	UP18	o	1,730,000	29,000	11,000	Poltava
Rivne	RV	56	UP19	o	1,142,000	20,000	8,000	Rivne
Sevastopol' City	SC	40	UP20	m	— —	— —	— —	Sevastopol'
Sumy	SM	59	UP21	o	1,450,000	24,000	9,000	Sumy
Ternopil'	TP	61	UP22	o	1,167,000	14,000	5,000	Ternopil'
Transcarpathia	ZK	21	UP25	o	1,183,000	13,000	5,000	Uzhhorod
Vinnytsya	VI	05	UP23	o	2,012,000	26,000	10,000	Vinnytsya
Volyn	VO	07	UP24	o	1,030,000	20,000	8,000	Luts'k
Zaporizhzhya	ZP	23	UP26	o	1,993,000	27,000	10,000	Zaporizhzhya
Zhytomyr	ZT	18	UP27	o	1,578,000	30,000	12,000	Zhytomyr
					50,307,000	604,000	231,000	

Status: These divisions are oblastey (o, sing. oblast': regions), mista (m, sing. misto: independent city), and a respublika (r, republic).

Abv: Two-letter code for international compatibility (defined by the author).

ISO: Codes from ISO 3166-2.

FIPS: Codes from FIPS PUB 10-4.

Population: 1982-01-01 estimate.

Area-km: Square kilometers.

Area-mi: Square miles.

Further subdivisions: The regions are divided into rayony (districts).

Territorial extent: Crimea includes Kosa Tuzla, an island in the Strait of Kerch.

Kherson includes the barrier islands of Tendrivs'ka Kosa and Dzharylhach; the northern end of the long promontory Kosa Arabats'ka Strilka; and some islands in "Lake" Syvash, the bay enclosed by that promontory, such as Chut'uk Island.

Origins of names:

Crimea: Greek *kremnoi*: escarpments

Dnepropetrovs'k: Dniepr (River) + (Grigoriy Ivanovich) Petrovskiy, Soviet politician

Kharkiv: possibly from Tatar *karak*: bandit, the city of bandits

Khmel'nyts'kyy: probably after Bogdan Khmel'nyts'kyy (1593–1657), Ukrainian warlord

Kirovohrad: after Sergei Mironovich Kirov (1886–1934), Russian politician

Transcarpathia: Latin *trans*: beyond + Carpathian (Mountains), as seen from Kiev

Change history: At the turn of the century, nine guberniy (governments) of Russia approximately matched the eastern and central parts of present-day Ukraine: Chernigov, Kharkov, Kherson, Kiev, Podolia, Poltava, Taurida, Volhynia, and Yekaterinoslav (see Russia for more details). The governments were divided into uyezdi (counties), which were subdivided into volosti (districts). The western parts of Ukraine were in the Austrian provinces of Galicia and Bukovina, and the Hungarian counties of Bereg, Máramaros, Ugocsa, and Ung (see Hungary for more details).

1918-01		Russian part of Ukraine declared independence. Later that year, Ukrainians in East Galicia formed their own republic in federation with Ukraine.
1918-03-03		By the Treaty of Brest-Litovsk, Russia acknowledged the independence of Ukraine. The region of Chelm was transferred from Poland to Ukraine.
1919		Paris Peace Conference made East Galicia a protectorate of Poland. Russia and Germany had both renounced the Treaty of Brest-Litovsk.
1919-12		Ukrainian Soviet Socialist Republic established.
1921-03-18		Poland and Russia signed the Riga Treaty, ending the Russo-Polish War. Poland gained the western part of Volhynia from Ukraine.
1921		Crimea became an A.S.S.R. within the Russian S.F.S.R. The rest of Taurida guberniya was split between Odessa and Yekaterinoslav guberniy.
1922-12-30		By the Treaty of Union, Ukrainian S.S.R. became a constituent republic of the newly formed Union of Soviet Socialist Republics, with its capital at Kharkov. It contained the nine guberniy, excluding the Crimea, four counties in northern Chernigov, and territory lost to Poland, but including one county from the guberniya of Kursk.
~1923		Donets guberniya split from Yekaterinoslav. Its capital was Bakhmut (later Artemovsk).

1924	Moldavian A.S.S.R. split from Ukraine, consisting of Bessarabian territory on the left bank of the Dniestr River.
1925	Ukraine reorganized into 53 okruhas (provinces), subdivided into raiony (districts).
~1927	Taganrog and Shakhty provinces transferred from Ukraine to Russia.
1932	Ukraine reorganized again, this time into seven oblastey (regions), subdivided into raiony.
1934	Capital of Ukrainian S.S.R. moved from Kharkov to Kiev.
1935	Name of Lugansk region and its capital changed to Voroshilovgrad, in honor of Marshal Kliment Yefremovich Voroshilov (1881–1969).
1939	Splits had increased the number of regions to sixteen.
1939-09	Soviet conquests in Galicia annexed to Ukrainian S.S.R.
1940-06	Northern Bukovina transferred from Romania to Ukrainian S.S.R. by treaty. It became Chernovtsy region.
1940-08-02	Soviet Union assimilated Bessarabia, a former guberniya of Russia, which it had retaken from Romania. From parts of Bessarabia and the Moldavian A.S.S.R., the Moldavian S.S.R. was created. The remaining parts merged with the Ukraine (the Moldavian part joined with Odessa, and the Bessarabian part becoming the new region of Izmail). The annexation was formalized on 1947-02-10.
1945-06-29	Soviet Union acquired Subcarpathian Ruthenia, also called Carpatho-Ukraine, from Czechoslovakia. It became Transcarpathia region within the Ukrainian S.S.R.
1945-07-16	Potsdam Conference began. As one outcome, the Soviet Union recovered territory lost in the Russo-Polish War up to approximately the Curzon Line, annexing it to the republics of Byelorussia, Lithuania, and Ukraine. This territory became the regions of Drogobych, L'vov, Rovno, Stanislav, Ternopol', Transcarpathia, and Volyn.
1954-02-19	Crimea (now an oblast) transferred from Russian S.F.S.R. to Ukrainian S.S.R.
~1955	Cherkassy region formed from parts of Kiev and Poltava. Izmail merged with Odessa. Names of Kamenets-Podol'skiy region and its capital Proskurov both changed to Khmelnitsky.
1958	Name of Voroshilovgrad region and its capital changed back to Lugansk.
1961	Name of Stalino region and its capital changed to Donetsk.
1962	Name of Stanislav region and its capital changed to Ivano-Frankovsk.
~1963	Drogobych region merged with L'vov.
1991-12-25	Soviet Union officially dissolved. Its 15 constituent republics became independent countries. Many of them had already unilaterally declared independence in the preceding few months. Ukrainian names of regions and cities became official.
1992	Status of Crimea oblast changed to autonomous republic.

Other names of subdivisions: During the Soviet era, the Russian names were considered standard. Now, the Ukrainian language is official. Both languages are written in the Cyrillic alphabet, but they use certain individual letters that are different. Their transliterations into the Roman alphabet are also different. To compound the confusion, in Ukrainian or Russian, the name is usually given in adjective form, followed by the generic (usually Oblast'). For example, Chernihiv would be Chernigovskaya Oblast' in Russian, Chernihivs'ka Oblast' in Ukrainian; its capital is Chernigov or Chernihiv, respectively. Kyyiv is now the preferred English name for the capital, but the Russian-based spelling, Kiev, is still well established.

Cherkasy: Cherkas'ka Oblast' (Ukrainian); Cherkasskaya Oblast', Cherkassy (Russian)

Chernihiv: Chernigov (Russian); Tschernigow (German)

Chernivtsi: Chernivets'ka Oblast' (Ukrainian); Chernovitskaya Oblast' (Russian); Chernovtsy (Russian); Czernowitz, Tschernowzy (German); Tchernovtsy (French)

Crimea: Crimée (French); Criméia (Portuguese); Krim (German); Krymskaya Respublika (Russian); Respublika Krym (Ukrainian)

Dnipropetrovs'k: Dnepropetrovsk (Russian); Dniepropietrovsk (variant); Dnjepropetrowsk (German)

Donets'k: Donetskaya Oblast' (Russian); Donezk (German, Italian); Stalino (obsolete)

Ivano-Frankivs'k: Ivano-Frankovsk, Ivano-Frankovskaya Oblast' (Russian); Stanislav (obsolete)

Kharkiv: Charkow (German); Jarkov (Spanish); Karkov (Italian); Khar'kov (Russian)

Kherson: Cherson (German); Khersons'ka Oblast' (Ukrainian)

Khmel'nyts'kyy: Chmelnizkij (German); Hmelnicki (variant); Kamenets-Podol'skaya Oblast' (obsolete); Khmel'nyts'ka Oblast' (Ukrainian); Khmel'nitskaya Oblast' (Russian)

Kiev: Kiew, Kijew (German); Kiiv, Kijev, Kiyev, Kyiv, Kyjiv, Kyyiv (variant); Kyyivs'ka Oblast' (Ukrainian)

Kiev City: Grad Kiev (Russian); Misto Kyyiv (Ukrainian)

Kirovohrad: Kirovograd, Kirovogradskaya Oblast (Russian)

Luhans'k: Lugansk (Russian); Luhans'ka Oblast' (Ukrainian); Voroshilovgrad (obsolete)

L'viv: Lemberg (obsolete); Llvov (Spanish); L'vov (Russian); Lwow (German); L'vivs'ka Oblast' (Ukrainian)

Mykolayiv: Nikolajew (German); Nikolayev (Russian)

Odessa: Odesa, Odes'ka Oblast' (Ukrainian); Odesskaya Oblast' (Russian)

Rivne: Rivnens'ka Oblast' (Ukrainian); Rovenskaya Oblast', Rovno (Russian)

Sevastopol' City: Misto Sevastopol' (Ukrainian); Sebastopol (variant); Sebastopoli (Italian); Sewastopol (German)

Ternopil': Ternopol' (Russian)

Transcarpathia: Ruthenia (obsolete); Zakarpats'ka Oblast' (Ukrainian); Zakarpatskaya Oblast' (Russian)

Vinnytsya: Vinnitskaya Oblast (Russian); Vinnyts'ka Oblast' (Ukrainian); Winniza (German)

Volyn: Volhynia (variant); Volyns'ka Oblast' (Ukrainian); Volynskaya Oblast' (Russian); Wolynien (German)

Zaporizhzhya: Saporoshje (German); Zaporiz'ka Oblast' (Ukrainian); Zaporojie (French); Zaporozhskaya Oblast', Zaporozh'ye (Russian); Zaporožje (variant)

Zhytomyr: Jitomir (French); Shitomir (German); Zhitomir, Zhitomirskaya Oblast' (Russian)

UNITED ARAB EMIRATES

ISO = AE/FIPS = TC   Language = Arabic   Time zone = +4   Capital = Abu Dhabi

During the 19th century, Great Britain made a series of agreements with seven independent sheikhdoms on the Persian Gulf. As a result, the area became known as the Trucial Coast. There was no formal union until 1971, although stamps were issued in 1961 under the name Trucial States.

Other names of country: Arabiemiirikunnat (Finnish); De forente arabiske emiratene (Norwegian); Emirados Arabes Unidos (Portuguese); Emirati Arabi Uniti (Italian); Emiratos Árabes Unidos, Omán de la Tregua (Spanish); Émirats arabes unis (French); Förenade Arabemiraten (Swedish); Forenede Arabiske Emirater (Danish); Ittihad al-Imarat al-Arabiyah (formal); Sameinuðu arabísku furstadæmin (Icelandic); Trucial Coast, Trucial Oman, Trucial States (obsolete); Vereinigte Arabische Emirate (German); Verenigde Arabische Emiraten (Dutch).

Origin of name: descriptive: formed by union of several Persian Gulf city-states ruled by emirs.

division	ISO	FIPS	population	area-km	area-mi
Abu Dhabi	AZ	TC01	670,125	67,350	26,000
Ajman	AJ	TC02	64,318	250	100
Dubay	DU	TC03	419,104	3,900	1,500
Fujayrah	FU	TC04	54,425	1,200	500
Ras al Khaymah	RK	TC05	116,470	1,700	700
Sharjah	SH	TC06	268,722	2,600	1,000
Umm al Qaywayn	UQ	TC07	29,229	800	300
			1,622,393	77,800	30,100

Status: These divisions are emirates.

ISO: Codes from ISO 3166-2.

FIPS: Codes from FIPS PUB 10-4.

Population: 1985 census.

Area-km: Square kilometers.

Area-mi: Square miles.

Capital: Capitals have the same names as their emirates.

Territorial extent: Each of the emirates lies mainly on the Arabian Peninsula. There is a small neutral zone between Abu Dhabi and Dubay.

Abu Dhabi includes numerous Persian Gulf islands, including Abu al Abyaḍ, Şir Bani Yas, Dalma, and Şir Abu Nu'ayr.

Ajman consists of three enclaves. The one containing the capital lies on the Persian Gulf; one is on the border between Fujayrah and Sharjah, and the last is partly shared with Oman.

Dubay has one large section, plus a small enclave next to Oman.

Fujayrah has two sections. The one containing the capital is partly shared with Sharjah.

Ras al Khaymah consists of two sections separated by Fujayrah. It claims the Tunb Islands in the Persian Gulf.

Sharjah consists of a large section on the Persian Gulf, plus two enclaves on the Gulf of Oman (one of which is partly shared with Fujayrah). It shares the administration of Abu Musa Island with Iran.

Origins of names:

Abu Zabi: Arabic: Zabi's father

'Ajman: Arabic: foreigner, Persian

Ras al-Khaymah: Arabic *ra's*: head or cape, *khayma*: tent

Change history:

1952	Kalba and Sharjah merged, taking the name Sharjah and Kalba (later shortened to Sharjah). That same year, Fujayrah was recognized as a Trucial State.
1971-12-02	Abu Dhabi, Ajman, Dubay, Fujayrah, Sharjah, and Umm al Qaywayn formed the United Arab Emirates, an independent federation.
1972-02-01	Ras al Khaymah merged with the United Arab Emirates.

Other names of subdivisions:

Abu Dhabi: Aboû Dabî (French); Abu Dabi (Portuguese); Abū Ẓabī, Abū Ẓaby (variant)

Ajman: 'Adjmân (French); Ajmā (Portuguese); 'Ajmān (variant)

Dubay: Dibay (French, Spanish); Doubaï (French); Dubai, Dubayy (variant)

Fujayrah: Al Foudjaïrah, Fudjayra (French); Al Fujayrah, Fujaira, Fujairah, Fujeira (variant)

Ras al Khaymah: Ras al Khaima, Râs al Khaïmah (French); Rā's al Khayma, Rā's al Khaymah (variant)

Sharjah: Ach Chârdjah, Chārdja (French); Ash Shāriqah, Ash Shārjah, Sharjah and Dependencies, Sharjah and Kalba (variant)

Umm al Qaywayn: Oumm al Qaïwaïn, Umm al Qi'īwayn (French); Qaiwan, Umm al Qaiwain, Umm al Qayqayn, Umm al Qaywayn, Umm el Quwain (variant); Um al Qaiuan (Portuguese)

UNITED KINGDOM

ISO = GB/FIPS = UK   Language = English   Time zone = +0 ^{d} Capital = London

The United Kingdom has been independent for the entire 20th century. The name Great Britain properly refers only to the island shared by England, Scotland, and Wales; however, it is often casually used to refer to the whole United Kingdom. The official name was the United Kingdom of Great Britain and Ireland until 1927, when it was changed to the United Kingdom of Great Britain and Northern Ireland, recognizing the separation of the Irish Free State in 1922. The United Kingdom has had many dependencies and possessions during the 20th century that are listed in this book as separate countries.

Other names of country: Bretland (Icelandic); Grossbritannien (Swiss-German); Iso-Britannia (Finnish); Regno Unito (Italian); Reino Unido (Portuguese, Spanish); Reino Unido de Gran Bretaña e Irlanda del Norte (Spanish-formal); Royaume-Uni (French); Royaume-Uni de Grande-Bretagne et d'Irlande du Nord (French-formal); Storbritannia (Norwegian); Storbritannien (Danish, Swedish); United Kingdom of Great Britain and Northern Ireland (formal–English); Vereinigtes Königreich (German); Vereinigtes Königreich Großbritannien und Nordirland (German-formal); Verenigd Koninkrijk (Dutch).

Origin of name: descriptive: formed originally by union of Kingdoms of Great Britain and Ireland.

division	abv	ISO	FIPS	NUTS	reg	typ	conv	population	area-km	area-mi	capital
Antrim	AN	ANT	UK52	UKB	N	ds		46,600	563	217	Antrim
Ards	AD	ARD	UK53	UKB	N	ds		63,600	369	142	Newtownards
Armagh	AM	ARM	UK54	UKB	N	ds		50,700	672	259	Armagh
Avon	AV	AVN	UK01	UK61	SW	cn		962,000	1,338	517	Bristol
Ballymena	BL	BLA	UK55	UKB	N	ds		56,100	637	246	Ballymena
Ballymoney	BY	BLY	UK56	UKB	N	ds		23,800	419	162	Ballymoney
Banbridge	BB	BNB	UK57	UKB	N	ds		32,000	445	172	Banbridge ➤

division	abv	ISO	FIPS	NUTS	reg	typ	conv	population	area-km	area-mi	capital
Bedfordshire	BD	BDF	UK02	UK51	SE	cn	Beds	534,300	1,235	477	Bedford
Belfast	BF	BFS	UK58	UKB	N	ds		303,800	115	44	Belfast
Berkshire	BK	BRK	UK03	UK52	SE	cn	Berks	752,500	1,256	485	Reading
Borders	BO	BOR	UK78	UKA1	S	rg		103,881	4,672	1,804	Newtown Saint Boswells
Buckinghamshire	BU	BKM	UK04	UK52	SE	cn	Bucks	640,200	1,883	727	Aylesbury
Cambridgeshire	CM	CAM	UK05	UK4	EA	cn	Cambs	669,900	3,409	1,316	Cambridge
Carrickfergus	CF	CKF	UK59	UKB	N	ds		29,300	87	34	Carrickfergus
Castlereagh	CS	CSR	UK60	UKB	N	ds		57,900	85	33	Belfast
Central	CE	CEN	UK79	UKA1	S	rg		268,000	2,631	1,016	Stirling
Cheshire	CH	CHS	UK06	UK81	NW	cn	Ches	966,500	2,328	899	Chester
Cleveland	CV	CLV	UK07	UK11	NO	cn	Cleve	557,000	583	225	Middlesbrough
Clwyd	CD	CWD	UK90	UK91	W	cn		413,800	2,426	937	Mold
Coleraine	CL	CLR	UK61	UKB	N	ds		47,700	485	187	Coleraine
Cookstown	CK	CKT	UK62	UKB	N	ds		27,700	623	241	Cookstown
Cornwall	CO	CON	UK08	UK62	SW	cn	Corn	475,200	3,546	1,369	Truro
Craigavon	CR	CGV	UK63	UKB	N	ds		76,600	382	147	Craigavon
Cumbria	CU	CMA	UK09	UK12	NO	cn	Cumb	489,700	6,810	2,629	Carlisle
Derbyshire	DB	DBY	UK10	UK31	EM	cn		939,800	2,631	1,016	Matlock
Devon	DV	DVV	UK11	UK62	SW	cn	Dev	1,040,000	6,711	2,591	Exeter
Dorset	DS	DOR	UK12	UK63	SW	cn		662,900	2,654	1,025	Dorchester
Down	DW	DOW	UK64	UKB	N	ds		56,400	647	250	Downpatrick
Dumfries and Galloway	DG	DGY	UK80	UKA2	S	rg	D & G	147,100	6,370	2,459	Dumfries
Dungannon	DN	DGN	UK65	UKB	N	ds		43,900	780	301	Dungannon
Durham	DH	DUR	UK13	UK11	NO	cn	Dur	604,300	2,436	941	Durham
Dyfed	DF	DFD	UK91	UK91	W	cn		350,900	5,766	2,226	Carmarthen
East Sussex	ES	ESX	UK14	UK53	SE	cn		716,500	1,795	693	Lewes
Essex	EX	ESS	UK15	UK54	SE	cn		1,548,000	3,675	1,419	Chelmsford
Fermanagh	FE	FER	UK66	UKB	N	ds		50,300	1,876	724	Enniskillen
Fife	FI	FIF	UK81	UKA1	S	rg		339,300	1,307	505	Glenrothes
Gloucestershire	GC	GLS	UK16	UK61	SW	cn	Glos	538,800	2,643	1,020	Gloucester
Grampian	GP	GMP	UK82	UKA4	S	rg		493,200	8,704	3,361	Aberdeen
Greater London	GL	GTL	UK17	UK55	SE	mc		6,803,100	1,580	610	London
Greater Manchester	GM	GTM	UK18	UK82	NW	mc		2,561,600	1,287	497	Manchester
Guernsey	GU	GSY	GK		C	bw	Guern	61,739	78	30	Saint Peter Port
Gwent	GW	GNT	UK92	UK92	W	cn		446,900	1,376	531	Cwmbran
Gwynedd	GD	GWN	UK93	UK91	W	cn	Gwyn	240,100	3,869	1,494	Caernarvon
Hampshire	HA	HAM	UK19	UK56	SE	cn	Hants	1,578,700	3,777	1,458	Winchester
Hereford and Worcester	HW	HWR	UK20	UK71	WM	cn	H & W	686,000	3,926	1,516	Worcester
Hertfordshire	HT	HRT	UK21	UK51	SE	cn	Herts	989,500	1,634	631	Hertford
Highland	HI	HLD	UK83	UKA3	S	rg		209,400	25,391	9,804	Inverness
Humberside	HS	HUM	UK22	UK21	YH	cn		874,400	3,512	1,356	Beverley
Isle of Man	IM	IOM	IM		I	cd	I o M	64,282	572	221	Douglas
Isle of Wight	IW	IOW	UK23	UK56	SE	cn	I o W	126,600	381	147	Newport
Jersey	JE	JSY	JE		C	bw	Jer	84,082	116	45	Saint Helier
Kent	KE	KEN	UK24	UK57	SE	cn		1,538,800	3,732	1,441	Maidstone
Lancashire	LA	LAN	UK25	UK83	NW	cn	Lancs	1,408,000	3,063	1,183	Preston
Larne	LR	LRN	UK67	UKB	N	ds		28,700	338	131	Larne
Leicestershire	LE	LEC	UK26	UK32	EM	cn	Leics	890,800	2,553	986	Leicester
Limavady	LM	LMV	UK68	UKB	N	ds		29,600	587	227	Limavady
Lincolnshire	LI	LIN	UK27	UK33	EM	cn	Lincs	592,600	5,915	2,284	Lincoln
Lisburn	LB	LSB	UK69	UKB	N	ds		92,900	444	171	Lisburn
Londonderry	LD	DRY	UK70	UKB	N	ds		97,500	387	149	Londonderry
Lothian	LO	LTN	UK84	UKA1	S	rg	Loth	723,700	1,721	664	Edinburgh
Magherafelt	MF	MFT	UK71	UKB	N	ds		33,300	572	221	Magherafelt
Merseyside	MS	MSY	UK28	UK84	NW	mc		1,441,100	652	252	Liverpool
Mid Glamorgan	MG	MGM	UK94	UK92	W	cn	M Glam	541,600	1,018	393	Cardiff
Moyle	MY	MYL	UK72	UKB	N	ds		15,200	495	191	Ballycastle
Newry and Mourne	NM	NYM	UK73	UKB	N	ds		87,100	895	346	Newry
Newtownabbey	NW	NTA	UK74	UKB	N	ds		72,300	150	58	Newtownabbey
Norfolk	NF	NFK	UK29	UK4	EA	cn	Norf	759,400	5,368	2,073	Norwich
Northamptonshire	NA	NTH	UK31	UK32	EM	cn	Northants	587,100	2,367	914	Northampton ➤

division	abv	ISO	FIPS	NUTS	reg	typ	conv	population	area-km	area-mi	capital
North Down	ND	NDN	UK75	UKB	N	ds		70,700	73	28	Bangor
Northumberland	NB	NBL	UK32	UK13	NO	cn	Northumb	307,100	5,032	1,943	Morpeth
North Yorkshire	NY	NYK	UK30	UK22	YH	cn	N Yorks	720,900	8,316	3,211	Northallerton
Nottinghamshire	NT	NTT	UK33	UK31	EM	cn	Notts	1,015,500	2,164	836	Nottingham
Omagh	OM	OMH	UK76	UKB	N	ds		45,800	1,129	436	Omagh
Orkney	OR	ORK	UK85	UKA3	S	ia		19,300	976	377	Kirkwall
Oxfordshire	OX	OXF	UK34	UK52	SE	cn	Oxon	579,700	2,608	1,007	Oxford
Powys	PO	POW	UK95	UK91	W	cn		118,700	5,076	1,960	Llandrindod Wells
Shetland	SH	ZET	UK86	UKA3	S	ia	Shet	22,400	1,433	553	Lerwick
Shropshire	SP	SHR	UK35	UK72	WM	cn	Salop	412,500	3,490	1,347	Shrewsbury
Somerset	SM	SOM	UK36	UK63	SW	cn	Som	469,400	3,458	1,335	Taunton
South Glamorgan	SG	SGM	UK96	UK92	W	cn	S Glam	405,900	416	161	Cardiff
South Yorkshire	SY	SYK	UK37	UK23	YH	mc	S Yorks	1,292,700	1,560	602	Barnsley
Staffordshire	ST	STS	UK38	UK72	WM	cn	Staffs	1,047,400	2,716	1,049	Stafford
Strabane	SB	STB	UK77	UKB	N	ds		35,700	870	336	Strabane
Strathclyde	SC	STD	UK87	UKA2	S	rg		2,218,200	13,537	5,227	Glasgow
Suffolk	SF	SFK	UK39	UK4	EA	cn	Suff	661,900	3,798	1,466	Ipswich
Surrey	SR	SRY	UK40	UK53	SE	cn		1,035,500	1,677	647	Kingston upon Thames
Tayside	TA	TAY	UK88	UKA1	S	rg		385,300	7,493	2,893	Dundee
Tyne and Wear	TW	TWR	UK41	UK13	NO	mc	T & W	1,125,600	540	208	Newcastle upon Tyne
Warwickshire	WR	WAR	UK42	UK71	WM	cn	Warks	489,900	1,981	765	Warwick
Western Isles	WI	WIS	UK89	UKA3	S	ia		31,000	2,898	1,119	Stornoway
West Glamorgan	WG	WGM	UK97	UK92	W	cn	W Glam	368,700	816	315	Swansea
West Midlands	WM	WMD	UK43	UK73	WM	mc		2,619,000	899	347	Birmingham
West Sussex	WS	WSX	UK44	UK53	SE	cn		713,600	1,989	768	Chichester
West Yorkshire	WY	WYK	UK45	UK24	YH	mc	W Yorks	2,066,200	2,039	787	Wakefield
Wiltshire	WL	WIL	UK46	UK61	SW	cn	Wilts	575,100	3,481	1,344	Trowbridge
								57,699,984	243,215	93,907	

Abv: Two-letter code for international compatibility (defined by the author).

ISO: Codes from ISO 3166-2.

FIPS: Codes from FIPS PUB 10-4.

NUTS: Nomenclature of Territorial Units for Statistics. The first three characters of the NUTS code identify a statistical region of the United Kingdom.

Reg: Statistical region (two letters) or "country" (one letter), keyed to the table below.

Typ: These divisions are counties (cn), districts (ds), islands areas (ia), metropolitan counties (mc), regions (rg), bailiwicks (bw), and a crown dependency (cd).

Conv: Conventional abbreviation. These are usually punctuated with a period after each element except the ampersand (&). Some of them, like Lancs, have been in regular use for hundreds of years and are almost automatic; others, like Warks, are not very firmly established, and admit of variants (e.g. War). In a 1969 guide, the British Post Office said that only 24 counties had postally acceptable abbreviations. Not even all of those are listed here; for example, Co. Durham is the Post Office abbreviation for Durham.

Population: 1991 census.

Area-km: Square kilometers.

Area-mi: Square miles.

Capital: Note that there are two different capitals named Newport. The capitals of Castlereagh, Mid Glamorgan, and Surrey are in different counties (Belfast, South Glamorgan, and Greater London respectively). The capitals are usually referred to as county towns.

The United Kingdom defined Standard Statistical Regions (SSRs) in 1965, and modified them slightly when county boundaries were redrawn in 1974. Eurostat, the Statistical Office of the European Community, used these divisions when setting up its own statistical regions for Europe. Three of them match the historical countries that form the United Kingdom; eight others are subdivisions of England. This division is extended for the present listing by the addition of the Channel Islands and the Isle of Man. Note: In 1994-04, Government Offices for the Regions (GORs) were established, based on a division of England into ten regions which don't always match the SSRs.

reg	statistical region	NUTS	population	area-km
EA	East Anglia	UK4	2,091,200	12,575
EM	East Midlands	UK3	4,025,800	15,630 ►

reg	statistical region	NUTS	population	area-km
NW	North West	UK8	6,377,200	7,330
NO	Northern Region	UK1	3,083,700	15,401
SE	South East	UK5	17,557,000	27,222
SW	South West	UK6	4,723,400	23,831
WM	West Midlands	UK7	5,254,800	13,012
YH	Yorkshire and Humberside	UK2	4,954,200	15,427
C	Channel Islands	— —	137,196	194
I	Isle of Man	— —	64,282	572
N	Northern Ireland	UKB	1,575,200	14,125
S	Scotland	UKA	4,960,781	77,133
W	Wales	UK9	2,886,600	20,763
			57,691,359	243,215

Reg: One- or two-letter statistical region code (defined by the author).

NUTS: Nomenclature of Territorial Units for Statistics level-1 code.

Further subdivisions: The United Kingdom comprises England, Wales, Scotland, Northern Ireland, the Channel Islands, and the Isle of Man, which may be considered the major divisions. The British sometimes refer to them as countries, especially the first four. They have various and complex status. Each of these six divisions has a different history of subdivision, which is examined under Change history below.

Territorial extent: Except for the "islands areas," all divisions of England, Scotland, and Wales lie mostly on the island of Great Britain; all divisions of Northern Ireland lie mostly on the island of Ireland.

Ards includes Copeland Island.

Central includes some of the islands in Loch Lomond: Inchcailloan, Inchcruin, Inchfad, etc.

Cornwall includes the Isles of Scilly (Sorlings).

Cumbria includes the Isle of Walney.

Dyfed includes Skomer, Ramsey, Skokholm, and Caldy Islands.

Essex includes Foulness Island, Mersea Island, and other coastal islands.

Fife includes Inchkeith and the Isle of May.

Guernsey includes the islands of Guernsey, Sark, Alderney, Herm, Brechou, Jethou, and Lihou.

Gwynedd includes Anglesey, Holy, and Bardsey Islands.

Highland includes the islands of Skye, Rhum, Raasay, Scalpay, Eigg, Soay, Rona, Muck, Canna, Sanday, Ewe, and Handa. It also includes Stroma, just off John o' Groats House.

Isle of Man consists of the Isle of Man and the much smaller Calf of Man, both in the Irish Sea.

Isle of Wight consists of an island off the south coast of Britain.

Jersey consists of the island of Jersey and the tiny Îles Ecréhou.

Kent includes the Isle of Sheppey and islands in the mouth of the River Medway.

Mid Glamorgan includes Tusker Rock in the Bristol Channel.

Moyle includes Rathlin Island.

Northumberland includes Holy Island (Lindisfarne) and the Farne Islands.

Orkney includes the islands of Orkney Mainland (Pomona), Hoy, Westray, Rousay, Sanday, South Ronaldsay, Stronsay, Eday, Shapinsay, North Ronaldsay, Papa Westray, Flotta, and numerous others.

Shetland includes the islands of Shetland Mainland, Yell, Unst, Fetlar, Foula, Bressay, Fair Isle, Whalsay, Muckle Roe, Papa Stour, the Out Skerries, and many other small islands. Muckle Flugga is said to be the northernmost of the British Isles.

Strathclyde includes the islands of Mull, Islay, Jura, Arran, Bute, Coll, Tiree, Colonsay, Lismore, Ulva, Scarba, Kerrera, Luing, Iona, Oronsay, Gigha, Great and Little Cumbrae, and Sanda. It also includes some of the islands in Loch Lomond: Inchlonaig, Inchmurrin, Inchconnachan, etc.

Western Isles consists of the island group known as the Outer Hebrides. (The Inner Hebrides are in Highland and Strathclyde.) It includes the island of Lewis and Harris, a single island with two names. Formerly Lewis and Harris was divided between the counties of Inverness and Ross & Cromarty. The part in Inverness was Harris, and the rest was Lewis. Western Isles also includes the islands of South Uist, North Uist, Barra, Benbecula, Great Bernera, Pabbay, Eriskay, Vatersay, Mingulay, Berneray, Taransay, Scarp, Scalpay, and the Shiant Islands. Farther from the mainland are Saint Kilda, Boreray, Flannan, Rockall, and North Rona.

Prior to 1974, several counties had enclaves. The most noticeable were an enclave of Flintshire lying amid Cheshire, Denbighshire, and Shropshire, and part of Dunbarton between Lanark and Stirling.

Origins of names: The suffix -shire comes from Old English *sciran*: to cut.

Channel Islands: descriptive: islands in the English Channel

England: Land of the Angles (people from Angeln in Germany)

Northern Ireland: northern part of the island of Ireland (see the country entry for Ireland)

Wales: Germanic *walho*: stranger

Armagh: Old Irish *ard magh*: high plain

Avon: from river name, from Celtic word for river

Ayr: from river name, which probably came from Indo-European root *ar-*: water

Bedford: Beda's ford, possibly a man's name

Belfast: Irish *Beal*: opening, *Feirste*: sandbank, i.e. ford on a sandbank

Berkshire: from Celtic *bearroc*: hilly, applied to a birch forest

Borders: on the border between England and Scotland

Buckingham: Old English: from Bucca (personal name) + -ing (ethnic suffix) + *ham* (farm)

Cambridge: Norman French *Cantebruge*: bridge over the Cante (Cam) River; Cam is from Celtic for winding

Carrickfergus: Gaelic *carraig Fhearghasa*: rock of Fergus

Cheshire: shire of Chester, from Latin *castra*: camps

Cleveland: the cliff land

Cornwall: from ethnic name Cornovii + Anglo-Saxon *walh*: foreigner; Cornovii comes from Latin *cornu*: horn

Cumbria: from Welsh *cymry*: Welsh

Derby: from Old Norwegian *diur*: stag, *by*: village

Devon: Medieval Latin Dumnonia, from ethnic name Dumnonii

Dorset: Abbreviation of Medieval Latin Durnovaria: Dorchester + *sæton*: colonist

Down: Irish *dun*: fort

Dumfries: possibly Gaelic *dum fres*: fort of the Frisians

Durham: Old English *dun*: hill, *holmr*: island

Essex: Old English for Eastern Saxons

Glamorgan: Welsh *glanna Morgan*: Morgan's shore

Gloucester: Latin *glevum*, from Brittonic *glouiu*: bright place + *castra*: fort

Gwent: from Welsh *gwen*: smile

Gwynedd: after Cunedda, sixth-century king of northern Wales

Hampshire: Old English *hamm*: water meadow + *tun*: farm + *scir*: county

Hereford: Old English *here*: army, *ford*: ford (i.e. the army's ford)

Hertfordshire: Old English *heorot*: hart, *ford*: ford, *scir*: county

Humberside: land beside the Humber estuary.

Jersey: corruption of Latin Cæsarea (dedicated to Caesar)

Kent: Latin Cantium, possibly from Celtic *canto*: edge; *caint*: open country; or *kant*: rock (referring to the cliffs along the shore)

Leicester: Leire + Latin *castra*: fort (fort on the River Leire)

Lincoln: from Latin *Lindum Colonia*: colony on Lindum lake; Lindum is from Celtic *ilyn*: lake + *dun*: fort

London: possibly from man's name Londinos, from Celtic *londo-*: bold

Manchester: Celtic *mam*: breast, Latin *castra*: fort (original settlement near a breast-shaped hill?)

Norfolk: land of the northern people (north folk)

Northampton: from Old English North + *ham*: farm + *tun*: town

Northumberland: land north of the Humber estuary

Nottingham: from Snot (personal name) + -ing (ethnic suffix) + *ham*: farm

Oxford: ford of the oxen

Shropshire: shortened from Shrewsburyshire; Shrewsbury comes from Latin *civitas scrobbensis*: city of the scrub folk (civitas later translated as burgh)

Somerset: from Sumortun (modern Somerton) + *sæton*: colonist

Stafford: from Old English *steath*: landing place + ford

Suffolk: land of the southern people (south folk)

Surrey: Old English *suthrige*: south region (south of the Thames)

Sussex: land of the South Saxons

Warwick: Anglo-Saxon *war*: subsidiary farm + *wic*: weir

West Midlands: western part of the English Midlands, midway between the English Channel and Scotland

Western Isles: descriptive

Wiltshire: from Wilsætan, West Saxon settlers along the Wylye river; *sætan*: settlers

York: from Latin Eboracum: estate of Eburos, modified by Angles to Eoforwic (*wic*: dwelling) and by Danes to Jorvik

Change history: The histories of England, Wales, Scotland, Northern Ireland, the Channel Islands, and the Isle of Man are discussed individually, in that order.

England:

Prior to 1888, England was divided into 38 counties. (I exclude Monmouthshire, which was sometimes counted with England, and sometimes Wales. The territory of Monmouthshire is contained in the modern Standard Statistical Region of Wales.) They had existed for hundreds of years with little change. Their significance was geographical, historical, and social, but not administrative. The Local Government Act of 1888 created county councils with executive powers. By the same stroke, seven of the counties were split into two or three parts each, corresponding to traditional subdivisions. A new county, London, was formed from parts of Kent, Middlesex, and Surrey. In addition, 57 county boroughs were created. These were administratively on a par with the counties, but consisted of the urban areas of the larger cities. Informal lists of divisions often showed only the counties, implicitly combining each county borough with the geographical county it had come from. The counties were divided into districts of several types: non-county boroughs (cities too small to become county boroughs), urban districts, and rural districts. The rural districts were subdivided into parishes. London county was an exception: it consisted of 28 metropolitan boroughs and one city, the City of London (the historical center of London, about one square mile around Saint Paul's).

As time went by, more cities were split from their counties to become county boroughs, until there were 79 in 1931. Also, the county boroughs annexed adjacent land as the cities grew. The eventual result was that the counties had to provide a constant level of service with a diminishing tax base. This was one of the problems addressed by the 1974 reform.

These were the 47 administrative counties of England between 1900 and 1974.

name	1901	1911	1921	1931	1951	1961	1971	area-km	capital
Buckinghamshire	197,046	219,551	236,171	271,586	386,291	505,130	586,211	1,940	Aylesbury
Cambridgeshire	120,264	128,322	129,602	140,004	166,887	193,390	302,507	1,275	Cambridge
Isle of Ely	64,495	69,752	73,817	77,698	89,049	89,420		971	March
Cheshire	835,941	954,779	1,020,257	1,087,655	1,258,507	1,392,220	1,542,624	2,628	Chester
Cornwall	322,334	328,098	320,705	317,968	345,442	340,880	379,892	3,513	Truro
Cumberland	266,933	265,746	273,173	263,151	285,338	294,130	292,009	3,938	Carlisle
Derbyshire	599,694	683,423	714,634	757,374	826,437	890,180	884,339	2,604	Matlock
Devonshire	662,196	699,703	709,614	732,968	797,738	825,340	896,245	6,764	Exeter
Dorsetshire	202,063	223,266	224,731	239,352	291,323	319,800	361,213	2,521	Dorchester
Durham	1,187,474	1,369,860	1,479,033	1,486,175	1,463,868	1,530,170	1,408,103	2,628	Durham
Essex	1,083,998	1,350,881	1,470,257	1,755,459	2,044,984	2,324,120	1,353,564	3,957	Chelmsford
Gloucestershire	708,439	736,097	756,574	786,000	939,433	1,013,740	1,069,454	3,257	Gloucester
Hampshire	717,164	862,393	913,681	1,014,316	1,197,170	1,384,030	1,561,605	3,892	Winchester
Isle of Wight	82,418	88,186	94,666	88,454	96,625	93,090	109,284	381	Newport
Herefordshire	114,125	114,269	113,189	111,767	127,159	132,670	138,425	2,181	Hereford
Hertfordshire	258,423	311,284	333,195	401,206	609,775	857,200	922,188	1,637	Hertford
Huntingdonshire	54,125	55,577	54,741	56,206	69,302	85,520	202,337	· 947	Huntingdon
Peterborough	41,122	44,718	46,959	51,839	63,791	77,400		216	Peterborough
Kent	961,139	1,045,591	1,141,666	1,219,273	1,564,324	1,726,280	1,396,030	3,950	Maidstone
Lancashire	4,378,293	4,767,832	4,932,951	5,039,455	5,117,853	5,160,660	5,106,123	4,864	Preston
Leicestershire	437,490	476,553	494,469	541,861	631,077	691,530	771,213	2,154	Leicester
Holland	77,610	82,849	85,870	92,330	101,555	104,030	105,643	1,084	Boston
Kesteven	103,962	111,324	107,634	110,060	130,717	140,260	232,215	1,876	Sleaford
Lindsey	318,450	369,787	408,698	422,199	473,550	512,210	470,526	3,938	Lincoln
London	4,536,267	4,521,685	4,484,523	4397,003	3,347,982	3,185,770	7,379,014	303	London
Middlesex	792,476	1,126,465	1,253,002	1,638,728	2,269,315	2,239,770		602	London
Norfolk	476,553	499,116	504,293	504,940	548,062	568,420	616,427	5,319	Norwich
Northamptonshire	294,506	303,798	302,404	309,474	359,690	405,870	467,843	2,368	Northampton
Northumberland	603,119	696,893	746,096	756,782	798,424	825,650	794,975	5,228	Newcastle upon Tyne
Nottinghamshire	514,459	604,098	641,149	712,731	841,211	916,520	974,640	2,185	Nottingham
Oxfordshire	186,460	199,269	189,615	209,621	275,808	317,880	380,814	1,939	Oxford
Rutlandshire	19,709	20,346	18,376	17,401	20,537	26,390	27,463	394	Oakham
Shropshire	239,783	246,307	243,062	244,156	289,802	306,150	336,934	3,488	Shrewsbury
Somersetshire	434,950	458,025	465,691	475,142	551,453	609,410	681,974	4,178	Taunton
Staffordshire	1,231,113	1,328,644	1,353,511	1,431,359	1,621,034	1,765,550	1,856,890	2,989	Stafford
East Suffolk	255,800	277,155	291,073	294,977	321,909	353,290	380,524	2,256	Ipswich
West Suffolk	117,553	116,905	108,985	106,137	120,652	135,080	164,201	1,582	Bury Saint Edmunds
Surrey	893,920	1,123,569	930,086	1,180,878	1,602,483	1,744,690	999,588	1,869	Kingston upon Thames
East Sussex	450,979	489,070	532,187	546,864	618,516	673,190	750,312	2,147	Lewes
West Sussex	151,276	176,308	195,810	222,995	318,823	418,470	491,020	1,627	Chichester
Warwickshire	940,879	1,040,409	1,394,741	1,535,007	1,861,670	2,058,950	2,079,799	2,545	Warwick
Westmorland	64,409	63,575	65,746	65,408	67,383	32,550	72,724	2,043	Kendal
Wiltshire	271,394	286,822	291,838	303,373	386,692	439,260	486,048	3,483	Trowbridge
Worcestershire	458,565	545,699	397,910	420,056	522,846	581,270	692,605	1,812	Worcester
East Riding	144,748	154,768	460,880	482,936	510,904	530,170	542,565	3,036	Beverley
North Riding	377,338	419,546	456,436	469,375	525,481	565,080	724,463	5,510	Northallerton
West Riding	2,839,235	3,127,659	3,265,241	3,437,368	3,691,645	3,677,220	3,780,539	7,227	Wakefield
	30,090,689	33,185,972	34,728,942	36,827,067	40,550,517	43,060,000	44,773,112	127,246	

There were 38 geographical counties. They were the same as above, except for the seven which were divided into two or more administrative counties: Cambridgeshire and the Isle of Ely, Hampshire and the Isle of Wight, Huntingdon and the Soke of Peterborough, Lincolnshire (consisting of the Parts of Holland, Kesteven, and Lindsey), Suffolk (East and West), Sussex

(East and West), and Yorkshire (consisting of the East, North, and West Ridings). (Note: the word riding is a corruption of thirding, i.e. a third of the county.)

The following list shows county boroughs according to their geographical counties. Names in parentheses are alternate names or obsolete names. Some of these county boroughs were created or eliminated at some time during the period covered (1900–1974).

Bedfordshire: Luton. Berkshire: Reading. Cheshire: Birkenhead, Chester, Stockport, Wallasey. Cumberland: Carlisle. Derbyshire: Derby. Devonshire: Devonport, Exeter, Plymouth, Torbay. Durham: Darlington, Gateshead, Hartlepool (West Hartlepool), South Shields, Sunderland. East Suffolk: Ipswich. East Sussex: Brighton, Eastbourne, Hastings. Essex: East Ham, Southend (Southend-on-Sea), West Ham. Glamorganshire: Cardiff, Merthyr Tydfil, Swansea. Gloucestershire: Bristol, Gloucester. Hampshire: Bournemouth, Portsmouth, Southampton. Kent: Canterbury. Lancashire: Barrow-in-Furness, Blackburn, Blackpool, Bolton, Bootle, Burnley, Bury, Liverpool, Manchester, Oldham, Preston, Rochdale, Saint Helens, Salford, Southport, Warrington, Wigan. Leicestershire: Leicester. Lindsey: Grimsby, Lincoln. Monmouthshire: Newport. Norfolk: Great Yarmouth (Yarmouth), Norwich. Northamptonshire: Northampton. Northumberland: Newcastle upon Tyne (Newcastle), Tynemouth. Nottinghamshire: Nottingham. Oxfordshire: Oxford. Somerset: Bath. Staffordshire: Burton upon Trent, Stoke-on-Trent, Walsall, West Bromwich, Wolverhampton. Surrey: Croydon. Warwickshire: Birmingham, Coventry, Solihull. Worcestershire: Dudley, Smethwick, Warley, Worcester. Yorkshire, East Riding: Kingston upon Hull (Hull). Yorkshire, North Riding: Middlesbrough (Teesside). Yorkshire, West Riding: Barnsley, Bradford, Dewsbury, Doncaster, Halifax, Huddersfield, Leeds, Rotherham, Sheffield, Wakefield, York.

~1958	Capital of Derbyshire moved from Derby to Matlock.
1964	The London Government Act of 1963, effective in 1964, created Greater London. It consisted of the former counties of London and Middlesex, and parts of Essex, Hertfordshire, Kent, and Surrey, including the county boroughs of Croydon, East Ham, and West Ham. It was subdivided into 32 boroughs and the City of London. Its governing body was the Greater London Council.
1964-04-01	Luton county borough split from Bedfordshire.
1974-04-01	The Local Government Act of 1972 took effect. County boroughs were eliminated. England was reorganized into 39 counties, six metropolitan counties, and Greater London (which is sometimes numbered with the metropolitan counties). The non-metropolitan counties were subdivided into 332 districts, which were further subdivided into parishes.

The following counties were unchanged in territory: Bedford, Berkshire, Buckingham, Cornwall, Derby, Devon, Dorset, East Sussex, Essex, Greater London, Hampshire, Hertford, Kent, Norfolk, Northampton, Nottingham, Oxford, Shropshire, Suffolk, Surrey, West Sussex, and Wiltshire. The administrative counties which were contained in counties on this list (Isle of Ely, Isle of Wight, East and West Suffolk) disappeared. Name of Shropshire changed to Salop.

The following counties lost part of their territory, and occasionally gained a little, in the formation of new counties: Cambridge, Cheshire, Durham, Gloucester, Lancashire, Lincoln, Northumberland, Somerset, Stafford, and Warwick. In particular, Huntingdon was annexed to Cambridge, and Rutland to Leicester.

In addition, Avon was formed from parts of Gloucester and Somerset; Cleveland, from parts of Durham and North Riding; Cumbria, from Cumberland, Westmorland, and parts of Lancashire and West Riding; Greater Manchester, from parts of Cheshire, Lancashire, and West Riding; Hereford and Worcester, from Hereford and most of Worcester; Humberside, from part of Lindsey and most of East Riding; Merseyside, from parts of Cheshire and Lancashire; North Yorkshire, from most of North Riding and parts of East and West Ridings; South Yorkshire and West Yorkshire, from parts of West Riding; Tyne and Wear, from parts of Durham and Northumberland; and West Midlands, from parts of Stafford, Warwick, and Worcester.

1974-10	Isle of Wight county split from Hampshire.
1980	Name of Salop county changed back to Shropshire.
1988	Local Government Act of 1985 abolished county councils in the seven metropolitan counties (including Greater London).
~1989	Capital of Humberside moved from Kingston upon Hull to Beverley; capital of Northumberland moved from Newcastle upon Tyne (Tyne and Wear) to Morpeth.
~1992	Another reorganization was proposed. A new concept in this plan was the unitary authority, so called because it would provide all of the services formerly divided between two levels of government, the county and the borough or district. The plan was enacted, and implemented in four annual phases, from 1995 to 1998. The resulting

structure is complex. As I interpret it, the top level consists of counties and ceremonial counties. Only the top-level changes are shown here.

1995-04-01 Isle of Wight became the first unitary authority. It is also a county.
1996-04-01 Avon county split up into Bristol unitary authority (a ceremonial county) and two sections which were annexed to Gloucestershire and Somerset; Cleveland split between
Durham and North Yorkshire; Humberside split between East Yorkshire and Lincolnshire; name of East Yorkshire changed to East Riding of Yorkshire.
1997-04-01 Rutland (ceremonial) county split from Leicestershire.
1998-04-01 Hereford and Worcester split into counties of Herefordshire (ceremonial) and Worcestershire.

The results of this reorganization are not shown in the table of divisions of the United Kingdom for several reasons. The
reorganized divisions are enormously complicated. The standards have not yet been adjusted to reflect them. Good data are not
yet available. The author's interpretation of the complex authority structure, two-tiered in some places and one-tiered in others, may not prove to be the standard interpretation.

Wales:

Wales was never a united, independent kingdom. It was conquered gradually by England. The conquest was complete by
1282. The Act of Union of 1536 brought the two countries under one law. Wales was defined as a region by language and class,
not by government. Before the Local Government Act of 1888, Wales consisted of thirteen geographical counties (counting
Monmouthshire). As in England, the act created county councils for the counties, and split off four cities as county boroughs:
Cardiff, Merthyr Tydfil, and Swansea from Glamorganshire, and Newport from Monmouthshire.

county	1901	1911	1921	1931	1951	1961	1971	ar-km	capital
Anglesey	50,590	50,928	51,744	49,029	50,660	51,430	59,705	715	Llangefni
Brecknockshire	59,906	59,287	61,222	57,775	56,508	54,460	53,234	1,899	Brecon
Caernarvonshire	126,385	125,043	128,183	120,829	124,140	120,460	122,852	1,473	Caernarvon
Cardiganshire	60,237	59,879	60,881	55,184	53,278	53,390	54,844	1,794	Aberystwyth
Carmarthenshire	135,325	160,406	175,073	179,100	172,034	167,110	162,313	2,381	Carmarthen
Denbighshire	129,935	144,783	157,634	157,648	170,726	174,180	184,824	1,732	Ruthin
Flintshire	81,727	92,705	106,617	112,889	145,297	150,430	175,396	663	Mold
Glamorganshire	860,022	1,120,910	1,252,481	1,225,717	1,202,581	1,236,980	1,255,374	2,117	Cardiff
Merionethshire	49,130	45,565	45,087	43,201	41,465	38,360	35,277	1,709	Dolgellau
Monmouthshire	292,327	395,719	450,794	434,958	425,115	449,370	461,459	1,403	Newport
Montgomeryshire	54,892	53,146	51,263	48,473	45,990	43,690	42,761	2,064	Welshpool
Pembrokeshire	88,749	89,960	91,978	87,206	90,906	93,050	97,295	1,590	Haverfordwest
Radnorshire	23,263	22,590	23,517	21,323	19,993	18,430	18,262	1,219	Llandrindod Wells
	2,012,488	2,420,921	2,656,474	2,593,332	2,598,693	2,651,340	2,723,596	20,759	

1974 The Local Government Act of 1972, mentioned above, created eight counties, subdivided into 37 districts and further into parishes. The old counties contained in each
new county are as follows.

Clwyd	Flint, Denbigh (most), Merioneth (part)
Dyfed	Cardigan, Carmarthen, Pembroke
Gwent	Monmouth
Gwynedd	Anglesey, Caernarvon, Denbigh (part), Merioneth (most)
Mid Glamorgan	Glamorgan (part), Brecknock (part)
Powys	Montgomery, Radnor, Brecknock (most)
South Glamorgan	Glamorgan (part)
West Glamorgan	Glamorgan (part)

~1989 Capital of Gwent moved from Newport to Cwmbran.
1996-04-01 Wales reorganized into 22 unitary authorities. District councils abolished. The new unitary authorities created from each of the counties are listed here. Seven pre–1974
county names reappeared on the map, but only four of them had the same extent as
before: Anglesey, Cardigan, Carmarthen, and Pembroke.

name	population	area-km	capital	former
Aberconwy and Colwyn	110,700	1,130	Colwyn Bay	Clwyd, Gwynedd ➤

name	population	area-km	capital	former
Anglesey	68,500	719	Llangefni	Gwynedd
Blaenau Gwent	73,300	109	Ebbw Vale	Gwent
Bridgend	130,900	246	Bridgend	Mid Glamorgan
Caerphilly	171,000	279	Hengoed	Gwent, Mid Glamorgan
Cardiff	306,600	139	Cardiff	South Glamorgan
Cardiganshire	69,700	1,797	Aberaeron	Dyfed
Carmarthenshire	169,000	2,398	Carmarthen	Dyfed
Denbighshire	91,300	844	Ruthin	Clwyd
Flintshire	145,300	437	Mold	Clwyd
Gwynedd	117,000	2,548	Caernarvon	Gwynedd
Merthyr Tydfil	59,500	111	Merthyr Tydfil	Mid Glamorgan
Monmouthshire	84,200	851	Cwmbran	Gwent
Neath Port Talbot	140,100	441	Port Talbot	West Glamorgan
Newport	137,400	191	Newport	Gwent
Pembrokeshire	113,600	1,590	Haverfordwest	Dyfed
Powys	121,800	5,204	Llandrindod Wells	Powys, Clwyd
Rhondda Cynon Taff	239,000	424	Cardiff	Mid Glamorgan
Swansea	230,900	378	Swansea	West Glamorgan
Torfaen	90,600	126	Pontypool	Gwent
Vale of Glamorgan	119,200	337	Barry	Mid and South Glamorgan
Wrexham	123,500	499	Wrexham	Clwyd
	2,913,100	20,798		

Population: 1993 estimate.

Capital: Two unitary authorities have capitals which are outside of their territory: Monmouthshire (Cwmbran is in Torfaen) and Rhondda Cynon Taff (Cardiff is in Cardiff).

Former: county or counties from which this unitary authority was formed.

~1997   Name of Cardiganshire unitary authority changed to Ceredigion.

Scotland:

Scotland was united with England by the Act of Union of 1707, constituting Great Britain. The Local Government Act of 1889 created county councils, as had been done in England and Wales in 1888. Underneath was a complex structure of burghs and parishes. The Local Government Act of 1929 brought Scotland more into line with England and Wales by abolishing parish councils and creating four burghs (also called counties of a city), analogous to county boroughs. The burghs were Aberdeen (in the geographical county of Aberdeen), Dundee (Angus county), Edinburgh (Midlothian), and Glasgow (Lanark).

county	1901	1911	1921	1931	1951	1961	1971	ar-km	capital
Aberdeen	303,889	312,177	301,016	300,436	308,008	321,783	324,574	5,105	Aberdeen
Angus	283,729	281,417	271,052	270,190	274,876	278,399	281,131	2,262	Forfar
Argyll	73,166	70,902	76,862	63,050	63,361	59,390	59,926	8,092	Lochgilphead
Ayr	254,133	268,337	299,273	285,217	321,237	342,822	369,636	2,932	Ayr
Banff	61,439	61,402	57,298	54,907	50,148	46,454	43,767	1,631	Banff
Berwick	30,785	29,643	28,246	26,612	25,086	22,437	21,224	1,184	Duns
Bute	18,659	18,186	33,771	18,823	19,283	15,170	12,743	565	Rothesay
Caithness	33,619	32,010	28,285	25,656	22,710	27,370	27,901	1,776	Wick
Clackmannan	31,991	31,121	32,542	31,948	37,532	41,394	46,611	141	Alloa
Dumfries	72,562	72,825	75,370	81,047	85,660	88,440	88,540	2,777	Dumfries
Dunbarton	113,660	139,831	150,861	147,744	164,269	184,559	244,354	637	Dumbarton
East Lothian	38,653	43,254	47,487	47,338	52,258	52,677	56,966	692	Haddington
Fife	218,350	267,739	292,925	276,368	306,778	320,692	337,690	1,307	Cupar
Inverness	89,901	87,272	82,455	82,108	84,930	83,480	91,698	10,907	Inverness
Kincardine	40,891	41,008	41,779	39,865	47,403	48,810	27,188	989	Stonehaven
Kinross	6,980	7,527	7,963	7,454	7,418	6,702	7,090	212	Kinross
Kirkcudbright	39,359	38,367	37,155	30,341	30,725	28,870	27,761	2,330	Kirkcudbright
Lanark	1,337,848	1,447,034	1,539,442	1,586,047	1,614,363	1,626,424	1,456,151	2,278	Glasgow
Midlothian	437,553	507,666	506,377	526,296	565,735	580,329	603,615	948	Edinburgh
Moray	44,757	43,427	41,558	40,806	48,218	49,170	54,833	1,234	Elgin
Nairn	9,291	9,319	8,790	8,294	8,719	8,423	8,906	422	Nairn
Orkney	27,723	25,897	24,111	22,077	21,255	18,747	17,462	975	Kirkwall
Peebles	15,066	15,258	15,332	15,051	15,232	14,156	13,584	899	Peebles
Perth	123,255	124,342	125,503	120,793	128,029	127,056	128,692	6,458	Perth ➤

county	1901	1911	1921	1931	1951	1961	1971	ar-km	capital
Renfrew	268,418	314,552	298,904	288,586	324,660	338,872	366,485	621	Paisley
Ross & Cromarty	76,149	77,364	70,818	62,799	60,508	57,642	61,464	8,002	Dingwall
Roxburgh	48,793	47,192	44,989	45,788	45,557	43,183	42,255	1,724	Newtown St Boswells
Selkirk	23,339	24,601	22,607	22,608	21,729	21,052	20,743	691	Selkirk
Shetland	27,755	27,911	25,520	16,114	19,352	17,812	18,445	1,426	Lerwick
Stirling	141,894	160,991	161,719	166,447	187,527	194,878	211,994	1,169	Stirling
Sutherland	21,389	20,179	17,802	16,101	13,670	13,507	12,728	5,252	Golspie
West Lothian	64,787	80,155	83,962	81,431	88,577	92,768	112,833	311	Linlithgow
Wigtown	32,591	31,998	30,783	29,331	31,620	29,124	27,410	1,263	Stranraer
	4,412,374	4,760,904	4,882,557	4,837,673	5,096,433	5,202,592	5,226,400	77,212	

Note: The following counties have alternate names: Angus (Forfar), Dunbarton (Dumbarton), East Lothian (Hadding-ton), Midlothian (Edinburgh), Moray (Elgin), Shetland (Zetland), and West Lothian (Linlithgow). In most cases, the alternate names continued in occasional use long after they had been officially replaced.

1975-05-16   Local Government (Scotland) Act of 1973 became effective, replacing the counties and burghs with nine regions and three island areas. The regions were further subdivided into 53 districts. Each region, island area, and district had its own council. The old counties contained in each new region (or ia = island area) are as follows.

Borders	Berwick, Midlothian (part), Peebles, Roxburgh, Selkirk
Central	Clackmannan, Perth (part), Stirling (most), West Lothian (part)
Dumfries and Galloway	Dumfries, Kirkcudbright, Wigtown
Fife	Fife
Grampian	Aberdeen, Banff, Kincardine, Moray (most)
Highland	Argyll (part), Caithness, Inverness (most), Moray (part), Nairn, Ross and Cromarty (most), Sutherland
Lothian	East Lothian, Midlothian (most), West Lothian (most)
Orkney (ia)	Orkney
Shetland (ia)	Shetland
Strathclyde	Argyll (most), Ayr, Bute, Dunbarton, Lanark, Renfrew, Stirling (part)
Tayside	Angus, Kinross, Perth (most)
Western Isles (ia)	Inverness (part), Ross and Cromarty (part)

~1989   Capital of Fife moved from Cupar to Glenrothes.

1996-04-01   Local Government etc. (Scotland) Act of 1994 took effect. Scotland reorganized into the 29 unitary districts and three island areas (ia) shown here, each with a unitary council. The division was made mostly, but not entirely, along district boundaries. District councils were abolished. Angus, Clackmannan, East Lothian, Fife, Orkney, and Shetland were restored to essentially the same name and territory that they had before 1975.

unitary authority	population	area	former
Aberdeenshire	223,630	6,318	Grampian (part)
Angus	111,020	2,181	Tayside (part)
Argyll and Bute	90,550	6,930	Strathclyde (part)
City of Aberdeen	218,220	186	Grampian (part)
City of Dundee	153,710	65	Tayside (part)
City of Edinburgh	441,620	262	Lothian (part)
City of Glasgow	623,850	175	Strathclyde (part)
Clackmannan	48,660	157	Central (part)
Dumbarton and Clydebank	97,790	162	Strathclyde (part)
Dumfries and Galloway	147,900	6,439	Dumfries and Galloway
East Ayrshire	123,820	1,252	Strathclyde (part)
East Dunbartonshire	110,220	172	Strathclyde (part)
East Lothian	85,640	678	Lothian (part)
East Renfrewshire	86,780	173	Strathclyde (part)
Falkirk	142,610	299	Central (part)
Fife	351,200	1,323	Fife
Highland	206,900	25,784	Highland
Inverclyde	89,990	162	Strathclyde (part)
Midlothian	79,910	356	Lothian (part)
Moray	86,250	2,238	Grampian (part) ▶

unitary authority	population	area	former
North Ayrshire	139,020	884	Strathclyde (part)
North Lanarkshire	326,750	474	Strathclyde (part)
Orkney Islands (ia)	19,760	992	Orkney
Perthshire and Kinross	130,470	5,311	Tayside (part)
Renfrewshire	176,970	261	Strathclyde (part)
Shetland Islands (ia)	22,830	1,438	Shetland
South Ayrshire	113,960	1,202	Strathclyde (part)
South Lanarkshire	307,100	1,771	Strathclyde (part)
Stirling	81,630	2,196	Central (part)
The Borders	105,300	4,734	Borders
West Lothian	146,730	425	Lothian (part)
Western Isles (ia)	29,410	3,134	Western Isles
	5,120,200	78,134	

Population: 1993 estimate.

Former: Regions or island areas from which the unitary authority was formed.

~1997   Name of Dumbarton and Clydebank changed to West Dunbartonshire; name of Western Isles changed to Eilean Siar.

Northern Ireland:

The 1801 Act of Union merged Ireland with Great Britain, forming the United Kingdom. By 1900, Ireland was subdivided into 32 counties, which were grouped into four provinces with no administrative function. After a long and painful independence struggle, Ireland became an independent country with dominion status by the Anglo-Irish Treaty, on 1921-12-06. However, a referendum was held, and on 1922-12-12, six of the nine counties, and two county boroughs, in the northern province of Ulster voted to revert to the United Kingdom. The county boroughs were Belfast (in the geographical county of Antrim) and Londonderry (in Londonderry county).

county	1901	1911	1937	1951	1961	1971	area-km	capital
Antrim	545,270	580,811	635,352	674,820	692,500	717,798	2,907	Belfast
Armagh	125,392	120,291	108,815	114,254	117,900	133,969	1,266	Armagh
Down	205,889	204,303	210,687	241,181	270,200	311,876	2,465	Downpatrick
Fermanagh	65,430	61,836	54,569	53,044	52,400	50,255	1,701	Enniskillen
Londonderry	144,404	140,625	142,736	155,540	167,900	183,094	2,083	Londonderry
Tyrone	150,567	142,665	127,586	132,082	134,500	139,073	3,155	Omagh
	1,236,952	1,250,531	1,279,745	1,370,921	1,435,400	1,536,065	13,577	

1973   By the Local Government (Boundaries) Act (Northern Ireland) of 1971, Northern Ireland was reorganized into 26 districts, each with its own district council, and further subdivided into 526 wards. The new districts formed from each of the old counties are listed here.

Antrim	Antrim, Ballymena, Ballymoney, Belfast, Carrickfergus, Castlereagh (part), Coleraine, Craigavon (part), Larne, Lisburn (part), Moyle, Newtownabbey
Armagh	Armagh, Craigavon (part), Dungannon (part), Newry and Mourne (part)
Down	Ards, Banbridge, Castlereagh (part), Craigavon (part), Down, Lisburn (part), Newry and Mourne (part), North Down
Fermanagh	Fermanagh
Londonderry	Limavady, Londonderry, Magherafelt
Tyrone	Cookstown, Dungannon (part), Omagh, Strabane

Channel Islands:

The Channel Islands are not a single administrative unit; this phrase is just a convenient grouping of the bailiwicks of Guernsey and Jersey, which have been vassal states of the British crown since the Norman Conquest. A French dialect is a second language there. The other inhabited islands (Alderney, Brechou, Herm, Jethou, Lihou, and Sark) are dependencies of Guernsey. The Channel Islands are not, properly speaking, a part of the United Kingdom. Jersey is divided into 12 parishes. Here is the population history of the two bailiwicks.

bailiwick	1901	1921	1931	1951	1961	1971	1991
Guernsey	42,888	40,529	42,743	45,496	47,178	53,728	61,739
Jersey	52,636	49,701	50,462	57,310	57,200	72,691	84,082

Isle of Man:

Although the Isle of Man is tributary to the British crown, it is not in fact part of the United Kingdom. It is listed here in emulation of the standards. It is divided into six sheadings. Its population in successive censuses was 60,284 (1921); 49,308 (1931); 55,253 (1951); 48,151 (1961); 56,289 (1971); 64,679 (1981); 64,282 (1991).

Other names of subdivisions:

Major divisions:

England: Angleterre (French); Engeland (Dutch); Inghilterra (Italian); Inglaterra (Portuguese, Spanish)

Channel Islands: Îles Anglo-Normandes (French); Ilhas do Canal (Portuguese); Islas Anglonormandas (Spanish); Isole del Canale, Isole Normanne (Italian); Kanaal Eilanden (Dutch); Kanal-Inseln, Normannische Inseln (German); Kanalöarna (Swedish); Kanaløyene (Norwegian); Normannaeyjar (Icelandic)

Isle of Man: Île de Man (French); Ilha de Man (Portuguese); Insel Man (German); Isla de Man (Spanish); Isola di Man (Italian); Man (Norwegian); Mön (Icelandic)

Northern Ireland: Irlanda del Nord (Italian); Irlanda del Norte (Spanish); Irlanda do Norte (Portuguese); Irlande du Nord (French); Noord-Ierland (Dutch); Nord-Irland (Norwegian, Swedish); Nordirland (German); Norður-Írland (Icelandic)

Scotland: Écosse (French); Escocia (Spanish); Escócia (Portuguese); Schotland (Dutch); Schottland (German); Scozia (Italian); Skotland (Icelandic); Skottland (Norwegian, Swedish)

Wales: Gales (Portuguese, Spanish); Galles (Italian); Pays de Galles (French)

Minor divisions: The suffix -shire can be dropped from county names, except for Berkshire, Cheshire, Hampshire, Lancashire, Shropshire, Wiltshire, and Yorkshire. However, when there is a city of the same name, the preferred usage is either "county of Lincoln" (e.g.) or "Lincolnshire."

Cornwall: Cornouailles (French); Cornovaglia (Italian); Cornualha (Portuguese); Cornualles (Spanish); Cornwall and Isles of Scilly (formal)

Durham: County Durham (variant)

Greater London: Grande Londres (Portuguese); Grand Londres (French); Gran Londra (Italian)

Hampshire: Southampton (obsolete)

Londonderry: Derry (variant)

Newry and Mourne: Mourne (variant)

Orkney: Orcadas (Spanish); Orcades (French); Orcadi (Italian); Orkneyöarna (Swedish); Orknøyene (Norwegian)

Shetland Islands: Zetland (obsolete)

Shropshire: Salop (obsolete)

UNITED STATES

ISO = US/FIPS = US　　Language = English　　Time zone = (see table)　　Capital = Washington

The United States has been an independent country throughout this century. There are established procedures whereby its possessions become first territories, then states, or are granted independence. The territories and dependencies at present are all treated as separate countries by the standards, so they are listed individually in this book.

Other names of country: Bandaríki Norður-Ameríku (Icelandic); De forente stater (Norwegian); Estados Unidos (Portuguese); Estados Unidos (de América) (Spanish); États-Unis (d'Amérique) (French); Forenede Stater (Danish); Förenta staterna (Swedish); Stati Uniti d'America (Italian); United States of America (formal–English); Vereinigte Staaten (German); Vereinigte Staaten von Amerika (formal–German); Verenigde Staten (Dutch); Yhdysvallat (Finnish).

Origin of name: descriptive: formed by union of separate states in North America. America (originally referring only to South America) was named by Martin Waldseemüller (pseud. Hylacomylus) after Florentine navigator Amerigo Vespucci.

name	ISO	FIPS	conv	tz	population	area-km	area-mi	d	capital	adjective	ZIP
Alabama	AL	US01	Ala.	-6 d	4,040,587	133,916	51,705	2	Montgomery	Alabamian	350-369
Alaska	AK	US02		-9 d	550,043	1,530,700	591,007	6	Juneau	Alaskan	995-999
Arizona	AZ	US04	Ariz.	-7	3,665,228	295,260	114,001	4	Phoenix	Arizonan	850-865
Arkansas	AR	US05	Ark.	-6 d	2,350,725	137,754	53,187	9	Little Rock	Arkansan	716-729
California	CA	US06	Calif.	-8 d	29,760,021	411,049	158,707	6	Sacramento	Californian	900-966
Colorado	CO	US08	Colo.	-7 d	3,294,394	269,596	104,092	4	Denver	Coloradan	800-816
Connecticut	CT	US09	Conn.	-5 d	3,287,116	12,997	5,018	5	Hartford	Nutmegger	060-069
Delaware	DE	US10	Del.	-5 d	666,168	5,294	2,044	7	Dover	Delawarean	197-199
District of Columbia	DC	US11	D.C.	-5 d	606,900	179	69	7	Washington	Washingtonian	200-205 ➤

name	ISO	FIPS	conv	tz	population	area-km	area-mi	d	capital	adjective	ZIP
Florida	FL	US12	Fla.	-5 d	12,937,926	151,940	58,664	7	Tallahassee	Floridian	320-349
Georgia	GA	US13	Ga.	-5 d	6,478,216	152,577	58,910	7	Atlanta	Georgian	300-319
Hawaii	HI	US15		-10	1,108,229	16,760	6,471	6	Honolulu	Hawaiian	967-968
Idaho	ID	US16		-7 d	1,006,749	216,431	83,564	4	Boise	Idahoan	832-838
Illinois	IL	US17	Ill.	-6 d	11,430,602	145,934	56,345	1	Springfield	Illinoisan	600-629
Indiana	IN	US18	Ind.	-5	5,544,159	93,719	36,185	1	Indianapolis	Hoosier	460-479
Iowa	IA	US19		-6 d	2,776,755	145,752	56,275	8	Des Moines	Iowan	500-528
Kansas	KS	US20	Kans.	-6 d	2,477,574	213,097	82,277	8	Topeka	Kansan	660-679
Kentucky	KY	US21	Ky.	-5 d	3,685,296	104,659	40,409	2	Frankfort	Kentuckian	400-427
Louisiana	LA	US22	La.	-6 d	4,219,973	123,678	47,752	9	Baton Rouge	Louisianian	700-714
Maine	ME	US23	Me.	-5 d	1,227,928	86,156	33,265	5	Augusta	Downeaster	040-049
Maryland	MD	US24	Md.	-5 d	4,781,468	27,091	10,460	7	Annapolis	Marylander	206-219
Massachusetts	MA	US25	Mass.	-5 d	6,016,425	21,456	8,284	5	Boston	Bay Stater	010-027
Michigan	MI	US26	Mich.	-5 d	9,295,297	151,585	58,527	1	Lansing	Michigander	480-499
Minnesota	MN	US27	Minn.	-6 d	4,375,099	218,601	84,402	8	Saint Paul	Minnesotan	550-567
Mississippi	MS	US28	Miss.	-6 d	2,573,216	123,515	47,689	2	Jackson	Mississippian	386-397
Missouri	MO	US29	Mo.	-6 d	5,117,073	180,515	69,697	8	Jefferson City	Missourian	630-658
Montana	MT	US30	Mont.	-7 d	799,065	380,849	147,047	4	Helena	Montanan	590-599
Nebraska	NE	US31	Nebr.	-6 d	1,578,385	200,349	77,355	8	Lincoln	Nebraskan	680-693
Nevada	NV	US32	Nev.	-8 d	1,201,833	286,353	110,562	4	Carson City	Nevadan	890-898
New Hampshire	NH	US33	N.H.	-5 d	1,109,252	24,033	9,279	5	Concord	New Hampshirite	030-039
New Jersey	NJ	US34	N.J.	-5 d	7,730,188	20,168	7,787	3	Trenton	New Jerseyite	070-089
New Mexico	NM	US35	N.Mex.	-7 d	1,515,069	314,926	121,594	4	Santa Fe	New Mexican	870-884
New York	NY	US36	N.Y.	-5 d	17,990,455	127,190	49,108	3	Albany	New Yorker	100-149
North Carolina	NC	US37	N.C.	-5 d	6,628,637	136,413	52,669	7	Raleigh	North Carolinian	270-289
North Dakota	ND	US38	N.Dak.	-6 d	638,800	183,118	70,702	8	Bismarck	North Dakotan	580-588
Ohio	OH	US39		-5 d	10,847,115	107,044	41,330	1	Columbus	Ohioan	430-459
Oklahoma	OK	US40	Okla.	-6 d	3,145,585	181,186	69,956	9	Oklahoma City	Oklahoman	730-749
Oregon	OR	US41	Oreg.	-8 d	2,842,321	251,419	97,073	6	Salem	Oregonian	970-979
Pennsylvania	PA	US42	Pa.	-5 d	11,881,643	117,348	45,308	3	Harrisburg	Pennsylvanian	150-196
Rhode Island	RI	US44	R.I.	-5 d	1,003,464	3,139	1,212	5	Providence	Rhode Islander	028-029
South Carolina	SC	US45	S.C.	-5 d	3,486,703	80,583	31,113	7	Columbia	South Carolinian	290-299
South Dakota	SD	US46	S.Dak.	-6 d	696,004	199,730	77,116	8	Pierre	South Dakotan	570-577
Tennessee	TN	US47	Tenn.	-6 d	4,877,185	109,153	42,144	2	Nashville	Tennessean	370-385
Texas	TX	US48	Tex.	-6 d	16,986,510	691,030	266,808	9	Austin	Texan	750-799
Utah	UT	US49		-7 d	1,722,850	219,888	84,899	4	Salt Lake City	Utahn	840-847
Vermont	VT	US50	Vt.	-5 d	562,758	24,900	9,614	5	Montpelier	Vermonter	050-059
Virginia	VA	US51	Va.	-5 d	6,187,358	105,586	40,767	7	Richmond	Virginian	220-246
Washington	WA	US53	Wash.	-8 d	4,866,692	176,480	68,139	6	Olympia	Washingtonian	980-994
West Virginia	WV	US54	W.Va.	-5 d	1,793,477	62,758	24,231	7	Charleston	West Virginian	247-268
Wisconsin	WI	US55	Wis.	-6 d	4,891,769	145,436	56,153	1	Madison	Wisconsinite	530-549
Wyoming	WY	US56	Wyo.	-7 d	453,588	253,325	97,809	4	Cheyenne	Wyomingite	820-831
					248,709,873	9,372,615	3,618,781				

^{d} = *states where daylight saving time is observed.*

Status: These divisions are states, except for the District of Columbia, which is a district.

ISO: Codes from ISO 3166-2. These codes were developed by the Post Office Department along with the ZIP code system in 1963, although it was some time before they came into common use. They are also designated as two-letter FIPS State Alpha Codes in FIPS PUB 5-2.

FIPS: Codes from FIPS PUB 10-4. The two-digit codes after the "US" are also designated as two-digit FIPS State Numeric Codes in FIPS PUB 5-2.

Conv: Conventional abbreviations, standard before 1963 and still frequently used. States with short names were spelled in full.

Tz: Offset from GMT in hours for standard time. Many states have more than one time zone; in those cases, the majority time zone is shown.

Population: 1990-04-01 census.

Area-km: Square kilometers.

Area-mi: Square miles.

D: Division, as defined by the census bureau. Numbers are an arbitrary code keyed to the table below. The census bureau also defines four regions, which are groups of divisions. There are many other ways of dividing the United States into regions. This one merely has the sanction of the census bureau in its favor.

d	division name	region
1	East North Central	North Central
2	East South Central	South
3	Middle Atlantic	Northeast
4	Mountain	West
5	New England	Northeast
6	Pacific	West
7	South Atlantic	South
8	West North Central	North Central
9	West South Central	South

Adjective: Adjectival form of the state name.

ZIP: The Post Office Department introduced a system of postal codes for the U.S., effective as of 1963-07-01. They were designated ZIP codes, for Zoning Improvement Program. The codes are hierarchical. The first digit represents a group of states, usually contiguous. The first three digits represent part of a state. The full five digits represent a post office or urban delivery area. (Subsequently, an optional four-digit extension called ZIP+4 was added to identify a small block of addresses.) This column shows the range of three-digit ZIP codes used in each state (although border areas may be served from a different state).

Further subdivisions: Underneath the states there are counties, parishes (in Louisiana), boroughs (in Alaska), and independent cities (mixed in with counties in Maryland, Missouri, Nevada, and Virginia). The District of Columbia is its own only division. Territory in Alaska which lies outside the limits of any of the boroughs is referred to as the unorganized borough. For statistical purposes, the unorganized borough is divided into census areas. Counties, parishes, boroughs, independent cities, census areas, and the District of Columbia are generically known as "county equivalents." Counties in Connecticut and Rhode Island no longer serve any administrative purpose. Underneath the county equivalents, 29 states have further subdivisions, which may be called towns, townships, cities, boroughs, villages, districts, plantations, etc.; the generic term is minor civil divisions.

FIPS PUB 55-2 defines a three-digit code for every county equivalent in the United States. They are only unique within their state, but if either the two-letter or two-digit FIPS State Code is prefixed to them, a five-digit number is obtained which uniquely identifies the county equivalent. There is also a file of seven-digit codes for populated places, in which the first two digits of each codes identify the state. This file includes codes for minor civil divisions.

Territorial extent: There is one point where four states meet: Arizona, Colorado, New Mexico, and Utah.

Colorado, Wyoming, and Utah appear on a small- or medium-scale map to be bounded only by parallels of latitude and meridians of longitude. In fact, most of their borders deviate by a mile or so, because of early surveying errors that were perpetuated by law.

Alabama: includes Dauphin Island and the eastern tip of Petit Bois Island.

Alaska: includes Forrester, Dall, Long, and Prince of Wales islands at the southeastern end; in the southwest, the Aleutian Islands, extending to the Near Islands (Attu, Agattu, and some smaller ones); in the Bering Sea, Saint Lawrence, Nunivak, Saint Matthew, King, Little Diomede, and the Pribilof Islands (Saint Paul and Saint George); in the Gulf of Alaska, Kodiak, Chirikof, and Middleton islands; and many other coastal islands.

California: includes the Channel Islands (Santa Cruz, Santa Rosa, San Miguel, and Anacapa), Santa Catalina, San Clemente, and San Nicolas islands off Los Angeles, and the Farallon Islands off San Francisco.

Connecticut: despite appearances, its territory is not adjacent to the open sea. New York and Rhode Island have a water boundary which encloses Connecticut.

Delaware: part of its boundary with Pennsylvania is an arc of a circle. Its radius is twelve miles. Includes Pea Patch and Reedy islands in the Delaware River estuary.

Florida: includes the Florida Keys, stretching past Key West to the Marquesas Keys and Dry Tortugas.

Georgia: includes coastal islands from Cumberland in the south to Tybee in the north.

Hawaii: consists of the islands of Hawaii, Oahu, Maui, Kauai, Molokai, Lanai, Niihau, Kahoolawe, and a chain of islets extending as far west as Kure Island, but excluding Midway and Sand islands.

Kentucky: has an enclave surrounded by Tennessee and Missouri. It is formed by the southern border of Kentucky, approximately a straight east-west line in that vicinity, which is crossed three times by the Mississippi River which forms Kentucky's western border. There are no towns in the enclave, which lies across the Mississippi from New Madrid, Missouri.

Louisiana: includes islands in the Mississippi delta as far north as Grand Island, Isle au Pitre, and the Chandeleur Islands.

Maine: includes many coastal and offshore islands, as far south as the Isles of Shoals, of which Duck, Appledore, Smuttynose, and Cedar belong to Maine.

Maryland: includes the northern part of Assateague Island, and many islands in Chesapeake Bay, ranging south to Smith Island, which it shares with Virginia.

Massachusetts: includes Nantucket, Martha's Vineyard,

Nomans Land, the Elizabeth Islands, and other islands off Cape Cod, as well as many small islands in Massachusetts Bay.

Michigan: consists of two peninsulas and many islands in the Great Lakes. The islands closest to Canada are Isle Royale in Lake Superior, Drummond, Sugar, and Neebish islands on the Saint Marys River, Harsens Island in Lake Saint Clair, and Grosse Isle and Belle Isle in the Detroit River. Closest to Wisconsin is Saint Martin Island in the mouth of Green Bay.

Minnesota: includes islands in Lake of the Woods, which belongs partly to Canada. The northernmost point in the 48 contiguous states is near Angle Inlet. It's part of the mainland, but the only way to reach it from the rest of Minnesota by land is to go through Canada.

Mississippi: includes islands in the Gulf of Mexico from Cat Island to most of Petit Bois Island.

New Hampshire: includes White, Lunging, and Star islands in the Isles of Shoals group, and New Castle Island in Portsmouth Harbor.

New Jersey: includes many barrier islands on the Atlantic coast, but none in the New York City area.

New York: has two enclaves in New Jersey. The border between the two states followed the middle of the Hudson River. Liberty and Ellis Islands, lying west of that line, constituted small patches of New York land surrounded by New Jersey water. Recently a court awarded partial control of Ellis Island to New Jersey, so the situation may be changing. Four of New York City's five boroughs are on islands: Staten Island, Manhattan, and Brooklyn and Queens on Long Island. New York also includes Fishers Island at the end of the Long Island Sound; Grand Island in the Niagara River; some of the Thousand Islands (Wellesley, Grindstone, Carleton, Croil, etc.) in the Saint Lawrence River; and Valcour and Schuyler islands in Lake Champlain.

North Carolina: includes the barrier islands of the Outer Banks.

Ohio: includes Kelleys Island and the Bass Islands (North, Middle, and South) in Lake Erie.

Rhode Island: includes Block Island and numerous islands in Narragansett Bay.

Texas: includes some barrier islands, such as Padre, Matagorda, and Galveston.

Vermont: includes Grand Isle, Isle La Motte, and other islands in Lake Champlain.

Virginia: includes barrier islands and Chesapeake Bay islands south of Maryland's territory.

Washington: includes islands in Puget Sound and Haro Strait. The islands lying closest to Canada are San Juan, Stuart, and Waldron. Point Roberts, Washington, is the tip of a peninsula from Canada, cut off from the rest of Washington by water.

Wisconsin: includes the Apostle Islands in Lake Superior, and up to Chambers, Washington, and Rock islands in the mouth of Green Bay.

American Samoa, Guam, Northern Mariana Islands, Puerto Rico, U.S. Minor Outlying Islands, and Virgin Islands of the U.S. are United States possessions covered under their individual entries.

Origins of names:

Alabama: from Alabama River, from an ethnic name

Alaska: from an Aleutian word for mainland

Arizona: Papago *ali shonak*: place of a small spring

Arkansas: from Arkansas River, from an ethnic name

California: Named by Hernan Cortez in 1535 after a fictional island in the poem "Las Sergas de Esplandián," by Garcí Ordóñez de Montalvo

Colorado: from Colorado River, Spanish *colorado*: red

Connecticut: Algonquian *kuenihtekot*: long river

Delaware: after Thomas West, Lord de la Warr, first governor of Virginia

District of Columbia: named for Christopher Columbus

Florida: Spanish *Pascua Florida*: Palm Sunday, because discovered on 1513-03-20, Palm Sunday

Georgia: Named for King George II of England

Hawaii: Polynesian *Owhyhii*: place of the gods

Idaho: from a native word which means either "eaters of fish" or "stone of the mountains"

Illinois: from Illinois River, from Algonquin *illini*: warriors

Indiana: land of Indians

Iowa: from Iowa River, from native word *ay-ah-wah*: the sleeper

Kansas: from Kansas River, from an ethnic name, Sioux for south wind people

Kentucky: probably from Iroquois *kentake*: meadow land

Louisiana: named for King Louis XIV of France on 1681-08-22

Maine: the mainland, to distinguish it from the islands along the coast

Maryland: named for Queen Henrietta Maria of England, consort of Charles I

Massachusetts: from Massachusetts Bay, from an ethnic name, from Algonquian for big hills

Michigan: from Lake Michigan; Algonquian for big lake

Minnesota: from Minnesota River, from a Dakotan word for cloudy water

Mississippi: from Mississippi River, from Algonquian for big river

Missouri: from Missouri River, from an ethnic name

Montana: from Spanish *montaña*: mountain

Nebraska: from an old name for the Platte River, from Dakotan for flat water

Nevada: from the Sierra Nevada, from Spanish *nevada*: snowy

New Hampshire: named in 1629 after Hampshire county in England

New Jersey: named in 1664 after Jersey, a Channel Island

New Mexico: from Spanish Nuevo Mexico, applied to new lands north of the Mexican provinces

New York: after the city and county of York in England, but explicitly in honor of the Duke of York

North Carolina: Northern part of Carolina, named for King Charles I (Latin: Carolus) of England

North Dakota: Northern part of Dakota, from an ethnic name

Ohio: from Ohio River, from Iroquoian for beautiful river

Oklahoma: Choctaw for red people (originally applied to a smaller region)

Oregon: possibly from a mistaken identification of the Columbia River with a conjectural Ouaricon River on old maps

Pennsylvania: Penn (William Penn, grantee of land) + Latin *silva*: forest + -nia (suffix for country)

Rhode Island: from the island now known as Aquidneck, likened by Giovanni da Verrazano to Rhodes in the Mediterranean

South Carolina: Southern part of Carolina, q.v.

South Dakota: Southern part of Dakota, from an ethnic name

Tennessee: from Tennessee River, which was named for a Cherokee town near its headwaters

Texas: from a group of natives known as teyas or tejas, meaning friends

Utah: from Utah River, from an ethnic name (Utes)

Vermont: a coined name, intended to represent French *monts verts*: green mountains

Virginia: named by Queen Elizabeth I of England using an epithet which alluded to her unmarried state

Washington: named in honor of George Washington

West Virginia: descriptive; separated from Virginia in 1862 to adhere to the Union

Wisconsin: from Wisconsin River, possibly from Alonquian for big long river

Wyoming: after the Wyoming Valley in Pennsylvania, which was named from Algonquian for big flats

Change history:

1900-06-14	Hawaii organized as territory.
1907-11-16	Oklahoma territory merged with Indian Territory to form Oklahoma state.
1910	Capital of Oklahoma moved from Guthrie to Oklahoma City.
1912-01-06	Status of New Mexico changed from territory to state.
1912-02-14	Status of Arizona changed from territory to state.
1912-08-24	Alaska organized as territory.
1959-01-03	Status of Alaska changed from territory to state.
1959-08-21	Status of Hawaii changed from territory to state.

Other names of subdivisions: Formal name is "State of [state name]" unless otherwise noted.

California: Califórnia (Portuguese); Californie (French); Kalifornien (German)

District of Columbia: Distrito de Columbia (Portuguese, Spanish)

Florida: Floride (French)

Georgia: Géorgie (French)

Hawaii: Havaí (Portuguese); Hawaï (Dutch)

Kentucky: Commonwealth of Kentucky (formal)

Louisiana: Luisiana (Spanish); Louisiane (French)

Massachusetts: Commonwealth of Massachusetts (formal)

Mississippi: Misisipi (Spanish)

Missouri: Misuri (Spanish)

New Hampshire: Nova Hampshire (Portuguese); Nueva Hampshire (Spanish)

New Jersey: Nova Jersey (Portuguese); Nueva Jersey (Spanish)

New Mexico: Neu-Mexiko (German); Nouveau-Mexique (French); Novo México (Portuguese); Nuevo Mexico (Spanish)

New York: Nova York, Nova Iorque (Portuguese); Nueva York (Spanish)

North Carolina: Carolina del Norte (Spanish); Carolina do Norte (Portuguese); Caroline du Nord (French); Nord-Karolina (German)

North Dakota: Dakota del Norte (Spanish); Dakota do Norte (Portuguese); Dakota du Nord (French); Nord-Dakota (German)

Oregon: Oregón (Spanish)

Pennsylvania: Pennsylvanie (French); Pennsylvanien (German); Pensilvania (Spanish); Commonwealth of Pennsylvania (formal)

Rhode Island: State of Rhode Island and Providence Plantations (formal)

South Carolina: Süd-Karolina (German); Carolina del Sur (Spanish); Caroline du Sud (French); Carolina do Sul (Portuguese)

South Dakota: Dakota del Sur (Spanish); Dakota do Sul (Portuguese); Dakota du Sud (French); Süd-Dakota (German)

Virginia: Virginie (French); Virgínia (Portuguese); Commonwealth of Virginia (formal)

West Virginia: Virginia del Oeste, Virginia Occidental (Spanish); Virgínia Ocidental (Portuguese); Virginie occidentale (French); West-Virginia (German)

Population history:

name	1900	1910	1920	1930	1940	1950	1960	1970	1980	1990
Alabama	1,828,697	2,138,093	2,348,174	2,646,248	2,832,961	3,061,743	3,266,740	3,444,354	3,894,025	4,040,587 ➤

name	1900	1910	1920	1930	1940	1950	1960	1970	1980	1990
Alaska	63,592	64,356	55,036	59,278	72,524	128,643	226,167	302,583	401,851	550,043
Arizona	122,931	204,354	334,162	435,573	499,261	749,587	1,302,161	1,775,399	2,716,546	3,665,228
Arkansas	1,311,564	1,574,449	1,752,204	1,854,482	1,949,387	1,909,511	1,786,272	1,923,322	2,286,357	2,350,725
California	1,485,053	2,377,549	3,426,861	5,677,251	6,907,387	10,586,223	15,717,204	19,971,069	23,667,764	29,760,021
Colorado	539,700	799,024	939,629	1,035,791	1,123,296	1,325,089	1,753,947	2,209,596	2,889,735	3,294,394
Connecticut	908,420	1,114,756	1,380,631	1,606,903	1,709,242	2,007,280	2,535,234	3,032,217	3,107,564	3,287,116
Delaware	184,735	202,322	223,003	238,380	266,505	318,085	446,292	548,104	594,338	666,168
D. C.	278,718	331,069	437,571	486,869	663,091	802,178	763,956	756,668	638,432	606,900
Florida	528,542	752,619	968,470	1,468,211	1,897,414	2,771,305	4,951,560	6,791,418	9,746,961	12,937,926
Georgia	2,216,331	2,609,121	2,895,832	2,908,506	3,123,723	3,444,578	3,943,116	4,587,930	5,462,982	6,478,216
Hawaii	154,001	191,909	255,912	368,336	422,770	499,794	632,772	769,913	964,691	1,108,229
Idaho	161,772	325,594	431,866	445,032	524,873	588,637	667,191	713,015	944,127	1,006,749
Illinois	4,821,550	5,638,591	6,485,280	7,630,654	7,897,241	8,712,176	10,081,158	11,110,285	11,427,409	11,430,602
Indiana	2,516,462	2,700,876	2,930,390	3,238,503	3,427,796	3,934,224	4,662,498	5,195,392	5,490,214	5,544,159
Iowa	2,231,853	2,224,771	2,404,021	2,470,939	2,538,268	2,621,073	2,757,537	2,825,368	2,913,808	2,776,755
Kansas	1,470,495	1,690,949	1,769,257	1,880,999	1,801,028	1,905,299	2,178,611	2,249,071	2,364,236	2,477,574
Kentucky	2,147,174	2,289,905	2,416,630	2,614,589	2,845,627	2,944,806	3,038,156	3,220,711	3,660,324	3,685,296
Louisiana	1,381,625	1,656,388	1,798,509	2,101,593	2,363,880	2,683,516	3,257,022	3,644,637	4,206,116	4,219,973
Maine	694,466	742,371	768,014	797,423	847,226	913,774	969,265	993,722	1,125,043	1,227,928
Maryland	1,188,044	1,295,346	1,449,661	1,631,526	1,821,244	2,343,001	3,100,689	3,923,897	4,216,933	4,781,468
Massachusetts	2,805,346	3,366,416	3,852,356	4,249,614	4,316,721	4,690,514	5,148,578	5,689,170	5,737,093	6,016,425
Michigan	2,420,982	2,810,173	3,668,412	4,842,325	5,256,106	6,371,766	7,823,194	8,881,826	9,262,044	9,295,297
Minnesota	1,751,394	2,075,708	2,387,125	2,563,953	2,792,300	2,982,483	3,413,864	3,806,103	4,075,970	4,375,099
Mississippi	1,551,270	1,797,114	1,790,618	2,009,821	2,183,796	2,178,914	2,178,141	2,216,994	2,520,770	2,573,216
Missouri	3,106,665	3,293,335	3,404,055	3,629,367	3,784,664	3,954,653	4,319,813	4,677,623	4,916,766	5,117,073
Montana	243,329	376,053	548,889	537,606	559,456	591,024	674,767	694,409	786,690	799,065
Nebraska	1,066,300	1,192,214	1,296,372	1,377,963	1,315,834	1,325,510	1,411,330	1,485,333	1,569,825	1,578,385
Nevada	42,335	81,875	77,407	91,058	110,247	160,083	285,278	488,738	800,508	1,201,833
New Hampshire	411,588	430,572	443,083	465,293	491,524	533,242	606,921	737,681	920,610	1,109,252
New Jersey	1,883,669	2,537,167	3,155,900	4,041,334	4,160,165	4,835,329	6,066,782	7,171,112	7,365,011	7,730,188
New Mexico	195,310	327,301	360,350	423,317	531,818	681,187	951,023	1,017,055	1,303,302	1,515,069
New York	7,268,894	9,113,614	10,385,227	12,588,066	13,479,142	14,830,192	16,782,304	18,241,391	17,558,165	17,990,455
North Carolina	1,893,810	2,206,287	2,559,123	3,170,276	3,571,623	4,061,929	4,556,155	5,084,411	5,880,095	6,628,637
North Dakota	319,146	577,056	646,872	680,845	641,935	619,636	632,446	617,792	652,717	638,800
Ohio	4,157,545	4,767,121	5,759,394	6,646,697	6,907,612	7,946,627	9,706,397	10,657,423	10,797,603	10,847,115
Oklahoma	790,391	1,657,155	2,028,283	2,396,040	2,336,434	2,233,351	2,328,284	2,559,463	3,025,487	3,145,585
Oregon	413,536	672,765	783,389	953,786	1,089,684	1,521,341	1,768,687	2,091,533	2,633,156	2,842,321
Pennsylvania	6,302,115	7,665,111	8,720,017	9,631,350	9,900,180	10,498,012	11,319,366	11,800,766	11,864,720	11,881,643
Rhode Island	428,556	542,610	604,397	687,497	713,346	791,896	859,488	949,723	947,154	1,003,464
South Carolina	1,340,316	1,515,400	1,683,724	1,738,765	1,899,804	2,117,027	2,382,594	2,590,713	3,120,729	3,486,703
South Dakota	401,570	583,888	636,547	692,849	642,961	652,740	680,514	666,257	690,768	696,004
Tennessee	2,020,616	2,184,789	2,337,885	2,616,556	2,915,841	3,291,718	3,567,089	3,926,018	4,591,023	4,877,185
Texas	3,048,710	3,896,542	4,663,228	5,824,715	6,414,824	7,711,194	9,579,677	11,198,655	14,225,513	16,986,510
Utah	276,749	373,351	449,396	507,847	550,310	688,862	890,627	1,059,273	1,461,037	1,722,850
Vermont	343,641	355,956	352,428	359,611	359,231	377,747	389,881	444,732	511,456	562,758
Virginia	1,854,184	2,061,612	2,309,187	2,421,851	2,677,773	3,318,680	3,966,949	4,651,448	5,346,797	6,187,358
Washington	518,103	1,141,990	1,356,621	1,563,396	1,736,191	2,378,963	2,853,214	3,413,244	4,132,353	4,866,692
West Virginia	958,800	1,221,119	1,463,701	1,729,205	1,901,974	2,005,552	1,860,421	1,744,237	1,950,186	1,793,477
Wisconsin	2,069,042	2,333,860	2,632,067	2,939,006	3,137,587	3,434,575	3,951,777	4,417,821	4,705,642	4,891,769
Wyoming	92,531	145,965	194,402	225,565	250,742	290,529	330,066	332,416	469,557	453,588
	76,212,168	92,228,531	106,021,568	123,202,660	132,164,569	151,325,798	179,323,175	203,302,031	226,542,203	248,709,873

Census dates were 1900-04-15, 1910-04-15, 1920-01-01, and 04-01 (April 1) in subsequent years.

UNITED STATES MINOR OUTLYING ISLANDS

ISO = UM/FIPS = UM   Language = English   Time zone = (see table)   Capital = none

These islands were acquired haphazardly by the United States, and because of their isolation, they were administered separately from the states. Some of them were occupied by the Japanese during World War II.

Other names of country: Amerikanisch-Ozeanien, Amerikanische kleinere abgelegene Inseln im Pazifik (German); Îles Mineures éloignées des États-Unis (French).

Origin of name: descriptive.

division	FIPS	ISO	FIPS#	tz	population	area-km	area-mi
Baker Island	FQ	81	050	-12	0	3	1
Howland Island	HQ	84	100	-12	0	3	1
Jarvis Island	DQ	86	150	-10	0	4	2
Johnston Atoll	JQ	67	200	-10	1,325	3	1
Kingman Reef	KQ	89	250	-11	0	1	0
Midway Islands	MQ	71	300	-11	453	5	2
Navassa Island	BQ	76	350	- 5	0	5	2
Palmyra Atoll	LQ	95	400	-11	0	10	4
Wake Island	WQ	79	450	12	195	8	3
					1,973	42	16

Status: These divisions are unincorporated territories.

FIPS: Codes from FIPS PUB 10-4, in which these entities are treated as separate countries.

ISO: Codes from ISO 3166-2. They originated in a FIPS Standard. In table 2 of FIPS PUB 5-2, U.S. Minor Outlying Islands is listed as a state-level division of the United States. As such, its State Numeric Code is 74 and its State Alpha Code is UM. In table 3, its nine divisions are listed. They are assigned the codes in this column, under the heading "FIPS State Numeric Code."

FIPS#: Three-digit county codes from FIPS PUB 55-2, where these entities are treated as counties and United States Minor Outlying Islands is treated as a state or territory.

Tz: Offset from GMT to local time in hours. Daylight saving time is not observed.

Population: 1990-04-01 census.

Area-km: Square kilometers.

Area-mi: Square miles.

Capitals: These islands, even when inhabited, don't have named cities on them.

Territorial extent: Johnston Atoll includes Johnston, Sand, Hikina, and Akan islands.

Midway Islands includes Sand and Eastern islands.

Palmyra Atoll is a cluster of islands, of which Cooper is the largest.

Wake Island includes Wake, Peale, and Wilkes atolls.

Origins of names:

Johnston Island: named for Charles James Johnston, who discovered the island in 1807.

Kingman Reef: discovered by Captain W. E. Kingman in 1853.

Midway Islands: about midway between California and Japan.

Wake Island: discovered by Captain William Wake in 1796.

Change history:

1912	The United States annexed Palmyra Atoll to Hawaii. It had previously been claimed by both Great Britain and Hawaii.
1922	U.S. annexed Kingman Reef.
1935	Baker and Howland Islands, formerly claimed by Great Britain, became U.S. territories. United States laid claim to Jarvis Island.
1959-08-21	Palmyra Atoll split from Hawaii when the latter became a state.

Other names of subdivisions:

Jarvis Island: Jervis Island (variant)
Midway Islands: Îles Midway (French); Ilhas Midway (Por-

tuguese); Islas Midway (Spanish); Midwayinseln (German); Brooks Islands (obsolete)

Population history:

division	1930	1940	1950	1960	1970	1980	1990
Baker, Howland, and Jarvis Islands	N/A	10	0	0	0	0	0
Johnston Atoll	N/A	69	46	156	150	327	1,325
Midway Islands	36	437	416	2,356	2,220	453	453
Wake Island	N/A	N/A	349	1,097	1,647	302	195

URUGUAY

ISO = UY/FIPS = UY   Language = Spanish   Time zone = -3   Capital = Montevideo

Uruguay has been independent throughout the 20th century.

Other names of country: Eastern Republic of Uruguay (formal–English); República Oriental del Uruguay (formal); Republik Östlich des Uruguay (formal–German); Uruguai (Portuguese); Úrúgvæ (Icelandic).

Origin of name: possibly from *irugua*: chief channel + *y*: river, or Guarani *uru*: bird, *huguay*: tail (one source interprets the name as "river of the beautifully colored birds").

division	ISO	FIPS	population	area-km	area-mi	capital	postcode
Artigas	AR	UY01	74,968	11,928	4,605	Artigas	55000
Canelones	CA	UY02	443,660	4,536	1,751	Canelones	90000
Cerro Largo	CL	UY03	82,452	13,648	5,270	Melo	37000
Colonia	CO	UY04	121,185	6,106	2,358	Colonia (del Sacramento)	70000
Durazno	DU	UY05	55,644	11,643	4,495	Durazno	97000
Flores	FS	UY06	24,835	5,144	1,986	Trinidad	85000
Florida	FD	UY07	66,366	10,417	4,022	Florida	94000
Lavalleja	LA	UY08	61,192	10,016	3,867	Minas	30000
Maldonado	MA	UY09	127,257	4,793	1,851	Maldonado	20000
Montevideo	MO	UY10	1,330,405	530	205	Montevideo	10000
Paysandú	PA	UY11	111,040	13,922	5,375	Paysandú	60000
Río Negro	RN	UY12	51,620	9,282	3,584	Fray Bentos	65000
Rivera	RV	UY13	98,875	9,370	3,618	Rivera	40000
Rocha	RO	UY14	70,200	10,551	4,074	Rocha	27000
Salto	SA	UY15	118,013	14,163	5,468	Salto	50000
San José	SJ	UY16	98,161	4,992	1,927	San José (de Mayo)	80000
Soriano	SO	UY17	81,377	9,000	3,475	Mercedes	75000
Tacuarembó	TA	UY18	85,018	15,438	5,961	Tacuarembó	45000
Treinta y Tres	TT	UY19	49,394	9,529	3,679	Treinta y Tres	33000
			3,151,662	175,008	67,571		

Status: These divisions are departamentos (departments).
ISO: Codes from ISO 3166-2.
FIPS: Codes from FIPS PUB 10-4.
Population: 1996 census.
Area-km: Square kilometers.
Area-mi: Square miles.
Capital: The informal name is the part not in parentheses.
Postal code: Uruguay uses five-digit códigos postales. The numbers given in the table appear to be the start of the range for each department. Note the fitting number used for Treinta y Tres.
Territorial extent: The departments of Colonia, Flores, San José, and Soriano appear to meet in a single point.
Origins of names:

Montevideo: Spanish *monte*: mountain + Latin *video*: I see
Treinta y Tres: Spanish for thirty-three, the number of patriots under Lavalleja who invaded from Buenos Aires,

raised an army, and gained Uruguay's independence in 1825–1828.

Change history:

1927-12-22 Name of Minas department changed to Lavalleja.

Other names of subdivisions:

Montevideo: Montevidéu (Portuguese)

Population history:

division	1911	1941	1953	1963	1975	1985	1996
Artigas	31,380	55,748	63,589	52,093	57,528	69,145	74,968
Canelones	97,719	199,232	201,359	255,326	318,858	364,248	443,660
Cerro Largo	49,307	96,488	110,339	71,222	73,204	78,416	82,452
Colonia	63,732	129,322	135,038	104,795	110,860	112,717	121,185
Durazno	47,253	94,291	99,063	56,070	54,990	55,077	55,644
Flores	19,030	35,835	35,565	23,446	24,684	24,739	24,835
Florida	51,202	105,932	106,284	64,186	66,092	66,474	66,366
Lavalleja	33,168	115,181	115,852	65,560	65,240	61,466	61,192
Maldonado	57,036	66,539	67,933	61,548	75,617	94,314	127,257
Montevideo	338,125	536,533	836,165	1,173,114	1,229,748	1,311,976	1,330,405
Paysandú	48,419	83,490	92,417	86,988	98,733	103,763	111,040
Río Negro	27,622	47,147	51,954	46,741	49,816	48,644	51,620
Rivera	39,413	74,746	91,740	75,826	79,331	89,475	98,875
Rocha	39,038	82,156	86,334	55,006	59,952	66,601	70,200
Salto	54,159	99,754	108,030	92,595	100,407	108,487	118,013
San José	51,785	97,301	96,848	77,284	88,281	89,893	98,161
Soriano	44,720	92,671	99,927	74,749	80,114	79,439	81,377
Tacuarembó	51,505	104,889	119,658	76,255	84,829	83,498	85,018
Treinta y Tres	32,897	68,371	72,063	43,216	45,680	46,869	49,394
	1,177,510	2,185,626	2,590,158	2,556,020	2,763,964	2,955,241	3,151,662

1941 and 1953 are official estimates.

UZBEKISTAN

ISO = UZ/FIPS = UZ   Language = Jagatai Turkish   Time zone = +5   Capital = Tashkent

In 1900, the area which is now Uzbekistan was partly contained in Imperial Russia, the remainder being under Russian protection. The Emirate of Bukhara and the Khanate of Khiva had been protectorates since 1868 and 1873 respectively. The part that was in Russia proper was contained in the general government of Turkestan. Turkestan was divided into oblasts (regions), and the part that became Uzbekistan lay mainly in the Syr-Daria, Ferghana, and Transcaspian oblasts. In the years following the Russian Revolution, all of Turkestan joined the Soviet Union. Uzbekistan appeared on the map in 1924. When the Soviet Union collapsed in 1991, it became an independent country.

Other names of country: Oezbekistan (Dutch); Ouzbékistan (French); Ozbekiston Respublikasy (formal); Republic of Uzbekistan (formal–English); Usbekistan (Danish, German, Norwegian); Uzbekistán (Spanish); Uzbequistão (Portuguese); Úsbekistan (Icelandic).

Origin of name: land of the Uzbeks, from Turkish *uz*: free, *bek*: completely.

division	ISO	FIPS	population	area-km	area-mi	capital	Russian
Andijon	AN	UZ01	1,444,000	4,000	2,000	Andijon	Andizhanskaya Oblast' ➤

division	ISO	FIPS	population	area-km	area-mi	capital	Russian
Bukhoro	BU	UZ02	947,000	39,000	15,000	Bukhoro	Bukharskaya Oblast'
Farghona	FA	UZ03	1,814,000	7,000	3,000	Farghona	Ferganskaya Oblast'
Jizzakh	JI	UZ04	563,000	21,000	8,000	Jizzakh	Dzhizakskaya Oblast'
Khorazm	KH	UZ05	813,000	6,000	2,000	Urganch	Khorezmskaya Oblast'
Namangan	NG	UZ06	1,196,000	8,000	3,000	Namangan	Namanganskaya Oblast'
Nawoiy	NW	UZ07	542,000	111,000	43,000	Nawoiy	Navoiyskaya Oblast'
Qashqadaryo	QA	UZ08	1,241,000	28,000	11,000	Qarshi	Kashkadar'inskaya Oblast'
Qoraqalpoghiston	QR	UZ09	983,000	164,900	64,000	Nukus	Karakalpakskaya A.S.S.R.
Samarqand	SA	UZ10	1,789,000	16,000	6,000	Samarqand	Samarkandskaya Oblast'
Sirdaryo	SI	UZ11	481,000	5,000	2,000	Guliston	Syrdar'inskaya Oblast'
Surkhondaryo	SU	UZ12	986,000	21,000	8,000	Termiz	Surkhandar'inskaya Oblast'
Toshkent	TO	UZ14	3,792,000	16,000	6,000	Toshkent	Tashkentskaya Oblast'
			16,591,000	446,900	173,000		

Status: These divisions are wiloyatlar (sing. wiloyat: regions), except for Qoraqalpohgiston, which is a respublikasi (autonomous republic).

ISO: Codes from ISO 3166-2.

FIPS: Codes from FIPS PUB 10-4.

Population: 1982 estimate.

Area-km: Square kilometers.

Area-mi: Square miles.

Russian: Russian name of region/republic under former Soviet administration.

Territorial extent: Ferghana includes four enclaves within Osh region of Kyrgyzstan. The largest is around Sokh; the next-largest contains Iordan and Shakhimardan; and the other two are negligibly small.

Many sources say that there is also a division called Toshkent Shahri (FIPS = UZ13), or Tashkent City, within and separate from the Toshkent region. The ISO draft standard doesn't list it.

Origins of names:

Bukhoro: possibly from Sanskrit *vihara*: monastery

Qoraqalpoghiston: after the inhabitants, from Turkic *kara*:

black, *kalpak*: hat

Change history: A.S.S.R. = Autonomous Soviet Socialist Republic; S.S.R. = Soviet Socialist Republic. An S.S.R. was a constituent republic, or first-level division of the Soviet Union.

1920-04-04	Khanate of Khiva became Khwarazman People's Soviet Republic, also translated People's Republic of Khorezm.
1920-10-05	Emirate of Bukhara became Bukharan People's Soviet Republic.
1921-04-11	Turkestan A.S.S.R. formed from Amu-Darya (Petro-Alexandrovsk, modern Turtkul'), Ferghana (Skobelev), Pamir, Samarkand (Samarkand), Semirechensk (Verniy), and Syr Darya (Tashkent) regions, and the southern part of Transcaspian. (Capitals in parentheses.)
1922-12-30	By the Treaty of Union, Bukhara and Khorezm were linked to the newly formed Soviet Union. Turkestan A.S.S.R. was part of the Russian Soviet Federated Socialist Republic, one of the constituent republics.
1923-03	Bukhara and Khorezm merged with Turkestan A.S.S.R. Khorezm became an S.S.R. in 1923-10; Bukhara followed suit in 1924-09.
1924-10-27	Turkestan A.S.S.R., Bukhara S.S.R., and Khorezm S.S.R. reorganized into several entities, ostensibly to match ethnic groups. One of the new entities, formed from most of Bukhara and Khorezm along with parts of Turkestan, was the Uzbekskaya S.S.R. The Tadzhikskaya A.S.S.R., in turn, was part of the Uzbekskaya S.S.R.
1929-10-15	Tadzhikskaya A.S.S.R. split from Uzbekskaya S.S.R.
1936-12-05	Kara-Kalpak autonomous oblast merged with Uzbek; status of Kara-Kalpak changed to A.S.S.R.
1963-02-16	Syr-Darya oblast split from Samarkand.
1963-09-19	40,000 sq. km. transferred from Kazakh S.S.R. to Uzbek S.S.R.
1973-12-29	Dzhizak oblast split from Samarkand.

~1981   Navoi oblast split from Bukhara.
1991-08-31   Uzbekistan declared independence from the Soviet Union. Westerners began to use the
                   Jagatai Turkish, rather than the Russian, version of place names.

Other names of subdivisions: Before the dissolution of the Soviet Union, western sources normally used transliterations from Russian rather than indigenous names. There are various methods for transliterating from the Cyrillic to the Roman alphabet. The most common variant uses h instead of kh, c for ts, j for consonantal y, č for ch, š for sh, and ž for zh.

Andijon: Andijan (variant)

Bukhoro: Bukhara (variant); Mawarranahr, Transoxania, Turan (obsolete)

Farghona; Fergana, Ferghana (variant)

Khorazm: Khiva, Khwarazm (obsolete); Khorezm (variant)

Nawoiy: Navoi (variant)

Qashqadaryo: Kashka-Dar'ya, Kashkadar, Kashkadar'ya (variant)

Qoraqalpoghiston: Kara-Kalpakia, Karakalpakstan (variant); Qoraqalpoghiston Respublikasi (formal)

Sirdaryo: Syr-Dar'ya (variant)

Surkhondaryo: Sukhan-Dar'ya, Surkhan-Dar'ya (variant)

Toshkent: Taschkent (German), Tashkent (variant)

VANUATU

ISO = VU/FIPS = NH   Language = English, French   Time zone = +11   Capital = Port-Vila

At the beginning of the 20th century, the New Hebrides were an Anglo-French protectorate. On 1906-02-27 an agreement was reached making them a condominium of Britain and France. Thus they remained, until they attained independence on 1980-07-30 and took the name of Vanuatu.

Other names of country: New Hebrides (obsolete); Nouvelles Hébrides (obsolete–French); Republic of Vanuatu (formal–English); Ripablik blong Vanuatu (formal); Vanúatú (Icelandic).

Origin of name: native phrase for "our land."

division	ISO	FIPS	dist	capital
Ambrym	AM	NH05	C2	Eas, Ambrym I.
Aoba/Maéwo	AO	NH06	N	Longana, Aoba I.
Banks/Torres	BA	NH07	N	Sola, Vanua Lava I.
Éfaté	EF	NH08	C1	Port-Vila, Éfaté I.
Épi	EP	NH09	C1	Ringdove, Épi I.
Malakula	MA	NH10	C2	Lakatoro, Malakula I.
Paama	PA	NH11	C2	Liro, Paama I.
Pentecôte	PR	NH12	C2	Loltong, Pentecôte I.
Santo/Malo	SM	NH13	N	Luganville, Espíritu Santo I.
Shepherd	SH	NH14	C1	Morua, Tongoa I.
Taféa	TA	NH15	S	Isangel, Tanna I.

Status: These divisions are island councils.

ISO: Codes from ISO 3166-2.

FIPS: Codes from FIPS PUB 10-4.

Dist: Former district to which this area belonged under the condominium, keyed to table below.

Capital: Name of city, followed by the island it's on.

Territorial extent: Alternate names given in parentheses are usually older or rarer forms of the island name.

Ambrym includes Ambrym (Ambrim) island.

Aoba/Maéwo includes Aoba (Oba) and Maéwo (Aurora) islands.

Banks/Torres includes the Banks Islands (Santa María (Gaua), Vanua Lava, Mota Lava (Saddle), Uréparapa (Norbarbar), Vatu Rhandi, etc.) and the smaller Torres Islands (Hiu, Tégua, Toga, and Loh).

Éfaté includes Éfaté (Vate), Nguna, Moso (Verao), Lélépa, Émao (Mau), and other islands.

Épi includes Épi island.

Malakula includes Malakula (Malekula), Tomman (Ur), and the Maskelyne Islands.

Paama includes Paama and Lopévi islands.
Pentecôte includes Pentecôte (Pentecost) islands.
Santo/Malo includes Espíritu Santo (Marina), Malo, Aoré, Tutuba, Mavéa, Lathi (Sakao), and other islands.
Shepherd includes the Shepherd Islands: Tongoa, Émaé (Mai), Tongariki, Makura, Mataso, and others.
Taféa includes Erromango, Tanna, Anatom (Aneityum), Aniwa, and Futuna islands.
Change history:

~1985   Vanuatu reorganized from four districts into eleven island councils. The old districts were:

district	abv	capital
Central District Number 1	C1	Vila, Éfaté I.
Central District Number 2	C2	Lamap, Malakula I.
Northern	N	Luganville, Espíritu Santo I.
Southern	S	Lenakel, Tanna I.

(*Note:* Vila is now more often known as Port-Vila. The name of Lenakel has changed to Isangel.)

1994   Vanuatu reorganized from eleven island councils into six provinces: Malampa, Penama, Sanma, Shefa, Taféa, and Torba. No further information on the provinces is available yet.

VATICAN CITY

ISO = VA/FIPS = VT   Language = Italian, Latin   Time zone = +1 d   Capital = Vatican City

The Vatican City is widely recognized as sovereign territory under the rule of the Pope. After the reunification of Italy in the 19th century, this area, plus the Lateran Palace and Castel Gandolfo, was all that was left of the Pope's temporal domain. A treaty of 1929-02-11 formalized the relationship between the Vatican City and Italy.

Other names of country: Città del Vaticano (Italian); Heiliger Stuhl, Staat Vatikanstadt (German); Holy See, Vatican City State (formal–English); Saint-Siège, État de la Cité du Vatican (French); Santa Sede, Vaticano (Spanish); Stato della Città del Vaticano (formal); Vaticaanstad (Dutch); Vatikaanivaltio (Finnish); Vatíkanið (Icelandic); Vatikanstaten (Danish, Norwegian, Swedish).

Origin of name: named for the hill and surrounding area called Vaticanus by the Ancient Romans, from Latin *vates*: diviner.

division	abv	population	area-km	area-mi	capital
Vatican City	VA	802	0	0	Vatican City

Status: This division is the whole of the country, treated as a division for compatibility.
Abv: Two-letter code for international compatibility (defined by the author).
Population: 1992 estimate.
Area-km: Square kilometers.
Area-mi: Square miles.
Territorial extent: The Vatican City consists of less than half a square kilometer, surrounded by Rome, making it the smallest country in the world in area.

VENEZUELA

ISO = VE/FIPS = VE   Language = Spanish   Time zone = -4   Capital = Caracas

Venezuela has been independent during the entire 20th century. In 1953, a new constitution changed the name of the country from Estados Unidos de Venezuela to República de Venezuela.

Other names of country: Republic of Venezuela (formal–English); República de Venezuela (formal); Venesúela (Icelandic).

Origin of name: Spanish for little Venice, because early explorers found inhabitants living in stilt houses in lakes.

division	abv	ISO	FIPS	OCEI	typ	population	area-km	area-mi	capital
Amazonas	AM	Z	VE01	2	ty	55,717	180,145	69,550	Puerto Ayacucho
Anzoátegui	AN	B	VE02	3	st	859,758	43,300	16,720	Barcelona
Apure	AP	C	VE03	4	st	285,412	76,500	29,540	San Fernando (de Apure)
Aragua	AR	D	VE04	5	st	1,120,132	7,014	2,710	Maracay
Barinas	BA	E	VE05	6	st	424,491	35,200	13,590	Barinas
Bolívar	BO	F	VE06	7	st	900,310	238,000	91,890	Ciudad Bolívar
Carabobo	CA	G	VE07	8	st	1,453,232	4,650	1,800	Valencia
Cojedes	CO	H	VE08	9	st	182,066	14,800	5,710	San Carlos
Delta Amacuro	DA	Y	VE09	10	st	84,564	40,200	15,520	Tucupita
Dependencias Federales	DP	W	VE24		fd	2,245	120	50	
Distrito Federal	DF	A	VE10	1	df	2,103,661	1,930	750	Caracas
Falcón	FA	I	VE11	11	st	599,185	24,800	9,580	Coro
Guárico	GU	J	VE12	12	st	488,623	64,986	25,090	San Juan (de los Morros)
Lara	LA	K	VE13	13	st	1,193,161	19,800	7,640	Barquisimeto
Mérida	ME	L	VE14	14	st	570,215	11,300	4,360	Mérida
Miranda	MI	M	VE15	15	st	1,871,093	7,950	3,070	Los Teques
Monagas	MO	N	VE16	16	st	470,157	28,900	11,160	Maturín
Nueva Esparta	NE	O	VE17	17	st	263,748	1,150	440	La Asunción
Portuguesa	PO	P	VE18	18	st	576,435	15,200	5,870	Guanare
Sucre	SU	R	VE19	19	st	679,595	11,800	4,560	Cumaná
Táchira	TA	S	VE20	20	st	807,712	11,100	4,290	San Cristóbal
Trujillo	TR	T	VE21	21	st	493,912	7,400	2,860	Trujillo
Yaracuy	YA	U	VE22	22	st	384,536	7,100	2,740	San Felipe
Zulia	ZU	V	VE23	23	st	2,235,305	63,100	24,360	Maracaibo
						18,105,265	916,445	353,850	

Type: These divisions are estados (st: states), territorios (ty: territories), dependencias federales (fd: federal dependencies), and a distrito federal (df: federal district).

Abv: Two-letter code for international compatibility (defined by the author).

ISO: Codes from ISO 3166-2.

FIPS: Codes from FIPS PUB 10-4.

OCEI: Codes used by the Oficina Central de Estadística e Informática (OCEI) to identify states and territories. Within each state, OCEI numbers the municipios from 1 to n, and so on. By concatenating the codes for state, municipio, parish, and populated place, you can get a unique code, such as 23/4/1/5, for each populated place in Venezuela.

Population: 1990-10-21 census.

Area-km: Square kilometers.

Area-mi: Square miles.

Capital: Formal name includes the part in parentheses.

Further subdivisions: The states are divided into municipios (municipalities), or, in the case of territories/federal district, into departamentos (departments). The municipios are further subdivided into parroquias (parishes).

Territorial extent: Delta Amacuro includes many islands in the deltas of the Orinoco, Amacuro, and other rivers.

Dependencias Federales consists of the Caribbean islands, other than those belonging to Nueva Esparta, between 62° and 68° W. and south of 12°15' N., as well as Isla de las Aves, which is nearer to Guadeloupe. The largest of these islands are La Tortuga, La Blanquilla, and Los Roques.

Nueva Esparta consists of Margarita, Cubagua, and Coche islands.

Zulia is divided into three parts by Lake Maracaibo. Traveling clockwise around the lake shore from its opening to the sea in the north, you pass through Zulia, Trujillo, Zulia, Mérida, and Zulia.

The city of Caracas is divided roughly in half between Distrito Federal and Miranda. It is quite unusual for a city to lie in two different primary administrative divisions of a country.

Origins of names:

Carabobo: named for a village, from an ethnic name   Caracas: from an ethnic name

Change history: In 1900, the divisions of Venezuela were Amazonas Territory, Bermudez, Bolívar, Carabobo, Colon Territory, Delta Territory, Falcón, Federal District, Lara, Los Andes, Miranda, and Zamora. Bolívar was further subdivided into Armisticio, Caura, and Yuruari Territories, plus Bolívar proper. By ~1924 the modern divisions were in place, although the old ones continued in use for some time. Bermudez (capital Barcelona) was roughly equivalent to Anzoátegui, Monagas, Nueva Esparta, and Sucre. The Armisticio Territory of Bolívar was equivalent to Apure. Colon Territory was about the same as Dependencias Federales. Delta Territory became Delta Amacuro. Falcón (capital Maracaibo) contained Falcón and Zulia. Lara (capital Barquisimeto) contained Lara and Yaracuy. Los Andes (capital Mérida) was roughly equivalent to Mérida, Táchira, and Trujillo. Miranda (capital Caracas) contained Aragua, Guárico, Miranda, and most of the modern extent of Distrito Federal. Zamora (capital Guanare) was about equal to Barinas, Cojedes, and Portuguesa.

1933-12-13	Land around Turiamo transferred from Carabobo to Aragua; several municipios exchanged between Aragua and Guárico, amounting to a net gain of 1,414 sq. km. for Aragua.
~1940	Name of Zamora state changed to Barinas.
1991-03-08	Status of Delta Amacuro changed from territory to state.

Other names of subdivisions:

Amazonas: Amazone (French)   (formal); Federal Dependencies (variant)
Dependencias Federales: Dependencias Federales de Alta Mar

Population history:

division	1941	1950	1961	1971	1981	1990
Amazonas	3,728	10,582	11,757	21,696	45,667	55,717
Anzoátegui	155,746	242,058	382,002	506,297	683,717	859,758
Apure	70,560	88,939	117,577	164,705	188,187	285,412
Aragua	138,235	189,891	313,274	543,170	891,623	1,120,132
Barinas	62,959	79,944	139,271	231,046	326,166	424,491
Bolívar	94,522	127,436	213,543	391,665	668,340	900,310
Carabobo	191,442	242,923	381,636	659,339	1,062,268	1,453,232
Cojedes	49,769	52,111	72,652	94,351	133,991	182,066
Delta Amacuro	28,165	33,648	33,979	48,139	56,720	84,564
Dependencias Federales	852	779	861	463	850	2,245
Distrito Federal	380,099	709,602	1,257,515	1,860,637	2,070,742	2,103,661
Falcón	232,644	258,759	340,450	407,957	503,896	599,185
Guárico	135,089	164,523	244,966	318,905	393,467	488,623
Lara	332,975	368,169	489,140	671,410	945,064	1,193,161
Mérida	192,994	211,110	270,668	347,095	459,361	570,215
Miranda	227,604	276,273	492,349	856,272	1,421,442	1,871,093
Monagas	122,901	175,560	246,217	298,239	388,536	470,157
Nueva Esparta	69,195	75,899	89,492	118,830	197,198	263,748
Portuguesa	87,151	122,153	203,707	297,047	424,984	576,435
Sucre	291,452	333,607	401,992	469,004	585,698	679,595
Táchira	245,722	304,181	399,163	511,346	660,234	807,712
Trujillo	264,270	273,919	326,634	381,334	433,735	493,912
Yaracuy	127,030	132,436	175,291	223,545	300,597	384,536
Zulia	345,667	560,336	919,863	1,299,030	1,674,252	2,235,305
	3,850,771	5,034,838	7,523,999	10,721,522	14,516,735	18,105,265

VIETNAM

ISO = VN/FIPS = VM   Language = Vietnamese   Time zone = +7   Capital = Hanoi

Vietnam was part of French Indo-China in 1900. It attained partial independence in 1949. In 1954, the French, tired of fighting the Communists in the north, but unwilling to abandon the country to them, agreed to partition it along the 17th parallel. The parts were North Vietnam (capital Hanoi) and South Vietnam (Saigon, now Ho Chi Minh City). Conflict continued until the two countries were formally united on 1976-07-02.

Other names of country: Công Hòa Xã Hôi Chu Nghia Viêt Nam (formal); Socialist Republic of Vietnam (formal–English); Viêt Nam (French); Viet-Nam (Italian); Víetnam (Icelandic).

Origin of name: Vietnamese *viet*: foreigner, *nam*: south, applied by Chinese to foreigners from the south.

division	abv	ISO	FIPS	capital	old	former
An Giang	AG	44	VM43	Long Xuyen	S-C	An Giang
Bac Thai	BC	08	VM02	Thai Nguyen	N-T	Bac Can, Thai Nguyen
Ba Ria-Vung Tau	BV	43	VM53	Vung Tau	S-C	Phuoc Tuy
Ben Tre	BR	50	VM03	Ben Tre	S-C	Kien Hoa
Binh Dinh	BD	31	VM54	Qui Nhon	S-A	Binh Dinh
Binh Thuan	BU	40	VM55	Phan Thiet	S-A	Binh Thuan, Binh Tuy
Can Tho	CT	48	VM56	Can Tho	S-C	Chuong Thien, Phong Dinh
Cao Bang	CB	04	VM05	Cao Bang	N-T	Cao Bang
Dac Lac	DL	33	VM44	Buon Ma Thuot	S-A	Daklak, Darlac, Quang Duc
Dong Nai	DN	39	VM45	Bien Hoa	S-C	Bien Hoa, Long Khanh, Phuoc Thanh
Dong Thap	DT	45	VM46	Sa Dec	S-C	Kien Phong
Gia Lai	GL	30	VM57	Pleiku	S-A	Phu Bon, Pleiku
Ha Bac	HB	12	VM11	Bac Giang	N-T	Bac Giang, Bac Ninh
Ha Giang	HG	03	VM58	Ha Giang	N-T	Ha Giang
Hai Hung	HH	16	VM12	Hai Duong	N-T	Hai Duong, Hung Yen
Haiphong	HP	17	VM13	Haiphong	N-T	Kien An
Hanoi	HN	11	VM51	Hanoi	N-T	Hanoi
Ha Tay	HY	15	VM59	Ha Dong	N-T	Ha Dong, Son Tay
Ha Tinh	HT	23	VM60	Ha Tinh	N-A	Ha Tinh
Hoa Binh	HO	14	VM61	Hoa Binh	N-T	Hoa Binh
Ho Chi Minh	HC	42	VM52	Ho Chi Minh City	S-C	Bien Hoa, Gia Dinh, Hau Nghia
Khanh Hoa	KH	34	VM62	Nha Trang	S-A	Khanh Hoa
Kien Giang	KG	47	VM47	Rach Gia	S-C	Kien Giang
Kon Tum	KT	28	VM63	Kon Tum	S-A	Kontum
Lai Chau	LC	01	VM22	Lai Chau	N-T	Lai Chau
Lam Dong	LD	35	VM23	Da Lat	S-A	Lam Dong, Tuyen Duc
Lang Son	LS	09	VM39	Lang Son	N-T	Lang Son
Lao Cai	LO	02	VM64	Lao Cai	N-T	Lao Cai
Long An	LA	41	VM24	Tan An	S-C	Long An, Hau Nghia, Kien Tuong
Minh Hai	MH	53	VM48	Ca Mau	S-C	An Xuyen
Nam Ha	NH	19	VM65	Nam Dinh	N-T	Nam Dinh, Phu Ly
Nghe An	NA	22	VM66	Vinh	N-A	Nghe An
Ninh Binh	NB	18	VM67	Ninh Binh	N-T	Ninh Binh
Ninh Thuan	NT	36	VM68	Phan Rang-Thap Cham	S-A	Ninh Thuan
Phu Yen	PY	32	VM69	Tuy Hoa	S-A	Phu Yen
Quang Binh	QB	24	VM70	Dong Hoi	N-A	Quang Binh
Quang Nam-Da Nang	QD	27	VM29	Da Nang	S-A	Quang Nam, Quang Tin
Quang Ngai	QG	29	VM71	Quang Ngai	S-A	Quang Ngai
Quang Ninh	QN	24	VM30	Hong Gai	N-T	Quang Yen, Hai Ninh
Quang Tri	QT	25	VM72	Dong Ha	S-A	Quang Tri
Soc Trang	ST	52	VM73	Soc Trang	S-C	Ba Xuyen
Song Be	SB	38	VM49	Thu Dau Mot	S-C	Binh Duong, Binh Long, Phuoc Long, Phuoc Thanh
Son La	SL	05	VM32	Son La	N-T	Son La
Tay Ninh	TN	37	VM33	Tay Ninh	S-C	Tay Ninh
Thai Binh	TB	20	VM35	Thai Binh	N-T	Thai Binh
Thanh Hoa	TH	21	VM34	Thanh Hoa	N-A	Thanh Hoa
Thua Thien	TT	26	VM74	Hué	S-A	Thua Thien
Tien Giang	TG	46	VM37	My Tho	S-C	Go Cong, Dinh Tuong ▶

division	abv	ISO	FIPS	capital	old	former
Tra Vinh	TV	51	VM75	Tra Vinh	S-C	Vinh Binh
Tuyen Quang	TQ	07	VM76	Tuyen Quang	N-T	Tuyen Quang
Vinh Long	VL	49	VM77	Vinh Long	S-C	Vinh Long
Vinh Phu	VP	10	VM50	Viet Tri	N-T	Vinh Yen,Phu Tho,Phuc Yen
Yen Bai	YB	06	VM78	Yen Bai	N-T	Yen Bai

Status: These divisions are tinh (provinces), except for Haiphong, Hanoi, and Ho Chi Minh, which are thu do (formerly called thanh pho; municipalities).

Abv: Two-letter code for international compatibility (defined by the author).

ISO: Codes from ISO 3166-2.

FIPS: Codes from FIPS PUB 10-4.

Population and area not yet available for new provinces.

Old: Key to division of country in 1960, 1920. First letter in each pair is N for North Vietnam or S for South Vietnam. Second letter is A for Annam, C for Cochin China, T for Tonkin.

Former: Provinces in 1965 which occupied *approximately* the same territory.

Territorial extent: Vietnam claims the Paracel and Spratly islands in the South China Sea.

Ba Ria-Vung Tau includes the Con Dao islands.

Kien Giang includes the islands Phu Quoc, Rai, Tre, and others in the Gulf of Siam.

Origins of names:

Haiphong: Vietnamese *hai*: sea, *phong*: room

Hanoi: Vietnamese *ha*: river, *noi*: interior

Ho Chi Minh City: named for North Vietnamese leader Ho Chi Minh (pseudonym of Nguyen Ai Quoc, 1890–1969)

Change history: By 1900 the French had established a protectorate (tantamount to a colony) over Indo-China, known as the Indochinese Union or French Indo-China. It was divided into the territories of Anam (French name Annam; capital Hué), Cambodia (Cambodge; Phnom Penh), Cochin China (Cochinchine; Saigon), Laos (Laos; Louang Prabang), and Tongking (Tonkin; Hanoi). Anam, Cochin China, and Tongking were essentially equivalent to present-day Vietnam. The Vietnamese names for them were Trung Bo, Nam Bo, and Bac Bo respectively, meaning Center, South, and North. They were subdivided into provinces.

1954-07-21	Cease-fire agreement signed between France and the Viet Minh rebels, partitioning Vietnam into North Vietnam and South Vietnam at the parallel 17° North.
1954-12-29	North and South Vietnam became independent.
1959	South Vietnam consisted of 22 provinces of Cochin China and most of 13 provinces of Annam; North Vietnam consisted of 4 provinces of Annam and 29 provinces of Tonkin (?)
1976-07-02	North and South Vietnam merged to form Socialist Republic of Vietnam. Name of Saigon changed to Ho Chi Minh City.
~1981	Cao Lang province split into Cao Bang and Lang Son.
~1983	Vung Tau-Con Dao dac khu (special zone) formed by taking the area around Vung Tau (Cape Saint Jacques) from Dong Nai, and the Con Dao islands from Hau Giang. Before this change, the FIPS codes of Dong Nai and Hau Giang were VM08 and VM18, respectively. Name of Gia Lai-Cong Tum province changed to Gia Lai-Kon Tum. At this time, the provinces were as follows:

province	FIPS	population	area-km	area-mi	capital
An Giang	VM01	1,980,000	4,140	1,598	Long Xuyen
Bac Thai	VM02	980,000	8,615	3,326	Thai Nguyen
Ben Tre	VM03	1,275,000	2,400	927	Ben Tre
Binh Tri Thien	VM04	2,120,000	19,048	7,354	Hué
Cao Bang	VM05	595,000	13,731	5,302	Cao Bang
Cuu Long	VM06	1,850,000	4,200	1,622	Vinh Long
Dac Lac	VM07	735,000	18,300	7,066	Buon Me Thuot
Dong Nai	VM40	1,690,000	12,130	4,683	Bien Hoa
Dong Thap	VM09	1,430,000	3,120	1,205	Cao Lanh
Gia Lai-Kon Tum	VM10	785,000	18,480	7,135	Kontum
Ha Bac	VM11	2,110,000	4,708	1,818	Bac Giang ➤

province	FIPS	population	area-km	area-mi	capital
Hai Hung	VM12	2,625,000	2,526	975	Hai Duong
Haiphong	VM13	1,500,000	1,515	585	Haiphong
Ha Nam Ninh	VM14	3,315,000	3,522	1,360	Nam Dinh
Hanoi	VM15	3,170,000	597	231	Hanoi
Ha Son Binh	VM16	1,850,000	6,860	2,649	Hoa Binh
Ha Tuyen	VM17	975,000	13,519	5,220	Ha Giang
Hau Giang	VM41	2,735,000	5,100	1,969	Can Tho
Hoang Lien Son	VM19	950,000	14,125	5,454	Lao Cai
Ho Chi Minh	VM20	3,685,000	1,845	712	Ho Chi Minh City
Kien Giang	VM21	1,245,000	6,000	2,317	Rach Gia
Lai Chau	VM22	432,000	17,408	6,721	Lai Chau
Lam Dong	VM23	580,000	10,000	3,861	Da Lat
Lang Son	VM39	580,000	— —	— —	Lang Son
Long An	VM24	1,195,000	5,100	1,969	Tan An
Minh Hai	VM25	1,900,000	8,000	3,089	Bac Lieu
Nghe Tinh	VM26	3,655,000	22,380	8,641	Vinh
Nghia Binh	VM27	2,600,000	14,700	5,676	Qui Nhon
Phu Khanh	VM28	1,465,000	9,620	3,714	Nha Trang
Quang Nam-Da Nang	VM29	1,810,000	11,376	4,392	Da Nang
Quang Ninh	VM30	870,000	7,076	2,732	Hong Gai
Song Be	VM31	805,000	9,500	3,668	Thu Dau Mot
Son La	VM32	635,000	14,656	5,659	Son La
Tay Ninh	VM33	830,000	4,100	1,583	Tay Ninh
Thai Binh	VM34	1,790,000	1,344	519	Thai Binh
Thanh Hoa	VM35	3,010,000	11,138	4,300	Thanh Hoa
Thuan Hai	VM36	1,220,000	11,000	4,247	Phan Thiet
Tien Giang	VM37	1,505,000	2,350	907	My Tho
Vinh Phu	VM38	1,805,000	5,187	2,003	Viet Tri
Vung Tau-Con Dao	VM42	98,000	— —	— —	Ving Tau
		64,385,000	329,416	127,189	

FIPS: Codes from FIPS PUB 10-4.
Population: 1988 estimate.
Area-km: Square kilometers.
Area-mi: Square miles.

~1990   Binh Tri Thien province split into Quang Binh, Quang Tri, and Thua Thien. Nghia Binh province split into Binh Dinh and Quang Ngai. Phu Khanh province split into Khanh Hoa and Phu Yen.

~1992   Ha Nam Ninh, Ha Son Binh, and part of Hanoi provinces reorganized to form Ha Tay, Hoa Binh, Nam Ha, and Ninh Binh. Ha Tuyen province split into Ha Giang and Tuyen Quang. Hoang Lien Son province split into Lao Cai and Yen Bai. Nghe Tinh province split into Ha Tinh and Nghe An. Gia Lai-Kon Tum province split into Gia Lai and Kon Tum. Part of Dong Nai province annexed to Vung Tau-Con Dao special zone to form Ba Ria-Vung Tau province. Thuan Hai province split into Binh Thuan and Ninh Thuan. Hau Giang province split into Can Tho and Soc Trang. Cuu Long province split into Tra Vinh and Vinh Long.

1997   The CIA World Factbook says that Bac Thai, Ha Bac, Hai Hung, Minh Hai, Nam Ha, Quang Nam-Da Nang, Song Be, and Vinh Phu provinces *may* have been reorganized to form Bac Can, Bac Giang, Bac Lieu, Bac Ninh, Binh Duong, Binh Phuoc, Ca Mau, Ha Nam, Hai Duong, Hung Yen, Nam Dinh, Phu Tho, Quang Nam, Thai Nguyen, and Vinh Phuc provinces, and Da Nang municipality.

VIRGIN ISLANDS, BRITISH

ISO = VG/FIPS = VI   Language = English   Time zone = -4   Capital = Road Town

A British territory throughout the 20th century.

Other names of country: Britische Jungferninseln (German); Britse Maagdeneilanden (Dutch); Îles Vierges britanniques (French); Ilhas Virgens Británicas (Portuguese); Islas Vírgenes Británicas (Spanish); Isole Vergini Britanniche (Italian).

Origin of name: Named by Columbus for the 11,000 virgins of Saint Ursula, because discovered on her feast day.

division	abv	population	area-km	area-mi	capital
British Virgin Islands	VI	16,749	153	59	Road Town (Tortola Island)

Status: This division is the whole of the country, treated as a division for compatibility.
Abv: Two-letter code for international compatibility (defined by the author).
Population: 1991 census.
Area-km: Square kilometers.
Area-mi: Square miles.
Territorial extent: The Virgin Islands are divided between the Virgin Islands (U.S.) and the British Virgin Islands. The latter comprises islands north and east of The Narrows. The main islands are Anegada, Jost van Dyke, Tortola, and Virgin Gorda. Other islands in the British territory near the border with the U.S. territory are Little Tobago, Great and Little Thatch Island, Frenchman Cay, Pelican Island, and Norman Island.

VIRGIN ISLANDS, U.S.

ISO = VI/FIPS = VQ   Language = English   Time zone = -4   Capital = Charlotte Amalie

The Danish West Indies were purchased from Denmark on 1917-01-25, and became an unincorporated territory of the United States, and so they remain now.

Other names of country: Amerikaanse Maagdeneilanden (Dutch); Amerikanische Jungferninseln (German); Danish West Indies (obsolete); Îles Vierges américaines, Îles Vierges des États-Unis (French); Ilhas Virgens Americanas (Portuguese); Islas Vírgenes Americanas, Islas Vírgenes de los Estados Unidos (Spanish); Isole Vergini U.S.A. (Italian); Virgin Islands of the United States (formal–English).

Origin of name: discovered by Columbus and named Santa Ursula y las Once Mil Vírgenes: Saint Ursula and the Eleven Thousand Virgins.

division	abv	FIPS	population	area-km	area-mi
Saint Croix	SC	010	50,139	218	84
Saint John	SJ	020	3,504	52	20
Saint Thomas	ST	030	48,166	73	28
			101,809	343	132

Status: These divisions are the main islands. They have no administrative significance. The census bureau uses them as enumeration districts.
Abv: Two-letter code for international compatibility (defined by the author).
FIPS: Three-digit county codes from FIPS PUB 55-2. When prefixed with 78, which is the two-digit state code for Virgin Islands from FIPS PUB 5-2, they form a five-digit county code (e.g. 78010 for Saint Croix) which is unique within the United States. As a state-level division of the United States, the Virgin Islands has 78 as a State Numeric Code and VI as a State Alpha Code, according to Table 2 of FIPS PUB 5-2.
Population: 1990 census.

Area-km: Square kilometers.

Area-mi: Square miles.

Further subdivisions: The islands are divided into cities and rural districts.

Territorial extent: The Virgin Islands consist of the three main islands named above, and numerous adjacent islets.

Saint Croix includes Buck Island and Green Cay.

Saint John includes islands east of Pillsbury Sound and south of The Narrows, which separates it from the British Virgin Islands. The largest adjacent island is Lovango Cay.

Saint Thomas includes islands west of Pillsbury Sound. Some of the larger adjacent islands are the Hans Lollik Islands, Water, Brass, Savana, and Thatch Cay.

Change history:

1921	Name of capital changed from Charlotte Amalie to Saint Thomas.
1936-06-22	Organic Act set up two municipalities: Saint Croix, and Saint Thomas and Saint John. Name of capital changed back to Charlotte Amalie.
1954-07-22	New Organic Act passed, abolishing the municipalities in favor of a central administration.

Population history:

island	1911	1917	1930	1940	1950	1960	1970	1980	1990
Saint Croix	15,467	14,901	11,413	12,902	12,103	14,973	31,892	49,013	50,139
Saint John	941	959	765	722	749	925	1,743	2,360	3,504
Saint Thomas	10,678	10,191	9,834	11,265	13,813	16,201	29,565	44,218	48,166
	27,086	26,051	22,012	24,889	26,665	32,099	63,200	95,591	101,809

WALLIS AND FUTUNA

ISO = WF/FIPS = WF   Language = French   Time zone = +12   Capital = Mata Utu

The Wallis and Futuna Islands have belonged to France throughout the 20th century, and now have the status of overseas territory.

Other names of country: Îles Wallis et Futuna (French); Islas Wallis y Futuna (Spanish); Territory of the Wallis and Futuna Islands (formal–English); Wallis e Futuna (Portuguese); Wallis en Futuna (Dutch); Wallisøyene og Futunaøyene (Norwegian); Wallis und Futuna (German).

Origin of name: discovered in 1767 by Captain Samuel Wallis (1728–1795).

division	abv	population	area-km	area-mi	division	abv	population	area-km	area-mi
Alo	AL	3,000	85	33	Uvéa	UV	10,000	96	37
Singave	SI	2,000	30	12			15,000	211	82

Status: These divisions are royaumes (kingdoms).

Abv: Two-letter code for international compatibility (defined by the author).

Population: 1995 estimate.

Area-km: Square kilometers.

Area-mi: Square miles.

Further subdivisions: Uvéa is divided into three districts.

Territorial extent: Alo consists of the eastern part of Futuna Island. For the purpose of this book, I have also assigned to it the island of Alofi, which is uninhabited, on the basis of proximity. Futuna and Alofi together are known as the Îles de Horne (Hoorn).

Singave consists of the western part of Futuna Island.

Uvéa consists of Wallis (Uvéa) Island and adjacent reefs. The country's capital, Mata-Utu, is there.

Change history:

1961-07-29　Status of country changed from French dependency, administered from New Caledonia, to French territoire d'outre-mer (overseas territory).

Other names of subdivisions:

Singave: Sigave (variant)　　　　　　　　　　　Uvéa: Wallis (variant)

WESTERN SAHARA

ISO = EH/FIPS = WI　Language = Arabic　Time zone = +0　Capital = El Aaiún

In 1900, Spanish West Africa was a Spanish possession. It comprised four districts on the west coast of Africa: Ifni, Río de Oro, Saguia el Hamra, and Southern Protectorate of Morocco. Río de Oro was the area from Cape Blanco and about latitude 21°20' north to latitude 26°; Saguia el Hamra reached from there to about latitude 27°40' north (Cape Juby); and the Southern Protectorate of Morocco extended from there to Oued Draa, the border with French Morocco. Ifni was a coastal enclave around the town of Sidi Ifni. Spanish Sahara referred to Río de Oro and Saguia el Hamra. (In fact, the different names were used somewhat indiscriminately. Río de Oro was often applied to the whole colony, excluding Ifni.) In 1976, Spain relinquished Spanish Sahara. Mauritania and Morocco promptly divided it between them. However, Mauritania ceded its portion to Morocco three years later. Morocco has administered the region since then. The former Southern Protectorate is fully integrated into Morocco. As for Spanish Sahara, now known as Western Sahara, other governments have withheld recognition of Morocco's sovereignty pending a referendum.

Other names of country: Africa Occidental Española, Sahara Español (Spanish-obsolete); Saara Ocidental (Portuguese); Sahara Occidental (Spanish); Sahara occidental (French); Sahara Occidentale (Italian); Spanish Sahara, Spanish West Africa (obsolete); Väst-Sahara (Swedish); Westliche Sahara (German).

Origin of name: descriptive: located at the west end of the Sahara Desert (Arabic *sahara*: desert).

division	abv	ISO	population	area-km	area-mi
Boujdour	BO	BOD	8,481	100,120	38,660
Es Semara	ES	ESM	20,480	61,760	23,850
Laayoune	LA	LAA	113,411	39,360	15,200
Oued el Dahab	OD	OUD	21,496	50,880	19,640
			163,868	252,120	97,350

Status: These divisions are wilayas (provinces).
Abv: Two-letter code for international compatibility (defined by the author).
ISO: Codes from ISO 3166-2.
Population: 1994 census.
Area-km: Square kilometers.
Area-mi: Square miles.
Capitals have the same names as their provinces, except for Oued el Dahab (capital Dakhla).
Origins of names:

Laayoune: Arabic *el aaiún*: the springs
Río de Oro: Spanish for river of gold, referring to the bay on which Dakhla lies.

Change history: La Agüera was a district in southern Río de Oro during the 1920s. Cape Juby was a district in the Southern Protectorate of Morocco from 1916 to ~1948. The districts during the colonial period, with their capitals, were Ifni (Sidi Ifni), Río de Oro (Villa Cisneros, renamed Dakhla in 1976), Saguia el Hamra (El Aaiún), and Southern Protectorate of Morocco (Villa Bens, renamed Tarfaya in 1958).

1956-04-07   When Morocco became independent, it resumed control of the Southern Protectorate of Morocco.

1969-06-30   Ifni restored to Morocco by Spain.

1976-02-20   Spain relinquished Spanish Sahara (now consisting of Río de Oro and Saguia el Hamra). Mauritania and Morocco partitioned it, the southern half of Río de Oro going to Mauritania. The Moroccan sector was reorganized into the provinces of Boujdour, Laayoune, and Es Semara. The Mauritanian sector became the region of Tiris el Gharbia.

1979-08-14   Mauritania ceded Tiris el Gharbia to Morocco, which renamed it Oued el Dahab province.

Other names of subdivisions: Names are originally written in the Arabic alphabet, so they may be transliterated in various ways.

Río de Oro: Zona Meridional, Sur (obsolete)

Saguia el Hamra: Saguiet el Hamra, Sekia el Hamra, Zona Central, Norte (obsolete)

Southern Protectorate of Morocco: Zona Septentrional (obsolete)

Boujdour: Bojador (variant)

Es Semara: Smara (variant)

Laayoune: El Aaiún, La'youn (variant)

Oued el Dahab: Ed Dakhla (obsolete); Oued Eddahab (variant)

YEMEN

ISO = YE/FIPS = YM   Language = Arabic   Time zone = +3   Capital = Sanaa

In 1900, modern Yemen consisted of the Turkish vilayet of Yemen along the Red Sea, and a collection of territories on the Gulf of Aden and Arabian Sea which were in the British sphere. The border between them was delimited starting in 1902. This border remained in place through several changes in government, until 1990, when the two countries merged.

Other names of country: al-Jamhuriya al-Yamaniya (formal); Iêmen (Portuguese); Jemen (Dutch, Finnish, German, Icelandic, Norwegian); Republic of Yemen (formal–English); Yémen (French).

Origin of name: from Arabic for right-hand, its position relative to Mecca as seen from Africa.

division	ISO	FIPS	old	population	capital
Abyan	AB	YM01	YS03	416,271	Zinjibar
'Adan	AD	YM02	YS01	564,335	Aden
Al Bayda'	BA	YM07	YE01	505,751	Al Bayda
Al Hudaydah	HU	YM08	YE02	1,754,493	Al Hudaydah
Al Jawf	JA	YM09	YE11	169,440	R'aydah
Al Mahrah	MR	YM03	YS06	112,615	Al Ghaydah
Al Mahwit	MW	YM10	YE08	402,992	Al Mahwit
Dhamar	DH	YM11	YE09	1,049,120	Dhamar
Hadramawt	HD	YM04	YS05	871,202	Al Mukalla
Hajjah	HJ	YM12	YE03	1,265,845	Hajjah
Ibb	IB	YM13	YE04	1,963,975	Ibb
Lahij	LA	YM06	YS02	632,674	Lahej
Ma'rib	MA	YM14	YE10	183,053	Ma'rib
Sa'dah	SD	YM15	YE05	484,063	Sa'dah
San'a'	SN	YM16	YE06	1,907,968	San'a'
San'a' [City]	SA			973,548	San'a'
Shabwah	SH	YM05	YS04	375,541	'Ataq
Ta'izz	TA	YM17	YE07	2,198,871	Ta'izz
				15,831,757	

Status: These divisions are muhafazah (governorates), except for San'a' [City].

ISO: Codes from ISO 3166-2, except for SA for San'a' [City], which I added for completeness.

FIPS: Codes from FIPS PUB 10-4.
Old: FIPS codes used before the union of North and South Yemen.
Population: 1994 census.
Further subdivisions: The governorates are subdivided into districts.
Territorial extent: Aden includes the islands of Socotra, Perim, and Kamaran, along with Socotra's neighbors, 'Abd al Kuri and The Brothers (Samha and Darsa).

Yemen also owns the Hanish Islands and other islands in the Red Sea.

Origins of names:

Aden: probably from Akkadian *edinnu*: plain

Hadramaut: possibly from Hebrew Hatsarmawet, Biblical per-

son (Genesis 10:26)

Change history: In 1900, North Yemen was the vilayet of Yemen in the Ottoman Empire. Aden was a British possession, administered from Bombay. The rest of South Yemen, including Socotra, Perim, and Kamaran islands, was loosely under British protection in various forms.

1918-11	Yemen vilayet became independent as the Imamate of Yemen.
1932	Aden province split from Bombay presidency of India.
1934	Yemen and Saudi Arabia concluded Treaty of Taif, delimiting some of Yemen's northern boundary and assigning some disputed territory to Asir in Saudi Arabia.
1937-04-01	Aden split from India as a crown colony. The crown colony itself was only about 195 sq. km. Socotra, Perim, and Karaman were administered from Aden. The rest of the mainland was divided into the Eastern Aden Protectorate and the Western Aden Protectorate.
1958-03-08	Imamate of Yemen joined a loose federation with Egypt and Syria, which had recently merged as the United Arab Republic. The federation was called the United Arab States. Yemen pulled out in 1961.
1959-02-11	Federation of Arab Amirates formed from some of the sheikhdoms of Aden Protectorate.
1962	Following a coup, Imamate of Yemen became Yemen Arab Republic. At about this time, its divisions were Al Hudaydah, Hajjah, Ibb, Rida', Sa'dah, San'a', and Ta'izz governorates.
1963-01	Name of Federation of Arab Amirates, now including more sheikhdoms (mostly from the Western Aden Protectorate) and Aden itself, changed to Federation of South Arabia. The remaining part of the Aden Protectorate became the South Arabian Protectorate.
1967-11-30	Britain pulled out of Aden. People's Republic of Southern Yemen formed. Kuriya Muriya Islands transferred to Oman. Soon afterward, Southern Yemen was divided into six governorates, identified by Roman numerals from I to VI, increasing from west to east.
1970-12-01	Name of People's Republic of Southern Yemen changed to People's Democratic Republic of Yemen. To avoid confusion, this was commonly known as South Yemen, and the Yemen Arab Republic as North Yemen.
~1980	Rida' governorate split into Al Bayda' and Dhamar.
~1984	Al Jawf, Al Mahwit, and Ma'rib governorates split from other governorates in North Yemen.
1990-05-22	The two Yemens merged to form Republic of Yemen.
~1994	San'a' city split from San'a' governorate.

Other names of subdivisions: The Arabic definite article Al is sometimes omitted at the beginning of a name.

'Adan: Aden (variant)
Al Bayda': Al Beida (variant)
Al Hudaydah: Al Hodeida (variant)
Al Mahrah: Al Ghaydah (obsolete); Mahra (variant)
Hadramawt: Hadhramaut, Hadhramawt, Hadramaut (variant)

Lahij: Lahej (variant); Tuban (obsolete)
Sa'dah: Sa'ada, Saidah (variant)
San'a': Sana'a (variant)
Ta'izz: Taiz (variant)

YUGOSLAVIA

ISO = YU/FIPS = YO*   Language = Serbo-Croatian   Time zone = +1 ^{d} Capital = Belgrade

* = retired (see explanation of FIPS codes below)

Yugoslavia was born as the Kingdom of the Serbs, Croats, and Slovenes. In 1900, this area was fragmented. The Ottoman Empire still retained a foothold in Europe. Its vilayet of Kosovo later became part of Yugoslavia, as did northern Monastir and a corner of Saloniki vilayet. Bosnia-Herzegovina and the sanjak of Novibazar, both nominally Ottoman, had been occupied by Austria-Hungary since 1878. Serbia and Montenegro were independent kingdoms. The rest of the area that would eventually become Yugoslavia was in the Austro-Hungarian Empire, including the Austrian provinces of Carniola and Dalmatia, parts of Coastland and Styria, the Hungarian provinces of Fiume and Croatia and Slavonia, and parts of the Hungarian counties of Bács-Bodrog, Csongrád, Temes, and Torontál. In 1908, Austria-Hungary formally annexed Bosnia-Herzegovina. Following the Second Balkan War, by the Bucharest Peace Treaty (1913-08-10), Serbia annexed lands from the Ottoman Empire including its present southern section and what is now the Former Yugoslav Republic of Macedonia. The sanjak of Novibazar was split between Serbia and Montenegro. On 1918-12-04, the Kingdom of Serbs, Croats, and Slovenes was proclaimed. This kingdom was soon being called Yugoslavia, although the name didn't become official until 1929. The peace treaties which ended World War I sanctioned the fait accompli. They left the exact border with Italy open for negotiation (see Croatia and Slovenia for full details about this border, which was again shifted after World War II). Yugoslavia was occupied by the axis powers in World War II. After it was liberated, on 1945-11-29, it proclaimed itself the Federal People's Republic of Yugoslavia, formed as a federation of six constituent republics: Bosnia and Herzegovina, Croatia, Macedonia, Montenegro, Serbia, and Slovenia. Within Serbia there were two autonomous divisions: Kosovo region and Voivodina province. When the Communist bloc fell apart, starting in 1991, the republics began declaring themselves independent. Finally, only Montenegro and Serbia remained in the federation. They claim to be the successor state to Yugoslavia. The United Nations and the United States reject this claim, and treat them as two separate unrecognized states. Kosovo and Voivodina have been stripped of their autonomy.

Other names of country: Federal Republic of Yugoslavia (formal–English); Iugoslavia (Italian); Iugoslávia (Portuguese); Joegoslavië (Dutch); Jugoslavien (Swedish); Jugoslawien (German); Savezna Republika Jugoslavija (formal); Yougoslavie (French).

Origin of name: Serb *jugo*: south + ethnic name Slav.

division	ISO	FIPS	population	area-km	area-mi	capital
Montenegro	CG	MW	616,327	13,812	5,333	Titograd
Serbia	SR	SR	9,721,177	88,361	34,116	Belgrade
			10,337,504	102,173	39,449	

Status: These divisions are republics.

ISO: Codes from ISO 3166-2.

FIPS: Codes from FIPS PUB 10-4. Before the breakup of Yugoslavia, the country code was YO. The FIPS standard no longer recognizes Yugoslavia as a country. Instead, each of the republics has been given a FIPS country code.

Population: 1991 census.

Area-km: Square kilometers.

Area-mi: Square miles.

Further subdivisions: Yugoslavia, before it broke up, was divided into socialist republics. One of them, Serbia, was further divided into Serbia proper and two autonomous divisions. All of them — republics and autonomous areas — were in turn divided into opčine (communes). The communes are presumably still in place now.

The main divisions of Serbia are:

division	FIPS	population	area-km	area-mi	capital
Serbia proper	SR00	5,753,825	55,968	21,609	Belgrade
Kosovo	SR01	1,954,747	10,887	4,203	Priština
Vojvodina	SR02	2,012,605	21,506	8,304	Novi Sad

Origins of names:

Kosovo: field of the black birds

Montenegro: Italian calque of Serbo-Croat *crna*: black, *gora*: mountain

Serbia: land of the Serbs

Change history:

1918-12-04	Kingdom of the Serbs, Croats, and Slovenes proclaimed.
1920-06-04	Croatia, Slavonia, and western Banat annexed from Hungary by the Treaty of Trianon.
1920-07-16	Austrian provinces of Coastland, Carniola, Dalmatia, the southern part of Styria, and a small section of Carinthia incorporated into Kingdom of Serbs, Croats, and Slovenes by the Treaty of Saint-Germain.
1929	Name of the country officially changed to Yugoslavia.
1945-11-29	Yugoslavia became the Federal People's Republic of Yugoslavia, comprising six republics: Bosnia and Herzegovina, Croatia, Macedonia, Montenegro, Serbia, and Slovenia.
1991-01-25	Macedonia declared independence from Yugoslavia.
1991-10-08	Slovenia declared independence from Yugoslavia.
1992-01-15	Croatia's claim to independence recognized by the European Union.
1992-04-05	Independence of Bosnia and Herzegovina proclaimed.

Other names of subdivisions:

Kosovo: Autonomous Kosovo and Metohia Region (formal); Kosmet (informal); Kosova, Kossovo (variant); Kosovo-Metohija (French, Serbo-Croat); Kossowo-Metohija (German)

Montenegro: Crna Gora (Serbo-Croat); Kara Dag (Turkish); Monténégro (French)

Serbia: Serbía (Icelandic); Serbie (French); Serbien (Danish, German, Swedish); Servia (obsolete); Servie (French-obsolete); Srbija (Serbo-Croat)

Voivodina: Vojvodina (Italian); Vojvodine (French); Wojwodina (German)

Population history:

republic	FIPS	1948	1953	1961	1971	1981	1991
Bosnia and Herzegovina	YO01	2,561,961	2,847,459	3,277,948	3,746,000	4,124,256	4,365,639
Croatia	YO03	3,749,039	3,936,022	4,159,696	4,426,000	4,601,469	4,784,265
Macedonia	YO05	1,152,054	1,304,514	1,406,003	1,647,000	1,909,136	2,038,847
Montenegro	YO02	376,573	419,873	471,894	530,000	584,310	616,327
Serbia	YO07	6,523,224	6,979,154	7,642,227	8,447,000	9,313,676	9,721,177
Slovenia	YO06	1,389,084	1,504,427	1,591,523	1,727,000	1,891,864	1,974,839
		15,751,935	16,991,449	18,549,291	20,523,000	22,424,711	23,501,094

FIPS: Codes from FIPS PUB 10-4 before the dissolution of Yugoslavia.
Census dates, where known: 1953-03-31, 1961-06-30, 1981-03-31.

ZAMBIA

ISO = ZM/FIPS = ZA   Language = English   Time zone = +2   Capital = Lusaka

At the start of the 20th century, North-East Rhodesia and North-West Rhodesia were administered, with regard to British interests, by the British South Africa Company. In 1911, they merged to form the protectorate of Northern Rhodesia. The country took the name Zambia when it became independent in 1964.

Other names of country: Northern Rhodesia (obsolete); Republic of Zambia (formal–English); Sambia (German); Sambía (Icelandic); Zâmbia (Portuguese); Zambie (French).

Origin of name: from Zambezi River.

division	abv	ISO	FIPS	population	area-km	area-mi	capital	old name
Central	CE	02	ZA02	725,611	94,395	36,446	Kabwe	Broken Hill
Copperbelt	CO	08	ZA08	1,579,542	31,328	12,096	Ndola	
Eastern	EA	03	ZA03	973,818	69,106	26,682	Chipata	Fort Jameson ➤

division	abv	ISO	FIPS	population	area-km	area-mi	capital	old name
Luapula	LP	04	ZA04	526,705	50,567	19,524	Mansa	Fort Rosebery
Lusaka	LS	09	ZA09	1,207,980	21,898	8,455	Lusaka	
Northern	NO	05	ZA05	867,795	147,826	57,076	Kasama	
North-Western	NW	06	ZA06	383,146	125,827	48,582	Solwezi	
Southern	SO	07	ZA07	946,353	85,283	32,928	Livingstone	
Western	WE	01	ZA01	607,497	126,386	48,798	Mongu	
				7,818,447	752,616	290,587		

Status: These divisions are provinces.
Abv: Two-letter code for international compatibility (defined by the author).
ISO: Codes from ISO 3166-2.
FIPS: Codes from FIPS PUB 10-4.
Population: 1990 census.
Area-km: Square kilometers.
Area-mi: Square miles.
Old name: Name of capital before independence.
Further subdivisions: The provinces are divided into 57 districts.
Origins of names:

Copperbelt: site of a belt of copper mines

Change history:

1911-08-17   North-East Rhodesia (capital Fort Jameson) and North-West Rhodesia (capital Kalomo) merged to form Northern Rhodesia (capital Livingstone).

~1933   Capital of the country moved from Livingstone to Lusaka.

1953-07-14   British Parliament passed the Rhodesia and Nyasaland Federation Act, by which Northern Rhodesia protectorate, Nyasaland protectorate, and Southern Rhodesia colony were joined in the Federation of Rhodesia and Nyasaland (capital Salisbury, Southern Rhodesia).

1963-12-31   Federation of Rhodesia and Nyasaland dissolved into its original components.

1964-10-24   Northern Rhodesia became independent under the name Zambia.

~1973   Lusaka province split from Central province. Lusaka city, formerly the capital of Central, became the capital of Lusaka. Capital of Central moved to Kabwe. Initially Lusaka province was only 360 sq. km. around Lusaka, but by 1988 it had been enlarged to its present size.

~1977   Name of Barotseland province changed to Western; name of Western province changed to Copperbelt.

Other names of subdivisions:

Copperbelt: Western (obsolete)

Western: Barotseland (obsolete)

ZIMBABWE

ISO = ZW/FIPS = ZI   Language = English   Time zone = +2   Capital = Harare

Southern Rhodesia was a territory administered by the British South Africa Company at the start of the 20th century. It became a British colony in 1923. It joined in the Federation of Rhodesia and Nyasaland during that entity's term of existence (1953–1963), and then returned to colony status. In an attempt to retain a European-dominated government, it declared independence unilaterally. After some 14 years as a pariah state, it gave up the attempt and became fully independent as Zimbabwe.

Other names of country: Republic of Zimbabwe (formal–English); Simbabve (Icelandic); Simbabwe (German); Southern Rhodesia (obsolete).

Origin of name: named for ancient capital in ruins, whose name is Bantu *zimba*: palace, *bwe*: stone.

division	ISO	FIPS	population	area-km	area-mi	capital	alt/old
Manicaland	MA	ZI01	1,099,202	35,219	13,598	Mutare	Umtali
Mashonaland Central	MC	ZI03	563,407	29,482	11,383	Bindura	
Mashonaland East	ME	ZI04	1,495,984	26,813	10,353	Harare	Salisbury
Mashonaland West	MW	ZI05	858,962	55,737	21,520	Chinhoyi	Sinoia
Masvingo	MV	ZI08	1,031,697	55,777	21,536	Masvingo	Fort Victoria
Matabeleland North	MN	ZI06	885,339	76,813	29,658	Bulawayo	
Matabeleland South	MS	ZI07	519,606	54,941	21,213	Gwanda	
Midlands	MI	ZI02	1,091,844	55,977	21,613	Gweru	Gwelo
			7,546,041	390,759	150,874		

Status: These divisions are provinces.
ISO: Codes from ISO 3166-2.
FIPS: Codes from FIPS PUB 10-4.
Population: 1982 census.
Area-km: Square kilometers.
Area-mi: Square miles.
Alt/old: Earlier or alternate name for capital.
Origins of names: Manica, Mashona, and Matabele are all ethnic names.
Change history:

1923-10-01	Southern Rhodesia became a British colony.
1953-07-14	British Parliament passed the Rhodesia and Nyasaland Federation Act, by which Northern Rhodesia protectorate, Nyasaland protectorate, and Southern Rhodesia colony were joined in the Federation of Rhodesia and Nyasaland (capital Salisbury, Southern Rhodesia). At this time, the divisions of Southern Rhodesia were Mashonaland and Matabeleland.
1963-12-31	Federation of Rhodesia and Nyasaland dissolved into its original components.
1965-11-11	Southern Rhodesia declared independence unilaterally, taking the name Rhodesia.
~1974	Matabeleland split into Matabeleland North and Matabeleland South.
1979	Rhodesia began to style itself "Zimbabwe Rhodesia" as it moved toward integration.
1979-12-12	Zimbabwe Rhodesia returned to the status of a British colony.
1980-04-18	The country attained independence and changed its name to Republic of Zimbabwe. Name of the capital changed from Salisbury to Harare. The names of Victoria province and its capital, Fort Victoria, began to fall out of favor and be replaced by the native name Masvingo.
~1981	Mashonaland North split into Mashonaland Central and Mashonaland West (part); Mashonaland South split into Mashonaland East and Mashonaland West (part). Part of Matabeleland South around the city of Zvishavane annexed to Midlands.

Other names of subdivisions:

Masvingo: Victoria (obsolete)

Bibliography

In compiling the information in this book, I used a wide variety of reference works, trying to confirm every fact by the rule of "best two out of three." The standard references I used included various editions of the *Encyclopædia Britannica*, the *Statesman's Year-Book*, the *CIA World Factbook* (widely available on the World Wide Web), *Webster's Geographical Dictionary*, and many different atlases. The *Almanaque Abril*, published yearly by Editora Abril of São Paulo, included fairly comprehensive lists of administrative subdivisions of nations for a number of years. The *Almanaque Mundial*, published by Editorial America, Virginia Gardens, Florida, has subdivision lists for Latin American countries. The *Atlante Enciclopedia Geografica Garzanti*, published in Milan, has lists for the larger countries. A number of almanacs and statistical yearbooks are published for individual countries. *Whitaker's Almanack* has information on the United Kingdom and many of its former colonies. The United States and its possessions are well covered by the *World Almanac*, the *Information Please Almanac*, and many other sources. I found useful information in back issues of the *Almanach Hachette* (France), *Il Leonardo* (Italy), *Hvem Hva Hvor* (Norway), *När Var Hur* (Sweden), *Hvem Hvad Hvor* (Denmark), the English-language *Iran Almanac* and *Japan Almanac*, and others too numerous to mention.

The World Wide Web is the best source for recent changes. It must be used with caution, because there is no authority over or control of the information presented there, by any individual who wishes to present it, for whatever reason. I have tried especially hard to verify any information that came from the Web. My experience was quite favorable. It seems that no one has anything to gain by putting false or misleading lists of nations' subdivisions on the Internet. The main drawback of the Web is that information may be obsolete or undated.

The Web pages I used included country maps, especially the CIA maps available from the Web site of the Perry-Castañeda Library of the University of Texas; sites maintained by the statistics agencies of at least fifty countries; post office sites showing postal codes, and telecom sites showing telephone prefixes; the Library of Congress country studies; and the Arthur David Olson time zone archive (available by FTP, not on a Web page at this time). The Oddens's Bookmarks page points to on-line maps and other relevant sites.

URLs change so quickly that it would be futile to cite them here. Most of the sites mentioned can easily be found using a search engine. As of mid–1999, I am continuing to maintain updated links to worthwhile Web pages on what I have named the Statoids Web Page at <http://www.mind spring.com/~gwil/statoids.html>.

Here are some useful books on political geography and toponymy.

Aurousseau, Marcel. *The Rendering of Geographical Names*. London: Hutchinson University Library, 1957.

Bennett, Robert, ed. *Territory and Administration in Europe*. London: Pinter Publishers, 1989.

Deroy, Louis, and Marianne Mulon. *Dictionnaire de Noms de Lieux*. Paris: Dictionnaires Le Robert, 1992.

Dutt, Ashok K., and M. Margaret Geib. *Fully Annotated Atlas of South Asia*. Boulder: Westview Press, 1987.

Eastern Europe and the Commonwealth of Independent States 1992. London: Europa Publications Ltd., 1992.

Fifth United Nations Conference on the Standardization of Geographical Names. Vol. II. New York: United Nations, 1991.

Fisher, Morris. *Provinces and Provincial Capitals of the World*. New York: Scarecrow Press, 1967; second edition, 1985.

Fourth United Nations Conference on the Standardization of Geographical Names. Vol. II. New York: United Nations, 1987.

Groupe de Démographie Africaine. *L'Évaluation des Effectifs de la Population des Pays Africains*. Vol. I. Paris: Le Groupe, 1982.

Gustaffson, Agne. *Local Government in Sweden*, tr. Roger Tanner. Uddevalla: Swedish Institute, 1983.

Keith-Lucas, B. *English Local Government in the Nineteenth and Twentieth Centuries*. London: Historical Association, 1977.

Mardešić, Petar, and Zvonimir Dugački. *Geografski Atlas Jugoslavije*. Zagreb: Znanje, 1961.

Masson, Jean-Louis. *Provinces, Départements, Régions.* Paris: Éditions Fernand Lanore, 1984.

Matthews, C. M. *Place Names of the English-Speaking World.* New York: Charles Scribner's Sons, 1972.

Pounds, Norman J. G. *Political Geography.* New York: McGraw-Hill, 1963.

Schack, Jørgen. *Statsnavne og Nationalitetsord.* Oslo: Nordisk Språksekretariat, 1994.

Schmidt, Karl J. *An Atlas and Survey of South Asian History.* Armonk, N.Y.: M.E. Sharpe, 1995.

Stanyer, Jeffrey. *County Government in England and Wales.* London: Routledge and Kegan Paul, 1967.

Stewart, George R. *Names on the Globe.* Oxford: Oxford University Press, 1975.

_____. *Names on the Land.* Boston: Houghton Mifflin, 1967.

Wellich, Hans H. *The Conversion of Scripts.* New York: Wiley, 1978.

Index

This index lists all administrative divisions in the book except those that are, or were, countries. The latter will be found in the Registry of Countries on page nine. When a division is listed under two or more countries, page references to each country are given. However, when the same name is used for different divisions, there will be one entry for each occurrence of the name, followed by a comma and the respective country name.

Alphabetization is letter-by-letter, with commas considered as a break. All accent marks were ignored in determining alphabetical order. A few special characters were alphabetized as if they were digraphs: **æ** as **ae**, **ð** as **dh**, **œ** as **oe**, **ß** as **ss**, and **Þ** as **th**. For example, Þelamörk is listed as if it were spelled Thelamork.

The page references represent the first mention of that name under its country. For example, the Denmark article is on pages 104–107. When the index says "Aabenraa 106," it means that the name Aabenraa should definitely appear on page 106, and possibly on 107, but not on pages 104 or 105.